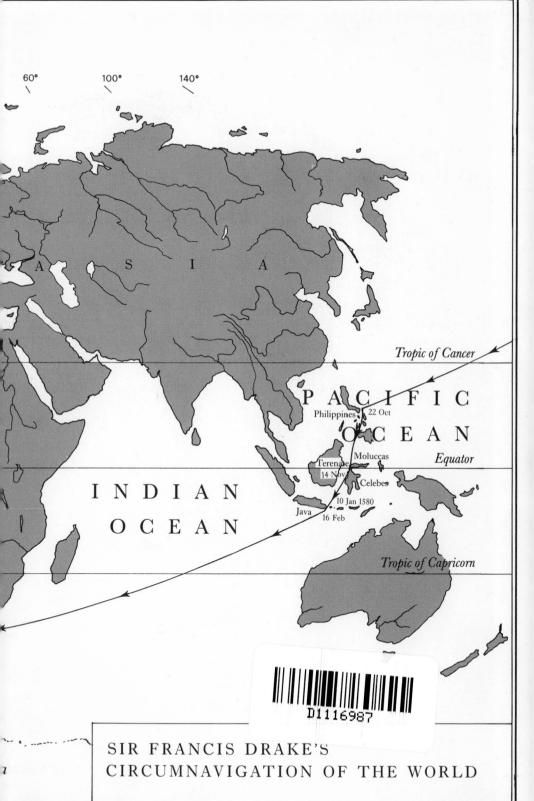

60°   100°   140°

A S I A

Tropic of Cancer

P A C I F I C

Philippines   22 Oct

O C E A N

Moluccas   Equator

Terenate
14 Nov.

Celebes

INDIAN

10 Jan 1580

OCEAN

Java   16 Feb

Tropic of Capricorn

D1116987

SIR FRANCIS DRAKE'S
CIRCUMNAVIGATION OF THE WORLD

FREEDOM'S OWN ISLAND

By the same author

MACAULAY
THE NATIONAL CHARACTER
THE LETTERS AND SPEECHES OF CHARLES II (editor)
THE ENGLAND OF CHARLES II
THE AMERICAN IDEAL

The Story of England
MAKERS OF THE REALM B.C.–1272
THE AGE OF CHIVALRY 1272–1381
THE ELIZABETHAN DELIVERANCE
KING CHARLES II 1630–1685
RESTORATION ENGLAND 1660–1702
ENGLISH SAGA 1840–1940

Samuel Pepys
THE MAN IN THE MAKING 1633–1669
THE YEARS OF PERIL 1669–1683
THE SAVIOUR OF THE NAVY 1683–1689
PEPYS AND THE REVOLUTION

The Napoleonic Wars
THE YEARS OF ENDURANCE 1793–1802
YEARS OF VICTORY 1802–1812
THE AGE OF ELEGANCE 1812–1822
NELSON
THE GREAT DUKE

The Alanbrooke Diaries
THE TURN OF THE TIDE 1939–1943
TRIUMPH IN THE WEST 1943–1946

English Social History
THE MEDIEVAL FOUNDATION
PROTESTANT ISLAND

A History of Britain and the British People
SET IN A SILVER SEA

THE FIRE AND THE ROSE
THE LION AND THE UNICORN
JIMMY
JACKETS OF GREEN
A THOUSAND YEARS OF BRITISH MONARCHY
SPIRIT OF ENGLAND

A HISTORY OF BRITAIN
AND THE BRITISH PEOPLE

VOLUME II

FREEDOM'S OWN ISLAND

The British Oceanic Expansion

Arthur Bryant

with a chapter by Professor John Kenyon

"Be of good comfort, Master Ridley, and play the man.
We shall this day light such a candle by God's grace
in England as I trust shall never be put out."
Bishop Latimer

"This England never did, nor never shall,
Lie at the proud foot of a conqueror."
Shakespeare

COLLINS
8 Grafton Street, London W1
1986

William Collins Sons and Co Ltd
London · Glasgow · Sydney · Auckland
Toronto · Johannesburg

BRITISH LIBRARY CATALOGUING IN PUBLICATION DATA

Bryant, Arthur
    Freedom's own island: the British oceanic expansion
    —(A History of Britain and the British People v.2)
    1. Great Britain—History—Modern period 1485.
    2. Great Britain—History—Lancaster and York, 1399–1485.
    I. Title   II. Kenyon, J.P.   III. Series.
    942   DA300

ISBN 0–00–217411–1

Some of the material in this book was first published
in 1942, 1944, 1950 and 1980.

Copyright in this edition
© The Estate of Sir Arthur Bryant 1986
Chapter 13 © John Kenyon 1986

Photoset in Monophoto Imprint by Ace Filmsetting Ltd, Frome Somerset
Made and printed by William Collins Sons and Co Ltd, Glasgow

CONTENTS

ILLUSTRATIONS

To
CHRISTINA FOYLE

Publisher's Note

Sir Arthur Bryant CH died in February 1985 shortly before his 86th birthday. This book, the second volume in his *History of Great Britain and the British People*, was found to be substantially complete. The only period for which Sir Arthur left incomplete indications of his intentions was that of the Revolution of 1688. The Publishers would like to thank Professor John Kenyon for filling this gap.

They would also like to thank Lady Bryant, Mrs Pamela McCormick, Mr Christopher Falkus and Mr Alan Macfadyen for their constant help in preparing the book for publication.

The third volume of the *History, The Search for Justice*, which was also left almost ready for publication, will follow in 1987.

CHAPTER ONE

Threshold to a New Age

'Leaving the old, both worlds at once they view
Who stand upon the threshold of the new'
Edmund Waller

DURING THE DISASTERS which befell England in the latter fourteenth century – the Black Death, the loss of her French conquests
and of her kings' former hereditary dominions, the Peasants'
Revolt and the dethronement of Richard II – there lived, surviving
them all, a court official named Geoffrey Chaucer. Son of a
London vintner supplying the luxurious court of Edward III, he
grew up in it as a page and, a favourite among the ladies as a story-
teller, marrying one of the Queen's women-in-waiting – a sister
of the mistress, and later morganatic wife, of the great John of
Gaunt, duke of Lancaster, father of the usurper, Bolingbroke, who
in 1399 became Henry IV. Chaucer rose to be Controller of the
London Customs and Clerk of Works to the royal palaces, and sat
as a knight of the shire in one of Richard II's parliaments. In his
earlier years he had often been employed on diplomatic missions,
in the course of which he visited Italy, where, being a poet and
maker of stories, he studied the works of the great Florentines,
Dante, Petrach and Boccaccio, and the new metrical forms they
had adapted from the classics.

Had he been born half a century earlier he would have written
his poetry in French. But he happened to live just when an England
long at war with France was turning her back on the French
tongue. In 1362, about the time he reached manhood, English
became the official language of the Law Courts and soon after-

I

wards of Parliament and the university schools. Chaucer, therefore, wrote in English, choosing the dialect of his own part of the
country, that of London and the east Midlands. Treating ideas
which had evolved in France and had never before been expressed
in an English vernacular, he enriched his verse freely with French
words, just as his contemporary, Wycliffe, and the translators of
the Lollard Bible enriched it with Latin. Being a highly original
man, many of these words* Chaucer coined himself.

Yet, great as his contribution to the development of the English
language, his contribution to English literature was far greater. In
his *Troylus and Cryseyde*, whose theme he borrowed from Boccaccio, he wrote not only one of the world's most beautiful love poems,
but created the first living woman character of English fiction. His
Cryseyde was not a mere symbol for woman's virtue or weakness
or a passive object of man's love or desire, like the heroines of the
French romances which were the staple reading of the time, but a
real creature, most delicately compounded of tenderness, sensitivity and timidity. Her tragedy, and her lover's, arose, not from
the operation of fate, but from the reaction of human character to
it and from the liberty of the individual soul to shape its own fate
which was central to the Christian church's creed.

In this, though because of his archaic spelling and language the
full magnitude of his achievement has never been popularly
realised, Chaucer's work ranks with Dante's as the supreme literary
expression of what Christianity had done for the Gothic peoples of
Europe. Out of the tribe and folk – anonymous save for its leaders –
was created in the course of the fourteenth century by an Englishman the literary conception of a separate individual, free to shape
his own character and, through it, his destiny.

In Chaucer's great poem, *The Canterbury Tales*, all his characters are real human beings, drawn from every walk of contemporary
English life. We see them riding through the Kentish countryside,
past the little town 'which the i-clepd is Bob-up-and-Down',
towards the towers of Canterbury and the shrine of 'the holy,
blissful martyr': the big, drunken, boastful miller with his bristly

* Among them *position*, *duration*, *attention*, *fraction*, *diffusion*, which, before the
sixteenth century, can be found nowhere except in his writings.

red beard and the tufted hairs on his nose, noisily playing the bagpipes at the approach to every village; the merry, frank-spoken host of the Tabard Inn who acted as compère and chaffed and cajoled everyone into telling his story; the merchant with his forked beard talking of his winnings, and the gaunt clerk of Oxford so ready to learn and teach; the wanton friar familiar with all the thriving householders along the road and their wives and daughters, and his foe the fiery summoner, with his pimples and garlic-laden breath. Every pilgrim is shown as a complete and separate being, with his or her own idiosyncracies and outlook, though bound together by a common quest.

To each of them, sketched in a few brilliant lines in the Prologue, is given a story to tell so exquisitely in part that it unfolds both the teller's story and his or her own soul. In this Chaucer was wonderfully original; the founder of a completely new form of literature in which characters reveal themselves. Before the first individual commoners emerge from the flat, two-dimensional horizon of recorded history, this unassuming civil servant, with his observant, humorous eye and all-embracing Christian charity, proclaimed their existence and separate identity. The Wife of Bath is as great a historical phenomenon as Thomas à Becket or Robert Bruce, even though in one sense she never existed.

In *The Canterbury Tales*, instead of the conventionalized types of knights and ladies, virtues and vices, which had been the common stock of literature before his time, Chaucer created a whole world of imaginary, yet living, characters drawn from life. In this he was the forerunner of Cervantes and Shakespeare, of the European novel and drama. He portrays the dainty, finicky, ladylike Prioress, Madame Eglentyne, who entuned the services so prettily through her nose and who, as G. K. Chesterton observed, wafts across the ages that 'delicately mingled atmosphere of fuss and refinement' peculiar to the English lady; the rustic reeve from Norfolk, with his cropped head and long, lean legs, who always rode at the tail of the cavalcade and whose talk was of the country:

> 'But I am old; me list not play for age,
> Grass time is done; my fodder is now forage.'

3

the white-bearded franklin, with his red face and love of good fare, who had served so often as sheriff and knight of the shire and in whose house 'it snowed of meat and drink'; and the brave, gentle, modest knight, who had fought all his days for chivalry, truth and honour:

> 'At many a noble landing had he been,
> At mortal battles had he been fifteen,
> And foughten for our faith at Tramassene . . .
> And though that he was as worthy he was wise,
> And of his port as meek as is a maid.
> He never yet no villainy had said
> In all his life unto no manner of wight.
> He was a very parfit gentil knight.'

Yet perhaps the most English of all his characters was Chaucer himself, with his self-deprecating manner, his unassuming elusiveness, his capacity for liking people because they seemed to him rather a joke; his ability to laugh, without being obtrusive, at himself and everyone else. There is something very personal about his poetry; he is always ready for a private aside, as when he apologises to the ladies for Chaunteclere's hard words about them:

> 'These be the cockë's wordë's and not mine,
> I can no harm of no woman divine.'

Or his curious reflection about the next world of which his contemporaries appeared to know so much:

> 'A thousand times I have heard men tell
> That there is joy in Heaven and pain in Hell,
> And I accord right well that it is so.
> And yet indeed full well myself I know
> That there is not a man in this countrie
> That either has in Heaven or Hell y'be.'

Superficially one of the happiest and most cheerful poems in the whole range of literature – a comic epic of a company of English pilgrims setting off on horseback on a spring morning from the

Tabard Inn at Southwark and beguiling the way to Canterbury by telling stories – *The Canterbury Tales* is something more. Into this unfinished masterpiece, this great artist compressed a vision of the world which ranks with that of Dante in its completeness too. Through his knowledge of it, so earthly in his miller or cook, so subtle in his graver characters, he portrays a whole nation of Christian men and women, linked together by a common faith in the all-seeing, all-embracing wisdom of God, binding everything in the universe from the highest to the lowest:

> 'The first Mover of the Cause above,
> When He first made the fairë chain of Love,
> Great was the effect and high was his intent,
> Well wist He why, and what thereof He meant.'

Like nearly all the men of his time Chaucer believed – not unnaturally considering the disasters through which he lived – that the world was declining, and that it was doomed to pass through a series of disasters culminating, sooner or later, in its extinction. Nor was his own life a particularly happy one. Yet his poetry, read in retrospect, is full of the vitality and gaiety of morning; of 'Aprille with his showers sweet' and of 'younge, freshe folkes,' and of a deeply rooted Christian faith transcending all the follies and disasters, however, grave, of existence. The greatest of all his characters, the wide and loud-mouthed Wife of Bath, had taken five husbands to the church door and mastered and buried them all; it tickled about her 'heartë's root' to think that she had had 'her world as in her time.' Yet the youth she looked back upon with such pleasure must have been passed, like Chaucer's own, under the shadow of the great plague which during her lifetime slew one out of every three of her contemporaries.

Chaucer's first and last word is of courage; of taking the world as one finds it, with all its tragedies and imperfections, and making it somehow a fine and brave thing:

> 'That thee is sent, receive in buxomness;
> The wrestling for this world asketh a fall.
> Here is no home, here is but wilderness:

5

Forth, Pilgrim, forth! Forth, beast, out of thy stall!
Know thy countree, look up, thank God of all;
Hold the high way, and let thy ghost thee lead,
And truth shall thee deliver, it is no dread.'

*   *   *

More even than his contemporary Wycliffe challenging the
authority of the universal medieval Church, Chaucer was the first
modern Englishman. A hundred years before private subjects
(other than princes, hereditary lords and prelates) began to figure
in the forefront of history, he foreshadowed, in his pictures of
contemporary life, the emergence of individuals from the anonym-
ity of the royal and ecclesiastical past. Nor, in the aftermath of the
great pestilence which uprooted national society in the second half
of the fourteenth century, was he the only English poet to draw
back the curtain which concealed from posterity the individual
figures of the working multitude that peopled it. Living in a very
different and socially far inferior milieu than that of the well-
placed, privileged author of *The Canterbury Tales*, the poor West
Country chantry clerk William Langland, in his great religious
allegory, *The Vision of William concerning Piers the Plowman*,
gazing out from his visionary viewpoint on the Malvern hills over
a vast 'field full of folk,' makes the whole workaday multitude
among whom he lived and laboured pass before us as separate,
clearly distinguished, men and women, 'bakers, brewers and
butchers, weavers of wool and of linen, tailors, tinkers and tax
collectors, Peter the pardoner, Bertie the beadle of Buckinghamshire, Reginald the reeve of Rutland, and Mumps the miller.'

'Some were putting out to plough, had little play-time,
In setting seed and sowing, sweated at their labour,
Winning wealth that the worthless wasted in gluttony,
Some pranked themselves in pride preciously apparelled,
Coming under colour of costly clothing . . .
Beggars and blackguards went busily about
With their bellies and bags all brimming with bread,
Feigning sick for food and fighting in the ale-house . . .
Cissy the sempstress sat on a bench,

6

Robin the rabbit-catcher and his wife with him,
Tim the tinker and two of his apprentices,
Hickey the hackney-man and Hodge the huckster,
Clarice of Cock's Lane and the clerk of the parish,
Parson Peter Proudie and his Peronella,
Davy the ditcher and a dozen others.
A fiddler, a rat-catcher, a Cheapside crossing-sweeper,
A rope-maker, a road-man and Rosy the dishwasher,
Godfrey the Garlick-hithe and Griffin the Welshman . . .
Jack the juggler and Janet of the stews,
Daniel the dice-player and Denis the bawd.'

Here is the real geneology of the English people who in the reign of the last Tudor queen, Elizabeth, were to challenge entry into the closed seas dominated by the great imperial hierarch, King Philip of Spain, shatter his invincible invading Armada and lay the foundations of an island state which, uniting under a common crown and a reformed religion, carried their love and practise of freedom into every ocean of the world in the course of what, in his great book, *The English Reformation*, Professor A. G. Dickens has called 'those three great centuries during which Britain placed her stamp upon world history.'

*   *   *

Hitherto, as I have described in the first volume of this *History*, English history had been shaped by a succession of achievement of Alfred of Wessex and his atheling successors, had made the Anglo-Saxon and Danish realm of Canute and the Confessor the best-governed kingdom in Christendom. The stark Norman Conqueror, his son Henry I – 'the Lion of Justice' – and his Angevin great-grandson, Henry II, who established the rule of law and the supremacy of the royal courts; Edward I, conqueror of Wales and creator of the continuing place in the realm of representative Parliaments; his grandson, Edward III, victor of Crécy and founder of the Order of the Garter; and the warrior heroes, Coeur de Lion and the Black Prince – all left behind them institutions or traditions which were to continue to shape the English future.

7

Yet there was one more occasion – perhaps the most memorable of all – when the grey goose feather wrought out of seeming-certain defeat a miraculous English victory. It happened in 1415, sixteen years after Richard II was dethroned in favour of his Lancastrian cousin, Henry Bolingbroke, and when, on the grounds that Richard had broken the fundamental laws of the realm, a Parliament conferred the Crown on his supplanter and cousin who was not the hereditary heir. But in doing so it did not end further conflict, for no sooner had Henry IV ascended the throne than the magnates, who had helped to put him there, intrigued against him as they had done against his predecessor. In 1403, after defeating a Scottish invasion backed by France, the Lancastrian king was faced by a formidable rebel coalition led by his former chief supporter, Henry Percy, earl of Northumberland, allied with the Scots nobles the latter had captured and a Welsh patriot leader, Owen Glendower, who, taking advantage of England's dynastic divisions, had raised most of the Principality against him. With the help, however, of his sixteen-year-old son and heir, Henry of Monmouth – 'Prince Hal' – the King defeated the insurgents at the Battle of Shrewsbury, where Northumberland's famous warrior son, Harry Hotspur, was killed. But it took Henry five more years to reduce the warlike North, while his son and heir restored peace to an insurgent Wales. It was in fighting Glendower and the Welsh tribesmen that the young prince learnt the business of war, mastering the arts of training, discipline and supply, and winning the confidence of his rough men and archers.

Succeeding, on his father's death in 1413, at the age of twenty-five to a doubtful title and a debt-ridden realm, Henry V had to defend his capital from an attempt to overthrow his rule within weeks of his accession. He suppressed the insurrection with inexorable resolution. Nor was he only bent on restoring the authority of the Crown at home. To enforce his rights abroad and unite his people behind him, he laid claim to the vast Aquitaine dominions ceded to his great-grandfather, Edward III, by the Treaty of Bretigny, or, in default, to the crown of France itself, derived, as he maintained, from his great-great-grandmother, Edward II's queen, Isabella. A soldier of genius, chaste, fearless and passionate for justice – or for what he considered justice – he was ruthless in enforcing his kingly rights and obedience to his will. His vision was intense, but narrow and backward-looking; he thought in terms of the vanished conquests of Edward III and Henry of Lancaster, and of a still older ideal – for he was a devout, even fanatic, Christian – of the Crusade to free the Holy Land.

By the summer of 1415 everything was ready for his venture. The crown jewels and the vestments from the Chapel Royal had all been pawned to pay for it. Sailing from Portsmouth with a small professional army, he landed on August 15th on the north shore of the Seine estuary and, after five weeks, stormed and captured the fortress of Harfleur, intending to make it an English town as his great-grandfather had made Calais. By now he had lost a third of his little force from dysentry. Leaving 2,600 of the remainder to garrison the captured town, he set out on October 8th with less than 6,000 men – five-sixths of them archers – along the Norman coast to Calais, 160 miles to the north, intending to cross the Somme by the submerged ford at Blanchtaque which Edward III had used before Crécy. But, finding that a French force had forestalled him on the far bank, he was forced to make a long detour almost to the headwaters of the river before he could find an unguarded passage.

Resuming his northward march across the downlands, where five centuries later so many of his countrymen were to die in the Battle of the Somme, on October 24th he found his path barred by an enormous French army, at least four times the size of his own. So certain did the destruction of his little force seem that, on the morrow – St Crispin's Day – the French leaders, who had spent the night dicing for the ransoms they expected to win the next day, made no haste to attack, expecting the trapped invaders to surrender as the only alternative to starvation or annihilation. Worn out after their march of 250 miles in 17 days, and with their rations almost exhausted, few of the English and Welsh – of whom there were many in that little band of fighting men – expected to live another day. Yet, as they moved silently through the soaking night to their battle stations, all were animated by their leader's unifying resolve.

9

At eleven o'clock in the morning as the French, confident of an English surrender, did not trouble to attack, the indomitable king gave the order, 'Advance Banner'. Leading his handful of dismounted knights and men-at-arms forward in three divisions, he directed the archers, behind their protective barriers of stakes, to open covering fire. Then, as the massed French cavalry bore down on them in a tumultuous and precipitous counter-attack, another vast host of French knights on foot, marching in dense columns towards the advancing English, seemed about to engulf and overwhelm them by sheer weight of numbers.

Once more, certain of victory, the French went down under that blinding hail of arrows. Since Crécy and Poitiers massive protective armour-plate had taken the place of the lighter armour of the past, leaving the horses – more vulnerable than their riders – to take the full force of the storm of winged death. Plunging wildly, and pressing together, as at Halidon Hill, into the narrowing funnel between the flanking salients of archers, horsemen and footmen alike were flung to the ground and suffocated, unable to move in their heavy cages of steel as they slithered and writhed together on the miry, rain-soaked ground. Their bodies quickly formed the base of an ever-rising wall of dead, wounded and dying men and horses, as each new wave of attackers, meeting the same fate, piled up on top of their predecessors.

It was the King who ended the impasse by ordering the archers, who had now exhausted their sheaves of arrows, to throw aside their bows and, with dagger, mallet and sword, reinforce the battle-axes of their fellow knights and men-at-arms in hacking a way through that huge rising wall of living and dying men and horses. For nearly three hours they were engaged in prising open helmets and knocking, hammering and unriveting plate-armour, consigning their prone and helpless wearers, if still alive, either to ransom or immediate death.*

By three o'clock in the afternoon the fighting ceased, and what remained of the French army scattered and faded into the October

---

* Among them was the duke of York, the nearest Yorkist heir to the usurped throne, who, fighting in the front line of English knights, lost his balance, slipped and was suffocated.

landscape. The English way to Calais was now wide open. Close on ten thousand Frenchmen lay dead on the field, including the Constable of France and three dukes. Among the prisoners were the Commander-in-Chief, Charles d'Albret, and the dukes of Orléans and Bourbon. When, a month later, the young victor – whose resolution and the news of whose triumph had united England – returned to his capital, he was met on Blackheath by the Mayor and Alderman of London in their robes of scarlet and white, at the head of 20,000 mounted citizens bearing the banners and devices of their guilds and trades. Escorted, amid pealing bells and chanting choirs, through streets filled with painted towers and pavilions and windows hung with cloth of gold, to St. Paul's, where a victory Te Deum was sung, it was characteristic of the grave young King, that, ascribing all the glory to God, he refused to don the dented armour and broken crown of gold he had worn on the battlefield. The splendour of that far day of triumph still comes down to us in the words and music of the Agincourt Song, written in his honour:

'Our King went forth to Normandy,
With grace and might of chivalry:
There God for him wrought marv'lously,
Wherefore England may call and cry,
    Deo gratias.

'Their dukes and earls, lords and baron,
Were taken and slain and that well soon,
And some were led into London,
With joy and mirth and great renown.
    Deo gratias.'

Two years later Henry returned to France. This time it was no cut-and-run raid to re-temper the blunted sword and spirit of England, but a carefully planned scheme of conquest. Laying siege systematically to every city of Normandy in turn, by January 1419 he had starved its capital, Rouen, into surrender. Then, having used the prestige of Agincourt to make an alliance with the greatest of the French king's vassals, the duke of Burgundy – lord of the rich cloth-manufacturing towns of Flanders, Artois and

Brabant – he demanded the French crown and, by a treaty negotiated at Troyes in 1420, secured the hand of the mad King of France's daughter and the right to rule his kingdom as Regent until he or the heir born to him by her should succeed to the French crown. With his victorious troops and his Burgundian allies driving the disinherited Dauphin's defeated and dispirited forces beyond the Loire, and with Paris in his hands, by 1421 all Henry's objectives seemed achieved. A year later the Lancastrian hero-king, still only thirty-five, was dead, worn out by dysentry and the continuous hardships of his campaigns.

For in the second half of the fourteenth century had come a rapid decline in the English kingdom's political power and cohesion, only temporarily arrested by Henry V's miraculous but anachronistic victory of Agincourt, his conquest of Normandy and marriage to the heiress of France. Within three decades of his death in 1422, with the final loss of all the country's conquests except Calais, and the outbreak in 1455 of the dynastic 'Wars of the Roses', the England of the royal Plantagenets 'that was wont to conquer others' had made a shameful conquest of itself, sinking into nadir of civil strife superficially reminiscent of the 'nineteen long winters' of Stephen's reign three centuries before.

Yet, unlike earlier internecine wars, the Wars of the Roses involved comparatively little interference with the lives of ordinary Englishmen. A matter of life or death to the great dynastic princes, the feudal lords and their armed retainers who precipitated and waged them, they were of no direct concern to the merchant at his counter, the stapler with his woolpack, the shipman in his boat and the husbandman in the field, unless by ill chance the latter's timber and clay shack happened to lie in the line of march of one of the little armies – Yorkist or Lancastrian – contending for the throne or on the site of one of their battles. By now ordinary Englishmen had already evolved a life of their own independent of the actions of princes and prelates.

For by the fifteenth century the division of medieval society into two rigidly separated classes was ceasing to exist in England. No longer was her population divided – as elsewhere in medieval Christendom outside the trading and manufacturing cities of

Italy and Flanders – into an armed, French-speaking, feudal and knightly ruling minority and a subordinate, servile and unarmed dialect-speaking rustic majority tilling the soil, and linked only by their allegiance to the Crown and to a common Christian faith expounded in Latin and administered by a Rome-directed priest-hood. For England's astonishing victories during the second quarter of the fourteenth century, over the feudal armies of a France with three times her population, had been due to the presence in her armies of growing numbers of rustic yeoman archers of humble birth and native Anglo-Saxon descent armed with a weapon which, demanding a high degree of skill and bodily expertise, they alone could wield. Drilled, disciplined and directed by such great commanders as Henry of Grossmont, Edward III and the Black Prince, they had proved themselves capable, in victory after victory, of shooting out of the field and annihilating the largest, most strongly-armoured and mounted knightly hosts in western Christendom. Fighting without armour side by side with dis-mounted lords and knights, they had even come by the time of Agincourt to constitute more than three quarters of England's field armies.

No Englishman, whatever his birth, who fought in those victorious bands could any longer think of himself, or be thought of, as servile. As Shakespeare, paraphrasing Henry V's speech before Agincourt, was to put it:

> 'For he today that sheds his blood with me
> Shall be my brother, be he ne'er so vile
> This day shall gentle his condition.'

And when, a generation after Crécy and Poitiers and a generation before Agincourt, two peasant armies from Essex and Kent rose against their knightly and ecclesiastical landlords and seized possession of the capital and Tower, their ranks must have included hundreds of bowmen who had fought, or whose fathers and sons had fought or were to fight, in these astonishing victories, and had learnt their hereditary skill at the archery butts after Sunday church in their native villages.

Even more had the relationship between feudal landlord and labouring serf been transformed by the devastating waves of bubonic plague which, between its first terrible onslaught in 1348/9 and the end of the century, almost halved the population of England, giving the worker of the land a temporary economic advantage as revolutionary, if less spectacular, as that won on the battlefield over France's knightly chivalry. For instead of there being a rising peasant population in need of land and subsistence, after the depopulation caused by the great plagues, the feudal owners of land could no longer dictate terms to its cultivators and were forced instead to offer anyone able and willing to till their otherwise useless land whatever conditions for doing so they chose to ask. It had been the attempt of a Parliament of landlords, by such legal enactments as the Statute of Labourers of 1349, to halt the liberating tide and enforce the continuance of serfdom which precipitated the Peasants' Revolt of thirty years later and cost many a lawyer – the landlord's hated agent – his life. Nor did the suppression of the rebellion, and the government's repudiation of the charters of freedom which it had been forced to grant in its hour of peril, halt the steady erosion of serfdom. For, continuing at an ever-quickening pace, as suited the interests both of the owners and cultivators of the half-empty, plague-depopulated land, villeinage was everywhere being replaced by a yeoman class of farmers and husbandmen who held their land, if not by a freehold or leasehold protected the Common Law courts – whose bias always ultimately tended to favour greater freedom – or by what was called copyhold, whose prescriptive rights were evidenced by copies of the entries in the rolls of the manorial courts, which themselves gradually came within the cognizance and protection of the Common Law.

It was not only in the lower reaches of English society that serfs were turning into yeomen, but far higher up the social scale. During the fourteenth and fifteenth centuries the proud ranks of the feudal nobility were continually being breached by newcomers of formerly ignoble descent – rich city merchants, judges and minor royal functionaries, and successive generations of franklins extending their estates by prudent and gainful marriages. As we have seen, the son of the favourite poet of the court of Richard II, Geoffrey Chaucer, himself the son of Edward III's wine merchant, served three times as Speaker of the House of Commons in the reigns of Henry IV and V, and fought by the latter's side at Agincourt, while his grand-daughter became by marriage first a countess and later a duchess. England was becoming a land where individuals, rising out of the common mass, could make a mark for themselves, while the mass itself was little by little varying and bettering its condition.

Though for eighteen more years after Henry V's death the English in France struggled to retain what they had won, they had been fatally handicapped by their lack of numbers and the growing inadequacy of their financial resources. They were even more fatally handicapped by the indiscipline of their soldiers. Henry V had hanged every plunderer, forbidden offences against women and monks, and even forced his troops to mix water with their wine; and, such was the terror instilled by this inflexible man, that he was obeyed. But once his hand was withdrawn the little army of occupation made the name of England stink in every French nostril. And when in 1429 an inspired French peasant girl of faith and genius miraculously breathed a new spirit into the defeated chivalry and manhood of France, every Frenchman felt that the war of national independence was his own cause. Though Joan of Arc was betrayed to the English and burnt as a heretic, five years after her martyrdom the Burgundians repudiated the English alliance to throw in their lot with their fellow Frenchmen. With the defeat and surrender at Castellon in 1453 of the last English force still fighting in France, a discredited government, bankrupt and exhausted, accepted the *fait accompli* and made peace. It did not end the fighting. It merely transferred it to England, with Englishman fighting Englishman.

For it was not only in France that the English had lost the habit of feeling and acting together in national matters which their long line of kings had given them. They had lost it at home, and with it the unity Henry V had temporarily restored. During the long minority of his weak-minded infant son Henry VI, the magnates, including the King's kinsmen, contended against one another and plundered the Crown. Judges and juries refused to convict the strong; elections were fought by rival lords and knights with the help of armed mobs; and those who offended the great were hunted down by gangs of murderers in their employers' livery. 'Get you lordship,' a country squire was advised, 'hereon hangs all the law and the prophets.'

Nor did matters improve after the young king came of age. He had inherited his father's piety and love of the Church, but none of his ruthlessness or strength of will. A gentle, saintly, yielding creature, of touching selflessness and humility, he was powerless in the hands of whoever of his relations or counsellors had access to him. Faced by the necessities and cruelties of an iron age, with all England's remaining possessions in France lost save Calais, and with his Lancastrian and Yorkist kinsmen contending openly after 1455 – first for the administration of the realm, and ultimately for the Crown itself – his feeble reason failed and he became, first temporarily, and then permanently, insane.

Yet before his warlike French queen, Margaret of Anjou, and her Lancastrian adherents were finally defeated by the better led and more substantially supported Yorkists, and Henry himself was supplanted on the throne in 1461 by his young warrior cousin, Edward of York, the hapless King, in the chaos of his time, bestowed on his country something at least which was to endure – the twin educational foundations of King's College, Cambridge, and its sister college, the King's College of Our Lady of Eton – where his gentle name is still held in remembrance.

'Here in his realm a realm to found
Where he might stand for ever crown'd.'

*　　*　　*

Henry VI's Yorkist supplanter Edward IV was the son of Richard duke of York, whose own father, a grandson of Edward III, had been beheaded for treason against Henry V before Agincourt. Richard of York himself had been not only the richest magnate in England, but, until the unexpected birth of a son to Henry VI in

1453, Heir Presumptive. He was also, as the eldest descendent through the distaff of Lionel of Clarence, the 'legitimate' heir of the pre-Lancastrian Plantagenets. After making himself, by a display of force, Regent of poor, pious Henry VI's chaotic England, and later claiming the throne by 'right of descent' – this proud, demanding prince, in the winter of 1460–1, suffered defeat and death at the Battle of Wakefield at the hands of the Lancastrians. But his nineteen-year-old son, Edward, with the powerful help of his cousin, the great north country magnate, Richard Neville, earl of Warwick, secured possession of London and had himself proclaimed King. Later that year he avenged at Towton the Lancastrian victories of Wakefield and St. Albans, and forced Henry and Margaret to seek refuge in Scotland.

For nearly a decade, with growing success, Edward IV governed England which, though it had been passively loyal to the Lancastrian line, welcomed his strong rule and restoration of public order. In 1465 his rival, the crazed, devout, fugitive Henry, was captured in the northern wilds and exhibited as a public spectacle before being incarcerated in the Tower. The young Yorkist king was a magnificent-looking man, nearly six feet four tall, strong, vigorous, handsome and amorous, with princely charm which won the hearts of men and women. His success with the latter all but proved his undoing, for at the age of twenty-two he bitterly offended his most powerful supporter, the earl of Warwick – then engaged in negotiating a marriage for him with the French king's sister-in-law – by secretly marrying the widow of a Lancastrian knight, Elizabeth Lady Grey. The subsequent elevation of this beautiful woman's Woodville relations so enraged Warwick that in 1469 he entered into an unnatural alliance with the King's treacherous brother, the duke of Clarence, and the exiled Lancastrians under Queen Margaret. For a short time 'the King Maker, as this ambitious dynast was called, drove Edward from the throne and set up in his place the imbecile Henry, resurrected from his Tower cell. But Edward, a brilliant soldier, returned to England early in 1471 with the help of his brother-in-law, the duke of Burgundy, and routed, first Warwick, at Barnet, and then, at Tewkesbury, Queen Margaret and her young son whom he put to death after his victory.

For the next twelve years Edward IV reigned without opposition. An excellent administrator and man of business, he was particularly popular with the trading classes of London to whom the murderous dynastic struggles of the nobility and rival royal houses meant nothing compared with the maintenance of peace and law. Even the nostalgic English desire for revenge against France he shrewdly turned to his own and his kingdom's financial advantage, raising in 1474–5 in conjunction with his ally, the duke of Burgundy, a powerful invading army and then, instead of embarking on another long, ruinous war like his Lancastrian predecessors, accepting from the French king, in return for his peaceful return to England with his army, a payment of 75,000 gold crowns and a pension for life.

Edward, who kept great royal state, was a cultured patron of the arts, like his magnificent brother-in-law. It was while residing in the latter's dominions, that a London mercer named William Caxton became interested in the new German and Dutch technique of reproducing books by printing. Born in the year of Henry V's death of Kentish yeoman stock and apprenticed at sixteen to a London mercer who served as Lord Mayor, he was a member of the richest of the great city merchant Companies, the Mercers, who, with the Grocers, Drapers, Fishmongers and Goldsmiths, virtually ruled the economic life of the capital and, throughout the fifteenth century, provided most of the occupants of the civic chair and aldermanic bench. Pursuing his highly profitable trade in the Low Countries and domiciled for thirty years at Bruges, he was *persona grata* at the rich cultured Burgundian court. Serving there as governor of a branch of the Company of Merchant Adventurers – founded in 1462 to market the country's growing export of manufactured cloth, which was now beginning to rival that of the raw wool which had long been England's staple commodity – he was a man of keen literary tastes and a typical representative of the new educated class of rising laymen who had broken the Church's age-long monopoly of learning. Translator into English of two French romances, to further his literary hobby he had studied at Bruges and Cologne the newly invented techniques or 'mystery' of reproducing manuscripts from movable types, and in 1474–5 printed two of his own translations – the first books ever to be printed into English. On his retirement from business two years later he brought his printing press to England. Setting it up in the precincts of Westminster Abbey, during the last fourteen years of his life he printed under royal patronage, with wonderful enthusiasm and assiduity, nearly eighty English books, including *The Canterbury Tales* and other works by Chaucer. When he died in 1491 he left behind him a means – whose possibilities were as yet unguessed at – of revolutionizing his countrymen's beliefs and ideas.

*   *   *

In 1483, prematurely worn out, it was believed, by his amorous excesses, Edward IV died of a fever at the age of forty, and the Crown descended to his twelve-year-old son, Edward V. This sensitive, intelligent boy, who had been living at Ludlow under the care of his Woodville uncle, Earl Rivers, while on his way to London to join his mother, fell in with the two greatest magnates of the realm – also on their way to London – his father's brother, Richard duke of Gloucester 'the King's lieutenant in the North', and the duke of Buckingham. Both, being of royal blood, detested the Queen Mother and her upstart Woodville relations and were determined to wrest the young king from their charge. Gloucester, Edward IV's last surviving brother – for Clarence, attainted for treason, had perished in the Tower – had none of the dead king's flamboyant bonhomie, and was small, introvert, secretive and austere. But he had the same administrative and military skill and courage, and was universally regarded as loyal and trustworthy. He had made himself highly popular in the wild and formerly Lancastrian North, whose warlike folk he had won over by his firm, but just, rule. Like them, he was reputed to be ruthless and was even said by some – probably wrongly – to have murdered Henry VI with his own hands, when in the Tower with him on the night of that saintly king's death.

This reputation Gloucester now enhanced by summarily

arresting, and sending to his northern fastness of Pontefract for subsequent execution, the young King's uncle, Rivers, his half-brother, Lord Richard Grey, and his Chamberlain, Sir Thomas Vaughan. Then, with his royal nephew a virtual prisoner, he marched on London, which he and Buckingham entered on May 4th 1483, four weeks after Edward IV's death, causing the Queen Mother with her daughters and younger son, the nine-year-old duke of York, to seek sanctuary in the Abbey. At a meeting of the Council Richard then had himself confirmed Protector, Defender of the Realm and Guardian of the King's person.

So far his high-handed proceedings had met with popular approval. For the Woodvilles were much disliked, and Gloucester seemed far better qualified by his rank and experience to rule during the King's minority than anyone else. But it soon appeared that it was not only the Woodvilles of whom he wished to be rid. On June 13th, nine days before the day fixed for the young King's coronation, at a Council meeting in the Tower Richard arrested and had summarily beheaded, without trial, his best friend and his dead brother's most trusted adviser, Lord Hastings. Then, having employed a pliant archbishop of Canterbury to persuade the Queen Mother to allow the little duke of York to leave sanctuary and join his brother in the Tower, he proceeded to bastardize both brothers by circulating stories that the late king had biga-mously married the queen and was even himself illegitimate, thereby casting a slur on his own mother, who was still living.

With the help of his ally Buckingham and a number of suborned London preachers, having thus represented himself as the sole remaining legitimate representative of the House of York, on June 26th Richard rode to Westminster Hall and took possession of the throne in the Court of King's Bench. Then, backed by an armed force from the wild north, he was crowned King on July 6th. So what little there was of the boy Edward V's brief reign was spent in the grim old Tower which William the Conqueror had first raised four centuries before. Nor were he and his brother ever to leave it. For a short while they could be glimpsed by passers-by, playing in the garden; then they disappeared into its inner recesses and were never seen again.

Soon after his coronation Richard III went on progress to settle his usurped kingdom. From Warwick that August, according to Sir Thomas More – who in his youth had known some of the chief actors in Richard's reign – he despatched one of his henchmen, Sir James Tyrell, to the Governor of the Tower with orders to deliver its keys to him for twenty-four hours. During that time, it was said, two ruffians smothered the royal children and buried them 'at the stair foot . . . under a heap of stones.' The account is open to some doubt, but in 1674, two centuries later, during alterations at the Tower, the skeletons of two boys were found lying on top of one another in this very place. What is certain is that, in the autumn of 1483, ugly rumours began to circulate in both England and France that the princes had been done to death.

If their murder was at Richard's orders, as was widely believed at the time, this otherwise able and astute king had committed, not only a shocking crime, but a major political blunder. For though, after thirty years of spasmodic civil war, Englishmen had grown accustomed to their rulers slaughtering one another, the murder of innocent children was something which they could not stomach. For the rest of Richard's brief reign his very real ability was bedevilled by the horror and distrust which the princes' disappearance had aroused, and which he could easily have dispelled had he only been able to produce them – the one thing he had apparently precluded himself from doing. So disastrous was the effect of his inability to do so that he had to face the enmity, not only of the Lancastrians, but of his fellow Yorkists. Before the autumn was out, he was confronted by a rising in all the southern counties from Kent to Cornwall. The Woodvilles and Courtenays, the Yorkist bishop of Salisbury, and the Lancastrian bishops of Exeter and Ely all took part in it. At the end of September they were joined by Richard's former fellow-conspirator, the duke of Buckingham, who declared himself, not for the displaced boy king he had helped to dethrone but who was now presumed dead, but for the heir of the Lancastrian Beauforts, Henry Tudor, earl of Richmond – an almost unknown twenty-six-year-old Welshman living in exile in Brittany – to whom an invitation to assume the throne was now sent in the name of both Yorkists and Lancastrians.

Yet Richard III, who never lacked courage, was a formidable opponent. That October, while unprecedented floods prevented the rebels from joining forces, with accustomed speed and daring he struck down each of his adversaries in turn. Buckingham was executed in Salisbury market-place, and for twenty more uneasy months Richard enjoyed a reprieve. But though he showed himself a generous, munificent and most capable ruler, nothing went right for him. In the spring of 1484, his only son died; in that of 1485 his queen. That summer some doggerel lines on his hated lieutenants, Catesby, Ratcliffe and Lovell, and his own heraldic congnizance of the Wild Boar, circulated through the country like wildfire.

'The Cat, the Rat and Lovell our dog
Ruleth all England under a Hog.'

Early in August 1485 the long-awaited Henry of Richmond landed in Wales with a tiny force, which was enthusiastically reinforced by his fellow Welshmen before marching into England. Before the month was up, though the royal army still out-numbered the invader's by two to one, Richard, fighting desperately, met his death on Bosworth Field while half his troops stood idly by or changed sides during the battle because they and their leaders refused to fight for a man they believed had murdered a helpless child, his own liege lord and brother's heir, whom he had sworn to protect. That night, tradition has it, the dead king's crown was picked up from the thorn bush where it had fallen and set upon Henry Tudor's head.

*   *   *

In thirty years that crown had been forcibly seized no fewer than five times, twice by a Yorkist from a Lancastrian, twice by a Lancastrian from a Yorkist, and once by a Yorkist from a Yorkist. Of four successive English kings all but one had died from violence. And throughout the fifteenth century, ever since the dethronement of Richard II, the succession had remained in dispute and no-one could feel sure who the next wearer of the Crown would be. This state of affairs now ended – though no-one realised it at the time – with Henry VII's accession. No king of England ever had a weaker hereditary claim to the throne. Yet he remained on it for nearly a quarter of a century, defeating, with very little bloodshed, every attempt to dethrone him, without the help of either a standing army or police force save for his private, and partly Welsh, household Yeoman of the Guard and Chamber.

First of the Tudor dynasty, Henry VII was perhaps the cleverest, and certainly the hardest-working, monarch ever to sit on the English throne. He started his reign heavily in debt and ended it, long after he had repaid all his creditors, richer than any king before him. He used his wealth, so industriously accumulated and carefully husbanded – for he audited and signed almost every page of his accounts himself – to restore the broken royal power and free it from incumbrances and restraints. To end the tyranny of 'the overmighty subject', especially the overmighty subject with royal blood in his veins who had been the bane of England during the Wars of the Roses, Henry invested the Crown with a new mystique, setting it in lonely majesty as a thing apart from every subject, even the highest. With only one duke and one marquis left after the holocausts and attainders of the Wars of the Roses, he chose his councillors mostly from new men who depended solely on himself, and used his Council, the Court of Star Chamber and the regional Councils of the Marches and North, to discipline the rich and powerful who employed their wealth and power to pervert the course of justice. Under these courts he governed an England, long used to turbulance, through the unpaid local magistracy drawn from the landed gentry, which Edward I had created two centuries earlier and on which, by successive Commissions of the Peace, Henry laid ever-increasing burdens.

His reign was the last of the English Middle Ages. It saw the building of many splendid Perpendicular churches in the country's new cloth-making regions, and the final flowering of its Gothic ecclesiastical architecture. The noblest of all were Henry's two royal foundations – for, like all the Lancastrian Kings, he was devout and orthodox – of the magnificent chantry chapel in West-

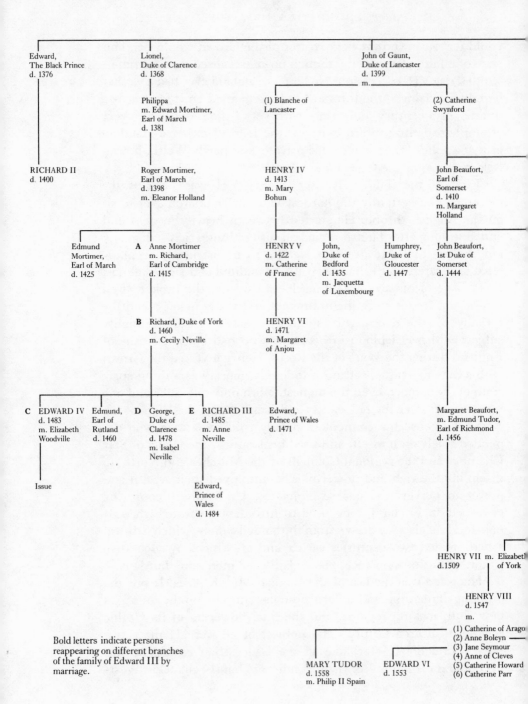

Edward,
The Black Prince
d. 1376

Lionel,
Duke of Clarence
d. 1368

Philippa
m. Edward Mortimer,
Earl of March
d. 1381

John of Gaunt,
Duke of Lancaster
d. 1399
m.

(1) Blanche of
Lancaster

(2) Catherine
Swynford

RICHARD II
d. 1400

Roger Mortimer,
Earl of March
d. 1398
m. Eleanor Holland

HENRY IV
d. 1413
m. Mary
Bohun

John Beaufort,
Earl of
Somerset
d. 1410
m. Margaret
Holland

Edmund
Mortimer,
Earl of March
d. 1425

A Anne Mortimer
m. Richard,
Earl of Cambridge
d. 1415

HENRY V
d. 1422
m. Catherine
of France

John,
Duke of
Bedford
d. 1435
m. Jacquetta
of Luxembourg

Humphrey,
Duke of
Gloucester
d. 1447

John Beaufort,
1st Duke of
Somerset
d. 1444

B Richard, Duke of York
d. 1460
m. Cecily Neville

HENRY VI
d. 1471
m. Margaret
of Anjou

C EDWARD IV
d. 1483
m. Elizabeth
Woodville

Edmund,
Earl of
Rutland
d. 1460

D George,
Duke of
Clarence
d. 1478
m. Isabel
Neville

E RICHARD III
d. 1485
m. Anne
Neville

Edward,
Prince of Wales
d. 1471

Margaret Beaufort,
m. Edmund Tudor,
Earl of Richmond
d. 1456

Issue

Edward,
Prince of
Wales
d. 1484

HENRY VII m. Elizabeth
d.1509   of York

HENRY VIII
d. 1547
m.

Bold letters indicate persons
reappearing on different branches
of the family of Edward III by
marriage.

(1) Catherine of Aragon
(2) Anne Boleyn
(3) Jane Seymour
(4) Anne of Cleves
(5) Catherine Howard
(6) Catherine Parr

MARY TUDOR
d. 1558
m. Philip II Spain

EDWARD VI
d. 1553

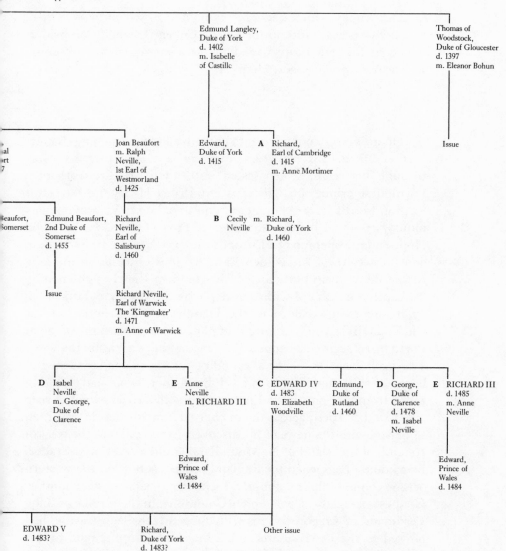

RD III m. Philippa of Hainault

Edmund Langley,
Duke of York
d. 1402
m. Isabelle
of Castille

Thomas of
Woodstock,
Duke of Gloucester
d. 1397
m. Eleanor Bohun

al
rt
7

Joan Beaufort
m. Ralph
Neville,
1st Earl of
Westmorland
d. 1425

Edward,
Duke of York
d. 1415

A Richard,
Earl of Cambridge
d. 1415
m. Anne Mortimer

Issue

Beaufort,
Somerset

Edmund Beaufort,
2nd Duke of
Somerset
d. 1455

Richard
Neville,
Earl of
Salisbury
d. 1460

B Cecily m. Richard,
Neville Duke of York
d. 1460

Issue

Richard Neville,
Earl of Warwick
The 'Kingmaker'
d. 1471
m. Anne of Warwick

D Isabel
Neville
m. George,
Duke of
Clarence

E Anne
Neville
m. RICHARD III

C EDWARD IV
d. 1483
m. Elizabeth
Woodville

Edmund,
Duke of
Rutland
d. 1460

D George,
Duke of
Clarence
d. 1478
m. Isabel
Neville

E RICHARD III
d. 1485
m. Anne
Neville

Edward,
Prince of
Wales
d. 1484

Edward,
Prince of
Wales
d. 1484

EDWARD V
d. 1483?

Richard,
Duke of York
d. 1483?

Other issue

THE ENGLISH MONARCHY
FROM EDWARD III TO ELIZABETH I

ZABETH I
503

minster Abbey which bears his name and in which he is buried, and the wonderful interior of King's College Chapel, Cambridge, which in his will he provided for as a memorial to his saintly Lancastrian predecessor, Henry VI.

*   *   *

Henry's reign coincided with immense and far-reaching changes further afield. Twelve years after his accession and half way through his reign, which lasted until 1509, the life-work of a Portuguese prince of English descent, Prince Henry the Navigator – a grandson of John of Gaunt and cousin of Henry V – was posthumously crowned by the rounding in 1497 of the Cape of Good Hope and the opening of a European sea-route to the Indian Ocean and the wealth of the golden East. By thus outflanking the centuries-old Moslem blockade of Christendom – lately tightened by the capture in 1453 of Constantinople by the Ottoman Turks and, by it and their advance to the Danube the destruction of the Christian Byzantine Empire completed – a generation of great Portuguese seamen changed the fate of the world. In the same year as Vasco da Gama's rounding of the Cape, a Genoese-born Bristol merchant named John Cabot, who had recently sailed from that port in an English ship with a royal patent to seek a way to the Orient across the uncharted North Atlantic, returned to Bristol with the news of his discovery, 3000 miles to the west of Ireland, of the island of Newfoundland and the coast of Labrador. By so doing he opened for England prospects beyond the western ocean comparable to those which five years earlier another Genoese navigator, Christopher Columbus, in the service of King Ferdinand of Aragon and his wife, Queen Isabella of Castile, had offered to the newly-united crusading kingdom of Spain by his discovery of the West Indies. In the same year John Colet, pioneer in England of the new humanistic or Renaissance scholarship brought by Greek scholars from captured Byzantium, returned from Italy to deliver his germinative Oxford lectures on St. Paul's Epistle to the Romans a generation before the German monk, Martin Luther, based on the same text his revolutionary doctrine of Justification by Faith alone which lay at the core of the Protestant Reformation.

In a famous passage in his Tudor *History of England* the Victorian historian, J. A. Froude, wrote of that dawn of new horizons for western man and of the mental and imaginative gulf so created between ourselves and our medieval ancestors.

'A change was coming upon the world, the meaning and direction of which even still is hidden from us, a change from era to era. The paths trodden by the footsteps of ages were broken up; old things were passing away, and the faith and the life of ten centuries were dissolving like a dream. Chivalry was dying; the abbey and the castle were soon to crumble into ruins; and all the forms, desires, beliefs, convictions of the old world were passing away, never to return. A new continent had risen up beyond the western sea. The floor of heaven, inlaid with stars, had sunk back into an infinite abyss of immeasurable space; and the firm earth itself unfixed from its foundations, was seen to be but a small atom in the awful vastness of the universe. In the fabric of habit in which they had so laboriously built for themselves, mankind were to remain no longer.

'And now it is all gone – like an unsubstantial pageant faded; and between us and the old English there lies a gulf of mystery which the prose of the historian will never adequately bridge. They cannot come to us, and our imagination can but feebly penetrate to them. Only among the aisles of the cathedral, only as we gaze upon their silent figures sleeping on their tombs, some faint conceptions float before us of what these men were when they were alive; and perhaps in the sound of church bells, that peculiar creation of medieval age, which falls upon the ear like the echo of a vanished world.'

Since Froude wrote, during our own century a succession of great English scholars have dispersed the mists and broken down the mental barriers which had partly concealed from modern minds those of our medieval ancestors and their enduring contribution to the institutions, laws and beliefs which still govern our polity today. Yet, in another and very real sense, the reign of Henry VII was a watershed between one age and a very different one in which the impact of England's institutions and beliefs ceased to be merely domestic and became global. Another and greater historian, my master G. M. Trevelyan, writing his *History of England* sixty years ago, and summarizing the changes which followed the Black Death and Hundred Years War, foreshadowed the new age to come.

> 'In the fifteenth century we see all the conditions of medieval society silently dissolving, sure prelude to the coming revolution. The villain is achieving his emancipation under a new economic order. New middle classes in town and country are thrusting themselves between lord and serf, the two isolated pillars of the old feudal structure. Commerce and manufacturing are growing with the cloth trade and are bursting the boundaries of medieval borough and guild. Laymen are becoming learned and thinking for themselves. Caxton's press is replacing the monastic scribe. The longbow of the English yeoman can stop the charge of the feudal knight, and the King's cannon can breach his donjon wall. As climax to all these profound changes, slowly at work through many passing generations, the mist is suddenly rolled back one day off the Atlantic waves, revealing new worlds beyond the ocean. England, it seems, is no longer at the extreme verge of all things, but is their maritime heart and centre.'

The story to follow is of how, finding a new faith and impetus from the hitherto forbidden translated and printed Scriptures, individual Englishmen and their fellow Britons who later became joined with them in their island polity, sought a new destiny for themselves on the oceans, and of how their pursuit of that destiny during the coming centuries left its mark on a wider world.

CHAPTER TWO

The Tudor Monarchy

'For Harry our King
Is gone hunting
To bring his deer to bay.'
Old Song

WHERE HENRY VII WAS CIRCUMSPECT, secretive, parsimonious and
unceasingly industrious, his son Henry VIII was an extrovert,
bursting with self-confidence, extravagant and avid for pleasure.
Succeeding to the throne at eighteen, he was a superlatively handsome, accomplished, and at first immensely popular Renaissance
prince.

Longing to shine, he at once started to spend his father's
accumulated treasure by engaging in costly foreign adventures,
including war with France. Against the latter's allies, the Scots,
whose king, James IV, invaded Northumberland in keeping with
his country's traditional policy, the English under the earl of
Surrey won in 1513 at Flodden an annihilating – and for Scotland
cataclysmic – victory, in which the Scottish king and the flower of
his nobility fell, so bringing to an end the harrassing raids on
England's northern counties which had continued, on and off, for
the past two centuries. But in France, unlike an earlier 'King Hal',
Henry sought the palm without the dust, and the highlight of his
campaigning was the Field of the Cloth of Gold in 1519, a parley at
which he vied with the French king, Francis I, in extravagant
magnificence. Intent on his pleasures, for the first twenty years of
his reign he left the management of his kingdom's affairs to a
brilliant and immensely ambitious churchman of humble birth,

Thomas Wolsey, who rose to be the richest, most magnificent and powerful man in the country – Lord Chancellor, archbishop of York, a Cardinal and, later, Papal Legate.

Yet there was one problem to which, even in those years of pleasure and display, the King was forced to give his mind – that of the succession. For his Spanish wife, Catherine of Aragon – to whom his father had affianced him after the death of her boy husband, Henry's elder brother – gave him only one surviving child, a daughter born in 1515. When it became clear that she could never bear another, Henry, who had to provide for the country's future security, sought a papal annulment of his marriage. Accustomed to having his way in all things, he was also deeply in love – 'stricken' as he put it, 'with the dart of love' – with a *femme fatale*, Anne Boleyn, grand-daughter of a rich London merchant, whose price was marriage.

For several years Henry and his minister, Wolsey, importuned the Vatican for the annulment. An orthodox champion of the Roman Church against the new Protestant anti-papal heresies now raging on the Continent and author of a book against Luther for which he had been granted the papal title of Defender of the Faith, he would have had little difficulty in obtaining one had not his queen been aunt to the most powerful Catholic monarch of the time, the Emperor Charles V, on whose goodwill the Pope was dependent against the French invaders of Italy. Thwarted, Henry finally got his way by breaking with the Papacy, dismissing Wolsey, then appointing as archbishop of Canterbury a married churchman, Thomas Cranmer, who set up an ecclesiastical court which pronounced Catherine divorced, so enabling the King to make Anne his queen.

During the 1530s Henry and his new minister, Thomas Cromwell – a lawyer of Protestant sympathies trained by Wolsey as his secretary – carried through, with the help of a strongly anti-clerical Parliament, one of the most drastic revolutions in English history. A century and a half after Wycliffe had denounced the corruptions of the medieval Church and sixteen years after Luther nailed his thesis against papal Indulgences to the door of Wittenburg church, Henry VIII and his Parliament repudiated the authority of the Pope. Declaring, in an Act against Appeals to Rome, that the realm of England was 'an empire . . . governed by one supreme Head and King', they ended all links with the Papacy, constituted the King supreme Head of the Church in England, and later dissolved the monasteries, confiscating their enormous wealth, most of which passed, in that corrupt and chaotic age, into private hands. Yet though Henry broke with Rome and ruthlessly suppressed the Pilgrimage of Grace, a North Country rising in support of the Cistercian monasteries, he never himself accepted the doctrinal and theological tenets of the more drastic Continental religious reformers. He executed both Anne Boleyn, who failed to give him a son, and his Protestant minister Cromwell, as he also did another of his six successive wives, Catherine Howard, a Catholic, and persecuted as heretics all who deviated from orthodox belief.

During his last years Henry was sole and absolute master of his kingdom, and, though striking terror into all who dared oppose him remained, despite his personal despotism, immensely popular with his subjects. He was a great patron of seamen, like his father Henry VII. Yet though, unlike the sunlit crusading kingdoms of the Iberian Peninsula, still a backward half-island in the Atlantic mists England established no trans-oceanic settlements for more than another century, Henry VIII prepared a way for her oceanic future by founding the nucleus of a regular Royal Navy. Its ships, built or bought instead of hired for employment by the Crown, carried between them more than two thousand guns. Firing no longer from boarding castles in the bows and stern but discharging broadsides from portholes in their hulls, they constituted a revolutionary innovation in warship design for sea warfare in ocean waters. And to supply, administer and man them Henry established a permanent Navy Board.

Yet the chief legacy of this able but terrifying monarch's thirty-eight years' reign was a social revolution in whose throes he left his country struggling. Like all revolutions it brought with it a trail of destruction, sweeping away, with much that had become outworn, sterile and unproductive, much also that was beneficial in social cohesion, time-honoured charity, personal virtue and artistic achievement, including the products of great schools of native painting, sculpture and music which were all but totally destroyed in an orgy of brutal and ignorant iconoclasm. Its immediate beneficiaries were a breed of grasping opportunists, as hard-hearted as they were hard-headed, whose grim, unpleasing faces look down from the portraits of Holbein, the brilliant German painter first introduced into England by the great Catholic humanist and Lord Chancellor, Sir Thomas More, who was later executed by Henry for denying the royal supremacy.

When the King died in 1547 the chickens hatched under his despotic and wilful rule came home to roost on the throne of his nine-year-old son, Edward VI. These were an empty Treasury, inflation engendered by reckless expenditure on foreign wars and an unscrupulous debasement of the currency with all its attendant injustice to individuals, and widespread popular unrest, vagrancy and pauperism, no longer relieved by religious and monastic charity. Bishop Ridley of London told William Cecil, then secretary to the young king's Lord Protector, that Christ was lying in the streets of his diocese, 'hungry, naked and cold.' A generation of enclosure by get-rich-quick land-grabbers and money-makers acting without regard to social justice, was only redeemed by the fine Latin grammar schools which the better among them, seeking immortality, endowed or re-founded in cities and market towns all over the country from the plundered spoils of the chantries, guilds and monasteries; by the end of the century there were more than three hundred and fifty such schools. These were to transmit to the young of a new and rising middle-class, recruited from the clever sons of the poor as well as from the yeomanry and lesser gentry, a working knowledge of Latin – then essential for all professions. And for the more scholarly they offered the fruits of that revival of classical learning known as the Renaissance. Westminster, Sherbourne, King's School Canterbury and St. Paul's – secular re-foundations of former abbey or cathedral schools – Shrewsbury, Merchant Taylors, Uppingham, Repton, Tonbridge, Gresham's, Rugby, Blundells, Harrow and the great London charity school, Christ's Hospital, were all products of this revolutionary age, transmitting, with the help of the rod, discipline and a bent for categorical thought and action to England's future rulers.

Above all, there remained from Henry's reign the growing religious differences unloosed by an as yet purely loyal and parliamentary Reformation which had destroyed the links and disciplines of long Catholic habitude while retaining an enforced conformity to outworn, and increasingly questioned, religious assumptions and beliefs. The outstanding problem Henry had settled was the succession, but that only precariously. For though by one of his wives, Jane Seymour, who died in childbirth in 1537, he had at last achieved a son, he bequeathed him but a feeble constitution. Of his two daughters, the elder, Mary, was a devoted Catholic, eager to undo what her father had done, while the younger, Elizabeth – child of Anne Boleyn – inclined to the reformed beliefs. And though their succession, in the event of Edward predeceasing them without heirs, was provided for by Henry's Act of Settlement, both were women, and therefore considered by most people at that time incapable of ruling a turbulent and divided realm.

The old King, seeking to rule from the grave, had hoped to preserve the religious *status quo* he had established. But the councillors he appointed to act during his son's minority allowed the reforming elements in the Church and laity a freedom hitherto denied them. Chief among them was the boy king's uncle, Edward Seymour duke of Somerset – a hero of the Scottish and French wars – who constituted himself Lord Protector. Under his tolerant aegis English Protestants in exile were allowed to return from the Continent and the clergy to marry, while Communion in both kinds took the place of the Mass, and Henry's anti-heresy laws were repealed by Parliament. In the hope of checking the clandestine circulation of unauthorized translations of the scriptures, King Henry had in the last years of his reign licensed the publication of an English Bible – translated by a former Austin friar, Miles Coverdale, and partly based on an earlier and forbidden translation by the exiled and martyred, William Tyndale, whose beautiful English and fine scholarship were to remain an inspiration for the Authorized Bible of the next century. Tyndale's controversy with his Catholic opponent and fellow scholar and martyr, Sir Thomas

More, crystallized the issues between the English reformers and
the defenders of the old faith, the former appealing to scripture and
individual judgment, conscience and inspiration, and the latter to
the authority and transmitted ritual and cumulative wisdom of the
Church and its apostically descended episcopacy. 'If they shall
burn me,' Tyndale wrote before his death as a heretic at the hands
of the Imperial authorities in the Netherlands, 'they shall do none
other than I looked for . . . There is none other way into the Kingdom of Life than through persecution and suffering of pain and
of very death after the ensample of Christ.' 'If God spare my life,'
he had told a priest at the outset of his great work of translating the
New Testament, 'ere many years I will cause a boy that driveth
the plough shall know more of the scripture that thou dost'. It
was this direct introduction in the vernacular to the Hebrew,
Greek and Latin scriptures – 'the Word of God' – which was to
make the English a Protestant people and turn what until now had
been a political Reformation into a popular one. Thirteen years
after Tyndale's martyrdom at the stake, in the first year of Edward
VI's reign, the archbishop of Canterbury, Thomas Cranmer, put
the seal on the translators' work of the past thirty years by issuing
in 1549 his Book of Common Prayer, which endowed the Church
of England and the English people with the lovely cadences and
consoling wisdom of its incomparable liturgy.

Though, like everyone else in power, the Protector Somerset
feathered his own nest, he was probably genuinely anxious to redress the social wrongs from which the poor were suffering through
enclosure, inflation and the dissolution of the monasteries. Unfortunately by attempting to do so too quickly he aroused such unruly
hopes in the rough, uneducated common people that they rose in
rebellion, so provoking a violent coup which led to his supersession,
and ultimate execution, by a more ruthless and ambitious dictator, John Dudley duke of Northumberland, a son of Henry
VII's hated financial agent, Edmund Dudley. But though during
the last three years of the reign this able and unscrupulous careerist, so typical of the new lords thrown up by the Henrician revolution, enjoyed complete control of the Council and young king – a
brilliantly precocious boy but, as his diary showed, a cold and

reserved prig too – his plans for excluding the Catholic princess Mary from the succession in favour of Lady Jane Grey, a sixteen-year-old Protestant great-granddaughter of Henry VII affianced to his son, were thwarted by Edward's death of consumption in 1553 at the age of fifteen.

Mary Tudor's brief reign was almost the saddest in English history, both for herself and her people. The daughter of Henry VIII and his divorced Spanish wife, she had suffered deeply from her father's treatment of her mother and his schismatical breach with the Church of her forbears. Child of a princess of Spain, she was cousin to the greatest European monarch since the days of Charlemagne – the Hapsburg Emperor Charles V, king of a united Spain, which by the marriage of the crowns of Castile and Aragon now rivalled France as the dominant power in Europe, ruler of the Netherlands, Germany and half Italy, and master of the immense mineral wealth of the New World. When after years of insults and humiliations Edward's failing health made her accession to the English throne imminent, Mary, who had once been bastardized by her own father, became at thirty-seven a match even for Charles V's heir, Philip of Spain. For one who had suffered so many years of loneliness and whose dearest wish was to restore her erring country to its former faith, marriage to the young crusading champion of the Catholic Counter-Reformation and the earth's richest monarch seemed a dazzling prospect.

Mary was kindly, charitable, affectionate, scrupulously honest – an un-Tudor-like trait – and excessively devout. She was also, like all her family, brave and stubborn, most of all in defence of her religion. When, in the days of the Protestant triumph after her brother's accession, the bishop of London – whom afterwards she burnt at the stake – had called on her to adopt the new Prayer Book and expressed the hope that she would not 'refuse God's word,' she replied, 'I cannot tell what ye call God's word; that is not God's word now that was God's word in my father's days . . . You durst not for your ears have avouched that for God's word in my father's days.'

At the time of her accession, Mary enjoyed the loyalty of her people, even of those who had embraced the new religion – still then, because for the mass of the people change was taken up only slowly, a minority. When the duke of Northumberland had raised rebellion and proclaimed his Lady Jane Grey in her place, the country rallied instantaneously to its legitimate and Catholic Queen, despatching the ambitious Northumberland and his innocent protégé to the scaffold.

The enthusiasm soon evaporated. Mary's marriage in 1554 to Philip of Spain, against the advice of her counsellors and Parliament, proved intensely unpopular with an insular people. For Mary it was a barren and cruel disappointment. Having performed his matrimonial duty to enlarge his dynastic empire, her youthful king and husband stayed little more than a year in England with her. At thirty-seven, with failing health, she was prematurely old, and the cold, correct Philip and his arrogant Spanish hidalgos made no bones about it. 'What,' asked one of them, 'shall the king do with such an old bitch?' Her hopes of a child, desperately sustained until time and her husband's prolonged absence made it impossible, proved a chimera. His one and only brief return for a few months in 1557 was solely to involve her and England in a disastrous war with France, in which, unlike Philip, she had nothing to gain and everything to lose.

All the Queen had left was her religion and her fierce Tudor resolve to re-impose it on her heretic subjects. Innocent of the world out of which she had so long lived, and ill advised, she went about it in the worst possible way. As well as having the leading Protestant churchmen, archbishop Cranmer and bishops Ridley of London and Latimer of Worcester,* burnt at the stake, she authorized, during her last three years, the burning of some three hundred humble Protestants, more than fifty of them women. For though she chose her administrators with care, and presided over a tightening of the machinery of government which would have been a credit to her meticulous grandfather, Henry VII, this atrocious business, carried out in public, had an effect on the English very different from that which their Queen intended, colouring her whole reign. For if – the only tangible result of the Spanish marriage

---

* 'We shall this day,' said Latimer to Ridley, 'light such a candle by God's grace in England as, I trust, shall never be put out.'

and alliance – the capture in 1558 by France of Calais, England's last Plantagenet conquest, was engraved on Mary's heart, when, in that year, she died, the memory of the Smithfield martyrs, more than any single factor, was to make the English people for the next three centuries undeviating enemies of Rome.

CHAPTER THREE

The Virgin Queen

'She shall be, to the happiness of England,
An aged princess; many days shall see her,
And yet no day without a deed to crown it.'

Shakespeare

ON NOVEMBER 17TH 1558 at the age of twenty-five, Elizabeth succeeded to the vacant throne of her father, brother and sister. Born on September 7th 1533, at the riverside palace of Greenwich – the first heir to the English revolution against the rule of the international Church – she had been christened, with Archbishop Cranmer as godfather, in the arms of Henry VIII while, to the sound of trumpets, Garter King-of-Arms proclaimed, 'God in his infinite goodness, send prosperous life and long to the high and mighty princess of England, Elizabeth!'

Yet within three years of her birth she had been disowned and disgraced. Before she was out of her cradle, her terrifying father had had her mother, Anne Boleyn, executed for alleged infidelity and herself – her child – bastardized. Banished the court, Elizabeth had been brought up in the country with her half-sister Mary, nineteen years her senior, whose mother's marriage had also been annulled. Much of her youth was spent at Ashridge, the old monastery of the Bonhommes in the Chiltern beechwoods, which after the Dissolution of the Monasteries the King used as a retiring place for the children of his successive queens. Restored by her father's wish in 1544 to the junior place in the succession by Act of Parliament, she had lived after his death with the Queen Dowager, Catherine Parr, in Chelsea. 'Schooled in danger and dis-

38

cretion,' when she was only fifteen the latter's husband, the Lord Admiral, an ambitious, thrustful man of forty and brother to the Lord Protector Somerset, had been executed for treasonously courting her – a lesson which taught her how dangerous it was for a woman in her position to indulge her affections. In an age of treachery and violence, when an occupant of, or aspirant to, the throne had every incentive to eliminate rivals, her life during the reign of her Catholic sister had been in constant danger. Soon after Mary's accession, when hardly out of her teens, the young princess had been thrown into the Tower and subjected to almost daily cross-examination. Only her cool head and stout heart saved her. But for her Spanish brother-in-law's hope of marrying her after her childless sister's demise, so bringing England into his Atlantic empire, with her known Protestant sympathies she would never have been allowed by England's Catholic rulers to live to inherit the Crown.

Superbly educated – she was widely read and mistress of six languages, including Latin and Greek* – her accession came as a providential deliverance to her Protestant subjects and herself. For both they and she faced tremendous risks. Her kingdom was near bankrupt and defenceless, divided by bitter religious differences in an age of increasingly embattled faiths, with unscrupulous profiteers battening on the spoils of the monasteries, the ruins of the feudal state and of the medieval Church. She inherited an exhausted treasury, a depreciated currency, a society vitiated by lawlessness and vagabondage, and a countryside impoverished by a run of bad harvests. Abroad the prospect was still darker. Dominating half Europe, imperial Spain, with its invincible infantry, its dazzling conquests in central and south America and its world-

---

* 'She has just passed her sixteenth birthday,' her tutor, the great Greek scholar, Roger Ascham, reported of her, 'and shows such dignity and gentleness as are wonderful at her age and in her rank. Her study of true religion and learning is most eager. Her mind has no womanly weakness, her perseverance is equal to that of a man, and her memory long keeps what it quickly picks up. She talks French and Italian as well as she does English . . . When she writes Greek and Latin nothing is more beautiful than her handwriting. She delights as much in music as she is skilful in it.'

wide oceanic power, had all but absorbed England through Philip's short-lived, but childless, marriage with Mary Tudor. Nearer home the traditional alliance between a giant France and Scotland, the upper and lower millstones, threatened to crush Protestant England and substitute for Elizabeth her half-French Catholic cousin and heir presumptive, Mary Stuart, now Queen both of France and the Scots. There were many in a still divided country who would have welcomed such an event. 'The Queen poor,' a contemporary wrote, 'the realm exhausted; the nobles poor and decayed; good captains and soldiers wanting; the people out of order; justice not executed; the justices unmeet for their offices; all things dear; division among ourselves; war with France and Scotland; the French king bestriding the realm, having one foot in Calais the other in Scotland; steadfast enmity but no steadfast friendship abroad.' England was a weak, unimportant half-island on the fringe of a continent dominated by two great Catholic powers, shut out from the trade and wealth of the transatlantic New World and the oppulent East by papal decrees and the might of Spain and Portugal, to whom, as their discoverers and colonizers, the Pope had granted an eternal monopoly. To most Englishmen the great days of their country and its one-time military glory seemed altogether things of the past. The vast continental possessions of the Plantagenet and Lancastrian kings had gone like a dream and with the loss of Calais, the last of the old landmarks had vanished.

It was such a realm and such a situation that Elizabeth was called upon to master. To her subjects, Protestant and Catholic alike, she seemed a weak, inexperienced woman; they would naturally have much preferred a man to rule them. Yet, unlike her predecessor with her Spanish ancestry and sympathies, she was, in her own words, 'mere English'. With her flaming hair, commanding will and gift of telling oratory, she was King Harry's daughter, while, through her beheaded mother – a great granddaughter of a London mercer – there was bourgeois blood enough in her veins to enable her to share her people's feelings. Everything turned on her ability to win their confidence and love, and so unite them behind her.

From the start she seized every opportunity of courting them. Her entry into London three weeks after her proclamation was the first act of a drama which was to continue to her dying day. 'To all that wished her well,' wrote one who witnessed it, 'she gave thanks. To such as bade "God save her Grace," she said in return, "God save you all," and added that she thanked them with all her heart. Wonderfully transported were the people with the loving answers and gestures of their Queen . . . How many nosegays did her Grace receive at poor women's hands. How often she stayed her chariot when she saw any simple body approach to speak to her. A branch of rosemary given to her Majesty, with a supplication, by a poor woman about Fleet Bridge was seen in her chariot when her Grace came to Westminster.'

'If ever any person had the gift or style to win the hearts of people,' another recalled, 'it was this Queen, and if ever she did express the same it was at that present, in coupling mildness with majesty as she did, and in stately stooping to the meanest sort. All her faculties were in motion, and every motion seemed a well-guided action: her eye was set upon one, her ear listened to another, her judgment ran upon a third, to a fourth she addressed her speech. Her spirit seemed to be everywhere, and yet so entire in herself as it seemed to be nowhere else. Some she pitied, some she commended, some she thanked, at others she pleasantly and wittily jested; contemning no person, neglecting no office, and distributing her smiles, looks and graces so artificially that thereupon the people again redoubled the testimony of their joys, and afterwards, raising everything to the highest strain, filled the ears of all men with immoderate extolling their prince.'

A magnificent actress who knew well how to hide her thoughts and feelings, there was no doubt of the sincerity with which she identified herself with her people. 'Have a care over them,' she told her judges in her first address to them; 'do you that which I ought to do. They are my people. Every man oppresseth and spoileth them without mercy. See unto them, see unto them, for they are my charge. I charge you even as God hath charged me.' 'Far above all earthly treasures,' she was to declare many years later, 'I esteem my people's love.' 'You may well have a greater prince,' she told them; 'you shall never have a more loving one.'

Elizabeth and her ministers, whom she chose with great shrewdness, had to play for time: time for the nation to resolve its religious discords, to reform the currency, to solve the problems of poverty and vagabondage, to recover national unity, above all to grow strong enough to meet the challenge of the immense foreign forces threatening it. She played with cunning, equivocation, parsimony, constant delays and every womanly and queenly art with which she was endowed, and, when the attack could no longer be evaded, with magnificent courage. 'I thank God,' she told one of her Parliaments, 'that I am imbued with such qualities that if I were turned out of the realm in my petticoat, I were able to live in any place in Christendom.'

*   *   *

Her first task after her accession was to resolve the bitter ideological divisions wrought by the religious changes of the past quarter of a century. Under her father they had cut the country's links with Rome and secularized the wealth of the monasteries and chantries; under her brother had carried England into the revolutionary camp of the Continental reformers, and under her sister back again to Catholicism – and a reformed, intolerant, persecuting Catholicism at that. Before the Marian persecutions, a hard conservative core, sustained by the rule of a Catholic Queen, had clung to the old Catholic Faith and acknowledged the supremacy and disciplines of Rome. A smaller, but vehement minority of 'Puritan' extremists had passionately denounced as idolatrous superstitions all the leading tenets and practices of the medieval Church – transubstantiation, the confessional, the efficacy of indulgences and papal remission of sin, pilgrimages, relics, and the intercession of saints. The majority of ordinary English men and women, including the heir presumptive, the Princess Elizabeth, while repudiating the authority of Rome, were instinctively traditionalist and like her father felt no great enthusiasm for doctrinal and theological abstractions. For though the sale of monastic and chantry lands had given English landowners of all classes an irreversible vested

42

interest in the secular results of the Henrician Reformation, there had been as yet no clear border-line in most men's hearts between the priest-led ritualistic, candle-lit worship of the past and the congregational and private scripture-reading and impromptu prayers and sermons of Protestant piety.

But the Smithfield fires and the inhumanity of Mary's reactionary advisers had decided the issue. With a young Protestant princess on the throne, and with as her principal adviser and minister, William Cecil – once the reforming Protector Somerset's secretary – England was set again on a Protestant course.

In breaking with Rome, however, Elizabeth moved with characteristic caution. For in the near bankrupt and ill-armed state of her small, vulnerable and still divided kingdom, she dared not do anything that could precipitate an attack by either of her giant Catholic neighbours, France and Spain. Her first and decisive step, though accompanied by every expression of friendship and affection, was to delay – until he grew impatient of waiting and betrothed himself to a French Catholic princess instead – acceptance of a proposal of marriage from her lately bereft brother-in-law, Philip, the 'most Catholic King' of Spain and arch-champion of the Counter Reformation. But at the opening of her first Parliament on January 25th, when the abbot and monks of Westminster met her with tapers burning in broad daylight, she waved them aside and all that they stood for with a firm, 'Away with those torches! We can see well enough!' Then, having made sure of her ground, she absented herself from Mass and, at Easter 1559, publicly received Communion in both kinds. Using Parliament as her father had done to secure national assent for her policies, but deliberately declining the title of 'Head' of the Church assumed by him and her brother, and acting instead, in the words of her new Act of Supremacy, merely as 'supreme Governor of all persons and causes, ecclesiastical as well as civil', this wise, temporizing and clement young ruler firmly opted for a moderate Protestant episcopacy with an English Liturgy and a seemly ritual, not too novel or difficult for those who had been brought up under the old Catholicism.

For in her church reforms, Elizabeth's purpose was not primarily doctrinal but political. It was to reunite her people behind a religious belief and prayer to which their character, temperament and experience inclined them to conform. She made her choice for a clear, simple, middle way, easy for moderate men to follow and, therefore, typically English. Idolatrous practices on the one hand and private preaching on the other were discouraged, as were 'contumelious and opprobrious words such as heretic, schismatic and Papist'. 'To unite the people of the realm in one uniform order' all were to attend their parish church on Sunday, while non-attendance was to be punished by a modest fine, though, only if ostentatiously persisted in, by imprisonment. At the same time a curb was placed on the verbal extravagances of Puritan extremists, intoxicated by the polemics of continental theologians and the new wine of the translated and printed scriptures. In Elizabeth's Act of Uniformity and in the Thirty-nine Articles which laid down guidelines for the Anglican Church, there was no abuse of Pope or Rome, while the words of the gentle, martyred Cranmer's restored Communion Service left communicants free, in their own minds, to accept or reject as they pleased the old Catholic dogma of the transubstantiation of the bread and wine of the Eucharist into the Real Presence of Christ's body and blood. Elizabeth's pragmatic attitude towards the furious controversies which raged round this beautiful but unprovable conception – ideological controversies which, with others like them, were about to plunge Europe into a century of persecution, massacre and civil and international war – was neatly expressed in some lines often attributed to her:

'Twas Christ the word that spake it,
He took the bread and brake it;
And what the word did make it
That I believe and take it.'

Or, as she was to put it many years later, when only England was free from the welter of religious strife dividing almost every other Christian land: 'If there were two Princes in Christendom who had good will and courage, it would be easy to reconcile the differences in religion, for there was only one Jesus Christ and one faith, and all the rest they dispute about but trifles.'

Within the Anglican Church, Catholic and Apostolic but not Roman – reaching back, in the view of its apologists, to the pristine traditions of early Christianity – there was room for all who accepted the outward forms of unity laid down by its royal Governor. And, at first, within the country at large, there was room too for those who, worshipping in the privacy of their own homes, did not try to propagate or impose divisive views on others. 'The law touches no man's conscience so as public order be not violated by external act or teaching,' Elizabeth told the Holy Roman Emperor, whose Catholic son, the Archduke Charles, was a suitor for her hand. In a universally intolerant age this broad-minded, merciful young Queen set a rare example of moderation and good sense, insisting only – though that in no uncertain terms – on total loyalty to the Crown and the ideal of national unity which all her life she strove to foster. That the settlement reached was broadly acceptable is shown by the fact that of 9,400 English clergy only a few hundred refused the new Oath of Supremacy, compared with a sixth who had resigned or been ejected from their livings when Mary had restored the Roman supremacy. Thanks to the hard work and administrative zeal of Elizabeth's three archbishops of Canterbury – the scholarly Matthew Parker, son of a Norwich weaver, his rather less successful successor, Edmund Grindal, and John Whitgift, whom, honouring for his celibacy, she used to call her 'little black husband' – parochial order was restored and the educational standards of the clergy raised out of all recognition during her forty-five years' reign. But it was from the Queen's humanity, breadth of vision and good sense, and the noble and inspiring Book of Common Prayer, with its glorious Collects, supervized and bequeathed to England by her godfather, the martyred Archbishop Cranmer, that the reformed Anglican Church derived its continuing spirit and soul. 'It is impossible,' the great Elizabethan historian, A. L. Rowse, has written, 'to over-estimate the influence of the Church's routine of prayer and good works upon society: the effect upon imagination and conduct of the Liturgy with its piercing and affecting phrases, repeated Sunday by Sunday . . .

They provided a system of belief, making a whole world of experience within which to live, giving satisfaction to the inmost impulses of the heart while not disturbing the critical standards of the mind, setting a guide to conduct in all the concerns of life, instructing in duty to God, one's neighbour and oneself, offering such consolation as nothing else in grief, in sickness and in the hour of death.' Nearly three hundred years later the duke of Wellington was to declare that it was the Church of England which had made England what she was, a nation of honest men.

The speed and magnanimity of Elizabeth's comprehensive religious settlement gave the country the unity essential to preserve it from the external perils threatening it. By the Treaty of Cateau-Cambresis signed in the spring after her accession, the rival dominating powers of Europe, France and Spain, made peace, leaving the latter's satellite, England, to whistle in vain for her lost Calais. That they might now combine against her at the instance of a fanatic Pope, eager to redeem a little lapsed island kingdom from heresy, was a possibility the Queen and her ministers could not safely ignore. For with the rapid growth of Catholic strength and conviction following the reforms of the Roman Church, set in train by the Council of Trent and the foundation in 1540 of the great international crusading Society of Jesus to combat heresy and win back souls – and nations – to the Faith, the position of the heretic ruler of a little state of barely five millions was becoming increasingly precarious. Facing England across the Channel and Biscay Bay, with their orthodox sovereigns both committed by their religion to root out heresy in their dominions, and with only the sea separating their powerful armies from her shores, lay the immense global empire of Spain, with its oceanic discoveries and conquests, and a France with more than three times England's size and population, now joined with Scotland under a single Crown.

For the 'auld alliance' between England's ancient enemy beyond the Channel and her restless, marauding northern neighbour had recently taken a new and menacing form. Eleven years earlier, following the death in 1542 of James V of Scotland after a shattering defeat by the English at Pinkie, the former's widow,

Mary of Guise – a French princess – had joined in 1547 with the Scottish Estates in sending her five-year-old child, Queen Mary Stuart, away from Scotland to be educated at the French royal court, out of reach of English invaders and her own feuding and kidnapping nobles. Here, a few months before Elizabeth's accession, the young Scottish Queen had been married at the age of fifteen to the even younger Dauphin of France, with a secret agreement, unknown to her distant subjects, that in the event of her dying before him without issue, he and his successors should inherit the Scottish Crown. Meanwhile French troops had been sent to Scotland to garrison the capital and royal castles. They both helped its French-born Dowager Queen and Regent, Mary's mother, to keep the English at bay and suppress the growing outbreaks of heresy which, as in every northern land, including France itself, were seeping into the country from the reformed Lutheran and Calvinist strongholds in Germany and Switzerland.

Less than a year after his marriage of Mary Queen of Scots, her young husband succeeded to the French throne. Originally intended, by Scotland's then would-be conquerer, Henry VIII, for his son, Edward, and Queen now of both France and Scotland, the sixteen-year-old Mary Stuart as a great-granddaughter of Henry VII now also claimed the English Crown, to which she was Heir Presumptive. For under Catholic law, its heretic new wearer, Elizabeth, was illegitimate and, therefore, a usurper.

Yet in the very summer in which the young Queen of Scots – who on Mary Tudor's death had assumed the royal arms and titles of England – found herself Queen of France, and while her Protestant cousin was laying with her Parliament the foundations of the Anglican Church, dramatic events were taking place in Scotland. In the Easter which saw Elizabeth avowing her Protestant sympathies by publicly receiving Communion in both kinds, the French Regent, Mary of Guise, now a very sick woman, alarmed by the spread of heresy among her daughter's subjects, ordained a compulsory enforcement of the religion of their fathers. Her edict was openly defied by a strong group of dissident nobles, who, calling themselves the Lords of the Congregation of Jesus Christ in Scotland, had recently subscribed to a Covenant renouncing the idolatry of the Roman faith – that of the established Church of their country. They now assembled at Perth with a number of defiant Protestant preachers whom the Scottish bishops had summoned to answer for their heresy. Here they were joined by John Knox, a fanatic and highly eloquent veteran reformer, who had just returned from self-imposed exile in the stronghold of Calvinist Protestantism, Geneva. Knox, who had suffered for his heretical preachings in the galleys of his country's French invaders and whose austere and uncompromising beliefs were well attuned to the dour, unrelenting humours of Scottish character, had played a leading part in fomenting opposition to Scotland's corrupt, effete and over-endowed ecclesiastical establishment. He now, on May 11th 1559, preached a sermon in Perth so inflammatory and 'vehement against the idolatry' of 'dumb dogs' and 'idle bellies', as he called the endowed priests and monks of the Roman Church, that the mob rose in enthusiastic response and sacked every monastic and religious house in the town.

Until this time the pent-up Protestant heresy, which had been raging for two generations on the continent, had so far only simmered in Scotland. It now exploded with the force of a tornado. A substantial part of the greedy and lawless nobles and lairds – like their fellow land-owners in England, 'lusting for kirklands' – joined with the more vocal elements of its poverty-stricken people in repudiating the ancient faith of their country in favour of a congregational or presbyterian system of church government, ruled by parish ministers and lay elders, and based on the ecclesiastical and civil discipline of Knox's friend and master, the great French-born scholar and prophet of Predestination, Grace and Election, John Calvin of Geneva. Everywhere Scottish Protestants took up arms in defiance of the dying Regent's attempts to repress the rebellion of her daughter's heretical subjects.

But the Protestants proved no match for the trained, disciplined troops of the French garrisons of Edinburgh Castle and Scotland's key port, Leith. As the indecisive campaign of that summer and autumn wore on, knowing that reinforcements from France would soon be arriving to crush them, Knox and the Lords of the Congregation appealed to Scotland's ancient enemy, England, and its young Protestant queen to save the nascent Scottish Reformation and free their country 'from the bondage and tyranny of strangers'. Elizabeth had no love for rebels and none whatever for John Knox, who shortly before her accession had published from Geneva a highly scurrilous and offensive attack on the then female Catholic rulers of Scotland, France and England entitled *A Blast of the Trumpet against the Monstrous Regiment of Women*. Yet, though the risks for her, both political and military, of armed intervention were daunting, the consequences of letting Scotland be forced back into the French and Catholic fold seemed even graver. Acting as secretly and unprovocatively as possible, and using every expedient to conceal her plans, she and her Secretary of State, William Cecil, sent first money and then, greatly daring, in the winter of 1559/60, a fleet to blockade Leith and the Firth of Forth. Finally in April 1560, they scraped together an army to enter Scotland and help compel the blockaded French garrisons to leave it. And when she had done so, by subsequently withdrawing her own forces from Scotland without asking any recompense, Elizabeth, in that crucial summer, not only won the gratitude of the Scots – something no English ruler had ever done before – but closed a vital gap in her country's defences against potential Catholic enemies in Europe. Henceforward they would have to reckon not, as until now, with a small Protestant half-island, out-flanked by another and hostile Catholic half-island traditionally allied to France and offering a foothold from which to attack England in the rear, but with a single island bound together by a common Protestantism.

What had happened changed the course of history. It was a first and, as it proved, decisive step in the creation of a new political entity in the world – Great Britain. It had been brought about by three factors – the cool courage and patient statesmanship of a young queen and her wise counsellor, Cecil; the realization of far-sighted Scots, like William Maitland of Lethington, that what he called 'the earnest embracing of religion' would inevitably cause the old hereditary enemies of Scotland and England to 'join straitly together'; and the fine seamanship and hereditary skill of English sailors. For it had been young Admiral William Winter's midwinter voyage to Scotland and his blockade of the stormy Firth of Forth, in an age when ships of war were not built, or expected, to remain at sea at such a season in northern waters, which had broken the French stranglehold on Scotland. Two attempts by French fleets and transports, first to forestall and then to raise Winter's blockade, had ended in disaster for them with the loss of half a dozen ships and several thousand soldiers in tempests. Cecil's and the Queen's subsequent refusal to relax their naval grip had decided the issue. For so long as the French garrisons of the Scottish royal castles could be supplied and reinforced by sea, they could never have been taken by storm or reduced by the untrained and undisciplined ragged Scots levies and their allies the equally ineffective English militia men. As it was, they were forced to accept, in the summer of 1561, the terms of the Treaty of Edinburgh, as the only means of getting their besieged and starving troops back to France in English bottoms. In return for that concession – the only alternative to starvation – the French troops were to leave at once, their fortress at Leith was to be dismantled, the government of Scotland to be transferred to the Council of Protestant nobles, and the French king and queen were to abstain from any further challenge to Elizabeth's right to her throne. For her and Cecil it was a tremendous triumph.

Yet it had been a near-run thing, and right up to the end it had not been clear whether the French would give in and leave Scotland free and Protestant. At one moment during the campaign it had even looked as though Philip of Spain might intervene to suppress the Scottish heretics while protecting his English sister-in-law – whose kingdom he still hoped to redeem from heresy – against any attack across the Channel by his rival France. As it was, England's slender financial resources had been strained to the utmost to supply her own and the Scottish insurgents' fighting forces.

Nor had her rustic militia – for she had no other army – shown any sign that it could compete with the professional armies of the Continent, armed as it still was with bills and bows, and raised from the rag, tag and bobtail of the countryside. Since the days, less than a century and a half before, when England's archers had been the arbiters of every battlefield, the nature of land warfare had changed out of all recognition. The masters of the field were now the huge regiments of highly paid Spanish, German, French and Italian mercenaries, with a discipline and esprit de corps based on professional pride and comradeship and the lively hope of gain, rape and plunder. Advancing in huge phalanxes of massed pikes, under the supporting fire of arquebusiers, musketeers and artillery, they dominated and broke the ranks of any opponent. They had sprung originally out of the little indentured 'retinues' or companies of English archers, who, armed with a devasting weapon which they alone could yield – the long bow of Gwent – under Edward III, the Black Prince and Henry V, had laid low the armoured and mounted feudal chivalry of France and western Christendom. Thereafter, taking service under elected captains as so-called 'free companies', they had sold themselves to any petty tyrant or walled corporate Italian or German city able to afford their services. Gradually, absorbed in their own civil wars, the English had dropped out of the European battle league and receded into their remote and misty island. Meanwhile mercenary soldiering had become a highly lucrative profession for the toughest and most aggressive members of society, for whose services the great dynastic monarchies of Spain, France and Austria, who alone could afford to pay them, competed. From them they drew their unchallengeable military strength, supporting them with the powerful and costly new weapons which European Renaissance technology had evolved. The most famous of all were the huge Spanish three thousand strong regiments or 'tercios' recruited from the hardy peasants of the Castilian plains. Once landed on England's shores, the invincible veterans of St Quentin and Muhlberg would be certain to overwhelm, 'with push of pike', her little ill-trained and ill-armed companies of balotted county militiamen. Under her archaic local military system these were recruited by corrupt muster-masters who, falsifying their returns, let off the able-bodied and well-to-do for bribes, and filled the ranks with criminals, cripples and beggars. 'Tattered prodigals, ragged as Lazarus,' Shakespeare was to describe them in the latter years of Elizabeth's reign, 'such as were never soldiers, but discarded unjust serving men, younger sons to younger brothers, revolted tapsters and ostlers trade-fallen, the cankers of a calm world and a long peace.'* Nor could England, with her Treasury drained dry by the extravagance of Henry VIII and the financial bankruptcy of his two successors, afford to hire armies of disciplined mercenaries like wealthy France and Spain.

For the moment her only defence lay in playing off these powerful rivals against one another and taking advantage of their internal difficulties. Eighteeen months after the expulsion of the French from Scotland, roused by a massacre of their co-religionists by a Catholic mob who had surrounded a church filled with worshippers and set it alight, Huguenots – as the French Protestants were called – took up arms and, like the Scots, appealed to Elizabeth to help them. Promised by their leaders the return of their lost Calais and offered in the meantime the port of Havre as a pledge for it, in September 1562 by the Treaty of Hampton Court, the Queen, under strong pressure from the more Protestant members of her Council, undertook to do in France what she had done in Scotland two summers before.

Yet, though the West Country seamen joined with the Huguenot deep-sea fishermen of La Rochelle and Brittany to sweep that Catholic kingdom's commerce from the Channel, the war on land went ill for the French Protestants. Unlike the Scottish reformers outnumbered by their orthodox countrymen, they were driven that winter out of their strongholds in Normandy. While the English were still assembling at Havre, the Prince of Condé, the Huguenot leader, surrendered to his royalist and Catholic country-

---

* Born six years after Elizabeth's accession, Shakespeare, writing six years before the end of her reign, drew in his *Henry IV* a picture of the time-honoured recruitment for war of England's county militia. 'I have misused the King's press damnably,' he made his fraudulent captain, Sir John Falstaff, confess. 'I have got, in exchange of a hundred and fifty soldiers, three hundred and odd pounds . . . A mad fellow met me on the way and told me I had unloaded all the gibbets and pressed the dead bodies. No eye hath seen such scarecrows. I'll not march through Coventry with them, that's flat; -- nay, and the villains march wide betwixt the legs, as if they had gyves on; for, indeed, I had the most of them out of prison. There's but a shirt and a half in all my company.' Not till 1595, seven years after the defeat of the Armada and two years before Shakespeare's play did the Privy Council decide that musketeers, instead of archers, should be enrolled in the country's Trained Bands.

men. Thereafter abandoned and attacked by both Catholics and Protestants, the English defenders of Havre, after a three months' siege in the summer of 1563, were forced to lay down their arms after a third of the garrison had perished in an outbreak of bubonic plague. Brought back to England by them, it swept the country, carrying off in 1564, the year of Shakespeare's birth, one in six of the population of Stratford-upon-Avon.

* * *

This costly and humiliating experience cured the young English Queen of what little taste she ever had for war. Henceforward, she did everything she could to avoid it, and by doing so, gave her people twenty-two years of much needed peace, during which time they grew richer and stronger, while her own slender financial resources, like those of her frugal grandfather, Henry VII, increased. Yet if, to protect her country, Elizabeth shunned man's costly expedient of war, she relied instead on her instinct and art as a woman to achieve the same ends. The weapon she used was marriage, and, by denying rather than giving it, held out herself and the dowry of her kingdom as a bait for the ambition, greed and vanity of her fellow princes.

In the sixteenth century international diplomacy moved in two main channels, war and dynastic marriage. For the first Elizabeth had nothing but dislike, not so much because it was cruel – though she hated cruelty – but because it was wasteful, uncertain and, in the universally corrupt state of public administration, disastrously expensive. Her mind revolted at it. But for the diplomacy of courtship she was perfectly fitted by temperament. Hers was a genius for intrigue, a taste for coquetry and a passion for flattery. As the heiress of England, open to offers from the highest bidder, and free to carry into international politics all the bewildering ways of a maid with a man, she was in her element. With as her dowry a kingdom, which though as yet of little account by itself, could bring a major accession of strength to any European power allied to it, she had a diplomatic and matrimonial card to play of the highest consequence, so long as it remained unplayed.

During the early years of the reign, she received at least fifteen proposals of marriage from Spanish, French, Swedish, Austrian, German and Danish, as well as Scottish and English, suitors. Two were from kings, two from hereditary princes, seven from dukes, two from earls, and two from her own subjects, a courtesy lord and a knight. After her rejection, by deliberate procrastinating, of her brother-in-law, Philip of Spain, the most powerful monarch on earth, in order to retain his friendship during the crisis with France over Scotland, Elizabeth had continued to keep a foot in the Spanish camp by favouring the suit of his cousin, the young Archduke Charles of Austria. For several years he seemed the most likely foreign aspirant for her hand. Later, at different times, she invited and encouraged proposals of marriage from a succession of young French princes. For, so long as she remained unmarried, France and Spain each nursed hopes, heretic though she was, of bringing her country into its dynastic orbit and herself and her people back to the Roman fold. It was the essence of her policy to keep alive the hopes of both rivals and use her virgin state and her woman's art of procrastination to play one against the other until such time as England was strong enough to stand on her own feet without the friendship of either.

At first it seemed inevitable – to everyone, that is, except herself – that she would marry, both to secure for her throne the guidance, strength and wisdom of a man, and to provide her kingdom with a male heir, so averting the dangers of a disputed succession. 'It is inconceivable that she should wish to remain single and never marry,' wrote the Austrian ambassador to his royal master, the Holy Roman Emperor. Nor could her counsellors understand the repeated changes of heart. The multiplicity of her suitors and the encouragement she gave them all puzzled and scandalized them. 'God send our mistress a husband, and in time a son, that we may hope our posterity shall have a masculine succession,' was Cecil's repeated prayer. 'Here is great company of wooers,' the poor man complained; 'would to God the Queen had one and the rest honourably settled . . . This song hath many parts, and I am skilled only in plainsong.'

The Queen suffered from no such inhibitions. She encouraged

them all. Her reluctance to marry – however carefully concealed, at first, possibly even from herself – may have been due to many reasons: to her desire for liberty, to inability to make up her mind, to a womanly preference for delay, to the embitterment in which her first girlish love affair had closed, above all, and always, to a sense of the true interests of her country and her supreme means of serving it – her hold on her subjects' hearts.

Only one suitor at this time seems to have touched her heart. Lord Robert Dudley was a younger son of the upstart duke of Northumberland who had supplanted the Lord Protector Somerset in Edward VI's reign and – like his own father before him, Henry VII's hated financial agent, Edmund Dudley – had been beheaded for treason. This tall, dark, handsome, distinguished looking and forceful young man of Elizabeth's own age – 'the gipsy' to the contemptuous older nobility – had shared her captivity in the Tower during Mary's reign. Robin, she called him, keeping him never far from her presence while he, with an eye on the throne, courted her assiduously. But he was married, and during the second year of the reign ugly rumours began to circulate that he meant to do away with the lonely wife, Amy Robsart, whom he kept languishing in the country while he attended the Queen and Court. Then in September 1560, the horrifying news reached Windsor that she had been found dead with a broken neck at the bottom of a flight of stone stairs at Cumnor Hall in Oxfordshire.

Faced by a scandal that could have shaken the throne, Elizabeth placed the trust and love of her subjects above her passion as a woman and the dictates of her heart. Though she never doubted his innocence, her Robin was banished from the Court until an inquest and a legal inquiry had shown that the cause of his wife's death must have been either accident or suicide. And though he resumed his affectionate intimacy with the Queen, his hopes of a royal marriage were never realized. For, while she continued to reward his devotion and her love for him with gifts, including the great castle of Kenilworth and, later, the earldom of Leicester, she kept him, like all her suitors, firmly in his place. 'God's death,' she is reported to have rebuked him for his jealousy of a rival, 'I have wished you well, but my favour is not so locked up in you that others shall not participate thereof . . . I will have here but one mistress and no master.' 'Which so quailed my Lord Leicester,' her earliest biographer, Sir Robert Naunton, added, 'that his feigned humility was long after one of his best virtues.'

Subjects who tried to dictate to their imperious royal mistress suffered the same fate. Throughout the first decade of her reign, conscious that her life alone (a life almost lost in October 1562 in an attack of smallpox) stood between them and the perils of a disputed succession – civil war, anarchy and invasion – successive Parliaments kept petitioning her either to marry and provide the kingdom with a male and, as they hoped, Protestant heir, or, in default, name a successor. To her intense indignation they once went so far as to refuse to vote her urgently-needed financial supply until she married. At this she turned on them with fury. 'It did not become,' she said, 'a subject to compel the Sovereign.' 'Was not I born in this country?' she asked. 'Were my parents born in any foreign country? Is there any cause that should alienate myself from being careful over this country? Is not my kingdom here?' 'I marvel,' she rated the Commons on another occasion, showing the Coronation ring on her finger, 'that ye have forgotten the pledge of this my wedlock and marriage with my kingdom . . . And do not upbraid me with a miserable lack of children; for every one of you, and as many as are Englishmen, are children and kins-men to me.' It was for her, their anointed Queen, she told them, not for some unknown and unpredictable heir to provide for the succession and safeguard the country's future. 'For though I be never so careful of your well-being and mind ever so to be, yet may my issue grow out of kind and become, perhaps, ungracious. And in the end this shall be for me sufficient that a marble stone shall declare that a Queen, having reigned such a time, lived and died a virgin.'

Yet though – to use her dynamic phrase – she would 'never be by violence constrained to do anything' and left the Commons in no doubt that, in this as in other matters, she would abate no jot of her royal prerogative and England's immemorial constitutional practice under which the wearer of the Crown initiated policy, like her father she regarded the 'counsel and consent' of the

"Perhaps the most English of all his characters was Chaucer himself, with his self-deprecating manner, his unassuming elusiveness, his capacity for liking people because they seemed to him rather a joke; his ability to laugh, without being obtrusive, at himself and everyone else. His work ranks with Dante's as the supreme expression of what Christianity had done for the Gothic peoples of Europe."

Henry VIII seeks to rule from the grave. But the councillors he appointed to act during his son's minority (from Edward VI's left here Seymour, Dudley, Cranmer and Russell) allowed the reforming elements in the Church a freedom hitherto denied them. In this allegorical painting of 1548, the Pope is crushed by the weight of the English Prayer Book and in the background soldiers destroy religious statues.

nation's representatives in their parliamentary Estates of Lords and Commons as an essential part of that constitutional practice. For it preserved and ensured that unity of the realm which was the supreme purpose of her reign. When, womanwise, outraged by the insolent language of a more than usually outspoken member of the Commons, she clapped him into the Fleet prison, she bowed at once to the House's outraged protest at this infringement of its right of free speech, and apologized handsomely, ordering his immediate release and declaring that nothing had been further from her intention than to impugn the rights of parliamentary debate. In the reconciliation between her and Parliament which followed, the Commons voted supply without any further attempt to make it dependent on her promise to marry, while she, in her turn, her prerogative admitted, graciously waived a third of the subsidy voted her. 'Do not think,' she told them in the speech from the throne which closed the session, 'that I am unmindful of your surety by succession, wherein is all my care, considering I know myself to be mortal. No, I warrant you. Or that I went about to break your liberties. No, it was never in my meaning, but to stay you before you fell into the ditch.' That declaration of January 2nd 1567 marked a decisive moment in the relations between the Queen and her Parliaments. Henceforward, whatever rifts arose between them, there was never any question but that it was she who directed the ship of state, while Lords and Commons, the hereditary and elected representatives of her people, meeting periodically at her summons to authorize and grant fiscal supply, gave her, through proved and custom-hallowed channels of consultation and debate, their counsel, advice and consent.

*   *   *

During her late twenties, while Elizabeth was keeping both foreign suitors and her own people guessing her intentions, she ceased to be the only marriageable queen in the European matrimonial stakes. For in December 1560, three days before her eighteenth birthday, Mary Stuart, Queen of France and Scotland and Catholic heir presumptive to England's childless throne, found herself a widow. With her sickly boy husband died her hopes of presiding over the brilliant sophisticated French royal court – the most cultivated in Europe – in which she had grown up. Instead, it became her fate to reign over a barren, divided, half barbaric, northern kingdom of barely a million people, half of whom, including a majority of its nobles, had passionately repudiated their, and her, ancient faith, which they now reviled as an idolatrous superstition. Apart from her claim to the English succession, which her Protestant cousin would not allow herself or her subjects to acknowledge, all she had to rely on when, a lonely girl of eighteen, she landed at Leith in August 1561, was her appealing beauty, her fascination to men, and an unshakeable belief in her right to sovereignty. In the course of the next four years, with her courage, gaiety and vivacity, she contrived to win for herself a following among Scotland's feuding and fickle nobility and to preserve intact her Catholic faith and worship. Warily watched by Elizabeth – who, in the hope of binding her and Scotland to England, offered her her own favourite, Leicester, as a consort – she made several attempts to negotiate a match with one of Europe's leading Catholic princes, including Don Carlos, the epileptic and repulsive son and heir of the King Philip of Spain. In the end, before Don Carlos's mysterious death – murdered, it was widely believed, by his own despairing father – she followed her fancy by marrying, in July 1565, according to Catholic rites, her nineteen-year-old cousin, Lord Darnley, with whom she had fallen in love. Heir to the earldom of Lennox, and, like Mary herself, a descendant of Henry VII with a reversionary claim to the English throne, he was a handsome, but as it soon turned out, spoilt and dissolute weakling.

Though the marriage broke down almost at once through his vices, it brought her, in the summer of 1566, a son and heir. Less than eight months after the wedding, refused the crown matrimonial which he coveted and bitterly resentful of the influence of a low-born Italian musician, a former boon companion and favourite of his own named David Riccio, whom, to the general scandal, Mary, with her love of music and gaiety, had made her private secretary, the jealous husband allied himself in return for their political support with a gang of disgruntled Protestant nobles. Together they broke into the palace of Holyroodhouse, where the pregnant Queen was supping with Riccio, her lady-in-waiting and friends, and, dragging the terrified Italian from the room as he clung to her skirts, hacked him to pieces in the doorway.

Held prisoner by the murderers, with splendid courage Mary planned her revenge. Wheedling her weak, cowardly husband into deserting his fellow conspirators, she escaped, heavy with child, from her captured palace in a wild midnight ride to Dunbar. Here, rallying her supporters, she resumed her reign. Nine months later, at midnight on February 9th 1567, despite an apparent reconciliation, her unwanted husband, the titular King, was murdered under horrific circumstances which brought her under grave suspicion of being party to the crime. For the man universally regarded as its instigator, the earl of Bothwell – a reckless Border baron with a fatal facility with women – was widely believed to be the Queen's lover and was known to be divorcing his wife, apparently with a view to marrying her. Suspicion turned to near certainty when, a few weeks after the murder of her husband, he abducted Mary, and, immediately afterwards, pardoned by her for the rape, married her.

In the ensuing popular outcry and fury Bothwell had to fly the country, while Mary, with mobs crying 'Burn the whore', was forced to abdicate in favour of her infant son, James VI, and accept a regency under her bastard Protestant half-brother, the earl of Moray. Imprisoned in the lake castle of Loch Leven for nearly a year, she escaped at the beginning of May 1568, only to be at once defeated by the Regent's forces at Langside. After a desperate flight through the heather, she crossed the Solway in a fishing boat and, almost penniless, sought refuge in England. 'I am now forced out of my kingdom,' she wrote to Elizabeth, 'and driven to such straits that, next to God, I have no hope but in your goodness.'

These terrible events in Scotland – saved only eight years earlier by Elizabeth's intervention from French domination and an enforced return to Rome – placed the English queen in a grave dilemma. On the one hand she wished to succour her unfortunate cousin and restore her to her throne, for she regarded the rights and duties of anointed sovereigns, and their responsibility to God for the governance of their realms as sacrosanct and not to be impugned or abrogated by subjects. On the other hand – for, unlike Mary, she was ruled by her head and not her emotions – she needed for her people's safety to preserve the Scottish Reformation and maintain friendly relations with the Regent Moray and Scotland's new Protestant rulers. These were now all the more important to England's future as the guardians of Mary's infant son James VI – Elizabeth's own godchild and the next legitimate successor after Mary to the childless English throne. For these reasons, and, in view of the dangers threatening both countries from the religiously riven Continent, she dared not let her fugitive and unwelcome guest out of her keeping. There had long been a love-hate relationship between the royal cousins, the one – so much a Tudor, resenting the other's early attempt to impugn her legitimacy and claim her throne, the other – so much a Stuart, equally resenting the other's understandable reluctance to acknowledge her claim to the succession. But Elizabeth was profoundly shocked by the Scots' dethronement and imprisonment of their hereditary sovereign. 'They had no warrant nor authority by the law of God or man,' she wrote, 'to be as superiors, judges or vindicators over their prince and sovereign, howsoever they do gather or conceive matter of disorder against her.' And when Mary indignantly declared herself guiltless of the crimes her rebellious subjects charged against her, she replied, 'O Madam! there is no creature living who wishes to hear such a declaration more than I, or will more readily lend her ears to any answer that will acquit your honour.'

Ignoring, therefore, the protests of her Ministers and Council, who regarded Mary's presence as a threat to the realm's peace and safety, Elizabeth, though keeping her captive, treated her as an honoured royal guest, offering her the hospitality of her northern castles and hunting forests but declining to receive her at Court until she had been cleared of the charge of murdering her husband. Mary, however, indignantly demurred at the idea of her cousin adjudicating between her and her rebel subjects. But, assured by

Elizabeth's promise to restore her to her kingdom, by force if necessary, should their charges against her be disproved, she acceded, reluctantly, to an English Commission of Enquiry being set up in York in October 1568. Almost at the same time, she began to make secret overtures through the Spanish ambassador to King Philip and the Pope, offering, with the help of a foreign invasion, to raise the English North in favour of a restoration of the Catholic faith. For, ignoring her cousin's warning at her first coming that 'those who have two strings to their bow may shoot stronger but rarely shoot straight,' and indignant at her captivity, Mary could not refrain from intriguing to regain her freedom and lost power, using her fatal charm to win men's hearts to her ends. And as northern England – remote, underpopulated and backward-looking – was still by far the most Catholic part of the country, she soon became, as Elizabeth's ministers had feared, a romantic rallying point for all who longed to restore the old faith under a Catholic, instead of a Protestant, Crown. Nor, with her sanguine, emotional nature, did she find it difficult to persuade those of her English neighbours of a like way of thinking to share her hopes.

CHAPTER FOUR

O Peaceful England

'In her days every man shall eat in safety
Under his own vine what he plants; and sing
The merry songs of peace to all his neighbours.'
Shakespeare

IT SO HAPPENED that in the fall of the year in which Mary sought refuge in England the relations between that country and Spain – in the past traditional allies against their common enemy, France – were coming under growing strain. For a clash of interest had lately arisen in two quarters gravely affecting both England's trade and her people's feeling. One was in the Netherlands – the rich industrial and commercial community of cloth towns in the continental alluvial plain facing the Thames estuary which from time immemorial had provided the country's, and London's, principal trading outlet to Europe. Formerly part of the powerful independent Burgundian dukedom – 'waterish Burgundy' as the greatest of Elizabethan poets was to call it – it had passed by marriage into the Spanish-Hapsburg dynastic empire of Charles V and, on his abdication in 1555, to his son, Philip II of Spain.

King Philip's character and outlook, unlike that of his internationally minded father, had been formed by the stark, uncompromising Iberian land in which he had grown up and to which, after his father's death, he withdrew, never again to leave it. And as, like his country, he was intensely and devotedly pious and, by temperament and occupation, a dedicated bureaucrat with a passion for uniformity, he and his distant easy-going Netherlander subjects soon found themselves at loggerheads.

More particularly in their northern, trading seaboard a growing number of them disagreed with their distant Iberian King over the matter dearest to his heart, Catholic religious orthodoxy.

For the opening years of Philip's reign had coincided with a rapid escalation of heretic preaching in the Netherlands, as in the adjoining territories of the Holy Roman Emperor, Germany and France. They also witnessed, with the final conclusion in 1564 of the Council of Trent, the full force of the new Catholic Counter-Reformation against the subversionist and divisive doctrines of Luther, Zwingli and Calvin. In no country was that great campaign for the faith welcomed more whole-heartedly than in Spain. Her whole history for five centuries had been a continuing crusade to win back by the sword formerly Christian lands from Moors and infidels. For, to a Spaniard, a heretic and an infidel were one.

Though still predominantly Catholic, particularly in its richer southern provinces, the peoples of the Netherlands, who were of several races, cultures and languages, did not feel in this way. When a Flemish heretic, who had trampled on a consecrated wafer, had his offending hand and foot wrenched off by red-hot irons and his tongue torn out before being publicly roasted to death in chains over a slow fire, the citizens of Bruges and the Estates of the Catholic province of Flanders petitioned their Spanish sovereign against the Inquisitor who had inflicted such a punishment. And the country's leading princes and nobles, many of whom had served and fought under Philip's father, and even his own Regent, his illegitimate half-sister the duchess Margaret of Parma, pleaded for less drastic methods of securing religious orthodoxy and uniformity in such a comparatively sophisticated and civilized society as Renaissance Burgundy – the land of Memling and Van Eyck.

But to the autocrat Philip, such appeals smacked of treasonable weakness, putting those who made them in the category, if not of heretics, of rebels. And when such criminal, as he viewed it, leniency on the part of the provincial authorities resulted in a fanatic minority of Protestant zealots breaking into Antwerp Cathedral and other churches to smash sacred statues, pictures and ornaments as idolatrous and superstitious baubles, the 'Most

Catholic' Majesty, as Philip's proud title was, resolved to teach the Netherlanders, leaders and people alike, a much-needed lesson they would never forget.

During the summer of 1567, when the marriage of Mary Queen of Scots with her husband's murderer was being expiated by her dethronement and imprisonment, armed with King Philip's commission as Captain-General of the Netherlands a man as stern and inflexible as himself and far more ruthless and cruel – the Castilian grandee and veteran military commander, the duke of Alva – was marching north through the Mount Cenis pass at the head of an army of 10,000 crack mercenaries from Spain's Italian provinces to discipline the Low Countries. Reaching Brussels on August 22nd, he wasted no time. Within a fortnight he had arrested the country's two leading Catholic princes – one of them, Count Egmont, the Stadtholder of Flanders and hero of the great Spanish victories against the French of St Quentin and Gravelines. At the same time he instituted a court of summary justice, with overriding powers of life and death, entitled the Court of Tumults, but soon to be known popularly as the Court of Blood. Through it he inaugurated a reign of terror, under which hundreds of Netherlands nobles perished on the scaffold or were sentenced to imprisonment.

Stunned at first by the magnitude of the calamity which had befallen them, the unwarlike peoples of the Low Countries watched in horror the extinction of their provincial liberties. But in May 1568, the month in which the Queen of Scots fled to England from the wrath of her subjects, a rising, impelled by desperation, broke out against the alien tyrant under the leadership of William Prince of Orange – the one magnate who, by leaving the country, had escaped Alva's initial arrest. Though joined by his brother, Count Louis of Nassau, it was short lived and mercilessly crushed by the Spanish army of occupation. Meanwhile thousands of helpless Protestants – for the most part humble artisans and craftsmen – fled by sea to the only refuge open to them, England, their old commercial customer and supplier. Their coming, and the pity aroused by their plight, caused a wave of popular feeling against Spain and Catholicism. So did the dislocation brought about by the persecution to England's long-established trade-links with the Netherlands. Of particular concern to the Queen and her Ministers was the disastrous effect it had on the highly sensitive money-market of Antwerp – then Europe's chief banking centre – on which the English Government, like most other governments at the time, depended for credit and supplies of specie.

That December a convoy carrying bullion from Genoese bankers, urgently needed for the payment of Alva's army in the Low Countries, was scattered by storms and took refuge in Plymouth and other south coast ports from the pirates and privateers swarming in the English Channel as a result of a new outbreak of religious civil war in France. Itself short of bullion through the collapse of the Antwerp money-market, the English government refused to allow the gold to proceed while they entered into negotiations with the Genoese bankers, whose property it legally was until delivered to its Spanish borrowers, with a view to borrowing it for themselves. This high-handed action had the dual effect of precipitating a furious complaint from Spain and ultimately, of causing a mutiny among Alva's mercenary troops. But it so happened that at that moment Elizabeth was able to counter it by complaining of a far more high-handed action against her subjects and property by Philip's officers on the other side of the Atlantic.

For another cause of difference between the two countries had arisen four thousand miles away, where Spain's intolerance in matters of faith was matched by her equal rigidity in matters of commerce. Her claim to a monopoly of all trade with America and the Indies, beyond the arbitrary ocean line drawn by the papal grant of 1493 to Spain and Portugal, had always been contested by England even before she repudiated the papal authority. For it constituted a threat to interests even more vital to her than the trade and markets of the Netherlands. And that Christmas news reached England of a shocking outrage committed by a Spanish Viceroy and his troops against English seamen and traders in the harbour of San Juan de Ulloa, the chief port of colonial Mexico.

Earlier that year John Hawkins, a thriving shipowner and merchant of Plymouth, had sailed for the West Indies with ten small ships, two of them owned by the Queen, bearing a consignment of negro slaves from the Guinea coast for sale to the Spanish colonists in the Caribbean, who, needing labour for their plantations, offered a ready and remunerative market for them. It was the third of such voyages made by him since 1562, when, learning of the colonists' demand for slave labour while trading with the Spanish Canaries, he had followed up his father's, William Hawkins's, pioneer voyages of twenty years earlier to the Guinea coast of Africa, in search of gold and ivories. Breaking into this far more lucrative trade and purchasing from local chieftains and slave-raiders a consignment of negroes – the cheapest and easiest-come-by commodity of that barbarous continent, where slave-owning, slave-trading and slave-raiding had flourished from time immemorial – he shipped them across the Atlantic to the Caribbean and Spanish Main.

In September 1568, having disposed of his cargo of slaves and made a highly profitable mutual exchange of goods with the Spanish colonists – whose easy-going local officials turned a blind eye to this forbidden but providential commerce with interlopers and heretics – Hawkins, his ships battered by a storm in the Gulf of Mexico, put into San Juan de Ulloa to refit and revictual before returning to his native Devon. It so happened that he had hardly anchored in the harbour, when the annual Plate Fleet arrived from Spain with the new Viceroy of Mexico aboard, Don Martin Enriquez. Unlike the colonial authorities, this stately functionary could not be expected to overlook any open breach of his royal master's orders. Though much inferior in tonnage and numbers, the superior gunnery of the English traders could have enabled Hawkins to keep the newcomers out of the port until he was ready to leave it. But, deeply conscious that he claimed to hold a commission from his Queen and even to be acting in the interests of King Philip himself – who only ten years earlier had been England's titular king and closest ally – and that any act of violence, even in self-defence, could involve war for his royal mistress who had strictly enjoined him not to harm any Spanish subject, he made a pact with the Viceroy. In return for allowing his fleet to enter the harbour, he secured from him an undertaking that the English ships should be allowed to complete their revictualling in peace before proceeding on their way home.

Having gained admission to the port, instead of honouring his word the Viceroy secretly summoned by night a thousand soldiers from the nearby garrison of Vera Cruz and used them to surprise and board the English trading vessels, whose crews they imprisoned and sent to the galleys or dungeons of the Inquisition. Only two ships managed to escape, the little *Judith* of 50 tons, whose commander, a twenty-five-year-old salt named Francis Drake, by fine seamanship cleared the harbour in time and returned home with her crew intact, and the scarcely larger *Minion*, a Queen's ship, which evacuated two hundred men, including Hawkins himself, from his doomed flagship. But, bereft of food and water on the long voyage home, after indescribable sufferings only fifteen survivors reached England in January 1569.

That act of black treachery – and the subsequent torture and martyrdom of helpless seamen – aroused feelings among their fellow west countrymen against Spain and the Roman Church even more bitter than those of the Londoners who had witnessed the Smithfield fires. Coming on top of the pitiful flood of fugitives from Alva's persecutions and Elizabeth's retention of the bullion intended to pay his mercenaries, its immediate impact was to exacerbate relations between England and Spain. The latter placed an embargo on English trade with the Netherlands and arrested English traders and travellers, while the islanders retaliated in kind. It was an exchange in which the latter were much the gainers, since, with their strategic position athwart Spain's sea communications with the Netherlands, they were able to play havoc with all Spanish merchandise and shipping using the English Channel.

*　　*　　*

It was under these circumstances that the captive Queen of Scots was able to repay the shelter Elizabeth offered her from her rebellious Protestant subjects by fomenting a rebellion of her English hostess's Catholic ones. 'Tell the Ambassador,' she informed an emissary from that diplomat, 'that if his master will help me, I shall be Queen of England in three months, and Mass shall be said all over the country.' And as the warlike Catholics of the North flocked to pay court to this romantic and beautiful exile of their own faith, herself the heir presumptive to the English throne, rumours of coming change began to circulate from mouth to mouth throughout the fells and dales of Westmorland, Yorkshire, Durham and Northumberland. Among those who succumbed to her charm was the chairman of the Court of Enquiry set up to investigate the criminal charges brought by the Scots against her – the duke of Norfolk. To him – England's sole remaining duke and a member of the Queen's Council – Mary secretly addressed affectionate letters implying that, if her marriage with Bothwell could be set aside, he might aspire to her hand. Warned by her ministers' intelligence agents of the purport of this clandestine correspondence, Elizabeth summoned Norfolk to Court. When he failed to take the chance offered him of making a full disclosure, she clapped him into the Tower.

That autumn it became known that, anticipating an English rising in Mary's favour, the Pope was preparing to pronounce Elizabeth excommunicate, releasing her Catholic subjects from the duty of obeying her. Before he could do so, the feudal North was already in arms. The church bells were rung backwards – the ancient summons to war of the Marches – and the Catholic farmers and shepherds of the dales turned out in their thousands with their fathers' arms. Too late to draw back from the treasonable brink into which Mary's tragic beguilements had led them, the earls of Northumberland and Westmorland, with their armed Percy and Neville retainers, marched into Durham on November 14th. At their head was the aged Catholic Sheriff of Yorkshire, Richard Norton, bearing the banner of the Five Wounds. It was the Pilgrimage of Grace of thirty years earlier over again. And, while already removed in haste from Bolton Castle in Wensleydale to Tutbury Castle in Staffordshire, Mary was hurried away still further south to Coventry, the rebels heard Mass in Durham Cathedral, burnt the English prayer book, and, seizing the port of Hartlepool for Alva's hoped-for landing, marched on York.

Yet though rumours circulated in London that Alva had sworn to pay his soldiers their arrears in Cheapside and make England's heretic Queen hear Mass in St Paul's at Candlemas, the rising collapsed as quickly as it had begun. Throughout the entire south and midlands the forces of the Crown and countryside, both Catholic and Protestant, remained solid in loyalty. Within a month of taking up arms the northern rebels, hopelessly outnumbered, dispersed without giving battle, their leaders flying across the Border to join Mary's sympathizers in southern Scotland. It was the last tragic chapter in the long feudal saga of Neville and Percy. The earl of Northumberland, captured by the Scottish Protestants, was handed over to justice in England and beheaded, while his fellow earl of Westmorland, finding no shelter in Scotland, fled abroad and lived out his life in exile as a pensioner of Spain. There was a brief recrudescence of fighting early in 1570, when another great northern magnate, Leonard Dacre, having failed to come out with his tenants in November owing to a personal quarrel with Norfolk, belatedly rose in the New Year. But he received his quietus at the battle of the Gelt on February 19th, when the Queen's cousin, Henry Carey, Lord Hunsdon, encountered him with only half his numbers and totally routed him. 'I much doubt, my Harry,' Elizabeth wrote to the gratified victor, 'whether that the victory were given me more joyed me, or that you were by God appointed the instrument of my glory; and I assure you that for my country's good the first might suffice, but for my heart's contentation the second more pleased me.'

Nor did any invasion from Spain follow the rising. For neither Alva in the Netherlands nor his distant master in Madrid were prepared to entrust an army to the mercy of the elements and of English seamen so long as England herself stood four square in loyalty to her Queen. As the rising had failed and there was no invasion, the Pope's excommunication of Elizabeth, when it came in February 1570, proved a damp squib. And though that January Elizabeth and the Scottish Protestants suffered a setback when the Regent Moray was assassinated, the Queen, striking swiftly back, put new heart into the adherents of the boy king, James VI and the Calvinist reformers. Using the flight of the rebels across the Border as a pretext, she sent a force after them under the President of the North, the earl of Sussex. It struck such terror throughout the Marches that, from the great English border fortress at Berwick to the Solway Firth, a peace, such as that restless region had scarcely ever known, reigned there for months. As a historian of the raid put it, it was 'the honourablest journey that ever was made into Scotland, with so few men, with so safe a return'.

The romantic Scottish queen's attempt to plunge England into the murderous internecine religious strife sweeping the Continent had ended in failure and tragedy for her adherents. For, under the martial law which accompanied the pacification of the wild dales and moors of the North, hundreds perished on the gallows or suffered forfeiture and exile. But it did not end either the Queen of Scots' intrigues to win her freedom and, with it, the English crown, nor the persistent refusal of her royal cousin to accede to the now almost universal demand of her ministers and people for her death.

Among those operating on Mary's behalf that summer was a Florentine banker named Roberto Ridolfi. Well known socially in City, and even government circles, as an undercover papal intermediary, he had been a principal party in secretly smuggling the Pope's bull of excommunication into England. An ardent Catholic, he entered that summer into a clandestine correspondence with Norfolk, whom, giving him the benefit of the doubt as to the degree of his involvement in the late rising, the Queen had just released from the Tower. Persuading that nobleman, to whom Mary was still writing love-letters, to resume his hopes of marrying her, he unfolded a wild plan of his own devising, blessed by the Pope and favoured, so he assured him, by King Philip, his ambassador in England, and Alva. Under this a Spanish invasion force of 10,000 men from the Netherlands was to land at either Portsmouth or Harwich, and, overturning the government, place Mary on the throne with Norfolk as her consort and king.

Armed with the names of forty supposedly dissatisfied peers who, in his sanguine belief, would take up arms for Mary, this self-important financier set off in the spring of 1571 for the continent to prime Alva, the Pope and the King of Spain. With his hands fully employed eradicating rebellion and heresy in the Netherlands, Alva, a military realist, had no intention of risking his army in an invasion of England until either Elizabeth was dead or a successful rising of Mary's followers had first secured, and held for forty days, a bridgehead for his troops. With his plotter's list of names of potential rebels, Ridolfi struck him as a dangerous babbler. But the Pope and Philip proved of more credulous stuff, and at Madrid Ridolfi proposed that, as a prelude to the rising and invasion, Elizabeth should first be assassinated.

All this he reported at length in elaborately concealed cipher letters to his fellow conspirators in England, including Mary and Norfolk, who, dazzled by the hope of exchanging a ducal coronet for a matrimonial crown, weakly lent himself to Ridolfi's temptingly ambitious but perilous dream. But the watchful and omnipresent spies of Cecil's intelligence network and that of its unresting organizer, Francis Walsingham, intercepted Ridolfi's messengers and eventually broke his ciphers, the keys to which were found hidden under the tiles of Norfolk's London house. The duke's arrest and return to the Tower followed immediately, and in January 1572 he was tried by his peers in Westminster Hall, found guilty and sentenced to death for treason.

A popular figure at Court and in the country, and, as England's solitary duke and, though himself only lately a convert to Rome, head of the nation's leading Catholic family, Norfolk survived for a further five months before the merciful and temporizing Queen could finally bring herself to sign his death warrant. 'The Queen's Majesty,' wrote Cecil – now promoted to the peerage as Lord Burghley – 'hath always been a merciful lady, and by mercy she hath taken more harm than by justice, and yet she thinks that she is more beloved in doing herself harm – God save her to his honour long among us.' It took the combined pressure of her anxious Council and of a new Parliament, which met in May 1572, to bring her to the sticking point and let Norfolk die, the first noble of the reign to perish on the scaffold.

Yet, though horrified by the Ridolfi plot, the entire country clamoured for Mary's death – 'the bosom serpent', as Walsingham called her – nothing could bring Elizabeth to sacrifice her to public clamour. She agreed to her closer surveillance and restraint in the northern castles where, under the watchful eye of one nobleman or other, she kept her phantom court, and for the moment – though not permanently – the English queen abandoned the hope of restoring her, either alone or in conjunction with the boy King James, to the Scottish throne. But when, in the summer of 1572, a joint committee of both Houses of Parliament, specially summoned to make provision for Elizabeth's safety, petitioned for Mary's immediate death, describing their request as 'a call and cry to God of all good subjects against the merciful nature of the Queen,' they were met by a firm royal refusal. It was couched in terms of such loving gratitude for their care and loyalty that one member even proposed voting her thanks for the good opinion she had of them. Frustrated in its attempt to bring in an Act of Attainder against Mary, Parliament passed a bill, depriving her of all claim to the English throne and making it a treasonable offence for anyone to advocate it, even legalizing lynch law against her if she should ever again plot against Elizabeth's life or throne. But the compassionate Queen again refused to give it the royal assent.

*　　*　　*

The country's rage against Mary was the measure of Elizabeth's popularity. This now seemed boundless. To Protestants abroad, struggling against the terrifying force of the persecuting Counter-Reformation or flying in their thousands to England for shelter, the queen appeared as a Deborah raised by God to save His faithful. To her own people her frail, irreplaceable, indomitable life alone stood between them and a repetition of the horrors which had overwhelmed the continent – the massacres, rapes, tortures and burnings of a brutal soldiery and a merciless Inquisition. After the defeat of the Northern Rebellion the anniversary of Elizabeth's accession – November 17th – was kept as a day of national thanksgiving and rejoining, with pealing church bells, feasts and bonfires – the answer of a free people to the Pope's excommunication and anathemas and the Smithfield fires of the divisive Marian past. 'We have cause daily to praise God,' the Speaker of the House of

Commons addressed her, 'that ever you were given us!'

For in fourteen years of ruling, in the face of all perils and problems, Elizabeth had made a united nation. And, as it grew in
wealth and strength, it was becoming a confident one. To make it
so had from the start been her aim and that of her ministers. Chosen
by her from the new, non-feudal middle class, their strength, like
hers, lay in their understanding of England and of its people's
needs and feelings. High and resplendent office the Queen conferred on her favourites and on the figureheads of the old aristocracy, but real power she reserved for a little group of men who made
statecraft and her service the business of their lives. Their fidelity
she ensured by seeing that they were committed up to the hilt to
the success of her policies, and by rewarding them enough – but
no more – to raise in them the expectation of further favours to
come.

At their head was the great Secretary of State, William Cecil,
who for forty of the forty-five years of the reign, until his death in
1598, was the Queen's *fidus Achates*. On the death of the old
marquis of Winchester in 1572, she made him Lord Treasurer.
In him, though she gave him many anxious moments, she reposed
a noble trust; her 'spirit', she called him. No prince in Europe, she
once said, had such a counsellor as she had of him. 'This judgment
I have of you,' she had told him on his appointment to her Council,
'that you will not be corrupted with any manner of gift, and that
you will be faithful to the State, and that without respect of my
private wish you will give me that counsel that you think best, and
that, if you know anything necessary to be declared unto me of
secrecy, you shall show it to myself only, and assure yourself I will
not fail to keep taciturnity therein.' Never was mutual trust better
justified.

At the start of the reign, faced by the bankruptcy of the
Treasury and the country's almost total defencelessness, the
Queen's and Cecil's first care had been to buy from abroad the
arms and munitions it so desperately needed, and to restore the
purity of the currency, debased by the dishonourable clippings of
the last three reigns. To restore public confidence in the medium of
exchange, they called down the value of all the base money minted

in the past fifteen years and issued in its place a completely new silver currency. In both operations they were aided by the genius and immense experience of the Crown's financial agent at Antwerp, Sir Thomas Gresham – a man of infinite resource after Elizabeth's own heart. 'As the exchange,' he wrote to her, 'is the thing that eats out all princes to the whole destruction of their common weal if it be not substantially looked into, so likewise the exchange is the chiefest and richest thing only, above all others, to restore your Majesty and your Realm to fine gold and silver, and is the means that makes all foreign commodities and your own commodities with all kinds of victuals good cheap, and likewise keeps your fine gold and silver within your Realm.'

Operating from Antwerp – before Alva's persecutions the financial centre of Europe – by foresight, meticulous attention to detail and unfailing punctuality in meeting the Crown's obligations, Gresham, with the Queen's backing, brought down the rates of interest, at which English governments had been forced to borrow, from thirteen and fourteen per cent to half and less than half that rate. Other European rulers with far larger resources, as a result of their procrastination in repaying, were forced to go on borrowing at ruinously high rates. 'It will not be a little spoken of through all the world,' Gresham noted proudly, 'that Her Majesty in her wars both make payment of her debts, when neither King Philip, the French king nor the King of Portugal in peacetime payeth nothing, who oweth no small sums of money.' It was his contention that the Queen should borrow, not from foreigners, but from her own subjects, 'whereby,' he claimed, 'all other princes may see what a Prince of power she is.' It was a situation which he did much in his lifetime to bring about. Before Alva's arbitrary taxes and the sack of Antwerp by his unpaid soldiery had driven its bankers and capitalists to seek in Protestant London a new and more secure international money and credit market, Gresham had built at his own expense an English Bourse or Exchange in Lombard Street, crowning it with his crest of the frugal and industrious grasshopper. Here, in the year after the Northern Rising, the Queen, after dining with him in his magnificent Bishopsgate mansion, caused her heralds to proclaim the new institution he had created – the Royal Exchange – to the sound of trumpets, so setting her seal on a process which in the fullness of time was to make the City of London the financial capital of the world.

With the economy operating now on a sound monetary basis the royal and Cecilian policy was to encourage every activity which could strengthen a small nation dependent, in a world of vast Powers, on quality rather than quantity. It rested on a recognition that England's real wealth lay in the character – the virtue, integrity, industry and enterprise – of her people. Building on its natural resources of corn, wool, timber, coal and iron and its strategic position athwart northern Europe's ocean trade-routes, Cecil sought to make England self-sufficient, first in the means of defending itself and then of creating enduring riches.

Serving both these ends was his encouragement of fishing, the trade which bred and trained seamen to carry the nation's merchandise, both coastwise and across the broad seas, and, in war, to man the Royal Navy. With her long, deeply indented coastline, something like half her four or five million people depended for their livelihood, directly or indirectly, on the sea. To encourage fishing, after agriculture England's chief source of wealth, Cecil in 1563 increased from two to three the number of compulsory weekly fish days – originally established by his former chief, the Lord Protector Somerset, to replace the medieval Church's enforcement of Lent, Fridays and fast-days. 'Let the old course of fishing,' he wrote in a memorandum for Parliament, 'be maintained by the straightest observation of fish days for policy's sake, so the sea coast should be strong with men and habitations, and the fleet flourish.' With Ember days and Lent this policy ensured a protected market for fish for half the year, so providing, with the help of bounties on shipbuilding, a livelihood and training for the country's hardiest, most daring and adaptable sons, giving point and purpose to the old fishermen's song:

> 'The husbandman has rent to pay,
> Blow, winds, blow!
> And seed to purchase every day,
> Row, boys, row!
> But he who farms the rolling deeps,

Though never sowing, always reaps,
The ocean's fields are fair and free,
There are no rent days on the sea.'

In other directions Elizabeth and her ministers pursued the
same protective, fostering and socially cohesive policy. The crying
problems of unemployment and vagrancy – so menacing since the
dissolution of the monasteries – were met by a succession of Poor
Laws. These, in the course of the reign, made the parish the unit of
relief, dividing those in need of assistance into two classes. For
those willing and able to work, but unable to obtain it, work and
the necessary tools and working materials were to be found by the
parish. The aged and impotent who were unable to work were to be
supported by outdoor relief in their own homes. Those who could,
but would not, work were, as in the past, to be branded as 'idle
rogues and vagabonds', whipped and sent back to the parish of
their origin or 'settlement', or, in larger units of population, to
Houses of Correction, there to be made to work 'as a true man
should do'. But the great principle of a statutory provision for the
poor – to be defined by Dr Johnson as the test of a civilized society –
was by the end of the reign part of the permanent law of England.
A compulsory poor rate, enforced by the Privy Council, levied by
Justices of the Peace and payable, in proportion to their means, by
all rate-payers, was the ultimate Elizabethan administrative legacy
to England, comparabie in importance to the supremacy of the
King's courts and Common Law bequeathed to it by Henry II,
and to the legislative power of the Crown in Parliament established
by Edward I. No other country in Europe as yet possessed such a
socially stabilizing institution. To operate it annually appointed
Overseers of the Poor were added to the existing constables and
churchwardens of the parish, whose responsibility to the Justices
of the Peace appointing them was to provide work or relief for all
who, through no fault of their own, were in need. Evolved, as was
the English way, out of pragmatic experiment and proved experience, it was based, like the country's ancient jury system, on the
knowledge, judgment and responsibility of the neighbourhood.

All this, like the Statutes of Labourers, Artificers and Apprentices, was part of Cecil's triple strategy of fostering and safeguarding employment by protective monopolies and tariffs; of ensuring quality of workmanship by a compulsory seven years' apprenticeship for all skilled crafts; and – in search of the ancient Christian ideal of the 'just price' – of regulating wages to meet the inflationary rise caused by the fortuitous influx of precious metals from the Spanish mines in America. Yet, such were the moderation and careful nature of the man and his royal mistress, that this paternalistic policy was combined with a far greater freedom from internal tolls and interference with trade than existed anywhere else in Europe, whose great rivers – Rhine, Rhone, Loire and Elbe – were studded with princely and feudal fiscal obstructions to the flow of commerce. Nor was any country so lightly taxed as Elizabeth's and Cecil's England. Like Gladstone long after them, they believed in letting the subjects' wealth fructify in his own hands, realizing, in an age of corrupt and inevitably inefficient administration, that the individual was far more capable of augmenting his income and wealth for his own and the general good than any government, however well-meaning.

Frugality in administrative costs and public expenditure – 'parsimony', as Elizabeth's critics called it, but, in effect, the only realistic way of combatting and checking corruption at a time when cheating the Crown was a universal practice – served the ends both of Cecil's patient, far-sighted, conservative and conserving policy and the Queen's natural bent and conviction. It was under the fostering care and with the encouragement of such a government – careful, prudent yet cautiously experimental – that, during the long Elizabethan peace of close on a quarter of a century, Englishmen of all classes, shaking off the lethargy, inertia and fears of the past, set themselves to make their island home a more comfortable one, and to win, by hard work and venturing, a higher standard of living for themselves and their children. Freed by their sovereign's tolerant and unifying ecclesiastical settlement from the ideological and religious frenzies which had formerly divided their country and which were now devastating the Continent, and sustained by a strong personal faith in God and the revealed and translated Scriptures, an insular Protestant people embarked, individually and collectively, on a prolonged period of growing prosperity and accumulation of wealth.

It was during Elizabeth's reign that the villages of southern England began to assume the appearance which was to characterize them for the next three centuries. Beautifully built farmhouses and cottages of half timber and brick or half-cast, and, in the limestone belt, of stone, began to take the place of the rude mud and wattle shacks of the medieval peasantry, while stone manor houses, with lattice-windows, porches, and panelled rooms, set among formal gardens, rose to partner the stone church towers of the older Catholic England. And, before the reign ended, much grander houses, many on the site of dissolved abbeys, took their place in the English landscape, built in the new classical style of the Italian Renaissance but with homely English differences, vast oriel windows and long galleries and gateways.

All the three main sources of English wealth – agriculture, seafaring and the cloth trade – flourished under the stimulus of individual ownership, freed from the shackles of the medieval clerical past, and within the framework of a stable and united kingdom whose ruler's objective was to make her people self-sufficient, confident and prosperous. In little more than sixty years after her accession, shipments of sea-coal to London from the Northumbrian mines multiplied roughly tenfold, the size of the country's merchant fleet five-fold, while, in the course of the reign, receipts from Customs on overseas trade doubled. 'If I should say the sweetest speech with the eloquentest tongue that ever was in man,' the Queen told Parliament, 'I were not able to express that restless and care which I have ever bent to govern for the greatest wealth.'

Confident of being able to transmit their lands to their posterity, the owners of the monastic acres which had passed into private hands in the reign of Elizabeth's father and brother now embarked on long term improvements of the soil – liming, marling, composting, draining, hedging and enclosing. 'Their hearts, hands, eyes and all their powers,' John Norden, the map-maker, wrote of the improving squires and yeomen of the West Country, 'concur in one, to force the earth to yield her utmost fruit.' Nothing was wasted, everything used to enrich themselves and their families.

78

Works like John Fitzherbert's *Book of Husbandry* and Thomas Tusser's rhyming *Five Hundred Points of Good Husbandry* enjoyed a popularity second only to the translated Bible and Foxe's *Book of Martyrs.*

Nor was it only in agriculture that Englishmen sought to improve their environment and turn it to private and public enrichment. Released from the stultifying tyranny over thought and imagination of the medieval Church in decay – in its youth and prime the teacher and civilizer of Christendom – English minds in search of material betterment began to explore the possibilities of exploiting the physical phenomena of the land they inhabited. Elizabeth's reign saw the dawn – a first faint flush across the virginal rustic landscape – of an industrial revolution which in coming centuries was to transform England, and, following her lead, Europe and America. Interrupted after Elizabeth's death by the tragic struggle between Crown and Parliament, its course was resumed after the Restoration and the Revolution of 1688.

During her reign, aided by the credit facilities afforded by Gresham and his fellow financiers of London's new money-market, England began to take the lead in industrial technology, hitherto enjoyed by Germany – split and fragmented now by the terrible internecine strife of the Reformation and Counter-Reformation. Mining and processing not only iron and tin, as in the past, but also for the first time copper and brass, by the end of the century the output from the coalfields of Northumberland and Durham, stimulated since the Henrician dissolution by the enterprise and inventiveness of their new private owners, far exceeded that of the rest of the continent put together. Much of the advance in mineral technology and production was due to Elizabeth's and Cecil's determination to make the country, in view of the perils facing it, independent of foreign arms and armaments. Under their encouragement and that of the Navy Board, the foundries of Sussex and Kent made long-range guns whose quality gave England's armed trading ships and privateers an ascendency, ship for ship, over those of every other nation, while John Evelyn, the diarist's grandfather, given a monopoly for manufacturing gunpowder, supplied from his mills in the wooded Surrey valleys the force and flame which enabled them to survive and prevail in every sea of the widening ocean world.

The very intolerance and inhumanity with which, in the years while Elizabeth was cultivating her peaceful English garden, the rulers of Spain, France, Portugal and Austria suppressed heresy in their dominions helped, too, to enrich England, as thousands of skilled workers fled across the Channel and North Sea to seek refuge under the Protestant Deborah's protecting wing. They brought with them the jealously guarded secrets and mysteries of their lucrative crafts. To the hereditary skill of the native smiths, nailors, scythe and harness-makers of the Black Country and the tin-miners of Cornwall – 'as hard and diligent labourers in that kind of trade as are to be found in Europe,' as one of their countrymen put it – there was added, in the second decade of the reign, an ever-growing stream of Flemish, Dutch and French craftsmen flying from the persecutions of the Counter-Reformation. German steel workers were settled in Sussex and paper-makers at Dartford in Kent, Huguenot glassmakers in Sussex, Dutch sugar-refiners from Antwerp in London, and Dutch engineers, brought into Cambridgeshire to drain the vast, watery, half-tidal Fens. Most beneficial of all to the country's economy were the thousands of Flemish weavers with their specialist skills who poured into the country to escape Alva's holocausts. They added a new impetus to England's thriving cloth trade, now widespread across the country from Yorkshire to East Anglia, and westwards into Gloucestershire, Wiltshire and Devonshire.

Much of the credit for the restored and flourishing state of the English economy belonged to Elizabeth's great minister, now Lord Burghley, who had so carefully nursed and nourished it. Yet it was the Queen who had appointed and sustained him, and without whose support he could have done little or nothing. And it was she who, by her dazzling and magnetic personality, and her love for her people, had infected the whole nation with her confidence, sense of purpose and awareness of its unity and destiny. Throughout her reign she continued the wooing of them begun at her accession and coronation and which, together with her diplomatic and political achievements, evoked such an astonishing response.

For she did not govern only from cabinet, council and presence chamber, but from her people's hearts, and in this lay her strength and magic. Moving from palace to palace – from riverside Greenwich to Whitehall, Richmond to Hampton Court, and Windsor – she was continuously on display, seeing and being seen by her subjects and communicating to them 'the affability', as well as splendour and majesty, of their prince. Every summer she went on progress, travelling with her enormous Court on horseback or raised high in an open litter. At the border of every county she was met by the sheriff and a train of local notables, and, wherever the common people thronged to see her, she would order her coach or litter to be taken to where the crowd was densest, there to address and talk familiarly with them. It was a dialogue between Queen and people, more informal but no less meaningful than between Queen and Parliament. And it was conducted in the language of love. At Coventry where the Mayor presented her with a purse of £100, she observed gratefully, 'It is a good gift, I have but few such, for it is £100 in gold.' 'If it please your Grace,' replied the Mayor, 'it is a great deal more.' 'What is that?' asked the Queen. 'It is the faithful hearts of all your loving subjects,' was the answer. 'We thank you, Mr Mayor,' she replied, 'that is a great deal more indeed.'

At other times she would honour one of her richer subjects by staying in his house or castle – a costly favour, though one for which many vied. It was probably in the summer of 1575, at one of these elaborate sojourns, held at her favourite, Lord Leicester's newly rebuilt Kenilworth Castle – a visit which lasted three weeks and, attended by an entire countryside, was marked by the most splendid entertainments, masques and pageants, 'princely pleasures', as they were called – that the young William Shakespeare, then a grammar schoolboy of eleven and son of an alderman and cornfactor of the neighbouring town of Stratford-upon-Avon, first set eyes on the Queen, before whom in her old age he was to act in his own plays in one or other of her royal palaces. And at the end of the autumn's progress, when she and her glittering Court returned to keep their wonted Christmas feast at Whitehall, they would be met by the Lord Mayor, alderman and liverymen in their ceremonial finery, with the customary exchange of greetings, 'God save your Grace!' and 'God save my people!' amid jubilant shouting and the roll of drums and blare of trumpets.

'It is difficult,' Sir John Neale wrote in his great biography of Elizabeth, 'to convey a proper appreciation of this amazing Queen, so keenly intelligent, so effervescing, so intimate, so imperious and regal. She intoxicated Court and country, keyed her realm to the intensity of her own spirit. No one but a woman could have done it – and no woman without her superlative gifts.' 'Her mind,' recalled her godson, Sir John Harington, 'was oftime like the gentle air that cometh from the westerly point in a summer's morn; 'twas sweet and refreshing to all around. Her speech did win all affections, and her subjects did try to show all love to her commands. . . . Again she could put forth such alterations when obedience was lacking as left no doubtings whose daughter she was.' Sir Christopher Hatton was wont to say, 'The Queen did fish for men's souls, and had so sweet a bait that no one could escape her network.'

Such was this great woman. Her character was a series of amazing contradictions; indeed, there were few attributes, good or bad, which she did not in some measure possess. She could make supreme decisions at moments, and in the long run nearly always arrived at the right conclusion, and yet it often seemed to her ministers that she was incapable of making up her mind or of pursuing a consistent course. 'For in truth,' wrote Cecil, 'she was more than a man, and sometimes less than a woman.' 'Now I see,' said the carter whom she had kept waiting while the royal plans for a journey were changed and rechanged a dozen times, 'she is a woman as well as my wife!'

Her vitality was amazing. She would do business with her ministers for hours before breakfast, walk in garden and gallery with the learned, showing off her wide knowledge and remarkable linguistic attainments, hunt all day and feast with music and dancing till long into the night. Like all persons of outstanding personality, she had the power of imparting her vitality to others, and her Court was a very lively place. Poor old Sir Francis Knollys complained he could not sleep because of the Maids of Honour, 'that they used, when retired for the night, to frisk and hey about so'. Behind her fierce, energetic nature was a strong sense of humour, and good humour at that. 'Keep your arithmetic to yourself,' she bade the tactless divine who preached to her in her old age on the text, 'Teach us so to number our days.'

Though she could be queenly beyond dreams, she could at other times unbend and, without losing her majesty, abandon all formality. When, creating her favourite earl of Leicester so that he could woo the proud Queen of Scots, she could not refrain at the height of the investiture from slipping her hand down his neck to tickle him. Once, in the midst of her court, a noble lord, bowing low before her, inadvertently let out a most uncourtly report and, ashamed beyond measure, fled the country in self-disgrace. Returning some years later after being assured that all was forgiven, he was received most graciously by the Queen, who held him long in conversation. As he was withdrawing, she called him back and whispered in his ear, 'My Lord, the fart's forgot!'

Greatest of all the Queen's services to England was the peace she gave her. When a divided Christendom was wracked by cruel ideological passions, within their watery bounds the English were at peace and unity. It was of this Elizabeth was most proud, and deservedly, for it was she who had saved them from the maelstrom by her diplomacy, her womanly dissimulation and cunning and, after her brief initial intervention in the religious wars of Scotland and France, her determination to spare both her people and purse from the waste, folly and destruction of war. She loved to receive, in the presence of foreigners, testimonies of the regard in which she and her Catholic subjects held one another, and when the outbreak of the Northern rebellion in 1569 for a moment shook her faith in her people's loyalty – before their overwhelming response, Catholic and Protestant alike, showed how little reason she had to doubt it – the French ambassador found her in tears.

*   *   *

Yet events in Europe were now moving fast, threatening the continued peace of her realm. In 1572, shortly after the exposure of the Ridolfi Plot, the people of the Netherlands once more rose in arms against Alva's intolerable tyranny and taxation. Powerless in the open field against the Spaniards' new weapon, the musket, but letting in the dykes to flood their land and taking to their boats, the sailors and fishermen of Holland and Friesland, calling themselves the Sea Beggars, made common cause with the Huguenot seamen of La Rochelle and the French western ports to wage merciless war against Spanish shipping in the North Sea and Channel. During the summer of that year they surprised and captured the outlying ports of Brill and Flushing – key to the Netherlanders' sea links with England and their best future hope of freeing themselves. For once again a wave of passionate sympathy for their co-religionists swept the English people, and hundreds of volunteers crossed the sea to serve under the Prince of Orange who had placed himself at the head of the rebellion.

That August, on St Bartholomew's Day, the menace of the Counter-Reformation in arms took a new and unexpected turn in a massacre of Huguenot leaders and followers, gathered in Paris for the wedding of the young Protestant King of Navarre to the French Queen Mother's daughter, Margaret de Valois – union which it had been hoped would end the ideological civil wars which had been tearing France apart and lead to a live-and-let-live religious settlement, not dissimilar to that which Elizabeth had achieved for England. Thousands perished in the holocaust, caused by a sudden hysteria and fanaticism, which, magnified by rumour, appalled English Protestants, whose own Queen, as part of her deliberate balancing act against Spain, had earlier that year negotiated a treaty of alliance with the French Queen Mother, Catherine de Medici, and her young son, Charles IX – a former aspirant to her hand.

Still more horrifying news for Protestant ears followed from the Netherlands where Alva and his soldiers now embarked on a campaign of deliberate terror and massacre. The town of Zutphen, which refused to admit his troops, was sacked and its inhabitants put to the sword. In his *Rise of the Dutch Republic* the historian Motley graphically described the fate which befell the people of Naarden when, hoping to escape the fate of Zutphen, its terrified burghers opened their gates to the Spaniards, only to be shot down without mercy.

> 'The town was then fired in every direction, that the skulking citizens might be forced from their hiding places. As fast as they came forth they were put to death by their impatient foes. Some were pierced with rapiers, some were chopped to pieces with axes, some were surrounded in the blazing streets by troops of laughing soldiers, intoxicated, not with wine but with blood, who tossed them to and fro with their lances . . . Those who attempted resistance were crimped alive like fishes and left to gasp themselves to death in lingering torture. The soldiers, becoming more and more insane as the foul work went on, opened the veins of some of their victims and drank their blood as if it were wine. Some of the burghers were for a time spared, that they might witness the violation of their wives and daughters, and were then butchered in company with those still more unfortunate victims.'

It was small wonder than an English member of Parliament – contrasting the fate of his co-religionists in Europe with what he called the 'peaceable government of Her Majesty' who 'doth make us to enjoy all that is ours in more freedom than any nation under the sun at this day,' – spoke of 'depopulations and devastations of whole provinces and countries, overthrowing, spoiling and sacking of cities and towns, imprisoning, ransoming and murdering of all kind of people.'

The feelings aroused by these happenings made it more difficult for Elizabeth both to keep England out of war and preserve the balance of her own tolerant and unifying church settlement. As religious persecution abroad intensified, she was subjected to increasing pressure from the growing body of Puritan activists in the country, and their demands for extreme measures against what they regarded as 'papist' ceremonies and idolatry – vestments, crucifixes, candles, the wearing of surplices, caps and gowns, and even kneeling at Communion. But though she was unable to control the wave of iconoclastic vandalism which, at the instigation of fanatics, was robbing the country's parish churches, like the abbeys before them, of England's rich inheritance of medieval statuary, painting and art, she persisted in retaining in her chapel royal the outward forms of worship and ritual music with which she had been familiar since childhood. Nor would she suffer gladly what she described as 'domine doctors with their long orations' or their dogmatic insistence on the theological tenets of Calvinist Geneva and of the new Protestant 'popes' who had succeeded the former Roman ones. And though she put no obstacles in the way of those who volunteered for service under the rebel patriot leader, William of Orange, and so won experience in the military art – of which her realm had been so perilously lacking at the time of her accession – she did her best to mediate between her old admirer, King Philip, and his rebellious Dutch and Flemish subjects. While trying to persuade him to grant them the same religious tolerance that she allowed her own – a freedom of conscience nothing would induce that most devout of princes to allow – she would have no truck with proposals to deprive him of their allegiance, and rejected out of hand William's offer to her in 1575 of a protectorate or sovereignty of the revolted provinces. For what she sought for herself and her people was not dominion over the territories and subjects of a fellow sovereign, but merely peace and freedom to trade where trade had been before.

Instead, she fell back on the matrimonial diplomacy by which she had sought to save her realm from the rival Catholic giants of France and Spain in the early years of her reign, setting the hopes and fears of one against the other. Now, as then, she had to keep a balance between two conflicting perils, doing what she could to help the struggling Netherland provinces recover their ancient liberties without goading her brother-in-law, King Philip, into war, while simultaneously discouraging their expanionist southern neighbour, France, from taking advantage of their revolt to free them from its old enemy, Spain, and absorb them itself. In pursuit of this aim, the preservation of the independence of the Low Countries – which was to remain a major principle of English foreign policy for the next three centuries – as soon as Elizabeth and her government had recovered from the shock of the Massacre of St Bartholomew's Day, she resumed her devious negotiations for a possible future marriage with a French prince. It was her way of insuring against both the risks that faced her and what to her was the biggest risk of all, the destructive and costly evil of war. And this in spite of the fact that she was now well into her forties and past the age when child-bearing was considered safe for a woman who had never borne a child. So that while in her twenties, when she had dangled the crown matrimonial before the fascinated eyes of Europe, her ministers and people, passionate to ensure their future safety by the birth of a suitable male heir to the throne, had viewed what Cecil called her 'prolonging and mincing' with ill-concealed impatience, they were now far from enthusiastic over the prospect of her marriage, especially as the foreign suitor favoured by her was a Catholic – though not a particularly devout one – with a bulbous nose and more than twenty years her junior. Her 'frog' she affectionately called him, and for nearly a decade until his death in 1584, the little duke of Alençon – a younger brother of the French king and later, as duke of Anjou, his heir – was, on and off, her official wooer, visiting England, first by proxy and then in person, and, with the dazzling prospect of its crown matrimonial before him, proving an eager and even, to her apparent delight, ardent one.

But by the time of his passing the great Queen had transformed her virginity, long used by her as an instrument of state, into a national patriotic emblem. Attended by every concomitant of romantic courtship and flowery bejewelled phrase, in which all her leading courtiers engaged, using the language of lovers to express their loyalty and adoration, the ageing royal vestal had become the inspiration of a resurgent nation. All her lovers, including her old and now elderly flame, Lord Leicester, were treated, and expected to behave, as devoted aspirants to her unattainable hand. In their exploits, her sailors, soldiers and explorers thought of themselves as her knights, serving an adored lady and mistress, and, when her favourites bestowed their attentions on – or married – anyone else, it was as suppliant lovers that they had to seek her forgiveness. 'How can I live alone in prison, when she is afar off,' wrote the bold adventurer, Sir Walter Ralegh, Captain of her Guard, after she had clapped him into the Tower for getting one of her Maids of Honour with child and, even worse offence in her eyes, marrying her; 'I that was wont to behold her riding like Alexander, hunting like Diana, walking like Venus, the gentle wind blowing her fair hair about her pure cheeks like a nymph, sometimes sitting in the shade like a Goddess, sometime playing like Orpheus.' In Edmund Spenser's romantic allegorical poem, *The Faerie Queene*, published in the fourth decade of the reign, she figured as Britomart, Queen of Chastity. To foreign Catholic onlookers, it almost seemed as though a nation of heretic iconoclasts had unconsciously reverted to the Mariolatry of their devout medieval forebears, who had been famed throughout Christendom for the honour they paid to the Virgin Queen of Heaven.

"All she had to rely on when, as a lonely girl of eighteen, she landed at Leith in August 1561, was her appealing beauty, her fascination to men, and – so much a Stuart – an unshakeable belief in her right to sovereignty." Mary, Queen of Scots.

FRANCISCVS DRAECK NOBILISSIMVS EQVES ANGLIÆ ANᵒ ÆT SVE 43

"Truly Sir Francis Drake is a fearful man to the King of Spain." Drake "the noblest English warrior" at the age of 43.

"God blew and they were scattered." The Armada medal, struck to commemorate the victory.

CHAPTER FIVE

Captains Courageous

'Sir Drake, whom well the world's end knew,
Which thou did'st compass round,
And whom both poles of heaven once saw,
Which north and south do bound,
The stars above would make thee known,
If men here silent were,
The sun himself cannot forget
His fellow traveller.'

Anonymous

WHILE ELIZABETH was still pursuing her aim of keeping her subjects out of the continental wars of religion, so enabling them to
grow rich and strong, some of them were beginning – not wholly
unbeknown to her – to enrich themselves by waging private war
at sea on their own account, thousands of miles away on the other
side of the Atlantic. Before Hawkins's three trading voyages to the
West Indies, the English had made no attempt to enter the forbidden Caribbean through which the fabulous Spanish wealth of
Central and South America poured into Europe. Though, even
before Henry VIII's breach with Rome, they had refused to
recognize the Spanish and Portuguese monopoly of the newly-
discovered lands and oceans allocated by Pope Alexander VI, they
had taken little advantage of the global opportunities offered to the
countries of Europe's Atlantic seaboard. Apart from the hardy
West Country fishermen who, in the wake of Cabot's discoveries,
annually followed their Breton and Norman counterparts to the
misty cod-haunted banks of Newfoundland, English ventures outside European waters before the 1560s had been mainly confined

to the efforts of a few enterprising Bristol and Plymouth merchants. One of the latter, John Hawkins's father William, had broken into the fringe trade of the Guinea coast, first opened up by the Portuguese navigators of the fifteenth century on their exploratory way round Africa and the Cape of Good Hope to the far golden treasures of Indian Goa and the spice islands. Some abortive attempts by London and Bristol merchants to find a way round the frozen northern shores of Russia to the fabled riches of Cathay had led, following a shipwreck, to an overland journey to Moscow and the Kremlin by Hugh Willoughby. Still more remarkable were the adventures at the court of Ivan the Terrible of a humble agent of the Muscovy Trading Company – founded in 1555 to promote the sale of English cloth in Russia – one Anthony Jenkinson, an ancestor of the future Prime Minister, Lord Liverpool. His friendship with the terrifying Czar and his travels across the camel routes of central Asia to the Oxus, Caspian and Persia, peddling English wares in the markets of Astrakhan, Bokhara and Kasbin, was a saga of fairy-tale romance and successful sales promotion. Another Elizabethan bagman, John Newbery, travelling at risk of his life for his country's trade, crossed the Syrian desert in a camel caravan, went down the Euphrates to Babylon, reached Goa in India, where he was imprisoned by the Portuguese, escaped, and by way of Golconda arrived at the court of the Great Mogul at Agra. His fellow traveller, Ralph Fitch, even got as far as Burma, Siam and Malacca.

What English merchants in search of trade could do by land they could do far more effectively by sea. Following the loss to the French of their staple port of Calais, and their gradually increasing difficulty in exporting cloth through Antwerp, which forced them to seek new markets in the wider world opened up by ocean discovery. Their experience of navigating and building ships for the stormy Atlantic and North Sea waters round their shores fitted them even better for this than the brave Portuguese, Spanish and French mariners who had preceded them. For France, too, though its ambitious rulers' eyes were focused on European rather than American conquests, had also entered the ocean field before England, exploring the St Lawrence estuary and annexing its vast empty Canadian hinterland. Further south Huguenot dissidents had founded a colony in Florida – later destroyed by the jealous Spaniards – while French pirates of the same persuasion, carrying their warfare against Catholic shipping in the English Channel to the other side of the Atlantic, had taken to preying on Spanish coastal vessels in the Caribbean and Gulf of Mexico.

As the ports of Europe became increasingly closed to their trade, more and more English merchants and seafarers set out to break the economic blockade around them by seeking a passage to Cathay and the Indies through the frozen polar seas round northern Europe and America. And when the inexorable ice continued to bar them, during the second decade of Elizabeth's reign, 'like salmon leaping at a fall too high for them,' as one historian put it, they ultimately turned westwards and, flinging down the gauntlet, drove their cockle boats into the heart of the Spanish Caribbean and Main.

It was a young sea-captain of genius who first pointed the way. Son of a poor Protestant bible-reader who had left his native Devon for Kent to escape Catholic persecution, Francis Drake had learnt his seamanship as a boy in small coasting vessels in the stormy tidal waters of the Thames estuary, Dover Strait and North Sea. In his middle twenties, having taken service with his kinsman, John Hawkins – Plymouth's leading merchant and ship-master – he had sailed under him on the ill-fated trading expedition to the West Indies which ended as we have seen in the disaster of San Juan de Ulloa, and from which, thanks to his quick wits and presence of mind, he had escaped unscathed.

The experience left him with a burning hatred of Spanish treachery and cruelty and a resolve to avenge the fate of his companions in the dungeons of the Inquisition and recoup Hawkins's and his own losses by attacking King Philip's apparently impregnable but, as he was quick to see, strategically vulnerable trans-atlantic empire. After two exploratory voyages to the Caribbean, he sailed from Plymouth in the early summer of 1572 with two small ships of seventy and twenty-five tons, manned by seventy-three picked young seamen, including two of his own brothers. His destination was the Darien Isthmus, the narrow mountainous land-link across which – in mule-trains from Panama on their closed Pacific Ocean to the Atlantic port of Nombre de Dios – the Spanish conquerors and exploiters of South America carried the fabulous Peruvian treasures of silver, gold and jewels from the mines of Peru, and which subsequently a huge, heavily-armed Plate Fleet from Spain bore back every year to Europe in order to finance King Philip's armies.

The army with which this obscure English sailor armed himself for his duel with the Spanish authorities was minute. Yet it was of the highest human quality. And in embarking on his crusade against Spain, Drake took precautions against every foreseeable contingency. For it was one of his characteristics that, while ready to challenge almost inconceivable odds, like England's other supreme sailor after him he never took risks until he had done everything possible to ensure success. It was this which gave him, and communicated to those under him, such immense confidence.

Drake was the first Englishman of England's great age of enterprise. Beginning in Elizabeth's reign and continuing until that of Queen Victoria, its hallmark was the belief that there was nothing which a man of courage and resolution, sustained by individual Christian conscience, might not accomplish if her were convinced it was his duty. There is no more amazing story than that of Drake and his seventy young seamen setting out in four small pinnaces, brought from England in sections and assembled by his ships' carpenters in a secret harbour on the Spanish Main which he had prepared as a base during an earlier visit. Landing before dawn, with drums beating and trumpets blaring, he and his handful stormed the fortified Spanish city of Nombre de Dios and all but succeeded in taking it. Then, when all hell broke loose as the sleeping town awoke, they advanced in two converging columns, amid volleys of musketry and the ringing of church bells, to the market place. Thence, though severely wounded, Drake led the way, first to the Governor's residence and then to the King's Treasure House where the silver and gold from the Pacific were stored. 'I have brought you to the Treasure House of the world,' he told his men; 'blame nobody but yourselves if you go away empty.'

But when they tried to break open the door, a sudden storm of tropical intensity descended, quenching the priming matches without which their muskets could not fire. While Drake was trying to rally them, he fainted from loss of blood. Attacked by growing numbers of Spanish soldiers – now recovering from their initial panic – the little band of Devonshire seamen, deprived of Drake's leadership and fearful of being cut off from their boats, carried their unconscious captain back to the waiting pinnaces and put off, defeated, for their hidden base.

Yet it was not in Drake's nature to admit defeat. As soon as he had recovered from his wound, having failed in his attempt to seize the treasure from under the noses of the garrison set to guard it, he resolved to obtain it another way. Living in the forest interior of the Isthmus were the half-caste descendants of the negro slaves whom the sugar planters of the Spanish Main had imported from Africa earlier in the century but whom they had treated so badly that they had escaped and, taking refuge in the jungle, intermarried with the Indian aborigines. Both, having suffered so much from the Spaniards, were relentless enemies of them and all their works.

It had been an attack on Nombre de Dios by the Cimaroons, as they were called, shortly before Drake's arrival that had caused its hitherto inadequate garrison to be reinforced and so brought about the failure of the English assault. Because of the reputation for friendliness and generosity he had won in his exploratory visits to the Isthmus and his habit of releasing, instead of killing, his prisoners, Drake was already known to the Cimaroons, and had no difficulty in forming an alliance with them against their hated foes and oppressors. Making a show of force, two hundred miles to the east, against the capital of the Spanish Main, Cartagena – from whose harbour he ostentatiously carried off two merchant ships, so leaving the enemy under the impression that he was on his way back to England – he completely vanished. Having found a new harbour and hiding place in the Bight of Darien, he spent the next five months there, keeping up the morale of his men by hunting and playing games, while living off the fat of the land from captured Spanish coasters. Meanwhile he perfected his plans for a joint operation with the Cimaroons, as soon as the winter rains should end, against the hundred-mile track from Panama to Nombre de Dios, along which the mule-trains bore the Peruvian treasure across the Isthmus to await the arrival from Europe of the annual Plate Fleet.

This time Drake planned his attack where he would be least expected, on the far side of the Isthmus, somehere between the Pacific port of Panama and the little Spanish mountain garrison station of Venta Cruces, half way along the forest track to Nombre de Dios. Before laying his ambush he was taken by his allies to the highest point of the forest, where from a bower built in a giant tree he and his lieutenant and fellow Devonian, John Oxenham – 'silent upon a peak in Darien' – set eyes on the far Pacific Ocean, the first Englishman ever to do so. Then, having ascertained when the first treasure train was expected to leave Panama, with eighteen Englishmen and thirty Cimaroons he carefully laid his ambush.

Once more his plans, so meticulously prepared, miscarried. The shout of a drunken sailor, who had been fortifying his courage from a flask, aroused the suspicions of a passing horseman. Suspecting an ambush and keeping back the treasure, the captain of the convoy sent his baggage train ahead to spring the trap. Disappointed of his prey, in order to escape being caught between the troops coming up from Panama behind him and the Spanish garrison of Venta Cruces on the track ahead, Drake, with instant presence of mind and quick decision, 'plucking the flower, safety, from the nettle, danger,' led his men and the Cimaroons in a sudden surprise attack on the little hill town. Yet, having driven its defenders into the jungle, before making good his escape to the coast and his waiting pinnaces he restrained his half-savage allies from avenging themselves on the Spanish civilians, and chivalrously found time to visit and calm the fears of some Spanish ladies convalescing there.

By now the seventy-three men with whom he had left Plymouth ten months before he had been reduced by wounds and jungle-fever to thirty-one. Yet he remained, as always, cheerful and determined to accomplish what he had come to do. 'Before I depart,' he had told a Spanish prisoner after the failure of his initial assault on Nombre de Dios, 'if God give me life and leave, I mean to reap some of your harvest which you get out of the earth and send into Spain to trouble all the earth.' And on the last night of March 1573, as yet another mule-train laden with gold and silver jingled through the forest, he achieved it almost at the gates of Nombre de Dios where he had begun. A chance encounter with the captain and crew of a Huguenot privateer, from whom he learnt of the Massacre of St Bartholomew, brought a timely addition of force, and together the English and their French fellow Protestants surprised and routed in open fight a strong escort of Spanish troops. The spoil they shared between them, it is now known from Spanish sources, amounted to £40,000 in the money of that day, or, at least ten millions in ours.

Drake had done what he had intended. For more than a year he had lived at the expense of the Spanish in the waters and forests of the Caribbean and had treated the authority of their government with contempt and, with his tiny handful of seamen, made their supposedly invincible military forces dance to his tune, eluding, like the legendary Robin Hood, all attempts to capture him. And, in the end, he had made Spain's rulers pay in full for their treachery at San Juan de Ulloa, seizing under their very noses the treasure he had come to take. Yet, though he knew he could expect no mercy if captured, he had waged his private war on the enemies of his country and religion by his own humane and chivalrous standards, taking no life save in open fight and showing courtesy and generosity to his captives, all of whom he subsequently released.

It was characteristic of Drake that, before he returned to England, he paid a final visit to Cartagena, where the Spanish plate fleet lay at anchor, and, with St George's Cross at his maintop and streamers flying, made a ceremonial cock of the snoot at the Goliath he had flouted and plundered. His subsequent arrival home at Plymouth, after a fifteen months' absence, on Sunday 9th August 1573, was a red-letter day in West Country history. As his ship, laden with treasure, anchored in the Cattewater, and the rumour ran round the town that Drake was home, everyone hurried to the waterside to greet the young hero, the congregation pouring out of St Andrew's church during sermon time, 'so filled with desire and delight to see him, that very few or none remained with the preacher.'

The value of the treasure which, with the help of his Huguenot partner, Drake had seized at gunpoint from Spain amounted to nearly a sixth of the then annual revenue of the English Crown (estimated by Sir John Neale, including the amount raised by parliamentary and other taxation, at about £250,000 a year); and, of the half-share of it brought back to England, nearly a twelfth. At the time of his arrival Elizabeth was engaged in one of her diplomatic balancing acts, trying to negotiate a rapprochement with her royal brother-in-law of Spain, who, like her, was reluctant, when it came to the point, to commit himself to the unpredictable extremities and expenses of war. The heroic resistance being put up under William of Orange and the Protestant northern and coastal provinces of the Netherlands and their fierce 'Sea Beggars' to Alva's increasingly costly campaign of frightfulness, as well as the revulsion felt at it by many Catholics, had by now caused King Philip to contemplate a less drastic means of reducing his rebellious subjects. At the end of 1573 he replaced the pitiless and uncompromising duke by a gentler and more politic Viceroy, Don Luis Requesens. And this had awoken in Elizabeth hopes, never wholly dormant, that her fanatically devout brother-in-law might, after all, be persuaded to accept the reasonable compromise over the Netherlands she had so sensibly been proposing. It was scarcely surprising therefore, that in view of the indignant protests of the Spanish authorities who were demanding Drake's head, the triumphant end of the opening round of his private war with Spain was viewed with considerably less favour in the Queen's Council than in his native Devon. For some months, for all his sudden accession of wealth, Drake found it advisable to disappear almost as completely as he had done in the palm-fringed shores of the Caribbean. And, though during the next three years many of his fellow countrymen, hoping to make their fortunes as he had done, set out on privateering expeditions of their own in that sea, Drake was not among them.

It was the new Secretary of State, Sir Francis Walsingham – champion, with Leicester, of the war party in the Council and a fanatical Protestant – who introduced him to the Queen. The meeting was an immediate success, for the two, as has been said, were of a kind. 'Drake,' she is reputed to have told him, 'I would gladly be revenged on the King of Spain for divers injuries I have received.' What exactly was agreed between them is uncertain, for the full royal instructions for Drake's mission were never committed to paper. But he was to sail with the Queen's commission in command of a secret semi-official joint stock venture in which she herself, together with Leicester, Walsingham, Sir Christopher Hatton – captain of her Bodyguard – John Hawkins and Lord Howard of Effingham, the hereditary Lord Admiral, were all shareholders.

It was given out that the destination of the expedition was Egypt, to open a new overland trade in East Indian spices through the Turkish port of Alexandria, in rivalry to the existing Venetian land and Portuguese sea routes. Yet though the seamen and soldiers enlisting for the voyage were told this, the gentlemen volunteers, who flocked to serve under Drake with his Midas touch, were led to understand that the voyage's real objective was the discovery of a vast new southern continent – Terra Australis. Rumoured to be rich in gold, it was believed to lie somewhere south of the stormy straits into the Pacific Ocean which the great Portuguese circumnavigator, Magellan, had found and negotiated for Spain sixty years earlier. Owing however to their immense distance from Europe and their navigational dangers, no one had since used them, the Spanish masters of Peru preferring the far shorter overland route across the Panama and Darien Isthmus. Now, by following Magellan's course through these remote and perilous straits, Drake was to find and annex this undiscovered continent and its fabled riches for the English Crown.

Though it was the essence of the partnership between the Queen and her avenging corsair that she should be free to disown him if reasons of state demanded – a condition unquestioningly and proudly accepted by him – there seems no reason to doubt that all alternatives for the expedition were discussed between them, though not all were committed to paper. Among these were a voyage of a plunder-ripe Pacific coast and the arrival of his little

fleet off Panama, 4,000 miles north of the Magellan Straits, to help
Cimaroons and the English corsairs from the Atlantic, drive the
Spaniards from the Isthmus, so compelling King Philip, deprived
of his chief source of military revenue, to desist from his despotic
courses in the Low Countries. Already John Oxenham had invested his share of the captured Darien treasure to equip a ship
for the Isthmus and had sailed in it from Plymouth with fifty-seven
men and equipment to build and launch a pinnace in the un-
defended waters of the Pacific – an intention of which Drake, who
conferred with him before he left, was almost certainly aware.

Yet the sling and stone with which the English David was once
again preparing to challenge the Spanish Goliath seemed ridicu-
lously small. It consisted only of Drake's flagship, the *Pelican*, of
little more than a hundred tons with eighteen guns, the *Elizabeth*
of eighty tons with sixteen guns, commanded by Captain John
Winter – a nephew of the Queen's veteran Admiral-at-Sea, Sir
William Winter – and three even smaller vessels, the *Marigold*,
Swan and *Christopher*. With this minute force and a company of
one hundred and fifty men and fourteen boys, Drake sailed from
Plymouth on November 15th 1577. Driven into Falmouth by a
storm and forced to return to Plymouth to refit, it was not till the
middle of December that he finally got away from England. After
watering on the Barbary coast and calling at the Cape Verde
Islands, where an invaluable captured Portuguese pilot elected to
join him, he was sixty-three days without sight of land before
striking Brazil on April 5th. 'During which long passage where
nothing but sea beneath us and air above us was to be seen,'
recalled one of the company, 'our eyes did behold the wonderful
works of God in his creatures, which He hath made innumerable,
both small and great beasts, in the great and wide sea.' Afterwards
the voyagers were becalmed in a dense fog on the coast of what
today is the Argentine, where at one point, taking soundings in a
dinghy, Drake himself was nearly lost. Here they encountered
dancing giants and flocks of ostriches and were attacked by savages
with poisoned arrows. Twice scattered by storms, it took the little
fleet many weeks, beating against adverse winds and assailed by
nameless terrors, before it was able to reassemble at the end of

June, in the wild, desolate bay of St Julian, 10,000 miles from England. Here, sixty years earlier, Magellan had refitted before entering the straits which bear his name, after quelling a mutiny and hanging two of its ringleaders.

Drake now faced the same experience. Among the gentlemen adventurers who had sailed with him was a former member of the earl of Essex's household with whom he had become friends while serving together in Ireland. A courtier of distinguished manners, who had fought as a soldier in the Low Countries, Thomas Doughty belonged to a world of culture and sophistication which Drake, a simple provincial sailor, had never before encountered. With all his charm, however, like many courtiers Doughty was an adventurer and intriguer. Drake had trusted and loved him, but during the long voyage south had found his trust misplaced. For Doughty tried to undermine his authority, stirring up trouble between the gentlemen adventurers and the rough sailors they despised. While amid the storms and darkness of a Patagonian midwinter, the expedition prepared for the passage of the Straits, Drake came to believe that his false friend was fomenting a mutiny with the intention of changing its destination or forcing it to return to England. Drake had him arrested and, impanelling a jury, tried and sentenced him to death for mutiny. Yet before Doughty paid the penalty for his treachery on an improvised block close to the remains of Magellan's gallows, the two old friends dined and took the Sacrament together, bidding each other farewell in Christian reconciliation.

After the execution, Drake addressed himself to restoring the morale and discipline of his command, shaken as it was by doubts and factions. One day, when all hands were assembled for Sunday service, he announced that he himself would preach the sermon. Rating the sailors for their contempt of the gentlemen adventurers, and the latter for shirking the work of the ship, he continued, 'I must have the gentleman to haul and draw with the mariner, and the mariner with the gentleman. I would know him that would refuse to set his hand to a rope, but' – after a pause – 'I know there is not any such here.' Then he revealed the full purpose of the voyage, stressing its immense difficulties and dangers, and offered a ship to all whose hearts failed them and who wished to return to England. Then, as no one took advantage of his offer, he went on: 'You come, then, of your own will: on you it depends to make the voyage renowned or to end a reproach to our country and a laughing-stock to the enemy. Let us show ourselves to be all of a company.' Twenty years later Shakespeare – at that time still a Stratford grammar schoolboy – paraphrased Drake's sermon in the speech he put into the mouth of Henry V before Agincourt:

> 'What's he that wishes so? . . .
> Rather proclaim it, Westmoreland, through my host,
> That he which hath no stomach for this fight,
> Let him depart; his passport shall be made,
> And crowns for convoy put into his purse:
> We would not die in that man's company
> That fears his fellowship to die with us.'

On August 17th 1578, with his three fighting ships, *Pelican*, *Elizabeth*, and *Marigold*, the small fry having been broken up for firewood during the fleet's midwinter sojourn in the Patagonian wilderness, Drake entered the Magellan Straits. Before doing so, he renamed his flagship the *Golden Hind*, after the crest of Sir Christopher Hatton, one of his chief backers at the Queen's Court. Negotiating, with the loss of six men, the intricate and perilous three hundred and sixty miles of icy mountain-bound Straits, in sixteen days – half the time taken by Magellan – he reached the Pacific on September 6th, only to be struck by a tremendous storm, which, scattering his little squadron, drove him far to the south. For fifty-six days the gale persisted. During its course the *Marigold* was engulfed with all hands and the *Elizabeth* driven back into the Atlantic and forced to return to England. Only the flagship remained, its indomitable commander and her crew subsisting on a diet of putrid penguin meat with which they had fortunately victualled the *Golden Hind* from an island during her passage through the Straits.

In the aftermath of the storm, Drake made two discoveries. One was that the fabled southern continent *Terra Australis* did not exist, at least where the cartographers supposed; the other that the mountains and islands south of the Magellan Straits ended only in ocean and that, beyond the southern extremity of America, the Atlantic and Pacific flowed into one another. When he had revictualled and refitted his solitary and storm-battered ship, he set out northwards up the four thousand mile Pacific coast of South America. In January 1578, he reached the most southerly Spanish settlement at Valparaiso Bay, where he surprised and plundered the unsuspecting shipping lying in the little roadstead and took on board a consignment of gold and Chilean wine.

Then began that amazing voyage up the Peruvian coast where no English ship had ever sailed before, with all the wealth of Spanish South America dropping like ripe plums into his hold. It was a revolutionary demonstration of what sea-power could do in an oceanic age – a new force to be reckoned with, of which Drake was the first pioneer. For at that moment in time and place it required only one ocean-going ship with a double broadside – the microcosm of a fleet-in-being in an ocean where few vessels mounted so much as a single gun – to make Drake temporarily master of the Pacific, rather as Cortes and Pizarro, and their few hundred conquistadores, with their unfamiliar weapons and horses, had conquered for Spain, half a century earlier, the empires of the Aztecs and Incas. Being free to strike wherever he chose, and enjoying completely initiative and surprise, he took care, as he moved up the coast, to sink or immobilize every vessel which could carry warning of his coming. Capturing ship after ship and helping themselves to whatever they chose or needed, his crew entered into the spirit of the game, laughing and frolicking their way northwards, the playboys and terror alike of the western world.

In the middle of February they reached Callao, the port of Lima, capital of Peru, and seat of its Viceroy. Here they plundered and set adrift, as the Spanish crews fled ashore, every ship in the harbour. Here, too, from their prisoners – all of whom Drake treated with his habitual kindness and released unharmed before he left – they learnt that Oxenham's adventure had ended in disaster, and that he and his two chief officers were awaiting death in the dungeons of the Inquisition at Lima.

With only a single ship left and no hope of co-operation from the Cimaroons, any idea of an attack on Panama from the Pacific was at an end. But before he left Callao, Drake learnt that a heavily-laden treasure ship had sailed for the Isthmus fourteen days before. While the Viceroy, hurrying down from Lima, mobilized every soldier on the coast for an attack on the intruder, the *Golden Hind* vanished over the northern horizon. A fortnight later, on March 1st 1579, Drake's fourteen-year-old page and cousin, keeping a look-out from the maintop, won the golden chain promised to the first seaman to sight the quarry. That night, with her mizzen mast brought down by a warning shot and her crew overpowered by a swarm of English sailors with cutlasses, the astonished captain of the *Nuestra Senora de la Concepcion* surrendered to a broad-shouldered, short-bearded man with magnetic eyes who, doffing his casque with grave courtesy, bade him 'accept with patience what is the usage of war'. For the next six days the two ships lay side by side on the calm sunlit Pacific, while emeralds, jewels and precious stones, thirteen chests full of reals of plate, eighty pounds weight of gold, and twenty-six tons of silver were transferred to the *Golden Hind*. Meanwhile, the Spanish captain was entertained in Drake's cabin as an honoured guest and, when the operation was over, he and his crew, with many little acts of kindness and courtesy from their captors, were allowed to resume their voyage in peace, less, however, as the Spanish authorities ruefully informed their sovereign, 362,000 pesos worth of treasure.

Three weeks later, on April 4th, far to the north off the Guatemalan coast, Drake captured another vessel, laden with Chinese silks and porcelain and owned by a Spanish nobleman of high birth, Don Francisco de Zarato, a cousin of Spain's senior grandee, the Duke of Medina Sidonia. From him we have a picture of Drake, by whom he was entertained for three days, in a letter sent after his release to the Viceroy of Mexico, describing his experiences at the hands of this strange corsair who boasted that he carried the Queen of England's commission and wore a gold sea-cap given him by her and a green silk scarf embroidered by her Maids of Honour with the words, 'The Lord guide and preserve thee until the ende'.

'He received me with a show of kindness and took me to his cabin where he bade me be seated and said, 'I am a friend of those who tell me the truth, but of those who do not I get out of humour.' . . . He is about thirty-five years old, of small size, with a reddish beard, and is one of the greatest sailors living, both from his skill and his power of commanding. He ordered me to sit next to him and began giving me food from his own plate, telling me not to grieve, that my life and property were safe. I kissed his hands for this . . . Certain trifles of mine having taken his fancy, he had them brought to his ship and gave me, in exchange for them, a falchion' – a broadsword – 'and a small brazier of silver, and I can assure your Excellency that he lost nothing by the bargain. On his return to his vessel he asked me to pardon him for taking the trifles, but that they were for his wife.'

Don Francisco also described the excellent discipline Drake kept:

'When our ship was sacked, no man dared take anything without his orders. He shows them great favour, but punishes the least fault. . . . Each one takes particular pains to keep his arquebus clean. He treats them with affection and they him with respect. He also carried painters who paint for him pictures of the coast in exact colours. He carries trained carpenters and artisans, so as to be able to careen the ship at any time. He has with him nine or ten gentlemen, younger sons of leading men in England who form his council. He calls them together on every occasion and hears what they have to say, but he is not bound by their advice . . . He has no privacy: those I mentioned all dine at his table. He is served on silver dishes with gold borders and gilded garlands, in which are his arms. He carries all possible dainties and perfumed waters: he said that many of these had been given him by the Queen. He dines and sups to the music of viols . . .'

By this time the entire Pacific coast of Spanish America was in uproar, its outraged authorities hastily casting cannon and repairing immobilized ships in order to seek the heretic intruder in the Gulf of Panama or, alternatively, intercept his homeward voyage, thousands of miles to the south, on the way back to the storm-swept Magellan Straits. But Drake – 'the master thief of the unknown world' as the Spaniards called him – was at neither. For,

having taken from a ship, engaged on their new China trade between Mexico and the Philippines, charts and sailing directions
for the Pacific passage, he had resolved to complete his mission by
circumnavigating the globe like Magellan, and return home by way
of the rich spice islands and the Portuguese seaway round Africa.

First, however, leaving Spanish waters far behind, he sailed
north up the American coast for a brief perfunctory search for the
Pacific entrance to the supposed North-West passage or Strait of
Anian – so dear to contemporary English cartographers, like the
equally imaginary Terra Australis. Then, buffeted by icy storms,
he turned back into the sunshine.

Before leaving America, somewhere north of the coast of what
today is California, and hundreds of miles from the nearest Spanish
settlement, Drake found a 'fair and good bay' whose white cliffs
reminded him of England. Here, to careen and give the *Golden
Hind* a much needed overhaul, he built a make-shift dock in which
to unload and reload the treasure from her crowded hold. While
doing so he established his usual happy relations with the native
Indians. 'Our General,' wrote the young gentleman adventurer,
Francis Preedy, to whom we owe the chief first-hand account of
the voyage, 'according to his natural and accustomed humanity,
courteously entreated them and liberally bestowed on them
necessary things to cover their nakedness.' They seem to have
regarded the 'palefaces' who had descended on them from the sea
as visitants from a higher plane, listened entranced to their psalm
singing and scripture reading, and invested Drake, whom they
tried, to his embarrassment, to worship, with a chieftain's crown
of feathers and the lordship of their country, which he accepted on
behalf of his royal mistress, proclaiming it an English dominion in
her name. He christened it New Albion and erected a monument
and inscription for the guidance of future settlers and voyagers.
Then, towards the end of July, the refreshed circumnavigators set
out on the long haul across the Pacific. 'The natives,' wrote Preedy,
'frequented our company to the hour of our departure, which
departure seemed so grievous unto them that their joy was turned
to sorrow. They entreated us that, being absent, we would remember them.'

It was sixty-eight days before the heavily-laden little ship first sighted land again in the Philippine Sea and nearly three months before she reached the Moluccas, centre of the sea-borne European spice-trade – at that time a closely guarded monopoly of the Portuguese, who had established a fort and factory in the islands. But at Ternate Drake found a friendly sultan who was at war with them, purchased from him six tons of cloves – even more valuable on the European market at that time than gold or silver – and negotiated a verbal treaty which was to become regarded as a starting-point for English sea-borne trade with the Orient. Then on January 9th 1580, while still negotiating the intricate maze of uncharted equatorial islands and swift treacherous currents which lay between the Pacific and Indian oceans, the *Golden Hind*, and the expedition with it, all but came to an end on a submerged reef on which, for twenty hours, she lay grounded. But, always cheerful and resolute in adversity, Drake refused to despair; 'as he had always hitherto showed himself courageous and of good conscience in the mercy and protection of God,' wrote one of his officers, 'so now he continued in the same.' After he had called all hands to prayer and lightened the ship by jettisoning half the guns and three tons of cloves, the wind suddenly changed, and the *Golden Hind* slid gently off the reef unharmed.

It was not till March, after a refit in Java, that Drake and his crew at last got clear of the treacherous Floris Sea and Indonesian archipelago and reached the open Indian Ocean. The first Englishman ever to cross it, as, in the course of his miraculous voyage, he had been of both the South Atlantic and Pacific, he rounded the Cape of Good Hope on June 18th – 'a most stately thing and the fairest cape we saw in the whole circumference of the earth'. Stopping only to water at Sierra Leone on July 22nd, and reaching far out into the Atlantic to pick up the westerlies, he cast anchor in Plymouth Sound on September 26th, 1580. Of the one hundred and sixty-four who had sailed with him from Plymouth nearly three years before, only fifty-one remained. Yet in the whole of his avenging foray in Spanish waters, not a single Spanish life had been taken.

But a vast amount of Spanish treasure had been – enough to

support Philip's armies in the Netherlands for many months and even more, taking into account the fantastic interest rates Spain had to pay for the loans borrowed, on the strength of her bullion shipments, from Italian, German and Flemish bankers under its extravagant and procrastinating financial system. It seemed a heavy punishment and penalty to suffer for the treacherous attack on Hawkins and his crews at San Juan de Ulloa. Philip's ambassador had demanded his piratical head in the, as he supposed, unlikely event of his ever getting back to England.

When therefore the triumphant circumnavigator arrived safe and sound with his captured treasure, Mendoza's fury doubled. Nor did Drake himself know what sort of reception he was likely to receive from the Queen, with whose enigmatic commission he had sailed before robbing her fellow sovereign so outrageously. He did not even know whether she was alive and reigning until a fishing boat, hailed off Cawsand, reassured his fears, for he had no news from home for nearly three years. What were Elizabeth's present relations with Spain and what the balance of forces in her councils he had still to learn. Using the pretext, therefore, of an outbreak of plague in Plymouth, he lay for a week off St Nicholas Island without landing until a messenger, despatched post haste to his friends at Court, together with some jewels for the Queen, could let him know how he stood.

He need not have worried. For he could not have arrived at a more opportune moment. Mendoza's complaints about his misdeeds in the outer oceans had merely been met by the Queen's bland insistence that Spain had no right to forbid, under pain of imprisonment or death, their use to her subjects who were therefore perfectly entitled in self-defence to take the law into their own hands, 'seeing,' as she put it, 'that the use of the sea and air is common to all.' Moreover, as she had made it abundantly clear to the ambassador, she had far more serious grievances of her own about Philip's interference in the affairs of her Irish kingdom, where a rising in Munster had been fomented by papal emissaries and Jesuits with Spanish arms and backing. And in the very week of Drake's arrival she had received news that six hundred Spaniards had landed there, presumably with her brother-in-law's authority, as part of an expedition sent by Rome to aid her rebellious Catholic subjects. She flatly refused to discuss the subject of Spanish injuries in the Pacific so long as a single Spanish soldier remained on Irish soil and until she had received a full apology for their being there.

Moreover, King Philip had committed a far more serious breach of international propriety that summer. Following the fall of the young King of Portugal in the disastrous battle of Alcazar-el-Kebir in the Moroccan desert, and the death, only a year later, of his aged celibate successor, the direct line of the House of Aviz had come to an end in January 1580 while the *Golden Hind* was still edging her course through the islands of the Portuguese East Indies. Among those with a claim to the vacant throne was Philip of Spain. But Portugal had been a separate kingdom for more than four centuries, and her people were jealous of their independence and proud of the rich trading and colonial empire their explorers had founded on the shores of Africa, Brazil and the Orient. It seemed, therefore, as morally questionable as high-handed for the ruler of Spain to invade his little crusading neighbour with a huge army under the dreaded duke of Alva and forcibly expel the successful claimant, Don Antonio, from the throne, of which, with popular Portuguese assent, he had taken possession six months earlier.

For Elizabeth and England, Philip's annexation of Portugal had tremendous implications. It all but doubled the size and wealth of Spain's already huge global empire, making it by far the most powerful state in Christendom, and carrying King Philip far along the road to universal dominion. And it brought him, not only the riches of the spice islands, the mines of Brazil and the sea-borne trade round Africa with the East, but a means of commanding the oceans which, as Drake had proved, had hitherto eluded Spain – a military but not as yet, save in the enclosed galley-ruled waters of the Mediterranean, an invincible naval power. For Portugal possessed an ocean-going fleet of twelve of the world's finest fighting galleons, the great Atlantic port of Lisbon and the ocean-staging islands of Cape Verde and the Azores. All these were now at Spain's command.

Coming in the same month as the news of this prodigious Spanish *fait accompli*, Drake's return with his treasure, his treaty with the Sultan of Ternate, and the wonderful story of his world-encircling voyage seemed providential. A resounding answer to Alva's sinister march on Lisbon, it made every English heart glow with pride. Never in international relations had so much been achieved by the resource and daring of one man. When, with a long train of packhorses laden with jewels, Drake arrived in London that October, he found himself the hero of the Court and nation. The value of his treasure in the money of the day amounted to a million and a half sterling or more than a third of the annual produce of King Philip's American mines. Those who had invested in his voyage, including its principal shareholder the Queen, received a fourteen-fold capital return. Before having the treasure in the *Golden Hind* officially valued to be shipped to London and lodged in the Tower, a grateful Elizabeth – in a letter under her sign-manual 'to be kept to himself alone' – instructed the royal Commissioner in Devon to allow Drake to retain £10,000 worth of bullion, equivalent to roughly four millions in present-day money, so making him one of the richest men in the kingdom and ensuring that, even if Philip succeeded in reclaiming any part of his lost hoard, her little privateer should keep what his courage and genius had earned him. Meanwhile depositions were taken from every survivor of the crew to prove that no Spaniard had suffered unnecessary violence during the voyage, unlike the unfortunate English seamen who had been hanged or sent to the galleys by King Philip's officers or burnt by the Spanish Inquisition, as John Oxenham was that October at Lima.

Such was Drake's popularity with his royal mistress – like everyone else agog to hear the story of his adventures – that, on his arrival at Court, she gave him a private audience lasting six hours and, on another occasion, sent for him no fewer than nine times in the course of a day. Poor Mendoza was beside himself with rage, describing, in vivid letters to his master, the Queen walking in the garden in deep converse with the offending pirate or appearing in Court on New Year's Day in a new crown set with five magnificent – Peruvian – emeralds. The climax to the infamous voyage came on April 4th 1581, when, coming down the river in her gilded barge, Elizabeth was entertained by Drake, 'a right magnifico now,' to a superb banquet – 'finer than any had ever been seen in England since King Henry,' the ambassador reported – in the state cabin of the *Golden Hind* at her moorings at Deptford. Afterwards, telling her host that she had brought a golden sword with which to cut off his head, she handed it to the French Ambassador – so implicating that diplomat and his country in her defiance of King Philip's demands for redress – bidding him knight the erring circumnavigator on his own quarter deck.

*　　*　　*

Drake's voyage round the world was a climacteric in the evolution of England as a nation. It was the starting-point for the next three and a half centuries of her history. Already, thanks to her Queen's inspired leadership, the champion of the threatened Protestant cause in Europe, her roving sea-captain's miraculous achievement had staked her little kingdom's claim to the freedom of the world's oceans. Together, in their very different ways, Elizabeth and Drake had raised it from the nadir of weakness, disunion and peril into which it had fallen to a repute greater than any it had known since the days of Henry V, when its archers had laid low the chivalry of Europe's mightiest kingdom. Like them, coming from outside the warlike feudal and knightly caste which for half a millennium had monopolized command of arms in the Christian West, the humbly-born Drake had proved himself both a fighting commander and a strategist of the highest genius. Almost alone he had seen how to win control of the outer oceans and realized the fatal communications gap between Spain's monopolist empire in the Americas and its arid, poverty-stricken homeland. Never commanding much more than a hundred men, and seldom that, he had made rings round her proud and stately colonial aristocrats and, despite her prodigious conquests of the past sixty years, had held her pretensions to military invincibility up to ridicule. With his practical experience of fighting Spain at sea, he saw how her imperial power could be broken for ever. In the summer after his return, he sought permission to fit out a new expedition to repeat, with a whole fleet instead of a single ship, his plundering voyage up the defenceless Peruvian coast, to rouse Spain's conquered helots to throw off her hated rule before, once more encircling the globe and joining forces with his remote ally, the Sultan of Ternate, to wrest the trade of the spice islands from King Philip's Portuguese vassals.

Till now, both the shrewd stateswoman on the throne and the self-made seaman of genius who had sailed to the ends of the world in her name had been seeking the same thing: the rejection of Spain's arrogant claim to a monopoly of trade in the outer oceans. Yet to the Queen the ultimate end she sought was not the destruction of the Spanish empire – something far beyond her means or ambition – but the preservation of the unifying peace which for close on a quarter of a century she had given her realm and on which its reviving strength and wealth depended. She wished to avoid war – not, as the event was to show, at all costs, but at all reasonable costs. And as she believed that, in the last resort, her fellow sovereign in the Escorial had the same distaste for the uncertainty and waste of war as her frugal and sensible self, she had no wish to goad him to extremities. A woman, a realist and a politique, by nature tolerant and open-minded and totally dedicated to the peace and well-being of her country, she found it hard to believe that to Philip, the peace and well-being of his subjects mattered less than the enforced imposition on all mankind of the orthodox Faith with which he had increasingly come to identify his own exclusive right to rule and ordain.

It was inevitable that the Queen's judgment, not Drake's, should prevail, for her control of foreign policy was absolute. Even the wise Burghley, though he might doubt and caution, could never challenge it. There was talk for a time in Court and City circles of sending the great corsair on a less ambitious voyage to take over the Portuguese island of Terceira in the Azores, which had declared for Don Antonio, as a future base from which to cut the platefleet's communications with America. But nothing came of it, for the Portuguese pretender, wearying of Elizabeth's delays and hesitations, decided to rely on French aid, instead of English, to restore him to his lost dominion. And, with the people of Portugal submitting, however reluctantly, to Alva's occupying army, a major, and seemingly irreversible, step had been taken towards the fulfilment of the Spanish poet, Hernando de Acuna's dream of *un Monarca, un Imperia y una Espana.*

Instead, Elizabeth continued as before to thwart her brother-in-law in such small ways as lay within her power. In August 1581 he was still threatening her with war to recover his plundered treasure. But she reduced him to reason, or, at least, hesitation, not by using Drake to harry his distant ocean realms again and enrage him still further, but by playing her old diplomatic card of an Anglo-French marriage treaty. That October Alençon – 'François the Constant' – revisited England at Elizabeth's invitation to renew his courtship, upon which Philip withdrew his threats, proposed a mutual forgiveness of all past offences and offered the incorrigible Queen a renewal of their ancient friendship. To both monarchs the war in the Netherlands seemed far more important than anything that could happen in the remore waters round America; Philip because his father's favourite patrimony and the triumph of the Catholic cause in Europe were at stake, Elizabeth because a Spanish victory there would not only finally close her people's traditional continental export market for their cloth, but release a victorious army for an invasion of her realm across the narrow seas. Seeing in Antwerp, like Napoleon two centuries later, a pistol pointed at the head of England, she continued to supply her restless French suitor with large, though not over-large, loans – financed out of Drake's Pacific plunder – to induce him to pluck her chestnuts out of the fire and sustain the Protestant cause in the Low Countries without her having to intervene herself and so provoke her Spanish brother-in-law into war.

So it came about, as a result of this precarious stalemate, that for the next few years England's greatest sea-captain remained on shore, purchasing from Sir Richard Grenville the great monastic estate of Buckland Abbey, representing a Cornish constituency in Parliament, and, later, serving as Mayor of Plymouth, in which capacity, with his usual enterprise and generosity, he later helped to provide the port with a piped water supply from Dartmoor.

When in 1582 a privately promoted expedition – to which both he, Leicester, Burghley, Walsingham, Hatton and the Muscovy Company all subscribed – sailed for the Moluccas to set up a trading factory to exploit his unwritten treaty with the Sultan of Ternate, its command was entrusted to a brother-in-law of John Hawkins, Edward Fenton. A courtier and soldier of fortune, Fenton had been engaged under the Yorkshire explorer and ex-privateer, Martin Frobisher, in some much publicized but unsuccessful, searches for gold on the frozen shores of northern Canada, where the latter had been trying to find the elusive North-West passage to the Pacific. But Fenton was no Drake, and the expedition proved a dismal failure, never getting further than Brazil. Meanwhile, consolidating their new Portuguese possessions and their control of Portugal's ocean-going navy, the Spaniards under their most experienced admiral, the Marquis of Santa Cruz – a hero of the great Mediterranean galley victory of Lepanto – won off Terceira in the Azores a decisive engagement against a French fleet seeking to restore Don Antonio to his throne. It left Spain with no rival in the Atlantic but England, and encouraged the victorious admiral to urge his royal master to prepare a massive invasion armada to overwhelm the troublesome islanders.

With France split by civil war, England now alone stood between King Philip and the dominion of western Christendom. But, still at peace under their pacific Queen, the islanders were already beginning to buckle on the wooden armour of their sovereign's fleet of war. Ever since Elizabeth's accession in England's forlorn and defenceless state after the fall of Calais – lost through her then weakness at sea – the growth of her naval strength had been a slow but continuous process. 'Bend your force and credit and device to maintain and increase your Navy,' the English ambassador in Paris, Sir Nicholas Throgmorton, had written as long ago as 1560 'for in this time, considering all the circumstances, it is the flower of England's garland'. And in the very month in which Drake had set out on his voyage round the world, his former chief and partner, John Hawkins of Plymouth, the most experienced ocean-going trader of his generation, succeeded his father-in-law, Benjamin Gonson, as Treasurer of the Navy

Board – the official body which, since its creation by Henry VIII, administered the royal ships and dockyards. His appointment was the result of a paper which he had prepared for Lord Treasurer Burghley entitled 'Abuses in the Admiralty touching Her Majesty's Navy'. In it he had exposed the time-honoured cheats which were causing the Crown to spend twice as much in building and maintaining its ships as was necessary. In many cases the Queen was paying officers and dockyard officials for vessels whose timbers she herself had already provided from the royal forests. Naval stores were habitually sold to line the pockets of officers and dockyard officials; clerks were paid double wages; worn out and decayed materials charged as though they were new. For almost everything the Navy needed the Queen was grossly overcharged. By eliminating all this corruption, or as much of it as was possible in a universally corrupt age, Hawkins – a practical and businesslike administrator with a lifelong experience of ships and the sea – was able during the next few years to double the efficiency of the Navy without increasing the amount this frugal-minded royal mistress was prepared and able to devote to it.

The underlying purpose which inspired Hawkins's paper and his subsequent work as Treasurer of the Royal Navy was the transformation of what was still a home-waters fleet, built and maintained to protect and patrol the seas immediately around England and Ireland, into one capable of operating, and remaining at sea, like Drake and his fellow buccaneers, thousands of miles from her shores. For this purpose, as he knew from personal experience, the huge castellated carracks, with their heavy superstructures of towering poop and forecastle, which had been the pride of the early Tudor Navy and its continental rivals, could be almost as dangerous in Atlantic gales to their own crews as to the enemies they were designed to overpower. The most effective warships in heavy weather were those offering as small a target to wave and shot as possible – slim, seaworthy, fast, handy and easy to sail and manoeuvre. In place of the thousand ton and even fifteen-hundred ton floating castles of the past, made for summer campaigns in gentler seas, which till now had been the pride of royal ship-wrights, Hawkins and the new English deep-water seamen favoured much smaller craft, 'not of so great bulk,' as Francis Bacon put it, 'but of a more nimble motion, and more serviceable'. Long in proportion to their beam in a ratio of three-and-a-half to one on the water-line, they could stay at sea in any weather and, because of their smaller size, were easier to maintain in dock, being so much the less liable to conceal dry rot in their timbers. Hawkins's ideal was the *Revenge*, of 450 tons, laid down in 1575, which, with its speed and hitting power, Drake regarded as the perfect fighting galleon and was, in war, to choose as his flagship. Its last fight in 1591 under Sir Richard Grenville was to constitute one of the great sea-epics of all time.

> 'Ship after ship, the whole night long,
>   their high-built galleons came,
> Ship after ship, the whole night long,
>   with her battle-thunder and flame;
> Ship after ship, the whole night long,
>   drew back with her dead and her shame.'

Apart from shipbuilding, supplies and dockyards, there were two other matters with which John Hawkins concerned himself during the ten crucial years when, as Treasurer of the Navy Board, he fought to overcome the inertia and excessive conservatism of the past and the time-honoured knavery and corruption of royal officers and contractors. One was guns, than which there had been none better in the world than those made in England under Cecil's fostering care of her native industry. In those years the gun-founders of Sussex, Kent and Surrey were acknowledged to be the best in Europe. So good were their guns that during Hawkins's Treasurership their export had to be forbidden to prevent their falling into Spanish hands. The gun most favoured by Hawkins and his colleagues was the culverin – lighter to carry, quicker in firing and with a longer range than the heavier cannon hitherto in use. Firing an iron shot weighing seventeen pounds, it had an extreme, if far from accurate, range of from a mile to a half to two miles – little less than that of the guns of Nelson's fleet at Trafalgar. And the English gunners were as famous as their guns – 'sober, wakeful, lusty, hardy, patient and quick-spirited.'

The other branch of naval administration where Hawkins's reforms proved revolutionary was that of manning. Instead of crowding as many men into the Queen's ships as possible, his experience, like Drake's, of ocean voyages had taught him the advantages of sailing and fighting with as few as possible. One of the handicaps imposed by the top-heavy superstructures in ship design of the past was the overcrowding involved in manning fore and aft towers with soldiers and gunners in readiness to board or sweep the crowded decks of their opponents with their small-arms. The broadside fire of long-range culverins made such floating towers as unnecessary and useless as the shore-warriors who filled them. The ships Hawkins built or converted were cheaper to man and victual and freer from the fevers, dysentery and typhus which swept through the overcrowded insanitary decks of their predecessors. The ideal complement of the *Revenge* and her successors was one hundred and fifty sailors, twenty-four gunners and seventy-six soldiers, or two hundred and fifty in all – a manning scale of a man for every two tons, or enough to sail and fight with maximum efficiency, compared with almost a man for every one and a half tons in the past. This allowed ships to remain at sea for much longer without having to revictual, and helped to reduce the incidency of scurvy. It also made it possible for Hawkins – who by now was financing the maintenance of the Royal Navy for a fixed annual contractual sum of £5,714 a year – to secure in 1585 a rise of the seaman's basic pay from 6s 8d to 10s a month. Above all, it enabled England to use to the full her supreme naval asset – a highly skilled hereditary seafaring population, bred from boyhood to navigating stormy waters, without having to dilute it with unnecessary soldiers and the untrained flotsam and jetsam of inland towns.

Little of this escaped Ambassador Mendoza's watchful eye. During the years following Drake's return from the Pacific, he warned his master that the English were building new war ships without cessation. Nor was it only at sea that the islanders were looking to their arms – hitherto so powerless on land against the disciplined Spanish, Swiss, Italian and German mercenaries employed by the great supranational dynasties of Hapsburg and Valois, with their sophisticated weapons and new battle techniques.

Since the outbreak of the rebellion in the Netherlands, growing numbers of young English and Welsh volunteers had been fighting beside their Dutch and Flemish co-religionists. In 1572 Sir Humphrey Gilbert, who had learnt his soldiering in Ireland – and ten years later was to go down in an Atlantic storm to death and history as the pioneer of North American colonization – formed the first English regiment in the Low Countries with the aid of a staunch, but unassuming, warrior from Glamorgan named Thomas Morgan. It was the first time English soldiers had fought together in any larger unit than a company against the huge dreaded Spanish *tercios* which had so long, 'at push of pike', carried all before them on the battlefields of the Continent.

They were followed by others, like the six Norris brothers, sons of Lord Norris of Rycote, all but one of whom were to die in the Queen's service. Though their Dutch employers and fellow fighters for freedom were receiving little support as yet from the cautious and frugal Queen, who was now once more trying to negotiate a peaceful settlement with Philip's commander-in-chief, the courteous young duke of Parma, these volunteers helped, in a melancholy terrain of rivers and marshes, to prove that, given the right military framework, their native isle still bred soldiers second to none in hardihood, valour and stoical humour. 'This is the hand which cut the pudding at dinner,' jested John Carey, throwing it on the mess-table after it had been severed by a cannon-ball. Such men formed a bridge in time between the archers of Crécy and Agincourt and their scarlet-coated descendants who fought and conquered under Marlborough and Wellington. And, during the late 1570s and 1580s, while young Englishmen, many of them cadets of famous families, were learning to be soldiers in a foreign war, at home the first frail attempts were being made to transform the primitive organization of the country's local militia – still armed with bills and bows – into some semblance of a modern fighting force.

Yet it was neither naval armada nor invading army which presented the greatest threat to England's peace as her Queen, in the autumn of 1582, entered on her fiftieth year. It was the threat to her life. That spring, an all but successful attempt by Spanish agents had been made to assassinate William of Orange – the chief obstacle, after Elizabeth herself, to the triumph of the Counter-Reformation in Europe. Though for weeks his life was despaired of, the prince recovered. But while the prize offered by Spain on William's head was high, that for the assassination of the childless Queen of England was even higher. For if she were to fall to an assassin's knife or bullet, her Catholic cousin, the Queen of Scots, would automatically succeed to her vacant throne. And during that summer a messenger of Mendoza, the Spanish Ambassador, disguised as a dentist, had been stopped crossing the Scottish frontier. A letter, hidden at the back of a mirror, was found among his possessions, which, in the hands of Secretary Walsingham's cipher-breakers, during a year of following clues and tapping Mary's secret correspondence, led to the discovery of a conspiracy – in which Mary herself, the Spanish Ambassador, King Philip and the Pope were all involved. As the prelude to a joint Catholic rising and Spanish invasion – designated by the code name, 'Enterprise of England' – Elizabeth was to be struck down by a devoted former retainer of Mary Queen of Scots, a young Catholic of good family named Francis Throgmorton, nephew of the former royal ambassador to France, Sir Nicholas Throgmorton.

Arrested and put to the torture, Throgmorton confessed all, reproaching himself before his terrible traitor's death that he had disclosed the secrets of her who was 'the dearest thing to him in the world'. For, in her correspondence with those who were plotting to kill Elizabeth, Mary had implicated herself to the hilt. Nor did Throgmorton's death remove the standing threat to the Queen's life and, with it, of the country's peace and security. At any moment some other unknown hand might set in motion the fearful train of consequences which the kingdom's foes, external and internal, had been planning. Only a week or two before Throgmorton's arrest a young Warwickshire Catholic gentleman – also caught and hanged – had set off to London with a pistol, boasting in his cups that he was about to compass the death of the Queen and 'hoped to see her head set on a pole, for she was a serpent and a viper'.

For in the year in which Drake returned from the Pacific the first Jesuit missionaries landed in England, sworn to face martyrdom in their dedicated task of winning back their countrymen to the faith. Most of those who, bravely defying Parliament's ban on Catholic priests, returned to England, did so, not to kill its Protestant sovereign, but to minister to their fellow Catholics – deprived by law of the offices and consolations of their faith. But two successive Popes had let it be known that merit for the faithful could be won by ridding the world of a heretic Queen. Ten years after Pius V had issued his Bull excommunicating Elizabeth and releasing her subjects from their allegiance, in December 1580 his successor, Gregory XIII, authorized an unequivocal reply by the Papal Secretary to an enquiry about the permissibility of taking her life. 'Since that guilty woman of England rules over two such noble kingdoms of Christendom and is the cause of so much injury to the Catholic faith and loss of so many million souls, there is no doubt that whosoever sends her out of the world, with the pious intention of doing God service, not only does not sin, but gains merit.'

The result of this dedicated priestly invasion was twofold. The laws against the practice of Catholic rites in England – at first, in a universally intolerant age, so mildly interpreted by her young Queen – were far more strictly enforced. The very existence of a Roman priest in England was now made treason by Parliament and punishable by death. As a result, the home of many a loyal and law-abiding Catholic subject became an illegal fortress where, sheltered in minute hiding places or priest holes made behind panelling or under floor-boards, visiting priests could lie concealed while carrying out their perilous ministrations of spiritual comfort and guidance to the local Catholics or 'recusants', as they became called. For the immediate effect of the exposure of the Throgmorton plot against the Queen's life was to spark off a national panic. In its course, to allay and canalize Protestant fears, the Council drew up a Bond of Association by which, in the event of the Queen's assassination, all loyal subjects were asked to pledge themselves to take the life, by any means available and without benefit of law, of any person claiming succession to the throne by virtue of such treasonable crime – that is, of Mary Queen of Scots. This Bond, with its resort to lynch law and the blood hunt, was widely subscribed to – in Yorkshire alone over seven thousand seals were received. It was subsequently submitted to Parliament for legalization when it met in November. Only as a result of Elizabeth's refusal to countenance the death of anyone, even her own murderer, without due trial was it modified by a provision for the setting up instead of a special tribunal to try any claimant to the vacant throne benefiting by the Queen's assassination. And all Jesuits and Catholic priests were ordered by Parliament to leave the country within forty days and their presence in England thereafter to be punished as treason.

*   *   *

Long before Parliament met, the revelations of the Throgmorton plot had led to a drastic tightening of the ring round the hapless but incorrigibly intriguing Mary who, with her little court and household, was removed from the chivalrous custodianship of the earl of Shrewsbury to Tutbury Castle and the close charge of a stern Puritan, Sir Amyas Paulet. It caused, too, the departure from England of her fellow conspirator, the Spanish Ambassador. On January 9th 1584, Mendoza was given fifteen days to leave the country whose sovereign he had sought to destroy. 'The insolence of these people,' he wrote indignantly to the Spanish Secretary of State, 'has brought me to a state in which my only desire to live is for the purpose of avenging myself upon them. I pray that God may let it be soon and will give me grace to be His instrument of vengeance.' Yet though his parting words, as he ended his ten years' diplomatic mission, were 'Don Bernardino de Mendoza was not born to disturb countries but to conquer them,' neither King Philip nor Elizabeth were yet fully prepared to resort to the final arbitrament of war.

Instead, the undeclared war between them in the Netherlands continued, with Elizabeth, in order to keep it alive, continuing to give the necessary minimum of financial aid to the rebel Protestant cause while the young Spanish Governor General, Alexander Farnese of Parma, by a combination of conciliatory diplomacy towards the southern and mainly Catholic provinces and of successive victories in the field, gradually narrowed the area controlled by William of Orange and the Dutch Calvinists and sea-faring northern irreconcilables. In March 1584, he won back the capital, Brussels, and, during the spring and early summer, the rich Flemish cities of Ypres and Bruges. Then, on July 10th at Delft, in response to the reward offered for William of Orange's life, an assassin's bullet, fired at point-blank range, won the King of Spain his greatest, and, as it seemed, culminating, triumph over the patriot leader and statesman whose twelve years' defiance of tyranny as Stadtholder of Holland, Zeeland, and Utrecht, had alone kept the rebellion in being.

With the death of William 'the Silent' – the faithful Father Wilhelmus of Dutch legend and national memory – the Protestant cause in the Netherlands seemed doomed. For with his army of 60,000 mercenaries, its discipline now restored, Parma was driving ever deeper into the heart of Flanders and Brabant, taking town after town, either by battle and siege or by the politic lenience he offered to all but persistent heretics. Thanks to the young Governor-General's wisdom, the revolt of the once United Provinces was ceasing to be national and becoming again merely Protestant, and, as such, increasingly confined to the north and seaboard. No help for the failing rebel cause could any longer be looked for from Elizabeth's old suitor, the French duke of Anjou – the former Alençon – whom she had subsidized to keep the rebellion alive without her own and England's intervention and whom Orange had installed as duke of Brabant and count of Flanders. For, an inveterate intriguer and double-dealer, Anjou had long alienated the Protestant elements in the country, and, succumbing to typhus, had died, a discredited man, only a few weeks before the tragedy of Delft. His death ended the possibility of any further help from a bitterly divided France, leaving, as it did, the reversion of its crown to the Huguenot Henry of Navarre. To Anjou's brother, the weak and frivolous Philip III, last of the Valois line, the despairing Netherlanders vainly offered their throne, only to have their offer rejected. For, with the threat of a Protestant succession precipitating a new French civil war, effective power in France for the moment passed to the Catholic champion, the duke

of Guise, who, making a secret alliance with Philip of Spain, called
in a Spanish army to keep out the heretic heir-presumptive, Henry
of Navarre.

With Ghent, last of the rebel Flemish cities of Flanders, falling
to Parma in September 1584, the Spaniards closed in on the great
port and commercial centre of Antwerp. That winter, while in
England Parliament debated the measures to deter would-be
assassins of the Queen, Parma built an enormous dam across half a
mile of tidal water to cut off all access to the doomed city from the
sea and any hope of its relief by the Dutch 'sea-beggars' from the
north. By the summer of 1585, as starvation began to bite and the
last appeal to the French king failed, it became clear that nothing
could save the Protestant cause in the Netherlands but the open
intervention of England. And no one in Europe believed that the
English would dare to challenge the immense military and – with
the Portuguese navy joined to Spain's – naval power of Philip's
all-conquering empire.

Yet as the summer drew on, it was beginning to look as though
the English might do so after all. At the end of May relations
between the two countries were exacerbated by a sudden and
treacherous embargo placed by the Spanish king on English grain
ships unloading in the ports of northern Spain, where a failure of
the previous year's harvest had caused a famine. The master and
crew of one of the ships ordered to be seized had resisted and,
overcoming the boarding party, sailed for England, carrying with
them the Spanish functionary supervising the arrests. On arrival,
papers concealed in his boots revealed that the seizure of the ships
had been made on King Philip's personal orders, in order to provide shipping for a future invasion of England. The indignation
provoked by this revelation of Spain's intentions coincided with
the arrival of commissioners from the Netherlands to beg Elizabeth's help for besieged and starving Antwerp.

The sovereignty they offered and implored her to take she
rejected, as she had done William of Orange's offer of ten years
before. But Antwerp was at its last gasp, and, once it fell, only
Holland and Zeeland, behind their sea barriers, would be able to
hold out against Parma's triumphant armies. Unless England's

help was speedily forthcoming, the resistance of the remaining United Provinces and, with it, of the reformed faith in the Netherlands, would be at an end, and Parma's victorious troops could be freed for an invasion of England. Reluctant as her queen was to commit her country to war, and all that it implied, she saw that the consequences for her people of a refusal to do so would be worse. Just as she and Cecil had faced the enormous risk of war in their country's hour of extreme weakness a quarter of a century before to save Scotland's Reformation and independence, they now acted to save those of the Low Countries, and for the same reason. Burghley summed it up in a memorandum to his royal mistress:

> 'Although her Majesty should thereby enter into a war presently, yet were she better to do it now, while she may make the same out of her realm, having the help of the people of Holland and before the King of Spain shall have consummated his conquests, . . . whereby he shall be so provoked with pride, solicited by the Pope and tempted by the Queen's own subjects, and shall be so strong by sea and so free from all other actions and quarrels, yea, shall be so formidable to all the rest of Christendom, as that her Majesty shall no wise be able with her own power . . . to withstand his attempts, but shall be forced to give place to his insatiable malice.'

So at her riverside palace, where fifty-two years earlier Elizabeth had been born, the die was cast. Though it was too late to save Antwerp, which capitulated from starvation on August 7th, by the terms of the Treaty of Greenwich, signed three days later, England agreed to provide an army of 4,000 foot – later raised to 5,000 – and 1,000 horse. In addition she undertook to advance the United Provinces £125,000 a year to support the war, more than half, that is, the ordinary revenue of her Crown. In return, the States were to allow the English to occupy the ports of Flushing and Brill as pledges for the loan.

In a formal 'Declaration of the courses moving the Queen of England to give aid to the Defence of the People afflicted and oppressed in the Low Countries' issued that autumn, Elizabeth and Burghley set out the reasons for their intervening. It expressly refrained from any formal declaration of war, even referring to King Philip as the Queen's 'ally' and paying a noble tribute to his Viceroy, the duke of Parma, as one 'who hath dealt in a more honourable and gracious sort in the charge committed unto him than any other that hath ever gone before him or is likely to succeed after him.' Disclaiming any wish to extend the Queen's dominions, it maintained that her sole purpose in sending aid 'to the natural people of those countries' with which England had so long been associated in trade and friendship, was 'to defend them and their towns from sacking and desolation, and thereby to procure them safety . . . to enjoy their ancient liberties for them and their posterity'. She had acted only because 'we did manifestly see in what danger ourselves, our countries and people might shortly be if in convenient time we did not speedily otherwise regard to prevent or stay the same'.

In this famous Declaration – compared by C. R. Markham to the American Declaration of Independence as 'one of the noblest state papers ever written' – Elizabeth laid down what was to remain a ruling principle of English policy for three and a half centuries: the independence of the Low Countries and a 'common cause' with all prepared to defend it against any despotic power seeking to absorb it. 'All this time of my reign,' she was to recall in Parliament a decade later, when the war with Spain she had tried so long to avoid had become the inescapable background of her life, 'I have not sought to advance my territories and enlarge my dominions . . . My mind was never to invade my neighbours or to usurp over any. I am contented to reign over mine own and to rule as a just prince.' For what was right for her own people, she held, must be right for other peoples. Against the supranational claims of imperial Spain to succeed, and extend, the supranational claims of the medieval Church, Elizabeth set herself and England as the champion of all 'natural' peoples who wished to govern themselves through their own laws and princes.

CHAPTER SIX

Preparations for Invasion

'The first article of the Tudor creed was that a united
England was an invincible England.'

S. T. Bindoff

'Come the three corners of the world in arms,
And we shall shock them. Nought shall make us rue
If England to itself do rest but true.'

Shakespeare

THE FREEDOM OF THE NETHERLANDS was not the only principle for
which Elizabeth's England contended. The other was the freedom
of the seas against Spain's claim to deny the use of outer ocean and
its shores beyond an arbitrary line drawn by papal decree. In 1584,
after the expulsion of Mendoza, the Queen had at last given the
arch opponent of that claim, Sir Francis Drake, leave to undertake
a second circumnavigation of the world, for which he had vainly
pleaded three years earlier. Financed by a joint stock subscription
by the Queen and other leaders of the Court and City, a fleet of
eleven warships, four barks and twenty pinnaces, manned by
1,600 picked sailors and soldiers, was to sail under Drake's command to ravage once more the Pacific coasts of Peru and Panama,
recross that ocean and, following up his treaty with the Sultan of
Ternate, take over from Spain the Portuguese 'factories' in the
East Indies, so securing for England the trade of the spice islands.

Had the expedition sailed and succeeded it might have anticipated by fourteen years the foundation of the East India Company
and, possibly by a century, the beginnings of England's commercial
ascendancy in the Far East. But King Philip's seizure of the

English grain ships in the Basque ports in the summer of 1585 changed its destination. Instead, it was deflected to release the captured ships and, then by way of the Cape Verde Islands, descend on the Spanish possessions in the Caribbean to cut the flow of American treasure across the Atlantic which was financing the suppression of the Dutch rebellion and the projected invasion of England. Before sailing from Plymouth in September, it was reinforced by twelve companies of soldiers, bringing its total complement to 2,300 men. Under Drake, as the Queen's Admiral and General, was the Yorkshire ex-privateer and Arctic explorer, Martin Frobisher, as vice-admiral, and Walsingham's son-in-law, Christopher Carleill – a brilliant young veteran of the Netherlands and French wars of religion – as lieutenant-general.

Up to the last moment it was feared that the Queen, still hoping to avoid a final breach with Spain, might stop the voyage. Even the usually cautious Burghley sent a secret warning to Drake to act quickly. He need not have worried, for, without waiting for the completion of the fleet's victualling, the great seaman was already off the Spanish coast. With only a fraction of England's naval strength, he occupied Vigo bay and proceeded, as though in his native Devon, to provision his ships at the expense of the Spanish authorities who, with their slow and cumbersome communications, were powerless to prevent him. Then, having dealt a shattering blow to King Philip's prestige, he sailed for the Cape Verde Islands, whose capital, Santiago, he sacked and burnt. During the Atlantic crossing, however, a fatal fever, contracted in the islands, caused the death of three hundred of his men, or nearly a seventh of his scanty force. Yet, it did not prevent him, in two brilliant amphibious operations, from storming and capturing – on New Year's Day 1586 – the capital of the West Indies, Hispaniola, and then, in February, in the face of a strong garrison, the supposedly impregnable fortress and harbour of Cartagena, capital of the Spanish Main. Both operations were superbly directed, raising Drake's reputation to a new height, most of all among his enemies who now regarded him as invincible – a man, as one of them put it, 'equal to any undertaking'. By the simple subject peoples whom Spain had conquered or enslaved he was regarded as liberator and saviour;

a captured Spaniard reported that 'Drake behaved with such humanity to the Indians and negroes that they all love him.'

As in his Pacific voyage of seven years before, owing to the manpower losses sustained on its outward course Drake was unable to achieve his supreme ambition of capturing the Panama isthmus and so cutting at its weakest point the supply-line between Spain's silver mines in Peru and her conquering armies in Europe. To have taken, let alone held, it with the few hundred soldiers left him would have strained his slender resources far too far. Nor did he succeed in capturing a single treasure ship, still less the Plate Fleet which it had been hoped in England might have fallen into his hands. For, having taken advantage of the respite afforded by his long enforced sojourn at home, the Spaniards were now much better able to defend themselves in their ocean colonies than they had been. As a result the expedition brought no financial profit to its promoters, who recovered only three-quarters of the capital they had invested in it. Yet the damage inflicted by Drake on King Philip's preparations for invading England was incalculable. Among the trophies he brought home were 240 captured cannon, at a time when the Spaniards were still only learning to make their own. And when the news of the capture of Hispaniola and Cartagena reached the money-markets of Europe, King Philip's credit plummeted. 'The Bank of Seville is broke,' noted Lord Treasurer Burghley, formerly so dubious about the consequences of Drake's ocean ventures, 'the Bank of Valencia also very likely. It will be such a cooling to King Philip as never happened to him since he was King of Spain.' For that monarch's financial problems of paying Parma's 60,000 mercenaries and buying naval stores, provisions and munitions from half the countries of Europe for an invasion of England had been increased out of all measure by the action of a few hundred men under a great naval commander four thousand miles away. What Drake had regained for his country was the initiative at sea which his royal mistress had thrown away by keeping him so long on shore. It was its recovery which caused Spain's 'General of the Ocean Sea', the Marquis of Santa Cruz, to hasten with the flower of his navy across the Atlantic to save the Caribbean from Drake's ravages, so shutting, at his master's urgent command, the stable door after the horse was out. 'Truly,' wrote Lord Burghley, 'Sir Francis Drake is a fearful man to the King of Spain.'

* * *

Yet King Philip was not to be deterred from his purpose. It had taken long to bring him to the sticking-point, and he was now resolved to deal, once and for all, with the menace of England and its heretic Queen. Yet the Queen who so plagued him was still hoping for peace with him, both for herself and the Netherlands. The cost and frustrations of the defensive war she had so bravely, but reluctantly, undertaken in the one place where, to a lands-woman's eye, (so far as is known the nearest she had then been to the sea was her riverside palace at Greenwich) it could alone be decisive, was proving all she had feared and more. She was vexed out of patience by the factious and greedy demands of the intolerant and ever-quarrelling Dutch magnates and burghers and the Calvinist fanatics, who together formed the hard core of resistance to Parma's armies and for whose sake she was making such onerous financial sacrifices. And the commander of the forces she had sent to their aid – her old flame, Lord Leicester, now grown stout and choleric – was not only no match for Parma in the field, but had caused her deep distress by flying in the teeth of her instructions and, intoxicated by the enthusiastic reception at his first landing in the Netherlands, had accepted from the States General the grandiloquent title of 'His Excellency' and the nominal Governor-ship of the rebellious Provinces – an authority which, for her country's sake, Elizabeth herself had deliberately refused. That 'a creature' of hers, as she wrote in an indignant letter to Leicester, 'raised up by ourself, and extraordinarily favoured by us above any other subject,' should flout her commandments in this way was intolerable and, after her public Declaration, had gravely impugned her honour with her fellow sovereigns. To make matters worse, his wife, Lettice, whom Elizabeth detested, was reported to be about to join him 'with such a train of ladies and gentlewomen and such rich coaches, litters and side-saddles, as her Majesty had

none such, and . . . as should far surpass her Majesty's court.' Only
Burghley's entreaties to his infuriated royal mistress saved Leicester
from the humiliation of having to renounce his offending titles
publicly.

Nor was Leicester's insubordination and the ill-success of his
arms the only problem facing the Queen that summer. A few days
after Drake's return from the Caribbean, a new storm broke round
the head of her embarrassing captive, Mary Queen of Scots. In
July 1586 a treaty had just been signed at Berwick under which
Mary's twenty-year-old son, James VI, accepted a pension from
the English queen in return for a permanent Scottish alliance.
Early that August it became known that his mother had been implicated in yet another plot against Elizabeth's life. The public
fury and panic knew no bounds; the church bells were rung, bonfires lit, and mobs, singing Protestant psalms and demanding
Mary's immediate death and that of the 'hellish priests' believed
to be plotting Elizabeth's assassination, paraded the London
streets. In a sense it had all been partly brought about by the ultra-
Protestant Secretary of State, Sir Francis Walsingham, who, a
few months earlier, had apprehended a secret Catholic agent sent
to English to try to re-open a correspondence with the captive
Mary, then under strict surveillance at Chartley in Staffordshire.
Faced by the rack, the agent had been 'turned round' by his
English captors and employed by them to open a 'secret' way for
Mary to receive and send letters, all of which were now intercepted and, before being sent on to their destinations, deciphered
by Walsingham's code-breakers. Through the medium of a
small waterproof case slipped through the bung-hole of the in-
going and outgoing kegs which supplied Mary's household with
beer, a voluminous cipher correspondence developed between
the captive Queen and her Catholic sympathizers at home and
abroad, every word of which became immediately known to the
government. It led to the discovery of an elaborate plot to assassinate Elizabeth as the prelude to a Catholic rising and a Spanish invasion – all part of King Philip's secret 'Enterprise of England' and
centring round a seminary priest and a rich young Derbyshire
landowner of ancient family, named Anthony Babington, formerly

a page of Mary's at Sheffield Castle. A dozen or more young Catholic gentlemen, under Babington's lead, had made a pact to win a martyr's crown by despatching Elizabeth and rescuing Mary from captivity. They had even had their picture painted together to commemorate their impending heroism, while Mary herself, favoured with a long letter from Babington describing exactly how they proposed to dispose of her royal cousin, replied, enthusiastically approving and adding a few helpful suggestions of her own. Poor woman, after twenty years of imprisonment and frustration, she had little else on which to employ her time and her very considerable talents for intrigue.

Caught red-handed, the conspirators, amid wild scenes of popular rejoicing, suffered the terrible penalties for high treason in St Giles's Fields on September 20th and 21st. Accompanied by rumours that the French of the now triumphant Catholic League – the residuary heirs, as it were, of the Massacre of St Bartholomew – had landed in Sussex and that a Spanish invasion fleet was about to sail from a Breton port, the parliamentary commission of peers, privy councillors and judges appointed by Parliament after the Throgmorton Plot to try the beneficiary of any attempt to assassinate the Queen, arrived on October 11th at Fotheringay where Mary had been taken for trial. Her bold denial of guilt in face of her own damning correspondence availed her nothing, and, 'with one assent', the Commission adjudged her guilty. Yet it took more than three months, despite much impassioned petitioning by Parliament, which met on October 29th, and another outburst of popular panic, with widespread rumours of Elizabeth's death and a Spanish landing in Wales, before the Queen could bring herself to sign the death warrant and thus make herself guilty of her cousin's and fellow sovereign's blood. For, in the last resort, she alone, not Parliament, possessed the constitutional power to end poor Mary's life.

On the morning of February 8th, in the hall of Fotheringay Castle, the dethroned Queen of Scots, Dowager Queen of France and heir-presumptive to the English throne, paid the final penalty of her tragic life for having placed her feelings as a woman before her duties as a Queen. Her noble dignity in the hour of defeat and death foreshadowed that of another Stuart sovereign sixty-two years later, her grandson Charles I. As the axe fell, a small pet dog, concealed in her skirts, emerged whimpering and lay in a pool of blood between her severed head and body. Afterwards, as the news reached London and bonfires were lit for joy in every street, Elizabeth alone remained inconsolable, refusing to eat or sleep, and even repudiating the unfortunate official who had despatched the death warrant after she had signed it.

* * *

By transmitting to her Protestant son her hereditary claim to the succession of the English throne – which the dead Queen before her execution bequeathed to Philip – Mary's death removed the incentive for a Catholic assassination of Elizabeth. For, while protesting volubly at his mother's decapitation, the young King of Scotland, who was not Darnley's son for nothing, remained tacitly, but cannily, committed to the English alliance and the substantial pension from Elizabeth he had recently accepted for it. Disappointed of a rising of English Catholics and a diversion by Scottish ones against the heretic Queen's northern border, for his 'Enterprise of England' King Philip was now entirely on his own. 'As the affair is so much in God's service,' he had written when Babington's plan had been submitted to him, 'it certainly deserves to be supported, and we must hope that our Lord will prosper it.' As the Lord had not yet done so, the devout royal autocrat, in his crusade against the troublesome islanders, now claimed the cuscession to their throne for himself and his family as he had done that of Portugal. His descent from John of Gaunt's daughter Philippa, gave him a better right to it, he reckoned, than any other Catholic claimant, and no one in his eyes but a Catholic had any right to occupy it at all.

After his victories over the French in the Azores, the Marquis of Santa Cruz – Spain's General of the Ocean Sea – had placed before his royal master a plan for a titanic punitive Armada against Elizabeth's heretic kingdom. It was to consist of 556 vessels, including 196 battle or capital ships, together with forty fly boats and

200 flat-bottomed barges carried on board the larger ships, the whole manned by 94,222 men, more than two-thirds of them soldiers. With this immense force he guaranteed to sweep England's Navy from the seas and land an army or armies at any point on her shores. It would make Spain unchallenged mistress of the Atlantic, English Channel and North Sea, as her victory at Lepanto had made her of the Mediterranean.

But the estimated cost of this self-contained amphibious enterprise was staggering. It involved the provision of 373,337 cwt of biscuit, 22,800 cwt of bacon, 21,500 cwt of cheese, 16,040 cwt of salt beef, 23,200 barrels of tunny-fish, 66,000 bushels of peas, beans and rice, 50,000 strings of garlic, more than five million gallons of wine, with 20,000 pipes of water for the horses and mules. The ships – half of which had still to be built – and their guns, ammunition and stores had to be collected from every quarter of Philip's world-wide dominions. It would cost more than even all the treasures of Mexico and Peru and the monopoly of the East Indian spice trade could meet. Eager though he was to subdue England, it was too much for the King's careful, calculating mind to contemplate, or for his slow patience to bear. For he was no longer prepared to wait even a year before settling accounts with Elizabeth.

Instead, Philip decided to reduce the size of the naval part of the enterprise, where his existing resources were limited, and to increase the military part where they were relatively unlimited. He already had to his hand in Flanders the finest army in the world under the command of its first soldier, situated on the nearest coast to England and only a day's sail, or single tide, from her shores. And though, like his predecessor and fellow soldier, the duke of Alva, Parma was not in favour of a war against the English, who commanded his vital sea supply-route through the Channel – at least until he had completed his reconquest of the Netherlands and secured the use of the ports of Antwerp and Flushing – in order to please his royal uncle and master, on whose favour all his worldly hopes depended, he had once, as part of an earlier plan for releasing Mary Queen of Scots, rashly suggested the possibility of a sneak barge invasion of England across the narrow seas when conditions of weather and tide were favourable and its defenders' attentions were deflected elsewhere.

Recalling this, the King therefore opted for a smaller and more manageable Armada, striking up the Channel from the Atlantic under Santa Cruz, in conjunction with a simultaneous descent on England's low-lying south-eastern coast by 30,000 troops under Parma, who were to cross the North Sea in flat-bottom barges collected from the rivers and canals of Flanders. How these two widely separated forces were to co-operate in the face of weather and tide, not to mention the watching English fleet in the Dover strait, was never wholly clear, despite Philip's meticulous and detailed calculations and directions on every other point. But the numerical odds in their favour seemed overwhelming. And in every port, from the Mediterranean to the Baltic, shipyards were now set to work and vast quantities of naval stores and equipment bought and shipped to the Tagus, where Santa Cruz's armada was to assemble. For Philip was resolved at all costs to strike down England in the summer of 1587.

During the winter which saw Mary Queen of Scots' trial and death, it became impossible any longer to ignore the enormous concentration of naval force building up beyond the Bay of Biscay, or to doubt its purpose. 'The like preparation was never heard nor known,' Drake warned his royal mistress, 'as the King of Spain hath and daily maketh to invade England.' In the closing days of 1586, while the threat of assassination was still hanging over her head, the Council had authorized the immediate preparation of a preventative expedition to sail in the spring to impede and, if possible, delay the concentration of this vast threatening force. Financed in the usual English way as a private joint stock venture – for, with the war in the Netherlands on her hands, the Queen's normal income was strained to the utmost – its command was entrusted to Drake, who, like his old associate and fellow Devonian, John Hawkins, Treasurer of the Navy, was insistent – novel though the idea was – that the place to defend England was on the enemy coast and not on her own. Though untaught in any school save that of practical experience in seamanship, Drake was a creative genius who had formed in his mind strategic and tactical concep-

tions far in advance of his time, which, in coming centuries were to
govern the theory and practice of the great sea captains of the classic
age of British sea power. These were to defend their island base by
seeking out would-be invaders off their own ports and challenging
and destroying them wherever found.

Though the main body of such of her Navy as the Queen
could at present afford to man, mobilize and maintain, was based,
as in the past, in the Medway and Thames estuary to guard against
an invasion from the Netherlands, Drake's flying ocean force,
fitting out at Plymouth, was the most powerful yet entrusted to
him. It consisted of twenty-three warships and pinnaces, with ten
companies of soldiers for shore operations. Four of the finest ships
of Hawkins's new-built Navy, including Drake's flagship, the
Bonaventure, were provided by the Queen herself – the principal
shareholder. Other subscribers were the Lord Admiral, the London merchants of the Levant Company, who contributed seven
heavily-armed Levanters accustomed to fighting their way through
the pirate-ridden Mediterranean, and Drake himself, who added
three more auxiliaries. His instructions were exceptionally wide.
He was to intercept, capture or destroy all naval vessels or supply
ships found on the Spanish coast – 'to impeach,' as they put it, 'the
joining together of the King of Spain's fleets out of their several
ports, to keep victuals from them, to follow them in case they
should . . . come forward towards England or Ireland.' He was
even empowered to 'distress the ships within the havens themselves.'

He wasted no time. As two years before in his Caribbean expedition, he was off even before he had fully completed victualling,
sailing from Plymouth at the beginning of April 1587. It was well
that he did so, for his pacific Sovereign, once more hoping for a
negotiated peace in the Netherlands, was still refusing to believe in
the seriousness of her hitherto temporizing brother-in-law's intentions. Among the State papers in the Record Office is a draft of
a later order from the Council which seems to have just failed to
reach Drake before he sailed, going back on his previous instructions and ordering him to 'forbear to enter forcibly into any of the
King's havens, or to offer any violence to any of his towns or

shipping within his harbours, or to do any act of hostility upon the land.' Either it never reached him or, if it did, he acted as if it had arrived too late.

For by then Drake was already at sea. 'There was never more likely in any fleet of a more loving agreement than we hope the one of the other, I thank God,' he had written to Walsingham before sailing. 'I find no man but as all members of one body to stand for our gracious Queen and country against Anti-Christ and his members . . . If your honour did now see the fleet under sail and knew with what resolution men's minds do enter into this action, so you would judge a small force would not divide them . . . Each wind commands me away, our ship is under sail. God grant we may so live in His fear as the enemy may have cause to say that God doth fight for her Majesty as well abroad as at home.'

What Drake did there was daring in the extreme. The bulk of the vast battle fleet which was intended that summer to strike down England was already at Lisbon, awaiting new guns, behind the forts guarding the narrow entrance to the Tagus estuary. Any attack on this, even if possible, was expressly forbidden to Drake by a Government still not officially at war with the Spanish/ Portuguese empire and still hoping for a negotiated settlement in the Netherlands. But Drake knew that there was a secondary con-centration of shipping intended for the Armada still at Cadiz, Spain's chief Atlantic port, and, resolved to strike hard, he made straight for it. Arriving off the port on April 19th, after battling for five days with a south-westerly gale, he called an immediate Council of War. It was a long-established custom of the Navy for Councils of War to act only on a majority decision of the captains present, but Drake would have none of it. Ignoring the objections of his Vice-Admiral, William Borough — a highly experienced officer and a member of the Navy Board — he ordered an immediate attack and led the fleet straight into Cadiz road. Here a large con-centration was guarded by shore batteries and defended by what has always been regarded as invincible in enclosed waters — a squadron of long shark-like galleys, with heavy iron-shod rams for sinking any vessel which crossed their path, independent of wind and tide and propelled at incredible speed by the great sweeps of oars of chained galley-slaves spurred on by the overseer's whip.

With a favouring wind the English fleet bore straight down on the crowded shipping in the harbour. Immediately the galleys went into the attack, expecting to sink or board the rash intruders. Before they could reach them, they were met by a devastating fire from the massed guns of the *Bonaventure* which, sweeping their enslaved oarsmen's benches, quickly immobilized them and drove them back for shelter under the shore batteries.

There were about eighty Spanish ships in the port. Except for the smaller fry which were able to take refuge in shoal waters where the English could not follow them, all those ready to sail were seized and taken out to sea by prize crews, while the remainder, after being plundered, were burnt. So were the painfully collected stores destined for the Armada. Then the invaders fell on the inner harbour, where a huge galleon belonging to the General of the Ocean Sea himself was awaiting its complement of guns. It, also, was boarded and burnt.

Yet when the wind dropped, and the dreaded galleys, seizing their opportunity, returned to the attack, they were again driven back in rout by the English gunners. Altogether 13,000 tons of shipping were destroyed before Drake withdrew, having inflicted an intolerable humiliation on earth's greatest monarch in his own chief Atlantic harbour. 'We sank,' Drake wrote in his report, 'a Biscayan of 1,200 tons, burnt a ship of 1,500 tons belonging to the Marquis of Santa Cruz, and thirty-one ships more of from 1,000 to 200 tons, carried away with us four laden with provisions, and departed thence at our pleasure with as much honour as we could wish.'

Anticipating by more than two hundred years the classic naval strategy of Jervis and Nelson in the same waters, Drake now moved up the coast to Cape St Vincent, round which all traffic bound for Lisbon from the Mediterranean and the ports of eastern Spain and Italy was bound to pass. Here, to afford his fleet a protected anchorage, he landed his troops and, taking personal command, stormed the cliff castle of Sagres from where, in the fifteenth century John of Gaunt's grandson, Prince Henry the Navigator, had directed the Portuguese discoveries.

Here, while challenging and taunting the indignant Santa Cruz to come out and fight against his all-destroying guns, Drake maintained a close blockade of the Portuguese coast, seizing the catches of tunny fish which were to provision the waiting Armada and capturing and destroying 1,700 tons of hoops and pipestaves on which it was going to depend for supplies of water. Only when his ships, overcrowded with their complement of soldiers, ran out of victuals was he finally forced to desist, hunger driving at least one of his little fleet to mutiny. Then, with what force remained to him, he suddenly struck out far into the Atlantic and, on reaching the Azores, sighted and captured a huge Portuguese carrack returning from the East Indies with a cargo of silks and spices. Its subsequent sale in England doubled the capital invested in the expedition. When, after Drake's return to Plymouth on June 26th, rumour of the carrack's capture reached King Philip, it caused him, in his rage and anxiety, to send part of the great fleet arming in the Tagus half way across the Atlantic in order to save his threatened treasure ships. By doing so it made it impossible for the Armada to sail before the winter.

Drake's exploit made him the most famous man in the world. Men said he had singed the King of Spain's beard. The Spaniards believed him to be a wizard who had traded his soul to the Devil for a magic mirror which enabled him to see the movements of his enemies wherever they were and so destroy them at will. 'El Draque', the dragon, they called him, viewing him with a mixture of fear and admiration. Even the Pope, Sixtus V, praised him. 'Just look at Drake,' he commented when the news reached him. 'Who is he? What forces has he? . . . We are sorry to say it, but we have a poor opinion of this Spanish Armada, and fear some disaster.' 'She certainly is a great Queen,' he said of the heretic princess in whose name these deeds were done. 'Were she only a Catholic she would be our dearly beloved. Just look how well she governs! She is only a woman, only mistress of half an island, and yet she makes herself feared by Spain, by France, by the Empire, by all.'

'There must be a beginning of any great matter,' Drake had written from Cape St Vincent, 'but the continuing of the same to the end until it be thoroughly finished yieldeth the true glory.' Yet,

almost alone, the Queen refused to be impressed by his achievement. Far from letting him return to his commanding station off the
Iberian coast to finish the blockade he had begun, she not only
refused him permission, but berated him soundly for what he
had done at Cadiz. For that summer she had again opened
negotiations with the duke of Parma, not only in the hope of
relieving her over-strained Treasury from the bottomless cost of
maintaining an army in the Netherlands in support of her unco-
operative and ungrateful Dutch allies, but, even more, of inducing
her royal brother-in-law to overlook all the insults and injuries she
and her maritime subjects had inflicted on him, so reverting to their
old familiar diplomatic Box and Cox relationship of the past
twenty-nine years. For there seemed no other way left to preserve
for her realm and people the healing and enriching peace she had
given them for the past quarter of a century.

And though much glory, even when unwanted, had attended
her arms at sea, it was very far from having done so under Leicester's command on land. And it was proving infinitely more expensive. The long sequence of petty defeats and retreats at Parma's
hands had been redeemed only by the stubborn courage of individual English soldiers. A year earlier there had fallen in a cavalry
skirmish near Zutphen the most brilliant and universally admired
of all Elizabeth's younger subjects, the poet and courtier, Sir
Philip Sidney – Leicester's step-son and Walsingham's son-in-law.
Son of the Lord President of Wales and Lord Deputy of Ireland,
one of the most accomplished writers England had known since
Geoffrey Chaucer, and, in the eyes of the princely rulers of
Europe, almost one of their own exalted family circle – Philip
of Spain was his godfather – with his virtue, genius and scholarship he was, at thirty-two, the bright star of the English Protestant
Renaissance. Though Governor of Flushing – the vital port which
an English garrison was denying Parma – and Leicester's General
of Horse, he could not refrain from venturing his life in the field.
As, mortally wounded, he was borne from it, he won for himself
an immortality surpassing even that of his famous *Defence of
Poesie* and *Arcadia*. 'For being thirsty from excess of bleeding,'
his friend, Fulke Greville, wrote, 'he called for a drink, but, as

he was putting the bottle to his mouth, he saw a poor soldier
carried along, who had eaten his last at that same feast, ghastly
casting his eyes at the bottle. Which Sir Philip, perceiving, took
it from his hand before he drank and delivered it to the poor man
with these words, "Thy necessity is yet greater than mine". And
when he had pledged the poor soldier, he was presently carried
to Arnhem.'

As for the cost of that unrewarding campaign for another
people's liberty, there seemed no end to the corruption and inefficiency – universal in that age – of the military administration
and the waste of all the Queen's careful frugality. In its first year
alone the war in the Low Countries had swallowed nearly half her
peacetime revenue. And though she had already contributed far
more than she had promised and had sent a further 5,000 troops
to the Netherlands to take the place of those who had fallen or died,
such was the habitual fraud and dishonesty of nearly all engaged in
public administration, that the men were still unpaid and in rags.
'It is continually alleged,' she complained, 'that great sums are
due; yet why such sums are due, or to whom they are due, and
who are paid and who not paid . . . is never certified.' No wonder
she hated war, and, most of all, the wasteful and uncertain business
of land warfare. 'It is a sieve,' she said, 'that spends as it receives
to little purpose.'

Throughout the winter and early months of 1588, while the
waiting Armada in the Tagus was recovering from the wounds
Drake had inflicted on it, the peace commissioners, whom the
Queen had sent to Flanders to negotiate with Parma continued,
therefore, to maintain that those wounds had never been intended
and had only occurred because Drake had exceeded his instructions, incurring thereby her grave displeasure. All her hopes of
peace now centred on being able to persuade Philip's Viceroy to
end the war and rebellion by assuming, with her help and mediation,
the sovereignty for himself of a reunited and independent Netherlands. But tempting though her inducement was to Parma – for
all his vice-regal honours a petty Italian princeling and royal
bastard, to boot, to whom such sovereignty would have meant
much – he was first and foremost a loyal servant of his uncle and

employer, the King of Spain, who had no intention of allowing him to conclude a peace with Elizabeth on such terms or of letting her off the fate he had now prepared for her. The negotiations were therefore only permitted to continue until the Armada and Parma himself were ready to strike. And though Parma wanted nothing so much as to be free to complete his reconquest, so brilliantly begun, of the Netherlands, and had no faith at all in his inexorable master's unrealistic proposal to embark his fine army in an unseaworthy fleet of flat-bottomed canal barges, he continued obediently to spin out the peace negotiations with Elizabeth's commissioners. And all the while he continued secretly – or as secretly, that is, as was compatible with building and widening canals to link the country's waterways to the Flemish coast – to prepare and organize his part in the impending invasion.

For King Philip was now adamant. So it came about that, when the Captain General of the Ocean Sea returned from his Atlantic wild-goose chase to the Azores after the elusive Drake, his inexorable master – still resolved to launch his 'Enterprise of England' before the end of the year – ordered him to take the Armada to sea in the heart of the winter gales. Only when warned by Santa Cruz that this would be to court certain disaster, was he reluctantly persuaded to wait till the spring of 1588.

That February, worn out by so many discouragements, Santa Cruz died, possibly of typhus which was raging among the overcrowded crews and soldiery of the waiting Armada, but more probably of exhaustion – for he was sixty-three – and despair at his inability to meet his sovereign's demands. The country, to whom, since his exploits at Lepanto and Terceira, the old seaman had become something of a national hero, was deeply shocked. But the crusading King, undeterred, promptly replaced him as Admiral-in-Chief of the Armada by the senior Grandee of Spain, the Duke of Medina Sidonia – a man of the highest birth and character but without the slightest experience of the sea or naval affairs. After pleading his reluctance to accept an assignment for which he was so manifestly unfitted, he obeyed his sovereign's command in the spirit of devoted Christian dedication and obedience, which, with personal pride and honour, was the highest ideal of Spain's crusading chivalry. 'If you fail,' the King wrote, 'you fail, but the cause being that of God you will not fail.'

Yet, by any standards, it was a deeply impressive force, 'the greatest Navy,' in Francis Bacon's words, 'that ever swam upon the sea.' Of its hundred and thirty sail, twenty-four were the giant new galleons of the Castilian Indies Guard and the huge fighting carracks of the Portuguese Royal Navy. The largest warships in existence, they were supplemented by four Neapolitan galleasses, each propelled, as well as by sail, by three hundred slave oarsmen and capable, under the spur of the whip, of sudden and tremendous speed. Forty-one others were large converted merchantmen or line-of-battle auxiliaries, with new fighting superstructures and armouries of heavy guns.

For, though the number of battleships was less than half the number envisaged in Santa Cruz's estimate of two years before, in one respect the 1588 Armada was a more formidable force than the abandoned one of 1586. Paradoxically it owed this to Drake's very success in Cadiz in the previous spring. For, such was the devastation he wrought there with the guns of Hawkins's new *Bonaventure* that everyone, from King Philip downwards, had realized that it would be suicide for the Armada to take to sea without a far heavier armament than that originally contemplated. Instead, therefore, of 1,150 guns distributed among 556 ships, it was equipped with 2,341, including nearly five hundred large cannon firing roundshot of up to 60 lb, far heavier, that is, than any employed in the English navy. For whereas the latter relied on long-ranging culverins capable of firing a 17 lb iron shot a mile or more, the Spaniards, trusting to their vast superiority in soldiers and relying on the classic Mediterranean tactics of grappling and boarding their adversaries, had used the year of waiting by collecting, from every quarter available, every heavy gun they could secure. Their object was to batter the lighter and swifter English ships to a standstill by a tremendous bombardment at short-range of their masts, spars and sails, so depriving them of superior sailing-power and leaving them at the mercy of their grappling irons and boarding troops.

Meanwhile, as it grew clear that the negotiations in Flanders between the Queen's commissioners and Parma were merely a blind to conceal the imminence of Spain's intentions, the main English regular fleet, until now in cold storage to conserve the country's slender financial resources, was at last being mobilized and manned. At its head was the hereditary Lord Admiral, Lord Howard of Effingham – the fourth of his family to serve in that office. For in that intensely aristocratic age no one but a great nobleman accustomed to command and obedience was considered capable of controlling the jealousies and rivalries of the rough sea captains under him. A member of the Council and a cousin of the Queen, unlike Medina Sidonia he was not without some, though no great, naval experience. Fifty-two years of age and a Protestant, he was a modest, courteous but clear-headed and highly honourable man, with a strong sense of duty and responsibility to those under him.

Taking up his command in December, Howard quickly made his authority felt. At first, true to custom, he established his headquarters and that of his fleet in the Thames estuary in support of the squadron patrolling the Dover Strait and Flemish coast against Parma's threatened invasion. But he quickly came round to the view of the more experienced *avant garde* seamen who had learnt their business fighting Spain as privateers on the far side of the Atlantic, that the best defence for the country at sea was to attack. Their supreme prototype was Drake, now appointed Howard's Vice-Admiral and second-in-command, and at the moment in charge of an advance force of five Royal Navy warships and twenty or thirty armed West Country and London merchantmen at Plymouth. 'The opinion of Sir Francis Drake, Mr Frobisher and others that be men of the greatest judgment and experience,' Howard wrote to the Council, 'is that the surest way to meet with the Spanish fleet is upon their coast, or in any harbour of their own, and there to defeat them ... I confess my error at that time, which was otherwise, but I did, and will, yield ever to them of greater experience.'

All April, as the abortive Flemish peace negotiations drew to their inevitable conclusion, Drake, fretting with impatience at Plymouth, bombarded the Queen and Council with requests for leave to attack the Armada. 'I assure your Majesty,' he wrote on the 13th, 'I have not in my lifetime known better men and possessed with gallanter minds than your Majesty's people are for the most part which are here gathered together voluntarily to put their hands and hearts to the finishing of this great piece of work. Wherein we are all persuaded that God, the giver of all victories, will in mercy look upon your most excellent Majesty and us, your poor subjects, who for the defence of your Majesty, our religion and native country, have resolutely vowed the hazard of our lives.'

'The advantage of time and place in all martial actions is half a victory, which being lost is irrecoverable,' Drake continued, 'wherefore, if your Majesty will command me away with those ships that are here already and the rest to follow with all possible expedition I hold it in my poor opinion the surest and best course . . . Touching my poor opinion how strong your Majesty's fleet should be to encounter this great force of the enemy, God increase your most excellent Majesty's forces both by sea and land daily, for this I surely think: there was never any force so strong as there is now ready or making ready against your Majesty and true religion.' 'If a good peace for your Majesty,' he wrote again on the 28th, 'be not forthwith concluded (which I as much as any man desireth) then these great preparations of the Spaniard may be speedily prevented . . . by sending your forces to encounter theirs, somewhat far off and more near their own coast, which will be the better cheap for your Majesty and people, and much the dearer for the enemy.' But, fearful lest her too aggressive seamen, in their desire to attack the enemy on his own coasts, should leave hers unguarded, the Queen and her Council refrained from giving the required permission.

* * *

That April, in a splendid religious ceremony at Lisbon, the Cardinal Patriarch and Viceroy of Portugal, representing King Philip, presented to the duke of Medina Sidonia, as he knelt before the high altar of the Cathedral, the Standard of the Armada. Blessed by the Pope, it was afterwards, to a salute from three hundred guns, raised to the mainmast of the duke's flagship, the *San Martin*. Owing, however, to stormy weather, it was not till May 19th, more than a month later, that the great fleet finally got to sea with its hundred and thirty ships and 30,000 men.

Four days later, on May 23rd, Lord Howard of Effingham, leading in the *Ark Royal*, took the main English fleet of thirteen battleships and supernumaries into Plymouth, Drake, vested with the Vice-Admiral's standard, going out to greet him with his Western Squadron of five battleships and twenty-three other craft. Three hundred miles to the east, five other English battleships and sixteen smaller craft, under Lord Seymour and Admiral Sir William Winter, remained, reluctantly, in the Downs to patrol the Narrows and, with the help of the Dutch 'sea-beggars', blockade the Flemish invasion ports of Dunkirk and Sluys. 'Our ships doth show themselves like gallants here,' wrote stout old Sir William Winter, 'I assure you it will do a man's heart good to behold them. And would to God the Prince of Parma were upon the seas with all his forces, and we in view of them!' It was this squadron's presence which made nonsense of King Philip's sanguine hope that, during the main English fleet's absence in the west, Parma's troops, packed in their flat-bottomed river barges, might be able to slip across the North Sea to the Essex coast.

Here an amateur army under Lord Leicester was already waiting to receive them, while a boom and Thames defence works were being put urgently in hand. For the country was arming fast. In every southern county militiamen and volunteers were forming under the Deputy Lieutenants and the young veterans who had learnt their soldiering in the Netherlands. 'Black' Sir John Norris, who had won his spurs wherever Englishmen – in Flanders, France and Ireland – had fought in the past fifteen years, was in charge of the coastal defences from Kent to Dorset; 3,000 men under Sir George Carey were hurried to the Isle of Wight, believed to be a major Spanish objective; and the two West Country paladins, Sir Walter Ralegh and Sir Richard Grenville, laying aside their plans for colonizing Virginia, took over the joint defence of Devon and Cornwall. By June 25,000 troops were in being in Essex to defend the coasts against the dreaded *tercios*, while another 14,000 under

Lord Hunsdon had assembled in Kent for the personal defence of the Queen. The last, however, for all their enthusiasm, found some difficulty in exercising their function, as Elizabeth refused either to remove from her riverside palace at Greenwich or take notice of their presence. For she did not consider she needed protection.

Meanwhile the Armada had run into difficulties, as it was driven far to the south and then struggled northwards against adverse winds up the Portuguese coast. For the number of experienced seamen to work so large a fleet, compared with the multitude of soldiers, nobles, priests and friars and other passengers aboard, was insufficient to cope with the exceptionally stormy conditions of that early summer. The victuals, which had been assembled in such immense quantities, and with such difficulty as a result of Drake's blockade in the previous spring, were already going bad, the water butts leaking, the wine soured, the meat,cheese and fish putrid in their barrels of unseasoned wood. After three weeks of trying to keep his unwieldy ships in station and his crowded and dysentry-ridden crews in heart, Medina Sidonia had at last reached Finisterre by June 9th when his vast straggling fleet was struck by a heavy south-westerly gale. The admiral and his leading ships managed to round the cape and take shelter in Corunna, while the remainder were driven far off course, some as far north as the Scillies.

The poor duke was by now in such despair over his impossible assignment that, once ashore, he found the courage – and, in the face of that grave, resolved and inexorable despot in his remote fortress, it required a good deal – to advise the King to abandon his venture. Thirty-three of his ships or a quarter of his total force were at that moment missing on the high seas – a prey to tempest and, worse than tempest, fear of the dreaded sea-wizard, Drake. Stores were running out, and most of the duke's storm-tossed ships were in need of urgent repairs. 'I am bound to confess,' he wrote, and he included himself, 'I see very few, or hardly any, of those in the Armada with any knowledge or ability to perform the duties entrusted to them.'

But Philip, who was always at his best in adversity, remained imperturbable. Wracked with gout and in perpetual pain, he bade his faint-hearted lieutenant be of good heart, repair his ships, revictual the fleet and trust in God, who would never allow a work of such importance to fail, provided its human instruments were worthy of it. And to meet the emergency and overcome the shortages, he sent his executive secretary to Galicia, with over-riding powers to requisition everything needed to revictual and get the battered Armada out to sea again.

Meanwhile all England waited breathlessly for news. Not till June 18th, four weeks after it had sailed from the Tagus, was the nation officially informed through a proclamation to the Lords Lieutenant that it was at sea. All the country knew for certain was that a powerful army, which had long terrorized the Netherlands, was waiting, under the greatest commander of the age on the Flemish coast, for a chance to invade; and that the largest fleet ever assembled was at large in the Atlantic to enable it to do so. Actually, at that moment, its head was sheltering from storms at Corunna, and the remainder of the Armada was still scattered about the Bay of Biscay trying to reform. Those whom its movements most concerned, and whose business it was to find it, were themselves windbound at Plymouth under the Lord Admiral and the little group of world-famous sea captains who were his assistants. By his tact, consideration, firmness and courtesy, and complete selflessness, Lord Howard had already welded them into a band of brothers and a single directing command; all he and they needed was a chance to find the enemy. 'There is here,' Howard wrote to Burghley, 'the gallantest company of captains, soldiers and mariners that I think was ever seen in England.' Twice they had set out to attack the Armada on the Spanish coast, but had only been forced to return by gales and adverse winds, which were also holding up the victualling ships from London on which their ability to remain at sea depended. 'Such summer season saw I never the like,' wrote Seymour from his station in the Downs, 'what for storms and variable unsettled winds.' They were equally handicapped by the Queen's not unnatural reluctance, with the two invasion threats hanging over her realm, to let them go far from its shores lest the Armada should slip past them. What she preferred was to have them what she called 'plying up and down' the Channel and Western Approaches: 'a thing,' commented the Lord Admiral, 'impossible.' Yet, no more than she, was he able to know where the still invisible enemy intended to strike: in the Channel, in Ireland, in Scotland or even, encircling the British Isles, in the North Sea. So Howard cast his defensive net as wide as possible, spreading his patrolling forces across the hundred miles of the Soundings from Scilly to Ushant, whenever the southwesterly gales of that stormy June and the arrival at Plymouth of long-awaited victualling ships from the Thames enabled him to do so.

For uncertainty over the supply of provisions was proving as much a handicap to England's sea defenders as the putrid state of the Armada's long-assembled six months' store of food and drink had proved to the Spaniards. It arose partly from the difficulties experienced by the Royal Navy's inadequate victualling-system – geared to supplying a fleet traditionally based on the Thames estuary – in serving one based on far-away Plymouth. It sprang even more from the Queen's habitual parsimony and her reluctance to let her aggressively-minded seamen venture more than a day's sail from England's threatened shores. That they could only do so at the expense of being forced almost immediately to return to harbour to avert starvation, had already prevented Drake from forestalling the threatened invasion by doing to the Armada in its own harbours what he had partially done at Cadiz in the previous year.

For that quick imaginative perception, linked to a lifetime's experience of sea, ships and seamen, which the Spaniards attributed to his possession of a magic mirror, enabled him, even before the news reached England, to realize that the Armada, scattered and dispersed by storms, was sheltering and refitting in the havens of north-west Spain. If, with a northerly wind behind them, the English could catch it wind-bound in harbour before it resumed its interrupted voyage, with their fast, easily manoeuvreable and heavily gunned warships, they would be able to damage it beyond hope of repair and, by doing so, save their country from invasion before King Philip's fleet could even catch sight of its shores. Every piece of news reaching England confirmed Drake's belief as to what had happened. Late in June a Cornish bark, bound for

France, had sighted nine great ships between Scilly and Ushant
with huge red crusaders' crosses on their sails; the captain of
another West Country coastal trader was chased by a fleet of fifteen
sail and, escaping from them, had landed in Cornwall and ridden
post-haste with his tidings to Plymouth.

So it came about that when on July 7th – with the fleet strung
out across the northern entrance to the Bay of Biscay – the wind
suddenly changed to the north, Drake persuaded Howard to seize
the opportunity and strike south with all speed. They were short
of rations but he knew that, once on the Spanish coast, he would
be able to repeat his expedient of two years before and victual the
fleet from Galician farms and granaries. But when the English
were within a day's sail of Corunna the wind suddenly changed
again and blew strongly from the south. There was no point in
trying to beat against it, for in their unvictualled state, long before
they could hope to reach their target, they would run out of food
and starve. There would also be the appalling risk that the Armada,
taking advantage of the change of wind, might put to sea and reach
the English Channel before them. There was nothing for it but to
return to Plymouth at once to revictual. This, in no happy temper,
they accordingly did, reaching the Sound, after two days battling
with a gale, on July 12th.

Early on the day on which the battered English fleet reached
Plymouth, the Armada, reassembled, refitted and revictualled, put
to sea again after its month in harbour. For the next four days the
vast fleet, with a southerly wind behind it, sailed northwards in
calm sunshine across the Biscay bay. The sight of the huge concourse of ships stretching from horizon to horizon, and the complete absence of any enemy or, indeed, a ship of any kind, inspired
a new confidence in all aboard.

By the night of July 15–16th, the great fleet was off Ushant,
where it ran into lowering and heavy weather, which swamped its
four Mediterranean galleys, forcing them to run for safety to the
nearby French coast, where two of them were shipwrecked, their
Mohammedan and Protestant galley-slaves escaping in the general
confusion. Here, too, Medina Sidonia put ashore one of his captains to travel overland to the Netherlands – where he arrived

eight days later – to warn Parma that he was on his way. For the next two days the storm continued and the Armada was once more temporarily dispersed, about forty of its ships being driven to the north by the southwesterly gale.

But on the 18th, a Thursday, the weather came fair again, and the fleet resumed its northward journey towards the Scillies, all its missing ships rejoining it by nightfall. On the same day a letter from the Lord Warden of the Cinque Ports reached the Secretary of State, Sir Francis Walsingham, to warn him that Spanish and Italian troops of Parma's army had been seen embarking at Dunkirk. The Viceroy himself wrote on that very day to let King Philip know that his invasion boats and barges had all assembled at Nieuport by the canals which he had had dug that winter to carry them to the invasion coast. And, as on the 19th, the Armada continued its course northwards in calm and halcyon weather, at its Admiral's orders it closed into battle formation.

CHAPTER SEVEN

The Invincible Armada

'Attend all ye who list to hear our noble England's praise;
I tell of the thrice famous deeds she wrought in ancient days,
When that great fleet invincible against her bore in vain
The richest spoils of Mexico, the stoutest hearts of Spain.'

Macaulay : Ballad of the Armada

'To invade by sea upon a perilous coast, being neither in
possession of any part nor succoured by any party, may
better fit a man presuming on his fortune than enriched
with understanding. Such was the enterprise of Philip II
upon England in the year 1588, who had belike never heard
of this counsel of Artabanus to Xerxes, or forgotten it.'

Sir Walter Ralegh : History of the World

AT FIRST LIGHT on Friday July 19th, Captain Thomas Fleming, patrolling off the Lizard in the 80-ton pinnace *Golden Hind*, sighted on the far southern horizon an ever-growing haze of sails. Knowing well what it portended, he made as fast as he could for Plymouth, a hundred miles away. At about four that afternoon, he found the Lord Admiral on the Hoe playing bowls with Drake. 'We have time to finish the game,' the latter is reputed to have said as he stooped to bowl, 'and beat the Spaniards too.' But there was no time for was to finish the revictualling of the fleet, which meant that the English had to go into battle without sufficient food and water for a prolonged campaign. Yet disastrous as such a handicap could prove, to remain in harbour an hour longer than necessary with the Armada bearing down on Plymouth before a south-westerly wind was to court certain destruction. There was no alternative but to get to sea as fast as possible. About the same time as the English admirals were alerted to their danger, fifty miles away watchers on the Spanish flagship caught their first glimpse of the far line of the Lizard, three leagues to the north, and of the land they had come to conquer.

All that evening and night, caught revictualling in harbour on a lee shore, the English crews worked fiercely and unrestingly to warp their ships out to sea against wind and tide before the enemy could attack. As darkness fell, on every height along the Cornish and Devonshire coasts, and far inland, the warning beacons were lit. It was the awaited signal to carry to every part of England the news that the Invincible Armada was off her shores.

> 'Night sank upon the dusky beach, and on the purple sea,
> Such night in England ne'er had been, nor e're again
>   shall be . . .
> For swift to east and swift to west the ghastly war-flame
>   spread,
> High on St Michael's Mount it shone: it shone on Beachy
>   Head.
> Far on the deep the Spaniards saw, along each southern
>   shire,
> Cape beyond cape, in endless range, those twinkling points
>   of fire.'

They marked the end of the twenty-five years of halcyon peace and security which Queen Elizabeth had given a formerly divided and imperilled people. They expressed, too, the unity and proud sense of nationhood which her rule had evoked. In every shire, as the summons went out, a whole nation sprang to arms to defend its Queen and realm.

> 'With his white hair unbonneted, the stout old sheriff comes:
> Behind him march the halberdiers; before him sound the
>   drums;
> His yeomen round the market cross make clear an ample
>   space;
> For there behoves him to set up the standard of Her Grace.'

By dawn on that Saturday, July 20th, the wind being at south-west, almost the entire English fleet, by a superb exercise of professional skill and disciplined improvization, had got itself out of Plymouth. All morning, close-hauled against the wind, its ships beat from the Sound to the open sea, in the Lord Admiral's phrase, 'very hardly'. By midday he had fifty-four of them close to the Eddystone rocks. Only a few vessels, caught in the midst of victualling, were still warping themselves out of harbour. An irreparable disaster had been averted.

Meanwhile the Spaniards, still twenty miles to windward and unaware that the English fleet lay in their path, were debating whether to attack Plymouth and, with their massive boarding troops, overwhelm any helpless English vessels lying there. But though they did not know it, the opportunity had already passed. And, though his subordinate admirals were strongly in favour of an attack on the port, Medina Sidonia felt bound by King Philip's instructions to fight only if there was no other way he could secure the all-important passage of Parma's army to England. Avoiding all diversions, therefore, he proposed to press steadily up the Channel towards the Straits of Dover where, three hundred miles to the east, he believed the main English fleet was waiting to bar his junction with the Viceroy. There, and there only, was he empowered to fight except in self-defence.

That night the Armada anchored in the close battle formation in which it was to sail and defend itself until it reached its destination. To observers from the shore it resembled an enormous crescent stretching far out to sea. In reality it constituted a vast square or round floating laager, with the flagship and largest fighting galleons in front to sweep aside opposition, while other warships on either flank and in the rear protected its soft centre, which was packed with transports and store-ships as in some enormous mobile harbour. This was in keeping with traditional Spanish naval technique, based on long experience of fighting in the enclosed waters of the Mediterranean by combatants applying to battles at sea the military rules appropriate to those fought on land.

During the night, which was moonlit but hazy, shadowy forms

were observed passing across the Armada's front towards the open ocean beyond it. Others were seen moving westwards between its inshore flank and the Cornish coast. Only when day dawned was it realized that a surprised and outnumbered English fleet, after weathering it out at sea, had crossed the Spaniards' front without being seen, and then, in the hours of darkness, had outflanked and infiltrated behind them and was now cruising a mile or so to windward. By a feat of seamanship so remarkable that the Spanish pilots and sailors could hardly credit it, Drake and his fellow admirals, in the course of a brief summer's night, had captured the weather-gauge and, at the expense of leaving the Channel and southern English coastline open to the Armada, had placed themselves in a commanding and controlling position in its rear. Instead of defensively barring its course towards the Straits and Parma's waiting army, staking his country's survival on a novel principle of naval warfare, Howard had deliberately uncovered what he had been sent to defend. By doing so he had regained the initiative. Outnumbered in capital ships by nearly two to one – for part of the new-built battle-fleet was at the other end of the English Channel guarding the narrow seas against Parma – he was in a position to call the tune and make the Armada dance to it.

The two fleets confronting one another – or rather drawn up behind one another, both facing east up the English Channel – presented a remarkable contrast. Obscuring the sight of the sea's surface for several square miles lay a dense mass of a hundred and thirty Spanish ships, some of them of a thousand tons or more, with huge black hulls, towering masts and superstructures, and coloured sails emblazoned with the Catholic mythology of a thousand years. Their decks were packed with soldiers waiting to board, while great grappling-irons hung from their yard arms to enable them to do so. As the contemporary Elizabethan historian, William Camden, put it, 'the English descried the Spanish ships, with lofty turrets like castles in front, like a half moon, the wings thereof spreading out about the length of seven miles, sailing very slowly though with full sails, the winds being, as it were, tired with carrying them and the ocean groaning with their weight.'

In contrast, scarcely half their height, with white sails bearing

St George's Cross and hulls painted in geometrical patterns of green and white – their Queen's colours – the scattered English battleships, hovering in the Armada's rear, looked almost puny by comparison. Lying low in the water, with guns bristling from their portholes, they yet had a trim, business-like and, to Spanish eyes, rather sinister look.

The first action fought in mid-ocean between two major sailing fleets was now about to begin. Having the weather-gauge, the English began the engagement by attacking the weather division of the slow eastward-moving Armada. They did so not as a single fleet but in little groups of ships – led by Howard, Drake and Hawkins or often without a leader at all – making for the nearest enemy vessel or group of vessels and subjecting them to their gun-fire, firing about five shots to one of their adversaries. As ship after ship, sailing in line ahead, poured successive broadsides on to one after another of the outlying Spanish ships, and then, tacking and returning, repeated the same punishment with the other broadside, the weaker ships of the Spanish weather-squadron began to give ground and fall back on the Armada's crowded centre.

But at this point the English received an unwelcome surprise from the unsuspected power of the new heavy-shotted cannon with which the Armada had been secretly equipped during the waiting months after Drake's spectacular gunnery success at Cadiz. Two Spanish ships in particular, both commanded by grandees of high lineage, the *San Juan* – flagship of the veteran Don Juan Martinez de Recalde of Bilbao, commanding the Biscayan squadron of the rearguard – and that of his vice-admiral, though heavily outnumbered and resisting with great gallantry, made it clear, whenever their assailants came too near, that the 50 lb iron round-shot from their new heavy battering pieces were capable of totally destroying the rigging on which the English ships depended for their superior mobility, so leaving them at the mercy of the grappling irons and massed boarding troops to which the Spaniards traditionally looked for victory. It was for this, realizing the superiority of the finely-handled English culverins firing their 17 lb shot at long-range, that King Philip had re-equipped his fighting galleons with far heavier cannon and shot. 'It must be borne in mind,' he had written, 'that the enemy's object will be to fight at long distance in consequence of his advantage in artillery . . . The aim of our men, on the contrary, must be to bring him to close quarters and to grapple with him.' During the Armada's year of waiting in the Tagus he had therefore given its average fighting-ship a broadside, at short-range, of twice the weight of the average English long-range broadside, and provided the fleet with no less than 123,790 cannon-balls and 517,500 lbs of gunpowder.

Realizing that to press home their attack against such devastating – and unexpected – weight of fire-power would be suicidal, the English fell back on their hereditary skill in seamanship and the greater manoeuvrability of their ships to keep out of range, confining their own bombardment of their foes to the longer ranges at which their culverins, with their much lighter shot, could safely operate. At this distance, though out of reach of the destructive power of the short-range heavy Spanish cannon, the English, notwithstanding the greater accuracy and speed of fire of their practised gunners, could make no impact at all on the stout hulls of their adversaries. Both participants in the furious and isolated gun battles which raged all morning were thus unable to make any decisive impression on their opponents, despite a prodigious expenditure of noise and ammunition, particularly on the English side, whose rate of fire was far more rapid than that of the less skilful and experienced Iberian gunners. The Spaniards suffered more casualties, mostly among the soldiers drawn up on their crowded decks waiting to board; the English, keeping to a safe distance, hardly any at all.

While this was happening, some of the greatest fighting galleons of the unengaged Spanish vanguard, led by Medina Sidonia's flagship, the 1,000 ton *San Martin*, had been coming to the assistance of Recalde's hard-pressed ships. To do so they had had to leave their stations in the Armada's closely-packed formation, and travel round its circumference to reach the embattled rear-guard. Like the retreat of some of the weaker brethren into the Armada's soft and crowded centre, this caused a good deal of confusion, including a collision between two galleons of the Andalusian squadron, causing one of them – the *Nuestra Señora del*

Rosario, flagship of its admiral, Don Pedro de Valdez – to lose her foremast and bowsprit. About the same time, another great galleon, the *San Salvador*, vice-flagship of the Guipuscoan squadron, carrying the Paymaster-General of the Armada and part of the royal treasure, was rocked by an enormous explosion, which destroyed both its stern decks and killed two hundred of its crew, burning and wounding many more. It was rumoured that a con-scripted Dutchman had avenged himself and his countrymen by throwing a lighted fuse into a powder-barrel before jumping over-board. Rendered unmanageable by fire, the *San Salvador*, like the damaged *Nuestra Señora*, had to be towed into the Armada's safe centre, where its treasure and surviving crew could be taken off and trans-shipped.

At one o'clock, the Spanish formation proving virtually un-breakable, alarmed at the rapidity with which his gunners were exhausting his fleet's inadequate reserves of ammunition Howard wisely called off the action. Neither side could claim a victory. The nine hundred or so heavy battering-pieces with which King Philip had equipped the Armada had failed to immobilize a single English ship or subject it to the close in-fighting and boarding which had won the great Spanish galley victories of Lepanto and Terceira, and through which he had hoped to crush the English by sheer weight of numbers and courage of his highly-trained and disciplined soldiers. In the course of a four hours' engagement, the Spaniards had discovered the impossibility of getting to close grips with the elusive islanders. 'Their ships being very nimble,' Medina Sidonia reported to the King after the action, 'and of such good steerage, they did with them whatever they desired.'

On the other hand, the English had found the tenacity and endurance of Spain's proud martial chivalry far greater than that of the easy-going Spanish colonials whom they had encountered and routed in the tropics. Nor, though for a short while they had dented, had they been able to break the close defensive cordon round the Armada's soft centre, any more than their hitherto triumphant guns had proved able at long-range to penetrate its galleons' stout sides. 'As far as we can perceive,' Drake reported, 'they are determined to sell their lives with blows.' 'I will not trouble

you with any long letter,' Howard wrote that afternoon to Walsingham. 'We are at this present otherwise occupied than in writing.
At nine of the clock we gave them fight which continued till one . . .
We durst not venture to put in among them, their fleet being so
strong.' The sting of his letter lay in its tail. 'Sir, for the love of
God and our country, let us have with some speed some great shot
of all bigness and some powder with it; for this service will continue long.'

One thing at least the English had achieved by that morning's
exploratory and indecisive engagement. With the wind behind
them, they had imperceptibly pushed the Spaniards past the
entrance to Plymouth, to the great relief of its Mayor and people,
anxiously watching and listening to the battle from the Hoe. It was,
however, essential to keep the Armada moving and not allow it
to seize a harbour or bay where it could disgorge its ravaging troops.
For the English could not know that this was precisely what King
Philip had expressly forbidden his Commander-in-Chief until
he could reach the Flemish coast and effect his junction with the
duke of Parma.

Nor were they aware that on that very afternoon, at a Council
of War in the *San Martin*'s cabin, the Spanish admirals were
urging this very course on the duke of Medina Sidonia. One in
particular – the staunch old seaman, Juan Martinez de Recalde, a
hero of Terceira and a former commander of the Indies Fleet –
argued passionately for providing the Armada with a secure base
at the western end of the English Channel, where it could refit
and be reinforced for future operations. For both he and the
English admirals were well aware that one such potential base --
the broad sheltered anchorage of Torbay – lay only a short distance
ahead on the Armada's port bow. Yet the conscientious duke
would not deviate from his master's orders or contemplate any
halting place on his perilous crusade except, at the urgent instance
of his admirals, the Isle of Wight two hundred miles ahead, which,
in earlier instructions, King Philip – though it was still a hundred
miles short of Parma's waiting army on the Flemish coast – had
suggested the fleet might seize on its way.

During that afternoon and evening – one of Councils of War in both fleets – the vast Armada, followed and shepherded at a safe distance by the English, was moving slowly eastwards along the Devonshire coast. All attempts to take the crippled *Nuestra Señora* in tow had failed, and the crippled flagship of the Andalusian squadron had to be abandoned. As night was falling, a galleon and one of the fast galleasses, together with a pinnace, were detailed to stay with her and take off her treasure, crew and admiral. But the latter, Don Pedro de Valdez – a cousin of the flag officer of the same name who had advised Medina Sidonia to leave the luckless ship to her fate – refused to sully his honour by leaving her. So it came about that during the night, after being accidentally sighted by a small English auxiliary which proceeded to shadow the *Nuestra Señora* and her cluster of escorts, the latter, fearful of being found at daybreak and cut off by the pursuing English, abandoned her and made off to rejoin the Armada. It so happened that during that night Drake, following Howard's flagship in the *Revenge*, saw some shadowy ships moving in the opposite direction and, suspecting they might be Spaniards trying to repeat his manoeuvre of the previous night and regain the weather-gauge, slipped out of his place in the line to follow and thwart them. Dawn, however, showed them to be a convoy of German merchantmen proceeding down Channel on their lawful occasions. In seeking to regain his place in the pursuing fleet, he accidentally encountered the abandoned Spanish derelict. Upon which, summoned by the *Revenge* to yield, Don Pedro de Valdes surrendered without a fight to the one man – the dreaded 'El Draque' – to whom even the proudest and bravest Spaniard felt it no shame to submit. Thus, with Drake's usual good fortune, he was able, at the very outset of the campaign, to capture, complete with its treasure, admiral and crew of 460 and 46 guns, a major Spanish galleon. Frobisher, who hated him and his good fortune, subsequently maintained that he had deliberately left his place in the line to snap up the abandoned prize. But as Drake at the time could not possibly have known of her fate and whereabouts – for, unlike the Spaniards in their close disciplined formation, the English had no means of communicating with one another at night except by lanterns – the charge was manifestly ridiculous. Both the *Nuestra Señora* and the burnt out and abandoned *San Salvador* were subsequently towed into English ports, where the latter's hold unexpectedly yielded up a providential store of 1,000 iron shot and two hundred barrels of high-grade powder, which was sent post haste after the English fleet, then running dangerously short of both.

So precisely did Medina Sidonia and his chief naval adviser – a disagreeable martinet named Diego Flores de Valdez, much disliked by his fellow admirals but in high favour with King Philip – observe the royal instructions that they sent a pinnace of officers of the Provost's Corps round the fleet to ensure that every ship was keeping its exact station in the rigid military formation ordained for it, with orders, and a hangman and gallows in attendance, to string up summarily any captain who got out of alignment. None, however, did so. Nor at this stage did Providence – favouring the Armada's sacred mission with a week of flawless, storm-free weather – nor the heretic islanders, with their shortage of ammunition, put a spoke in the Escorial's wheel, the English following the huge, impregnable floating fortress, vainly hoping for further stragglers to attack, as it made its slow majestic way eastwards across Lyme Bay in the summer sunshine of Monday, July 22nd. All the time a continuous stream of small ships and boats poured out from the little Dorset ports of Lyme, Charmouth and Bridport, bringing the English fleet volunteers, supplies of food, fresh vegetables and ammunition, as fast as the shore authorities could collect or requisition them, while spectators, peering anxiously seawards through the summer haze, crowded the low hills above the Chesil Beach and West Bay.

During the short moonlit night of July 22nd the Armada and Howard's shadowing fleet passed to the south of the long projecting peninsula of Portland Bill, to the immediate east of which, as dawn broke on Tuesday the 23rd, both fleets found themselves becalmed. By then the south-west wind which had followed them from the Atlantic had dropped and was succeeded by a gentle breeze from the north-east, giving the Spaniards the windward station which Howard and Drake had seized from them three nights earlier. Half a dozen ships on the English inshore flank, lying close to the Portland cliffs and led by the hot-tempered Martin

Frobisher in the 1,000 ton *Triumph* – the largest vessel in the English fleet – were as a result dangerously exposed to attack. Seeing an opportunity to apply the battering and boarding process which was the Spanish recipe for victory at sea, Medina Sidonia sent in his four swift giant Neapolitan galleasses, each propelled by three hundred galley slaves, to encircle the wind-bound English ships and enable their waiting soldiery to board them. But Frobisher, who was never happier than in a fight, poured such an intensity of fire on the galleasses' rowing-decks, killing and wounding so many of their oarsmen and smashing their long sweeps, that they were forced to take to their sails, which made them so clumsy as to be virtually unmanageable.

Meanwhile the inshore fight between the two fleets became general. Both flagships were heavily engaged, the *San Martin*, which had gone to the galleasses' assistance, being attacked by the *Ark Royal* and six other English ships. Yet though the Spanish flagship lost fifty of her crew from the English gunfire, had her water butts holed and fifty shots lodged – but only lodged – in her huge sides, the range between the contestants, as more and more Spanish galleons joined the mêlée, grew steadily less. And, as the danger of close fighting and boarding increased, the overwhelming superiority of the invaders' military manpower pointed to only one, and that a disastrous, ending.

At that moment Drake, from the battle's seaward flank, entered the fight with dramatic effect. Knowing, from long experience of the English Channel winds and weather, how in a summer's day an early offshore breeze could suddenly veer at midday to a sea-wind from the south or west, he had anticipated the change by beating out to sea while Howard and Frobisher were so dangerously engaged near Portland Bill. Then, when the wind behind him changed, with fifty ships, great and small, he swept down on the mêlée out of the clouds of battle smoke to rescue his hard-pressed chief and comrades, threatening not only to break the embattled Armada in two, but to cut it off from the east and the open Channel up which it was moving towards its junction with Parma. At once, abandoning his attempt to close on Howard and Frobisher, Medina Sidonia reformed his fleet's ranks so as to resume its purely defensive role. The engagement continued till five o'clock, when, not daring to press home their attack to point-blank range against the retreating enemy's heavy guns, and themselves running increasingly short of ammunition – for they were even reduced to firing plough-chains from the Dorset farms instead of shot – the English called off the fight. With the battered, but proud, *San Martin* leading, the Armada resumed its progress eastwards.

During Wednesday the 24th the two fleets, the English still at a respectful distance behind the Spaniards drifted in the light south-west breeze past Lulworth and the Purbeck cliffs towards the distant Isle of Wight. Here, under its temporary Governor, Sir George Carey, the islanders, reinforced by three thousand militiamen and volunteers from the mainland, were preparing to sell their lives dearly on the beaches to save their farms and villages from the fate of the Netherlands. Meanwhile, determined at all costs to keep the Armada moving past the island anchorages and thwarted so far in every attempt to break up its close formation, at a Council of War in the *Ark Royal*'s cabin the English admirals decided to match the Spaniards' discipline in battle with a battle order of their own, though a naval, not a military one. Instead of leaving their ships to fight individually and group themselves as they pleased, as in the battles of Plymouth and Portland, they agreed to confront the Spaniards next day in four separate squadrons, commanded by Howard himself, Drake, Hawkins and Frobisher, and to which every ship, great or small, naval or auxiliary, should belong, and from whom all captains and masters should take orders by signal or word of mouth. It was the first time in England's sea history that such a course had been taken.

At dawn on Thursday July 25th both fleets were again becalmed near the south point of the Isle of Wight. Guarding the eastern entrance to the Solent and the flat north-east coast of the island most exposed to a large-scale landing – and where the French had landed forty years before – was Frobisher's squadron, led by him in the *Triumph*. Once more the fiery Yorkshireman put up a magnificent fight. At one moment the *Triumph* was attacked by three galleons and was in imminent danger of being boarded. Lowering eleven of his boats to tow his imperilled flagship into what wind there was,

Frobisher's gunners just managed to keep the attackers at bay until a light breeze from the west got up and the great ship, with all her guns blazing, escaped from the net closing round her.

During the calm the *Ark Royal*, which had gone to Frobisher's assistance, had also been attacked by three of the Neapolitan galleasses which, emerging from the Armada's centre at high speed, with all their hundreds of oars flashing, surrounded and tried to board her. But once again, as at Portland two days earlier, just as the Spaniards with their grappling-irons and massed storm-troops, saw victory almost within their grasp, the situation was again transformed by Drake's seaward squadron. Anticipating the midday change of wind, to avail himself of which he had beaten out to sea, he burst on the battle from the south, possibly with Hawkins's squadron to aid him, sweeping the Spaniards away from their prey and the island beaches and threatening to drive the Armada's weather flank on to the dangerous Ower Banks between the Isle of Wight and Selsey Bill. To prevent his embattled fleet from being cut in two, Medina Sidonia and his leading galleons were forced to abandon both their potential prey and the invasion beaches and withdraw, still fighting, eastwards.

A little before three in the afternoon the rival admirals by tacit agreement broke off the action. Both sides were glad of the respite. For the Spaniards had had all they could take, and the English were almost out of ammunition. One Spanish hulk, the *Santa Ana*, heavily holed and in serious difficulty, dropped away to the south, making during the night for the French coast, where she became a total wreck. Both fleets spent the rest of the day recovering, their crews making good the damage to sails, hulls and rigging, and the two commanders-in-chief writing urgently to their backers on shore. Howard wrote to the earl of Sussex, Governor of Portsmouth, imploring him to send him all the shot, powder and victuals he could command. Meanwhile Medina Sidonia was writing to the duke of Parma, warning him to be ready to embark his troops the moment the Armada appeared off the Flemish coast, and requesting two ship-loads of powder and shot and as many small fly-boats as possible to help him force the evasive English into close encounter so that he could board and overwhelm them with his superior weight and numbers.

With only eighty miles to cover before the Straits of Dover, King Philip's strategy was about to be put to the test. There a small but powerful English squadron, under Lord Seymour and Admiral Sir William Winter, was guarding the narrow tidal waters which lay between the approaching Armada and the little shallow North Sea ports of Dunkirk and Nieuport, where Parma's invasion troops and barges were blockaded by two patrolling flotillas of fierce Dutch 'sea beggars', eager to cut the throats of every Spanish soldier who ventured within reach.

Having failed in three successive battles to break the Armada's defensive formation and, despite a prodigious expenditure of ammunition, to sink a single Spanish ship, the English admirals knew that, unless they could now force a victory over what had so far proved invincible, nothing could save their country from invasion. They had little time left in which to strike, for, if the weather held and the wind stayed in the west, the Armada could be on the Flemish coast within the next two or three days. It was now a week since they had left Plymouth Sound, and, despite supplies continually hurried out to them in small craft from every Hampshire, Sussex and Kentish port, they were growing short of food and had only ammunition enough for one more battle on the scale of the last three. And they knew that, unlike Spain, with the inexhaustible wealth of the Indies and the Pacific behind her, their small country was without financial reserves. For all her Queen's careful parsimony, she could not continue indefinitely to maintain a fully manned fleet and militia army with an invasion Armada remaining intact in northern waters.

In the Spanish fleet, unknown to the English admirals, even graver doubts and anxieties prevailed. For, though none of their ships had been sunk in battle, they had suffered far heavier damage by long-range gunfire than their smaller, more weatherly and better handled opponents. And the morale of their officers and crews had suffered far more than their ships from their humiliating failure, despite their superiority in size and numbers, to bring the English to grips. The need for a port or some safe harbourage, in which to repair and refit, was clear now to every seaman in the Armada. When Medina Sidonia's despatches at last reached the Escorial, forgetting what he had so imperiously ordained and the impracticability of what Parma had repeatedly, so far as he dared, warned him, even King Philip minuted, 'I do not see how they are to effect a juncture if they have no port to do it in.'

It was, therefore, in anything but a hopeful frame of mind that Parma received at Bruges on Sunday July 28th an urgent summons from Medina Sidonia, despatched overland on the previous evening from the Armada off Calais, where, at the end of its ten days' voyage up the English Channel, it had just cast anchor. 'If you cannot bring out all your fleet,' the Admiral wrote, 'send me the forty or fifty fly-boats I asked for yesterday, as with this aid I shall be able to resist the enemy's fleet until your Excellency can come out with the rest, and we can then go together and take some port where this Armada can enter in safety.' For, having obediently brought his great fleet, with all its treasure and its thousands of invincible soldiers, to anchor off a neutral French port twenty miles short of the Flemish border, this hapless landsman-at-sea seemed to be expecting the Viceroy, who had no fleet but only an army, to help him find the non-existent port for lack of which all King Philip's carefully laid plans looked like foundering.

So it came about that, in the afternoon of Saturday July 27th, having covered the eighty sea-miles from the Isle of Wight and deliberately avoided the English side of the Dover Strait, warned by his pilots of dangerous shoals immediately ahead along the French and Flemish coast Medina Sidonia anchored off the French port of Calais. Here, by courtesy of its neutral but Catholic governor, he could communicate quickly and directly with the duke of Parma. Immediately afterwards the English fleet, which had continued to shadow the Armada, anchored about a mile to windward and seaward of it, having, with its habitual expertise, avoided overshooting its quarry and so losing the wind, as the Spanish admirals had vainly hoped it would. Shortly afterwards, just as dusk was falling, it was joined from England by the remainder of the Royal Navy under Lord Seymour and Sir William Winter.

After the Battle of the Isle of Wight, the Council, its mind concentrated on the menace of the invading army assembled opposite the Thames estuary, sent an urgent despatch to Seymour, then cruising off Dungeness, ordering him 'to bend himself to stop the issue of the duke of Parma's forces from Dunkirk'. But on Saturday afternoon, while he was revictualling in the Downs on his way to do so, he received an urgent summons from the Lord Admiral bidding him join him off Calais. This, spoiling for a fight, he and Winter immediately did, with their eight battleships and thirty or so armed merchantmen and auxiliaries.

The entire Royal Navy was now concentrated under the Lord Admiral. His new accession of strength brought the number, though not the size, of the ships under his command to even more than that of the Armada. As the two admirals went aboard the flagship for a Council of War, there was a nip of autumn in the air, and more than a hint that the lovely summer weather of the past ten days was about to change. With Parma's waiting army at Dunkirk only a few hours away there was no doubt in the minds of those present what had to be done. If only the Spanish fleet's defensive formation could be broken, there would be a chance of destroying or crippling it before it could take in Parma's invasion barges. There was no time to be lost. It was, therefore, decided that, if the Armada made no move next day, the English should rout it out at night with fireships – the classic way of moving a fleet of wooden ships anchored on a lee shore.

During the Sunday, July 28th, both fleets rested, their crews observing their Catholic and Protestant forms of worship. But among the English, who had now been joined by many members of the Queen's Court – including Sir Walter Ralegh, the young earls of Oxford, Cumberland and Northumberland, Charles Blount the future Lord Mountjoy, and both Burghley's sons, Thomas and Robert Cecil – all thoughts turned to the battle to be fought on the morrow for their country's existence, and to the preparations for launching the fireships. It had been intended to have them prepared at Dover, but when it was realized that these could not arrive in time, they were taken from the swarm of small ships which had joined the fleet from almost every port in southern England. Both Drake and Hawkins contributed vessels of their own. All eight, screened from Spanish view, were stacked high with firewood and barrels of pitch, and armed with guns, pointed at the enemy, which would go off simultaneously as soon as the flames reached their primings.

At midnight a single gun was fired from the *Ark Royal*. Manned by volunteer crews, with dinghies in tow to evacuate them, the fireships set off in line abreast, aimed at the centre of the Armada. With both wind and tide running fast behind them, as that raging forest of fire bore down on the Spanish flagship and the great fighting galleons around it, a wild panic broke out. Though Medina Sidonia himself kept his head an his own flagship took orderly evasive action, in most of his ships the frightened captains and crews cut their cables, abandoned their anchors and put to sea in utter confusion. Many collided in the dark, and the flagship of the Neapolitan galleasses broke her rudder and ran aground. She was subsequently stormed and sacked, as she lay helpless on the beach, by successive waves of English and French plunderers.

Daybreak, on Monday July 29th, found the Armada drifting a few miles to the east of Gravelines, its formation lost. Scattered over a large area of sea, unable to anchor, Medina Sidonia in the *San Martin* tried desperately to rally and reform its ranks. It was the moment for which the English had been waiting. Weighing anchor at first light, they went into the attack in four squadrons, led by Drake, Hawkins and Frobisher, and Seymour and Winter with the newly joined squadron of the Narrow Seas. Howard, for once, entered the battle late, having been delayed attending to the destruction of the galleasses' grounded flagship.

For fifty miles to the east of Calais there stretched off the Flemish coast a line of concealed sandbanks known as the Banks of Zeeland, which every Spanish pilot was now seeking to avoid. Along its northern and menacing fringe the Battle of Gravelines, as it became known to history, was fought. To Drake, whose seafaring life had begun at the age of eleven as an apprentice on a Thames estuary hoy trading with Newcastle and the Netherlands, the swirling tides, currents, shoals, winds and sudden fogs of this treacherous stretch of water had been his earliest teachers, remaining deeply impressed on his memory. It was he who led the attack from the west on the Spanish rear. Passing and repassing the defending galleons in line ahead, the ships of his squadron led by the *Revenge*, firing their deadly broadsides, subjected the enemy to the heaviest fire yet experienced by them. The main target of attack was Medina Sidonia's flagship, the giant *San Martin*, which, though the English were unable to sink her owing to the strength of her sides, they battered so long and mercilessly that nearly half her crew were killed and her decks strewn with dead and dying. In the end, despite the courage of her seamen and soldiers, she became almost incapable of replying – a fact which helps to explain the astonishing lowness of the English casualties. For in the whole campaign against the Armada, including the culminating Battle of Gravelines, less than a hundred Englishmen lost their lives in action, and, owing to their superb seamanship, not even a single ship of theirs was sunk or boarded.

In dense clouds of smoke and amid deafening noise, the other English commanders, Hawkins in *Victory*, Frobisher in *Triumph*, Seymour in *Rainbow*, Winter in *Vanguard*, Howard in *Ark Royal*, Fenton in *Mary Rose* and the eighty-nine-year-old captain of the *Dreadnought*, Cheshire's Sir George Beeston – knighted three days earlier on the deck of the Lord Admiral's flagship with Frobisher and Hawkins – fell on the Spaniards' shaken ships like a pack of famished wolves. The *San Martin*, her fellow flagships and the great galleons of Castile and Portugal, defending the unprotected hulks and transports of the now broken Armada, bore the brunt of the day's fighting. But their captains' and crews' heroism was in vain. For their supply of round-shot was running out, and, as it did so, their assailants, fighting furiously, shortened the range, and, for the first time since the campaign began, the light shot of the long English culverins began to penetrate the hulls of the Spanish battleships. One great galleon, holed, withdrew behind the half-breached screen of what remained of the Armada's protected centre and there sank, while three others in like plight became total wrecks, drifting out of the fight onto the Banks of Zeeland or the Flemish coast beyond, where they subsequently surrendered to the English garrison of Flushing, or were boarded and massacred by the merciless Dutch 'sea beggars'.

By the end of the day, not a single Spanish galleon remained capable of fighting. Their stout structures and the morale of their crews were alike shattered. Their hulls, repeatedly holed, were leaking, their sails torn to shreds, their stores and water-casks ruined or broken, and their holds a shambles of dying or wounded men, horses and sheep. At about six o'clock in the evening, after nine hours of battle, which for the Spaniards had long become a massacre, they bore away north-eastwards, a huddled and broken mass, to escape the terrible English guns.

By this time the victors, unconscious of what in their desperation they had achieved, had literally shot their bolt, having run completely out of ammunition. The sound of firing, which had continued all day, suddenly died away. Listeners on the Flemish coast, realizing that a victory had been won but not knowing by whom, awaited the expected appearance of the triumphant Armada. Parma's soldiers stood to arms all night beside their barges at Dunkirk and Nieuport, waiting all next day for the sight of that forest of masts on the horizon. And at Flushing, and in the islands fringing the mouth of the Scheldt, the anxious Dutch wondered if at any moment a victorious Spanish fleet would appear to seize the haven it needed and so break from the sea the resistance their watery provinces had maintained on land for more than sixteen years.

But, on that fateful evening of July 29th 1588, as the guns ceased to sound and the vanquished sought refuge in the open sea to the north, and the victors, their stores of shot and powder exhausted, fell asleep beside their guns, the wind, which had shifted into the north-west, freshened into gale and began to blow the broken Armada back towards the dreaded Zeeland Banks on to which the English had striven all day to drive them. All through the night their danger grew as the doomed and shattered galleons struggled to escape. When dawn broke on Tuesday, 30th, their crews could see the white waves breaking over the shoals, towards which they were being helplessly driven. Already their pilots, who had been sounding all night, reported that the depth beneath them was down to seven fathoms and diminishing every hour. As their larger ships drew only six fathoms, the whole Armada seemed certain to be dashed to pieces on the hidden sand banks. So grave was their situation that, as the only hope of saving the lives of the 20,000 men still on board, a pinnace was prepared to carry an offer of surrender from the battered *San Martin* to the English Commander-in-Chief. But this proved too much for the Spanish sense of honour, and, according to one account, one of the admirals at the Council of War, the valiant Don Miguel de Oquendo, threatened to throw his fellow admiral, the hated Don Diego Flores de Valdez who had proposed this shameful course, into the sea.

Then at eleven o'clock, a miracle occurred. It was St Lawrence's Day, and, as every Spaniard aboard believed, it was St Lawrence's doing which now caused the wind so suddenly to shift to the south-west. Miraculously the drift on to the sandbanks ceased, and, as the great ships, the wind filling their tattered sails, turned north-wards again towards the open sea, those, who an hour before had expected to die, thanked God and St Lawrence for sparing them to live to another day. How soon for most of them that day would come, and how horrifying the death reserved for them would be, was mercifully not revealed.

The English, who that morning had expected the wind to finish the work of destruction they had begun, but had been unable themselves to complete it for lack of shot and powder, watched with dismay their defeated enemy sail so unexpectedly out of the jaws of death into which they had so nearly driven them. There were still some hundred and twenty Spanish sail – only a dozen or so less than there had been when they were sighted near the Lizard. They were still afloat and free, if they could or would, to find a harbour and base, in Scotland, Scandinavia or North Germany from which to threaten England anew. Thwarted of their prey, sadly and hungrily the victors – for they were almost as bare of victuals as they were of ammunition – set out to follow and shadow them. For though they knew they had done their utmost, they still had no idea of the extent of the damage they had inflicted on their foes and how great a victory they had won.

On the evening after the battle the Lord Admiral wrote to Walsingham:

'We had chased them in fight until this evening late and distressed them much. But their fleet consisteth of mighty ships and great strength; yet we doubt not, by God's good assistance to oppress them. . . . Their force is wonderfully great and strong, and yet we pluck their feathers by little and little. I pray to God that the powers on the land be strong enough to answer so present a force.'

But Drake, who had a much clearer idea of the damage he and his ships had wrought, wrote more sanguinely:

'God has given us so good a day in forcing the enemy so far to leeward as I hope in God the Prince of Parma and the Duke of Sidonia shall not shake hands this few days; and whensoever they shall meet, I believe neither of them will greatly rejoice. . . . I assure your Honour this day's service hath much appalled the enemy.'

Still less did the rulers and people of England realize the magnitude of their sailors' victory. Alerted to their peril since the beginning of the year by news of the digging of canals and the concentration of invasion barges on the Flemish coast, the Armada's appearance off their shores and its unimpeded voyage up the Channel had awoken an intensity of alarm and patriotic fervour in every part of the country. The news in London of yet another battle which had left the Spanish fleet still at large, while Parma's victorious army of the Netherlands, bent on invasion, lay only a single tide away, made everyone feel that a landing was imminent and that the Armada's sortie into the North Sea was only a feint to allow the dreaded *tercios* to cross while the English fleet was following it. So probable did this seem that urgent orders were sent by the Council for Seymour's squadron of the Narrow Seas to leave the pursuing fleet and resume its watch off the Thames estuary and its blockade of Parma's invasion ports. Meanwhile Howard's ships, hungry and munitionless, followed Medina Sidonia northwards. For the latter still carried in his transports an army almost as large as Parma's able to land anywhere on the coast – in East Anglia, in Catholic Yorkshire, in Scotland, which, with its dissident Catholic nobles, had always seemed a possible target for the Armada.

But aboard the great fleet itself, there was no longer any thought of such adventures. On the evening of the day on which it escaped destruction on the Zeeland Banks, a Council of War was held in the flagship as to what should be done. Medina Sidonia and his admirals at first spoke of honour and of a return to Calais or the Channel. But, when it came to the moment of decision, all were unanimous. No prudent course seemed open to them but to take their damaged fleet back to Spain to refit and repair. Before them lay more than two thousand two hundred perilous sea-miles round the rocky coasts of Scotland and Ireland. But the only alternative was unthinkable. For no one aboard was prepared to face again the terrible English seamen and their guns. Yet by a strange paradox only one of those terrible seamen seemed able as yet to grasp the dire nature of the Spaniards' plight: their old tormentor, Francis Drake. The principal architect of their defeat, he wrote cheerfully on Wednesday July 31st, two days after the battle, 'There was never anything pleased me better than seeing the enemy flying with a southerly wind to the northwards . . . I doubt it not but ere be long so to handle the matter with the Duke of Sidonia as he shall wish himself at St Mary Port among his orange trees.'

So, with a brisk wind behind it, the Armada continued north-wards – past the approaches to the Thames and Harwich, past the great bulge of Norfolk, and far out into the German Ocean. Despite the many thousands of superlative soldiers, trained and ready for invasion, waiting unused in its transports, it turned neither west towards the ports and beaches of northern England nor east towards those of the North German estuaries, Denmark and the Baltic, seeking to find a haven in which, were it tempted to fight again, it could refit, repair and revictual. And, keeping just out of range, the English fleet followed it with no ammunition for its guns and no knowledge that its fleeing enemy had none either. 'We set on a brag countenance,' Howard reported to Walsingham, 'and gave them chase as though we wanted nothing.' Every time that Medina Sidonia in his battered flagship lay to, with a crippled galleon or two in support, to give his demoralized ships time to get away from their dreaded pursuers, the English also lay to and waited and watched until the hasty flight to the north was resumed, when they again followed them.

On Friday, August 2nd, four days after the victory of Gravelines, with the two fleets sixty miles out to sea in the latitude of Newcastle, the wind shifted to the north-east. The English, who had been on short rations ever since they left Calais and were now almost out of food and water, feeling that further pursuit was unnecessary, decided to return home at once with the wind to revictual and re-arm and help defend the country against the threat of Parma's invasion. From the trail of drowned horses, sheep and mules thrown overboard by the flying Spaniards, they knew that the latter must be very short of water and fodder, and that, with a gale shifting now to the north-west, there was no chance of their finding shelter in the Forth should King James of Scotland renege on his alliance with England. Leaving two small fast vessels to shadow the Armada, they turned about and made their way south as fast as possible.

*   *   *

Meanwhile all England braced itself for immediate invasion. Wednesday August 7th was the day of highest flood-tide at Dunkirk when ships could enter its harbour and embark the troops Parma had assembled. Had not Howard and Drake broken the Armada's formation with their fireships and defeated it at Gravelines, it could have been the day on which it made its rendezvous with Parma. The wildest rumours were circulating on the Continent: that, in a great battle off Harwich, Drake had been captured with many ships, that he had lost a leg, that, in another fight off Newcastle, the English flagship had been sunk, and 'the great sailor, John Hawkins, had gone to the bottom.'

But in England the only thought now was of the coming battle on land. After it had become known that the Armada has passed the Thames estuary, the panic in the capital subsided, where it had been feared that the fate of Antwerp was about to be visited on

London. Here more than 6,000 citizen soldiers, mainly apprentices, officered by merchants and shopkeepers enrolled in the City's Trained Bands, had been drilling twice weekly at Mile End. Now attention passed to the camps at Tilbury and Colchester, where the Militia of Essex had been standing to arms since the beginning of the summer. For in time of war every county raised, through the Justices of the Peace and the Head Constables of the Hundreds, its own local defence force. And as it was in Essex that Parma seemed most likely to land, volunteers and militiamen from other counties had been flocking there in their zeal to defend their Queen, Faith and country. 'It was a pleasant sight,' recalled one eye witness, 'to behold the soldiers as they marched towards Tilbury, their cheerful countenances, courageous words and gestures, dancing and leaping wheresoever they came.' It was, indeed, incredible, Leicester wrote to Walsingham, how many men had been raised in the past six weeks, more than at any time, he believed, since the Norman Conquest. Some put the figure at 20,000 while another 8,000 volunteers were in Kent, guarding the Queen – so far as she permitted – under her cousin, Lord Hunsdon. It was while so engaged during the Armada summer that, notwithstanding his advanced age, the old soldier had become the 'protector' of a nineteen-year-old girl – daughter of an Italian court musician – who later, as 'the dark lady of the sonnets', was to become the mistress of the actor, William Shakespeare, of whose licensed company of players Hunsdon, as Lord Chamberlain, was patron.

Yet neither the arms nor the organization of England's amateur military defenders matched their numbers or fervour. Raised for the emergency by the Justices of the Peace and commanded by the Lord Lieutenant and Deputy Lieutenants of the shire, some of the militiamen bore pikes or arquebuses, in the use of which they were being drilled by veterans of the Netherlands and Irish wars, while others were still armed with the bows and arrows of their country's famous, but now remote, military past. Nor did the militiamen from other counties, who flocked so enthusiastically into Lord Leicester's camp at Tilbury, always arrive with commissariat or rations. Four thousand of them, he complained, suddenly appeared after a twenty-mile march without as much as a loaf of bread or

barrel of beer between them, though they cheerfully announced
that 'they would abide more hunger than this to serve her Majesty
and the country'. Though no one doubted they would sell their
lives dearly, it was difficult to feel sure how amateur troops so
trained and organized would fare if attacked by the massive ranks
of the pikesmen and musketeers of Spain's world famous *tercios*.
With his not very happy experience against the latter in the Low
Countries, Leicester at that moment, was probably a better judge
of the matter than any non-seafaring subject of the Queen. 'If her
Navy,' he asked, 'had not been strong and abroad . . . what case
had herself and her whole realm been in by this time?'

* * *

It was at this juncture, on Wednesday August 7th, that Howard's
fleet, dispersed by heavy storms on its voyage south, struggled into
port at Yarmouth, Harwich and Margate, after its nine days' dis-
appearance and nearly three weeks after it had left Plymouth so
suddenly on short rations. 'I pray God,' the Lord Admiral wrote
from Margate to Walsingham, 'we may hear of victuals, for we are
generally in great want . . . If I hear nothing of my victuals or
munitions this night,' he added in a postscript, 'I will gallop to
Dover to see what may be got there, or else we shall starve.' Nor
was hunger and lack of powder and shot the Admiral's only problem. Epidemic typhus, scurvy and malignant disease, caused by
putrid food and water and primitive sanitary conditions, were
raging in his ships. 'With great grief I must write unto you what
state I find your fleet,' he informed the Queen next day from
Dover. 'The infection has grown very great and in many ships,
and now very dangerous. And those that come in are soonest infected. They sicken one day and die the next.'

But the royal mistress to whom he addressed his letter was no
longer at her riverside palace. 'We do instantly beseech Thee of
thy gracious goodness,' she had declared in the prayer she had
issued to her people when the Armada arrived in the Channel 'to
be merciful to the church militant here upon earth, and at this
time compassed about with most strong and subtle adversaries. O

let Thine enemies know that Thou hast received England into Thine own protection. Set a wall about it, O Lord, and evermore mightily defend it.' On August 6th she had gone down the river by barge to Tilbury, a day's march nearer the enemy, by whom, it was reported, 'she was not a whit dismayed.' Next morning – it was the day of high tide at Dunkirk and of Parma's expected sailing – mounted on a white charger, with Leicester at her side, she rode through the ranks of her army with a marshal's baton in her hand, nine trumpeters in scarlet and Garter King at Arms going before, while her ladies in attendance followed. Then, 'like some Amazonian empress,' she inspected her troops, the pikes, lances and colours of each company being lowered in homage as she passed. Afterwards she addressed them in words which, like Churchill's after Dunkirk, became part of the English heritage.

'My loving people,

We have been persuaded by some that are careful of our safety, to take heed how we commit ourselves to armed multitudes for fear of treachery. But I assure you, I do not desire to live to distrust my faithful and loving people. Let tyrants fear. I have always so behaved myself that, under God, I have placed my chiefest strength and safeguard in the loyal hearts and goodwill of my subjects. And therefore I am come amongst you, as you see, at this time, not for my recreation and disport, but, being resolved in the midst and heat of battle, to live or die amongst you all, to lay down for my God, for my kingdom, and for my people, my honour and my blood, even in the dust. I know I have the body of a weak and feeble woman, but I have the heart and stomach of a king, and of a king of England too, and think foul scorn that Parma or Spain, or any prince of Europe should dare to invade the borders of my realm.'

'This place,' wrote Walsingham who was there, 'breedeth courage.'

Yet no Prince of Parma and his army emerged from Dunkirk. A week earlier, unknown to the waiting English, the great soldier, like Napoleon two centuries later, quick to realize what had happened, had marched his troops away from the invasion coast, knowing that, without command of the sea, no conqueror could any longer hope to put a foot on English soil with impunity. And six hundred miles away to the north, while Elizabeth was speaking, the proud fleet of Spain was flying westwards, with a fair south-easterly wind, between the Orkneys and Shetlands, seeking the quickest way home to Spain and safety. For, in the words of the great naval historian Michael Lewis, 'in the running fight off Gravelines on Monday July 29th 1588, . . . the Invincible Armada was thrashed beyond redemption in body and spirit alike.'

CHAPTER EIGHT

Elizabethan Harvest

'Our late sovereign, Queen Elizabeth, (whose story hath no
peer among princes of her sex) being a pure virgin, found it,
set foot in it and called it Virginia.'

Sermon preached at Whitechapel April 1609
to the Adventurers and planters of the Virginia Company

'To seek new worlds for gold, for praise, for glory.'

Sir Walter Ralegh

ON THE DAY AFTER ELIZABETH'S GREAT SPEECH at Tilbury, the gale
which had driven the flying Armada far to the north abated, and
the fog which succeeded it, lifted, leaving the sun shining for a
brief while almost as brightly on those remote Scandinavian waters
as it had done on the Biscay Bay five weeks earlier. But the fleet
which had kept such magnificent fighting formation all the way
from the Western Approaches to Calais was already breaking into
fragments. Faulty navigation and the destruction wrought by the
English guns to sails, spars and rigging; abandoned anchors and
cables – more than a hundred of which had been lost at Calais;
broken pumps and holed water-butts, compelling the jettisoning
of thousands of sheep and cattle which, had water been available,
could have provided rations for the entire fleet and army for
several more weeks; three thousand sick and wounded in crowded
airless holds; above all a cumulative and rapid decline in morale
and discipline, had all helped to bring the proud fleet of Spain and
Portugal to its lamentable pass. Some of its ships had strayed off
course almost as far as the Norwegian coast and Iceland; another

grounded in Fair Isle; more than one galleon, holed between wind and water at Gravelines, had sunk under the North Sea waves never to be seen again.

Worse was to follow. For several days, sailing north-about in isolated detachments and then turning west towards the Atlantic, the broken Armada steered a course between the Orkneys and Shetlands, at first in almost halcyon weather, not unwonted in August in those remote waters. On the day after Howard's pursuing but starving fleet had turned back to England, an experienced pilot on Medina Sidonia's command had charted the homeward course over the two thousand and more sea miles which separated the fugitive fleet from its harbours in northern Spain. Sailing-orders were issued by the Admiral under which, after clearing the Northern Isles and Cape Wrath, all ships were to follow the *San Martin* westwards as far as latitude 58 deep in the Atlantic, shunning the shorter and more direct line to Spain south-westwards along the rock-strewn shores of Hebridean islands and the rugged northern and western coasts of Ireland. Only when they reached a point 400 miles west of the mouth of the Shannon were they to make a straight run south for home.

Yet the beaten Armada had to face a foe as deadly as the hidden rocks, shoals and currents and the murderous breakers sweeping out of the Atlantic towards its Celtic eastern coasts. So much of the provision made to feed the fleet and army had been destroyed by the English guns in the four battles fought in the Channel and North Sea that now only the barest rations were available to sustain life during the long voyage home. Sooner than subsist on a daily ration of four ounces of weevily biscuit and half a pint of sour wine per head – all that could be doled out if the fleet was to reach its destination before its stores gave out – many of its captains turned southwards towards home before clearing the perilous inshore waters of western Britain. Nor were the more bellicose among them without hope of avenging their defeat at sea by seizing a military base in Protestant England's restless Catholic dependency.

For on August 24th two despatches reached the Queen's Council in London. One was from Lord Seymour in the Downs confirming that Parma had marched inland and broken up his embarkation camp on the Flemish coast. The other was from Sir William Fitzwilliam, the Queen's Lord Deputy in Ireland, giving warning that the Armada was approaching the north Irish coast and that an invasion of Ulster – the most warlike, turbulent and ungovernable of all the island's half-savage provinces – was imminent. The Spanish threat had shifted from the southern seas and shores of Protestant England to those of the Queen's other and Catholic kingdom.

Yet, though an invasion of Ireland took place, it proved an involuntary one. Instead of choosing where and when they would land, the proud soldiers of Spain, who had conquered half America and driven their European rivals from every disputed foothold in Flanders and Italy, were flung in their unwieldy floating castles on to the Irish rocks and beaches by gigantic waves which drowned them in hundreds and left their ships shattered, holed and helpless. The sodden and half-dazed survivors, laden with treasure – gold chains, rings and jewellery, belt-purses and doubloons sewn into their clothing, velvet and silk cloaks, crucifixes and silver and gold handled daggers and Toledo swords – were set upon, as they lay helpless and famished on those savage, inhospitable strands, by greedy hordes of the poorest peasants in Europe, almost as hungry as themselves and merciless in their search for the fabulous Spanish treasure tossed so providentially onto their shores. For September was wild and gusty with great seas which would have caused little danger to well-found, fully-manned, seaworthy ships, but which threatened to swamp the battered, leaking galleons fighting their way home under Medina Sidonia far in the Atlantic deeps, and drove the little groups of isolated vessels, hopefully edging the Hebridean and Ulster and Connaught cliffs and headlands, inescapably to their fate. All the way south from Fair Isle and Tobermory, Rathlin and Lough Swilly, Sligo Bay and Eris Head, Achill and Clare Island, the lonely Arans in Galway Bay, Loop Head and the Blaskets, to far away Cape Clear and the Kerry and Munster coasts, lay signposts to death for that multitude of broken, storm-tossed sons of Spain.

Yet at least two attempts were made by gallant Spanish officers who, after shipwreck, reformed their men and, still in arms, tried to secure a foothold in Ireland for survival, and, at best, a base for conquest. The most important was that of Alonso de Leyva, the young commander of the Armada's original van and the doyen of Spain's military chivalry whom King Philip, who like everyone else loved him, had secretly appointed to take over supreme command of the expedition should anything happen to Medina Sidonia. Early in September de Leyva's flagship, *La Rata Coranada*, carrying cadets from almost every Spanish noble family, ran aground in Blacksod Bay on the Mayo coast. With 600 survivors he made a fortified camp round the ruins of an old Celtic castle and tried to establish relations with the mercurial native chieftains. Learning, however, that English forces were moving up to destroy him, and joined by the crew of another stormbound vessel, the *Duquesa Santa Ana*, which had somehow managed to escape shipwreck in the bay, de Leyva with the two ships' companies, now 800 strong, set out once more for Spain, only to be blown north by renewed south-westerly gales and driven ashore on the Ulster coast. Still refusing to accept defeat, he again made a fortified camp and prepared to defy the English, whose Lord Deputy, Fitzwilliam, and the Governor of Connaught, Sir Richard Bingham, had ordered every Spaniard who survived the sea, and the swarm of native plunderers and corpse-robbers, to be hanged or put to the sword. Then, hearing that the galleass, *Gerona*, was lying beached and rudderless in Donegal Bay some twenty miles away, de Leyva marched his hungry men to join her. After repairing her rudder and chivalrously declining the proffered hospitality of the chief local magnate, the enigmatic Hugh O'Neil, earl of Tyrone, lest their presence should compromise him with his English overlords, he set out again in mid-October in the patched up *Gerona* for neutral Scotland. After successfully negotiating the entrances to Lough Swilly and Lough Foyle, she struck a rock in the night near the Giant's Causeway and sank with all hands but nine.

Another attempt at military action after shipwreck was made by Don Alonso de Luzon, one of the *tercio* colonels. His ship, the Levantine *La Trinidad Valencera*, sprang a leak off the Ulster coast and only just reached it in time, grounding on a reef near the entrance to Lough Foyle. Marching with the combined crews of his own and of another vessel, to whose rescue he had gone before she foundered, he set off inland, but almost immediately ran into a strong English force marching north to clear the coast of invaders. A fierce engagement followed in which, though outnumbered, the Spanish commander put up a gallant resistance before surrendering on condition that he and his men should be taken unharmed into the presence of the Queen's Lord Deputy. Yet few in the column of unarmed men who set out next day under escort towards the Irish capital reached their destination save de Luzon himself, who was subsequently ransomed. The rest, officers and men alike, were plundered of their clothes and belongings, and made to run the gauntlet, many of them being shot or hanged by their escorting guards who, contrary to normal English practice, in the embittered conditions of Irish anarchy and tribal warfare showed little more mercy than that offered by the Spaniards to Protestant seamen captured beyond the oceans and consigned to the dungeons and torture-chambers of the Inquisition.

From the twenty-five or more Spanish ships known to have been wrecked on that cruel coast, only a handful of those who had sailed in them from Spain left Ireland alive. The few who did so, after indescribable sufferings managed, with the help of native Catholic sympathizers, to reach Scotland, where, the richer among them, ransomed by Parma, secured shipment to the continent in Flemish and North German trading vessels. Those, that is, who were not intercepted and slain out of hand by the merciless Dutch sea beggars who had long been conducting a blockade of terror against Spain and Spaniards off the Netherlands coast. Of the many more who remained in Ireland the English Governor of Connaught, equally set on eradicating every trace of the Spanish presence, wrote to the Lord Deputy, on September 21st, 'I dare assure your Lordship now that in the fifteen or sixteen ships cast away on the coast of this province, which I can on my own knowledge say to be so many, there hath perished at least 6,000 or 7,000 men, of which there hath been put to the sword, first and last, by my brother George, and executed one way and another, about seven or eight hundred or upwards.'

Eleven days before this uncompromising letter was written

there had crept into the port of Santander on the Basque coast twenty-four broken and rotting ships from the outer Atlantic, headed by Medina Sidonia's flagship, the *San Martin*. Their crews were gaunt scarecrows and seemed more like corpses than living men. Many died soon after from their sufferings, among them the fiery, impetuous admiral, Miguel de Oquendo, who, after Grave-lines, had challenged his colleagues' decision to fly to the Atlantic, and who now died of shame on the very day his flagship accident-ally caught fire and blew up at her moorings. Early in October he was followed to the realms of death and honour by his fellow admiral, Recalde, who, driven by storms onto the southern Irish coast, like the fine seaman he was had anchored his battered galleon, *San Juan*, under the lee of Great Blasket Island in the one position which protected her from every wind but the southerly one that later bore him back to Spain, where he died from his wounds and sufferings. Altogether more than half the Armada's ships and men never returned and, of those who did, probably only half ever recovered from their terrible voyage.

* * *

Such were the fruits of sixteenth-century warfare. The crusade which King Philip had prepared and launched to overwhelm England and which her Queen, with a persistence equal to his own, had tried so hard to avert, had ended for him in bitter and humili-ating defeat. It decided that England, and Britain with her, should not be absorbed in Spain's harsh orthodox Atlantic empire, but should remain independent and Protestant. Yet the war continued of its own volition until both principal protagonists were dead, Philip dying in 1598 and Elizabeth in 1603, when her Protestant godson, James VI of Scotland, succeeded peacefully to the English throne, so uniting the British isle under a single crown. England's one positive war-aim – apart from the all-important negative one, secured by the rout of the Armada, of preserving her national inde-pendence and religion – was finally achieved in 1609, when Philip III of Spain signed a Twelve Years' Truce with the United Pro-vinces, as the 'rebel' Protestant northern half of the Netherlands had now become, acknowledging their right to trade in Spanish waters and enjoy untramelled political and religious freedom. It was to secure this that Elizabeth had braved the intolerant dynast's wrath and risked open war a quarter of a century before.

For what followed the Armada's defeat was a long-drawn-out war of attrition in which neither side gained anything substantial but, for the sake of which, both paid heavily in human life and material wealth. With the mines of central and southern America and the sea-borne spice trade of the Portuguese East Indies, Spain was still immensely powerful and was able to equip three further Armadas, two against England in 1596 and 1597, and a third in 1601 against the English garrison of Catholic Ireland, then in open rebellion. All failed completely. For, though the Spaniards had learnt much from their maritime foes and had made their warships and the protection of their overseas possessions and trade far more effective than they had been before, all their attempts to overcome their island adversary ended in disaster. For, while they were, historically and geographically, a land and military power, the sea was England's natural element, while Spain was forced to rely largely on subject and allied countries for the supply equipment of her fleets.

Nor, with her much smaller population and power-base, was post-Armada England herself any more successful in her attacks on Spain and its empire and treasure fleets. Twice, in 1589 and 1596, she launched a major naval and military offensive against the Iberian mainland, the first a fiasco which failed to attract a hoped-for Portuguese patriot rising in Lisbon in its support, the second a brilliant success which reduced the great naval port of Cadiz to a smoking ruin. Yet nothing came of either or of repeated attempts to capture the Plate Fleet or shake Spain's hold on the Azores and Caribbean. It was England's longest war since her duel with medieval France in the fourteenth and fifteenth centuries.

The chronic shortage of money brought about by this continual warfare, not for the private citizen – whose wealth the Queen's pacific and fructifying policy had done so much to enhance – but to meet the public needs of the Crown, constituted the chief harm that Spain, sustained by the flow of specie from the

Peruvian mines, was able to inflict on Elizabeth's England during the last fifteen years of her reign. The defeat of the Armada had cost her more than half the total war-chest which she and her prudent Lord Treasurer, had built up during the long years of peace. It was soon all spent, leaving the Government for the rest of the long Spanish war with an average annual expenditure of nearly a third of a million, or more than twice the normal revenue of Elizabeth's early years. An Irish rebellion in 1598–1601 alone had cost a million. For the primitive administrative machinery of the time gave the subject almost unlimited opportunities for cheating the Crown in wartime. Falsified musters, swelling the ranks with imaginary or absentee soldiers, multiplied the numbers the Queen had to pay, clothe and feed; officers and soldiers vied with one another in selling the latter's clothing and even arms, often to those who had originally supplied them, leaving the fighting man half naked and a subject of reproach and public scandal. As for supplies for the Queen's ships, despite all Hawkins's vigilance and probity and the monarch's own sharp probings and remonstrances, they were sometimes paid for twice over. 'Watch and never look so narrowly,' a Justice of the Peace wrote, 'they will steal and pilfer.'

All this tended to nullify the Elizabethan peacetime financial policy of keeping taxation to an indispensable minimum and letting the nation's wealth fructify in the pockets of the industrious and frugal subject. To avoid the unpopular course of repeated requests to Parliament to make good the deficits in the revenue caused by wartime expenditure – so repugnant to a Queen who depended for power on the love of her subjects – the government was driven to selling off to private purchasers, little by little, almost the whole of the Crown's vast share of the monastic lands that had accrued to it at the Dissolution, leaving a legacy to future sovereigns of royal impecuniosity and need which was to imperil the political balance and unity of the realm. It was also increasingly driven to the easy expedient of using the royal prerogative to lease, to private persons, patents, monopolies and exclusive rights for the sale of essential commodities, many of them indispensible to everyday life, like coal, salt, soap, starch, iron and leather. In the last two Parliaments of the reign, public indignation at these, some of them granted to unpopular Court favourites, boiled over into overt attacks on the Queen herself.

Yet, despite old age, Elizabeth's sense of political realities never failed her. Nor did the touch of her shrewd finger on the public pulse. When in the autumn of 1601 royal monopoly after monopoly had been denounced in an indignant House of Commons, with her perfect sense of timing the Queen yielded without loss of dignity or grace. Letting it be known through the Speaker that 'she herself would take order of reformation' and that no monopoly would henceforth continue unless approved by a court of law, on November 30th 1601 she addressed a delegation of the House of Commons in the Council Chamber at Whitehall in words which epitomized her reign.

> 'Though God hath raised me high, yet this I count the glory of my crown that I have reigned with your loves. It is not my desire to live or reign longer than my life or reign shall be for your good. And though you have had, and may have, many mightier and wiser princes sitting in this seat, yet you never had, nor shall have, any that will love you better.'

In that noble series of books in which the greatest of all Elizabethan historians, Dr A. L. Rowse, has surveyed her reign, he draws from a contemporary letter a wonderful picture of this invincible Queen in the penultimate year of her life. An old soldier and veteran of the Flemish wars, Sir William Browne, was accorded an interview on an August morning in 1601, as she walked in the garden with her entourage of ladies and courtiers,

> 'She presently called for me and was pleased to say I was welcome with many good words . . . I had no sooner kissed her sacred hands but that she presently made me stand up and spoke somewhat loud and said, "Come hither, Browne!" and pronounced that she held me for an old faithful servant of hers and said, "I must give content to Browne," or some such speeches. And then, the train following her, said: "Stand, stand back! Will you not let us speak but ye will be hearers?" And then walked a turn or two, protesting of her

"Whatever rifts arose between them, there was never any question but that it was she who directed the ship of state, while Lords and Commons, the hereditary and elected representatives of her people, meeting periodically at her summons to authorise and grant fiscal supply, gave her, through proven and custom-hallowed channels of consultation and debate, their counsel, advice and consent". The Queen, with Burghley at her right hand and Walsingham at her left, presides over Parliament.

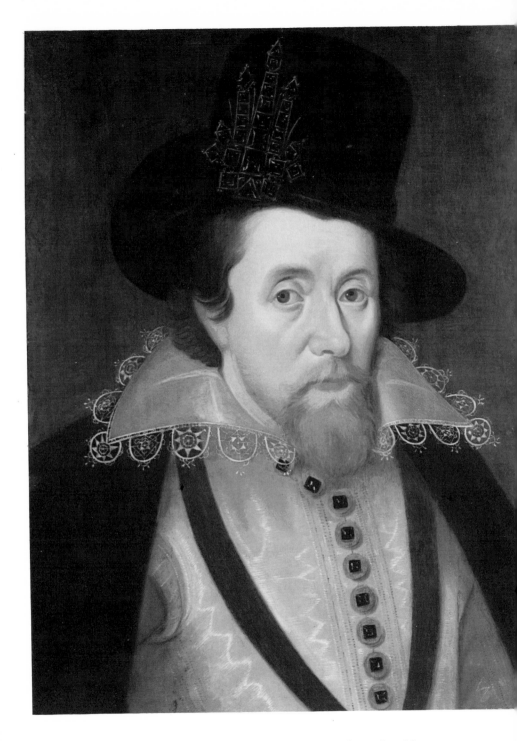

James VI and I, "the most learned sovereign ever to sit on a Scottish – or English – throne".

most gracious opinion of myself. "And before God, Browne,"
said she, "they do me wrong that will make so honest a
servant jealous that I should mistrust him" ... Having walked
a turn or two, she called for a stool, which was set under a
tree and I began to kneel, but she would not suffer me; in so
much that after two or three denials which I made to kneel,
she was pleased to say that she would not speak with me
unless I stood up. Whereupon I stood up and . . . she discoursed of many things.'

In the course of his audience the Queen took the opportunity
to disabuse the loyal veteran of the prejudice which she suspected
his fellow soldiers felt against her politic Secretary of State, Sir
Robert Cecil, who had succeeded his dead father, Lord Burghley,
in her supreme favour, 'Dost thou see that little fellow that kneels
there?' she asked. 'It had been told you that he hath been an enemy
to soldiers. On my faith, Browne, he is the best friend that soldiers
have.'

Though in her sixties Elizabeth still presented to the world the
same proud, imperious, if unpredictable, front as ever, the years of
war, unlike the earlier ones of peace and creative statecraft, were
for her inevitably years of loss and decline. One after another those
she had loved or worked with dropped away: Leicester only a few
weeks after her great speech at Tilbury when, as her Commander-
in-Chief, he had ridden by her side through the ranks of her cheering soldiery. (A letter to her, written in September from Rycote on
his way home from Tilbury to Kenilworth, only reached her after
he was dead. 'His last letter,' she endorsed it.) Her principal Secretary of State, the Protestant champion, Sir Francis Walsingham,
died in 1590; the great seamen, Drake and Hawkins, in their last ill-
fated West Indian voyage in 1595–6, from which neither returned
alive. They were followed by her cousins Lord Hunsdon, the Lord
Chamberlain, and his deputy, Sir Francis Knollys. And in 1598
had gone the closest and most trusted of all, Lord Treasurer
Burghley.

Those years of war, too, were checkered by public and social
disasters, like the long-drawn-out guerrilla war among the bogs
and mountains of northern Ireland; and the one day rebellion and

execution for High Treason of the earl of Essex, which was one of
its tragic consequences; the five successive bad harvests at the end
of the century which drove up the price of wheat from twenty to
nearly sixty shillings a quarter and caused a famine among the
urban poor; and the great epidemics of bubonic plague in 1592
and 1593–4, immortalized by Thomas Nashe's haunting threnody,
In Time of Pestilence.

> 'Brightness falls from the air
> Queens have died young and fair:
> Dust hath closed Helen's eye;
> I am sick, I must die –
> *Lord have mercy on me!*'

Though for Elizabeth herself nearly all the enduring work of
her reign had been done before the war, for her subjects the harvest
sown in those years was gathered in the years preceding and following her death. The confidence, vitality and sense of common purpose she had given her people inspired and sustained them in every
department of life. They were the years of the madrigals and the
music of William Byrd – pupil of the great Thomas Tallis – of
Tomkins, Weelkes, Morley, Orlando Gibbons and Dowland; of
Hilliard's miniatures and Isaac James's sculpture; of Spenser's
Faerie Queene, Camden's *Britannia* and Hooker's *Ecclesiastical
Polity,* of Bacon's *Essays* and *Novum Organum,* and the poems of
Walter Ralegh and John Donne; of the building of the great
Elizabethan and Jacobean houses that rose out of the ruins of the
monasteries – Burghley and Hatfield, Wilton and Knole and Long-
leat – and the fantastic palace of glass and towers which Bess of
Hardwick raised among the Derbyshire hills. Above all, they saw
the brief miraculous flowering of the Elizabethan theatre and its
supreme product, the genius of Shakespeare; and the publication
of the King James or Authorized Version of the Bible. Most far-
reaching of all in its effects on the future of the world were the
colonization by Englishmen of the eastern seaboard of North
America and, with it, the genesis of the future United States, and
the almost simultaneous foundation of the East India Company

and the beginning of English, and presently British, involvement in India and the Orient.

* * *

The challenge which began in Elizabeth's reign to Spain's and Portugal's monopolist claim to the ownership and use of the outer oceans and of all the unoccupied lands which bordered them, took three forms. One was that of English merchants, trading their wares by land and sea into every country into which they could infiltrate, even at the risk of their lives, from the frozen wastes of Hudson Bay and Greenland to the markets and caravan routes of Bokhara and Samarkand. More spectacular was that of Drake and his fellow privateers and his daring use of his country's hereditary skills in seamanship, shipbuilding and gunnery to win local command of whatever sea he sailed in order to levy a highwayman's toll on the mineral treasure with which the Spanish king financed his wars of conquest and oppression. And a third was that of Drake's fellow West Countrymen, the Devonshire cousins, Humphrey Gilbert, Richard Grenville and Walter Ralegh, whose imaginative minds were more obsessed with the idea of establishing 'plantations' or colonies of English settlers on the other side of the Atlantic than of avenging the oppressions and cruelties of imperial Spain and recouping their losses by raiding her ports and capturing her treasure ships. For, though Drake had always cherished the idea of striking at Spain's power by fermenting a rising of her oppressed subject peoples, his essentially practical and matter-of-fact mind, for all its phenomenal daring, never seriously contemplated planting a new England, with English settlers, laws, institutions and language, on the Atlantic shores of the North American wilderness.

Yet, while for nearly a hundred years England, as a nation, had lagged far behind its southern European neighbours in exploiting the great ocean discoveries of the latter fifteenth century, there had always been a few English minds which shared the expansive and romantic dreams of the Iberian, Gallic and Italian global navigators and conquerors. As early as the reign of Henry VIII John

Rastell, brother-in-law of Sir Thomas More, had expressed a
nostalgic wish that

> 'they that be Englishmen
> Might have been the first of all
> That there should have taken possession
> And made first building and habitation
> A memory perpetual!'

Still earlier, in the reign of Henry VII and in the very year in which
Vasco da Gama rounded the Cape of Good Hope and before
Columbus himself had penetrated beyond the West Indies, a
Bristol merchant of Italian origin, John Cabot, coasting the shores
of what were to become Newfoundland and Nova Scotia, had been
the first known European to discover the North American mainland. His son Sebastian, also sailing from Bristol, claimed to have
discovered a north-west passage through the polar ice from the
Atlantic into the Pacific.

But it was the Devonshire landowner, dreamer and fire-eater,
Sir Richard Grenville, and his fellow West Countryman, Sir
Humphrey Gilbert, who, in the second decade of Elizabeth's
reign first took practical steps to bring about an English settlement
on the coast of North America. Gilbert was an old servant of the
Queen's who, with her Welsh ancestry and Renaissance mind and
education, was deeply interested in everything pertaining to the
New World and its possibilities. Among her Celtic contacts was
the Welsh astrologer and clairvoyant, John Dee, at whose home at
Mortlake she would sometimes call on her journeys to and from
her palace at Richmond. Dee nursed enthusiastic dreams of a
'British' – not English – empire and was the first to use that name
in his unpublished 'Atlantical Discourses'. He loved to trace his
not unsympathetic sovereign's claim to a global empire based on
her descent from the legendary King Arthur. And it was he who
produced and submitted to her two rolls of evidence tracing her
title to sovereignty in North America. In October 1578, she and
her Council granted Letters Patent to Sir Humphrey Gilbert, 'to
search, find out and view such remote, heathen and barbarous
lands, countries and territories not actually possessed of any

Christian prince or people' and settle colonists there under laws 'agreeable to the form of the laws and policies of England'. It was in his Patent that the Queen openly challenged the arrogant claim of the Spanish monopolists who – in the words of Richard Hakluyt, the lifelong historian and chronicler of Elizabethan ocean discovery – 'account all other nations for pirates, rovers and thieves which visit any heathen coast that they have sailed by or looked on.'

Among those who served in Gilbert's first exploratory voyage to the coast of North America was his half-brother, Walter Ralegh – fifteen years his junior. The expedition achieved nothing, but was followed by others, including one in 1583 in which, after taking nominal possession in the Queen's name of the cod fishermen's island of call, Newfoundland, which thus became England's earliest overseas possession, Gilbert – 'a man noted,' as the Queen put it, 'of not good hap by sea' – lost his flagship in a storm with most of the stores she was carrying to found a transatlantic settlement. Observing that it was as near heaven by sea as by land, he transferred his flag to a ten-ton pinnace, the *Squirrel*, and was last seen calmly reading a book before the tempest swallowed him up.

'The first of our nation that carried people to erect an habitation in those northern countries of America,' as Hakluyt called him in his championship of the case of American colonization, Gilbert was succeeded by the brilliant Ralegh, by then the Queen's rising favourite. But though in 1584, at the latter's instance, she invested in a joint stock venture to plant a colony on the North American coast, contributing one of her royal ships, the *Tiger*, as flagship and £440 worth of gunpowder from the Tower, she declined to make the project official, no doubt for fear of offending Spain, with whom war had not yet broken out. Thus Ralegh's friend and protégé, the thirty-two-year-old Richard Hakluyt, vainly pleaded with her to do in his pamphlet, *A Discourse of Western Planting* – presented to her on his knees in an audience obtained for him by Ralegh – describing it as 'certain reasons to induce Her Majesty and the State to take in hand the western voyage and the planting therein.'

As Elizabeth would not let her new favourite, Ralegh, leave her side, the expedition was commanded in his absence by that even earlier enthusiast for colonization, his cousin, Sir Richard

Grenville. But she allowed the infant colony – whose hundred or so settlers, mostly from the West Country, Grenville planted in the summer of 1585 on Roanoke Island – to be named after her, Virginia. When Grenville arrived back in England in the autumn, after leaving his second-in-command, Ralph Lane – a former royal equerry – in charge of the infant colony and promising to return with reinforcements and supplies next year, he was greeted at Plymouth by Ralegh, who reported proudly to the Secretary of State, Walsingham, 'I have possessed and peopled the same to Her Majesty's use, and planted it with such cattle and beasts as are fit and necessary for manuring the country.'

So it came about that for a year, including a hungry winter in which they were forced to live on their stores, a minute colony of Englishmen made what they intended to be a permanent home in the North American wilderness. It was the winter in which Drake captured and ravaged the two capitals of the Spanish Main and Caribbean, returning home to England in triumph in the early summer of 1586. On his way he called at the little settlement on Roanoke Island in the Pamlico Sand. It so happened that the ship bringing provisions and reinforcements, which Grenville and Ralegh had promised should reach the colony in the spring, had not yet arrived, and, a sudden storm arising, the settlers, thinking themselves abandoned, lost heart and at the last moment decided to accept Drake's offer to take them home in his fleet. Hardly had they gone when a supply ship sent by Ralegh appeared, 'freighted with all manner of things in most plentiful manner for the supply and relief of his colony', followed soon after by Grenville himself, only to find the settlers gone.

It seemed a great opportunity lost, all the more so as the first reports from the young colony had been so hopeful. 'We have discovered the [main] land,' Lane had written to the enthusiastic Hakluyt in England, 'to be the goodliest soil under the cope of heaven, so abounding with sweet trees that bring such sundry and pleasant gums, grapes of such greatness yet wild, . . . so many sorts of apothecary drugs, such several kinds of flax, and one kind like silk, the same gathered of a grass as common there as grass is here . . . It is the goodliest and most pleasing territory of the world, for the continent is of a huge and unknown greatness, and very well peopled and towned, though savagely, and the climate so wholesome that we had not one sick since we touched the land here. If Virginia had but horses and kine in some reasonable proportion, I dare assure myself, being inhabited with English, no realm in Christendom were comparable to it.'

Because of this, Ralegh and Grenville were not deterred. 'Unwilling,' as Hakluyt put it, 'to lose the possession of the country which Englishmen had so long held', before returning to England Grenville left fifteen men on the island with two years' provisions. Meanwhile Ralegh fitted out another colonizing expedition of a hundred men and seventeen women, which sailed for Virginia in the following year with a charter to found a city on the Chesapeake estuary to the north. But when in the summer of 1587 they landed on Roanoke, they found the bones of only one of the fifteen men left behind by Grenville, and the little fort built by their predecessors razed to the ground by hostile Indians, with whom the English, unlike the conquering Spaniards in Central and South America, had tried to live in utopian peace and amity.

But though, in a Latin dedication to Ralegh, Hakluyt wrote that 'no terrors, no personal losses or misfortunes could or ever would tear you from the sweet embracements of your own Virginia, that fairest of nymphs ... whom our Sovereign has given you to be your bride', two small pinnaces despatched by Ralegh in the spring of 1588 to make contact with the Virginia settlers never managed to weather the Atlantic storms of that summer, while the expedition of seven ships – the largest yet planned for a transatlantic plantation – which he and Grenville were fitting out at Bideford, never sailed. Instead it was ordered to join the fleet Drake was assembling at Plymouth against invasion, while he and Ralegh, as Lords Lieutenant of Devon and Cornwall, took command of the levies raised to resist a Spanish landing. And in the following year, after the Armada's defeat, when all the country's resources were mobilized for the amphibious attack on Lisbon under Drake and Sir John Norris, no one could spare time for colonizing America. Meanwhile, busied in the Queen's business in Ireland, Ralegh assigned his rights in the city to be named after him on the Chesapeake to a syndicate of London merchants, who, reinforcing his own efforts to contact the lost planters, sent out in 1590 a relief expedition, only to find that the entire colony had disappeared without trace.

Yet, though as a result of its disappearance, the continuance of the war, Grenville's death in the last fight of the *Revenge* in 1591 and Ralegh's fall from royal favour in the following year, the Virginian project lapsed, England's maritime and commercial activities in the world's oceans and furthest shores continued. Frobisher's earlier attempts 'to ship a course for China' by finding new trading routes to the Pacific round the northern extremities of America and its encircling ice, were succeeded by those of three great navigators, John Davis – author of *The Seaman's Secrets*, the first practical work on navigation published by an Englishman – Henry Hudson and William Baffin. Living at Sandridge on the Dart, a close friend of Humphrey Gilbert and his family, between 1583 and 1587 Davis made three attempts to penetrate that steely corridor of dreams, the North-West Passage, greatly enlarging knowledge of the mysterious and baffling waters between Greenland, the Pacific and the North Pole. About the same time, a twenty-six-year-old East Anglian from Trimley in Suffolk, Thomas Cavendish, emulated Drake's voyage round the world by sailing in 1586 through the Magellan Straits into the Pacific, where he captured a rich Manila galleon, and, subsequently rounding the Cape of Good Hope, was the first Englishman ever to land at St Helena, returning victorious to England in the autumn of 1588 when he crossed the shattered Armada's homeward course.

All this, and much more, Richard Hakluyt recorded in his great book, *The Principal Navigations, Traffics and Discoveries of the English Nation*, which he had been preparing for press throughout the Armada year and published in 1589, proudly claiming that the English 'in searching the most opposite corners and quarters of the world and, to speak plainly, in compassing the vast globe of the earth more than once, have excelled all the nations and peoples of the earth.' 'For which of the kinds of this land before her Majesty,' he asked in his Epistle Dedicatory to Walsingham, 'had their banners ever seen in the Caspian Sea? Which of them hath ever dealt with the Emperor of Persia, as her Majesty hath done, and obtained for her merchants large and loving privileges? Who ever saw before this regimen an English lieger in the stately porch of the Grand Signior at Constantinople? Who ever found English consuls and agents at Tripolis in Syria, at Aleppo, at Babylon, at Basra and, which is more, who ever heard of Englishman at Goa before now? What English ships did heretofore ever anchor in the mighty river of Plate? Pass and repass the unpassable (in former opinion) strait of Magellan, range along the coast of Chile, Peru and all the backside of Nova Hispania, farther than any Christian ever passed, traverse the mighty breadth of the South Sea, land upon the Locones [Philippines] in despite of the enemy, enter into alliance, amity and traffic with the princes of the Moluccas and the Isle of Java, double the famous Cape of Bona Speranza, arrive at the Isle of St Helena, and last of all return home most richly laden with the commodities of China, as the subjects of this now flourishing monarchy have done?'

*   *   *

Over one route, the passage round the Cape to the Indian Ocean to break into the Portuguese monopoly of the seaborne spice and silk trade, the English were at first far less successful than in their forays into the Spanish Caribbean and Pacific a generation earlier. For the great Portuguese carracks of over a thousand tons were more than a match in those remote waters for the smaller English armed merchantmen, superior in gunnery and seamanship though the latter were. And before the end of Elizabeth's reign the enterprising merchants and seamen of the United Provinces, to preserve whose independence she had gone to war with King Philip, had themselves begun, not only to challenge, but to usurp for themselves the Portuguese monopoly, sending out powerful trading ships of their own built and equipped for long voyages in eastern waters. The first two English ventures to break into the Indian Ocean met with total disaster; of the three armed merchantment which sailed in 1591 only one successfully rounded the Cape of Good Hope, and, though it ultimately reached Cape Cormorin,

all it brought back to England, after a two years' voyage of indescribable hardships, was a cargo of sick sailors, victims of scurvy,
starvation and their own mutinies. A second expedition in 1596
fared no better, not a single survivor of its three ships returning
to England.

It was the success of the Dutch, and the ageing Queen's determination that her own subjects should not be outdone by them,
that led to the successful entry into the luxury trade of the Orient
of the English East India Company. Founded by a consortium of
London merchants under the title of 'the Governor and Company
of the Merchants of London trading into the East Indies', and
granted by a royal charter of December 31st 1599 a monopoly for
fifteen years of all trade with lands beyond the Cape of Good Hope
or Magellan Straits, it sent out its first fleet from Torbay in the
spring of 1600. Its moving spirit, and for many years its chairman,
as also of the Levant Company, was Sir Thomas Smythe, one of
the rich sons of 'Customer' Smythe – the immensely able and
shrewd financier who from 1570 to 1588 had farmed the royal
Customs to the benefit, thanks to his remarkable efficiency, both
of the Crown and, even more, of himself.

Though in the more distant spice islands the Dutch, super-
seding the easier-going Portuguese, had gained a long march on
their former protectors and allies, who, at the time of the Queen's
death, had established only a single trading 'factory' at Bantam in
Java, the English directed their efforts instead towards India,
where one or two daring Elizabethan merchants had already penetrated by land. Through Smythe's initiative the Company, early
in the reign of James I, established a permanent representative at
the court of the Mogul emperors at Agra – at that time virtual
rulers of the peninsula. Within six years of Elizabeth's death,
when her successor renewed the company's fifteen years' monopoly 'for ever', it was sending out regular voyages to the Indian
Ocean every year, establishing 'factories' on both India's eastern
and western coasts, and penetrating far beyond, to Siam in 1612
and Japan in the following year. The £72,000 of capital initially
invested in the Company earned in the course of a few decades a
return far greater than that of the most spectacular of Drake's
plundering voyages of the past.

Almost simultaneously this far-sighted Elizabethan merchant prince, operating from the City of London, sent out his country's tentacles across the North Atlantic to refound the lapsed Virginian settlement which Ralegh and Grenville had planted before the Armada and the long Spanish war. Here there were no hopes of rich trading argosies or quick – or even, at first, any – returns on the capital required to recruit, ship and maintain emigrants and establish homes and farms in a wilderness as yet only inhabited by savages. Even Ralegh, who in his darkest hour was still to write of Virginia that 'he would yet live to see it an English nation', had hitched his dreams to a new star – that of the legendary golden kingdom of El Dorado which he persisted in believing existed in the mountains of that vast and still unexplored tract of tropical South America which lay beyond the Spanish Main between the mouths of the Orinoco and Amazon. In 1595, in the desperate hope of winning back the Queen's lost favour by presenting her with a fabulously rich dominion surpassing even Spain's Peru, he fitted out and led an expedition to this elusive land, subsequently publishing a book about it entitled *The Discovery of the Large and Beautiful Empire of Guiana*. Thrown after Elizabeth's death into the Tower and sentenced to death for treason on dubious charges of plotting against the new King, he was to spend the rest of his life as a prisoner, the last great Elizabethan, writing his noble *History of the World* and only released on sufferance in 1616 – the year of Hakluyt's death – to prepare for a last and fatal voyage to Guiana to seek his illusory El Dorado, paying for it two years later with his head, at the instance and demand of his unrelenting enemies, the Spaniards who hated him and all he stood for.

It had been men of such soaring vision and imagination as Ralegh and Hakluyt who had first conceived the idea of making new Englands beyond the oceans. By their propagation of it, the one in the Council chamber and at sea, the other by his pen, they had caused it to germinate in the minds of their countrymen. But it required qualities of a different kind to turn their vision into everyday reality. Such were those of Sir Thomas Smythe and his fellow merchants in their city counting-houses who, pooling their knowledge and resources and sharing their risks, laid out their money, prudently but boldly, on a long-term investment in their country's future, with the patience, persistence and resolution to see the thing through. Calling all prepared to join them Adventurers, they used the capital raised from them to recruit planters and maintain plantations until these were able to support themselves.

As soon as Elizabeth's pacific successor had brought the long wasting war with Spain to a conclusion in 1604, two joint-stock companies were formed, one in London presided over by Smythe, and the other by West Country merchants and gentry at Plymouth, Exeter and Bristol. The London company, by far the richer of the two, sent out three ships – the *Susan Constant*, *Godspeed* and *Discovery* – in December 1606 with a hundred settlers to take the place of those who had vanished twenty years earlier. In the spring of 1607, landing on the shores of Chesapeake Bay, they built a fort and a little timber settlement which they named Jamestown after the new King. Though only thirty-eight of them remained alive at the end of the first winter, successive batches of settlers were sent out by Smythe and his partners every summer. At first their losses were enormous. Six years after the original landing Smythe told the Spanish ambassador that, of the thousand men and women sent out in the previous summer, eight hundred had already died. By 1622 of more than ten thousand who had landed in Virginia, fewer than two thousand survived.

Yet the colony itself survived. Two things enabled it to do so. One was the resolution and persistence of its promoters in London. 'With such very great losses as they have suffered,' the Spanish ambassador, who hoped the venture would fail, reported to his master, 'they still show so much courage.' For of the £80,000 which Smythe and his partners put into the colony in its first years, not one penny had been provided by King James and his government. It was their Elizabethan faith in the English future which sustained them and the colony. Building on the growing enthusiasm for the idea of American plantation which successive editions of Hakluyt's great work was generating, the Virginia Company sent supply ship after ship across the Atlantic to give the colonists the chance to establish themselves. 'Divine Providence,' it was claimed, 'having reserved for us this magnificent region and the discovery of this great world, which it now offers to us; and, since we have arms to embrace it, there is no reason why we should let it escape us.'

The other factor which enabled the colony to survive was the spirit of self-help and self-survival, replacing the first settlers' sanguine and idle dreams of utopia, with which the colonists themselves, under the spur of necessity, set to work to cultivate the ground. 'If any would not work neither should he eat,' was the rule which their self-appointed leader, Captain John Smith, a typical younger Elizabethan, had by the second winter established in the little colony, where every man was given an initial allotment of three acres to cultivate. 'When our people were fed out of the common store and laboured jointly together,' he reported, 'glad was he who could slip from his labour or slumber over his task, he cared not how; nay the most honest among them would hardly take so much true pains in a week as now for themselves will do in a day. Neither cared they for the increase, presuming that nowsoever the harvest prospered, the general store must maintain them, so that we reaped not so much corn from the labour of thirty as now three or four do provide for themselves.' Instead, from then onwards, self-help became the rule among the English pioneers in America. At their back was the ocean, and before them the forest. Every man had to 'root, hog or die'. 'I live a simple life,' one of them wrote a few years later, 'and hath builded a shop, and doth follow the weaving of linen cloth, and I have bought 450 acres of land in the woods.'

Untamed encroaching forest, feverish swamp and unfordable river, wild beast and wilder red men, cold, famine and disease were the realities which faced the early colonists in their new homeland. During the Indian massacre of 1622 more than three hundred and fifty of them perished, and a further five hundred in the year that followed. Yet in England determination to make the Virginian plantation succeed had now become a point of national pride. Among those who lent support to the London Virginia Company after the royal grant in 1609 of the colony's second Charter, were the archbishop of Canterbury, the earls of Pembroke, Montgomery and Southampton – Shakespeare's friend and patron – eighteen other peers, ninety-eight knights, including Sir Oliver Cromwell – uncle of the future Protector – and Fulke Greville, Sir Philip Sidney's friend and biographer, and fifty-six of the City Livery Companies. And the Poet Laureate, Michael Drayton, in his *Ode to the Virginian Voyage*, hailed the Adventurers and planters now streaming across the Atlantic to take possession of the new transatlantic England – the right to which the Elizabethans and their dead Queen had won through their long struggle with Spain.

> 'To get the pearl and gold
> And ours to hold,
> Virginia,
> Earth's only paradise.'

While attention was focused on the activities of the London Virginia Company, those of the West Country or Plymouth company, with its smaller financial resources, had passed largely unnoticed. In the opening years of the century some exploratory voyages south from the Newfoundland fisheries had been made along the northern part of the Atlantic littoral which was the Plymouth company's plantation area. These had roughly mapped out the future Maine and Massachusetts coastline and given names to some of its geographical features such as Cape Cod and Martha's Vineyard. Early in 1607, following the load of the London Company, the West Country Company's two chief promoters, Sir Ferdinando Gorges, governor of the fort at Plymouth, and Lord Chief Justice Popham, a former Recorder of Bristol, had sent out a hundred colonists in two ships, the *Gift of God* and *Mary and John*, the latter commanded by Ralegh Gilbert, a son of Sir Humphrey. They made a landing at Sagadahoc on the Kennebec River where they survived the winter. But when the supply ship arrived in the summer of 1608, the colonists had had enough and decided to return home. In the meantime Popham had died and, the Company's finances being temporarily exhausted, colonization of the eight hundred or so miles of coastline of what was still thought of as northern Virginia lapsed for another twelve years.

It was the enthusiasm of John Smith, whose vigour and common sense had done so much to save and establish the pioneer colony on the Chesapeake, that kept interest in this unexploited northern area of colonization alive. It was he who, cruising its coasts every summer, published in 1616 a *Description of New England*, which gave it its name. 'New England,' he wrote, 'is great enough to make many kingdoms and countries, were it all inhabited . . . As for the goodness and fine substance of the land, we are for the most part yet altogether ignorant of them, but only here and there where we have touched or seen a little, the edges of those large dominions which do stretch themselves into the main, God doth know how many thousand miles.'

Four years later in 1620, partly through the continued efforts of Sir Ferdinando Gorges – a simple soldier who had begun life fighting in Elizabeth's Netherlands wars and who devoted his modest fortunes and the portions of his two wives to the cause of colonization – two expeditions went out from the West Country. The nucleus of one was a small group of Nottinghamshire separatists, calling themselves the Pilgrims, who had earlier migrated to Holland in order to practise their own peculiar kind of worship. Sailing from Plymouth that September with other emigrants in a 130 ton ship, the *Mayflower*, they were driven by storms as far north as Cape Cod, where after a month's voyage they landed at what became known as New Plymouth. Though half of them died during that first terrible New England winter, the colony survived. In the next two decades they were followed by thousands of other emigrants who settled in growing numbers round the shores of Massachusetts Bay and in the town they had founded and named after Boston in Lincolnshire. They were mostly of a strong puritanical bent, born of the growing conflict between the Laudian Anglican church establishment at home, supported by the Stuart kings, and its critics backed by an increasingly intransigent Parliament. Elizabethans by birth though the founding father of New England were, they derived their ideology from those who had opposed the dead Queen's unifying efforts and refused to conform to her cherished Anglican settlement. They can therefore hardly be regarded, like the colonizers of Virginia, as part of the Elizabethan harvest. Theirs, as they proudly insisted, was 'a Bible Commonwealth', where, as one of them put it, 'the righteous are in authority'.

*   *   *

Yet the English Bible to which these authoritarian fanatics appealed as the justification of their beliefs, and on the literal interpretation of which they founded their commonwealth, was itself an essential part of the Elizabethan harvest. It was a measure of that harvest, reaped from the seed of national unity sown by Elizabeth in the germinative first years of her reign, that at the very moment when England's merchants and seamen were carrying her life and influence into every ocean and continent, her writers were creating, out of a formerly rude vernacular, a literature, not only potentially, but already in achievement, as great as any yet known to history, even that of ancient Greece. Three contributions of supreme literary genius – two of them, as befitted an intensely religious age, sacred in character and, the other secular – took their place at that moment in the continuing national consciousness and in that of all the lands overseas in which the writ of England ran or was to run. One was the liturgy of the Anglican Church, the other the Authorized Version of the Bible published under James I in 1611, following the Hampton Court Conference of divines called in the year after Elizabeth's death. The third contribution was the plays of William Shakespeare.

The Anglican Book of Common Prayer was originally conceived in the deeply receptive mind of Queen Elizabeth's godfather, the martyred Archbishop Cranmer, and was based on the traditional Catholic liturgical rite, purged of what to Protestants seemed idolatrous accretions. Never used by the whole nation like the James I Bible – for the more extreme puritanical precisians and their Nonconformist successors could never bring themselves to accept it as did the more conservative elements in the nation – the Anglican Prayer Book helped to shape and ennoble the thoughts and minds of generations of English folk, gentle and humble alike. For its resounding passages and phrases, and its translations from the lovely Psalms of David, sank deep into the national consciousness.

'We have erred and strayed from thy ways like lost sheep; we have followed too much the devices and desires of our own hearts; we have left undone those things which we ought to have done, and we have done those things which we ought not to have done, and there is no health in us.'

'Lord, who shall dwell in thy tabernacle, or who shall rest upon thy holy hill? Even he that leadeth an uncorrupt life, and doeth the thing which is right, and speaketh the truth from his heart . . . He that setteth not by himself, but is lowly in his own eyes, and maketh much of them that fear the Lord. He that sweareth unto his neighbour and disappointeth him not, though it were to his own hindrance.'

'The Lord is my shepherd; therefore can I lack nothing. He shall feed me in a green pasture, and lead me forth beside the waters of comfort. He shall convert my soul, and bring me forth in the paths of righteousness, for his name's sake. Yea, though I walk through the valley of the shadow of death, I will fear no evil; for thou art with me; thy rod and thy staff comfort me.'

One passage from the Psalms illustrates what the Elizabethan ideal of national unity meant for the English people.

'O pray for the peace of Jerusalem; they shall prosper that love thee. Peace be within thy walls and plenteousness within thy palaces. For my brethren and companions' sake I will wish thee prosperity.'

So, shaping the thoughts, feelings and speech of future generations, were the sayings, injunctions and definitions of the Elizabethan liturgy, as finalized in the great post-Restoration Anglican Prayer Book of 1662, re-issued after the Civil War and Interregnum, during which it had been temporarily interdicted. 'The fear of the Lord is the beginning of wisdom.' 'To strengthen such as do stand; and to comfort and help the weak-hearted and to raise up them that fall; and, finally, to beat down Satan under our feet.' 'The author of peace and lover of concord, in knowledge of whom standeth our eternal life, whose service is perfect freedom.' 'All sorts and conditions of men.' 'That peace which the world cannot give.'

What was true of the Anglican liturgy was even more true of the Authorized Version of the Bible. 'We never thought,' wrote Dr Miles Smith in his modest Preface to the King James Bible, 'that we should need to make a new translation, nor yet to make a bad one a good one . . . but to make a good one better, or, out of many good ones, one principal good one.' Distilled by English scholars and divines from the successive translations and versions of the past century, it became natural for English men and women of all classes – including the humblest and least educated – to lard their speech and thought with its phrases and analogies. The spiritual history, beliefs, traditions and legends of an ancient Christian people on the threshold of a new age were set out by the post-Elizabethan revisers and editors in language as simple as it was profound and in rhythm as moving as the greatest music. 'In the beginning was the Word and the Word was with God.' 'All things were made by him, and without him was not anything made that was made.' 'And the light shined in the darkness, and the darkness comprehended it not.'

Nowhere in the compass of a single volume have the great truths and mysteries of human existence been made more comprehensible to simple minds – or, for that matter, to sophisticated ones – than in the inspired language of great poetry and prophecy contained in this marvellous communal work of revision and recapitulation. 'The Kingdom of God is within you.' 'God is a spirit and they that worship him must worship him in spirit and in truth.' 'All things work together for good to them that love God.' 'For I am persuaded that neither death, nor life, nor angels, nor principalities, nor powers, nor things present, nor things to come, nor height, nor depth, nor any other creature shall be able to separate us from the love of God which is in Jesus Christ our Lord.'

*　　*　　*

The other supreme legacy of the Elizabethan harvest were the plays of William Shakespeare. They were not the only works of great English secular literature evoked by the age which the Queen had inaugurated; the prose of Hooker, Ralegh and Francis Bacon were all, in their different ways, masterpieces. So, was the arcadian, and in part archaic, poetry of Philip Sidney and of Edmund Spenser, and the anything but archaic poetry of the great late Elizabethan amorist, metaphysic and divine, John Donne, Dean of St Paul's. Yet these, unlike the Prayer Book and Bible, were written only for a very small literary, scholarly and virtually private readership. For at that time no general reading public existed for any but religious and theological works.

But the plays of William Shakespeare were composed for acting before audiences drawn from every class, were immensely popular in their day and, as no other secular literature of the time, represented the thoughts and feelings of the nation. As their posthumous fame was to prove, their appeal was not limited to their own time. Yet though, as Matthew Arnold was to write, Shakespeare was not for an age but for all time, he was by birth and environment an Elizabethan or Elizabethans. Born in 1564 in the little Warwickshire market town of Stratford-upon-Avon less than six years after Elizabeth's accession, and outliving her by little more than a decade, the bulk of his work – though not all the greatest – was written during her reign. Son of a glover and wool-dealer who became an alderman, and, in the crisis year of 1569, bailiff or mayor of his native Stratford, in his fifty-two years he experienced and shared in the social and cultural life of all three main classes into which contemporary England – at that time more homogeneous than at any period in her history – was divided. For growing up in the ranks of the rural trading middle class, with a good Latin education at the local grammar school, owing to his father's failing fortunes and debts and his own improvidence at the age of eighteen in getting a neighbour's daughter into trouble and having to marry her, he missed the chance of a university education and had to seek his fortunes in the rough and tumble tavern and slum life of the English capital. Here, as his plays reveal, he acquired a wonderful knowledge and understanding of the life and familiar speech of the poor and uneducated. Here, too, he became attached to one of the licensed companies of players competing for the favours of the theatre-loving London populace and, in his late twenties, while serving it as an actor, made a name for himself by writing for it three successful chronicle plays on the troubled reign and civil wars of Henry VI, as well as two modish Italian comedies, *The Two Gentlemen of Verona* and *The Comedy of Errors*.

At this point he seems to have won the affectionate friendship and patronage of the eighteen-year-old earl of Southampton, ten years his junior, a wealthy young nobleman of the highest fashion in whose household he lived, possibly as some kind of tutor, during the plague years of 1592–93 when the London theatres were shut. During this time, in addition to a long intimate sonnet sequence for his patron, he wrote two much admired courtly poems dedicated to him, *Venus and Adonis* and *The Rape of Lucrece*. All this, as well as his growing fame as a maker of plays, brought him before he was thirty to the notice and into the society of the royal Court and aristocracy.

In the first half of Elizabeth's reign a professional class of licensed actors, presenting plays with immense popular appeal, had grown out of the universal English love of acting and drama – a legacy of the medieval Church which had familiarized the Christian story and its legends through the dramatized ritual of its services and the Christmas, Resurrection and other seasonal plays acted in church and churchyard. Supplemented by the 'mystery' plays given by the trade and religious guilds of the cities and chartered towns, in an age without newspapers and popular books when very few could read, everyone had taken part in these, both as actors and spectators. When after the Reformation a Protestant Church discarded them in favour of sermons and extemporare prayers and readings from the translated scriptures, they continued to survive in the popular heart and habit in the shape of performances by troupes of strolling players, given in inn-courtyards, stage-wagons and barns in the towns, and by traditional mumming-plays and morris and country dances in the villages.

Frowned on by puritans addicted to long sermons and prayer-meetings and who, being themselves virtuous, wished there to be 'no more cakes and ale', attempts were made by the civic authorities in London and the larger towns to suppress such strolling players as 'sturdy rogues and vagabonds'. But the acting fraternity was supported, not only by the unpoliced urban populace of pleasure-loving artisans and apprentices, but by the Queen and Court, whose favourite entertainments were the seasonal dramatic performances enacted by the boys and choristers of the Chapel Royal and St Paul's at Christmas, Shrovetide and other holidays.

One feature of her reign was the patronage by drama-loving nobles of troupes or companies of actors who, in return for bearing the name and wearing the badge of their patronage, were protected by royal licence from the enactments of pietistical Parliaments and civic authorities. Their earliest patron was Elizabeth's first favour-ite and suitor, Lord Robert Dudley, who, it was said, 'loved a play and players'. In the opening year of her reign he formed his own company which, after his elevation to an earldom, became known as Leicester's Men. In 1574, faced by attempted restrictions on their freedom by the City, he helped to secure them Letters Patent under the Great Seal, giving them the right to act in London and all towns throughout England. Two years later, the leading member of his company, James Burbage, previously a joiner, built the first London theatre in the precincts of the former priory of Holywell in Shoreditch, just outside the City bounds; a second theatre, the Curtain, rose in the same year. Other licensed com-panies of players under aristocratic patronage were Lord Strange's, later the earl of Derby's the earl of Warwick's, the earl of Sussex's, Lord Chandos's, Lord Worcester's, the Lord Admiral's and the earl of Pembroke's, the company for which Shakespeare probably wrote his earliest plays. In 1583 five years before the Armada, the Queen's own company was formed, with the greatest clown in England, Richard Tarleton, the favourite alike of the London mob and of Elizabeth herself, who, it was recorded, once bade them 'take away the knave for making her laugh so excessively' as he fought against her little dog, Perrico de Faldas, with his sword and long staff.

The fare provided by such actors was declamatory, rhetorical and accompanied by highly dramatic action. Played on platforms closely surrounded by a jostling excited audience, the more important of whom sat not only in boxes above, but sometimes, on the stage itself, their appeal was even more to the ear than the eye. The contact between actor and audience was exceedingly close, the whole auditorium often rising and shouting in excited response to the words or actions of the leading players. As their art developed with practice, many of them acquired an extraordinary skill in arousing the emotions of their auditors. The plays they performed also evolved rapidly, from crude melodrama or rough and tumble, into a fine art, the best written by university graduates in declamatory blank verse from familiar Italian or classical tales. Among these were George Peele and John Lyly from Oxford, and Robert Greene, Thomas Nashe and Christopher Marlowe from Cambridge, the last, though short-lived, a poet of the highest promise, whose resounding lines in his *Tamburlane*, *Faustus* and *The Jew of Malta* aroused passionate excitement and admiration in his audiences.

After the plague years of 1592 and 1593, which broke up several of the old licensed companies and wrought havoc in the ranks of the university playwrights, Shakespeare, at the age of thirty, found himself, for the next decade, without a serious rival as a popular dramatist. In 1594, possibly with the help of his patron, Southampton, he bought a proprietary share in a new licensed company, the Lord Chamberlain's, formed under the patronage of the Queen's elderly cousin, Lord Hunsdon, who a few years earlier had been the 'protector' of Shakespeare's 'dark lady of the sonnets'. This company quickly outdistanced all rivals in the favour of both London audiences and the Court, its members including both James Burbage's son, the great tragedian, Richard Burbage – who made his name, like Garrick after him, playing the leading part in Shakespeare's *Richard III* – William Kemp, Thomas Pope, and John Hemmings who, with Henry Condell, collected and edited Shakespeare's plays for the folio edition published seven years after his death. On James I's accession, the company became the King's Company, its members wearing royal livery and becoming officers of the Household as grooms of the chamber-in-ordinary.

Shakespeare did not write his plays to be read or published; he wrote them to be acted. And since the effectiveness of speech in the densely packed proscenium theatres of the Elizabethan stage depended on declamation and sound, being a poet he used the language of poetry to mould and sway his auditors' feelings. Nurtured, like every Elizabethan through compulsory church attendance, on the noble rhythms and music of the Anglican Liturgy and the English translations of the Bible, he employed his natural sense of music – for no greater musician of words ever lived – to carry his audience with him into whatever mood the course of his play demanded. His was a genius for coining casual phrases whose use became universal. 'One touch of nature makes the whole world kin.' 'The slings and arrows of outrageous fortune.' 'The course of true love never did run smooth.' 'There's a divinity that shapes our ends, rough-hew them as we will.'

Having to make money for the company for which he worked and of which he was a shareholder, Shakespeare sought to give the public what it wanted. His first success, while still working for Lord Pembroke's company in the years after the defeat of the Armada, had been based on the patriotic fervour aroused by Spanish intervention in France in 1591 when, to aid the Huguenot king, Henri IV, English expeditions were sent to Britanny and Normandy under Sir John Norris and the dashing young earl of Essex, the popular hero of the London mob. Shakespeare's three chronicle plays about the reign of Henry VI and the Wars of the Roses, with their memories of 'brave Talbot' and his heroic defence of England's lost French dominions, were all appeals to the patriotism which Elizabeth's unifying reign had fostered. So were his later historical plays – founded on Holinshed's chronicle history of England – *King John* staged in 1596, the year of Essex's gallant exploits at Cadiz, *Richard II* and *Richard III*, the two parts of *Henry IV*, and *Henry V* in 1599, when amid scenes of tumultuous enthusiasm, as the Queen's Lord General and Viceroy of Ireland, the popular hero earl rode out of London, 'the people pressing exceedingly to behold him for more than four miles space, crying out "God save your Lordship" "God preserve your Honour."' Shakespeare's hope of his victorious return:

'Were now the General of our gracious Empress,
As in good time he may, from Ireland coming,
Bringing rebellion broached on his sword,
How many would the peaceful City quit
To welcome him.'

was to be tragically dashed. For it was the spoilt and neurotic favourite's reliance on his fatal popularity with the London mob that was to cause him, after his ignominious return from Ireland, to raise what the Queen contemptuously called his 'rebellion of one day', leading in February 1601 to his execution for High Treason, and his lieutenant Southampton's two years' incarceration in the Tower.

The features of Shakespeare's historical plays distinguished them from those of his contemporaries. One was his genius, anticipating that of Walter Scott in the Waverley novels, of peopling them not only with historic characters, but with imaginary ordinary men and women who figure in no history books but are the real stuff of contemporary life in any age. With these he created those wonderful scenes in Justice Shallow's Cotswold garden and Falstaff's haunts in the Boar's Head tavern and Mistress Quickly's Dolphin chamber, alternating with great scenes of state, give a sense of instant reality to his re-enactment of his country's past, as when he himself as Chorus introduced his *Henry V* to the excited audience at his company's new theatre, the Globe, on Bankside.

'Can this cockpit hold
The vasty fields of France? Or may we cram
Within this wooden O the very casques
That did affright the air at Agincourt?'

The other distinguishing feature of Shakespeare's historical plays was his political realism, rare in writers and intellectuals who in all ages tend to lack it in their obsession with ideals and abstractions. Like the Queen, he never forgot the fallibility which underlay the relations of human beings in society. For all his keen perception of the injustices and corruptions of the world, he was, therefore, a conformist and never a rebel or destroyer. With Dr Johnson he saw how precarious were the assumptions on which

civilization rests, and how easily they can be undermined. So in
the great speech on degree in *Troilus and Cressida* – written just
before Elizabeth's death with its renewed fears of a disputed
succession – Ulysses asks

'How could communities,
Degrees in schools and brotherhoods in cities,
Peaceful commerce from dividable shores,
The primogenetive and due of birth,
Prerogative of age, crowns, sceptres, laurels
But by degree, stand in authentic place?
Take but degree away, untune that string
And hark what discord follows! . . .'

Not all Shakespeare's plays were written for the London
theatre and its tough masculine audiences. Several were intended
for performances at Court, where he was a favourite playwright of
both Elizabeth and James I, or in some great country house. An
early example was his *A Midsummer Night's Dream*, produced in
May 1594 to grace the nuptials of Southampton's mother to Sir
Thomas Heneage, Vice Chamberlain of the royal household. In
this enchanting play, moonlit with exquisite poetry, Shakespeare
let his fancy loose, peopling the great hall, where his fantasy was
probably played, with the creatures, real and imaginary, of his
Warwickshire childhood: Snug the joiner, Snout the tinker, and
Bottom the weaver, with whom, so unaccountably, Titania, Queen
of the Fairies, fell in love. Her king, Oberon, and her attendant
fairies-in-waiting, Peasblossom, Cobweb, Moth and Mustardseed,
share the stage with the humans.

'Through the house give glimmering light,
By the dead and drowsy fire,
Every elf and fairy sprite
Hop as light as bird to briar.'

The same happy intrusion of the scenes and fauna of his native
countryside occurs in half a dozen of his plays, though intended
for the rough London theatre. Even in one of his earliest comedies,
the audience is suddenly transported from a royal palace in Navarre
to an English village, first in summer, then in winter.

Drama being constructed out of the clash and contact of human beings with one another, the basic work of an Elizabethan play-wright was to use the spoken word to delineate character. Where Shakespeare differed from nearly all his predecessors and con-temporaries was that, instead of using stock types as the personae of his plays, he made them real human beings with all the differ-ences and idiosyncrasies of individual human nature and charac-ter. In this he was aided by the extraordinary range of his sym-pathies which enabled him to enter into the inner feelings of every character he delineated.

It is this quality that informs his tragedies and raises them to a level unattained by even the Greek dramatists. The essence of classic pagan tragedy was the fall, from the height of power and fortune, of a great man, struck down by the inexorable workings of Fate or Nemesis. But in the Christian drama of Shakespeare the tragedy which befalls a great man arises primarily out of some flaw or weakness in an otherwise noble character which exposes him and others dependent on him to the buffets of Fate and mis-fortune – ambition, jealousy, passion, arrogance, indecision. The element of free will which lies at the heart of the Christian concept enters into and dominates the dramatic story.

After the great sequence of tragedies which Shakespeare wrote between his thirty-sixth and forty-fifth year – *Julius Caesar, Ham-let, Othello, King Lear, Macbeth, Antony and Cleopatra, Corio-lanus, Timon of Athens* – in his last plays he turned, like the great artist he was, to something new: to a theme which was neither comedy nor tragedy, but that of human repentance and forgive-ness. All three involved bringing in a new generation to redress the failure and folly of an old. And all three – *Cymbeline, The Winter's Tale* and *The Tempest* – are transfused with a gentle and elegiac music. The last of these pastoral romances, *The Tempest*, was inspired by the account of a hurricane which shipwrecked, on the then still unexplored island of Bermuda, the flagship of the expedition sent by the London Virginia Company in the spring of 1609 to put the infant American colony, as was hoped, on its feet. The account of the storm and shipwreck, in which everyone was miraculously saved, reached England in a news letter sent home by one of the survivors, William Strachey, Secretary designate to the

Virginia colony. From it, and his description of the island, Shakespeare reconstructed the story in this magical play, first produced
on Hallowe'en night 1611 at Whitehall before the King. It was one
of the fourteen plays, six of them by Shakespeare, played two years
later to celebrate the nuptials in 1613 of the Princess Elizabeth –
Wotton's 'Queen of Hearts' and ancestress of the present Queen –
to the Elector Palatine of the Rhine.

In its course, Shakespeare himself, in the person of the magi-
cian, Prospero, bade farewell to his art:

'Our revels now are ended. These our actors
As I foretold you, were all spirits, and
Are melted into air, into thin air:
And like the baseless fabric of this vision
The cloud-capp'd towers, the gorgeous palaces,
The solemn temples, the great globe itself,
Yea, all which it inherit, shall dissolve
And, like this insubstantial pageant faded,
Leave not a rack behind. We are such stuff
As dreams are made on, and our little life
Is rounded with a sleep.'

It was not, however, quite Shakespeare's last word. In 1612,
when he was forty-eight and four years before his death in April
1616, he contributed a final historical play on the reign of Henry
VIII. In it, describing the christening of Henry's daughter, the
Princess Elizabeth, he paid his tribute to the great Queen and her
reign, of which he and his work had been part:

'This royal infant – Heaven still move about her –
Though in her cradle, yet now promises
Upon this land a thousand thousand blessings,
Which time shall bring to ripeness: She shall be . . .
A pattern to all princes living with her,
And all that shall succeed . . .
In her days every man shall eat in safety
Under his own vine what he plants, and sing
The merry songs of peace to all his neighbours . . .
She shall be to the happiness of England
An aged princess; many days shall see her
And yet no day without a deed to crown it.'

CHAPTER NINE

The Wasted Heritage

'O thou, that dear and happy isle,
The garden of the world erewhile,
Thou Paradise of the Four Seas
Which Heaven planted us to please,
But – to exclude the world – did guard,
With wat'ry, if not flaming, sword:
What luckless apple did we taste
To make us mortal and thee waste?'

Andrew Marvell

WHEN THE LAST SURVIVORS of the Elizabethan age followed one another to the grave – Shakespeare and Hakluyt in 1616, Ralegh two years later, Francis Bacon and Bishop Andrewes, a saintly reviser of the King James Bible, in 1626, and John Donne, the great preacher poet Dean of St Paul's, in 1633 – England was already the parent kingdom of a cluster of minute plantations and trading stations on the far side of the world's oceans. And, for the first time in its history, the whole British island was under a single crown.

The dead queen's closing legacy to her country at the start of a new century was that England and Scotland were now joined under the same crown within the confines of a single isle. Thanks to the queen's far-sighted and patient statesmanship, the age-long enmity between England and Scotland had ended in a union of their crowns under her chosen – though never publicly acknowledged – heir, James VI of Scotland, son of her cousin and former prisoner, Mary Queen of Scots. From Britain's strategic position commanding the sea-lanes between the open Atlantic and the ports of northern France, the Low Countries, Germany and the Baltic, her merchants and seamen, under Elizabeth's unifying rule, had proved their ability to sail and trade in every ocean of the world. Theirs, if they chose to use it, was a key to ever-expanding future wealth and fortune. More even than her thriving agriculture and rich sheep pastures and cloth manufacture, the sea offered a field of opportunity for England's more adventurous and vigorous sons. For set in ocean, with 7,000 miles of deeply indented coastline longer than that of any European country, no town in the island was more than a hundred miles from salt water. In her brilliant survey of pre-Civil War England, Dame Veronica Wedgwood has calculated that in the 1630s at least half her people derived their livelihood, directly or indirectly, from the sea. Fisheries, coastal and river trade, ocean voyages, the manning of the king's ships in peace and war, privateering, and, outside the law, piracy, had become the sinews of a commercial nation's strength.

James Stuart, the VI of Scotland and I of England, who had succeeded to the throne of this young and vigorous maritime kingdom, was the only son of Mary Queen of Scots by her murdered bridegroom, Lord Darnley. After his Catholic mother's dethronement and flight to England, James had been brought up from babyhood as a Calvinist Protestant by the rigid fanatics who surrounded and controlled his throne. Faced, like all his predecessors of the House of Stuart by the agelong turbulence and treachery of the Scottish feudal nobility* – whose pursuit of family feud and greed so often transcended both their loyalty to the throne and their religious professions – he grew habituated to scenes of civil war and slaughter. On more than one occasion rival nobles carried their bloody broils into their young King's presence, kidnapping or holding him up to political ransom as they had done his hapless mother before him. Of the five Regents who governed Scotland during his minority only one died a natural death. Mal-

---

* Lord Melbourne, Queen Victoria's first Prime Minister and mentor, asked by his youthful sovereign to tell her something about her Scottish, as distinct from her English, royal progenitors, is said, after looking it up in a book, to have replied, 'It's all very sad, Ma'am, and very confusing. All of them were called James and all of them were murdered.'

formed in his mother's womb, possibly as a result of her heroic midnight ride to Dunbar after the gang murder, in her presence, of her secretary Riccio, the timid boy-king developed such a horror of cold steel that he could not bear the sight of a drawn sword. His early experiences made him a lover of peace at almost any price.

Yet from the stern Calvinist pedagogues who instructed him in their austere branch of the Protestant faith, he had received such a grounding in theological lore, that he proved as much an educational prodigy as had his cousin, Elizabeth, in the very different liberal and humanist climate of her father's Renaissance court. At the age of ten, he could translate extempore a chapter of the Bible from Latin into French and from French into English. An author at eighteen, before he succeeded to the English throne he had written and published seven learned theological works. There is a contemporary portrait of him in his nineteenth year, from the pen of a French agent at his court at a time when France, taking advantage of his obsession for a French-educated Catholic cousin, was trying to wean back Scotland – half of whose northern nobility still inclined to the old faith – from its new Protestant and English connection.

'He is wonderfully clever . . . full of honourable ambition and has an excellent opinion of himself. Though, owing to the terrorism under which he has been brought up, he is timid with the great lords and seldom ventures to contradict them; his special anxiety is to be thought hardy and a man of courage . . . He dislikes dancing and music and amorous talk and curiosity of dress and courtly activities. He eats, speaks, dresses and plays like a boor, and he is no better in the company of women.

'He is never still for a moment, but walks perpetually up and down the room and his gait is sprawling and awkward; his voice is loud and his words sententious. He prefers hunting to all other amusements and will be six hours together on horseback. His body is feeble, yet he is not delicate; in a word, he is an old young man . . .

'He is prodigiously conceited and he underrates other princes. He irritates his subjects by indiscreet and violent attachments. He is idle and careless, too easy and too much

given to pleasure, particularly to the chase, leaving his
affairs to be managed by others . . . He told me that, whatever he seemed, he was aware of everything of consequence
that was going on, and that he could afford to spend time in
hunting for that, when he attended to business, he could do
in an hour more than others could do in a day.'

When, twenty years later, he succeeded to the English throne,
the boy had proved father to the man. Hobbledehoy and prig he
may have been, but schooled in the strenuous pedantries and
logical athleticism of the Presbyterian Kirk, he had made himself
a master of dialectic. Nursed and disciplined on an uncompromising diet of tough, argumentative and interminable theological
dogma, he was an inveterate reader, with an international reputation for learning and scholarship. As a controversialist, in an age of
universal religious controversy, he had few masters. Passionately
addicted to the study of theology – a subject over which all his
contemporaries, learned and unlearned alike, were for ever contending – he loved to elucidate and expound its finer points.
Inordinately vain, he loved, too, to parade his learning and erudi-
tion. He was the most learned sovereign ever to sit on a Scottish –
or English – throne.

And for all his physical timidity he had somehow contrived,
not only to survive, but, little by little, to strengthen his hold on
his stark northern kingdom. By setting and balancing its brutal
feudal nobles against the equally arrogant plebeian ministers of the
Kirk, who – believing themselves God's elect and the sole reposi-
tary of the Gospel as revealed to them in all its simplicity and truth –
were for ever lecturing, finding fault with and rebuking him, he
gradually succeeded in moderating the more extreme pretences of
both his would-be masters. Against the insistence of Knox's
successor, Andrew Melville – who once called him, to his face,
'God's silly vassal' – that Scotland was a dual monarchy whose
titular king was himself a subject of another and higher King who
made His will on earth known and obeyed through the witness of
the Presbyterian Kirk, James in the end succeeded in getting its
General Assembly tacitly to accept some kind of constitutional
relationship with the Crown by agreeing that its individual

ministers should not attack and abuse him from the pulpit until their charges and complaints had been officially investigated and adjudicated. And three years before his accession to the English throne, for the first time since the leaders of the Scottish Reformation had renounced and repudiated episcopacy for ever, he was able to introduce three Protestant bishops, nominated by himself, into the ancient royal Parliament or Estates of the realm through which the kings of Scotland had traditionally governed their turbulent dominion.

An hereditary sovereign in an intensely monarchical and religious age, for all his shrewd and canny awareness of his stark northern countrymen's beliefs and prejudices – for he was every inch a Scot – James had reacted instinctively against their democratic Presbyterian form of Church government as incompatible with kingly authority. This had caused him to look with sympathy – and eager anticipation – towards his aged cousin Elizabeth's Anglican Church establishment, where ecclesiastical authority, in loyal subordination to and close co-operation with the Crown, was exercised by bishops of supposed apostolic descent, not from a perverted and degenerate Italian papal see, but from the early Fathers of a pure and still undefiled Christianity. For, in common with all contemporary kings and princes Protestant and Catholic alike, James believed that as an anointed sovereign he was entrusted with a task sanctioned by Heaven, and that an episcopal Church was the instrument through which such sacred royal responsibilities could best be exercised. And, unlike other princes, he had himself clearly defined his conviction in his writings. Kings, he wrote in his *The True Law of Free Monarchies*, were appointed by God to govern and subjects to obey.

So, when in March 1603, the long-awaited summons reached him – galloped in four days from the darkened palace where the dead Elizabeth lay, while her people, haunted by fears of a disputed succession and civil war, turned anxious eyes to the north – the 'British Solomon' hastened southwards to take possession of the glittering heritage now so providentially his. Greed, as well as the desire to exercise his kingly wisdom in a wider sphere impelled him. For the frugal resources of his barren northern kingdom had

Charles II, "disguised as the manservant of Jane Lane, who, riding postillion behind him carried for a week the crown of England in her hands during the King's flight after Worcester."

"Old George Monk, the first professional soldier of that unique school which believes that the military arm should be subordinate to the civil."

allowed little scope for princely liberality or for full indulgence in the costlier pleasures of the chase, the table and the bottle, to all of which he was addicted. For, as well as a kindly, he was also a greedy man. He wished his subjects well, but himself even more so. And as he proceeded southwards, in the happiest of Scotland's invasions of England, both the Scottish courtiers and favourites who accompanied him, and those of his new subjects who hurried north to greet him, encountered a shower of royal largesse. And while he scattered grants and honours as though from an inexhaustible source, he indulged himself freely, pursuing his favourite pastime of hunting all day in England's northern deer forests, and in feasting and drinking every night in the hospitable castles and country homes of the nobles and gentry along the road.

Nor was he unmindful of the benefits he intended to confer on England through his skill in kingship. Among these was to be an end to the long wasting war with Spain and the extension to his new realm, so long deprived of it, of the advantages of peaceful commerce with that rich and powerful country which, thanks to him, Scotland had long enjoyed. And, as earnest of his goodwill to the Escorial – still the crusading stronghold of Catholic orthodoxy – and of his tolerant and broad-minded approach to the doctrinal differences which so bitterly divided Christendom, firm and convinced Protestant though he was, he proposed to extend a new toleration to his English Catholic subjects by waiving the recusancy fines for non-attendance at Anglican services. Above all, he planned to confer on both his new and old subjects alike the removal of all legal, constitutional and fiscal barriers between their two countries, so creating a common British citizenship for all with a consequent enlargement of his own royal powers.

At York England's new sovereign was met by the dead Queen's principal adviser and Secretary of State, Robert Cecil – the younger son and political successor of the great Lord Burghley. Among others who flocked to greet him was Shakespeare's former patron, the young earl of Southampton, who, with his faithful cat, had been imprisoned for the past two years in the Tower as the chief lieutenant of the beheaded earl of Essex, one of whose offences against their jealous royal mistress had been a secret correspondence with the too expectant Scottish king.

These suitors to the rising sun were now able to assess their new sovereign in person. It proved, though at the moment a very gracious, somewhat grotesque one. For King James's tongue was too large for his mouth, and hung out while he spoke, causing him to slobber over his food and, even more, when he drank. Nor was he very cleanly in either his dress or person, seldom washing his hands or bothering to change his clothes which, padded against attempted assassination were often filthy, especially after hunting. For he had a curious and repellant habit, after the kill, of plunging his legs into the warm bowels of the dead stag, either out of superstition – for, despite his learning or perhaps because of it, he was intensely superstitious – or because he imagined he derived some physical benefit from the practice.

Yet, though lacking in the personal dignity which had distinguished his dead predecessor and her Tudor father and grandfather, he had an open and friendly nature. For all his boorish northern manners was clearly conscious of his regality, to which his learning and fame as a scholar added additional respect. His familiar speech was pungent and pawky, and replete with homely sense and wit. But it was too often a scholar's wit, of superior airs and demeaning to those against whom it was directed. His openness would be interpreted by his subjects and Parliaments as weakness; his learning as schoolmastery, his insistence on his royal dignity as vanity (for whereas Elizabeth would inspire respect when she stood upon regality, James had not the presence to do so), and his generosity as indulgence. It is sad to agree with Notestein's judgement that 'few kings have been so fitted by nature to call forth an opposition'.

One of his first acts, as befitted a man who believed himself an eminent theologian, was to convene, at the request of the Puritan clergy, an assembly of the Anglican Church at Hampton Court in 1604. It was this assembly which decided to produce the Authorized Version of the Bible, and to issue the revised edition of the Prayer Book which is now part of our national heritage. James confirmed his childhood hostility towards Puritanism, though agreeing with their wish 'to see Sunday more strictly observed', refusing to change the Anglican and Elizabethan confession of faith, or its ceremonies, its ritual, and above all its episcopal authority, whose limitation he refused even to discuss. On the contrary, he identified the bishops with monarchial authority, and stressing the supremacy of the Crown over that of the Church, second only to God, insisted on the use of the Book of Common Prayer by every holder of an ecclesiastical benefice, summarizing his thought in the later notorious phrase 'No bishop, no king'.

This disappointment to the Puritans, whose influence James undoubtedly underestimated, did not, on the other hand, give solace to those at the opposite religious persuasion, the Catholics. When Robert Cecil began to tighten the penalties for Catholic recusancy, and rumours circulated of yet more harsh penalties from the theologian king, there was made yet further evidence of James's inability to bind his subjects together, despite their widely different religious views, as Elizabeth had done. A Catholic faction identified the Privy Council and Parliament as the principal sources of this intolerant treatment, and resolved that the neatest way of disposing of the problem would be to assassinate as many Parliamentarians and Privy Councillors as possible. Robert Catesby, a shadowy figure, whose background allows for a variety of interpretations of madness and anarchy in his motives, plotted to capture the king's children and in the ensuing confusion seize power with the aid of a few armed men. On the evening of November 5th, 1605, as Catesby and most of his fellow conspirators were in the Midlands preparing the abduction of the royal children, Guy Fawkes filled one of the cellars of the Houses of Parliament, to which he had been given access by the earl of Northumberland's steward, with a huge quantity of gunpowder. As he lay there, waiting for the convening of Parliament the following morning, he was discovered by Cecil's men, whence he was led away, and in time, executed. Cecil had been warned by Lord Mounteagle, whose connection with the conspirators remains unclear, that desperate actions were afoot, and had been keeping watch on the movements of numerous Catholic suspects. The other conspirators were quickly rounded up, to later generations serving annually on November 5th, in their madcap enterprise, as the focus of the loyalty of the English people to their parliamentary tradition, and, rather unfairly, as evidence of the unreliability of Catholic adherence to such a tradition.

The swift action of the King's minister did nothing to allay the growing distrust between King and Parliament. They soon came to blows over the trivial matter of who should be the judge of disputed election returns. In 1610 they failed to agree on an imaginative scheme proposed by Cecil – now created earl of Salisbury – known as the Great Contract, which transferred to Parliament many of the sources of the King's ordinary revenue, in return for a fixed annual grant from Parliament of a size which would have been sufficient to clear his debts and cover much of his usual expenditure. But Salisbury's expedients since 1603 to try to raise revenue and cover James's gross extravagances – he spent more on jewels every year than he did on the army – had led some members to regard him as had been Henry VII's hated lieutenants, Empsom and Dudley, who had worked for a monarch much less lavish but with as great a need to increase his revenue. Salisbury had leased the customs out to tax farmers and introduced a new Book of Rates; he had tightened the administration of the Crown lands to such an extent that in some royal forests every tree was numbered to ensure that the Crown was not suffering from poachers. His wise scheme was rejected, and with it one of the methods of accommodation on financial matters which could have lessened the tension that led ultimately to the Great War in Charles I's reign. Exhausted by his efforts on James's behalf, Salisbury was forced to resort to the sale of titles, auctioning earldoms at £10,000 a piece before he collapsed in 1612. The Crown's credit declined so far that in 1615 a London brewer refused to supply beer to the royal household without payment in advance. It was a poor and far cry from the glorious days in which Elizabeth and Salisbury's father had managed and led Parliament, to fuse Crown and people together in a common, and mutually respecting bond.

Without Salisbury's hand, the government moved with more and more uncertainty. In the same year, 1615, James committed the folly which most justly earned him the title 'the wisest fool in Christendom'. Knowing his vicious attraction to personable young men, one of the jealous court factions pushed under James's eye George Villiers, who was advanced from place to place at court with an astonishing rapidity. Clarendon, in his *History of the Great Rebellion* said that no man 'rose in so short a time, to so much greatness of honour, fame and fortune, upon no other advantage or recommendation, than the beauty and gracefulness of his person.' James showered upon him the dukedom of Buckingham, the earldom of Coventry and countless lesser titles, made him chief of the army and the navy, Lord Warden of the Cinque Ports, Gentleman of the Bedchamber and a Knight of the Garter. His grip on patronage at court became seemingly watertight, and increasingly, he exercised control over Prince Charles, the heir to the throne, undertaking with him a foolhardy expedition to Spain in 1623 to indulge Charles's fantasies of romantic involvements at that court. His influence continued over the opening years of Charles's own reign, after his father's death in 1625. That it became impossible for the Stuart kings to see eye to eye with their Parliaments over matters of prerogative, dignity and finance is hardly surprising when the chief court favourite was a man of Buckingham's stamp, a man who could spend £3,000 per year on clothes and found his official income of £15,000 per year hardly enough to support his vanity.

CHAPTER TEN

Severed Crown and Restoration
1625–1665

'The King is a suitor to you . . . that you will join with him
in restoring the whole nation to its primitive temper and
integrity, its old good manners, its old good humour and its
old good nature; good nature a virtue so peculiar to you . . .
that it can be translated into no other language, hardly
practised by any other people.'

Lord Chancellor Clarendon's reconciliation Speech
to Parliament, September 1660

IN 1625, nine years after Shakespeare's death, Charles I succeeded
his father whose academic belief in the Divine Right of Kings he
shared with an almost mystical belief. During the first four years
of his reign he became embroiled with three successive Parliaments, whose claims to control policy and criticize his ministers
he regarded as treasonable, and whose reluctance to grant taxes he
bitterly resented. After 1629 he governed the country for eleven
years by proclamation without calling a Parliament. His intentions
were benevolent – for he was essentially a good man – but, unlike
the far more autocratic Tudors, he completely failed to appreciate
Edward I's dictum of three centuries before that that which touches
all should be approved by all, and that to govern England effectively
there must be 'counsel and consent'. By identifying the Crown
with the exercise of untrammelled administrative authority – in
that age frequently corrupt, occasionally unjust and nearly always
inefficient – and with ideological and religious beliefs antipathetic
to a vocal majority of his people, he undermined the instinctive
love of the nation for its hereditary monarchy. Though a Protestant, his ecclesiastical leanings, unlike those of his increasingly

Puritan subjects, were those of the high Anglican Church of which by law he was the Head. His love of seemly ritual and ceremonial, as well as a devoted marriage to a French Roman Catholic princess, Henrietta Maria, made them suspect him, however wrongly, of Popery.

A man of rare artistic feeling and perception – he was a great collector of paintings and sculpture – Charles was a thoroughly bad politician. A poor judge of character, he lacked flexibility and shrewdness and had little sense of timing. His favourite church-man, Archbishop Laud, described him as 'a mild and gracious prince who knew not how to be or to be made great.' Having blundered into an unnecessary war with his fanatically Presby-terian Scottish subjects by trying to impose bishops and an English, and therefore alien, prayer book on them, in 1640 he was forced by lack of money to call a Parliament. The cumulative undercurrent of criticism which he had so long dammed became a raging torrent and, backed by the London mob, his opponents who included John Hampden, the Buckinghamshire squire who had refused to pay ship money, under the leadership of the great parliamentarian, John Pym, compelled him, among other dis-tasteful things, to give up his right of dissolution and sign the death warrant of his faithful minister, Strafford. Finally, rather than surrender his control of the militia, in 1642 he appealed to arms, the conservative north and west of the country loyally supporting him, while the richer, more populous and more vigorous south-east and the capital backed Parliament.

In four years' civil war, helped by the Scots and later by a professional 'New Model' army, Parliament was ultimately vic-torious. It was the most divisive and most decisive war ever fought within these shores, ultimately ensuring the ascendancy of the rights of the people, as represented in Parliament, over the preroga-tive of the king. But though by 1646 a captive Charles was forced to concede every parliamentary demand, so fanatical was his belief in his divine right to govern that he would not be bound by any concession. And though the victorious Parliament, Presbyteri-an Scotland and the Army all fell out with one another and, as a result of the King's intrigues, became embroiled in 1648 in a second

Civil War, the ultimate victors – the Army chiefs – resolved on his death as the only way of preserving the war's gains. Yet by putting Charles on trial for his life in Westminster Hall, they enabled him to challenge, publicly and with great eloquence, their legal right to try him. By this, and his superb dignity on the scaffold, he ultimately saved – at the loss of his head – both the hereditary Crown and the Church of England, which by his earlier obduracy he had brought to the point of ruin. 'I do stand more for the liberty of my people,' he declared, 'than any here that came to be my pretended judges, and therefore let me know by what lawful authority I am seated here . . . For if power without law may make law, may alter the fundamental laws of the kingdom, I know not what subject he is in England can be assured of his life or anything he can call his own.'

After Charles's public execution in Whitehall on January 30th, 1649, on the balcony of his own banqueting Hall, Oliver Cromwell – a Huntingdonshire squire and member of Parliament, who had helped to found and train the all-powerful New Model Army and, at the decisive battles of Marston Moor and Naseby in 1644 and 1645, had proved himself a cavalry commander of genius – found himself increasingly called upon to direct the destinies of the new republic or Commonwealth. In 1649, as Commander-in-Chief in Ireland, he ended a cruel and interminable racial and religious war by storming Drogheda and Wexford and ruthlessly putting their stubborn papist garrisons to the sword. In 1650, when the Scots invited the young king in exile, Charles II, to Scotland, Cromwell routed them at Dunbar, and a year later, after they had invaded western England, at Worcester. In 1653 he intervened decisively in politics by turning out the corrupt and intolerant remnant or 'Rump' of the oft-purged Long Parliament, and assumed the title of Protector, seeing himself, as he said, as 'set upon a watch-tower to see what may be for the good of this nation, and what may be for the prevention of evil.'

For five years Cromwell – or Old Noll, as his opponents called him – was virtually dictator. Being an Englishman with a respect for legality, he was not happy. Nor, though he wished to see England the kind of land he and his Puritan soldiers had dreamed of and fought for, did he believe this could be achieved by letting unrealistic fanatics – Agitators, Levellers, Anabaptists – set up an egalitarian Utopia without rule, order or social stability. Despite the intensity of his Puritan idealism, Cromwell was a realist. The paradox of his position – and of the nation whose underlying instincts he represented – was that, having fought to destroy the unparliamentary rule of Charles I, he came eventually to realize that the only kind of state in which Englishmen could be happy was that of a constitutional monarchy in which personal liberty and property were assured under the rule of law. 'A nobleman, a gentleman, a yeoman,' he said, 'that is a good interest of a nation, and a great one.'

For Cromwell, the independent Puritan revolutionary who set out to

> 'cast the kingdoms old
> into another mould,'

proved at heart a conservative who wished to conserve and ultimately – though he did not realize it – restore the English polity which the Stuart kings and the nation's reaction against them had between them destroyed. All his attempts to end his own military dictatorship by setting up checks and balances – the 'Praise-God Barebones' Parliament of the Saints, the Instrument of Government, the rule of the Major-Generals – ended in failure. When in 1658 he died, after reluctantly refusing the proffered Crown, it became clear, during an eighteen months' anarchic interregnum of warring major-generals, that nothing could meet England's need but the restoration of Crown and Parliament.

*　　*　　*

The Restoration began, seven years before the great Lord Protector's death, on the evening of his 'crowning mercy' and final victory – Worcester. As the last streaks of daylight, September 3rd, 1651, fell on the Worcestershire landscape, a tall dark fugitive drew in his horse on a lonely heath. About him clustered some sixty lords and officers, whose looks told a tale of peril and defeat.

At that moment the shadow of the King of England and Scotland had touched a lower point than any to which his twenty-one chequered and poverty-stricken years had brought him. A few weeks before he had ridden at the head of a Scottish army along the moorland road by Shap Fell, watching, across the unclouded atmosphere of summer, the distant Derbyshire heights beckoning him on to London and his father's lost crown. Now his gallant gamble had ended in dust. All day he had fought at the head of outnumbered and despairing men as Cromwell's net closed in on Worcester. Only at evening, as the shattered Scots poured out through St Martin's Gate, had King Charles the Second, protesting he would rather die than see the consequence of so fatal a day, been swept by the rout from the doomed city.

At Barbourne Bridge, where the grass highway to the north was crowded with flying men, there had been a hasty consultation. Charles himself had wished to ride alone to London, trusting to arrive before news of the battle and so take ship to France. But the day was already waning, and his companions had dissuaded him from this desperate course. Leaving the main line of fugitives to the west, they rode with him across a land of wooded valleys and little hills, until at nightfall they reached Kinver Heath. Here the scout, who was leading, admitted that he was lost.

In the confusion that followed, the earl of Derby brought forward a Catholic gentleman, Charles Giffard, owner of a remote house in Shropshire, near which he had found shelter a few days before. To Giffard and his servant, Yates, a poor rustic skilful in the ways of that country, the fugitives entrusted themselves. So guided they came down into the hidden lands below. As complete darkness fell, romance spread her cloak over the king and hid him from the thousand eyes that sought him.

Nobody suspected the little party of Cavaliers who walked their horses through the streets of sleeping Stourbridge. At an inn near Wordsley the king stopped for a hasty tankard of ale: then rode on through the night, a crust of bread in one hand and meat in the other. Giffard rode at his side, telling him of the secret hiding-places of Whiteladies and Boscobel, while the broken lords and officers trotted behind. For some hours they followed a maze of winding lanes till they came to the edge of Brewood Forest. Here, fifty miles from the battlefield and a little before dawn, the tired king saw the dark outlines of the ruined monastery of Whiteladies.

The clatter of hooves and the whispered calls of Giffard brought down the Penderels, the poor Catholic woodcutters who tenanted the house. To these humble folk the great personages, crowding into the hall, turned for help and advice. While a hasty message was sent to bring William, the eldest of the five Penderel brothers, from Boscobel, the King, in an inner chamber, broke his fast on sack and biscuits. A few minutes later Lord Derby brought in William and Richard Penderel to him, telling them that they must have a care of him. To this they proudly and gladly assented. Richard went out to fetch some country clothes, while the King stripped and put on a rough noggen shirt. The first lines of dawn were appearing when Richard returned with an old sweaty doublet, a green, threadbare coat and a greasy steeple hat without band or lining. Lord Wilmot, the stoutest and merriest of the fugitives, began to cut the long royal locks with a knife, but did the job so badly that Richard was commanded to finish it, which he did in great pride with a basin and a pair of shears. Placing his hands up the chimney, Charles, who, despite peril and weariness, could not refrain from laughing, completed his make-up by blacking his face. Then, while his companions rode off to join the flying Scots, he went out into the dawn with Richard Penderel and a bill-hook.

It was raining. All day the King crouched in the damp undergrowth of a little wood, called Spring Coppice. About midday Penderel's sister-in-law, Elizabeth Yates, brought him a blanket to sit on and a mess of milk, butter and eggs. She told him news of the world outside the woods – of long streams of Scottish fugitives and pursuing Roundheads and of search-parties already at Whiteladies. Afterwards he fell into a broken slumber.

Charles had changed much since van Dyck had painted him amid the silken dresses, the flowing hair, the lace, the pearls, the roses of his father's court. Sent at fifteen to preside over the king's ruined fortunes in the west, he had spent a last year of boyhood on English soil, amid the squabbles and debaucheries of a broken army, driven back week by week towards the sunset until the royal banner floated in solitary loyalty above Pendennis castle. Thence, on a March night in 1646, he had passed out of England.

He had become king at eighteen – of an estate of broken men and women, dangers, debts and beggary. Nor had he had anywhere to lay his head, for the rulers of Europe, overawed by the 'powerful devils at Westminster', had little wish to shelter him. Then the tempter had appeared in the homely guise of an elder of the Presbyterian Kirk and offered him the Scottish Crown in return for the renunciation of the Anglican cause for which his father had died. After many pitiful evasions, to find bread for himself and his followers, he had taken the Covenant and sailed for Scotland. In the year which followed, he had learnt many things. He had been humiliated and catechised; subjected to an infinity of dull, tedious sermons, made to do penance for the sins of his father and the idolatry of his mother, and threatened with betrayal to his iron foes. Yet by patience and a certain gentle persuasiveness he had at last overthrown the supremacy of Argyll and the Kirk, and at the eleventh hour rallied a united Scotland behind him. But his triumph had come too late; half the country was in Cromwell's hands, and the sequel had been that bold, desperate march into England. Now an adventure, which had begun in shame, degredation and the sorrow of honest men, was ending in a little wet wood in a corner of the land he had come to conquer. But it was pleasanter to sleep under a hedge in England than in a palace in Scotland: even the rain and the weariness were better than that.

In the intervals of sleep the King talked to Penderel. He had still hopes of reaching London and there taking ship for France, but his companion knew of no one on that road who could assist him. It was therefore decided that he should make for Wales, where he had many friends, and that Penderel should escort him that night to Madeley, ten miles to the west, where a Catholic gentleman of his acquaintance might secure them a passage across the Severn.

A little before dusk the two left the wood and made their way across a heath to Hobbel Grange, the cottage where Richard lived

with his widowed mother. The old peasant came out to welcome
her king, blessing God that she had raised up children to succour
him in his time of need. She gave him bread, cheese and a fricassee
of bacon and eggs, and wondered to see his appetite, half regal and
wholly boyish. While she waited at the table, her son-in-law,
Francis Yates – who not long after was hanged at Oxford for his
share in the affair – came in with thirty pieces of silver, his all,
which he offered to the King. The latter who – though he perhaps
did not realize the full grandeur of the sacrifice – was not un-
acquainted with poverty, accepted ten of them in his necessity.

The night was pitch black, and Charles, after two days of
continuous action and exposure, was tired out. He and Penderel
made their way across country, avoiding the haunts of men and
clambering the wet fences and pales of remote enclosures. After
a few miles the trackway they were following dipped down to
bridge a stream, beside which stood a mill. The miller, hearing
footsteps, appeared at the door, and called on them to stop. Instead
of obeying, they ran blindly past him. The lane beyond the river
was muddy and steep, and the darkness was such that Charles had
nothing to guide him but the rustling of Penderel's breeches ahead
and the miller's footsteps behind. When his breath and courage
could carry him no longer, he flung himself into the hedge and
waited for the end. Here Penderel joined him, and the two lay
listening for their pursuer. But all was quiet, and after a time they
resumed their journey through the briary, dripping night. Poor
Charles was now in despair. His ill-made country shoes so racked
his feet that he threw them away and walked in his slashed stockings. His nose began to bleed, his head throbbed and his limbs
trembled with cold and weariness. 'Many times he cast himself
upon the ground with a desperate and obstinate resolution to rest
there till the morning, that he might shift with less torment, what
hazard so ever he ran. But his stout guide still prevailed with him
to make a new attempt, sometimes promising him that the way
should be better, sometimes assuring him that he had but a little
farther to go.' Shortly after midnight they came to Madeley.

At the edge of the village Penderel left the King in hiding and
made his way to Francis Wolfe's house. The old gentleman – he

was sixty-nine and lived to see the Restoration – came to the door. Penderel asked him if he would help a Royalist fugitive of rank to cross the Severn. Wolfe replied that the town was full of troops, and all the passages across the river guarded, and that he would not undertake so perilous a task for anyone but the King himself. But when Penderel blurted out the truth he expressed his readiness to venture his life and all that he had.

As the priest-holes in the house were known, the Wolfes and their daughter, Anne, sheltered the King all that day in a hayloft. In the evening they brought him food and money and new shoes and stockings. Then, as the passage of the Severn was judged impossible, the two travellers started on the return journey for Boscobel. At Evelith Mill, fearing their challenger of the previous night, they left the roadway, intending to ford the river above the bridge. Here Penderel's courage, for the first and last time, failed him. The heavy rain had swollen the little stream, and, child of the Midlands that he was, he confided that he could not swim and that it was a scurvy river. Thirty years afterwards Charles dictated the story of that passage to Pepys. 'So I told him that the river, being but a little one, I would undertake to help him over. Upon which we went over some closes to the river side, and I, entering the river first to see whether I could myself go over, who knew how to swim, found it was but a little above my middle, and, thereupon, taking Richard Penderel by the hand, I helped him over.' At about three o'clock that morning they passed the gateway of White-ladies and came into the woods between that place and Boscobel.

Leaving the King in the wood, Penderel went on to Boscobel to consult his brother as to the next step in their desperate enterprise. Here news awaited him. Lord Wilmot had found a refuge at the house of a neighbouring Catholic gentleman, Mr Whitgreave of Moseley Hall, through the offices of Father Huddleston, a priest who lived there. The other piece of news was that Colonel Careless, who two days before had led the last charge over the cobblestones of Worcester, was in hiding at Boscobel.

Careless accompanied Penderel back to the wood. He found the King, at the first stroke of dawn, sitting forlorn on a tree-stump, and could not refrain from weeping at the sight. The three men

walked together across the high ground towards Boscobel, looking
back, as the sun touched the Wrekin, on the far Welsh mountains
beyond the Severn.

At Boscobel, a black and white hunting-lodge amid a jumble
of barns and hayricks, the King breakfasted off bread, cheese and
small beer. Joan Penderel, William's wife, washed and dressed his
feet, cutting the blisters and inserting pads of paper between his
toes. Then, as it was probable that the house would be searched by
one of the numerous companies of soldiers in the neighbourhood,
Charles and Careless went out again into the wood.

At the edge of the copse, overlooking the highway, was an old
hollow oak. Into this, at Careless's suggestion, they climbed. The
road below was soon busy with passers-by, and through the veil of
leaves that concealed them they could see a party of soldiers searching the woods, where the Penderels, to allay suspicion, were 'peaking up and down' with their nut-hooks. After a time Charles, worn
out, fell asleep with his head in Careless's lap. As the hours passed
and the King's fitful slumber continued, Careless's supporting
arm became completely numbed. With infinite difficulty he awoke
him, motioning him to silence lest the troopers below should hear.

At nightfall, when the seekers had gone home to prepare for
the Sabbath, the Penderels brought a ladder to the tree, and Charles
and Careless, tired, cramped and hungry, returned to Boscobel.
They passed through the big parlour of the house – it still stands –
and up the stairs to a long attic gallery, used for storing cheeses.
Here Mrs Penderel, whom Charles christened Dame Joan, brought
them a supper of chickens. Afterwards, as the night was fine,
Charles sat for a while drinking wine in the garden, where Humphrey Penderel, the miller, came with news. While in the town that
day he had been questioned by a republican officer, who suspected
that he knew of the King's whereabouts. Humphrey had stoutly
denied all knowledge, whereupon the officer showed him a proclamation, threatening death to all who should aid 'Charles Stuart, a
long dark man above two yards high', and offering a reward of
£1,000 to anyone who should betray him. On hearing this Charles
could not help reflecting on the temptation to which the poor men
who sheltered him were exposed, but Careless, divining his

thoughts, assured him that had the reward been a thousand times as great it could not have shaken their fidelity.

Before the King retired to rest, Careless asked him what he would like for breakfast. Charles suggested mutton – a reply which caused the Penderels to exchange glances, for suspicion might be aroused should they attempt to obtain so unusual a luxury from their neighbours. He then made his way upstairs to a hiding-hole beneath the attic floor, where he spent the night on a straw pallet in a space little bigger than his own body.

He awoke early on Sunday morning, and the first sounds he heard were the church bells of Tong. Careless had been up before him and brought him his breakfast from Farmer Staunton's sheepcote. Together they fried the mutton collops before the fire.

Charles spent the greater part of the day reading in a 'pretty arbour' in the garden, where there was a stone seat and table. 'He commended the place for its retiredness,' and so rested. Here, as in other places, there is a touch of the *Pilgrim's Progress* in the narrative: one is reminded of the shepherd's boy in the Valley of Humiliation. The King's state was indeed very low. He was surrounded by his enemies, a price was set on his head, and his poor protectors were hard put to it to know where to turn for food for another day.

While the King spent that Sabbath in the garden John Penderel made his way to Moseley to consult Lord Wilmot and ask his help. He found Whitgreave and Father Huddleston, who informed him that Wilmot had left Moseley for Colonel Lane's house, Bentley, beyond Wolverhampton, intending thence to travel to the coast. As every hope of Charles's escape now depended on Wilmot, Penderel persuaded the others to take him to Bentley. Here Wilmot was found. In consultation with this cheerful, self-confident fugitive, who himself scorned any disguise but a hawk on his sleeve, it was decided that Charles should be brought that night from Boscobel to Moseley and that Wilmot should meet him there. On the way back Penderel revealed the identity of their intending guest to Whitgreave and Huddleston. Having fixed a rendezvous at the foot of the garden, he returned with the news to Boscobel.

From Boscobel to Moseley was eight miles: the night was

dark and stormy. Charles was still too lame to walk, and Humphrey Penderel's aged mill-horse, with a 'pitiful old saddle and rough bridle', was requisitioned for him. He bade farewell to Careless and set out, surrounded by the five Penderel brothers and Yates, who marched beside him armed with bill-hooks and pistols, ready to sell their lives in his defence. With this curious and devoted army the King crossed Chillington Park and the dark Staffordshire woods. At Pendeford Old Mill, two miles from his destination, he dismounted, leaving the horse with William, Humphrey and George Penderel. He had gone a few paces on his way when he turned back and, begging their pardon that his troubles had made him forgetful of his friends, gave them his hand to kiss. The peasant brothers kneeling before the King in the storm are the epitome of this night. It was the supreme moment of their simple and pious lives.

In a little grove of trees in the corner of a field called the Moor, Father Huddleston was waiting for the King. He led him down a long walk of trees, through a gateway and across a garden. At the darkened door of the house Whitgreave did not know before which of the eight shadowy figures, all habited alike, he should kneel, until the light of the hall fell on the pale, kingly boy with his cropped hair and shabby clothes, and Wilmot said: 'This is my master, your master, and the master of us all.'

* * *

For six weeks, hunted, penniless and with a price on his head, the young King remained as much a part of the English landscape as the bryony in the September and October hedges. Smuggled by a proscribed priest into the proud and willing custody of a ruined royalist house, and with a whole countryside searching for him, he rode to seek a boat at Bristol, disguised as the manservant of its daughter, Jane Lane, who, riding pillion behind him, carried for a week the crown of England in her hands – and never was trust more faithfully and delicately performed. Thence, unsuccessful, he passed to Trent House in Somerset, where another heroic girl, Juliana Coningsby, and a handful of devoted men and women braved death to preserve him and the English future. Narrowly escaping capture at Bridport on the Dorset coast and thence after returning to Trent, passing to Heale House in the Avon valley above Salisbury, where, after what must have seemed an eternity of peril, hardship and failure, and a final journey across Hampshire and Sussex a Brightelmstone coal brig, found by a loyal merchant, carried him to France.*

During the next eight years he was the mere shadow of a King – so thin and attenuated that his all-powerful enemies in England could almost forget him. His was a world of poor, ruined Cavaliers, wandering from one debt-haunted corner of the continent to another and begging their bread from contemptuous princes. 'Every bit of meat, every drop of drink,' wrote the Keeper of the royal purse, 'all the fire and all the candles that hath been spent since the King's coming hither is entirely owed for, and how to get credit for a week more is no easy matter.' 'I know of no other counsel to give you,' his faithful shadow Chancellor, Edward Hyde, enjoined a fellow exile, 'than, by the grace of God I intend to follow myself, which is to submit to God's pleasure and starve really and literally, with the comfort of having endeavoured to avoid it by all honest means . . . Indeed all discourse of submitting or compounding with those rogues in England hath so little sense or excuse in it that there needs no reply to it. You and I must die in the streets first of hunger.'

For all those hungry years – in Paris, Germany, Flanders – Hyde bore on his broad shoulders the burdens and afflictions of that forlorn Court. It was he who kept the 'family' from starving. 'I do not know that any man is yet dead for want of bread,' he wrote, 'which really I wonder at. I am sure the King owes for all he hath eaten since April; and I am not acquainted with one servant of his who hath a pistol in his pocket.' Hungry himself and sometimes so cold that he could scarcely hold a pen and too poor even to buy a faggot, in the darkest hours of their long exile Hyde kept hope alive for the little band of ruined cavaliers round the King, knowing in his heart that sooner or later the follies and oppressions

* A detailed account of the rest of Charles II's flight across England can be found in the first chapter of the author's, *King Charles II*.

of their enemies would bring about a natural reaction. 'If I did not assuredly believe that they will at last determine the confusion and be each other's executioners, I should be very melancholic,' he told his fellow courtier, Sir Edward Nicholas. 'We can but wait God Almighty's time.'

It was long in coming. Even after the news of Cromwell's death – that it had 'pleased God . . . to do that which He would not allow any man the honour of doing,' the familiar tale of debts and beggary closed round the exiles again.

Yet for all the debts and the closing in of another starving winter, things *were* happening in England. They buried the great Protector, and Evelyn saw the superb equipage, the effigy, the royal robes, the crown in life he dared not wear. 'But,' he added, 'it was the joyfullest funeral I ever saw, for there were none that cried but dogs, which the soldiers hooted away with a barbarous noise drinking, and taking tobacco in the streets as they went.' The Army was now supreme – but it was an army without a Head.

All through the spring of 1659 a great reaction was setting in for Charles. In the Commonwealth Parliament that February he seemed to have almost more friends than the new Protector, Cromwell's son – 'Tumbledown Dick' – and in the lobbies men whispered the dangerous conundrum, 'If a single person, why not the King?'. The extremer republicans fell much on the arbitrary acts of the Government, and Sir Henry Vane declared that he had not thought to have seen the day when free-born Englishmen should be sold as slaves by their own countrymen. In May the military – the 'men of buff' – dissolved the Cromwellian Parliament and restored the Rump, for out of five hundred members of the original Long Parliament, scarcely fifty of it by it were allowed to sit. By the end of May the Protectorate had ceased to exist, the new Council of State was busy demolishing Cromwell's monument in the Abbey, and its members were privately engaged in stocking their larders with the remaining deer from the royal parks. But the year 1659 ended with the King and his fellow exiles still at Brussels, cold, hungry and depressed in the gloom of a Flemish winter.

At the end of 1659 all the London apprentices, who had

grown up since the Civil War, were singing. They sang old ballads, printed on broadsides; of justice and the gallows, and the Rump and 'England's murthering monsters', under the very noses of the soldiers. And, added those cheerful prints:

> "tis hoped before the month of June
> The birds will sing another tune!'

And, though no one dared say it openly, everyone knew what they meant.

That October the Rump had cashiered General Lambert, the most able and ambitious of the generals who jockeyed to take their old commander Cromwell's place and Lambert, aping his former master, had turned out the Rump. These events had determined the army's Commander-in-Chief in Scotland to act. General Monk – 'Old George', as his soldiers called him – had been bred a Cavalier, and had only taken service under the Parliament when the royal cause was lost. Shrewd and Devonshire to the bone, he was the first professional English soldier of that unique school which believes that the military arm should be subordinate to the civil. With a rapidity strange in so slow a man, he now secured the strong places throughout Scotland and disarmed his Anabaptist officers. Then he assembled his troops and told them what he proposed to do – to march into England to assert 'the freedom and rights of three kingdoms from arbitrary and tyrannical usurpations.' On December 5th, with seven thousand men, he was at Berwick, and Lambert, his rival, was marching north to oppose him. 'They say the nation will be involved in a new and bloody war,' Hyde had written, 'I pray tell me what will be the end of that war?'

The rough youth of London, the City apprentices, had never a doubt. When on December 5th they rose and clamoured for 'a Free Parliament', and the wicked old one-eyed cobbler, Colonel Hewson of Drogheda fame, was sent to subdue them, they pelted his soldiers with old shoes and slippers, turnip-tops, stones and tiles. In the country the Army fared no better; Puritan Bristol rose against it, and at Southampton, when the garrison went out to drill, the townsmen locked the gates. Men dreamed of massacres and ruin; it was 'a crazy time everywhere'. By the end of December, the Army, hopelessly divided among itself, was being tossed on the surge of an angry countryside. Its rank and file, unpaid, had broken into mutiny, while its commander, the 'weeping Anabaptist' General Fleetwood, sat 'peaking in his chamber, as if it were moulting time with him and birds of his feather.' On Boxing Day, escorted by a vast crowd of soldiers and apprentices, Speaker Lenthall once more processed, with mace before and Rump behind, to take possession of Westminster.

Far away on the bleak border at Coldstream, Monk prepared to march. On a December night, between two and three, his chaplain, Price, roused him from the wooden form on which he was resting, and spoke to him of his duty – to restore the known laws of the land. 'Mr Price,' he replied, 'I know your meaning and I have known it. By the grace of God I will do it.' On January 1st 1660 he crossed the Rubicon. 'It was the Lord's day too, and it was His doing,' wrote Price. 'The frost was great and the snow greater, and I do not remember that we ever trod upon plain earth from Edinburgh to London. The air this day was very clear too, so that we could distinguish the very colours of the pebbles of the Tweed.'

As Monk marched, resistance crumbled. All Yorkshire came out in arms to aid him. Fairfax, the former Commander-in-Chief of the New Model Army and victor of Marston Moor and Naseby, forgetting his gout, left his heavy country life and raised his tenants: 'became another man, his motions so quick, his eyes so sparkling, giving the word of command like a general.' There was a great work to be done, though still none dared to call it by its name.

In London rumour ran riot. Wild excitement and depression followed in succession. Men were resolved to 'shake off the soldiers', and the young clerks, over their evening bowl at the Dog Tavern, spoke privately of . . . no one would say who. Merry doggerels – not very kindly, exceedingly lewd – about the Grandees of the Rump went the round of the town. And on January 30th Samuel Pepys, as he woke in the morning, fell a-singing of his song, 'Great, good and just,' and 'thereby put himself in mind that this was the fatal day, now ten years since, his Majesty died.' What did these things portend?

The hungry royalist exiles in Flanders, warming chilled fingers before starved fires, could scarcely imagine, and they dared not hope. Hyde pleaded patience: 'to sit still till they are in blood.' In his bones he could feel something stirring. But the debts and poverty were worse than ever, and it was bitterly cold. 'In this terrible weather,' he wrote on February 2nd, 'we have all some envy towards you that are in a place, where you can want no fire, which we all do; if, and when it will change, we yet know not.'

All the while Monk marched. At York he was deluged with petitions for a Free Parliament. He said nothing, 'was dark,' and when incautious men spoke of a king, frowned. But though he came ostensibly to protect the Rump, the members of that body were dubious and made secret efforts to undermine his authority. On February 3rd his troops entered London – likely men, with the officers wearing red and white favours in their hats and trumpeters going before in liveries of scarlet and silver. Next day the Rump offered him the Oath of Abjuration of the House of Stuart, and he refused to take it.

A decision of the City fathers to pay no taxes until a Free Parliament should be called gave the Rump its chance. On February 8th it ordered Monk to march into the city and pull down the gates and portcullises, thereby offering him the alternatives of disobeying the Civil power or incurring the hatred of London. Still obedient, he marched into a puzzled and angry city. Royalist hopes fell to zero. But on the night of the 9th, Monk called a council of his leading officers. With their aid he penned a letter to the Rump, demanding the issue of writs for filling up the House with excluded members and an early dissolution to make way for a Free Parliament. The letter was at once printed. Monk had done his work.

Again – it was Saturday, February 11th – once more Monk marched into the city, the people silent and watching. At the Guildhall he told the Mayor and Aldermen why. Within half an hour all men's faces had changed. That night was such a one as no man could remember. One observer counted thirty-one bonfires in a single street, and at every one a rump roasting; the butchers in the Strand rang a peal on their knives, 'and all the bells in all the

churches as we went home were a-ringing . . . The common joy
was everywhere to be seen . . . indeed it was past imagination, both
the greatness and the suddenness of it.'

By Monday all England knew, and from Hampshire John
Stewkeley, jumping to conclusions, wrote that Monk had declared
for 'a single person (you may imagine whom) and for a Free Parliament . . . We may all soon meet if the wind blows from Flanders,
which I pray for as a subject, as a member, as an Englishman.'
That week it was quite surprising how many times young Mr
Pepys, secretly in taverns and wine-vaults, drank the health of his
exiled sovereign. And as the news of these doings filtered across to
the Continent, there was a wild flutter of hope in the breasts of the
exiles and their landladies.

Yet still Monk showed no signs of recognizing that there was a
king across the water, and angrily reproved any who spoke to him
of Charles Stuart. In this he was wise, for the Royalist tide was
running so strongly that there was some danger of a reaction. Dispossessed Cavaliers in their cups spoke wildly of revenge and
restoration of property, and Monk was heard to observe that, if
there was a fanatic party on one side, there was a frantic one on the
other. Yet beneath the surface, he was going with the tide as fast
as any man. 'I cannot omit,' wrote a Royalist agent, 'that his little
son being asked who he was for, whether a King a Protector or a
Free State, he answered that he was for the King, and so was his
mother.' The good lady represented the feeling by now of almost
every woman in England. 'My head is so testicated with the times,'
wrote one of them, 'between hope and fear, that I know not what to
do; if things be not as I hope, my heart will break, I cannot outlive
it; but I do not despair, for I am confident it will be.'

On the afternoon of March 15th, just before the Exchange
closed, there appeared a humble workman 'with a ladder upon his
shoulder and a pot of paint in his hand, and set the ladder in the
place where the last King's statue had stood, and then went up and
wiped out that inscription, *Exit Tyrannus*,* and as soon as he had

---

* After Charles I's execution, the royal statue outside the Exchange was thrown
down by order of the Government, and over the empty niche the words inscribed:
'*Exit Tyrannus, Regum Ultimus*' – 'The tyrant is gone, the last of the kings'.

done it threw up his cap and cried, *God bless King Charles the Second*, in which the whole Exchange joined with the greatest shout.' Next day, by the votes of the excluded members, the Long Parliament brought its existence to an end, and Monk, judging the time ripe, gave a secret interview to the royal emissary, Sir John Grenville.

On March 30th Grenville reached the King at Brussels, where he delivered Monk's message, advising him to leave the territory of a state with whom England was still at war. Next morning, before it was light, or the Spaniards had time to stop him, Charles galloped across the frontier to Breda. Here, with Hyde at his shoulder, he signed the famous Declaration which secured at once a bloodless revolution and a restoration without conditions. The unquiet wraiths of twenty years, confiscated property, religious settlement, vengeance for bloodshed, were exorcised by Hyde's magic formula – the King would leave all to the will of a 'Free Parliament'. To the Declaration, Charles added letters to Monk, to the Speakers of both Houses, the Council of State and the City of London. For Monk he enclosed a commission as Captain-General of his forces and a blank warrant to appoint a Secretary of State. Grenville himself refused all honours, but before he left for England Charles slipped into his pocket a grant for the earldom of Bath – promised to his father, the great royalist Sir Bevil – and the posts of Groom of the Stole and First Gentleman of the Bedchamber.

When Grenville reached England in the middle of April, the elections for the new Parliament were still uncertain, and General Lambert, escaped from the Tower, was in arms in the Midlands. Monk therefore put the King's letter into his pocket and bade Grenville wait with the others till summoned by the Council of State. Then Lambert was defeated at Daventry, the successes of the Cavaliers at the elections became known, and 'every man began to be merry and full of hopes'. On the 25th the new Parliament met, the great Presbyterian, Dr Reynolds, preaching to the assembled members of St Margaret's from the text: 'Behold, unto you that fear my name shall the son of righteousness arise with healing in his wings.' Meanwhile 'plain, homely, downy' Mrs Monk was busy preparing Whitehall.

On Saturday, April 28th, Grenville officially handed the King's letter to the Council, who decided to pass it unopened to the House of Commons. The following Tuesday was the pleasantest of May Day mornings, and Pepys, with the Fleet off Deal as temporary secretary to its commander, his cousin, Sir Edward Montagu, wished himself in Hyde Park. As soon as the House assembled, Arthur Annesley, President of the Council, announced that Sir John Grenville was at the door with a letter. He was ordered to be brought in, and the Speaker took the letter and read it aloud, while the members stood bare-headed. Afterwards Monk's cousin, William Morrice, moved that the constitution of England lay in King, Lords and Commons. Without a dissentient voice the vote was carried. After that, all restraint went. They voted thanks to Grenville, and £50,000 to the King and that he should be invited to return at once and rule them. And Luke Robinson, the fanatic, 'all bathed in tears', stood up and spoke for an hour and a half, recanting all his former opinions and promising to be a good subject in future. But nobody paid much attention to him, for a thing had happened 'never read of in history, when monarchy, laid aside at the expense of so much blood, returned without the shedding of one drop.' 'This government was as natural to them as their food or raiment, and naked Indians dressing themselves in French fashion were no more absurd than Englishmen without a Parliament and a King.'

In the afternoon the whole nation went mad, with 'ringing of bells and drinking of the King's health upon their knees in the streets' – which Pepys thought a little too much – and loyal Mr Dobeson, a great sufferer for the cause, actually burnt the windmill at Charlton in his joy. There were, of course, a few dissentients: the minister of Gawthorpe, Lincs, kicked the local bonfire out, and a certain Captain Southwold remarked that if the king came in he would cut him up as small as herbs in a pot. But for the vast majority of the nation it was 'the happiest May Day that had been many a year to England.' And down at Deal lay a fleet in her pride with pennants loose, guns roaring, caps flying and the loud *Vive le Roys* echoing from one ship's company to another.

The subject of all this joy was at Breda, writing tenderly to his little sister Minette about the purchase of clothes and ribbons, and waiting to learn the terms upon which a Restoration would be admitted. When Grenville arrived with a letter from Monk, preceding by a few hours the official invitation from the House, Charles was at supper. After he had read the letter, he embraced Grenville, telling him that no man had ever been more welcome, for now he could say he was a king and not a Doge.

Thereafter life became an unbelievable dream. On the following day came eighteen deputies from the States-General to invite him to the Hague and offer £30,000 for his expenses. On May 14th, accompanied by his brothers, the dukes of York and Gloucester, his sister Mary, and her child, William of Orange, Charles set out from Breda. At the Hague, where he dined off covers of gold, he was waited upon by the Committee of the Lords and Commons, with a promise of £50,000 and an invitation from Parliament that he 'would return and take the government of the kingdom into his hands.' There followed fourteen London citizens with a trunk containing £10,000, round which the exiled family gathered to gaze with wonder at so much gold.

It was a busy and crowded time. All day long the King interviewed delegations and supplicants, and all night, since there was no other period available, wrote letters. To one delegation only he returned a short answer – a bevy of ministers who begged a pledge that he would forbid surplices and the Book of Common Prayer in his Chapel Royal – replying that, in giving liberty to others, he did not intend to surrender his own.

The only business that now remained was to bring the King to England. On May 15th the fleet under Admiral Montagu sighted the Dutch coast, all hands making ready painting royal coats of arms where formerly the Commonwealth Harp had been, getting out silk flags and cutting up yellow cloth to initial C.R. upon them. Next morning Samuel Pepys, made secretary to the Admiral by the Muse of History for the purpose of recording these events in his diary, visited the Hague and was much impressed by the neat, clean town with its maypole at every door and the burghers with their muskets as bright as silver. Indeed, after the drabness of Commonwealth London, he was unable to find words to express a full sense of its gallantry. In the afternoon, on the *Naseby*, the

Admiral, resplendent in gold and silver, sent for him, and the two had a most significant talk about religion, in which Montagu declared himself wholly sceptical, an enemy to enthusiasm and intolerance and a believer in uniformity of worship and prayer. When Pepys, being unable to stand, retired that night to his bunk, a new age had dawned for England.

On the 17th, a day of reception, the King wrote to Monk, fixing the place of his landing.

> 'I need say little to you since I have informed Dr Clarges of my purpose, and he will tell you with what difficulty I get one-quarter of an hour to myself. I have thought the best I can of the place where I should disembark . . . and have resolved, God willing, to land at Dover. . . . But you can hardly imagine the impatience I have to see you, for, till then, I shall take no resolution of moment. I pray bring Mrs Monk with you, and believe me to be very heartily your affectionate friend.'

The touch about Mrs Monk was characteristic, and showed a proper appreciation of a real power in the land.

On the night of May 22nd fifty thousand people waited for dawn on the sand-dunes. At 2 a.m. the drums beat, and the crowds stirred with excitement. Then the King, with his brothers, his sister and his aunt, the Queen of Bohemia, escorted by a great cortège came down to the waterside, where the Admiral awaited them. It was a lovely day, and Pepys had put on his linen stockings and white canons. As the royalties came aboard the crowded flagship, all the guns in the Fleet broke into thunder.

At eleven o'clock the royal party dined together, 'which,' thought Pepys, 'was a blessed sight to see.' Afterwards the *Naseby* was rechristened the *Royal Charles*, and the memory of many old sorrows and glories buried. The time came for the shore boats to leave, and the witty Queen of Bohemia, with shining eyes – Shakespeare's *The Tempest* had been written for her wedding day fifty years before – took her leave of the King, while Mary clung to him weeping. Then the anchor was weighed.

All afternoon the King walked up and down the deck, examining everything on the ship. Later he told to the wondering courtiers the tale of his miraculous escape from Worcester, and Pepys, clinging to the fringe of the listening crowd, wept to hear it. In the evening he supped alone in his cabin, glad to be away from the crowd and the stir for a little. Afterwards he stood on the moonlit poop, looking back at the vanishing coast-line. Such days are memorable and deeply stamped on the mind.

At dawn on the 25th, the Fleet anchored off Dover, close in-shore. Monk, summoned by horse, was hurrying from Canterbury, and a vast concourse was waiting in the little sea town. From the decks the exiles watched the scene. The King, active as ever, called his brothers to try the sailors' victuals, and the three break-fasted like true Englishmen off peas, boiled beef and pork.

About three o'clock Charles was rowed ashore in the Admiral's barge. Pepys followed in a smaller boat with the footman and 'a dog the King loved'. The beach was dense with spectators, and, as the barge ran across the shingle, the guns on all the forts and ships burst into flame. Other guns down the coast took up the echo, till four hours later the Tower artillery proclaimed to the listening citizens that the King had come into his own. As he stepped ashore, he knelt down and thanked God for this strange and wonderful deliverance. Then he rose and, drawing Monk to him, kissed him and called him father. As every eye in the multitude fixed its gaze on that little group by the water's edge, the soldier placed his sword in his master's hand and cried *God save the King*. All took up the mighty sound, but in the midst of it the young duke of Gloucester was heard crying *God save General Monk*.

The Mayor of Dover approached and presented his insignia of office (which was returned) and a fine Bible which the King declared he loved above all things in the world. Then while the people shouted continuously, Charles, under a canopy of state, passed through them to his coach. So, with all Kent running and riding after him, he drove towards Canterbury.

Two miles out, the King left the coach and mounted his horse to sniff the air. It was fifteen years since he had seen England in May. Then he rode across Barham Downs to Canterbury. The bells of the Cathedral were ringing as he passed through the narrow streets. That night, before he slept, he scribbled a line to his sister Minette: 'My head is so dreadfully stunned with the acclamations of the people, and the vast amount of business that I know not whether I am writing sense or nonsense.'

At Canterbury he spent the week-end; saw a multitude of suitors, invested Monk, Montagu and two great English cavaliers, Southampton and Hertford, with the Garter, and attended Anglican service in the Cathedral. On Monday, through roads lined all the way, he went on towards Rochester.

On Tuesday, May 29th 1660, the sun rose early to welcome the King's thirtieth birthday. Many thousands of his subjects rose earlier. On Blackheath, before the serried regiments of the fallen Army, with a rural triumph of morris dancers, with tabor and pipe, the Lord Mayor and a hundred and twenty thousand citizens were waiting. All the way to the capital the concourse grew. Then, amid an indescribable colour and din, 'with a triumph of above twenty thousand horse and foot, brandishing their swords and shouting with inexpressible joy; the ways strewed with flowers, the bells ringing, the streets hung with tapestry, fountains running with wine,' the long procession passed over London Bridge into the crowded streets. A hundred thousand heads looked down as Colonel Browne's regiment, in silver doublets and black scarves, trotted by, but the road drowned even the bells when the King rode into view. Here he was at last, 'the Black Boy', whom so many had secretly toasted and mentioned in bated breath and dreamt of. Tall, slim, and dark, he rode bare-headed between that dazzling crowd, bowing now to left, now to right, to the ladies in the balconies and windows. The smiling eyes looked with approval at the companies of 'proper maids all alike in white garments', and the long hands drew in his fine horse and took the Bible which the London ministers proffered him. And Evelyn, the diarist, remembering the long years of oppression, 'stood in the Strand and beheld it and blessed God . . . for it was the Lord's doing, and such a restoration was never mentioned in any history, ancient or modern, since the return of the Jews from the Babylonish captivity.'

Towards evening the King came to his Palace of Whitehall. The Houses of Parliament with their Speakers were awaiting him.

After a brief rest he received the Address of the Lords, and made his answer – 'disordered by my journey and with the noise still sounding in my ears (which I confess was pleasing to me because it expressed the affections of my people)' – promising them that he would endeavour by all means to restore the nation to its freedom and happiness, and ever defend its faith and laws. Then he went up to the Banqueting Hall to hear the long oration of the Speaker of his faithful Commons. 'I am so weary,' he answered, 'that I am scarce able to speak, but I desire you may know . . . that whatsoever may concern the good of this people I shall be as ready to grant as you shall be to ask.'

It had been the King's intention to attend a service of thanksgiving at the Abbey that evening, but the strain of the long day had proved too much for even his strength. Instead he offered his oblation in the Presence Chamber of the Palace. Yet, at that supreme moment, there was a glint of irony behind the tired, smiling eyes; he was foolish, he remarked, not to have come home before, since every man in England was protesting that he had always longed for his return. Down in Buckinghamshire, the rector of Maid's Moreton wrote with joy in the church register: 'This day, by the wonderful goodness of God, his Sacred Majesty King Charles II was peacefully restored to his martyred father's throne, the powerful armies of his enemies being amazed spectators and in some sort unwilling assistants in his return . . . And from this day ancient orders began to be observed. *Laus Deo!*'

CHAPTER ELEVEN

Carolean England

'For all that I have yet seen, give
me old England.'
Clarendon

APART FROM LONDON, which, at the time of the Restoration, housed
over half a million inhabitants, or about a tenth of the total population, outside its sea-fringe of ports and fishing villages, England
was still almost wholly rural. Its other towns, even the provincial
capitals like York, Norwich and Exeter were mere appendages of
the surrounding countryside, serving it as markets and, in the
winter, social centres for the local gentry. There was ample space
in it – elbow room for liberty, and solitude for thought and un-
sullied imagination. The French ambassador, travelling westwards, was surprised to see how empty it was, passing in a distance
of thirty leagues of fine land very few villages and scarcely a soul
on the road. Yet how lovely this open, lonely land was! In Devon
the folk clotted their cream with sugar to crown their apple-pies,
and, in the fields beside the Ouse in Huntingdonshire, the milk-
maids bore home their pails with music going before. In that
county, so rich was it in corn, it was the custom, whenever a king
of England came, to meet him with a hundred ploughs.

Here in the country quiet the old ways of life persisted. Parson
Moore of Horsted Keynes did his shopkeeping by barter, receiving
for a box of pills and sermons a ribspare and hog's pudding, and in
remote parts of Lancashire boon-services were still unsuperseded
by rents. The colliers of the Tyne rowed on their holy days by
verdant flats and woods, with trumpeters and bagpipes making

music in the stern, and west of the Pennines the country-people went bare-footed, leaping as if they had hoofs. Rich and poor alike talked and spelt in the dialect of their county, Cheshire Mrs Dobson writing to tell her husband:

> 'I leve here tow and twenty milke cous and a boll, three big hefers and a boleke and seven which are yer old bests; and one boll calfe which runs upon one of the coues and seven other calves which are this year rered, and one fat tegg.'

It was a world of hedge squires and parsons, of yeomen, cottagers and ragged squatters, making their wares and pleasures after the manner of their forbears with little news of or regard to what was happening elsewhere. For 'that great hive, the city', its vices and graces, country-folk had nothing but pity. To cousins there imprisoned they sent vast cheeses and pies of game; 'there was two very fat geese, eight wild ducks, and eight woodcocks, and in the box a pair of stockings' in one such that Lady Shakerley sent her son in London. 'When I came home,' wrote Robert Paston, 'which is the sweetest place in the world, I found my children and Mrs Cooper pretty well, and she and the gentleman are taking their pleasure to see an otter hunted in the pond.'

In the summer of 1667, seeking a respite from overwork and clamour, the Clerk of the Acts of the Navy, Samuel Pepys, took his family by coach for a day's outing to Epsom. Here on the downs, only fifteen miles from London, 'far from any houses or sight of people,' he encountered an old shepherd listening to his boy reading the Bible. 'He did content himself mightily in my liking his boy's reading and did bless God for him, the most like one of the old patriarchs that ever I saw in my life, and it brought those thoughts of the old age of the world in my mind for two or three days together.'

That age was nearer than the rising young official from London realized. For, though England had broken her last links with Rome a century before and was, politically speaking, militantly Protestant, her simple country folk were still instinctively rooted in the faith the medieval Church had taught them. Faith was the air its people breathed. To them it explained everything; even affliction was a visitation sent to test the spirit and teach patience and resignation. 'If you be taken away by this dreadful pestilence,' a correspondent wrote during the plague of 1665, 'you have had a fair warning and a very long time to prepare yourselves for Heaven. It seems that every day at London is now a day of judgment and that all our thoughts are placed on death, on Hell, on Heaven and upon eternity. Thy will be done on earth as it is in Heaven is the balsam that cureth all.'

Such faith sustained men in all the major crises of life, nerved them to bear pain worse than modern medical science permits us to know, and buoyed them in the hour of deprivation which, with early mortality and constant epidemic disease, was so often their lot. 'For the world,' the Norwich physician, Sir Thomas Browne, wrote, 'I count it not an inn but a hospital, not a place to live but to die in.' Death still seemed the climax of existence – the hour when a man reaped what he had sown.

In an age when religious feeling was so strong as to amount to an obsession, men saw the hand of God in every happening. 'It was an hideous and portending thing,' wrote Sir Edward Harley of a gale, 'I pray God we may learn the voices of these things.' Even the most ordinary occurrences seemed 'providences'. 'I got home,' a country parson recorded in his diary, 'and found my wife pretty hearty, having taken physic this day and it working very easily with her: a great mercy!'

Behind all this lay the universal reading of the Bible. Educated and uneducated alike spoke its direct and inspired English; official jargon had still to turn the phraseology of administration into a mystery, though Pepys in his vast and laborious naval memoranda was paving a way. An ambassador related in an official dispatch how, when a mob chased its victims to the water-front, 'it pleased Him who bridges the sea with a girdle of sand to put bounds to the fury of the people.' Familiarity with the Bible was the first step in all seventeenth-century education. The very children's alphabets were biblical, one beginning:

> 'In Adam's fall
> We sinned all,'

and ending ingeniously,

> 'Zaccheus he
> Did climb a tree
> Our Lord to see.'

The national religion as re-established by law in 1660 was Anglicanism – that temperate and homely blend of ancient Catholic ritual and Church government with Protestant tenet which expressed the English genius for compromise. During the Interregnum the Anglican Church had suffered severely – its priests expelled, its estates alienated, its cathedrals desecrated. With the Restoration it entered upon a golden period. Its parsons, in their black gowns, square hats and vast white bands, enjoyed a revenue which, though only a fraction of that of the rich possessioners of the medieval Church, gave its incumbents an assured place in society. And in the cathedral towns comfortable and dignified colonies of the higher clergy made themselves as much at home as the rooks in the elms above the prebendal houses they inhabited. At Wells there dwelt under the shadow of the cathedral no less than seven and twenty prebends and nineteen canons, besides a dean, a preceptor, a chancellor and an archdeacon. Here the high pomps of Anglicanism – for a generation banished as idolatry – were revived in all their glory. At Exeter the bishop sat beneath a crimson canopy in a seat covered with red cloth. It almost seemed to Catholic observers as though they were in the presence of their own ancient rites: only there was a difference. For as one of them observed, 'under the tabernacle, on a level with the floor of the church, in an enclosure of wood, stood the wife of the bishop and his children, no less than nine in number.' 'I have seen,' wrote another witness, 'the bishop and the bishopess, the little bishops and the little bishopesses.'

In the parish churches neither vestments nor images had any place: the royal arms, the tables of the Decalogue and the sepulchral monuments of the landed gentry were the only idols permitted. Everyone went to church once a week, many two or three times. Here the *pièce de résistance* was the eloquence of the clergy. A priesthood was still as essential to social life as in the Middle Ages, but it was now a Protestant priesthood teaching by sermons, the translated scriptures and a vernacular liturgy, instead of a Catholic one using images, dramatic representations and Latin incantations. Two sermons a day was the normal Sabbath fare (Pepys would sometimes drop into three or four City churches on a Sunday to sample the sermons) and an hour apiece not thought too long. Sermons were much read by the laity, and many a carrier's cart as it lumbered into the shires bore a folio of good Dr Sanderson's or Dr Cosin's sermons for the delectation of some country lady. 'The bishop this week,' wrote a London correspondent, 'comes down to you in the wagon, and I hope brings his blessing with him.'

In the towns and the rich eastern and south-western counties, Puritanism had taken root. After the Restoration it was christened by new names – fanaticism by its Anglican opponents, nonconformity the State. The rules and ritual of the established Church proved too narrow for many who had embraced the intense, though diverse, beliefs of Puritan revelation. To foreigners these presented a bewildering variety. There were Anabaptists who believed in the extinction of rank, Libertines who held that sin was only an opinion, Adamites at whose weddings bride and bridegroom wore only a girdle of leaves, Brownists who regarded church bells as popish inventions and broke into prophecy after sermons, and Sabbatarians who believed that divine revelation had been exclusively vouchsafed to Robert Dogs, the London coal-man. 'The common people,' observed an atonished foreigner, 'enjoy a liberty which is incredible, every man following that religion and those rites which most suit his fancy.' Yet the followers of all these varied creeds had two things in common: all loathed the Church of Rome and all believed implicitly that they alone were in the right.

Most powerful of the Nonconformist sects were the Presbyterians, whose quarrel with Anglicanism centred round the question of Church government. At the Restoration it was hoped that they might be induced to conform to a creed which in its essential beliefs differed little from their own, but their dislike of bishops proved too strong. In 1662 over a thousand clergy laid down their livings rather than conform to episcopal government and read the liturgy. Setting up as private teachers, some at least did rather better for themselves than had the Anglican clergy whom they had dispossessed during the Interregnum; for their congregations were drawn largely from the thriving middle class of the towns, who were ready to pay handsomely for their oratory. In London, Mr Cotton in the Great Almonry, Baxter in Great Russell Street, and the famous Manton in Covent Garden, preached to packed and fashionable congregations every Sunday.

The unlicensed preachers were a great thorn in the side of the royal Government, whose practices they constantly, and not unnaturally, attacked in their sermons. It seemed to loyal subjects as though they were planning a new revolution and second republic. But, to do them justice, they were probably quite unconscious of any ulterior purpose but a divine one; their gloomy and awful prognostications on the fate of Church and State seemed in their eyes as inspired and disinterested as the prophesying of Balaam. 'I preached,' recorded honest Oliver Heywood, 'to a pretty full congregation at the house of Jeffrey Beck; the Lord made it a refreshing night to many souls, though our adversaries watched and gnashed their teeth when they saw so many coming together. I had great liberty of speech in preaching and praying, though,' he added a little sadly, 'not such melting of heart as sometimes I have enjoyed.'

Yet the narrowness and pride that at times showed itself in the Puritan leaders was redeemed by the humility and seemly lives of their followers. Readers of the *Pilgrim's Progress* will remember the song the shepherd boy sang in the Valley of Humiliation. Less familiar is the description of the boatswain, Small, in John Sheffield's *Memoirs*. Small had been captured with the rest of the crew of the *Royal Katherine* at the battle of Southwold Bay, and, after the captain and officers had been sent off, had been stowed under hatches with the remaining survivors. Unarmed and urging them on with his whistle, he led them in a surprise assault on the Dutch guard and almost miraculously recaptured the ship. 'He was a Nonconformist,' added Sheffield, 'always sober, meek and quiet (even too mild for that bustling sort of employment) and very often gave me an image of those enthusiastic people who did such brave things in our late Civil War; for he seemed rather a shepherd than a soldier and was a kind of hero in the shape of a saint.'

Two Christian creeds were outside the pale of English public opinion – the Quaker's and Roman Catholicism. The Quakers had few friends. Despite the ultimate gentleness of their tenets, their outrages against contemporary manners won them enemies in all places. One of them, a woman, rose in the middle of the sermon in Windermere church and, 'with a loud inarticulate noise', shouted down the preacher; another made a practice of visiting market-places and rich men's houses, stark naked and smeared with excrement, informing all and sundry that the Lord God would besmear their religion as he was besmeared. Inevitably the poor man was subjected to 'many grievous whippings with long coach whips, stonings and diverse imprisonments.' Such excesses, though unfairly, were universally attributed to the Quakers. Until their sturdy integrity of life and constancy of purpose had won them the honoured place they later took in the national life, they suffered unceasing persecution.

The Catholics, or papists as they were called, were even more universally detested. They were suspected, quite erroneously, of perpetual machinations against the Government and people of England. Among the upper and middle classes no reading was more popular than that which exposed, usually at devastating length and with no mincing words, the fallacies of Rome. As for the common people, any demagogue who was unscrupulous enough to play on their anti-Catholic feelings could loose a murderous wild beast. Once a year the London mob processed through the city with effigies of pope, cardinals and devils stuffed with live cats to make them squeal realistically when burnt, amid shouts of delight, at Smithfield.

Composed almost entirely of members of certain ancient families and their tenantry, the English Catholics had shown con-spicuous loyalty to the King's cause during the Civil War and Inter-regnum. After the Restoration they received little reward, for, however much the King might incline to them, he was powerless in face of the universal hatred in which they were held. Fines for 'recusancy', which during the 'bad times' had sometimes reached as much as twenty pounds a month, were still imposed, though at a milder rate, and priests were forbidden to minister the rites of their religion under pain of death. Even the most common rights of justice were denied to Catholics, who dared not resort to litigation when an unscrupulous opponent could always enforce on them an oath incompatible with their faith or win the case by default. In times of national panic their lot became still more precarious, for then their houses were searched for arms and their liberty restricted by 'chains', which forbade them to travel more than a mile or two from their homes. During the 'Popish Plot' of 1678, the best advice a friendly Westmorland justice could give to a Catholic widow was to marry a Protestant who could protect her property and person. Yet persecution only strengthened their constancy. The sons mostly of ancient English Catholic houses, their priests were trained abroad at St Omer or one of the other English Catholic colleges, and then returned to their own country to pass secretly from house to house, ministering to their flocks in attics and secret oratories and faithfully discharging their duty in constant peril of death. Their epitaph was written by one of their flock, William Blundell of Crosby. "We'll hang them," sayeth a Lancaster jury. "We'll crown them," sayeth Christ.'

Intolerance was the ugly reverse of seventeenth-century piety. It could hardly be otherwise when heresy was still supposed, as in Catholic days, to involve eternal damnation. A neighbour of another religion seemed as great a peril to a man's children as the plague. All the political struggles of the age, culminating in the Revolution of 1688 and the triumph of Parliament over crown, sprang partly from the attempt of the last two Stuart kings – the one secretly, and the other publicly, a Roman convert – to grant to the Catholics a greater degree of tolerance than their other subjects would countenance.

*　　*　　*

The government of this bigoted land rested on triple supports – Crown, Law and People. The Crown was the executive and provided the element of decisive power. Yet it was a carefully tempered power. Its seat was the old Tudor palace of Whitehall. For nearly half a mile it stretched along the river, a warren of galleries, apartments and gardens, the home not only of the King but of the ministers of State, servants high and low, courtiers, chaplains, ladies and all the gilded army which encompassed the throne. One entered it either from the river or 'the lane' – that 'long dark dirty and very inconvenient passage' – which, spanned by two gateways, linked Charing Cross with Westminster. Its buildings were of all sizes and ages, from Inigo Jones's classic Banqueting Hall to the little octagonal Cockpit.

The centre of this courtly city was the long Stone Gallery, the hub of the Stuart government of Britain. On its walls hung the pictures which Charles I had collected and his enemies dispersed, and which his son had partly reassembled. Here they made a kind of national picture gallery, for the place was open to all comers. Yet few in the crowd that walked continuously up and down the galleries came for the pictures; places, preferment, sightseeing, above all, news, were the business of that place of rumours. 'It runs through the galleries,' was the prefix which sped the national gossip.

Well it might, for those who waited here saw the outward stir of all that was moving the wheels of State. The velvet curtains across the doors would part and the King himself pass through the crowd, followed by a group of ministers and suitors from Bed-chamber or Council Room, still contending for that royal ear whose retention was at once the hardest and most precious achieve-ment of a careerist's life. Here in the Gallery, for a moment, opportunity flitted by.

From the Stone Gallery guarded doors opened into the royal apartments. In the Robe and Council Chambers the principal committees of State in debate, while in the Withdrawing-room waiting gentlemen warmed their hands before the fire. Beyond was the holy of holies, the Bedchamber. In this great room, with its windows looking on to the tides and shipping of the river, the most secret affairs of State were transacted at all hours of the day 'between the bed and the wall'.

It was not here, or in his closet, that England saw the King, nor even in the Ante-room where the Foreign Ministers daily awaited his return from the park, but in perfumed banqueting hall and chapel. He dined in state, a little after midday, before a background of tapestry, while the massed lords of the household served him on bended knee and all England came and went in the galleries above to share the pageantry. The mysteries of State were performed against a setting of crimson and gold, with the royal trumpeters and kettledrummers marching in scarlet cloaks faced with silver lace, before fringed hangings, gilt mirrors and a world of gleaming fabric.

A few hundred yards down the muddy lane called King Street and across the cobblestones of Palace Yard was the Parliament House. Here sat the watchdog set by the nation to prevent the royal executive from overriding the law. At least that was how people saw it, for the theory of parliamentary sovereignty, first put forward by the extremists of the iron time, had been abandoned at the Restoration as repugnant to English Constitution and habit; the old view of England was that Parliaments met, not to govern, but to prevent others from misgoverning. The age of Charles II was the last age in which this was so; after 1688, when the people's representatives became themselves the rulers of the nation, the people, whatever else they gained, lost this traditional buffer between themselves and the executive.

Parliament represented not the masses but the privileged estates of the realm – those who were best able to safeguard ancient legal rights against an encroaching executive. The House of Commons was composed mainly of country magnates, with a sprinkling of merchants, officials and courtiers. They were chosen by a curious blend of nomination and limited election which varied from locality to locality; it was never easy to say who had the right to vote and who not. Their sittings were still spasmodic; twice in Charles II's reign long periods passed without any session at all, and there is little evidence that the people as a whole, as distinct from the politically interested minority, much resented the omission. It was only when the nation was in trouble or its religion threatened that Parliament was ardently desired by everyone. Its power lay in its right to withhold those additional aids to the customary income of the Crown without which the executive could not afford to embark on any new policy. Throughout the seventeenth century, owing to the continued decline in the value of money, the Crown was generally in need of such aid. This and the fear of Catholicism were the chief causes of national dissension.

* * *

Dwarfed by its neighbour France, with her 19,000,000 inhabitants, the population of England stood at about 5,000,000 at the beginning of Charles II's reign, and perhaps 500,000 more at the end. The statistician, Gregory King, reckoned that all but a million and a half lived in the country. According to him nearly a fifth of the heads of the nation's 1,360,000 households were yeomen owning their own land either by freehold or copyhold. More than half were agricultural labourers and cottagers, many of whom, though working for others, had a small stake in the land, if only a commoner's right of grazing and turfage. But the greater part of the soil – formerly vested in the Crown and the medieval Church – was now the hereditary property of a few thousand landowners. The primogenitary system evolved by the Plantagenet lawyers, the erosion of feudal tenures and the spoliation of the monasteries had combined to create an aristocracy of dynastic landed families whose estates and traditions were transmitted unbroken by the partition that occurred in other European countries. Though less than two hundred of the heads of such families were peers and, as such, hereditary legislators, it was from the general body of landed gentry that the Crown drew the unpaid local leaders who represented the shire in Parliament, enforced as justices of the peace the law in their native place, and in their courts of Quarter Sessions administered the counties.

Many of these county families had been founded by some yeoman, merchant or court official who had risen to wealth and power in the fifteenth and sixteenth centuries on the ruins of the medieval State and the dissolution of the monasteries. Others had grown rich from the expanding cloth-trade, as often as not marrying their heirs into aristocratic or knightly families. Yet, though the occupant of the Tudor manor house was frequently a hard man who had nails in his boots for those who climbed beneath him, as the magic of the English countryside closed around him and his children good humour revived and the grasp of greedy fingers relaxed. The courtier, merchant or lawyer, who had invested his gains in a country estate, oppressed his tenantry and harried his neighbours with lawsuits, was transmuted in a generation or two into the chivalrous loyalist who gave his life for a king with whose cause he had little sympathy but whom he supported because, as one squire put it, he had eaten his bread and would not do so base a thing as to desert him in his need. He was still often quarrelsome, but that was because most Englishmen at the time were. 'If you said any such thing,' wrote one of his kind, 'I would advise you to eat your words immediately, else – by the living God – I'll cram them down your throat with my sword – and that very shortly.' But when his temper was not aroused, the typical squire, like Addison's Sir Roger de Coverley, was good humoured and friendly: the kind of man who saluted everyone who passed him with a good morrow or good night and, 'when he entered a house, called the servants by their names and talked all the way upstairs to a visit.'

After religion – belief in the all-importance of which he shared with his contemporaries of all classes – the squire's ruling passions were the chase and the enlargement of his estate. He sought the latter in Parliament, in the courts of law and in matrimony – especially in matrimony. Few things, even the King's favour, could do so much to advance a dynastic family's fortunes as a rich and influential marriage. For this reason – though most seventeenth-century marriages occurred no earlier than those of to-day – the heirs and heiresses of large properties were sometimes contracted at a very early age. Thus Sir Ralph Verney wrote of 'a young wedding between Lady Grace Grenville and Sir George Cartwright's grandson' – a Buckinghamshire family uniting with a Northamptonshire one – 'she is six years old and he a little above eight years, therefore questionless they will carry themselves very gravely and love dearly.' Occasionally an heir kicked over the traces and chose for himself; when this happened, the defrauded father was justly indignant. 'Sir,' wrote Lord Cork to his son, 'I am informed that you are so miserably blinded as to incline to marry and so with one wretched act to dash all my designs which concern myself and house.' Few parents, however, expected a son or daughter to marry anyone who aroused active aversion. A right of veto was allowed, such as John Verney used when he had his prospective bride paraded up and down Drapers' Garden so that he might see if there were 'nothing disgustful' about her.

The marriage of daughters was seldom a profitable business. Young ladies with fortunes were, of course, easily disposable; 'Sir Ambrose Crawley's daughters go off apace, but £50,000 ladies will never stick on hand.' But no father would allow a son with expectations to marry a girl, however attractive, without a portion proportionate to his estate, and in the correspondence of the time the girls of landed families often present a somewhat pathetic picture, nervously anxious to marry and doomed to a life of dependence as companion to some rich relative if they failed. 'I think,' wrote one young lady in despair, 'my marrying very unlikely in any place and impossible in this.' Shortly afterwards she made a runaway match with a penniless curate; anything she felt was better than being left an old maid.

All this made a marriage settlement a complicated business. The parties' legal advisers would engage in interminable correspondence, and learned counsel in London would be feed, so that children and grandchildren unborn might be provided for and remote contingencies anticipated. Months, sometimes years, would pass before the final details were complete and the young people free to wed. In one case, when the latter took matters into their own hands and married before the legal formalities were completed, the father of the bride – who gained greatly by the bridegroom's impatience – wrote to his discomfited opposite, 'And to show you he is your own son, we had much ado to keep him from kissing his bride before matrimony was all read.'

Though occasionally genuine tenderness sprang up between the young people before the wedding, a conventional phraseology of courtship was *de rigeur*. They called themselves one another's 'servants' and wrote such letters as young William Blundell with his father's aid wrote to Mary Eyre: 'Oh! my most honoured dear lady, how shall I count those unkind hours that keep me from so great a joy? I told you once before (as I hope I did not offend) that your goodness hath cause to pardon what your virtue and beauty hath done.' Most of the love-letters of the time were written after, not before, marriage. There were exceptions like those of Dorothy Osborne. Forbidden to see her love, she wrote to him: 'I think I need not tell you how dear you have been to me, nor that in your kindness I placed all the satisfaction of my life; 'twas the only happiness I proposed to myself, and had set my heart so much upon it that it was therefore my punishment to let me see that, how innocent soever I thought my affection, it was guilty in being greater than is allowable for things of this world.' She waited for him for seven years and had him in the end without breaking any of the commandments of God or man.

From courtship and the making of settlements one passed into marriage through the ceremonies and junketings of an English wedding. On the bridal day in a well-to-do home the company put on coloured scarves, love-knots and ribbons, and fine gloves and garters. After the sack posset had been eaten and all were 'high-flown', the bride was undressed by her maids and the bridegroom by his male friends, the company coming up from their junketings below to see them to bed, scramble for ribbons and garters, fling the bride's stocking and draw the curtains on them. 'We saw Sir Richard and his fine lady wedded,' wrote Buckinghamshire Edmund Verney, 'and flung the stocking, and then left them to themselves, and so in this manner ended the celebration of this marriage à la mode; after that we had music, feasting, drinking, revelling, dancing, and kissing; it was two of the clock this morning before we got home.'

Honeymoon there was none, and among the landed gentry for the first few weeks after marriage the bride usually had the comfort of being surrounded by her own folk and friends. Then she passed into the possession of her husband's family and became as much the daughter of her father and mother-in-law as if she had been their own child. In most cases she was received with love and kindness, for in the seventeenth century the tie of kinship was very strong.

* * *

Whether the parties were rich or poor, marriage marked the beginning of a new household and the enrolment in the community of a new householder. The household was the economic and legal unit of life, and seventeenth-century society was organized in households. 'I am a wise fellow,' said Dogberry, 'and which is more an officer, and which is more, a householder.' The poorest household might consist of no more than the householder, his wife and children, but a large proportion accommodated more than the householder's family. A craftsman or shopkeeper when he set up house would have a journeyman and apprentices to share his roof and board, a schoolmaster pupils and an usher, a farmer 'servants-in-husbandry' – a farm boy 'to plough and hoe and reap and sow', a dairy maid or maids to milk the kine and ewes, and a serving one to help his wife prepare meals and make butter, cheese and whey. In days when everything had to be done by hand, probably as many as a quarter or even a third of England's families enlarged themselves in this way in order to earn their livelihood and get the work of the community done, while poorer families sent their children to serve in them and learn their trade until they, too, could marry and form households of their own. The cash wages of such servants was often minute, but they shared the same food and living conditions and, in the average decent Christian home, the affections of those for whom they worked. So did the day labourers who slept in their own cottages but worked on the land of their better-to-do neighbours and took their daily place at the family table. It was a patriarchal system that had existed from time immemorial, in which the father was the 'master' and the 'master' the father-figure of the household. Though subject to obvious abuse, so long as there was food for all – which there usually was unless the harvest failed for several seasons in succession – it made for a more contented and humane organisation of economic activity than was to exist later under factory conditions.*

Once married, even into the richest family, a bride had plenty to do. The management of a country house called for all a woman's energies. The smallest manor house was forced to maintain a large

* See Peter Laslett's remarkable work, *The World we have Lost* (Methuen 1965), based on group study and analysis of seventeenth-century parish registers.

household in an age when public services were non-existent and even letters had to be fetched by a servant from the nearest post-town. A country house was a factory for living, making its own food and drink from seeding to brewhouse and kitchen, its own fuel and candles, spinning flax and wool for clothing and uphol-stery, and even curing feathers to make mattresses and pillows. Of all this work the lady of the house was priestess and her maids the acolytes. 'I hear she looks to her house well,' wrote Lady Hobart of a newly wedded niece, 'and grows a notable housewife and delights in it.'

The end of seventeenth-century marriage was the procreation of children. 'I hope,' a husband wrote, 'that I shall yet live to see my little round wife come tumbling home to her brats with a brat in her belly.' For economic reasons the poor married and bred late, but better-to-do parents were always praying that God would 'fill the cradle with sweet brave babes.' 'Your mother,' wrote a ruined cavalier to his son, 'was well delivered of her tenth daughter (the thing is called Bridget), so that now you have had three sisters born in the space of thirty-two months. You may well think that is not the way to get rich.'

Few mothers were too grand to nurse their young. 'I wish you could see me sitting at table with my little chickens one on either side,' wrote one great lady; 'in all my life I have not had such an occupation to my content to see them in bed at night and get them up in the morning.' 'My boy is now undressing by me,' wrote another, 'and is such pretty company that he hinders me so I cannot write what I would.'

*   *   *

Education began early. Life was too uncertain to prolong child-hood unnecessarily; the sooner boys stood on their own feet and girls were married the better. Rich and poor alike learnt their catechism from the parson after Sunday morning service, while those who were taught to read studied the alphabet from the horn-book – a printed page pasted on a small wooden bat covered with talc, framed in horn and hung round a child's neck; it could also be used for battledore and shuttlecock. For most, however, there was no book-schooling save such as was given, at best, for a year or so in childhood at the village dame-school. The majority of the population was illiterate; Pepys tells of a mayor of Bristol who pretended to read a pass upsidedown. But there was education in craftsmanship and vocation, taught by father to son or master to apprentice; a master tailor's son became a tailor, and a carpenter's a carpenter. It was a training that, at best, utilized the imitative instinct in a boy, taught him to do one thing thoroughly, and that the trade which he was to follow, and to take pride in doing so.

For those destined for positions in Church and State – a minority, though by no means confined to a single class – a classical education afforded the mental discipline needed to make decisive minds. Bred on brown bread, cheese and small beer – drunk from a stone jar into which careful mothers would sometimes drop a little rhubarb – while the girls were set to sampler work and the arts of deportment and household management, the sons of the gentry, armed with goose-quill, slate and ink-horn, advanced against the first entrenchments of the classics. Leaving aside such prodigies as little Richard Evelyn, who could, before his fifth year, decline all the nouns, conjugate the verbs, regular and most of the irregular, and recite the entire vocabulary of Latin and French primitives, the average of attainment was surprisingly high. Thirteen-year-old Richard Butler, who had been brought up at home in the wilds of Ireland and was regarded as backward, could read Ceasar's *Commentaries* in Latin to his grandfather with ease. 'You may find us now and then,' wrote the latter, 'up to the ears in Plutarch, in a hot dispute whether Alexander or Caesar was the braver man; and perhaps within an hour or two this gallant young disputant will be up to the knees in the brambles, at the head of a whole regiment of pitiful tatterdemalions beating to start a hare.' For, reared in a communal household drawn from every rank in rural society, a seventeenth-century country gentleman was in little danger of growing up out of touch with those whom he was called upon to govern.

The country was still largely unenclosed and game was plentiful. Shooting, which was taking the place of the older sports of fowling and hawking, was becoming a science, and most squires kept and trained pointers, setters and retrievers. As for horse dealing, it provided a means of sport, travel and profit, as well as entertainment, for the whole nation. 'Had you seen or heard how Mr H. V. and Mr J. O. Risley cheated one another in the exchange of two admirable jades,' wrote one countryman to another, 'and with what confidence and craft it was carried, 'twould make you intermit a little of your serious thoughts.' Hunting was universally practised, but was still rather a miscellaneous sport, where every hedge squire kept his own hounds and went after anything that ran. The main pursuit was hare-hunting.

Love of field sports gave the nation bluff, cheerful, healthy rulers – men such as Lord Shaftesbury's friend, Squire Hastings of Woodlands in Dorset. Long, thin, fiery-haired, in aged clothes of green which even when new had never cost more than five pounds, he kept all manner of hounds that ran – buck, fox, hare, otter and badger – and his house was full of hawks, hounds and terriers. His walls were hung with gamekeepers' poles and the skins of foxes and martens, and the floor of his hall strewn with marrow-bones. 'He was well-natured, but soon angry, calling his servants bastards and cuckoldry knaves, in which he often spoke truth to his own knowledge, and sometimes in both, though of the same man. He lived to be a hundred and never lost his eyesight, but always wrote and read without spectacles and got on horseback without help. Until past four-score he rode to the death of a stag as well as any.'

Yet, despite their passion for field sports, the country gentry were far from all being gross, boorish nimrods. Their letters give a very different picture of their tastes and interests than those of contemporary plays and lampoons. Educated, the best of them, at famous Latin schools like Westminster, Eton and Winchester – 'the best nursery for learning for young children in the world' – and at Oxford or Cambridge colleges which drew their revenues from their native shires, they built commodious classical houses, filled them with artistic treasures and, encompassing them with walled gardens to catch the sunlight, made fountains, parterres and grottoes and walks of beech and sycamore. They stocked their libraries with finely printed editions of the classics and of history, theology and literature, and bound them in the seemly russet and gold of their age. And since there was no other secure form of investment but land, they looked after their estates with industry and good sense.

*   *   *

Yet England was no longer a purely agricultural country. Fostered by the Puritan virtues, trade was steadily growing. The poverty which followed in the train of the Civil Wars stimulated this expansion, for it drove many, whose early upbringing had accustomed them to a high standard of living, to see a return on their reduced capital that only enterprise could give. The costly tastes which the restored Court imported from France furthered this process. 'Venturing' was in the air. When young Dudley North made his first voyage to the Levant as apprentice to a Turkey merchant, his lawyer brother invested the whole of his slender savings with him, while his father gave him a hundred pounds and bade him live on it and make his fortune. He did so, peer's younger son though he was; a life of poverty would have been the only alternative. So also William Blundell of Crosby, struggling to keep his estate together under the pressure of fines and decimation scraped together £40 and risked it in a small share of 'an adventure to the Barbadoes in the good ship *Antelope* of Liverpool', to receive a year later a hundred per cent return on his investment. 'Keep your shop and your shop will keep you', was the prudent motto of the London trader; and this sober integrity was enhanced by a capacity for taking risks. A city merchant told Pepys how by doing so he had had credit for £100,000 at a time when his total wealth in hand was not more than £1,000.

Though the growth of luxurious tastes offered a premium to the trader who had the capital or credit to lay out on remote returns, there was scope for the small man with pluck and initiative. A universal spirit of enterprise prevailed, everyone seeming ready to supplement his earnings by setting up in some sort of trade. A foreign visitor in 1669 reported that there was not a rustic's cottage in Devon or Somerset that did not manufacture white lace; in Suffolk every housewife plied her rock and distaff at the open cottage door and in Gloucestershire the old women knitted stockings while they smoked their pipes and baked their puddings.

With industry went integrity of workmanship. Throughout the world the English were building a reputation for quality. It was symptomatic of their genius that they excelled in the making of instruments of precision. Every parish had its subsidiary population of masons, carpenters, smiths and wheelwrights, who made its houses and furniture, supplied its agricultural implements, shoed its horses and did its repairs. This rustic proximity of client to craftsman set a premium on thorough workmanship, which, handed down from father to son, survived in newer crafts where the local check was wanting. The typical English craftsman of the seventeenth century was old Jonas Shish, that plain, honest ship's carpenter whom Evelyn knew, and who, though he could hardly read and never could explain his trade to another, built many a fine ship, as his forbears had done before him.

The quiet years of Charles II's reign were marked by steady mercantile and colonial expansion. Men were laying up for themselves and their children treasure for the future. On every sea the adventurous ships of England sailed, returning with riches in their holds to enhance the wealth of a little island of squires, yeomen and homely merchants, and bringing silks and scents and delicate fabrics for their ladies. In a quarter of a century Evelyn's £250 invested in the stock of the East India Company multiplied threefold. Pennsylvania, where Charles dispatched the Quaker Penn in 1682; the Carolinas, New York and the shores of the Hudson; treaties with the Turks and Moors to make Englishmen free of the Mediterranean; trading settlements at Bombay and Fort William, and dusky ambassadors bringing gifts from the Great Mogul; companies to trade with Africa, Guinea and the coasts of Barbary; expeditions to find a new road to the East through the Arctic ice or discover the wonders of the South Seas: all these were milestones in the country's commercial and imperial development. 'This part of Africa is very fertile,' a pioneer reported, 'and wants nothing but English industry to improve it.' There was immeasurable confidence in what an outward-looking maritime community of five million could achieve. 'The thing which is nearest the heart of this nation,' wrote the King to his sister, 'is trade and all that belongs to it.'

The atmosphere of adventuring and experimenting was favourable to scientific discovery. During the Interregnum a little group of learned men had begun to meet in Wadham College at Oxford to discover something of the world they lived in. They were the nucleus of the Royal Society, which was founded in Christopher Wren's room in Gresham College shortly after the Restoration. At their weekly meetings the conversation was philosophical and cheerful, and the experiments ranged all nature. They employed an itinerant, who every year made a report of his discoveries, bringing back, not tales of new Messiahs or godly judgments on the wicked, but dried fowls, fish, plants and minerals. When Prince Rupert was about to lead a fleet against the Dutch on the Guinea coast the virtuosos requested him to employ his leisure in sounding the depths and fetching up water from the bottom of the sea. In their boundless curiosity they were blue-printing a new design for living. Even, when the plague of 1665 was at its height, Evelyn, calling at Durdans, discovered Dr Wilkins, Sir William Petty and Robert Hooke contriving chariots, new rigging for ships, a wheel to run races in, and other mechanical inventions.

Pneumatic engines, aeolipiles for weighing air, calculating machines, quench-fires, even a 'new fashion gun to shoot off often, one after another, without trouble or danger, very pretty,' all came alike to this remarkable generation. And with all this achievement these men were not specialists, but versatile beyond imagination. Wren, at twenty-four, was a professor of astronomy and the wonder of Europe for mechanical invention, and was over thirty before he ever thought of architecture. The learned Lord Keeper Guilford, beside attaining to an exquisite skill in music, devoted much time to the Torricelian experiments; his youngest brother, Roger North, barrister, musician, author and architect, mastered the theory of light. 'The very remembrance of these things,' he wrote in after years, 'is delight, and while I write methinks I play. All other employments that filled my time go on account of work and business: these were all pleasure.'

* * *

Mercantile enterprise was backed by the country's natural resources. With plenty of coal, iron, lead, lime and timber, and an easily accessible littoral, rich in harbours, England was ideally equipped for world trade. Her chief commodity was her woollen manufactures, but she also exported tin, pewter, brass, horn, leather, glass and earthenware. In return, her merchants brought home tobacco from the plantations of the New World, wine from France, Spain and Portugal, sugar and rum from Barbados and Jamaica, spices and silks from the Levant, timber and tar from the Baltic and cotton goods from India.

The Navigation Acts gave the carriage of most of these commodities to English shipowners. Those who manned their vessels served a rough and varied apprenticeship, often beginning their sea-life in the fishing trade before they took service in the merchantmen or, more occasionally, in the King's ships of war. All round the coasts the shipbuilders were busy – at Newcastle, Sunderland, Hull, Yarmouth, Aldeburgh, Harwich, Shoreham, Portsmouth and Bristol – while the whole of the Thames from London Bridge to Blackwall was a vast shipbuilding yard. And to feed the yards the rivers were filled with timber floating seawards from the more accessible woods.

This sea-borne trade was paid for by a heavy price in human suffering. The merchant captains and seamen who trafficked with the Mediterranean ports took their lives in their hands, and suffered more perils than those of the Atlantic waves. From Sallee, Algiers and Tripoli issued the Moorish corsairs, with whose governments the English Crown lived, at best, in a state of precarious peace, and whose swift vessels were a match for all but the strongest merchantman. Many English seamen captured by them passed the rest of their lives in loathsome captivity. Others, after years, were ransomed by the funds raised by the charitable in England for the redemption of slaves. So a tender-hearted gentleman wrote to the Secretary of the Admiralty to tell him how Captain Spurrill, who had endured nine years' cruel usage at Tangier, had been redeemed by his efforts. 'And now this poor suffering man is free,' he added, 'if you will thrust him into his Majesty's service that he may know how to live, I will publish your generosity to everybody.'

Of the freights that English ships bore outwards, cloth was still king. The three great districts of its manufacture were East Anglia, the South-West and Yorkshire. From the first came the baizes and serges of Colchester and Sudbury, all the villages round which span wool for Portugal and Italy. Colchester in 1662 boasted eight churches and employed 10,000 workers. As one travelled from Suffolk to Norfolk the signs of industry and prosperity became still more marked, a face of diligence being spread over the whole county, till the spires of Norwich rose before one, the greatest town in England for the making of stuffs and worsted stockings.

In the South-West was the quality trade. This was the broadcloth manufacture which clothed the fine gentlemen of half Europe. Fed by the wool of Salisbury Plain and the Cotswolds, almost every parish between upper Thames and Exe was learning to make fine cloth. From the towns of four counties – Somerset, Wiltshire, Dorset and Gloucestershire – the master-clothiers sent out wool to the villages, where women and children spun the yarn which later their packmen collected for their looms. Here a union of nascent capitalism and cottage industry was enriching a whole community. In the pleasant valleys of the Stroud and Wiltshire Avon the sides of the hills were covered with the paddocks of clothiers, each man in 'his fair stone house' and spending his £500 a year. Bristol for drugget and cantaloon, Taunton for serges, Wells for fine Spanish stockings, Frome for medley cloth, and Bradford-on-Avon and Stroud for dyes, were the household names of the West Country trade that Bristol, Barnstaple and Blackwell Hall exported to all the world. And farther west was Exeter of the serges, where thousands of artisans and all the country folk for twenty miles round were continuously employed in making baizes and light cloths for Spain, France, Italy and the Levant.

The cloth trade of the West Riding was as yet only concerned with the coarser manufactures. The Yorkshire kerseys of Leeds, Halifax, Huddersfield, Bradford and Wakefield supplied the needs of common folk who could not afford the fine medley and broadcloth of the west. The wool market at Leeds, which appeared miraculously twice a week down the broad main street of the town, was already resorted to by factors with letters from customers in places as distant as Russia and North America. It was fed by the industry of the Yorkshire clothiers, whose houses and stony enclosures lined the slopes of the West Riding valleys, so that, as one gazed down them, the eye was caught by the pale gleam of innumerable pieces of white cloth stretched upon the tenters. With coal and running water at their doors, they were able to complete in their own houses almost all the processes required for their trade.

All this manufacturing was rural in its setting, and most of those who practised it were also engaged in agriculture. The merchants and shopkeepers of the provincial towns kept farm and orchard in the adjacent meads. Only giant London, and to a lesser degree Bristol, were urban entities. The latter, with its crowded Tolsey, its tall bridge across the Avon, lined like London's with continuous houses, and its cobble-stones worn smooth by sledges, was the only place in England beside the capital which could market unaided the goods which its merchants brought home. Its carriers supplied all South Wales, the South-West, and the western midlands with sugar, wine, oil and tobacco. Liverpool, which with the development of the industrial north was to outdistance Bristol in the next century, was still only in process of transition from a ragged fishing village to a brick town, while Southampton was apparently dying of old age and London competition.

Straw hats from Dunstable, saddles from Burford, buttons and thread from Maidstone, salt from Worcester, Chester and Newcastle, were some of the lesser manufactures which rustic England produced in the last age before the Industrial Revolution. The geographical distribution of industry is best indicated by the annual excise returns; that for 1665 shows that while London, Middlesex and Surrey were together farmed for £140,000, the yield for Yorkshire, Kent, Norfolk and Devon was £16,000, £15,000, £13,800, and £9,500 respectively, and for Essex, Gloucester, Suffolk and

Lincolnshire from £8,600 to £7,200. None of the other counties was farmed for more than £4,600, with little Huntingdonshire, which was almost entirely rural, bringing up the rear with an excise rental of only £1,400.

In all this activity of the English breadwinner there was little hindrance from the State. Most of the old medieval restraints operated in theory rather than in practice, and were everywhere falling into disuse. After the crushing exactions of the Interregnum, taxes were low, and direct taxation, save in time of war, almost negligible. Most of the revenue was raised by the indirect impositions of Customs and Excise, and the former protected English industry as much as the latter penalized it. And wherever Customs duties proved excessive they were mitigated by the wholesale smuggling that immediately sprang up, for in those policeless days the laws of supply and demand easily overrode the paternal intentions of governments. On Romney Marsh the illicit export of wool, which was called 'owling', and the import of brandy, wine and tobacco so profitable that it maintained a whole population of armed smugglers, usually more than capable of intimidating the occasional soldiers sent to suppress them.

*　　*　　*

The domestic trader's chief handicap was the state of the roads. Subjected to an ever-growing volume of wheeled traffic, they were worse than they had been in the Middle Ages. So deep were the ruts on the main highways that in the spring it was customary for the parish authorities to plough them up with the road-plough kept under the church-porch. In some parts of the country, notably in the heavy midlands and the deep clays of Sussex, teams of oxen were used to draw carts and coaches, and in the west the hills were so full of rolling stones and the lanes so narrow that corn was carried, not in carts, but on the backs of horses, corded on wooden frames. The demands of the metropolis turned every highway near it into a quagmire, sodden with the ordure of a never-ceasing procession of beasts – cattle, sheep, pigs, turkeys, geese – marching to the London slaughter-houses. And on every heath and moor

271

suspicious-looking men, muffled up in great-coats and with pistols at their sides, might be observed speculating on the possible strength of passing travellers. Those who seemed to have small capacity for resistance they would approach and travel beside for a while, until opportunity offered for even closer acquaintance.

On such roads it was easy for travellers to lose their way. Sign-posts were almost unknown, and on the lonelier stretches travellers hired guides. Riding from Huntingdon to Biggleswade, Pepys had to employ the services of two countrymen to lead him through the waters. Every few miles travellers were forced to ford a stream, and every few hundred yards a watercourse. Bridges were few, and many of the broader rivers could only be crossed by ferry, an unpleasant proceeding which necessitated maddening delay and often, in winter, a severe cold.

For those who wished to travel quickly the post-horse was the surest medium. Post-horses could be hired from the Government postmasters along the main roads at threepence a mile, with an extra fourpence for the guide at each stage. But, though a single man riding post might cover the distance from Huntingdon to London in the inside of a day or from Chester to London in two, anything on wheels travelled far more slowly. Private coaches, drawn by teams of shire horses or Flemish mares, were an uncertain and expensive form of travel, especially when they began to grow old. 'I wish the new wheels had come up with my coach,' complained one magnate, 'for these old wheels break every time they go out.' 'I had a sad mischance coming from London with my wife and servants,' wrote another, 'for the coach overturned and fell on the side I sat on, and those in the coach fell on me and thereby put one hip out of joint and mightily strained the joint of my other hip and my back bones are displaced.'

Stage coaches were the chief contribution of the time to the amenities of travel. Clumsy, boxlike vehicles, usually made of black leather and swung on leather straps, with wooden shutters or flaps for windows, they jolted at thirty or forty miles a day up and down the main roads. To those who remembered the country before the Civil Wars they appeared almost unbelievably fast: 'in four days and a half from Garswood to London,' wrote Lancashire

William Blundell, 'it seems to be almost incredible.' Yet the printed bills advertising the 'flying coaches' which accomplished the journey from Oxford to the 'Greyhound' in Holborn in a single day, never failed to end with the cautious proviso, 'If God permit.'

Every coach had its inns of call in the towns along its route, where horses were changed. Innkeeping in England was regarded as a respectable profession; at The Crown, Mansfield, the landlord and his wife were gentlefolk. More often the former was 'an honest ingenious man' of the middle rank, who distilled 'incomparable strong waters' and kept good wine, a bowling-green and perhaps a cockpit for his neighbours. In many places after the Restoration he was an old soldier, who had fought for King Charles and loved to regale travellers with tales of Prince Rupert and Marston Moor. And since horses and inns went together, he was generally something of a jockey, and, like good Mr Hunt of The Three Cranes, Doncaster, was fond of talking horses. And with good fare for mind and body, it mattered little if an odd frog or two croaked in one's chamber, or if mine host, anxious not to foul more sheets than necessary, was over-apt to assume that his guests were ready to share a bed.

Heavy goods, if they went by land, did so without reference to time. Perishable wares could only be moved at heavy expense. Mackerel, which could be bought at a penny a hundred on the beach at Bridport, fetched twice as many shillings in the London market. Long strings of pack-horses, travelling in file with a bell tinkling from the leading horse, were the goods trains of the age; unless they went by water, coal, iron, wool and crates of clay for the potteries all travelled in this way. In many parts of the country narrow stone causeways, raised above the morass of the surrounding highway, were built to accommodate such traffic.

Since the roads were so bad, much of the heavier merchandise went by river. The wharves of Reading, Maidenhead and Henley shipped Berkshire and Oxfordshire malt and meal on to barges which fed London, taking in return oils, groceries, salt and tobacco for the neighbouring countryside. Every sizable river bore its share of freightage, and, as the century drew to a close, scheme after scheme came before parliament for making navigable some provincial river and opening up new trade.

One commodity in England travelled quickly – his Majesty's mails. Ever since the Crown had taken over responsibility for a postal service at the beginning of the century the speed at which letters moved had been increasing. Each of the main roads radiating from London had its regular service, with post-houses at all the principal towns. Here letters were distributed to the local carriers or fetched by the messengers of the country gentry. They were charged on delivery, and by the sheet and distance: a single sheet travelled from London for twopence for the first eighty miles, and a double sheet for twice as much. Envelopes being unknown, letters were elaborately folded, sealed and addressed on the outside, as

'To my honourable Friend
Sir Jeffrey Shakerley
at his house Hulme
Stone bag.'

Sometimes, especially in the case of Government dispatches, they were further superscribed with directions to local postmasters and postboys. 'Haste, haste, haste', was scrawled across one letter which must have aroused much excitement as it travelled down the Great North Road, 'for his Majesty's most important service. Ride for your life.'

The chief drawback of the postal service was its cost. An unsuccessful private scheme of 1659, and a successful one of 1680, attempted to overcome this by the establishment of a penny post in the capital. That of 1680, which conferred immortality on a not too reputable speculator named Dockwra, introduced the principle of dated postmarks. As, however, it infringed the Government's monopoly, the scheme was taken over by the State, which incorporated most of its other features, yet characteristically doubled the cost. But the high cost of postage was in part overcome by the privilege of franking, allowed to members of both Houses of Parliament. As legislators were exceedingly generous in providing their friends and constituents with signatures, few merchants of importance had any difficulty in getting their letters franked. Apart from the post there was no national public service except the courts of law, the revenue, the Navy and the newly formed standing Army of royal guards. All other administration was left to the parish, whose humble officers preserved the peace, enforced public order, maintained the highways and administered the poor law and public relief under the supervision of the justices of the peace, the sheriff and lord lieutenant. Those who did the dogsbody work of government at the lowest level were still drawn from the general body of the people. Except in the towns, where their duties were performed by paid deputies, they were unpaid. Every householder who was not a member of one of the classes specially exempted by parliament was expected to serve his turn in the parish offices or provide a substitute. Service was usually for a year; failure to perform its duties was punishable at law by fine and imprisonment. The principal parish officers were the churchwardens, the overseers of the poor, the overseers of the highways, and the petty constables. The first, in addition to the duties of church maintenance, still in theory exercised some of the moral functions of the medieval church, such as visiting ale-houses during the hours of divine service and driving malingerers to worship. The duties of the overseers of the poor were much more onerous. Appointed by the justices from a rota of householders, it was their business to give weekly relief to the aged and impotent, to keep a stock of raw material on which to set the able-bodied unemployed to work, to build houses on the common land for the houseless, to educate poor children and bind them as apprentices and to administer any lands or moneys left by the charitable for the poor of the parish. To provide such services they were empowered to levy a poor rate under cover of the signature of the local justices; for failure to perform them adequately they could be indicted at Quarter Sessions. Neglect of a destitute person might even bring them to the dock for manslaughter, while extravagance in the use of parish funds exposed them to the wrath of their neighbours.

The surveyor of the highways, sometimes called the boonmaster or waywarden, was appointed by the court of Quarter Sessions from a list of agricultural holders submitted by the vestries. It was his business to see that all whose property adjoined the public highways kept clear their gutters and drains, trimmed their hedges and refrained from stacking manure, timber or hay on the road. If they proved refractory it was his duty to name them in the parish church after the sermon, giving them thirty days' grace in which to make amends, after which he was entitled to do it himself at their expense. It was also his duty to waylay passing carts and wagons with more than the statutory number of horses or with wheels of less than the statutory width, and generally enforce the transport enactments of parliament and Privy Council. And three times a year he had to 'view' every road, watercourse, pavement and bridge in the parish and report their state to the justices, sub-sequently, with the latter's authority, levying a highway rate to bear the cost of repairs. His most arduous duty was the supervision of the statute labour which every householder, either in person or by deputy, was compelled by law to perform for six days in the year.

Apart from the small fry of parish officialdom – clerk, sexton, beadle and bellman – most of whom were paid, the oldest of the parish officers was the constable. He was appointed at the court leet and sworn by the justices. First and foremost it was his duty to preserve the King's peace. If any affray was made he had to pro-ceed to the spot and, bearing his staff of office, call upon the offen-ders to desist. 'Christopher Stubbs of Wath,' ran the record of a north-country court, 'presented at Richmond for making an assault and affray, on Christmas last in John Tanfield's house, on one John Stapleton and also for abusing James Harrison, constable of Wath, reviling him and pulling away a great part of his beard, when commanding the said Christopher to keep the peace.' In persuance of his duty the constable could call on any citizen to assist him, and it was an indictable offence to refuse. For in the village community, democracy was not a right but an obligation.

The constable's functions were so many that it must have been difficult for him during his year of office to earn his livelihood. It was his duty to enforce the statutes which a puritanically-minded parliament periodically passed against cursing and swearing, tippling in ale-houses, profaning the Sabbath and eavesdropping at neighbours' windows. In such matters, however, custom and the remoteness of central authority allowed him wide discretion. If in the execution of his duties he exceeded the law or trespassed on some private liberty, an action lay against him at the suit of the injured person; if he allowed a malefactor committed for trial to escape from the parish cage or lock-up, or his own house, he could be imprisoned. It must sometimes have been a relief to his feelings to execute the punishments meted out by the justices to erring citizens – to put a nagging woman in the ducking-stool or affix such a notice as Robert Storr and Christopher Smith, constables of Bedale, were ordered to attach to the person of Margery Metcalf of Crackall: 'I sit here in the stocks for beating my own mother.'

Most educative of all the constable's tasks was his attendance at the courts – to present an offender at petty sessions, to wait on the head constable of the hundred, to present a return or pay in the parish taxes, to journey to the county town to answer an indictment brought against his village for failure of some statutory duty. It brought him into contact with a wider world, showed him how public business was executed and taught him the practical difficulties of administration.

* * *

Such was the nursery of England's democracy. Her people were proud and independent, accustomed to manage their own affairs and resentful of interference. When a Court official tried to keep the common folk of Windsor out of the royal park they assembled in force, broke the gates and pales and announced that the park was their own. Foreign visitors were always testifying to the rude strength of English democracy; the king, wrote Sorbière, had to be free and easy with the nobility, the officers of the army with their soldiers, landlords with their tenantry.

For there could be no ruling such a people on any other terms. Fighting was their favourite pastime. In Moorfields, on holidays, the butchers, out of hereditary hatred, fell upon the weavers till they were glad to pull off their aprons and hide them in their breeches; or sometimes it would be the weavers who won, wounding and bruising all their rivals and calling out round the town: 'A hundred pounds for a butcher!' The very Inns of Court were riotous, and when the Lord Mayor elected to go to dinner in the

Temple with his sword borne before him, the students pulled it down and besieged him all day in a councillor's room. Even in Oxford a learned antiquary belaboured one of his fellow dons whenever he met him, giving him many a bloody nose and black eye.

This pugnacity the English carried into the concerns of State. In this they astonished foreigners; a Frenchman reported that the very boatmen wanted the milords to talk to them about State affairs while they rowed them to parliament. With those who disagreed with their views they had a short way. When the French ambassador omitted to light a bonfire at his door to celebrate an English victory over the Dutch, the mob smashed his windows and all but grilled him on his own furniture. His successor, after describing an attempt to kill the first Minister of the Crown in his own bedroom, could only comment: 'When I reflect that this land produces neither wolves nor venomous beasts, I am not surprised. The inhabitants are far more wicked and dangerous.'

Yet, widespread though the instinct for liberty was, the exercise of authority was equally so. If England was libertarian – even, within its aristocratic framework, democratic – it was also sternly and practically authoritarian. From time immemorial the Crown had ruled by delegating its authority at every level to local worthies and representatives whom it supervised through the instrument of royal functionaries and the law – privy councillors, judges of assize and eyre, sheriffs, high constables, coroners, lord lieutenants and deputy lieutenants, justices of the peace and many more. Few Englishmen of whatever rank to whom authority was entrusted seemed afraid of exercising it; those who failed to do so were little accounted. Part of the immense respect in which Cromwell was held by his countrymen – for all the opprobrium he suffered as a usurper and regicide – was that he was not afraid to use the full authority of a king. One sees the men of that age through the mists of time – the hot-blooded gentry who fought in their cups, the country tenants twisting words in their manor courts to cheat their lords, the unpoliced Londoners who plundered the very sweet-meats from the feasts of the great. Proud and unbending, their natures were tinged by melancholy and deep feeling that sometimes turned their pugnacity to strange enthusiasms and stranger oddities. 'Everywhere in England,' wrote a foreigner, 'you will meet with gloomy and fanatical humours, presumption and extravagance of thought.' Yet, there was something in them, he added, that was great and which they seemed to inherit from the old Romans. It was from their freedom that they derived it.

Encompassed with Wooden Walls

'It may be said now to England,
Martha, Martha, thou art busy about
many things, but one thing is necessary.
To the question, What shall we do to
be saved in this world? there is no
other answer but this, Look to your Moat.
The first article of an Englishman's political
creed must be, That he believeth in the sea.'

George Savile, Marquess of Halifax

SECOND ONLY TO JOHNSON, Samuel Pepys is the quintessential Englishman. Through the many volumes of his Diary, the greatest in the language, we have not only a detailed portrait of an endlessly fascinating man, but as exact a depiction of his age as of any in our history. Our vision of the reign of Charles II comes large as life from his pages. Three times in the course of a great naval war it fell to the lot of this rising young Navy Board official to record in his shorthand diary three shattering national disasters. In the summer of 1665, when alone among his colleagues in the nascent Admiralty, he had remained at his post in the stricken capital, he described vividly the horrors of London's last epidemic of bubonic plague. A year later he became for four hectic days the chronicler of the Great Fire which all but destroyed it.* And in the spring of 1667 he had, for the third year running, to record another national disaster which not only brought the three years' naval war against the Dutch – who, after concluding peace with Spain became our fierce competitors in trade – to an abject and humilia-

* A full account of Pepys's description of the plague of 1665 and the Great Fire of 1666 may be found in the author's *The Man in the Making*.

ting conclusion, but threatened him with the loss of office and even –
such was the public clamour it aroused against the Navy Office – of
his liberty and fortune. For that spring, in the face of the enormous
burden of naval debt and unpaid bills and wages brought about
by War, Plague and Fire, and the even more costly failure of
Parliament to vote adequate supplies to service, provision and
man the King's ships, the Government – relying on a speedy
end to the peace negotiations then in progress – adopted the
disastrous economy of laying up the battle-fleet. As a result,
during the second week of May 1667 the Dutch entered the
Thames estuary, broke through the chain guarding the mouth of
the Medway, where the unmanned English warships were moored,
and, after setting fire to some of them, carried away the flag-ship,
the *Royal Charles*, in triumph. The news, Pepys wrote, 'struck me
to the heart.'

It is conceivable that but for Pepys's work during the next two
decades Britain might never have achieved that permanent naval
ascendancy in the world's seas which she was to maintain until the
present century, and might have remained what she had been
before his time, a second-class European power without an overseas empire. In the year 1633, in which he had been born, English
villages on her south-western coasts were still being raided by
Algerian pirates who held in slavery thousands of her seamen
captured on trading voyages to the Mediterranean. For the boast
that England commanded even the narrow seas around her was
hardly borne out in fact. Pepys, a poor London tailor's son who had
won a Cambridge scholarship from St Paul's school and at the age
of 27 in 1660 was given the lucrative office of Clerk of the Acts of
the Navy Board through his kinship to the Commander-in-Chief
of the fleet which brought back Charles II. Before that there had
only been two recent periods in the country's history when she had
been feared at sea: in those wonderful three decades at the end of
Elizabeth's reign when Drake and his fellow West Country seamen
had defied the naval might of imperial Spain and her tyrannical
monopoly of the right to trade and colonize in the New World, and
in the even shorter space of time when, by dint of unprecedented
taxation and rigid discipline, Cromwell and his great admiral,

Robert Blake, had made the Commonwealth fleet a dominating factor in European politics. Apart from these two brief spells of victory and glory, since Henry VIII had first created a permanent naval establishment it is hardly an exaggeration to say that the main function of the King's ships had been to provide careers, estates and perquisites for corrupt officials and fradulent contractors.

When Pepys entered upon his new functions, he was ignorant of almost everything that belonged to them. During his first two years of office, apart from accepting, like every government official of his day, whatever discreeet bribes, commissions and perquisites offered themselves, his chief concern was to make the most of his new-found importance – the foremost pew in church, the four-poster bed to himself when he visited abroad – and to enjoy the highly convivial companionship of his more experienced colleagues, Admirals Batten and Penn. For the rest, as he put it, 'I did lie late abed'.

But early in 1662 there came the first signs of change. The colleagues whose bacchanalian habits and social position had made them at first so attractive began to prove irksome, and their rather natural insistence on their superior experience and status galled the pride of the young Clerk of the Acts. In his isolation, he sought for ways by which he could show himself their equal. He had not far to look, for his fellow officers were anything but attentive to their business. 'So to the office,' he wrote, 'where I do begin to be exact in my duty there and exacting my privileges and shall continue to do so.' It was the beginning of a new era in his life, and ultimately England's, Pepys had found his vocation.

It was not in his nature to do things by halves. Having resolved thenceforward to do his duty, Pepys set out to equip himself for its performance. In the summer of 1662 he occupied his leisure moments by learning the multiplication table, listening to lectures upon the body of a ship, and studying the prices of naval stores. 'Into Thames Street beyond the bridge, and there enquired among the ships the price of tar and oil, and do find great content in it, and hope to save the King money by this practice.'

Pepys's transcendent qualities as an administrator were first

displayed between the years 1664 and 1667, when the Second
Dutch War put the English naval administration to the test. The
summer campaign of 1665 began with a great victory, a triumph
for English gunnery; but its fruits were lost at a critical moment of
the year, when a Dutch fleet might have been destroyed, because
the British commander-in-chief was forced to withdraw his ships
to harbour owing to a breakdown in the victualling system. On
October 6th 1665, Pepys sat down and drafted a letter to the duke
of Albemarle outlining and proposing remedies, which is a model
of how an important administrative recommendation should be
worded. Starting from clearly stated premises, it unfolded in lucid,
compelling language, illustrated every now and then by phrases
which stick in the memory, both the pros and cons of his argument,
until its unanswerable logic had demolished all objections. Nor
does it detract from its merit that Pepys hoped, as he admitted in
his Diary, 'to do himself a job of work in it.' Few could grudge his
salary to the new Surveyor-General of Victualling, as he became,
knowing how dire was the need of such supervision and how well
equipped he was to give it.

For when he felt his pulse for pleasure beat too high, he set his
will against his erring heart and the frailties of his over susceptible
nature and conquered them. 'But Lord!' he wrote, 'what a conflict
I had with myself, my heart tempting me a thousand times to
go abroad about some pleasure or other, notwithstanding the
weather foul. However I reproached myself with my weakness in
yielding so much my judgement to my sense, and prevailed with
difficulty and did not budge; but stayed within and to my great
content did a great deal of business.' And as the summer of 1665
approached and the rival fleets prepared to put to sea, Pepys spent
his time setting all things to rights – getting his long-delayed
pursers' plan put into execution, making his report to the Lord
High Admiral's secretary, Sir William Coventry, on the state of the
victualling, and writing a solemn letter – this time to the Lord
High Admiral, the duke of York, himself – on the want of money,
stressing 'the excessive rates we are forced to give for everything
the service wants, the merchant resolving to save himself in the
uncertainty of his payment by the greatness of his price.' Nor,

when he could be spared from his desk, did he fail to take boat and so to his proper place 'by water among the ships'.

The Second Dutch War was the hard school in which Pepys learnt the lessons of maladministration and their correctives. Despite all his efforts, the supineness of his colleagues and the appalling want of money which crippled the Navy at every turn culminated in the humiliation of the Medway. Discouraged and disillusioned, for a time he even despaired, trifled away whole days on the pursuit of pleasure, both seemly and unseemly, and almost seemed to accept the inevitability of England's decline once more into a third-rate naval power. The sharp medicine of a parliamentary enquiry restored him. In February 1668 he shouldered the entire burden of defending himself and his incompetent colleagues from the charges brought against them. And as in the pages of his diary one watches that heroic fight, unsparing labour day and night, cool, courageous bearing, none the less noble because in his inner soul he was often afraid, one forgets the petty corruptions, the bullying days at home, the sly salacities of the secret hour in coach and tavern, and remembers only the great heart which dared to wage it and the cool head that triumphed over the enemies of his Office. Grumble he sometimes did, writing to the duke of York of the troublesome life he was forced to lead, dancing attendance on one Committee after another; retirement to country peace and quiet – 'a good book, and a good fiddle and I have a good wife' – he often contemplated; tired he was always, 'for I am weary,' he said, 'of this life.' But he stood fast.

On February 28th 1668 the angry Commons decided that the Principal Officers of the Navy should be ordered to answer for the crimes of which they were accused at the Bar of the House on the following Thursday. Pepys at the thought of that terrible ordeal wished himself a great way off – 'who am least able to bear these troubles, though I have the least cause to be concerned in it.' Then for five days he betook himself to the work of preparing the defence of the Office, for his colleagues were too busy excusing themselves to think of anything else. At ten o'clock on the eve of the dreaded day he went home, weary and dull and sick, feeling that he could do no more, and lay down on his bed. But sleep came but fitfully and after three hours he waked, 'never in so much trouble in all my life of mind, thinking of the task I have upon me . . . and what the issue of it may be.'

So he lay tossing restlessly till five in the morning, when he called to his wife Elizabeth to comfort him, which she at last succeeded in doing, making him resolve to resign his post and endure the trouble of it no more. Then at the Office with his clerks he huddled over a few more notes, took boat with his faithful assistants Hewer and Hayter to Westminster and joined his waiting colleagues. As the summons had not yet come he drank half a pint of mulled sack at the 'Dog' and added a dram of brandy bought from Mrs Howlett's stall in Westminster Hall. A little before midday they were called into the lobby. The House was full and alight with expectation.

There, when the Speaker had read the Report of the Committee, with his fellow officers standing taut and anxious about him and the Mace lying on the table before, Samuel Pepys began the defence of the Navy Office. And, as he stood there, a miracle happened; all doubts and fears fell from him and he spoke with a wonderful ease and certainty, 'most acceptably and smoothly and continued at it without any hesitation or loss but with full scope and all my reason free about me, as if it had been at my own table, from that time till past three in the afternoon, and so ended without any interruption from the Speaker'. Then they withdrew.

As they came out of the chamber, his colleagues whom he had saved and all those within hearing crowded around him, crying up his speech as the finest ever heard. It almost looked as if a vote acquitting the Principal Officers would be taken then and there, but Pepys had spoken so long that there was something of a stampede of members to their dinner, and the few who returned later were so drunk that such professed enemies of the Office as Sir Thomas Littleton were able to prevent the House from dividing. Yet nothing could rob Pepys of a wonderful triumph. When next morning he called on Sir William Coventry, the first word that statesman said to him was, 'Good morrow, Mr Pepys, that must be Speaker of the Parliament-house,' adding that the Solicitor-General had declared that he was the best speaker in England and that men were saying that he had but to put on a gown and plead at the Chancery bar and he could not fail to earn at least £1000 a year. His cousin George Montagu, outsoaring them all, embraced him, declaring that he had often before kissed his hands but now he would kiss his lips, for they were those of another Cicero. Even the King came up to him in the Park and congratulated him, and told his friends that he thought he might teach the Solicitor-General. Everywhere, at the Court, in the House, on 'Change, men spoke of his great performance. No wonder that the delighted, but prudent little man noted in his journal his resolution 'not to make any more speeches while my fame is good – for fear of losing of it'. Pepys had, in that speech, laid the foundation of confidence in the Navy Office on which he and his successors could build, and had exemplified by his honest competence the spirit of commitment to able public service on which the expansion of England's trade and dominion would come to rely.

*　　*　　*

Five years later, in the midst of another naval war against the Dutch, at the age of forty Pepys was called by Charles II to become Secretary of the Admiralty Commission which had been hastily set up to carry out the duties of the former Lord High Admiral, the duke of York, who had had to resign after having publicly declaring himself a Roman Catholic – in that fanatic age the most unpopular thing any Englishman could be. From 1673 to 1679 the former Clerk of the Acts became the virtual mainspring and controller of the Admiralty, establishing and enforcing administrative and disciplinary rules for the entire naval service and speaking and answering for it in Parliament. Acting as the sole interpreter of, as he was the sole link, between the limited and carefully defined functions of the new Admiralty Board and the more general powers which the King, who now trusted him implicitly, had retained in his own hands, he was able to establish order, method and precedent in every branch of the Service.

To apply to it the rules, first taught in his Puritan youth, by which he had gradually learnt to govern his own life, now became the essence of Pepys's work. 'Little care,' he jotted down among the rough notes on naval matters which he kept for his own guidance, 'goes to the making officers of the Navy for their own preservation to put in very wholesome words and cautions in their orders for any service to be done, such as words of Dispatch, Efficacy, Good Husbandry, etc.' He himself never failed to insert such words in his orders and to insist that they were observed. Henceforward, in the Service, there was to be a rule for everything, and an unsleeping authority to see that it was obeyed or punished when disobeyed.

For schoolmaster in sea matters to the nation in general, and the Navy in particular, was what Pepys became for the remainder of his official life. During it he was responsible for initiating, planning and securing from a reluctant and often hostile Parliament the necessary finance for the greatest shipbuilding programme ever undertaken in the country's history – the provision of 30 new battleships built on the most up-to-date lines, which was to give his country the strongest battle fleet in Europe. In doing so and in enforcing his rules on the highest, as well as the lowest, officer in the Service, he made many enemies. In 1679, during the hysterical national panic of the so-called Popish Plot, he was driven from office and, as a staunch supporter of his former master, the hated Catholic duke of York, was thrown into the Tower, falsely accused of popery and high treason and, for many months, was in danger of his life. During the next four years when he was out of office and the King, playing the political storm, was unable to make use of his incomparable services, the corrupt and inefficient politicians who mismanaged the Admiralty Service in Pepys's absence – the 'land admirals', as the contemptuous seamen called them – allowed the new battle fleet he had built to rot at its moorings in the neglected and plundered dockyards.

Then, as the political tide gradually turned in the King's favour in the autumn of 1683, Pepys was recalled to service and sent on a mission as chief adviser to his friend, Dartmouth, who was being sent with a fleet to evacuate the inhabitants and military garrison of England's costly North African colony, Tangier. While there, and during the homeward voyage in the winter gales of early 1684, he was able to see, at first hand, the crying need for the restoration of the rules and discipline he had been at such pains to establish in the naval Service.

As the fleet fought its way northward, Pepys talked much with the ship's officers about the affairs of the Navy. Sam Atkins, his old clerk, now acting as joint secretary to Lord Dartmouth, told him how openly the captains despised their orders, each man saying that it was better to get a few thousand pounds by a 'good voyage' carrying bullion and merchandise for private merchants, in defiance of orders than to obey them when at the worst the only punishment would be dismissal from an uncertain employment. Once rich, for all they cared, the Service might go to the devil. Atkins cited the case of Captain Russell – the future victor of La Hogue – who had made a vast fortune by ignoring all Pepys's rules, and could now never be tempted to sea again, though the best gentleman-commander in the fleet.

Pepys was a man of the pen, little accustomed to danger or monotony, a bureaucrat with a passion for rules of his own devising, a great condemner of the human failings of others, though one who had done very well for himself in his own time. He was growing old and, many may have thought, curmudgeonly. But his anger was not caused solely by the time-long corruption and laxity that seems to us the common air of his age. For he stood, as it were, on the threshold of his own sacked and broken house. If his past life had had any significance, he thought, it was that in his six years at the Admiralty he had achieved the unachievable and had driven corruption and laxity out of the chief of the State services. He had given the Navy of England what he had hoped would prove a permanent rule and harness. And now, after five more years of the inept control of his successors, everything he had striven for had vanished as though it had never been.

For almost alone among the men of his century Pepys grasped what the sea might come to mean to his country. More even than Ralegh before him or Halifax in his own day, though with only a tithe of their eloquence, he comprehended the future of England. The winds and tides that cradled her spoke to this landsman of her destiny. When most of his contemporaries were expanding all their powers in contending for particular forms of government and worship, he was scanning the horizons which have since grown familiar. Beyond the island mists, yet within reach of a little people of five or six millions, could they but be made to realize it, lay the shadowy outlines of a wealth and power such as no nation had ever before enjoyed in the history of the world. Bondsman of the pen and ledger as he was, comfortable materialist in peruque and fine linen, Samuel Pepys was yet sustained by vision. There was only one means by which that vision could be made a reality: the precepts he had spent his life in framing, and their observance by those who wrought the nation's destiny at sea.

It was this inner conviction that justified Pepys's indignation against the men of Tangier, though in later years many of them, schooled by his hard rules, were to do their country good service. He could not rest so long as the regulations on which he knew his dream depended were hourly flouted. Admiral Herbert publicly boasted that he had never kept a ship's journal in his life and never would. What the devil, he asked, was the use of remembering where the wind was when it was past? He did not even know the names of the ropes on his own ship so that he was perpetually having to bid his men 'Haul up that whichum there!' usually with some lewd jest to disguise his ignorance. It was so in everything he did.

Such was the result, Pepys reflected, of the fatal distinction between gentlemen and tarpaulins. These young men with their fine clothes and Court ways, who looked to Herbert as their natural leader, and drank, diced and whored in the face of the whole fleet, set a standard which better men were forced to follow, turning swaggerers and ruffians, drunkards and spendthrifts that they might be thought gentlemen. As Pepys looked out on the waste of waters, such distinctions seemed meaningless. In a ship the ordinary gradations of society were levelled to a bare, swaying deck, on which man stood, with nothing but his skill in seamanship to secure him from the terror and immensity of the seas. And save for that skill nothing mattered at all.

Pepys had too much respect for birth and breeding not to wish to see those who possessed them in the Navy. But first they must submit themselves to the stern training which alone could turn them into seamen. It was hard to expect a nobleman or courtier to make the sea his trade and share the conversation and company, diet and clothes of a rude sailor. 'Nor can he be neat and nice,' he reflected sadly, 'to make love in the fashion when he comes among the ladies.'

It was, indeed, the very tastes and inclinations of fine gentlemen that seemed to have banished all honour and decency from the Navy. Every captain intrigued, cheated and quarrelled to get money to maintain his expensive vices, a tenth part of which would make ten plain tarpaulins and their families happy who were now ready to starve. And for every penny the individual gained by such means, the King paid twice or threefold.

There was only one remedy. The opportunities for making easy fortunes by carrying bullion and merchandise which tempted courtiers and titled adventurers into the Navy must be taken away. And they must be replaced by regular, adequate salaries, such as could enable honest men to keep themselves and their families decently without having to cheat the Crown. 'Let the business of carrying money,' Pepys wrote, 'be taken away, and that will of itself take away the difference of gentleman and tarpaulin, for it is only for the sake of that that the difference is made and kept up.' Henceforward there should only be one distinction, that of rank, awarded after adequate training and experience. In all else those who served the King at sea should be brothers. In his egalitarian plea, so easy to comprehend in our day, so hard in his, the great Secretary of the Admiralty reached back to Drake, forward to Nelson.

Poor sailor as he was, Pepys, not without a certain unromantic heroism, continued to pursue his historical studies on the rolling deeps off the Portuguese and Spanish coasts where in time to come those dispensations of Providence which he coveted for his country were to be won by the broadsides of the men his rules had schooled. He pored over Hakluyt's Voyages of the Elizabethan era, wondering as he did so at the strange indifference of an island people who had left the chronicling of its sea annals to a poor country parson. More than ever his reading prompted him to practical ends: 'puts me again in mind of Sir W. Ralegh's advice for the laying down the discipline of the sea in writing as that of the land has by divers been done.' As he gazed at the encircling horizon. 'I know nothing,' Pepys wrote, 'that can give a better notion of infinity and eternity than the being upon the sea in a little vessel without anything in sight but yourself within the whole hemisphere.'

He knew now the dangers of the sea and understood its mystery. To the poor, illiterate and desperate men, brought into its service by harsh necessity, his heart went out in almost fierce sympathy. 'Let me also taste their beverage,' he wrote in his memo book, and the entry, one feels, was made with affection. They and their like were the ministers of the work to which all his experience and study were prompting him. And the hard trade which they adopted for lack of any other means of livelihood, they struck to in the end out of love, 'with a resolution to live and die in it and so make it their interest to make themselves masters of it by learning and doing and suffering all things.' By such indomitable instruments something great might one day be achieved.

Soon after he returned to England Pepys was asked by his Sovereign to resume his former charge at the Admiralty. What, under his new title of Secretary of the Affairs of the Admiralty he found when he took stock of the situation was enough to discourage even him. When he had been driven from his post five years earlier he had left his successors a fleet of 76 ships at sea and 12,000 men in pay, equipped for war and with stores enough to set out the remainder in an emergency. Now, apart from a small peace-time establishment of a score of frigates and two or three fire-ships, manned by just over 3,000 men, the Navy had ceased almost to exist as an effective force. For after five years of neglect, the battle fleet he had built was literally rotting in harbour. All the rules he had established had been forgotten. While vast sums had been squandered or pocketed by venal officials, the offices he had created to check corruption and extravagance had been abolished in the name of economy. The Admiralty and Navy, by far the greatest spending Department of State, was being run as a gigantic swindling concern by those who should have been its trustees, from the well-connected commanders who quarrelled among themselves as to which should enjoy the illicit benefits of the next 'good voyage', to the store-keepers and petty clerks who picked the yards bare. To such a pass had the wasted years of control by ignorant politicians reduced Pepys's administrative machine. To set it once more in motion, to overcome inertia and expel vested interest demanded the labours of a Hercules and the wiles of a Ulysses.

They were not wanting. During the next five years, first under Charles II, and, after the beginning of 1685, under his brother James II – Pepys's former chief, the duke of York – the great Secretary's quickening touch made itself felt in every part of the body naval. Nothing was too small for his attention. That every man's duty should be done to the King and right to all men had long been his own working motto; he made it once more the Service's.

As for the state of the great ships he had laid down before he left office they were more deplorable than anything he could have conceived. There, when he visited the neglected dockyards, they lay, the very flower and heart of his cherished Navy. Their buttocks, bows and quarters were soft with decay, their tree-nails burnt and rotten, the planks started from their transoms and ready to drop into the water. Some were in actual danger of sinking at their moorings. Patched with canvas and shotboard to hide their nakedness, they reminded Pepys of the battered ships he had so often seen returning from battle. Yet the only battle of their history had been that which he himself had waged on the floor of the House for their laying down. Such seemed the end of the stately ships of the line which he had conceived and planned to give his country an enduring ascendancy over her rivals and permanent command of the seas. His dream had dissolved into dust – powdered fine like a coating of sand over the rotting sides which could not even be breamed without danger of their taking fire.

Yet it was not in Pepys's nature to despair. In little more than two years the Special Commission – which he set up in 1686 after securing financial support from Parliament – completely restored, under his wise guidance, the all-but-abandoned thirty ships-of-the-line, largely through the brilliant technical skill of the great naval architect, Sir Anthony Deane, whom he had picked for the task and whose career he had long fostered.

During the four years of James II's brief reign – in many ways the most formative in the Navy's history – with the absolute authority entrusted to him by his sovereign, Pepys once more conceived, pronounced and recorded for his successors the rules which time and the long momentum of work and precept were to make the routine and spirit of a great Service. To obey orders punctually and without question and to hold the Regulations of the Admiralty as more sacred than the Ten Commandments, to do one's duty for one's bare wages without cavil and in the face of death, and to lay one's all in the keeping of the Navy in the belief that somehow, in this world or some other, the Service would care for and vindicate its own; such was the creed which the little scribe in the great wig taught the fighting men of the Stuart Navy. In this, unsympathetic as it seemed to the chaotic and tempestuous individualism of the seventeenth century, lay devotion, inspiration and the joy of sacrifice. Unguessed-at by its creator, a course was being charted that was to lead through the shoals of Quiberon and the deeps of Trafalgar to sea dominion and empire.

*   *   *

Yet the time for his achievement was short-lived. By his royal master's tactlessness, inability to compromise and the rigidity with which he sought to extend the rights of his persecuted fellow co-religionists, James II, who had many virtues, including a life-long devotion to the Navy, threw away all the advantages won by his brother's political skill. Acclaimed by the ruling High Tory party as the son of the martyred King who had died for the Church of England, he persisted in outraging its most cherished beliefs and prejudices by unilaterally suspending the laws in order to grant office to Roman Catholics and Dissenters, by governing without a Parliament – since no Parliament would endorse his policy – and by maintaining a standing army partly recruited from Irish Papists and destined, it was popularly believed, to enslave the nation so calling into question, justifiably in this case, his religious affiliations. When in the summer of 1688 a son was unexpectedly born to his second and Catholic queen, Mary of Modena, abandoning the hope that their dilemma was only temporary and putting their religion before their loyalty, James's disillusioned Tory supporters joined with their Whig opponents in secretly inviting his Protestant son-in-law, William of Orange, to invade England to save the religion and laws of the country.

For that autumn of 1688 the curtain was rising on a momentous drama. Beyond the Channel Louis XIV, the Catholic 'Grande Monarque', was preparing to extend his ever-widening boundaries, and his lifelong adversary, William of Orange, was assembling ships and troops for a dash on England while there was still time. For were he to wait till Louis turned his invincible legions against Holland, he knew he would have to wait for ever. Meanwhile his ambassador in London continued to deceive King James, and James to deceive himself as to his son-in-law's intentions. And all who had any stake in the Protestant Reformation – the nobles and gentry with abbey lands, the clergy of the threatened Established Church, the populace who hated Rome – looked to William. And for as long as he could King James looked resolutely away, refusing to hear what was being whispered in every coffee house and market place.

Between these contending forces stood Pepys, completing the last touches of his great work of restoring, consolidating and disciplining the Navy. On August 16th when he left London at 6 a.m. to attend his royal master at Windsor, an account, too alarming to be ignored, reached him there from the English agent at the Hague of William's preparations – of 23 ships of war at Amsterdam already rigged with topmasts, 11 more at Helvoetsluys fitting out with all possible speed, and others in the same state of preparation elsewhere, in all 90 ships, great and small.

The Admiralty could disregard the preparations on the other side of the North Sea no longer. On the night of August 17th Pepys countermanded all previous instructions, directing any naval shipping in the Downs to remain there 'in the best readiness that may be fore the execution of any orders'. Three days later leave was stopped and partial mobilization ordered. All available frigates were to be concentrated in the Downs, six ships-of-the-line to be fitted out for sea at once, and the 5th rates in harbour to be converted into fireships. All, as Pepys put it, was 'to be dispatched as for life or death'.

Dictating letters in the office at midnight, sitting with the King in Cabinet or hurrying between London and Windsor, Pepys was once more performing the task he had first essayed a quarter of a century before and had learnt to do better than anyone else on earth. By his side, as permanent chief of his London office, was Samuel Atkins, who during the Popish Terror had once faced death for his sake, while down the river his long-tried aides, Deane and Hewer, first chosen by him in the days of his administrative youth, were doing all that masters of their profession could do. Throughout the closing weeks of August and the first three of September mobilization went forward by cumulative steps. Down by the waterside and on Tower Hill the drums beat for volunteers, and at the ports the carpenters broke the Sabbath with their hammering, and the press-gangs waited for incoming merchant ships.

Before the end of September even the King became aware of the nature of the forces threatening him. On the 20th, after a visit to Chatham and Sheerness to view the fortifications, and naval preparations, he was brought back post-haste to London by news from Holland so authentic that it was no longer possible for him to doubt it. He is said to have turned white and speechless at the proofs of his son-in-law's treachery. To the bewilderment of an incredulous nation, the ship of state was seen to put helm about and go round to the opposite course. Thereafter the frightened King started to reconcile himself with the Church of England and the Tory Party he had so rashly alienated. On September 21st, the day after the royal return from Chatham, a proclamation was issued promising the exclusion of Catholics from Parliament. On October 2nd James informed the Lord Mayor and Sheriffs that he would restore the ancient Charter and privileges of the City, and ten days later made good the same promise to every borough in England. A flood of dismissals of Roman Catholics from the Lords Lieutenant and other key positions followed. But it was not in

King James's nature to make a bold simultaneous Elizabethan withdrawal from his past mistakes. Instead, after the manner of his father, Charles I, he fell back step by step, and always a step too late.

The King at least pinned hopes on the Navy where he knew he could count on the unshakeable fidelity of his Admiralty Secretary. And, sooner than offend the insular prejudices of his officers and seamen, he expressly refused an offer of French naval assistance. Though to set the battle fleet to sea just as winter was falling was a feat unknown to the seventeenth century, a general mobilization of all but the largest ships was ordered. On September 24th the senior officer in the Service, Lord Dartmouth – Pepys's old friend of Parliament days, George Legge, and his companion of the Tangier voyage – was appointed to the command. On September 28th orders were given to such part of the fleet as could be manned and kept to sea in autumnal and winter storms to assemble at the Buoy of the Nore. Other ships were to proceed to the rendezvous as soon as they could be got ready, from Orfordness, Yarmouth, Blackstakes, Chatham, the Hope, Long Reach, Deptford, Woolwich and Portsmouth. Even the Straits fleet at distant Gibraltar was laid under contribution. Nor were they to wait till they could be fully manned but to sail at the first opportunity before an easterly wind brought out the Dutch: if necessary they were to take soldiers aboard to make up their complements. On October 1st Fighting Instructions were issued to the Admiral.

In their attitude to the invasion, which was then hourly expected, Pepys and his sovereign showed themselves in advance of the strategical conceptions of their time. But their bolder sea counsels of August 26th were superseded by a more cautious plan. A Drake, a Blake, a Nelson, and perhaps, had he lived, a Narbrough might conceivably have dared all and met Orange's threat with a shock of frigates amid the Zeeland shoals while the battle fleet was making ready. Honest George Legge did not feel justified in taking so overwhelming a risk on a dead lee shore in a season of tempests. He preferred to keep his fleet in the Thames till he was able to meet the invader with equal or superior force. Recalling the limitations of seventeenth-century ships, it is hard to blame him.

The technique of long cruising, and still more of close blockade in winter storms, had still to be learnt.

For the moment, therefore, the work of defending England depended mainly on Pepys and his subordinates in York Buildings and the river shipyards. And so long as the wind blew hard from the west and William's ships lay bound in their harbours, it might avail. But what if the wind should change before the work was complete? On that question the fate of England depended for five anxious weeks until it was decided, not by a daring Admiral with his guns blazing amid crowded transports, but by the winds of Heaven. In the formal Fighting Instructions which Pepys by orders of the Council drafted on October 1st, Dartmouth was empowered to 'endeavour by all hostile means to sink, burn, take and otherwise destroy and disable' the 'armed force of foreigners and strangers', which a second William the Conqueror was preparing to launch against his country. Yet so long as Dartmouth remained in the Thames that was just what he could not do.

In that crowded hour the formal end of the work of Pepys's Special Commission passed almost unnoticed. In two and a half years, six months less than its originally estimated term, it had rebuilt almost wholly twenty ships, all of them line-of-battle, and repaired sixty-nine others. It had also built three new fourth rates and thirty-three storehouses, and laid down an eight months' reserve of sea stores for every ship; 'such a treasure of stores,' Pepys proudly claimed, 'as England was never before mistress of.' Nor, he might have added, such a treasure of ships. For her naval strategy of future years the Special Commission had provided her with a strength of fifty-nine capital ships of the first three rates. Henceforward for the next two and a half centuries her grand Fleet was to be a permanent influence in the counsels of Europe and the world.

CHAPTER THIRTEEN

The Search for Stability

by

Professor J. P. Kenyon

'What we did [in 1689] was in truth and
substance, and in a constitutional light, a
revolution not made, but prevented.'

Burke

IN THE EVENT all Pepys's elaborate preparations were in vain. On
October 30th the wind turned hard towards the west, a 'Protestant
Wind' which pinned the unfortunate Dartmouth in the Thames
Estuary, quite unable to round the North Foreland, while William's
unwieldy fleet, larger than Philip II's Armada a hundred years
before, sailed serenely down the Channel, past the fortified south
coast towns and the Isle of Wight, until it reached a safe landfall at
Torbay in Devon. It was November 5th, already a reverberant
anniversary for all true Protestants. The Prince disembarked his
army of 12,000 men, with their horses and all their equipment, in a
matter of two days, and sent his fleet on westward, to round Land's
End and take the long road back to Holland via the north of Scotland. It was an amazing feat of logistics, but it owed a great deal to
luck – or divine intervention. Gilbert Burnet, an exiled Scots divine
who had had many a theological tussle with William, had now
returned with him. 'As soon as I landed,' he tells us, 'I made what
haste I could to the place where the prince was, who took me
heartily by the hand, and asked me, if I would not now believe [in]
predestination. I told him, I would never forget that providence
of God, which had appeared so signally on this occasion'.

And the providence of God continued to shield him. William
was an invader, with a foreign mercenary army; two-thirds of it

was German or Danish, and it was said to contain more Catholics than the King's. James, the anointed and charismatic leader of the nation, had at his command about 20,000 men, the overwhelming majority of them English, with a few Irish and Scots. If it had come to a pitched battle William's position as England's Great Deliverer would have been fatally compromised, whatever the outcome. But, whether intentionally or not, William had chosen his landing place well; James had to try and dislodge him, though by mid-November the earl of Danby had seized control of Yorkshire in the Prince's name, the revolt spreading to Durham and Northumberland, Lord Delamere had raised Cheshire, and the earl of Devonshire and the earl of Shrewsbury between them had taken over the Midlands.

James ordered his army to rendezvous at Salisbury, and he arrived to take command on November 19th. News reached him there that the earl of Bath and the duke of Beaufort had surrendered the whole of the West Country to William, and with his rear secure William left Exeter on the 21st to begin the long march east towards Salisbury. There James dithered; this bold, simple-minded man was now afflicted by a disastrous infirmity of will, and plagued by an unstaunchable nose-bleed which incapacitated him for action. On the 25th he ordered a retreat on London, and that night John, Lord Churchill, second-in-command of the army, deserted to the Prince, followed by several high-born officers; Lord Drumlanrig, the duke of Ormonde and the duke of Grafton (a bastard son of Charles II); and two professional colonels, Percy Kirke and Charles Trelawney. On his way back to London his son-in-law, Prince George of Denmark, made his exit, closely followed by Princess Anne.

James now offered to negotiate, and his commissioners met the Prince on December 8th at Hungerford, where elaborate arrangements were made for the assembly of a freely-elected Parliament with William holding a watching brief. His position was still immensely strong, and it is difficult to see what effective restrictions Parliament could have imposed on him, bearing in mind that William and his army could not stay in England indefinitely now that war had broken out in Western Europe, involving the United

Provinces. But in fact he secretly sent his wife and his baby son, whose birth was already a matter of controversy, on ahead to France on December 10th, and he followed them twenty-four hours later, having destroyed the writs for a new parliament, thrown the Great Seal of England into the Thames and ordered the Army to disband. On the 12th Dartmouth, from Spithead, surrendered the Fleet to the man whose coming it had been designed to prevent.

William at once began a forced march on London, where public order was breaking down, and the people were panicking badly at the rumour that James's demobilized Irish regiments were coming to sack the city in revenge. A committee of peers hastily assembled at the Guildhall to form a provisional government were more irritated than anything by the news that James had in fact been arrested by some over-zealous fishermen in Kent. They sent four of their number down to Faversham to escort him back, but in their instructions they were careful to add that if he was 'resolved to withdraw himself from his people', then 'they were to see his Majesty on board any ship his Majesty shall command to transport his royal person whither he pleases'.

James did not take the hint, but his arrival in London once more on December 16th was a decided anti-climax. William peremptorily ordered him to leave Whitehall so that his army could enter the capital and restore order. His first thought was Ham House, near Richmond, but when James chose a mansion in Rochester, Kent, with a garden backing on to the river, he made no objections. James was off down the river on December 22nd and celebrated Christmas at Versailles, a pensioner of Louis XIV.

In these confusing and hectic circumstances the English governing classes were stampeded into a course of action which it is safe to say none of them had previously contemplated – not even the 'Immortal Seven' who had originally invited William over the previous June. In James's absence William had to be asked to take over the administration and summon a new parliament, which was elected with remarkable speed, and assembled before the end of January, 1689. Most of the new Commons, and nearly all the House of Lords, were decidedly 'un-revolutionary' in temper, but scarcely any of them wanted King James back – even some of his staunchest supporters hitherto – except on terms he was unlikely to accept. As for his son, James Francis Edward, it was clearly impossible to retrieve him from France, so his claims, already hotly disputed, could safely be ignored. Even so, any attempt actually to depose an anointed king would destroy what flimsy consensus existed, but on the other hand a quick settlement was imperative; Louis XIV, at the head of the strongest army in Europe, was firmly behind James, and Ireland had already declared in his favour; worse still, the radicals were ready with a republican solution, as they had been on the death of Charles I. In the end the Commons, and more reluctantly the Lords, adopted the flimsy pretence that James had abdicated, by inference if not by positive act, and the throne was therefore vacant. William was at once invited to fill it, and as a sop to the traditionalists his wife Mary, James II's elder daughter, was declared joint sovereign, queen regnant rather than queen consort. All this was accomplished at a formal ceremony in Westminster Hall on February 13th, 1689. At the same time the new king and queen were presented with a hastily-compiled Declaration of Right, which was later enacted into law as the Bill of Rights. This at once joined Magna Carta in the select pantheon of unalterable English law, but it was precise only in its condemnation of what was safely past, and extremely vague in its provision for the future.

That future was murky indeed. The Revolution of 1688 was the first to be dignified by that name – the Great Rebellion of the 1640s was not called a 'revolution' until the nineteenth century – and it is still regarded as the beginning of constitutional parliamentary monarchy in Britain; but it administered a traumatic shock to the constitution, which seemed unlikely in the next generation to survive intact. Scotland and Ireland at once rose in revolt: Scotland returned to her allegiance almost at once, for though King James's champion John Graham of Claverhouse, 'Bonny Dundee', defeated the government forces at Killicrankie in 1689, he fell at the moment of victory and Scots Jacobitism with him. The cause of Catholicism and national independence in Ireland was sustained by James II in person, assisted by French troops, and despite his defeat at the Boyne in 1690 after which he fled in discredit back to France, it took another two years to suppress the Irish Rebellion, leaving a legacy of discontent which persisted into the nineteenth and even the twentieth century.

But English society was also split right down the middle, and it was a split which as late as 1714 showed no signs of closing. Central was the question of allegiance; whether, in fact, a conscientious and Christian man could take an oath to two monarchs in succession, both still living. A few decided at once they could not; some, like Samuel Pepys, simply retired from public life, others actively conspired with the Old Regime, in exile at St Germain. Indeed for the first time since the eleventh century there was an alternative, and perfectly viable, royal family. Jacobite plotting, which reached its height in an assassination attempt on King William at Turnham Green in 1696, added a new element of tension and suspicion to the politics of the 1690s, especially since James II was now identified with the national enemy, and it was one of Louis XIV's avowed war aims to restore him to the throne of his fathers. On the other hand, Britain was now involved in a European war which grew more expensive every year, in terms of lives as well as money, simply to keep William on the throne, for though the war is usually known as 'The Nine Years' War' or 'The War of the League of Augsburg', it is sometimes more correctly described as 'The War of the English Succession' – certainly Britain's only plausible war aim was the maintenance of the Revolution settlement. Sir Keith Feiling speaks, melodramatically perhaps, but without undue exaggeration, of 'the atmosphere of evil mystery' which hangs over the middle years of the 1690:

> 'There are midnight meetings in Birdcage Walk, ex-officers of the Guards holding rendezvous in Covent Garden, deep drinkings at the George in Piccadilly, cabalistic limps and squeezing of oranges in half the inns round St James's. Off Dymchurch Flat government cutters are beating up to intercept the owling boat, which brings brandy and spies from Ambleteuse or Boulogne. Watch is being kept on the Sussex coast for "a pock-marked man, black-visaged, wears his own hair"; peers of England are hidden in the neighbouring farms, waiting on the tide; your neighbour in the coach may be a Jesuit, a government informer, or an assassin.

Oxford professors are employed by Lord Nottingham to decipher "invisible" letters, and as the lemon juice comes out in the heat or the cipher numbers yield their secret, another noble head may be shaking on its shoulders, or another home blasted and disgraced'.

Lord Nottingham, Secretary of State, did in fact use Dr John Wallis, Savilian Professor of Geometry at Oxford, as his code-breaker, and though no noble heads were ever removed, Jacobite peers like Dartmouth and Ailesbury spent long periods in the Tower. In 1692 the poison reached the royal family, when Anne's favourite John Churchill, created earl of Marlborough at the Coronation, was cashiered and imprisoned on suspicion. Anne and her sister Queen Mary never spoke to each other again.

But even those who supported the Settlement did so with varying degrees of enthusiasm and commitment. The Whigs, who had first emerged as a party in 1680, when they had made a resolute attempt to bar James from the succession, were naturally exultant that their worst prophecies had been fulfilled, and wholeheartedly embraced the Revolution as a welcome confirmation of the fact that Kings were subordinate to the People (whoever they might be), a pragmatic philosophy couched in intellectual terms by John Locke, whose *Two Treatises of Government* were published early in 1690. Some of them even argued that James should have been unequivocally deposed, (as he had been in Scotland, where the Estates had voted that he had 'forefaulted' the throne). This was anathema to the Tories, the old Church-and-King party of Charles II's reign. They regarded the Revolution as a necessary but deeply regrettable event, forced on them by King James's irredeemable folly; few of them indulged in active Jacobitism, but most of them regarded their allegiance to King William as conditional, and 'for the duration'. This attitude hardened with the unexpected death of Queen Mary from smallpox in December 1694, at the age of 32, taking with her to the grave the succession 'in the right line', and removing a consort whose simplicity and charm had done much to offset her husband's dour taciturnity. Successive attempts by the Whigs in Lords and Commons to insert the magic words 'rightful and lawful king' in the oaths to William all failed, even after the attempt on his life in 1696; in fact, it was not until the closing weeks of his reign, early in 1702, that Englishmen were required to abjure, or reject, King James's claim to the throne, or his son's, even though five years previously, at the Peace of Ryswick, Louis XIV himself had been obliged to recognize William as king *par la grace de Dieu*.

Financial pressure widened this ideological divide. Almost by accident the nation found itself committed to war on an unprecedented scale; in Flanders, the Mediterranean, the Caribbean and America. In fact, the war of 1689–97 could well be termed the first of the world wars, and the War of the Spanish Succession (1702–13) was worse. A war expenditure of £5 million a year could not be met by direct taxation, though a land tax at 4s. in the £ was introduced in 1692 and proved permanent. Otherwise the war was funded by public loans, secured on increased customs and excise duties, and more outre devices such as hackney carriage licenses and national lotteries. The result was the creation of a National Debt which had soared to £40 million by 1710.

Of course, the very fact of these loans, funded on a long-term basis, gave an increasing number of government creditors a vested interest in the preservation of the Settlement. The famous 'Million Pound Loan' of 1693, for instance, was secured on new excise duties imposed for ninety-nine years; this was no short-term expedient, merely for a generation. The following year the government established the Bank of England, with another loan of a million pounds at eight per cent. The day the books were opened, at Mercer's Chapel in the Poultry, £300,000 poured in; in the next forty-eight hours another £300,000; in ten days the books were full. This reflected the fact that the amount of 'floating' money in the economy was reaching a critical point, and safe investments were hard to find. Many men, from all walks of life, including the nobility, were now investing in the 'Funds', taking a regular income with no prospect of capital repayment; in fact they were becoming, in French terminology, *rentiers*. Trade was booming, in spite of or perhaps because of the war, and the tariff barriers raised against foreign imports protected suppliers and manufacturers who were already making fortunes by war contracts. The loss of the Smyrna convoy to French privateers in 1692 was a major disaster, for which three admirals were broken, but the Navy was growing stronger yearly, and William's decision to winter the Fleet at Barcelona in 1694-5 confirmed England's grip on the Western Mediterranean, first established by Cromwell's admirals in the 1650s but lost by default under Charles II. Huge fortunes were to be made in almost every branch of overseas trade, but especially from the import and re-export of colonial goods from the Caribbean and America, and the export of Indian cotton goods and silks to Europe, a trade so lucrative that by 1698 it was supporting not one but two East India Companies, with a combined capital of £3.9 million. As the power of the Dutch waned, the financial capital of the world, the centre of banking, insurance and credit facilities, moved inexorably from Amsterdam to London, where it was to remain for more than 200 years.

Lower down the social scale, the retail trade and small manufactures were flourishing, too. The mouthpiece of the small business man was Daniel Defoe, whose *Tour through the Whole Island of Great Britain*, written in 1708-10, though not published until 1724, was a paean of praise for the enterprise and competence of the lower middle classes. In agriculture, the English tenant farmer and small squire were the envy of the world. Rolling fields of wheat and barley proclaimed England's ability – rare in seventeenth-century Europe – to feed its people; and on the downs within a six-mile radius of Dorchester half-a-million sheep comfortably and profitably grazed. Sheep and cattle were still puny by modern standards, but the rotation of crops and the cultivation of the turnip to see cattle through the winter – a process usually associated with the 3rd Viscount Townshend, 'Turnip Townshend', in the 1730s – were already coming in. Working class wages, in town and country, were adequate, and unemployment low. Only in times of especial stress were the common people threatened; as in 1696, when an over-confident government took the alarming step of re-coining all its silver currency at the height of a major war; or in the Great Frost of 1709, which paralysed the whole of Europe from Christmas Eve, 1708, well into the following March. But increasing prosperity led to increasing social strain, for though most Englishmen were growing wealthier, some were manifestly wealthier than others. Entrepreneurs, merchants, large manufacturers and businessmen of all kinds were manifestly doing well out of the war, by government contracts and government patronage. They, together with the wealthier nobility, were also heavy investors in the Funds. Merchants and wholesalers faced increasing excise and customs duties, but these they could pass on to the public. The Land Tax could not be passed on, and it bore heavily on the small squire, like Addison's famous literary creation, Sir Roger de Coverley, with a modest estate let out to tenant farmers with whom he had a patriarchal relationship which forbad rack-renting. On the other hand, since the tax was not graduated, the great landowners had income in hand and the capacity to improve their property, quite apart from any income they might receive from government investment or the spoils of office. The great houses of the period, notably Vanbrugh's Blenheim, Castle Howard and Seaton Delaval, not to mention Talman's Chatsworth, testified to the splendour of uninhibited wealth. Of course, the Sir Roger de Coverleys of this world were nowhere near bankruptcy, nor was their life style much diminished, but they were conscious of the distinction between them and men whom they did not regard as their social superiors – who in the case of London merchants and bankers were very much their social inferiors – and for them and their kind participation in politics was becoming increasingly a luxury it was difficult to sustain.

For Parliament's unwillingness in 1689 to vote the King a regular annual income – with which his predecessor had run so disastrously amok – and the need to vote extra money for the war, not to mention the need to scrutinize how it was spent, meant that it had to re-assemble every autumn for five or six months, a habit which persisted thereafter, even in time of peace. This imposed unheard-of strains on a whole class of gentlemen to whom election to the Commons had previously been an honour designed to lend them dignity and influence in their own locality, which only involved occasional attendance at Westminster for a few short sessions stretched over many years. Now they had to leave their estates for half the year to the tender mercies of paid land agents, and, worse still, expose their wives and daughters to the heady and expensive temptations of the London Season. Most of them also had to lease or buy a town house consonant with their dignity as legislators, and so for that matter did many of the country lords.

It was doubly aggravating that this further enriched London property speculators and the great noble landlords of Belgravia and Bloomsbury. The drift of the *haut monde* westward, drawn to the King's palace of Whitehall and the law courts in the adjacent Westminster Hall, and repelled by the heavy industrial smog which hung over the City proper, had begun under James I and accelerated under Charles II. Charles's Lord Treasurer, the earl of Southampton, began laying out Southampton Square (later Bloomsbury Square) in the 1660s, and on his death in 1667 his daughter and sole heir Rachel carried his property by marriage into the great Whig family of the Russells, earls of Bedford, who already owned Covent Garden. The 5th earl (duke in 1694) gave his name to Great Russell Street and Bedford Square. The King himself led the way when he laid out St James's Park in 1661–2, and he was followed by his Lord Chancellor, Clarendon, who built a sumptuous mansion on the road running along the north side of the Park, exotically christened 'Piccadilly'. This was torn down in 1683 to make way for the development of the Albemarle Street and Bond Street complex. Meanwhile Lord Berkeley had built himself a house on the lane now called Berkeley Street, and in the 1680s and 1690s was busy laying out Berkeley Square, as well as Charles Street, Hill Street and Bruton Street. At the nearer end of Piccadilly that great connoisseur the earl of Burlington built the house of that name, which now houses the Royal Academy, and the development of St James's Street and St James's Square began in 1663 under the aegis of the earl of St Albans.

Further south Dr Nicholas Barbon, conformist son of the Puritan fanatic who had given his name to the 'Barebones Parliament' of 1653, was buying up the great palaces between the Strand and the river – Essex House, Devonshire House, Ely House, and so on – and tearing them down to build middle-class housing. It was also in the 1680s that Sir George Downing, the Treasury Secretary, laid out Downing Street and Horse Guards Parade, and in their external aspect Nos 10 and 11 Downing Street are very much as he left them. Soho came on a little later, developed in the late 1680s and 1690s by Gregory King, who laid out King Square (later Soho Square) and Gregory Street (soon shortened to Greek Street). These were all lined, of course, with quality gentlemen's residences and smart shops; the more dubious functions of twentieth-century Soho were fulfilled by Covent Garden and the New Exchange at the City end of the Strand, whose status had now deteriorated sharply. By 1700 the new 'Mayfair' district had reached the line of Bolton Street, where for the moment it stopped; beyond were green fields stretching away to Knightsbridge, interrupted only by the brick walls of Hyde Park. But many fashionable people were already retreating further, to the delightful villages of Battersea and Chelsea, and the asthmatic William III, unable to stand the polluted air of Whitehall, bought the earl of Nottingham's house in the village of Kensington, and began the refurbishing of the royal palace of Hampton Court, easily accessible from Whitehall by river. Occasional usage become regular habit when the old Whitehall Palace was burnt down in 1698, leaving only Inigo Jones's Banquetting House. By this time the size of London was quite monstrous. Paris was even larger, but it held only 5% of France's population, London 10% of England's; and whereas in 1524 London's population had equalled that of the next six English towns, in 1680 it equalled that of the next sixty combined.

The growth of London and the London monied interest fuelled a deep social resentment, which drove a wedge between 'City' and 'Country', replacing the old antagonism of the early seventeenth century between 'Court' and 'Country'. Many Sir Roger de Coverleys survived in Parliament right down the eighteenth century – witness those indomitable critics of any and every government between 1714 and 1740, Sir John Hinde Cotton and Sir Watkyn Williams Wynn – but many did not, and those who survived found their role as legislators and parliamentarians increasingly usurped by a new breed of political animal, the professional politician, who was looking to make his career in politics. Typical of this new breed was Charles Montagu, 'The Little Man', the Whig financial genius who evolved the tax structure which financed King William's War and founded, indeed invented, the Bank of England. A decidedly poor relation of the great ramified Montagu family, which numbered in its ranks two earls (of Manchester and Sandwich), a duke (of Montagu) and Lord Montagu of Boughton, he entered Parliament in 1689 under the aegis of Charles Sackville, earl of Dorset, who liked his satircal verse, and rose to be Chancellor of Exchequer, First Lord of the Treasury and Viscount (later earl of) Halifax.

Halifax is an extreme example of the way the post-revolution Whigs were evolving from a party of radical protest and reform into an establishment group which welcomed strong central government, financial expansionism and militarism. But for much lesser men than him the patronage at the disposal of a war-time government was increasing at an astonishing pace; not only the number of Army and Navy commissions, but all kinds of new posts, in the Commission for Sick and Wounded, for instance, the Commissions for Transport Ships and for Masts, the Victualling Commission, the Ordnance, and so on. Fortunes were to be made in the supply of clothing to the forces, or beer, not to mention guns and ammunition.

The potential for improper government influence on Parliament was obvious, and the new parliament elected in 1690 was soon dubbed the 'Officers' Parliament' or the 'Pension Parliament'. In fact the governments of William were very ill-organized in this respect, but when they had over 200 MPs under their wing, one way or another, out of 513, there seemed no reason they should be free to vote as they wished. As one agitated and fearful pamphleteer put it:

'What points might not such a number carry in the House, who are always ready and constantly attending, with more diligence to destroy our constitution that the rest have to preserve it? Who represent not their country but themselves, and always keep together in a close and undivided phalanx, impenetrable either by shame or honour, voting always the same way, and saying always the same things, as if they were no longer voluntary agents, but so many engines merely turned about by a mechanic motion, like an organ where the

great humming basses as well as the little squeaking trebles
are filled but with one blast of wind from the same sound-
board.'

Men's darkest suspicions were confirmed in 1695, when the
Secretary to the Treasury, the Speaker of the House of Commons
and the Lord President of the Council were detected in various
complex schemes of corruption involving army forage contracts,
the issue of hackney carriage licenses, East India Company shares
and even the Orphans' Fund of the City of London. The Speaker,
Sir John Trevor, was put to the humiliation of moving his own
expulsion from the House; Mr Secretary Guy was also expelled
and sent to the Tower, and the duke of Leeds was barred from
meetings of the Privy Council of which he was President. But so
complex was the knavery involved that the Commons were still
investigating Guy's conduct as late as 1704, as part of a diligent,
though entirely fruitless, attempt to convict Halifax of malpractice
at the Treasury between 1693 and 1699.

The immediate effect in 1695 was to smooth the passage of a
new Triennial Act, for which the Opposition had been compaigning
since 1692, which obliged the Crown to call a general election every
three years at least, thus in theory exposing corrupt MPs to regular
scrutiny by their constituents. Of course, it did not work like that;
nor was it much help that the Regency Act of 1706 excluded from
the Commons the holders of any new offices or posts created after
that year as well as those in receipt of government pensions. The
prospect of taking a real part in government, even on the fringes,
not to mention the chance of sinking one's snout in the ample
trough of patronage, enhanced the attractions of a seat in Parliament, and thus the competition for it. Bribery and corruption,
with their attendant drunkenness and mayhem, became a regular
feature of elections, and successive bribery acts, passed with due
piety and without the least controversy at Westminster, were
powerless to stop it. Immortalized in the acid penmanship of
Hogarth's four 'Election' scenes, in 1753, the violence and corruption of the hustings were carried over into Mr Pickwick's Eatan-
swill. Worse still, the excitement of election upon election – for
the Crown could dissolve parliament when it wished, and the

average life of any parliament between 1695 and 1715 was two years, not three – encouraged party animosity and hardened party attitudes. Many candidates had no choice but to stand on the crudest platform; Whigs denouncing Tories as crypto-Catholic Jacobites, Tories denouncing Whigs as anabaptist republicans; and support for this kind of stance was readily forthcoming in an 'electorate' which was becoming increasingly politicized, whether its members actually had a vote in a given constituency or not. Jonathan Swift, who went down to report a by-election in Leicestershire in 1707, wrote:

> 'They have been polling these three days, and the number of thousands pretty equal on both sides; the parties as usual, High and Low, and there is not a chambermaid, prentice or schoolboy in the whole town but what is warmly engaged on one side or the other'.

At a time when votes were cast in public, usually on a raised platform in full view, a voteless but violent mob was enfranchized effectively enough.

Moreover, in the wake of the Revolution of 1688 men scarcely appreciated, as historians now do, that Parliament had taken control of the King – rather the opposite. William III, this remote, mildly autocratic foreigner, now disposed of an annual income, and commanded fleets and armies, on a scale beyond the wildest dreams of his Stuart predecessors. With the conclusion of the Peace of Ryswick in 1697 dark suspicions, concealed during the war years, rose to the surface, and in a series of stormy sessions Parliament destroyed William's war time government and forced him to reduce the army from more than 30,000 men to 8000 – the peacetime establishment on Charles II's death in 1685. In fact, war-weariness and xenophobia dictated a policy of isolation; so much so that in 1701 Parliament even acquiesced in the accession of a French candidate to the throne of Spain, thus 'abolishing the Pyrennees', as Louis XIV exultantly claimed. Only Louis's megalomaniac folly in recognizing James II's son as King James III of England after his father's death in September 1701 forced a reluctant nation back into war in 1702, to preserve the Protestant

Succession all over again. On the eve of that war William died, of injuries received when his horse stumbled on a molehill and threw him, and the Jacobites gratefully toasted 'the little gentlemen in black velvet'.

*   *   *

But by this time the Church of England had weighed in to the party conflict, on the Tory side, of course. In fact, it gave the Tories an intellectual and moral weight which they had hitherto lacked in their opposition to government.

In the backwash of the Revolution the Church had been unmercifully battered and almost drowned. Her unity was shattered by the allegiance controversy, not only to James II but to his son, for as archbishop Sancroft of Canterbury pointed out, James Francis Edward had been prayed for as Prince of Wales in every parish church in the land for the last six months of 1688, and the promised investigation into the circumstances of his birth had never taken place. Sancroft refused the oaths to the new government and was eventually deprived, as were four of his most respected bishops and a number of other prominent churchmen. The stand made by these 'Non-Jurors' created a schism which, while insignificant in size, was ominous in its implications. The fact that the overwhelming majority of the clergy *did* take the oaths – most of them, it was suspected, merely to keep their jobs – was quite unexpected, and a cause for shame rather than congratulation.

Moreover, the fact that James II in 1687 and 1688 had made a determined effort to win the political support of the Protestant Nonconformists, or Dissenters, who had been expelled from the Church in 1662, on a platform of complete religious toleration, made some concessions in that direction inevitable; Sancroft himself agreed. The Toleration Act of 1689, allowing Dissenters freedom of worship in their own 'meeting-houses' (the term 'chapel' was not used in this context until much later), was the bare minimum, but it was enough. It broke the monopoly of English Protestantism which the established church had hitherto enjoyed,

"Second only to Johnson, Pepys is the quintessential Englishman. It is conceivable that but for his work, Britain might never have achieved that permanent naval ascendancy in the world's seas which she was to maintain until the present century, and might have remained what she was until his time, a second-class European power without an overseas empire." Pepys in the great portrait by Hayls, with a musical manuscript to display one of his greatest loves.

Frost on the Thames, 1677.

The "Protestant wind" blows William of Orange to Torbay.

embodied in the Uniformity Acts of 1559 and 1662, which made church attendance on Sundays compulsory.

Such attendance at once fell noticeably, and the Dissenters emerged 'from the closet' in alarming numbers, displaying great wealth, social cohesion and self-confidence, especially amongst the bankers and merchant princes of London. Deism and agnosticism were rife amongst the upper classes, and the spread of Unitarianism or 'Socinianism' which denied the divinity of Christ, caused understandable alarm. Meanwhile the 'Scientific Revolution' associated with the name of Isaac Newton tended to undermine belief in a Creator or a Creation, and when he died in 1691 the great theoretical chemist Robert Boyle left part of his fortune to found the annual Boyle Lectures, with the purpose of reconciling the discoveries of experimental science with the principles of the Christian religion. Critics also detected the general slump in personal moral standards, especially amongst the upper classes, which we tend to associate with the reign of Charles II. In fact, what we call 'The Restoration Drama' continued to flourish and develop in the hands of playwrights like Congreve, Farquhar and Vanbrugh well into Queen Anne's reign, and it was in 1698 that Jeremy Collier published his great philippic, 'A Short View of the Immorality and Prophaneness of the English Stage', in which he inveighed against the indifference of popular playwrights to the marital bond, their positive glorification of adultery and fornication, their emphasis on money as the basis of all human relationships. (It was ironic that Collier was a Non-Juror; so was William Law, the author of that great eighteenth-century best-seller, *A Serious Call to a Devout and Holy Life*.) Nor were spectacular examples of upper-class delinquency lacking. For instance, the long-drawn-out attempt of the 7th duke of Norfolk to divorce his wife for her adultery with Sir John Germain titillated the imagination of the House of Lords for much of the decade, ending only in 1701, and it is not surprising that to one honest Tory it seemed that:

> 'We are fallen into the dregs of time, wherein atheism and irreligion, sedition and blasphemy, seem to divide the world between them, and in which that generous honesty and religious loyalty which was once the glory and character of our nation is vanished.'

313

But even worse was the Church of England's sudden relegation to a subordinate role in national politics. At one stroke it had lost that 'special relationship' with the Crown which had sustained it ever since the Reformation. How could it have a special relationship with a king who, as a Dutch Calvinist, was effectively a Dissenter himself, and insisted on being excused from the proviso in the Bill of Rights which obliged all future monarchs to take the Anglican communion? Church and State were no longer co-equal; politics was no longer religious, nor religion political. Indeed, the influence of the clergy on Charles I and James II, preaching as they did the Divine Right of Kings and enjoining the people to unquestioning Passive Obedience, was now blamed in many quarters for the disasters which had overtaken those unhappy rulers. The clergy were even accused of unwittingly conspiring to subvert the constitution, and advised to withdraw altogether from a public role they had neither the ability nor the experience to sustain. As one of their critics observed:

'The clergymen (the English especially) being for the most part of mean birth, unimproved by travel, are the worst politicians in the world . . . The histories of all ages are filled with their miscarriages, yet they have seldom drawn a greater load of contempt upon themselves, than by their late violences, while the Court and they were well with one another; and nothing but the insolence of some of them could abate that pity, which was natural to the observation how they were carried hoodwinked to destruction, and were made tools to subvert their own religion, and the civil rights of the people'.

Or as Sir Joseph Jekyll put it in 1710, with the full weight of the House of Commons behind him:

'It is plain that religion hath nothing to do to extend the authority of the prince, or the submission of the subject, but only to secure the legal authority of the one, and enforce the due submission of the other, from the consideration of higher rewards and heavier punishments'.

In fact, the Church was to be a mere propaganda agency of the secular State.

The High Church Movement, which came to prominence in the late 1690s under the brilliant leadership of extremists like Francis Atterbury and Henry Sacheverell, was a violent reaction against this trend. Its aim was the re-instatement of the Church to a commanding position in national life and national politics, and such was the pressure they brought to bear on the King that in 1701 he agreed to summon Convocation, the Church's parliament, which had stood adjourned since 1689, and before that since 1664. The movement now had a public platform from which to broadcast its principles, which Henry Sacheverell outlined as follows. A High Churchman, he said

> 'is high for the Divine Right of episcopacy, high for the uninterrupted succession, high for the liturgies against extempore prayers, high for the primitive doctrine and discipline of the ancient church. He believes separation from the Church of England to be a damning schism, and the Dissenters to be in a very dangerous state, notwithstanding the Toleration Act'.

It was a message which had sinister implications for the Dissenters. If they were indeed in schism, then ultimately they must be suppressed, and indeed the rage against them grew year by year, provoked especially by the practice of occasional conformity; that is, occasional attendance at Anglican communion in order to qualify for office under the Test Act of 1673. This was spectacularly underlined in 1697 by the folly of Sir Humphrey Edwin, the new Lord Mayor of London, who on his first Sunday in office attended his parish church in the morning, and in the afternoon went in solemn procession to the local meeting house. Bills to outlaw this practice passed the Commons in 1702, 1703 and 1704, and their defeat in a Whig dominated House of Lords only exacerbated party resentment.

Of course, the Tories and High Churchmen were invigorated in 1702 by the accession of Queen Anne, not only a true daughter of the Established Church but a true daughter of the last legitimate monarch, James II. But by now the Succession was beginning to loom large on the horizon. Queen Anne's son, William, duke of Gloucester, had died in 1700 – the only candidate acceptable to all parties. By the Act of Settlement in 1701 Parliament had vested the succession after Anne's death in the Dowager Electress of Hanover, last surviving child of Charles I's sister Elizabeth, and in her son the Elector George Ludwig. But these remote and unknown German Lutherans were unattractive candidates, especially so to the High Church party, who now began to question the accepted interpretation of the Revolution. If, as they now argued, the events of 1688–89 had not involved the nation in resistance or rebellion then the doctrine of Passive Resistance was intact; and if James II had indeed voluntarily abdicated, then his decision did not bind his son, and though James Francis Edward was still, lamentably enough, a staunch Catholic, he might be restored on much stricter terms than could ever have been imposed on his father.

This brought party conflict to boiling point. The Whigs accused the Tories of undermining the Protestant Succession and surrendering the nation to Rome; the Tories accused the Whigs of atheism and even republicanism. Moreover, these divisions were widened and deepened by unrestrained printed propaganda. In 1695 Parliament had at last refused to renew the latest in a series of Press Licensing, or Censorship, Acts, and Anne's reign saw the emergence of nineteen newspapers, though many of them were short-lived, and only one of them, *The Daily Courant*, appeared daily. In the meanwhile the Whig *Observator* (1702), Defoe's *Review* (1704) and Swift's *Examiner* (1710), were the direct precursors of our own political weeklies. This was also the golden age of pamphleteering, when the great satirical journalists – Defoe, Swift, Addison, Steele – could claim to have a major share in the moulding of public opinion. Certainly Swift's *Conduct of the Allies* (1711), arguing for a separate peace, was one of the most influential political works of the century; but in the height of party passion playing cards, fans, even handkerchiefs, were pressed into service to carry Whig or Tory slogans. Even the sermons of the leading divines often achieved best-seller status, which is strange when we remember that these same divines never ceased to lament the growth of irreligion. But alas, most such sermons were concerned with the application of religion to politics: whether the Revolution, for instance, could be squared with St Paul's teaching on the obedience owing to the powers that be, or whether the nation's treatment of King James in 1688 was not akin to its treatment of his father in 1649, for which it lay under a sentence of perpetual humiliation? Indeed, the cult of the Blessed King Charles the Martyr had reached extraordinary proportions, and the annual fast on the anniversary of his execution, January 30th, was the occasion for some astonishing sermons. William Binckes, preaching to Convocation in 1702, compared his sacrifice to that of Christ at Calvary, and rather to Our Saviour's disadvantage, though it is true that he was severely censured by the House of Lords, which found that his sermon contained 'several expressions that gave just scandal and offence to all Christian people'.

The Tories could also point to the high cost of maintaining the existing Settlement; for if the war which opened in 1702 was ostensibly concerned with the Spanish Succession, it is doubtful if England would have entered it had not Louis XIV also put the English Succession at risk. Men were uneasily conscious that ever since 1689 England, despite regular protestations to the contrary, was developing into a militarist state, to the great benefit of the Whigs and their Dissenting cronies in the City. By 1694 she was employing 83,000 men in Flanders, more than half of them British. Parliament's attempt to reduce the army establishment after the Peace of Ryswick was only temporarily successful, and in 1702 20,000 men were sent with Marlborough to Flanders, rising by 1708 to 25,000. Over and above this, she despatched 8000 men to Spain in 1704, rising to 9000 in 1705, 10,000 in 1706. In 1708, in a desperate attempt to offset her defeat by the French at Almanza the previous year, she shipped out another 16,000, and a crude form of conscription had to be introduced. The Navy, too, steadily increased in size, though from a larger base; 109 ships of the line rose to 200 in 1697, and in 1702 she had 40,000 men in service.

Under William III, who for all his experience was not the best of generals, this sacrifice seemed in vain, and the butchery of British troops at Steenkirk in 1692 and Landen in 1693 was a shock to public opinion, especially since in Marlborough's absence they came under Dutch field officers. But at La Hogue (or Barfleur) in 1692 Admiral Russell mauled the French Atlantic squadron so badly that any prospect of a Jacobite-led invasion was scotched for good, and in the same way William's recapture of the great fortress-town of Namur in 1695 prevented an invasion of the Netherlands. Ryswick, in 1697, was therefore only a stalemate peace.

However, by the time the war was renewed in 1702 Marlborough had been restored to favour; in fact, he was William's designated successor as Captain-General of the Allied forces in Western Europe. The application of his genius was at once decisive. A bold march down the Danube and into Austria in 1704 ended at Blenheim, where he smashed the French and Bavarian armies and relieved the pressure on Vienna. His second great victory, at Ramillies in 1706, led to the fall of Brussels and the conquest of the Spanish Netherlands – roughly speaking, modern Belgium – and brought him to the frontiers of metropolitan France. Further victories followed, at Oudenarde in 1708 and Malplaquet in 1709. For the first time since 1588 England basked in the intoxicating glory of military supremacy. Year after year the banners of her defeated enemies were paraded through London before being hung in Westminster Hall, and year after year, sometimes month after month, the Queen made the solemn processional journey from Kensington to Wren's new cathedral of St Paul's, nearing completion at last, to offer thanks to God for the latest victories of her great captains. Dumpy little Anne, 'Great Anna', took her role as the nation's war leader with high seriousness; she modelled herself on her great predecessor, Elizabeth I, and even took over her motto, *semper eadem*.

The result was a transformation of national life; for the first time since the 1640s the soldier, and particularly the disabled veteran and the half-pay officer, became a common feature of the social scene, and even passed over into literature, notably in George Farquhar's play *The Recruiting Officer*. But not everyone found the change congenial; to Jonathan Swift the new military class was as one with the new monied class, and together they were undermining the good old social order of England, based on landed property. Of the London of 1710 he wrote:

> 'Let any man observe the equipages in this town. He shall find the greater number of those who make a figure to be a species of men quite different from any that were ever known before the Revolution, consisting of either generals or colonels, or of such whose whole fortunes lie in funds and stocks; so that power, which according to the old maxim used to follow land, is now gone over to money'.

All was well while the war went well, but after 1706 things began to go badly wrong. Wonderful as Marlborough's victories were, they brought him no nearer Paris and a dictated peace, and the allied losses at Malplaquet (1709) were denounced as unacceptable. The Whigs, now firmly in the saddle, refused to make a compromise peace while Louis XIV's grandson, Philip V, occupied the Spanish throne, but all attempts to dislodge him failed. True, after a fierce engagement off Malaga in 1704 the French Mediterranean fleet was bottled up in Toulon for good, and the British went on to seize Gibraltar, holding it after an epic siege lasting nearly a year, in which the Corps of Royal Marines first distinguished itself. This and the capture of Minorca in 1708 consolidated Britain's grip on the Mediterranean for another century. But on land a succession of patchwork armies came up against the same patriotic resistance which was to baffle Napoleon in a later Peninsular War; nor were they helped by the intrusion of party rancour even into the battlefield; of the two armies engaged at one time or another in the campaign one was headed by the Whigs' hero, the earl of Galway, the other by the darling of the Tories, the earl of Peterborough. They were resoundingly defeated by a French army under Marlborough's Jacobite nephew, James, duke of Berwick, at Almanza in 1707, and again at Brihuega in 1710, when the Whig general and future cabinet minister, James Stanhope, was captured. High taxation was an increasing burden, French privateers were making deeper and deeper inroads into English shipping, Louis XIV was ready to negotiate, and the Whigs' cry of 'No Peace without Spain' seemed increasingly unrealistic and irresponsible.

It was the last straw when Marlborough demanded that his captain-generalship be renewed for life: 'A General for life, and our lives for the General', was the bitter quip which went round the London coffee-houses.

The Whig ministers themselves put a match to the bonfire when they made the mistake of impeaching Henry Sacheverell for an inflammatory sermon delivered at St Paul's on November 5th 1709 – an anniversary now inflammatory in itself – in which he accused them of encouraging a fifth column of Dissenters within the ministry and presented the Revolution of 1688 'in black and odious colours'. The trial, in February 1710, generated enormous heat; the flow of propaganda on both sides became a torrent; the pulpits roared and threatened, pamphlet after pamphlet tumbled from the press. The offending sermon itself, "The Perils of False Bretheren', sold more than 100,000 copies, and was translated into Dutch, German and French. At the height of the trial, on the night of March 1st, London was taken over by the mob, baying for 'Sacheverell and Peace'; several prominent Dissenting meeting-houses were burnt down, and troops had to be brought in to defend the Bank of England. But the upper classes were not immune to hysteria. Sacheverell was 'a well-hung man', in the contemporary idiom, and titled ladies rallied to his cause with a will. The duchess of Cleveland locked her husband in his room lest he go down to Westminster Hall to cast his vote against the Doctor, and Lady Rooke, wife of the Tory admiral, Sir George Rooke, who took a packed lunch each day to sustain her through the proceedings, was mortified to find that she had offered a chicken wing to the gentleman next to her without first canvassing his opinion – 'But, it coming into her head to ask him if he was for Sacheverell, and he answering, No, by G–d, madam; then by G–d, sir, said she, I will have my wing again, and snatched it out of his hands'.

Sacheverell was duly convicted, but the Lords imposed a mere token punishment, and the damage was done. Hearkening to the cry for peace, Anne felt strong enough to dismiss the ministry *en bloc*, put Marlborough on a short rein – though he was not dismissed until the following year – and call a general election which returned a House of Commons dominated by Tory backwoodsmen, who at once founded the famous October Club, dedicated to the most extreme reaction as well as the hearty consumption of good October ale.

*   *   *

The last four years of the Queen were ones of bitter contestation, from which it seemed the nation could never emerge united. Her new ministers, Robert Harley, earl of Oxford, and Henry St John, Viscount Bolingbroke, insisted on pushing through the Peace of Utrecht, in 1713, though in so doing they 'dished' Britain's allies; not only the Emperor and the Dutch, but the future George I, Elector of Hanover. Having earned George's implacable enmity, and with the Queen's health clearly failing, they entered into secret negotiations with the Pretender.

Deeply suspicious and alarmed, and expecting the Pretender 'next oars', the Whigs found themselves helpless. Their majority in the Lords was destroyed in 1712, when Harley and the Queen took the unprecedented step of creating twelve new Tory peers overnight; they had high hopes of victory in the General Election of 1713, but these were cruelly dashed. Happy with the peace, and determined not to jeopardise it, the electorate returned the Tories with an increased majority. The Whig peers even began to arm their servants against a possible Jacobite *coup d'état* on the Queen's death.

But this long-awaited event, when it came in July 1714, was an anti-climax. The Pretender had already made the great refusal, and unless he would at least agree to 'take instruction' in Protestantism he was not a viable candidate. Nor did Anne so regard him, despite her hatred for the Hanoverians. Before she took to her bed for the last time she dismissed Harley and replaced him as chief minister by the neutral but staunchly Hanoverian duke of Shrewsbury. Bolingbroke was dismissed and fled in a panic to France. George I was proclaimed without incident, and he saw no reason to hurry to his new kingdom; in fact, he did not arrive until September 18th. When his barge came to rest at Greenwich steps one of the first to kiss his hand was Marlborough, Captain-General once more. 'My

Lord Duke', said the King, 'I hope your troubles are now all over'.

Not quite. The King's overwhelming and manifest support brought the Whigs a resounding victory in the Election of 1715, but such was their majority that it allowed them the dangerous luxury of quarrelling amongst themselves. On the other hand their decision to impeach Harley and Bolingbroke for high treason kept open old party wounds, and the Jacobite Rebellion of 1715, though it was mainly confined to Scotland, was accompanied by widespread rioting in England and surreptitious activity amongst the Tory nobility and gentry, resentful at their exclusion from power. The ministry passed the Riot Act in 1715, authorising the use of troops to quell civil disturbances, and the following year it pushed through the Septennial Act, which extended the life of the sitting parliament, and all future parliaments, from three years to seven. However, this only encouraged the ministers to carry their cabinet quarrels to extremes, and in 1717 Robert Walpole and Lord Townshend took their followers into opposition, leaving their erstwhile colleagues, James, earl Stanhope, and Charles, earl of Sunderland, at the head of a minority government. This unedifying episode only closed in 1721, when the King threatened to put his German ministers, Bernstorff and Bothmar, in power, but the Whigs had only cobbled together a re-united ministry when they were overwhelmed by the South Sea Bubble. This wild burst of stock market speculation centred on the South Sea Company drove the price of shares up to impossible heights on the London market, and in the inevitable crash which followed hundreds were bankrupted, thousands lost substantial sums of money they could ill afford, and the financial credit of the City of London and the moral credit of the Whig ministers were severely shaken. The Tories, and many of the more radical Whigs, were confirmed in their opinion that the monied interest was corrupt and rotten to the core. Robert Knight, the Cashier of the South Sea Company, fled to France, taking much vital evidence with him, not to return for twenty years. James Craggs the Elder, Postmaster-General, committed suicide, and his son of the same name, Secretary of State, died of smallpox, perhaps conveniently. Earl Stanhope, the other Secretary, suffered a fatal loss of temper while defending himself in the House of Lords and died of a brain haemorrhage. Sunderland, the First Lord of the Treasury, was exonerated but had to retire to the court post of Groom of the Stole. The main scapegoat was the Chancellor of Exchequer, John Aislabie; barred from public life he retired to Yorkshire to nurse his resentments in silence and lay out the magnificent gardens at Studley Royal, near Ripon. (He was never noticeably short of money.)

*　*　*

When the South Sea Bubble burst it seemed likely to blow eighteenth-century society apart. Stanhope even considered suspending the Septennial Act, so as to put off the next general election until after the King's death. But society found its saviour in the unlikely figure of Robert Walpole; bluff, rotund, cynical and rather vulgar, with more than a whiff of financial scandal about him, and a record of spiteful party in-fighting. Indeed, the pen picture painted by his latest biographer is far from flattering:

> 'A short, dumpy man, weighing rather more than twenty stone. His arms and legs were short; his heavy head sprang almost straight from his shoulders. His features were large and coarse – square double chin, strongly marked black eyebrows, straight thinnish mouth, with a thick protruding underlip, a sharp, emphatic nose'.

But he was a surprisingly effective orator and a master of parliamentary procedure; he knew the temper of the House of Commons as no other man, and his policy of peace, retrenchment and stability struck a chord in the hearts of the small landed squires from whose ranks he had sprung. The sudden death of the earl of Sunderland in 1722 left his way clear, and other potential rivals to his power were relentlessly excluded in the years ahead, even his brother-in-law Townshend in 1730. Secure in the confidence of King George II, wielding crown patronage without compunction to subdue and discipline the House of Commons, his power did not begin to totter until the late 1730s, and by the time he fell at last in 1742 the system he had fashioned could not easily be altered. Whether he was

Britain's first prime minister or not is an idle question; this was a simpler, cruder age. John Carswell likens him to 'one of those long-voyaging sea captains who were the agents of prosperity in his own great era of trade':

> 'The King was the owner; but on board Walpole was un-disputed master. He maintained discipline partly by appeals to the old esprit-de-corps still generated by the name of whig, and partly by threatening references to the old fears still stirred up by the word tory; rum and the rope's end. And in the last resort, whether the offender was officer or fo'c'sle hand, the sentence, systematically pronounced, was marooning'.

The drift of events, and the hardening structure of society, worked in his favour, of course. The commanding position Britain had attained in Europe by the Peace of Utrecht had been consolidated by Stanhope's diplomacy; Walpole did not face the prospect of another war until 1738 or 1739. The Tory Party, for reasons which are still far from clear, failed to regain its position as an alternative government; as for the High Church movement, it was tricked into suicide. In 1717 Benjamin Hoadly, the Whig bishop of Bangor, initiated the Bangorian Controversy when he preached before the King a revolutionary sermon on 'The Nature of the Kingdom and Church of Christ'. Taking as his text Christ's remark, 'My kingdom is not of this world', Hoadly argued that all Christian churches, with their priests and ministers, were merely an administrative convenience; they were by-products of man's carnal nature, and enjoyed no supernatural authority whatsoever. The resultant furore split the Church; Convocation had to be adjourned *sine die* (and in fact it did not meet again until 1852), and the discomfiture of the High Churchmen was complete when their acknowledged leader Francis Atterbury, now bishop of Rochester, was attainted, dethroned and exiled in 1723 for intrigue with the Pretender. This vacancy, and the death of five more bishops in the same year, enabled Walpole's clerical adjutant Edmund Gibson, bishop of London, to remodel the episcopal bench in the Whig image. By 1730 the Hanoverian Church was descending into that comfortable lethargy, that political subservience, which was to make it the mockery of future generations.

At the same time the fruitless intrigues of the Jacobite Court, plus a brief war with Spain in 1718 and another war scare ten years later, allowed the government to maintain a substantial standing army. Ironically, it was a Tory government which took the crucial decision, when it demobilised the greater part of the army in 1713, to retain most of the officer corps on half-pay. The Jacobite Rising of 1715 gave the Whig government an excuse to retain an army of 36,000, including garrisons abroad, and Walpole increased the home establishment alone to 18,000 in 1722, 26,000 in 1727, despite regular protests that this was against the spirit, if not the letter, of the Revolution Settlement.

In fact, the three great professions of the Victorian Age, the Army, the Church and the Civil Service, were already taking shape, and particularly the Civil Service. Samuel Pepys had been only one of the first of a new race of Under-Secretaries who were to fashion a new structure of permanent administration for a new age. He was unusual solely in his refusal to accept the Revolution; others had no such qualms. Henry Guy, for instance, served as Secretary to the Treasury from 1679 to 1695, when he was disgraced, and then his post went to his protege William Lowndes, who had entered the Treasury in the 1670s as a junior clerk. Lowndes survived into the reign of George I as a key figure in the transaction of Treasury business, inside as well as outside Parliament; he took the motto for his coat-of-arms from the Commons Committee for Ways and Means, and 'Ways and Means' is still the motto of the Selby-Lowndes family. When he died in 1724 Walpole told the Commons, 'This House has lost a very useful Member, and the public as able and honest a servant as ever the Crown had.' His successor, John Scrope, was even closer to Walpole, and was not expected to survive his fall in 1742, especially since he resolutely declined to give evidence against his old master. But he died in office ten years later. As William Pulteney admitted:

> 'Mr Scrope is the only man I know that thoroughly understands the business of the Treasury and is versed in drawing money bills. On this foundation he stands secure, and is immoveable as a rock'.

In their seventy years of service he, Lowndes and Guy had together served six monarchs and three dynasties.

Almost as remarkable was the career of William Blathwayt, who held the post of Secretary-at-War (we would say Under-Secretary of State at the War Office) from 1683 to 1704, and was deeply trusted by the cautious William III, who said he was 'dull, but had a good method'. Indeed he had; his reforms at the War Office took the department through the Napoleonic Wars. So did the reforms of William Bridgeman, who was appointed Secretary to the Admiralty in 1695 to clear up the mess left by Pepys's successors. The growing needs of a militarist state, the importance of a regular, properly-administered income from taxation, and not least the continual risk of having to account for their stewardship to a captious and critical House of Commons, led to the formation of permanent departments with permanent records, with a long-service salaried staff, whose standing was altogether different from that of Pepys's devoted clerk, Will Hewer. (Even then, there were mortifying lapses; in 1705, for instance, the Secretary of State's office could not turn up a copy of the Peace of Ryswick, signed only eight years before.) And naturally these Civil Service heads partook of the nation's growing wealth and self-assurance; their life style would have appeared incredible to Pepys, with his little tied house near the Navy Office in Seething Lane. Henry Guy had his own pocket borough, at Hedon in the East Riding, and entertained William III at his mansion at Tring in Hertfordshire on his way to Ireland in 1690. When Queen Anne took the waters at Bath she commonly stayed with William Blathwayt at nearby Dyreham Park, the house designed by Talman, the architect of Chatsworth, the gardens by Le Nôtre, who had laid out the gardens of Versailles for Louis XIV. In fact, such men were auxiliaries to that splendid governing aristocracy which Disraeli termed a 'Venetian Oligarchy', and one modern historian has called the 'Earls of Creation'.

The whole country by now was rotten with wealth, trade was still booming, and so was agriculture; in fact, the South Sea Bubble itself was symptomatic, betraying as it did the untouched reserves of capital floating loose in this affluent society. Amongst the lower classes there was a startling degree of violence and excess which could at times produce an equally violent reaction. The Waltham Blacks, a gang of rural poachers and desperadoes who ranged the southern counties in the early 1720s, provoked the notorious Black Act of 1723, which made it a capital offence to be found after dark with one's face blacked. Indeed, between 1688 and 1820 the number of offences, mainly against property, for which the death sentence could be imposed rose from about 50 to over 200. But despite the high crime rate, and the high level of violence, there is no suggestion of destitution, even in the towns. There was squalor and degradation enough, of course, and especially in London; after all, Walpole himself was mobbed on the steps of the House of Commons in 1733 and narrowly escaped with his life; his son Horace tells us in 1754 that he could not attend the theatre in the afternoon without an escort of two brawny manservants armed with cudgels; urban squalor is mercilessly exposed in Hogarth's famous etching 'Gin Lane'. But Hogarth was not arguing that squalor made for alcoholism, rather the opposite; the other half of the diptych, 'Beer Alley', is often ignored. Here Hogarth portrayed the rude good health, cheerful domestic life and social responsibility of a working-class family imbibing honest English ale instead of brain-rotting Dutch spirits. And the key point is that workers had the money to indulge in either.

Nor was this prosperity accidental. It owed everything to the excellence of the British Constitution and the blessings of Liberty, which set this fortunate nation apart from all others, and made her an example to the world. Poets never tired of hymning in execrable verse:

'Happy BRITANNIA, where the QUEEN OF ARTS,
Inspiring Vigour, LIBERTY abroad
Walks unconfin'd, even to thy farthest Cotts,
And scatters Plenty with unsparing Hand'.

And though it was acknowledged that the way had been prepared by King John's obstreperous barons, by Queen Elizabeth of ever-blessed memory and other early heroes, what had set the seal on England's greatness was 1688, that 'Glorious Revolution', the 'Year I of English Liberty'. The approval of such foreign luminaries as Voltaire and Montesquieu only confirmed the British in their stupendous complacency. In the balanced structure of King, Lords and Commons they had achieved the ultimate constitution, the Classical Constitution, on which virtually no improvement could be made.

The strange thing is, this constitution was headed by kings who had no popular appeal at all and enjoyed scant public respect, even in the inner circles of power. Moreover, the 'prime ministerial' form of government introduced by Walpole was regarded with the deepest suspicion, a suspicion which found violent expression in the opposition to his Excise Scheme in 1733, when he, George II and Queen Caroline were pilloried in the public prints in a way which would have been unthinkable a hundred years before or a hundred years after. In fact, though ministries could usually face a general election with confidence, they were extremely sensitive to public opinion and easily stampeded by any threat of social disorder. The Excise Scheme had to be withdrawn, firm legislation against gin abuse was frustrated again and again by the lobbying of the distillers and rioting on the part of their customers. In 1752 Henry Pelham's ministry was even shaken by the riots which greeted the belated introduction of the Julian Calendar, which involved dropping for that year the twelve days between September 2nd and 14th, and in 1754, in response to anti-semitic pressure, it cravenly repealed a Jewish Naturalisation Act it had passed only the previous year.

Never mind: the British excused the practice of the constitution and adored the theory. According to that theory the monarchical principle made for executive efficiency and continuity while the democratic principle, expressed through the House of Commons, and the aristocratic principle, expressed through the House of Lords, acted as a check upon each other and upon the King, while an independent judiciary, armed with those wonder-working weapons, Magna Carta and Habeas Corpus, dispensed an even-handed justice unaffected by political pressure and in theory available to the lowest in the land. And though Dissenters were still barred from central government the blessings of religious toleration – another boon conferred at the Revolution – meant that even the Quakers could aspire through business and manufacture to the aristocracy of wealth if not the aristocracy of rank. As Sir William Blackstone put it in his *Commentaries on the Laws of England*, a work of near-biblical authority:

> 'Of a constitution so wisely contrived, so strongly raised, and so highly finished, it is hard to speak with that praise which is justly and severely its due. The thorough and attentive contemplation of it will furnish its best panegyric'.

Of course, to a weaver toiling in the sweat shops of London or Leicester, to a ploughman or cowman working a fourteen-hour day seven days a week on the estates of the duke of Rutland or the duke of Devonshire, such considerations were highly abstract – when they were not entirely unknown. But the lower orders knew their place, and could be relied upon to keep to it. In the words of Edmund Burke, that eminent defender of the British *ancien régime*:

> 'They must respect that property of which they cannot partake. They must labour to obtain what by labour can be obtained; and when they find, as they commonly do, the success disproportioned to the endeavour, they must be taught their consolation in the final proportions of eternal justice'.

After all, that was what the Church of England was for.

CHAPTER FOURTEEN

Freedom's Own Island

'Good and evil will grow up in the world together; and they who complain, in peace, of the insolence of the populace, must remember that insolence in peace is bravery in war.'

Dr Johnson

IN THE *Spectator* papers, published in the reign of the last Stuart sovereign, Queen Anne, two writers of genius described the pride Englishmen felt in the expanding commerce and wealth of their country's capital at the start of the eighteenth century. 'As I moved towards the city,' wrote Steele, 'gay signs, well disposed streets, magnificent public structures and wealthy shops, adorned with contented faces, made the joy still rising till we came to the centre of the city and centre of the world of trade, the Exchange of London.' 'Our ships,' Addison boasted, 'are stored with spices and oils and wines; our rooms are filled with pyramids of china adorned with the workmanship of Japan; our morning's draught comes to us from the remotest corners of the earth; we repair our bodies by the drugs of America and repose ourselves under Indian canopies.'

For during Queen Anne's reign, Marlborough's victories of Blenheim in 1704 and Ramillies, Oudenarde and Malplaquet in 1706, 1708 and 1709, over the Grand Monarch's hitherto invincible armies, had made Englishmen, for the first time, conscious of an imperial destiny. A little island of six million people was learning to use its vantage-point at the ocean gates of Europe to gather tribute from every shore of earth. 'He calls the sea the British common,' Addison wrote of his imaginary merchant, Sir

Andrew Freeport: 'there is not a point in the compass but blows home a ship in which he is an owner.' The English – and the Scots with whom their Parliament, as well as throne, had now been joined by the Act of Union of 1707 – began to seize their opportunities with both hands.

For divided since the death of Elizabeth by violent religious and political controversies, with the Revolution of 1688 the English had achieved a working compromise and, with it, national unity. The essence of that so called 'glorious' and 'bloodless' Revolution, and of the settlement which followed it, was that Englishmen should cease to destroy one another for the sake of abstract theories and seek, under a parliamentary monarchy, a working compromise upon which they could agree to differ. Its philosopher was the grandson of a Somerset clothier, John Locke, who had grown up during the Civil War and Interregnum and lived to hear the news of Blenheim. He was the first – and English – prophet of the Age of Reason and the Rights of Man. His two cardinal principles were that it was an error to entertain 'any proposition with greater assurance than the proofs it is built upon will warrant,' and that no man should 'be subject to the inconstant, uncertain, unknown arbitrary will of another.' Moderation, toleration and liberty, preserved by rational laws and the sanctity of private property, were his recipe for human well-being. He voiced the experience of a generation which had seen all its religious and political ideals discredited by fanatics. His attitude was enshrined in the urbane *Spectator* essays of Joseph Addison whose self-proclaimed mission was to wean his countrymen from party rancour and spleen and teach them to co-exist with 'good-nature, compassion and humanity.' In his imaginary portraits of the slightly absurd but lovable old Tory squire, Sir Roger de Coverley, and his Whig adversary and fellow clubman, Sir Andrew Freeport – types of the rival landed and moneyed interests – he showed how arguments between fellow countrymen, which a generation earlier had been resolved only by sword and cudgel, need 'proceed no further than to an agreeable raillery' between friends. In this capacity for good-humoured controversy, in which political opponents could differ yet remain friends, lay the key, not only to the

331

English eighteenth century, but to more than two hundred years of peaceful parliamentary evolution.

Given permanence by an alliance between the Whig nobility and the City merchants and bankers, the Revolution of 1688 placed on the throne a Dutch, and later a German prince, both descended from James I, but gave the controlling direction of the kingdom to the greater owners of land – the principal architects and beneficiaries of that Revolution. Wiser than the Stuarts they had overthrown, they exercised power by shunning its outward forms. They governed in the King's name and legislated through an assembly of country gentlemen, lawyers and placeholders, more than equal to their own hereditary chamber in political status but indirectly subject to their social and territorial influence. In this they showed their shrewdness. For, after their experience of its exercise by Charles I and the military and doctrinal despots who had supplanted him, the English people did not like the appearance of power.

Nor did these supremely fortunate creatures exercise power for its own sake – these Russells and Grenvilles, Cavendishes, Talbots and Howards with their scores of thousands of acres, their hereditary titles and offices, their State sinecures and pensions for their younger sons and cousins and retainers. (As late as 1760, at the beginning of George III's reign, there were only 174 British peers.) They sought honours and riches with avidity and retained them with firm grasp, securing their continued enjoyment by elaborate entails on their elder children. But they valued them almost entirely for what they brought in freedom and ease to themselves. They extended and improved their domains and cheated the King's Exchequer for the glorious privilege of being independent.

The countryside was dotted with their lovely palaces and noble avenues, the fields and woods of the whole kingdom were open to their horses and hounds, the genius of man, past and present, was brought to decorate their houses and gardens, to fill their libraries with the masterpieces of the classical and modern mind, to cover their walls with paintings and tapestries and adorn their tables with exquisite silver and porcelain. Theirs was an ample and splendid design for living. Nor was it a purely material one. For such was the subtlety of their intelligences that they instinctively refused to be chained by their possessions and comforts. They encouraged freedom of expression and diversity of behaviour, preferring a vigorous existence and the society of equals to a hot-house tended by serfs. They sent their sons to rough, libertarian schools where strawberry leaves were no talisman against the rod (at Harrow, according to school tradition, the duke of Dorset was always beaten twice – once for the offence and once for being a duke) and afterwards to the House of Commons where men used plain words and likewise suffered them. And if by their English law of primogeniture they transmitted to their firstborn a wealth and freedom equal and if possible superior to their own, the same law endowed their younger sons with incentive and scope for action and adventure. They left the doors of opportunity open.

Nor did they ignore nature. They made no extravagant attempt to secure exclusive privilege for their blood, but frankly recognized the principle of change. They were realists. Though possessing almost unlimited power, the English aristocracy never attempted to make itself a rigid caste. The younger sons of a duke or marquis were by courtesy entitled lords; the younger sons of a viscount or baron, honourables. There their transmitted dignities ended. Save for the eldest male their grandchildren were all commoners with the same prefix as groom and gamekeeper. Kinship with them, though a social asset, was no defence to breach of the law: a man might be hanged though he were cousin to a marquis with 80,000 acres. The great lords looked after themselves and their immediate kin: they refused to endanger their privilege by extending it too widely.

Within the confines of their sensible ambition and the law there was no limit to their personal power and enjoyment. They did as they pleased. The world was their park and pleasance, and they never doubted their right to make themselves at home in it. 'Mr Dundas!' cried the duchess of Gordon to the Home Secretary at an Assembly, 'you are used to speak in public – will you call my servant'; Lord Stafford paid a Home Secretary a private retaining fee of £2000 a year to do his accounts. And if they chose to be naughty, naughty they were: his Grace of Norfolk – 'Jockey of

Norfolk' – who looked like a barrel and reeled like a drunken faun, broke up a fashionable dance he was attending by ringing the church bells and distributing cider to a mob under the ballroom windows to celebrate a false rumour that a fellow 'radical' had won the Middlesex election.

Because they enjoyed life and seldom stood deliberately in the way of others doing the same, they were popular. They took part in the nation's amusements and mixed freely with their neighbours. They were healthy, gregarious and generous and had little fear in their make-up. They governed England without a police force, without a Bastille and virtually without a civil service, by sheer assurance and personality. When the Norfolk militia refused to march to a field day unless a guinea a man were first distributed, their colonel, William Windham, strode up to the ringleader and, ignoring their oaths and raised muskets, carried him to the guard-house, standing at the door with a drawn sword and swearing to the mob about him that while he lived the man should not go free.

Wishing to be *primi inter pares* and not solitary despots, the higher aristocracy merged imperciptibly into the country gentry. The marquis of Buckingham in his white pillared palace at Stowe was only the first gentleman in Buckinghamshire, the social equal, if political superior, of the Verneys, Chetwodes, Drakes, Purefoys and other humbler squires. They went to the same schools, sat round the same convivial tables, rode together in the hunting field and took counsel with one another at Quarter Sessions. In each family the elder son was the independent lord of his own little world, whether it was a couple of thousand homely acres or a broad province such as fell to the lot of a Fitzwilliam or a Percy. The younger sons and their young sons after them quickly shaded off into the general body of lawyers and clergymen, Navy and Army officers, bankers and merchants. Proud blood and breeding flowed in a broad unimpeded current through the nation's veins.

So did the desire to live well: to dine and hunt and lord it like an elder son. Despite inequalities of wealth and status the English preserved a remarkable unity of social purpose. Even in their most snobbish occasions – and in their veneration for the 'quality' they seemed snobs to a man – there was something of a family atmosphere. On the continent, where noble blood was a fetish and caste a horizontal dividing line, a nobleman's house tended to be a vast barracks rising out of a desert and set against a background of miserable hovels in which ragged creatures of a different species lived an animal, servile existence. In England even the costliest mansion soon mellowed into something cosy and homely: more modest, more human than anything dreamed of by Polish count or Germon baron. French princes and princesses at Versailles built themselves sham cottages in their grounds and dressed up as shepherds and shepherdesses to feed their starved palates on homely pleasures; in England simplicity, with sturdy mien and broad bucolic joke, was never far off. The cottage, snug and thatched, with its porch, oven and tank and its garden warm with peonies and rambler roses, stood four-square against the mansion gates.

The thing that first struck foreign travellers about rural England was its look of prosperity. 'As always,' wrote the young Comte de la Rochefoucauld of a Norfolk journey in 1784, 'I admired the way in which in all these little villages the houses are clean and have an appearance of cosiness in which ours in France are lacking. There is some indefinable quality about the arrangement of these houses which makes them appear better than they actually are.' In *The Deserted Village* Goldsmith, by describing what sweet Auburn had been before the east wind of enclosure struck its Christian polity, idealised yet painted from a still living model common to England alone:

'How often have I loitered o'er thy green
Where humble happiness endeared each scene!
How often have I paused on every charm,
The sheltered cot, the cultivated farm,
The never-failing brook, the busy mill,
The decent church that topped the neighbouring hill,
The hawthorn bush, with seats beneath the shade
For talking age and whispering lovers made.'

Poverty there was an injustice – in many cases harsh, bleak and grinding. With the coming of large-scale enclosure in the last quarter of the century they began to increase fast, for the new methods of farming and land-tenure brought wealth to the few but debasement and suffering to the many. But though men were everywhere being dispossessed by mysterious parliamentary and legal processes beyond their understanding of rights their forbears had enjoyed, the countryside as a whole retained the air of well-being that had pervaded it for the past hundred years. The predominant type, soon to become a minority, was the cottager who laboured three or four days a week on his richer neighbour's land and two or three on his own. He still regarded the larger farmer who was beginning to be his employer as an equal: had lived in his house in his bachelor days as an unmarried farm servant, had perhaps aspired to his daughter, and shared his bread and cheese at the long oaken board and drunk his home-brewed beer or cider round his winter ingle-nook. In an unenclosed village he farmed three or four acres of his own in the common fields, holding them by a tenure – a copyhold or perhaps a lease for the longest survivor of three or more lives – which made him something more than a cap-touching tenant dependent on another man's will.

Such men could afford to feel independent: they were. 'If you offer them work,' wrote an improving farmer, 'they will tell you that they must go to look up their sheep, cut furzes, get their cows out of the pound or, perhaps, say that they must take their horse to be shod that he may carry them to the horse-race or a cricket-match.' It was, indeed, this independence which caused their better-to-do neighbours to disregard them in their attempt to enlarge their own freedom by opening new avenues to wealth. The tragedy of the enclosures was not that they changed the older basis of farming and land tenure, which was ill-suited to the needs of a growing country, but that they did so without making provision for that continuing stake in the soil for their neighbours which had made the English a nation of freemen. When the Parliamentary Commissioners offered a poor commoner a few years' purchase for his hereditary rights of grazing and turfing, they were depriving unborn generations of their economic liberty. This was forgotten by a vigorous gentry exercising untrammelled legislative power and possessed by an enlightened, if selfish, desire to improve on the wasteful and obstructionist farming methods of the past. In their impatience they overlooked the fact that freedom – their own most prized privilege – usually appears inefficient in the short run.

Yet, though decline and decay had set in, and during the last forty years of the eighteenth century nearly three million acres were subjected to Enclosure Acts, the typical village was still a microcosm of the greater England of which it was a part, whose members included every social type from the squire who administered the law to the barber who cupped veins and drew the rustic tooth. Here was the blacksmith whose smithy was at once the ironmongery of the community and the wayside repair-station of an equestrian age, the wheelwright with his cunning craft, the clockmaker, the tailor seeking orders from door to door, the upholsterer, glazier, miller, cobbler, farrier, maltster, reddleman and tranter. Arthur Young, writing in 1789, enumerated, in a Norfolk parish of 231 families 38 husbandmen, 26 spinners, 12 farmers, 12 publicans, 8 carpenters, with a total of 57 different classes of employment. Such employments were intricately interwoven. The farrier, the miller and the maltster usually also held or rented farms; the village craftsman had his garden and, in an unenclosed village, his holding in the common fields. Few were solely dependent on their craft. The rustic world, by geographical measure, was narrow, but there was choice in it.

In many counties a subsidiary form of employment was afforded by the cloth industry. Like other local crafts, such as the cottage lace industry and straw plaiting of Buckinghamshire, it afforded domestic occupation and employment not only to men, but to women and children. The wealth thus acquired, as Wilberforce said, was not obtained at the expense of domestic happiness but in the enjoyment of it. Such trades had their ups and downs, and with the expansion of machinery it was soon to be mostly downs. But in the last decades before the Napoleonic Wars, the weavers, especially in the North, were doing well, often employing journeymen and apprentices in addition to their families. The new mechanical spinning frames gave them cheap and plentiful supplies of yarn. They enjoyed well-furnished dwellings bright with clocks, prints, oak and mahogany furniture and Staffordshire ware, and plenty of butcher's meat, oatmeal and potatoes.

Good fare was regarded as an Englishman's birthright. Every cottage had its flitch of home-cured bacon hanging from the smoky beam and its copper for brewing ale. Eggs, geese, poultry and rabbits abounded, though the wild game which in earlier days had come easily to the peasant's pot was disappearing with enclosures and the growing passion of the rich for the chase. But although a term was being set to all this prosperity and a stormier horizon lay in the path of the 'poor, the age of comparative rustic plenty lingered into the 'eighties of the Hanoverian century. Rochefoucauld in 1784 noted how much greater the consumption of meat was in England than in any other country and even claimed that in East Anglia the labourer enjoyed butcher's meat every day. This was probably an exaggeration, but in contemporary France and Germany such a claim would have seemed fantastic.

With transport still dependent on the beast and the soft cart-track, the bulk of what was raised could only be consumed locally. Every place and season had its peculiar delicacies. 'My dinner (I love to repeat good ones),' wrote John Byng over his slippered ease in his inn at nightfall, 'consisted of spithcock'd eel, roasted pigeons, a loin of pork roasted, with tarts, jellies and custards.' Woodforde, a Norfolk parson with a modest living, entertained his neighbours to 'fish and oyster sauce, a nice piece of boiled beef, a fine neck of pork roasted and apple sauce, some hashed turkey, mutton stakes, salad, etc., a wild duck roasted, fried rabbits, a plum pudding and some tartlets, desert, some olives, nuts, almonds and raisins and apples.' Nor was such feasting confined to the days when the good parson entertained. He and his niece Nancy did themselves almost equally well on ordinary days. 'We returned home about three o'clock to dinner. Dinner to-day boiled chicken and a pig's face, a bullock's heart roasted and a rich plum-pudding.' Small wonder that Nancy sometimes felt ill of an afternoon 'with a pain within her, blown up as if poisoned'; that the parson was forced to complain after a somewhat restless night, 'mince pie rose oft.'

They drank as deep, even when it was only tea. Miss Burney's mother once made Dr Johnson twenty-one cups in succession. After dinner, bottles of spirits – brandy, rum, shrub – moved in ceaseless procession round the table. At Squire Gray's – 'a fine jolly old sportsman' – the cloth was not cleared until a bottle of port had been laid down before a mighty silver fox's head, out of which the squire filled a bumper and drank to fox-hunting preparatory to passing it about. Parson Woodforde did not scruple to entertain five fellow-clergymen with eight bottles of port and one of Madeira, besides arrack punch, beer and cider.

It was the hallmark of your true Englishman that he 'loved his can of flip'. In London alone there were more than five thousand licensed houses within the Bills of Mortality. From the royal family to the poor labourer 'being in beer' – a state so habitual that it was ordinarily held to excuse almost any excess – there was a general contempt for heeltaps. George III's sailor son, the duke of Clarence, whenever one of his guests stopped drinking, would call out, 'I see some daylight in that glass, sir: banish it.' 'We made him welcome,' wrote Ramblin' Jack of the fo'c'sle, 'as all Englishmen do their friends, damnabell drunk, and saw him safe home to Dean's Square, Ratclife way.'

Foreigners were much impressed, if sometimes appalled, by all this exuberant grossness. These robust islanders, with their guzzling and swilling, seemed like so many pieces of animated roast beef with veins full of ale. It appeared a point of pride with them – a mark of their superiority to other starveling nations – to fill themselves up. A farmer at the 'Wheel' at Hackington Fen ate for a wager two dozen penny mutton pies and drank half a gallon of ale in half an hour: then, remarking that he had had but a scanty supper, went on for the sheer love of the thing and consumed a 3d. loaf, a pound of cheese and a leg of pork. 'Sir,' said the great Dr Johnson, the very embodiment of eighteenth-century England, 'I mind my belly very studiously, for I look upon it that he who will not mind his belly will scarcely mind anything else.'

*　　*　　*

The foundation of this good living was the wealth of the English soil. Throughout the century a succession of remarkable men – aristocrats, hedge squires and farmers – devoted their lives to the improvement of crops and livestock. Bakewell's new breed of

Leicester sheep in the 1760s and 1770s gave his country two pounds of mutton where she had one before. From King George III – 'Farmer George' – who contributed to the *Agricultural Magazine* under the pseudonym of Robinson and carried a copy of Arthur Young's *Farmer's Letters* on all his journeys – to Parson Woodforde, who recorded daily his horticultural activities and observations on the weather, the pursuit of husbandry gripped the English mind. Great lords would pay £400 or more for the hire of one of Mr Bakewell's rams, and yeomen would club together to establish cart-horse and ploughing tests. The country gentleman who did not look after his estate lost as much caste as he who shirked his fences in the hunting field. Hardy and realist, the landowners of England were a source of astonishment to continental neighbours who did not know at which to wonder more: aristocratic absorption in clovers and fat cattle or the intelligence with which farmers and peasants, who abroad would have been regarded as no better than beasts of burden, conversed on the principles of their calling.

This common passion was one of the influences which tempered the aristocratic government of the country. By accustoming men of all classes to act together, it gave them national cohesion. It was not that the political constitution of the country was democratic: it was on the face of it overwhelmingly aristocratic. The House of Lords was hereditary. Of 558 members of the House of Commons, 294 – a majority – were returned by constituencies with less than 250 electors. Many of the newer and larger centres of population had no representation at all, while an under-populated county like Cornwall still returned a tenth of the English and Welsh members. 157 MPs were nominated by eighty-four local proprietors, mostly peers, and 150 more on the recommendation of another seventy. Yet the power of the great lords, who regarded the Whig rule of England as something permanently ordained by Heaven, did not prevent the younger Pitt from carrying the country against the prevailing parliamentary majority in the election of 1784. The effect of corruption, openly acknowledged and shamelessly displayed, largely cancelled itself out. Those who sought entry to Parliament were often childishly sensitive to what their fellow-countrymen – and particularly their neighbours – thought of them.

The very illogicality of the electoral system inclined them to bow to any unmistakable expression of public opinion; they felt the intellectual weakness of their position and claimed no sanctity for their point of view.

The ninety-two knights of the shire were the élite of the House and carried far more weight than could be explained by their numbers. When they were united – an event however which only happened in a time of national emergency – no Government could long withstand their opposition. This was because their election by forty-shilling freeholders gave them a real right to speak for England: they represented the substance of her dominant interest and industry. They were no placemen or carpet-baggers but independent gentlemen openly competing with their equals for the suffrages of their neighbours – of those, that is, best fitted to judge their character and stewardship. Before a county election sturdy freeholders rode into the shire town from every side to hear speeches from the rival candidates, to be canvassed by them in market hall and street, to march in bannered and cockaded processions behind bands of music, and to eat and drink at their expense in the leading inns and taverns. The most important of all county elections – because it represented the largest constituency – was that of the great province of Yorkshire: on the result of this the eyes of ministers and even of European statesmen were fixed.

In such contests, and even in those of the close boroughs, there was a wealth of homely plain speaking and even homelier conduct. The candidates, however splendid their lineage and estates, had to take their turn of lampoons, brutal jests and rotten eggs and run the gauntlet of a fighting, drunken, cheering, jeering crowd before they could hope to enter the portals of Westminster. One did not have to be an alderman or an hereditary burgess or even a forty-shilling freeholder to fling a dead cat at the hustings. The right to do so during an election was regarded as an inalienable privilege of every Englishman: the only check the right of every other subject to return the compliment. At the Wycombe election in 1794 Lord Wycombe was thrown down in the mud and Squire Dashwood, another candidate, lost his hat and almost his life. 'Elections are certainly of some use,' wrote radical John Byng, 'as affording lessons of humility and civility to a proud lord and a steeped lordling.'

The rowdiest of all elections was that of Westminster. Here, by one of the incalculable illogicalities of the English constitution, something approaching manhood suffrage prevailed. Every adult male with his own doorway and a fireplace on which to boil his pot had the right to record his vote. Like Yorkshire, Westminster was regarded by statesmen as a political test: in its noisy humours – its riots, its stuffed effigies, its grand ladies cajoling porters and draymen with kisses – one could feel the pulse of England.

Perhaps the most startling manifestation of English licence was the power of the mob. England had no police force, and it was regarded as a mark of effeminate namby-pambyism to wish there to be one. Facing a mob was like facing a fence or standing up to an enemy in the ring: a thing a gentleman took in his stride. One did it with courage and good humour, and then the monster – which, being English itself, respected courage and good nature – did no great harm. True in 1780 the London mob, out of an ignorant Protestant fanaticism, surrounded the Houses of Parliament, took drunken control of the capital for four days and burnt down a good deal of it. Yet even this excess was regarded as part of the price of popular freedom. And in its crude, barbarous way the mob did – under guidance – act as a kind of rough watchdog of the national liberties. Thus, when the House of Commons, in its dislike of the disreputable John Wilkes, outraged the principles of freedom of choice and speech which it was its duty to uphold, it was the constancy of the mob to the cause which had brought Strafford to the scaffold that shamed and finally defeated the advocates of despotism.

Liberty outside Parliament was reflected by liberty within. For all the power of the great nominating lords and borough-mongers and the allurements of the Treasury, there were more independent members in the House than is possible under the rigid Party machinery of to-day. In a major issue it was not the Whips but men's consciences that turned the scale in the lobbies. Minorities could make themselves felt. A great speech could decide a hard-fought debate: members were not the tied advocates of particular interests obeying mandates issued in advance. They gave their constituents unfettered judgment.

Nor did the complexion of the House discount the rise of talent. Within its narrow range the old parliamentary system fostered it. Again and again it recruited to the country's service the strongest motive power in the world – the force of genius untrammelled by the rule of mediocrity. A young man of brilliance, who had the good fortune to attract the notice of some great peer, might be set on the high road to the Front Bench. Pitt with £300 a year became Prime Minister at twenty-four, and Burke, a man of genius without any of the arts of the demagogue and lacking both birth and independent fortune and even English nationality, for he was Irish, entered Parliament by the back door of a rotten borough and a discerning aristocrat's approval.

Behind every English exercise of liberty was the conception of law. It did not coerce a man from acting as he pleased: it only afforded redress to others if in doing so he outraged their rightful liberty or the peace of the community. Every man could appeal to the law: no man could legally evade it. Not even the King: perhaps it would be truest to say, least of all the King. The squire who rebuked George III – in the latter part of his reign a very popular monarch – for trespassing on his land became a national legend.

In England there was no *droit administratif*; no sacred principle of State with which to crush the cantankerous subject. The official had to produce the warrant of law to justify his action. If he exceeded his authority, whatever his motives, he suffered the same penalty as though he had acted as a private citizen. There was no escape from the law: it was like divine retribution and might overtake the transgressor at any moment of his life. Joseph Wall, for all his fine connections, was hanged at Newgate in front of a cheering mob for having twenty years before, while Governor of Goree, sentenced a mutinous sergeant to an unlawful flogging which caused death.

Trial by law was conducted in public. Judges were appointed for life and were irremovable save for gross misconduct. Issues of fact were decided by a jury of common citizens. Any man arrested could apply to the courts for an immediate writ of *Habeas Corpus* calling on his custodian to show legal cause why he should be detained. In all doubtful cases the prisoner was given the benefit of the doubt and acquitted. These were the main pillars of English justice, together with an unpaid magistracy of local worthies, the absence of a paid constabulary,* and a traditional distrust of the standing army which was always kept by Parliament – alone capable of voting funds for its maintenance – at the lowest strength compatible with national safety, and often a good deal lower.

There was another safeguard for freedom – the legal sanctity of property. It was individual ownership, it was held, which enabled a man to defy excessive authority. Without a competence of his own to fall back on, the subject could be bribed or intimidated: a John Hampden without an estate seemed impracticable to the English mind. The guardians of her liberties were the gentlemen of England whose hereditary independence protected them from the threats and guiles of despotism. They were tyrant-proof.

Any interference with a man's property by the State which infringed what an eighteenth-century correspondent called 'the sweet majesty of private life' was regarded as pernicious. Free men were supposed to be free to do as they liked with their own. Taxation had to be kept as low as possible and the extent of a man's contribution to the kingdom's upkeep left, wherever practicable, to his own choice. Direct taxation was regarded as repugnant to English principles both on account of its compulsion and of the power of inquisition it involved. The taxpayer had the option of declining to purchase the taxed article and so avoiding the tax. For this reason many antiquated tariff barriers which would otherwise have been swept away in the rising tide of free trade were retained for revenue purposes.

'No taxation without representation' was the oldest battle-cry in the armoury of English freedom; it dominated the constitution.

---

* In London a small patrol of less than fifty thousand men was maintained to guard its highwayman-infested approaches, while a handful of professional Bow Street runners – popularly known as 'redbreasts' on account of their scarlet waistcoats – occasionally patrolled the more lawless districts. For the rest the public order of the capital was left to the medieval constables of the parishes, assisted by a race of venerable watchmen or 'Charlies' with traditional staffs, lanterns and rattles.

dew is on the grass and the sun is shining high over 'Old Winchester' as they take the field against All England. With her solid heart of sober, quiet folk, England had such reserves of strength that it was difficult to estimate her breaking point."

William Pitt the Younger, "the living example of the triumph of reason", addressing the House of Commons in 1793. "Unless we wish to stand by and suffer State after State to be subverted, we must now declare our firm intention effectually to oppose those principles of ambition and aggrandisement which have for their object the destruction of England, of Europe and of the world."

Those assembled in Parliament did not represent numbers but property: the greater landowners in the House of Lords, the lesser in the Commons, side by side with the burgesses who represented the nation's mercantile interest. Such an assembly was tender to the taxpayer, unsympathetic to the executive. Eighteenth-century England had been saved from a recurrence of the seventeenth-century struggles between Crown and Parliament by vesting power in a cabinet of Ministers who commanded the support of a majority in the House of Commons. Because of this, administration and justice were supported more cheaply than in any other country of equivalent size and importance. The cost of administration in Prussia was twice as much, in France many times that of Britain. The chief civil expenses were the sinecures and pensions which the ruling aristocracy, usurping the former perquisites of the Court, lavished on their relations and supporters. Even the Navy, in peacetime, was pared to the bone, particularly in the matter of seamen's pay. Yet economy on the Navy was at least kept within limits. For experience had taught the English that their commercial wealth depended on their fleet.

*   *   *

'Trade,' Addison had written, 'without enlarging the British territories has given us a sort of additional empire; it has multiplied the number of the rich, made our landed estates infinitely more valuable and added to them the accession of other estates as valuable as the lands themselves.' The development of commerce under the Hanoverians was prodigious. In 1720 the value of the country's imports was just over £6,000,000; by 1760 it was nearly £10,000,000, by 1789 over £37,000,000. During these years East Indian tea and West Indian sugar became part of the staple dietary of the people. Everything conspired to further this process: natural health and vigour, free institutions, aptitude for seamanship and colonisation and a unique geographical position.

Together they brought Britain the beginning of a global and territorial empire, acquired not through any deliberate design of conquest, but fought for and won by her sailors and soldiers as a

345

consequence of her merchants' search for markets. After the Treaty of Utrecht in 1713, which brought to a successful conclusion the wars with which William III and Marlborough, with their Dutch and Austrian allies had restrained and humbled the ambitions of the Grand Monarch of France, there had followed a quarter of a century's peace under the first two Hanoverian kings and the Norfolk squire, Sir Robert Walpole, with his parliamentary and financial skills, who for twenty years was their first, or 'Prime', Minister. They were years epitomised in the contemporary song about the Vicar of Bray who, through all the political changes and revolutions of the time, contrived to retain his plump living.

> 'When George in pudding time came o'er
> And moderate men looked big, Sir,
> My politics I changed once more
> And so became a Whig, Sir.'

But in 1739 Walpole could no longer restrain the indignation of the merchant community and a high-spirited nation at atrocities committed by Spanish revenue officers against English seamen at their agelong game of attempting to break Spain's rigid monopoly of trade with her South American colonies. A naval war broke out between the two countries,* fought mostly among the fever-haunted islands of the Caribbean, but distinguished by Anson's feat, emulating Drake, of circumnavigating the globe and returning with teeming holds filled with captured Spanish treasure. Later the war spread to Europe where, in 1742, an Anglo-German king, George II, fighting to preserve his Hanoverian electorate from the French, distinguished himself by his gallantry in the victory of Dettingen. Thence it spread to the Channel where the French, after vainly attempting to invade, put ashore in Western Scotland the last Stuart claimant to the English throne, the young Pretender – the dethroned James II's grandson – who, after a forlorn and abortive invasion of England with a Highland army in 1745, was subsequently routed by George II's brother, 'butcher'

---

* The War of Jenkins's Ear – the ear was that of a sea captain exhibited by an indignant member in the House of Commons.

Cumberland, at tragic Culloden. Temporarily ended by the Peace of Aix-la-Chapelle in 1748, but continuing unofficially between English and French colonists and traders in North America and India, the war between England and France broke out again in Europe in 1756. By the end of the so-called Seven Years War, which lasted till 1763, all but its first two years under the direction of the great and fiery war Minister, William Pitt, earl of Chatham, Britain found herself on a pinnacle of unexpected and unprecedented glory. 'No-one,' it was said, by one of his officers, of Chatham, 'can enter his closet without coming out of it a braver man.' In 1759 – the 'year of victories' – his inspired leadership and strategy culminated in the storming of the Heights of Abraham above the St Lawrence River by young General Wolfe, who falling in the hour of triumph, won for his country the citadel of Quebec from the French dominion of Canada.

All Britain's victories rested on the mastery of the oceans by the Royal Navy. Evolved as a regular force in permanent being under the later Stuart kings, and given a foundation of rule and discipline through the clerkly labours of Samuel Pepys, it was officered by hardy professionals of the highest competence and manned by an hereditary race of almost incredibly tough and deft seamen from England's coastal counties, supplemented in time of war, by the scum of London and the seaport towns conscripted by pressgangs. Its fleets were led in battle by a succession of great commanders – Edward Vernon, 'that provident great admiral'; the circumnavigator and far-sighted administrator and First Sea Lord, George Anson; and Edward Hawke, who, in a gale in November 1759, shattered the French Brest fleet among the rocks of Quiberon Bay. In two global wars, spanning sixteen of the twenty-four years between 1739 and 1763, they and their fellow admirals won for their country a virtually permanent command of the world's seas.

Meanwhile in India, the miraculous victory of Plassey – won in 1757 by a former East India clerk of genius, Robert Clive, with 800 British soldiers and 2000 native auxiliaries, over a powerful army of 50,000 under Surajah Dowlah, the wicked Nabob of Bengal – brought a London trading company mastery of that great Ganges delta province and, with it, the key to the future supremacy of India. Hitherto the British had been little more than casual factors trading from isolated coastal ports on the fringe of the half anarchical peninsula by precarious leave of friendly native princes and in armed rivalry with other European trading companies. Now, in the second half of the century, the East India Company found itself administering densely populated and fabulously rich possessions many times the size of England. At first it merely regarded this unlooked-for dominion as a financial windfall for its factors and shareholders: the imagination of Leadenhall Street could stretch no further.

It was not only in India that a nation of farmers and shopkeepers failed to visualize the magnitude of their political opportunity. Along the eastern seaboard of North America, freed now from fear of French aggression by the conquest of Canada, lived two million British settlers. These a patronizing Court and Parliament, insisting on its legal right to tax them, treated as if they lacked the stubborn independence of their kinsfolk at home denying them application of the maxim 'no taxation without representation' – for the colonies were not represented at Westminster – which was thought of as the right of all subjects of the British Crown. The result was a financial quarrel, persisted in with all the ferocious obstinacy and moral rectitude of the race and the rigidity of its home Treasury administrators until no alternative remained but a systematic reconquest of the colonies by British soldiers or the end of the imperial connection.

The issue was still undecided when, following the colonists' Declaration of Independence in 1776, Britain's outdistanced competitors for the race for empire seized their opportunity for revenge. France, Spain and Holland – the three chief maritime powers of the continent – supported by Russia, Sweden and Denmark, joined hands with the colonists. With her fleets outnumbered, her finances in temporary ruin and her army forced in 1781 to capitulate to the Americans at Yorktown, Britain's greatness seemed finished. Then the brilliance and tenacity of her seamen, Rodney's and Hood's great victory of the Saints off Dominica in April 1782, and the stubborn three years' defence of Gibraltar by

General Eliott, turned the scale. A disastrous war dwindled into stalemate. The British faced the facts and in 1783 made peace. Their former colonies became the United States of America.

Yet unperceived by the islanders, who thought their new imperial heritage lost for ever, the process which had made the first empire continued and at an accelerated pace. What had happened before happened again. In every corner of the world where ships could sail enterprising Britons appeared, begging concessions, planting factories and on occasion hoisting the imperial flag as a protection for their ventures. No sooner, in the poet Cowper's phrase, had the jewel been picked from England's crown, than other jewels blazed in the empty sockets. In 1768 a self-taught navigator of genius, James Cook – a Yorkshire agricultural labourer's son who had gone to sea at eighteen in a Whitby collier and enlisted in the Navy – was given a Lieutenant's commission, and, at the instance of the Royal Society and the Admiralty, sailed in the 368-ton *Endeavour* on the first of the three voyages which, thanks to his indomitable leadership and navigational skill, revolutionized knowledge of the Southern seas, charted the shores of New Zealand and Australia and prepared the way for British rule in the Antipodes. Within five years of the final loss of the American colonies, Captain Phillip had established the first British settlement on the Australian continent. An even vaster new Britain in America took embryonic shape amid the empty snows of Canada where 140,000 defeated French, 60,000 migrant loyalists from the United States and a few thousand rough Scottish emigrants contrived to live together under King George's writ. Elsewhere a chain of forts, naval bases and sugar and spice islands continued to afford British traders springboards of opportunity.

For the moment the chief imperial field for the aspirant to wealth was India, which was beginning to take the place of the West Indies. From this oriental El Dorado flowed an ever-widening stream of spices, indigo, ivory, sugar, tea, ebony, sandalwood, saltpetre, cotton, silks and calicoes and fabulously rich merchants who bought up English estates and rotten boroughs, married their children into the aristocracy and received from their less fortunate countrymen the envious name of nabob. It was due to them that Britain first became conscious of her eastern possession and began to assume a direct responsibility for its government. The India Act of 1784, subordinating the political power of the Directors of the East India Company to a Board of Control appointed by the Crown, and the impeachment of Warren Hastings, the great Governor-General of Bengal, in 1787 were symptoms of this new interest, half-humanitarian, half-imperial.

* * *

By the last quarter of the eighteenth century the commercial success of the nation was beginning to change its character. Already it was setting out on its long trek from country to town. Even at the start of the Hanoverian age, London had more than three-quarters of a million inhabitants within a circuit of twenty miles. By now it stretched from Millbank in the west to Limehouse and Poplar hamlet in the east and from Islington in the north to Newington south of the River. Elsewhere population was concentrating itself in urban entities of a kind unknown to the civic culture of the past. The capital was no longer Britain's only great town. By 1790 Manchester had 80,000 inhabitants, Liverpool and Birmingham over 70,000 and Leeds 50,000. The population of Lancashire, hitherto one of the most barren areas of England, had grown to 600,000.

For here on the humid western slope of the Pennines a new industry arose during the second half of the century to rival the cloth trade of Yorkshire. It grew out of the Indian demand for manufactured bright cottons. Raw cotton, it was found, could be grown with slave labour on the plantations of the southern American colonies. The Lancashire climate, the traditional skill of English spinners and weavers and the astonishing ingenuity of British inventors did the rest. In 1771 Richard Arkwright, a Bolton barber, improving on the earlier work of the handloom weaver, Hargreaves of Blackburn, set up the first water-propelled spinning frame in Derbyshire. Eight years later Samuel Crompton, a Lancashire farmer and weaver, invented his spinning mule. These changed the entire nature of the industry and ultimately of British domestic life. The factory with its myriad turning machines took the place of the cottage spinning wheel. In 1741 Britain exported £20,000 worth of cotton goods; in 1790 £1,662,369 worth.

The northern heaths with their water power and coal-seams became transformed. Gaunt buildings with rows of windows rose like giant wraiths on the wild Matlock hills and in misty Lancashire valleys, and around them rows of cheerless, squalid little houses. Within a few years quiet old market towns like Rochdale swelled into noisy, straggling cities, filled with unwashed, pagan spinners and weavers: they seemed to a Tory of the old school 'insolent, abandoned and drunk half the week.' The capital of this area, now given over to the service of Mammon, was the old Jacobite town of Manchester, whose new population huddled together in damp, stinking cellars. Its port, importing corn and raw cotton, was up-start Liverpool, home of the West Indian trade and its scandalous offspring, the slave trade, with windmills and warehouses full of flies, rum and sugar, crowding for a mile along the northern bank of the Mersey.

Farther south in a formerly wild countryside another industrial area was growing up round the coal and iron-fields of Staffordshire and north Warwickshire. This was the Black Country – by 1790 a land of forges, collieries and canals with grimy trees and hedges. The traveller, venturing into this little-trodden, satanic region, saw rows of blackened hovels swarming with ragged children, and, instead of church spires, tall chimneys belching metallic vapours and at night lit by flames. At its southern extremity was Birming-ham – a squalid overgrown village or manufacturing town afflicted with elephantiasis, where 'crusty knaves that scud the streets in aprons seemed ever ready to exclaim, "Be busy and grow rich!"' and where the head grew dizzy with the hammering of presses, the clatter of engines and the whirling of wheels. Here almost every man in the cobbled streets stank of train-oil, and many had red eyes and hair bleached green by the brass foundries.

A few miles from Birmingham, the 'toyshop of Europe', lay the great Soho manufactory of Boulton & Watt. Here over his own works lived the princely capitalist who in the course of thirty virtuous and laborious years turned the creative genius of a Scottish engineer, James Watt, into a dynamic force to refashion the world.

Here the first practical cylindrical steam-engines were placed on the market, and manufacturers, statesmen and princes flocked to see the first wonder of Europe and buy the commodity which all the world of Mammon needed – 'power'. Such men as Boulton were pioneers of a new race, serving and exploiting the needs of their fellow-creatures with an energy and disregard for all other objects that make them loom through the mists of time like Titans. John Horrocks, the Quaker spinner, beginning work in a horse quarry, within fifteen years amassed a fortune of three-quarters of a million pounds and entered Parliament as member for his native town. Josiah Wedgwood of Etruria, exploiting the contemporary love for the ceramic art, made £500,000 out of pottery and transformed a wild moorland into a hive of smoking ovens trodden by thousands of horses and donkeys laden with panniers and by men and women with faces whitened with potter's powder. Far below them in the social scale but travelling the same adventurous road were newer and ever newer capitalists: dispossessed yeomen venturing their little all in the fierce industrial hurly-burly, or spinners earning, perhaps 35s. a week, working what would be regarded to-day as inconceivable hours and denying themselves every comfort to purchase a mill where others should work as hard for them in their turn.

Moralists deplored what was happening and, in the spread of depravity and atheism, predicted revolution. Instead of thinking of national well-being, statesmen and men of substance, they argued, were becoming obsessed with sordid considerations of profit-making. By the last decade of the century there were 100,000 men and women and 60,000 children working in the cotton mills, many of the latter indentured by Poor Law Guardians to masters who treated them little better than slaves. Yet the national conscience was not asleep but only bemused by a multiplicity of new activities and openings for money-making. A great and vigorous people, firmly launched on the ocean of untrammelled enterprise, was bound to commit errors, even crimes. Liberty had her economic gales as well as political. Yet the sea of endeavour was wide, and it was open. There was room to correct mistakes.

For all the while a recurring transformation was taking place.

As popular energy, overwhelming the barriers of restriction, swept away obstructions to the free flow of trade and talent, the competition of ruder types tended to out-produce and undersell those already established. The genteel merchants of Bristol, mellowed by two centuries of wealth and refinement, were no match for the products of pushing, hungry Liverpool, whose merchant captains were content with a moiety of the wages paid to their haughtier rivals. Those who had their way to make by a natural process caught up and ultimately outdistanced those with an inherited start. At first sight this seemed to threaten a progressive debasement of culture and social standards: the tough and the shover tending to shoulder out the gentleman and the fair dealer. Yet, as one bucket in the well of commerce fell, the other rose. The national passion for emulation constantly replanted the standards of quality in fresh soil; the greasy, aproned, clog-footed mechanic of one generation became the worthy merchant of the next. And if the process of cultural rise was not so quick as that of fall, the artistic and intellectual reserves of society were so vast that they could afford a good deal of dilution.

For in culture England had never stood higher, not even in the age of Shakespeare or that of Wren and Newton. Samuel Johnson, the great lexicographer and moralist, had died in 1784 and his friend, Goldsmith, ten years earlier.* But in 1788 Reynolds Romney, Gainsborough, Opie, Rowlandson, Stubbs and the young Lawrence were all painting, Cowper, Crabbe and Blake were writing poetry, Boswell was putting the last touches to the greatest biography in the language, and Gibbon had just finished its most majestic history. Wordsworth was born in 1770, Coleridge in 1772, Turner, Jane Austen and Charles Lamb in 1775, Constable in 1776, Hazlitt in 1778, de Quincey in 1785 and Byron in 1788. North of the border, where Adam Smith of Glasgow had established an international reputation as the first political economist of the age, Edinburgh was entering upon her brief but glorious flowering of native wit as the northern Athens. Raeburn was beginning to paint, Dugald Stewart to lecture, Walter Scott was

* The author's biography of Samuel Johnson is forthcoming.

353

studying the romantic lore of his country, and an Ayrshire plough-man, Robert Burns, had published his first volume. And in the realm of science Britain's achievements were equally remarkable. Joseph Black, the chemist, Hunter the founder of scientific surgery, Priestley the discoverer of oxygen, and Jenner who conquered the scourge of smallpox are among its great names. It was an age of gold that had the Adam brothers as its architects, Cosway as its miniaturist, Hepplewhite and Sheraton as its cabinet-makers. In the drawing rooms of London and of the lovely pastoral mansions which looked out on to the dreaming gardens of Repton and Capability Brown, a society moved, brocaded, white-stockinged and bewigged, more gracious, more subtle, more exquisitely bal-anced than any seen on earth since the days of ancient Greece.

Yet this society was governed by no fixed and absolute laws, confined by no insurmountable barriers. Under its delicate polish lay a heart of stout and, as the event was to prove, impenetrable oak. Its people were tough to the core. 'I shall be conquered, I will not capitulate,' cried Dr Johnson as he wrestled with death, guiding the surgeon's blade with his own hand. The duke of Portland at sixty-eight underwent an operation for the stone, remaining seven minutes under the knife without a murmur. Diminutive Jacob Bryant, the great classical antiquary, asked by his sovereign what branch of activity he was most noted for at Eton, answered to the astonishment of his auditor: 'Cudgelling, sir, I was most famous for that.' Young girls wore sticks of holly in their bosoms to teach them to hold their heads high, old Edge of Macclesfield at sixty-two walked 172 miles in under fifty hours for a bet; King George III rose daily at 4 a.m. and spent three hours on his dispatch boxes before taking his morning ride in Windsor Park. And the common people were tougher, if it were possible, than their betters. At Shirley village in Bedfordshire the penny barber told a traveller that he never used a brush since his customers, complaining of the tickling, preferred to be shaved dry.

They were fighters to a man: a race as game as the cocks they backed in the crowded, stinking pits of Jewin Street and Hockliffe. 'Look you, sir,' cried old General Sherbrooke to a fellow-officer who had offended him, 'my hands are now behind my back, and I advise you to leave the room before they are brought forward, for, if they once are, I will break every bone in your body.' 'Why, my little man,' asked one of the East India Directors of twelve-year-old John Malcolm at his interview for a commission, 'what would you do if you met Hyder Ali?' 'Cut off his heid,' came the instant reply.

Yet, though passionately addicted to barbarous sports like bull-baiting and cock-fighting, the English led the world in humanitarian endeavour. It was an Englishman, John Howard, who, at extreme risk and personal inconvenience, travelled 50,000 miles visiting the putrid, typhus-ridden jails of Europe; and it was Englishmen who at the close of the century first instituted organised opposition to cruelty to children and animals. Nothing so well illustrates the slow but persistant national impulse to mitigate inhumanity as the popular condemnation of the slave trade. This movement ran directly counter to the immediate material interests of the country; it none the less steadily gained strength from its inception by a handful of Quakers in the 1760s until the end of the century it was espoused by the Prime Minister, William Pitt himself – son of the great Chatham – and the overwhelming majority of thinking Englishmen.

The transatlantic slave trade had grown up to meet the needs of Britain's plantations in the West Indies and American colonies. Its headquarters was Liverpool, whose merchants imported seven-eighths of the negroes brought from Africa to America. In return for the slaves sold to the planters, they brought back to England sugar, rum, cotton, coffee. Thus the whole of the country indirectly benefited from this horrible traffic. The slaves, many of whom were kidnapped and who were sold to the traders by their fellow African chiefs and neighbours, were taken from the West African coast across the 'Middle Passage' to the West Indies in crowded slavers, loaded three slaves to a ton, the poor chained wretches being packed so tightly between decks that they were often forced to lie on top of one another. The mortality both of human cargo and seamen was appalling, but the smaller the consignment of slaves that arrived, the better the price paid for the remainder.

Every reason was sought to justify the continuance of the traffic.

355

Liverpool merchants and their parliamentary representatives declared that, were a measure passed to regulate the miseries of the 'Middle Passage', the West Indian trade would be ruined, Britain's commercial supremacy lost and the Navy be denuded of trained seamen. Yet having once been brought to the notice of the British people, the slave trade was doomed. For, with all its barbaric survivals, Christian Britain was a land of decent folk: of men and women with conscience. And because of the blend of freedom with order in her political institutions, the dictates of that conscience, though slow to mature, were ultimately given effect. Barbarous laws and cruel customs – men hanged in public for petty crimes, lunatics chained to the wall knee-deep in verminous straw, animals tortured at Smithfield and in the bull-ring – of these and their like there were plenty, but they were continually being ameliorated by the advancing pressure of public opinion. Instinctively a nation of freemen turned towards the light. That age-long process was the justification of their freedom.

For by freedom the English meant something more than freedom for themselves, though they certainly meant that. Conventional and conservative in their prejudices, often thoughtless and mentally lazy, they yet genuinely valued freedom for its own sake: for others, that is, as well as for themselves. And their ideal of liberty was never an abstraction. It was based not on generalizing but on measuring: on a calculation of the comparative rights and wrongs of every individual case. Burke's dictum, 'If I cannot reform with equity, I will not reform at all,' was, for an Irishman, a curiously English saying. It expressed the intensely personal interpretation of the national idea of freedom.

Heretics in Catholic eyes, backsliders in those of Geneva, since ridding themselves of the Catholic Stuarts the English, while remaining stubbornly Protestant, had grown far more tolerant. Except for Holland, theirs was the only European country in which men might worship God in any way they pleased. It was true there was a State Church to which the majority of Englishmen belonged and whose membership conferred civic privilege. But the Church of England was supported by Parliament less because it had a monopoly of truth as because it seemed the most suitable medium for promulgating Christian and Protestant teaching.* With their genius for evolving institutions capable of withstanding the erosion of human nature the English had rejected both the Catholic and Calvinist conceptions of religious society. In place of a priesthood uncontaminated by the ties of marriage but in danger of undermining the mutual trust of the home, they had licensed a sober married clergy with the same family responsibilities as other men. In place of a theocratic caste untrammelled by secular obligations and therefore a source of political intrigue, they had established a Church subordinate to and allied to the State. But in their desire to give its ministers independence and social status, they had endowed many of them with more of the world's goods than was readily compatible with their spiritual vocation. After a century's monopoly of the loaves and fishes there was a good deal of pluralism, in cases amounting to downright scandal, much neglect of church and parishioner, and a general atmosphere of comfortable complacency. Almost a quarter of the country's nine thousand parishes were without resident incumbents, and in many churches there was an atmosphere of damp and decay: weeds grew in the graveyard and small boys played fives in the shady corner under the belfry.

Yet those whom the Church neglected, the rejected of the Church cared for. The missionary journeys of the early Methodists among the pagan outcasts of industrial Britain did God's work where well-endowed complacency had failed. Preaching a crusade, Wesley's disciples carried the Gospel into the dark corners of what, but for them, might have ceased to be a Christian land. In its remoter parts there sprang up a new Protestant religion of passion and poetry attuned to the simplicities and superstitions of the poor. Among the roughest of the rough – the lonely weavers of Yorkshire and Lancashire and the miners of Durham and Cornwall – thou-

---

* 'Gentlemen,' said Lord Chancellor Thurlow to the deputation of Nonconformists which waited on him in 1788 to ask for a repeal of the Corporation and Test Acts, 'I'm against you, by God. I am for the Established Church, damme! Not that I have any more regard for the Established Church than for any other church, but because it is established. And if you can get your damned religion established, I'll be for that too!' Crabb Robinson, *Diary*.

sands were to be found practising a faith as pure as that taught by Christ to the fishermen of Galilee. This noble work of conversion – the supreme triumph of eighteenth-century English individualism – served not only spiritual but political ends. As much as any single factor the faith and discipline of Methodism in the last terrible revolutionary and war-wracked decade of the century, helped to save Britain from the fate of revolutionary France.

*   *   *

For, with her solid heart of sober, quiet folk, England had such reserves of strength that it was hard to estimate her breaking point. To comprehend her secret one must probe beneath the variegated surface – the splendours of aristocratic salons and rural parks and palaces, the gambling dens and cockpits of the metropolis, the grim sores of factory and foetid slum – and seek it in the calm continuity of family life. The lessons handed down from mother to daughter, the hereditary craft taught the boy at his father's knee, the sturdy children playing together in the orchard, the clean-dressed, home-spun village people taking the road to church on Sunday morning, here were the enduring roots of national life. In the pages of John Nyren's *The Cricketers of My Time*, published in 1833, the author recalled the men of Hambledon with whom he had grown up in the 'seventies and 'eighties of the previous century. In his gallery of cricketing heroes we can see the fathers of the men who tended the guns at Trafalgar and manned the squares at Waterloo, making their way with curved bat and eager eye up the woodland road from Hambledon village to the downland pitch on Broad-Halfpenny on the first Tuesday in May. The dew is still on the grass and the sun is shining high over 'Old Winchester' as they take the field against All England. Here is little George Lear the famous long-stop, so sure that he might have been a sand-bank, and his friend, Tom Sueter, the wicket-keeper who loved to join him in a glee at the 'Bat and Ball'; Lambert, 'the little farmer', whose teasing art, so fatal to the Kent and Surrey men, had been mastered in solitude by bowling away hours together at a hurdle while tending his father's sheep; and 'those anointed clod-

stumpers, the Walkers, Tom and Harry' with their wilted, apple-
john faces and long spidery legs as thick at the ankles as at the hips.
'Tom was the driest and most rigid-limbed chap . . . his skin was
like the rind of an old oak, and as sapless. . . . He moved like the
rude machinery of a steam-engine in the infancy of construction
and, when he ran, every member seemed ready to fly to the four
winds. He toiled like a tar on horseback.'

What Wellington became to his Peninsular veterans and
'Daddy' Hill to Wellington, Richard Nyren was to the Hambledon
cricketers and John Small to Nyren. 'I never saw,' his son recorded,
'a finer specimen of the thoroughbred old English yeoman than
Richard Nyren. He was a good face-to-face, unflinching, uncompromising independent man. He placed a full and just value
upon the station he held in society and maintained it without
insolence or assumption. He could differ with a superior without
trenching upon his dignity or losing his own.' And his *fidus Achates*,
yeoman Small, was worthy of him. He loved music, was an adept
at the fiddle and taught himself the double bass. He once calmed
a bull by taking out his instrument and playing it in the middle of a
field. His fellow cricketer, the duke of Dorset, hearing of his musical talent, sent him a handsome violin and paid the carriage.
'Small, like a true and simple-hearted Englishman, returned the
compliment by sending his Grace two bats and balls, also paying
the carriage.'

In the English memory there are few more endearing scenes
than that famous pitch on the Hampshire down. When 'Silver
Billy' Beldham – the first bat of the age – was in or runs were hard to
get and the finish close, Sir Horace Mann, that stalwart patron of
the game, would pace about outside the ground cutting down the
daisies with his stick in his agitation, and the old farmers under the
trees would lean forward upon their tall staves, silent. 'Oh! it was
a heart-stirring sight to witness the multitude forming a complete
and dense circle round that noble green. Half the county would be
present, and all their hearts with us – little Hambledon, pitted
against All England, was a proud thought for the Hampshire men.
Defeat was glory in such a struggle – victory, indeed, made us only
'a little lower than angels'. How those fine brawn-faced fellows of

farmers would drink to our success! And then what stuff they had to drink! Punch! – not your new *Ponche à la Romaine*, or *Ponche à la Groseille*, or your modern cat-lap milk punch – punch be-deviled; but good, unsophisticated, John Bull stuff – stark! that would stand on end – punch that would make a cat speak! . . . Ale that would flare like turpentine – genuine Boniface!

'There would this company, consisting most likely of some thousands, remain patiently and anxiously watching every turn of fate in the game, as if the event had been the meeting of two armies to decide their liberty. And whenever a Hambledon man made a good hit, worth four or five runs, you would hear the deep mouths of the whole multitude baying away in pure Hampshire – 'Go hard! – Go hard! – Tich and turn! – tich and turn!'' To the honour of my countrymen . . . I cannot call to recollection an instance of their wilfully stopping a ball that had been hit out among them by one of our opponents. Like true Englishmen, they would give an enemy fair play. How strongly are all those scenes, of fifty years by-gone, painted in my memory! – and the smell of that ale comes upon me as freshly as the new May flowers.'

From the high hill which rose out of the woods beyond the pitch one could see on clear days half southern England – valley and down and forest. Over that wide countryside the sea winds never ceased to blow from every point of the compass, free as the hearts of oak the land bred. Waving trees and smoke fluttering like a ragged banner, feathery heath, lonely cottages at the edge of moor and forest, ragged cows and geese and ponies pasturing in the wild by ancient prescribed rights. Tidal rivers flowing through marshes to the ocean with black cattle grazing at their salt edges and wooden cobles and crab-boats tossing on their silver bosom; land of semi-nomads, gatherers of shellfish, fowlers, longshore fishermen and armed smugglers – of Slip-jibbet and Moonshine Buck tip-trotting by in the dark with tubs of Geneva for the parson and 'baccy for the clerk'. Sometimes travellers and shepherds near the coast would see the fleet of England riding at Spithead in one of the broad bays of the Channel shore; 'pleasant and wonderful was the sight as seen from Ridgeway Hill, with the West Bay and the Isle of Portland and Weymouth and Melcome Regis, all lying in the calm sunshine,' wrote Elizabeth Ham in after years, 'I see it now.'

Further inland were the familiar objects of the country scene: the reapers in the golden field, the cottages of wattle and timber with their massive brick chimneys and deep thatch, the mill with its weather-boarded walls and throbbing wheel amid willows and alders, the saw-pit with sweating craftsmen and stacked timber, the leafy lane with the great hairy-footed horses drawing home the wain laden with hay and laughing children. Along the high roads bright, liveried postilions glinted like jewels before swaying post-chaises, and postmen, riding or mounted high on coaches, passed in the scarlet livery of England. With infinite slowness, soon over-taken by these fast-moving ones, a vast tilted stage-wagon crawled like a snail behind its eight horses, their neck-bells making dis-cordant music while the carrier trudged beside idly cracking his whip in the air. Along the road were haymakers at their work, mansions with ancient trees and cropping deer, and at every village the blacksmith's forge with old Vulcan looking out from his open door, 'grey and hairy as any badger'. And perhaps as it grew dark and the lights were lit on the coaches, the traveller might overtake a neighbouring gentleman's hounds, as John Byng did one May evening, coming home from an airing.

Within the candle-lit windows of the wayside cottage and the farmhouse on the hill, old John Bull would sit dozing with his pot beside the kitchen fire, the dog and cat asleep at his feet, the good wife at her wheel, the pretty maid his daughter coming in with her pail, the children playing with the caged bird, the tinder-box on the shelf, the onions and flitches hanging from the ceiling. From this home he was presently to go out to face and tame a world in arms. For the moment he was content and at his ease, perhaps more so than was good for his continuing soul. In the tavern down in the village old England still lived on where over their pipes and bowls, gathered round the bare rude table, the local worthies, with russet, weather-beaten faces, cracked their joke and trolled their song. Though their summer was brief before winter aches and penury encompassed them, they knew how to be merry. Cricket matches and fives playing, the crowd at the fair gathered round the cudgellers' high wooden stage, the squeak of a fiddle or the shrill cry of a mountebank with his Merry Andrew on the village green on a warm summer evening, the carollers and the mumming players coming out of the Christmas snows, these were the outward symbols of a race of freemen taking their pleasures in their own way as their fathers had done before them. It seemed a far cry from these peaceful scenes to the rough humours and turbulent racket of London – the butchers of Shepherd's Market and May Fair elbowing their way through the dirty streets to a hanging at Tyburn, the footpads in the shadows of Park Lane, the foetid cells of Newgate – or the restless, sullen money-making of Manchester and Birmingham. Yet all were part of an English whole whose meaning it was hard to compass in a word, but whose people were in a greater or lesser degree adherents of two dominant ideals – justice and their own freedom.

> 'The nations not so blessed as thee
> Must in their turn to tyrants fall,
> While thou shalt flourish great and free,
> The dread and envy of them all.'

So sang the islanders in their favourite 'Rule Britannia', and the words expressed their firm, unalterable conviction. Their very versatility was part of their heritage of liberty. 'Now in as hot a climate as that of the East or West Indies and sometimes in winter feel the cold of Greenland,' wrote John Byng, 'up and down; hence we are precarious, uncertain, wild, enduring mortals. And may we so endowed continue, the wonder and balance of the universe.'

CHAPTER FIFTEEN

Heart of Oak

'We are in a war of a peculiar nature . . . We are at war with a system which by its essence is inimical to all other governments, and what makes peace or war as peace and war may best contribute to their subversion. It is with an armed doctrine that we are at war.'

Burke

A LITTLE BEFORE IT GREW LIGHT on a cold February morning in 1793, a crowd began to gather on the parade ground at Whitehall. Against the seventeenth-century facade of the Treasury and the grey classic stone of Kent's Horse Guards, the first battalions of the three regiments of Foot Guards were drawn up in long lines of scarlet and white. At seven o'clock precisely, a cortège of officers appeared riding down the Mall from the direction of Buckingham House. At their head was King George III of England with his two elder sons, the Prince of Wales and duke of York.

Mounted on a white charger, in General's uniform, the little, erect, blue-eyed man who represented in his person the idea of England rode down the lines. Then the men marched past in companies, moving in slow time. Two thousand strong, they swung out of Storey's Gate and crossing Westminster Bridge took the road to Greenwich, the King and the officers of his staff riding for a time after them and the Queen and the princesses following in carriages. All the way through the southern suburbs the troops were accompanied by a vast, enthusiastic crowd, who so overwhelmed the rearguard with embraces and loyal potations that many fell by the way and had to finish their journey in carts. Next day they embarked under the royal eye for Holland in overcrowded, seaworthy transports, without stores, medical appliances or reserves of ammunition. So the first expeditionary force of the longest war in Britain's history passed beyond the seas.

No man living could have guessed its duration. Before it was to end at Waterloo twenty-two years later, the youngest survivor of those who sailed that day was to be in his forties. The nature and purpose of the struggle were to change out of all recognition; those who were Britain's allies were to become vassals of her terrible adversary and to be aligned against her, and yet more than once, fired by her example, to shake off their chains and range themselves again by her side against the tyrants. Once, for a short while, Britain herself, victor on her chosen element the sea but wearied by the unending conflict, was to temporize with a momentarily exhausted foe, only to renew the fight within a few months when the faith reposed in despotic power had been violated. But on that cold February day nothing of this could be foreseen.

From 1793 to 1815 Great Britain remained at war with the greatest military power on earth, whose at first ragged but soon ruthlessly disciplined armies animated by a revolutionary fervour which gave its devotees the strength of men in a delirium, overran the territories of all its neighbours. Within three years of the outbreak of war France had thrown up in a twenty-seven-year-old colonial artillery officer, Napoleon Bonaparte, one of the great military geniuses of all time who, winning dazzling victory after victory, succeeded in making himself, first dictator, and then Emperor of the French and their conquered satellites. Yet neither the British government nor her patient rock-like people ever compromised, gave in or despaired. In the long struggle which followed there were only two constant factors, one the French resolve to impose a New Order on Europe by force – at first revolutionary and ideological and later Napoleonic and imperial; the other the British refusal to admit of any order not based on agreed international law. Other nations were tossed in and out of the storm like leaves. Only Britain, though she bent, never broke. For a whole generation, sometimes with powerful allies but as often alone, she fought on. At times she found herself fighting against the whole of Europe.

*　*　*

The war had arisen out of the violent disintegration of the ancient royal and aristocratic society of France, the Continent's most populous and powerful kingdom, bankrupted by a century of cumulative borrowing begun to finance Louis XIV's wars of conquest. Since then, in three further wars between 1740 and 1783, France had contended with Britain for maritime and colonial supremacy, but had never been able to shake off the burden of debt in which her attempt at European hegemony had involved her. Six months after the meeting of the States General – called in 1789, after long abeyance, to restore and reform the finances of a bankrupt kingdom – a popular explosion swept away the floodgates of crushing taxation and social inequality behind which the creative energies of France's virile and ingenious people had long been dammed by the aristocratic and bureaucratic incompetence of her *ancien régime*. On July 14th a ragged mob from the Paris slums attacked the Bastille, where a handful of State prisoners were guarded by thirty Swiss guards and eighty military pensioners. Behind it all Paris, surging through the narrow cobbled streets, was in revolution, the tocsin ringing from every tower and a great flag, which was not that of the French monarchy, borne above a raging, shouting, trampling human river. With its Governor and garrison massacred and their dripping heads borne in triumph on pikes, the Bastille became the symbol of a doomed society, its death throes the celebration of the birth of a new force in the world, terrible to all who opposed it, full of mysterious hope to those who accepted it.

In the revolutionary ferment which followed, France seemed like a giant awakening from sleep. The whole nation was gripped by a strange fanatic fervour. In England these events were greeted at first with sympathy. France, it was felt, was following the British example of reason, toleration and liberty, ushered in by the Glorious Revolution of 1688. Henceforward the two great civilized nations of the West would lead the world hand in hand. Pitt assured the French Ambassador 'that France and England had the same principles, namely not to aggrandise themselves and to oppose aggrandisement in others.' The Leader of the Opposition, Charles James Fox, in his generous enthusiasm described the fall of the Bastille as the greatest and best thing that had ever happened. Most enthusiastic of all were the young. 'Bliss was it in that dawn to be alive,' the poet Wordsworth recalled in after years, 'but to be young was very heaven!'

But when an armed mob marched on Versailles, carried the King and Queen to Paris in a seven hours' bacchanalian route amid obscene jests and cries of '*A la lanterne*', and established the rule of liberty by flinging drunken insults at their sovereign and butchering his retainers, sober Britons began to have doubts. Liberty was one thing; anarchy and confusion another. Yet the best of them continued to hope that good would come out of it and that the licence begotten of long despotism would be succeeded by ordered freedom.

No one was more convinced of this than the Prime Minister. A reformer and lover of peace, William Pitt at 30, after six years as the youngest Chief Minister in English history, was a living example of the triumph of reason. By his industry, sound judgement and financial acumen he had raised his country in a few years from the despairing aftermath of a ruinous war to an unrivalled prosperity. He had restored her finances, liberalized her commercial system and begun to rationalize her laws and parliamentary system. He had done, in fact, or begun to do, all those practical things about which the French theoretical philosophers and politicians never tired of boasting.

The last thing he wanted was war. Unlike his father, Chatham, he loathed the very thought of it. 'The present convulsions in France,' he told the House, 'must sooner or later culminate in general harmony and regular order, and, thus circumstanced, France will stand forth as one of the most brilliant Powers of Europe. She will enjoy just that kind of liberty which I venerate.'

Yet the events of the next two years belied his hopes. The contrast between the high ideals of the French leaders and the practice of their followers grew not less, but greater. A nation in which a community of nuns could be dragged by a mob from the hospital in which they were nursing and scourged naked through the streets was not redeemed from despotism because its National Assembly proclaimed its tolerance to be perfect, inalienable and absolute. Liberty, to have any meaning for Englishmen, had to be based on Law, and Law in its turn on Justice, as Edmund Burke pointed out in his *Reflections on the French Revolution*. For Burke brought to the French Revolution the historic English touchstone of every political pretension. 'Whenever a separation is made between liberty and justice,' he wrote, 'neither is safe.' In a book which swept England he put his finger on the central weaknesses of the Revolution and of the men of violence who directed it: that in their passion for logical abstractions, they refused to recognize the need for religion and morality. They maintained that under a perfect Constitution there was no need for religion or justice because an ideal State automatically created the ideal man.

Every excess of the French mob confirmed what Burke foretold. As the more extreme elements in France took charge of the Revolution, sympathy of educated Englishmen for it froze in its tracks. For the English instinct, confronted by something new and violent in the world, sensed danger. Yet Pitt refused to abandon the policy of peace on which he had restored his country's prosperity. In his Budget speech in February 1792, announcing new economies in Britain's fighting services, he declared his belief that there had never in the history of the country been a time when, from the situation of Europe, fifteen years of peace might reasonably be expected.

Yet within a year Britain was at war. It was when the French – proclaiming 'War to the tyrant's palace! Peace to the poor man's cottage!' – carried their crusade of terror and renewal into the territories of their neighbours that hopes of Britain remaining unaffected by the turmoil on the far side of the Channel began to fade. In April France declared war on Austria, and that summer a Prussian army, accompanied by French emigrés, crossed the frontier in September capturing the fortress of Verdun, while gangs of murderers swept through the Paris prisons, and slaughtered more than a thousand helpless men, women and children – an atrocity repeated in every major city in France. Then, on the 20th, at Valmy on the Champagne plain, a ragged French army repelled the Prussians causing them to retreat, two days before France was declared a Republic, while before the month ended, another ragged French army of enthusiasts entered the Rhineland. At the end of October the Republican general Dumouriez invaded Belgium at the head of 70,000 men, and on November 6th won the first great victory of the Republic at Jemappes, as a cloud of skirmishers, followed by columns of ragged fanatics chanting the 'Marseillaise', drove the white-coated Austrians from the low heights near Mons. A week later they were in Brussels.

The politicians in Paris went mad with joy. It seemed that nothing could now stop the advance of their armies and of their apocalyptic creed: nothing should be allowed to. On November 16th an excited Convention passed two Decrees, the first empowering their generals to follow the flying foe into neutral territory, the other declaring the navigation of the Scheldt estuary – granted exclusively to Holland by a long series of international agreements – open to all nations by the Law of Nature.

Britain was the principal guarantor of the Scheldt treaties. She was also the United Netherlands' ally. The rulers of Holland, now a rich and timorous merchant oligarchy, did everything within their power to avoid inflaming their powerful neighbour, and as long as it was possible, refrained from formally asking Britain to fulfil her treaty obligations. But after the fall of Antwerp on November 28th and a peremptory ultimatum demanding the passage of French troops through the frontier fortress of Maastricht, they begged that a British squadron should be assembled in the Downs.

Pitt, whose historic conception of European peace was founded on respect for international obligations, could only agree. The retention of the Dutch coastline and the great anchorage of the Scheldt in friendly hands was a vital British interest: the Dutch alliance the keystone of his foreign policy. He could not abandon them at the dictates of frenzied demagogues and of an imaginary 'Law of Nature' enforced by French guns.

The men of the Revolution believed that Britain's strength was a web of gossamer. They thought it depended on banknotes. They had only to cut off the trade of the London plutocrats and their power would vanish in a night. On February 1st the Republic declared war on Great Britain and Holland.

Far away, under the chandelier of the old House of Commons, Pitt was quietly speaking, the pale wintry sunlight falling on his paler face and the packed benches around him. 'They will not accept, under the name of liberty, any model of government but that which is conformable to their own opinions and ideas; and all men must learn from the mouth of their cannon the propagation of their system . . . Unless we wish to stand by and suffer State after State to be subverted, we must now declare our firm resolution effectially to oppose those principles of ambition and aggrandisement which have for their object the destruction of England, of Europe and of the world.'

*   *   *

England was answering a challenge. That challenge was the claim of violence to override law: the dominance of the unbridled will. The French were seeking to impose a new order on the world, not by reason and precept but by force. England was not, as Burke had wished, denying the validity of that new order: that was for the future to decide. What she was defying was, not the French Revolution, but the right of Jacobin fanatics to dictate by force what the rest of mankind must believe and do. Instinctively she was taking up arms against the most dangerous thing in the world: the lust for tyrannic power which grows on what it consumes.

That Britain was unprepared for war did not trouble her people. As a land power she was contemptible. Compared with France with half a million out of her twenty-five millions in arms or learning to bear arms, the United Kingdom had an effective peacetime strength of less than 15,000 troops. Apart from the Brigade of Guards, its line regiments, long reduced by peacetime economy, were mere administrative skeletons with a cadre of regular officers and a rank and file of ragged recruits. The rest of the Army, another 30,000, were scattered about the world, mostly in remote and unhealthy stations which constantly called for new drafts.

On the outbreak of war Pitt introduced a Bill for raising 25,000 recruits for the Army, and embodying 19,000 additional men in the Militia. But, as he shrank from compulsion, the former were easier

369

to vote than to raise. And the ancient militia, ballotted for annually
in every shire for four days exercise in arms a year and liable only
for home service, could not meet the nation's need for a striking
force. For this auxiliaries had to be sought from the smaller states
of Germany. According to custom 14,000 troops from the king's
Electorate of Hanover were therefore taken on the pay-roll, and
another 8,000 Germans hired, after much preliminary haggling,
from the Prince of Hesse-Darmstadt.

Had Britain had to rely on land power alone, her effort in a
European war would have been negligible. But though in 1792
only twelve battleships were in commission and there was no ship-
of-the-line at sea in either the Mediterranean or West Indies, the
Royal Navy remained what Pepys's labours had made it over a
century before – the first sea-power in the world. Against France's
seventy-six battleships Britain had a hundred-and-thirteen.

The difficulty was to find the men to man them. It was the
custom at the end of every war for a Government dependent on a
Parliament of taxpayers to discharge the bulk of the seamen. Only
the officers – a corps of the highest professional skill – were retained
permanently. The lower deck was recruited, as occasion required,
from the merchant and fishing fleets, whose hereditary seamen
supported by their labours and simple virtues the nation's maritime wealth and strength. In time of war by immemorial custom
pressgangs roved the streets and waterways of the coastal towns
and districts, seizing at will any young men bred to the sea or who
looked like a sailor.

In 1792 the personnel of the Navy, which had been 110,000 at
the end of the American war, was only 16,000. It was not till the
second half of February that the dreaded Press broke out on the
River, and several thousand seamen were dragged from incoming
merchantmen and colliers. After that the work of manning the
King's ships went on smartly. Yet months elapsed before the
battle fleet was fully manned. In the meantime the country had to
rely on its frigates.

Fortunately, for the moment, the enemy was not formidable at
sea. A dozen years before the Royal Navy of France had proved a
worthy adversary. But now, though eight of its ships mounted 110

guns or more to the 100 of the largest British class, the Revolution had deprived it of its best officers and reduced its crews to unruly mobs incapable of the intricate skill and unquestioning discipline needed to bring squadrons of large sailing vessels into action. The ships were dirty and neglected: the men remained in port and never went to sea. When the Convention ordered them out to fight, it found the 'audacity' it shrilly demanded a poor substitute for seamanship.

Such considerations caused Pitt to hope that the war he had striven so hard to avoid might not be so serious a matter after all. To the eye of reason the French were doing almost everything calculated to destroy their own country. They had slain or banished their moderate leaders, alienated every friendly state in Europe, undermined the discipline of their defenders and neglected the arts of life for windy abstractions. Their frantic boasts that they were about to 'dictate peace on the ruins of the Tower of London' and show up the weakness of Britain's 'corrupting wealth' did not impress Pitt at all. It was indeed on this very wealth that he relied. As the first financial statesman of the age, he had nothing but contempt for the reckless way in which the Jocobins were destroying France's credit and commerce. Thanks to his prudent management Britain was financially richer than ever in her history. Despite bad harvests revenue was again buoyant and trade expanding. An economic victory seemed assured.

So, at first, did a military one. For on the very day, after narrowly escaping shipwreck, that the Guards, 2000 strong, landed at Helvoetsluys to save the imperilled Dutch Republic, the ragged, enthusiastic Revolutionary army sent to overrun the Austrian Netherlands panicked before the guns of a disciplined Imperial force deployed in its path. For by now all the threatened kingdoms surrounding France were joined to resist her invasion.

Pitt's first plan for waging the war into which he had so reluctantly been drawn was to rely on the demoralization of France's navy and, using his scant military forces in amphibious expeditions against her ocean colonies, to employ the wealth won in the West and East Indies to finance Austrian and Prussian subsidies. This was the 'blue water' policy which his father, Chatham, had made so glorious and profitable during the Seven Years War. Its principle of limited liability naturally appealed to a Minister whose main object had always been to balance national accounts and whose hatred of war was based at least partly on its expense. It commended itself, too, to the City whose treasure lay in Caribbean sugar islands.

Yet even this conception of war required men. Nineteen, or nearly a quarter, of the eighty-one infantry battalions were already garrisoning those West Indian islands from which the main attack on France's colonies was to be launched. And so unhealthy was the climate that the normal wastage from disease was 25 per cent. To take the offensive an additional force of at least 20,000 was needed.

But no sooner had promises of reinforcements been sent to the Governors of Jamaica and Barbados than the Government's plan was superseded by the course of events in Europe. For the opportunity offered by the sudden collapse of the Revolutionary Armies, laying the plains of northern France wide open to an Allied advance, was too good to miss. Pitt and his chief lieutenant, the genial Scottish Secretary of State, Henry Dundas – who was as much a tyro in the art of war as he – agreed to postpone their West Indian projects and raise and put into the field a force of 40,000 British Hanoverians and Hessians alongside their Austrian and Prussian allies.

For the next eighteen months a polyglot British expeditionary force, slowly growing in strength and commanded by the King's second son, the twenty-eight-year-old duke of York, served in an international army under the Austrian generalissimo, the Prince of Coburg. When, in the summer of 1793, after wasting three months of opportunity, the latter took the offensive, he did so with all the stately deliberation of eighteenth military science. Though in the demoralized state of France, by now in the throes of the Terror, there seemed little to stop a swift march on an anarchic Paris, the military pedants of the Imperial Staff would do nothing contrary to the canons of their text-books. Every road by which a French raiding party might advance against flank or rear had to be guarded, every enemy outpost laboriously driven in, even the smallest fortress stormed or blockaded into starvation. The army advanced

with infinite slowness, spread out in an enormous cordon from
Mauberge to Ostend. As soon as it reached the frontier fortresses
of Condé and Valenciennes, it stopped to besiege them in form.
Nothing would induce Coburg to advance further until they had
been reduced.

While the Allied Army remained before them, trenching,
sapping and mining, and the guillotine in the French capital and
every provincial city spurted blood, hatred of the foreigner and the
foreigner's ally – the suspected traitor – was being forged into a
fearful weapon against France's foes. That August a forty-year-old
Burgundian captain of engineers, Lazare Carnot, was appointed to
the Committee of Public Safety and ordered to organize victory.
Two days after his appointment a *levée en masse* was ordered of the
country's entire manhood. It was a new conception of war, blend-
ing the modern nation with the embattled tribe of the remote past.
It was Carnot who made it work. Austere, unsparing, a student of
history and theology, with Roman virtues and Calvinistic ideals,
the tall ungainly captain, stretched out on the floor of his office
among his maps and green portfolios, unconsciously forged the
weapon of the future Caesarian Napoleon. During the next twelve
months he revolutionized the formation, discipline and training
of every unit, chose the officers, set the armies in motion according
to a single daring and methodical plan. Far away on the frontiers,
and in the great confused camps of the interior, the ragged armies
responded to their unseen touch, while in the sun-drenched squares
and narrow, evil-smelling streets of the cities, the murder gangs
went about their business of universal terror, and the guillotine
rose and fell. Wielding a power undreamt of by the Grand Monarch
of the Bourbon past, the Committee of Public Safety, whose word
was law, whose frown death, hammered France into a new shape
and discipline, for a particular purpose, centralized, hardened,
despotic.

* * *

It was the duke of York's forces, laboriously closing in on Dunkirk
from marshy towns and villages figuring not for the last time in

British history – Ypres, Furnes, Poperinghe – which first felt the tempo of Carnot's quickening hand. For here, in the opening days of September, he struck. Using the interior lines which France's position gave her, he assailed Coburg's classic cordon – weak at every point and strong at none – with the shock of hammer blow concentrated against a single spot. The French came on in the new order Carnot had prescribed: the picked men – the natural fighters – going before in fierce impetuous waves of sharpshooters, the remainder massed in columns whose density made up for lack of training and whose superior numbers, launched in endless waves, enabled them to penetrate the defenders' lines. A covering force of Germans at Hondschoote, though fighting back with the stubborn hardihood of their race, were quickly overwhelmed. Threatened with encirclement between the marshes and the sea, the duke of York was forced to retire in haste, abandoning his siege guns and most of his stores.

Pitt took it with calm courage. It was a severe shock, he wrote, but only, he trusted, a temporary one. 'It ought to have the effect of increasing, if possible, our exertions.' His faith seemed rewarded. Hard on its tail came astonishing news from the Mediterranean, where twelve British ships-of-the-line under Lord Hood, had been blockading the great naval arsenal of Toulon. On August 27th, terrified by the Jacobin holocaust of massacre, rape and arson which had just befallen Marseilles, moderate elements in the town ran up the white flag and invited Hood to take possession. The greatest arsenal in France, with thirty ships of the line, passed into the hands of a British fleet of only twelve.

It presented the Government with a heaven-sent opportunity, or would have done if only it had the resources to exploit it. With Hood appealing for troops, four courses were open to a parliamentary government of country gentlemen who still saw the war to crush the infant dynamic of armed Jacobinism in its terrifying cradle as a leisurely campaign of capturing places. They could send their entire available force to Toulon, so laying the foundation of a new offensive to destroy the Jacobin power from the south. This, however, would necessitate, not only withdrawing their troops from Flanders, but abandoning any idea of an expedition to the

West Indies, Brittany or La Vendée – the deep-wooded patriarchal
land south of the Loire where the simple peasantry had taken up
arms in their thousands against the scum of the cities sent to
massacre their priests. Or Britain could fall back on its original
'blue water' strategy and, eschewing continental adventures, dispatch an overwhelming force to the West Indies. What the
government could not do, but tried to do, was to carry out all four.
For it would not withdraw from Flanders because of its pledges to
its European allies and the King's anxiety for his Hanoverian
possessions. It could not abandon operations in the West Indies
because the City would not let it. It would not abandon the idea of
helping the western royalists, for whom it had begun to assemble a
small expeditionary force at Southampton because this would
alienate the Portland Whigs – a parliamentary group whom it
wished to appease. And it would not relinquish its unexpected
foothold at Toulon because the opportunity seemed too good to
miss.

The result was as might have been expected. The delayed
expedition sent to the West Indies in November was only half the
size planned and was inadequate either to conquer the French
colonies or hold them when taken. The scratchforce assembled to
help a French rising waited for artillery and stores until December
and then sailed without them to the Brittany coast, only to find
that the insurgents had already been driven from it, and that any
chance of a landing had passed. Meanwhile Toulon was starved of
troops, not because the Government did not wish to send any, but
because it had not left any to send.

While Pitt and his allies were gathering miscellaneous forces
to assail France from the furthest points of the compass, Carnot
was massing his forces to strike outwards. Unlike his enemies he
perfectly understood the art of war. His first blow fell in the Rhône
valley where, capturing a rebel Lyons, he removed all danger of
Austrian infiltration across the Alps into the Midi. Then he struck
again in Flanders, defeating the Austrians at Wattingnies, and a
week later broke the other end of Coburg's overstrained cordon in
a two-days' drive through Menin, Ypres and Nieuport which all
but cut the British off from their base at Ostend.

As soon as the armies in the north had gone into winter quarters Carnot concentrated his forces against the hapless Vendeans. By Christmas half the villages of the West were heaps of cinders and the fields strewn with thousands of corpses. As the blue-coated armies drove outwards like some mighty force compressed, the Jacobin bosses followed them, scotching dissension with unspeakable terror. By December Carnot was ready for Toulon. Here he had gathered 35,000 men and given the command of the artillery battery to a young Corsican captain named Napoleon Bonaparte. When the French attacked on the stormy night of the 17th the defending force of Piedmontese, Spaniards and French royalists, with a sprinkling of British soldiers and marines, were unable to make any effective resistance.

There was nothing for it but immediate evacuation. On the night of the 18th, with every gun firing on the blazing city from the surrounding heights, and the criminals, released from the jails, putting man, woman and child to the sword, a young British captain, Sidney Smith, endeavoured to destroy the French fleet which it was now too late to remove. In the resulting confusion only thirteen of the battleships were accounted for. Eighteen others survived to fight another day.

A week later the British fleet, crowded with nearly 15,000 refugees – 'fathers without families and families without fathers, the picture of horror and despair' – was joined in Hyères Bay by belated troops from Gibraltar intended for the defence of Toulon. Others lay idle in Moira's transports off the Isle of Wight, while more were in mid-Atlantic, tossing up and down on their way to West Indian graveyards. 'The misfortunes of our situation,' wrote the shrewd old King, 'is that we have too many objects to attend to, and our forces consequently must be too weak at each place.'

In the spring of 1794 the Allies re-opened their long delayed northern advance on Paris. From the heights above Le Cateau, where on April 16th the young Emperor of Austria inspected 160,000 troops, they advanced with steady leisure to besiege Landrecies. Their line, the cordon of steel that was to strangle revolutionary France, stretched from the sea to the Sambre. Carnot knew that France must break it or starve. All his hopes were pinned on the offensive – such an offensive as old Europe had never seen. His orders to his generals, whose only choice was victory or the guillotine, was to attack at all costs and go on attacking until they had broken through.

With both sides taking the offensive there followed a month of confused fighting in which the little contingent of British Regulars played a distinguished part. Three days after its cavalry had ridden over three French squares, and taken 400 prisoners and 13 guns, it was detailed by Coburg to take part, with four other corps, in an elaborately timed operation designed to cut off a French army. Alone among them, it carried out its part punctually. As a result 10,000 Britons, after taking all their objectives, found themselves in the heart of a French force four times as numerous. As a result, at dawn on May 18th the British, their flank exposed by the Austrian retreat, were compelled to fall back in haste, abandoning Tournai, Oudenarde and Ghent without a shot. On July 5th, at an allied council on the future field of Waterloo, the duke of York pleaded with the Allied commander, the Prince of Coburg, for a stand on the ridge of Mont St Jean. Yet, scarcely had a decision to fight been reached, than the Austrians, fearful for their communications, once more abandoned their allies and retreated eastwards towards their bases on the Rhine, leaving the road to Brussels open. By doing so they not only exposed the expeditionary force's flank but forced it to fall back, in isolation, northwards on its own base at Antwerp. 'The opinion which the British nation must have on the subject,' wrote the indignant duke of York to Coburg, 'is that we are betrayed and sold to the enemy.'

In this witches' cauldron of disaster, Arthur Wellesley served his first apprenticeship in war. It proved hard and discouraging. He landed at Ostend at the end of June 1794 with his regiment as part of a force hastily sent out from England under Major-General Lord Moira to save that indefensible port, and which only just escaped encirclement by a brilliant march across the French front to join the duke of York's army, as it retreated towards Holland. At Boxtel on September 15th 1794, the twenty-five-year-old former Dublin Castle A.D.C. received his baptism of fire when the enemy, crossing the Dommel in overwhelming force, drove the British from

377

their positions. A counter-attack under cover of darkness failed disastrously, largely owing to faulty command and the lack of training of newly-promoted youthful regimental commanders fresh from England. But Lieutenant-Colonel Wellesley's 33rd regiment proved an exception and, by its discipline and steady musketry, plugged a dangerous breach in the line and, when others were failing, firing volleys in extended line beat off a strong attack by a French column.

Sullenly the army retreated beyond the Waal. It felt neglected and forgotten. Its boots were worn out and its uniforms stained and ragged; the new recruits who filled its ranks arrived in thin linen jackets and trousers without waistcoats, drawers and stockings. The Wagon Corps, founded to supply its needs, seemed to have been raised from the thieves' kitchens of Blackfriars and Seven Dials, and was known to the troops as the 'Newgate Blues'; and the military hospitals proved shortcuts to the next world. A Dutch observer counted 42 bodies flung out of one barge of 500 sick, who had been left untended on the open deck without even straw to lie on. The surgeons' mates allowed the sick and wounded to starve, and spent the sums they claimed from Government in drinking and debauchery.

From top to bottom the military administration, tested by adversity, was rotten. 'I learnt more by seeing our own faults and the defects of our system in the campaign of Holland, than anywhere else,' the future duke of Wellington recalled. 'I was left there to myself with my regiment, the 33rd, on the Waal, thirty miles from headquarters, which latter were a scene of jollification, and I do not think that I was once visited by the Commander-in-Chief. The infantry regiments, taken individually, were as good in proper hands as they are now, but the system was wretched.' Everything which could make an efficient fighting force was lacking except courage. 'We want artillerymen,' wrote the duke of York's A.D.C., Captain Calvert, 'we want a general officer at the head of the artillery, we want drivers and smiths . . . we want a commanding engineer of rank and experience . . . we want, at least, two out of the four brigades of mounted artillery with which his Grace of Richmond is amusing himself in England. We want a total stop put to that pernicious mode of bestowing rank on officers without even the form of recommendation, merely for raising (by means of crimps) a certain number of men, to restore to the Army those independent and disinterested feelings and high principles which should actuate a soldier and form the basis of the military discipline of a free country.' The new Secretary at War, when he visited the front, commented bitterly on the shortage of artillery drivers. 'One sits at home quietly and overlooks such particulars,' he wrote, 'but the fate of armies and of kingdoms is decided often by nothing else.'

With more than half its 21,000 infantry down with typhus, wounds and exposure, and with Dutch traitors and French agents swarming through its lines, the army had only one hope – winter. The floods of November turned the Waal into an impassable barrier of desolate waters. Behind it a forlorn handful of redcoats preserved the last foothold of the *ancien régime* in the Low Countries, guarding the banks of Amsterdam and the Dutch fleet and naval stores. In a letter written that December, Arthur Wellesley, already a veteran campaigner, drew a picture of their plight. 'The French keep us in a perpetual state of alarm; we turn out once, sometimes twice, every night; the officers and men are harassed to death, and, if we are not relieved, I believe there will be few of the latter remaining shortly. I have not had my clothes off my back for a long time and generally spend the greatest part of the night upon the banks of the river.' He described how the enemy, who kept him and his men continually on the *qui vive* at night, would chatter to them by day across the river and even show off before them by dancing the *carmagnole*, occasionally scattering the spectators with a cannon-ball.

A week before Christmas the floating ice in the Waal began to pack. By the new year the frozen flood had ceased to be a barrier. Breaking every canon of eighteenth-century warfare and trusting for supplies to a barren and ice-gripped countryside, the French poured across the river. To avoid annihilation the outnumbered British and Hanoverians fell back hastily towards the Ysel.

The cold of that January was something which old men remembered fifty years afterwards. The retreat of the army across the icy wastes of Gelderland had the quality of a nightmare. There was no shelter against the arctic wind. Discipline vanished, and even the Brigade of Guards engaged in pitched battle round the bread wagons with their traditional foes, the Hessians. 'Those who woke on the morning of the 17th January 1795,' wrote Sir John Fortescue in his *History of the British Army*, 'saw about them such a sight as they never forgot. Far as the eye could reach over the whitened plain were scattered gun-limbers, wagons full of baggage, stores or sick men, sutlers' carts and private carriages. Beside them lay the horses, dead; here a straggler who had staggered on to the bivouac and dropped to sleep in the arms of the frost; there a group of British and Germans round an empty rum cask; here forty English Guardsmen huddled together about a plundered wagon; there a pack-horse with a woman lying alongside it, and a baby swaddled in rags peering out of the pack with its mother's milk turned to ice upon its lips – one and all stark, frozen, dead. Had the retreat lasted but three or four days longer, not a man would have escaped.' As it was, more than six thousand – a third of the expeditionary force – perished in four days.

The retreat completed the disintegration of Holland. The mob rose, set up trees of Liberty and flaunted the tricolour. On January 20th the French entered Amsterdam and proclaimed a revolutionary Republic. There was not even time to remove the fleet. A few smaller vessels got away to England, but a flying body of French horse and artillery galloped across the frozen Zuyder Zee and surprised the Dutch battleships ice-bound in the Texel.

All hope of any further stand now vanished. The starving and demoralized survivors of the British Expeditionary Force fell back into north Germany. That a remnant returned to England at all was largely due to young Lieutenant-Colonel Wellesley. In temporary command of a brigade covering the retreat, he was always on the spot, saw everything for himself, did everything. That his men were without overcoats in a freezing winter, that the commissariat on which their food depended failed utterly to function, was not his fault. Whatever he could do to remedy these defects, he did. Not that it brought him credit with the higher command, for those who do work their superiors leave undone are seldom thanked. But he saw how war should not be waged, and it was a valuable lesson. 'I learnt,' he said afterwards, 'what one ought not to do, and that is always something.'

CHAPTER SIXTEEN

Touch and Take

'I will try to have a motto, or least it shall be my watchword –
Touch and Take.'

Nelson

THE ROYAL NAVY had made its entry onto the world stage under
Drake and the Elizabethans, had sunk into insignificance under the
early Stuarts, recovered under Cromwell and the second Charles
to wrest the sceptre of ocean commerce from Holland, and, given
administrative discipline by the life-long labours of Pepys, became
during the eighteenth century the leading arbiter of human affairs
at sea. Yet until the age of Nelson its ascendancy was never un-
disputed. For over a hundred years monarchical France, with its
much greater population and resources, had contended with
Britain for command of the sea and, on more than one occasion,
all but attained it. Britain's danger was greatest when France and
the Atlantic empire of Spain joined hands against her, as they did
during the American War, when, from 1778–83, with her fleets
outnumbered, she had had to fight for her every existence.

Yet Britain had always triumphed in the last resort because the
sea was her whole being, whereas with her Continental rivals it was
only a secondary consideration. 'The thing which lies nearest the
heart of this nation,' Charles II had written, 'is trade and all that
belongs to it.' Being an island, her commerce was maritime and its
protection an essential interest of an ever-growing number of
people. They were ready to make sacrifices for the Navy which they
would never have done for the Army or any other service of the
Crown. For it was on the Navy, as the Articles of War put it, that

under the Providence of God the safety, honour, and welfare of the realm depended.

Because of these things the Navy touched mystic chords in the English heart which went deeper than reason. The far sails of a frigate at sea, the sight of a sailor with tarry breeches and rolling gait in any inland town, and that chief of all the symbolic spectacles of England, the Grand Fleet lying at anchor in one of her white-fringed roadsteads, had for her people the power of a trumpet call. So little Byam Martin, seeing for the first time the triple-tiered ships of the line lying in Portsmouth harbour, remained 'riveted to the spot, perfectly motionless, so absorbed in wonder' that he would have stayed there all day had not his hosts sent a boat's crew to fetch him away. From that hour his mind was 'inflamed with the wildest desire to be afloat.' Bobby Shafto going to sea with silver buckles on his knee was an eternal theme of eighteenth-century England: of such stuff were admirals made.

They had a hard schooling. Flung at twelve into an unfamiliar world of kicks and cuffs, crowded hammocks and icy hardships, or after a few months under 'Black Pudding', the omnipresent horse-whip of the Naval Academy, Gosport, apprenticed as midshipmen to the cockpit of a man-of-war, they learnt while still children to be Spartans, dined off scrubbed boards on salt beef, sauerkraut and black-strap, and became complete masters before they were men of a wonderful technical skill in all that appertained to the sailing and fighting of ships.

They were as inured to roughness and salt water as gulls to wind. Boys in their teens would spend days afloat in the maintop, ready at any moment to clamber to the masthead when top-gallant or studding sail needed setting or taking in. They grew up like bulldogs, delighting to cuff and fight: in some ships it was the practice while the officers were dining in the wardroom for the midshipmen to engage regularly in pitched battles on the quarter-deck, Romans against Trojans, for the possession of the poop, banging away, 'all in good part,' with broomsticks, handswabs, boarding pikes and even muskets.

These were the permanent cadre of the Navy; the officers of the establishment, 'born in the surf of the sea,' who, unlike the lower deck, coming and going as occasion demanded, lived in the Service and died in it. They were bound together by the closest ties of professional honour, etiquette and experience. Socially they were of all sorts: one high-born captain filled his frigate with so many sprigs of aristocracy that his first lieutenant – no respecter of persons – was wont to call out in mockery to the young noblemen and honourables at the ropes, 'My lords and gentlemen, shiver the mizen topsail!' The majority were of comparatively humble origin, occasioning Sir Walter Elliot's remark in Jane Austen's *Persuasion* that, though the profession had its utility, he would be sorry to see any friend of his belonging to it. Few had much of this world's goods nor, unless exceptionally lucky over prize money, could hope for much. Some were scholars – for it was a literary age – and read their Shakespeare or discoursed learnedly on the classical associations of the foreign ports they visited: more often they were simple souls, 'better acquainted with rope-yarns and bilge water than with Homer or Virgil'. But one and all were masters of their profession, proud in their obedience to King and country and ready to give their lives and all they had whenever the Service demanded. 'A bloody war and a sickly season!' was the closing toast of many a jovial evening in the wardroom: it was so that men rose in their calling.

Such men not only officered the fleet: they gave it their own tone and spirit. They were often rough teachers, too fond of enforcing their commands with the lash. But the men they commanded were rough too; hard-bitten merchant seamen and fishermen, brought into the Service for the duration by the press-gangs, with always a sediment in every ship of jailbirds and incorrigibles whose only chance of freedom was the hard life of the sea. The unresting, automatic discipline which the handling of wind-propelled warships in northern waters demanded could not have been enforced by gentler souls: it was that which gave Britain command of the waves and kept the Royal Navy from the slovenly, helpless degradation which befell that of revolutionary France. From the admiral, piped on board, to the boatswain's mate with his colt ready to 'start' the lower deck to action, strictly ordered subordination and readiness to obey were the hallmarks of the Service.

384

The life of the seamen was a life apart; something that was of
England yet remote from it. A king's ship was a little wooden
world of its own, with its peculiar customs and gradations unguessed at by landsmen; its proud foretopmen, the aristocrats of
the sea, and far down out of sight its humble waisters: pumpers and
sewermen, scavengers and pigsty keepers. In such a community,
often years together away from a home port, men learnt to know
each other as they seldom can on shore: to love and trust, to fear
and hate one another. There were ships that became floating hells,
ruled by some sadistic tyrant, with drunken, flogging officers
'crabbed as fiends', and savage, murderous crews such as that
which flung Bligh of the *Bounty* to perish in an open boat in a
remote sea. There were others commanded by captains like Nelson,
Pellew and Duncan, where the men looked on their officers as
fathers and were eager to dare and do anything for them.

The nation honoured its rough, simple seamen, as it had cause
to, though it usually saw them at their worst: ashore on their brief
spells of leave, with discipline relaxed and their hard-earned
money riotously dissipated on brandy and the coarse Megs and
Dolls of the seaports. But it saw too, as we also can glimpse from
the prints of the old masters, the fine manly faces, the earnest gaze,
the careless attitudes so full of strength and grace for all the gnarls
and distortions of weather, accident and disease: symbols of
rugged-headed courage, manly devotion and simple-hearted
patriotism. They were children – generous, suspicious, forgiving,
with the fortitude and patience of men: rough Britons tempered
by the unresting sea into virtue of a rare and peculiar kind. The
sight of a Monsieur's sails roused in them all the unconquerable
pugnacity of their race: the whine of Johnny Crapaud's shot
whipped their quick tempers to savagery. Though chivalrous and
generous victors, they were not good losers like the courtly
Spaniards and the aristocrats of the old French navy; they had to
beat their adversary or die. As they waited at quarters before a
fight, 'their black silk handkerchiefs tied round their heads, their
shirt-sleeves tucked up, the crows and hand-spikes in their hands
and the boarders all ready with their cutlasses and tomahawks',
they reminded an eye-witness of so many devils.

Yet from such scenes the British sailor could pass in a few hours
to the buffoonery and practical jokes dear to the lower deck, the
fiddler's lively air, the droll or pathetic ballads with their rhythm
of the waves, while the seas broke over the forecastle and the ship
pitched and rolled; and to those tenderer moments when, homeward bound, hearts panted with the anticipated happiness of
meeting wives and sweet hearts and the headwind's moping con-
trariness was lulled by the chorus of 'Grieving's a folly, boys!'

> 'And now arrived that jovial night
> When every true bred tar carouses,
> When, o'er the grog, all hands delight
> To toast their sweethearts and their spouses.'

History loves to linger over the good-humoured jollity between
decks when port was reached: the girls on the seamen's knees with
sturdy, buxom arms around their necks; the reels and gigs as
Susan's bright eyes promised her Tom Tough his long-awaited
reward; the grog and flip that passed about under the light of the
flickering lanterns. And judging by the popularity of Dibdin's
songs, the nation liked to think of such scenes too and took deep
comfort in the thought of the hearts of oak and jolly tars that kept
its foes at bay.

*   *   *

In 1797 – the fifth year of Britain's struggle against the militant
power of Revolutionary France – the Royal Navy alone stood
between her and defeat. One by one her continental allies had
collapsed before the élan of the ragged revolutionary armies;
Prussia and Holland had given up the fight and entered the enemy
camp, Piedmont had sued for an armistice and, in the autumn of
1796, the sudden defection to the French cause of Spain and its
powerful navy – lying athwart Britain's trade and ocean communications – had forced her to withdraw her fleet from the Mediterranean, where that summer Bonaparte had overrun northern
Italy in a series of dazzling victories over her ally, Austria. The
three chief naval powers of the continent – France, Spain and

386

Holland – were now aligned against her, outnumbering her ships of the line by nearly two to one. Ireland was on the verge of revolution, the working-class population of the industrial north was hungry and restless, and powerful invasion forces were waiting with transports at Brest and Texel for a chance to break the blockade and strike at England or Ireland. During the last fortnight of 1796, the Brest expedition got to sea and reached the Irish coast, only to be driven back by gales; in February, after an abortive attempt to burn Bristol, a raiding force made landings on either side of the Bristol Channel, causing a panic in the City, during which Pitt's Government suspended cash payments and seemed about to fall. Only a timely victory off Cape St Vincent on St Valentine's Day over a Spanish fleet gave the country a respite.

But nine weeks later, on the morning of April 17th, dreadful rumours began to percolate through the capital. The Navy, which had saved the country from invasion, was about to betray it to its enemies. The Channel Fleet had refused to sail and mutinied for an increase of pay. By nightfall the news was confirmed. And at that very moment the Austrians were on the point of asking a truce from the victorious Bonaparte, Ireland – almost denuded of troops – was defenceless, and a French army of liberation was waiting to embark at the Texel under cover of the Dutch fleet.

*　　*　　*

Naval pay, fixed by ancient enactment, had stood for nearly a century and a half at 10s. a month for an ordinary seaman and 24s. for an Able. But the price of the commodities on which the sailor's family depended had not remained constant. To the normal rising trend of prices had been added war inflation, now aggravated by a bank crisis. In the merchant's service the laws of supply and demand had raised the seaman's pay to four times the naval rate. Prevented by the pressgang from selling their highly skilled services in the open market and forced to let their wives and children starve while they served their country, the men of the Royal Navy were conscious of a grave injustice of which their rulers – ill-served by statistics – were blissfully unaware. Even the despised soldiers had

been given a small rise since the war. But the sailors – the pride
and defence of the nation – had had nothing done for them, though
certain of their officers had recently had increases. So strong was
their feeling that at the beginning of March before sailing for the
spring cruise the men of the Channel Fleet combined to send round-
robins to old Lord Howe, their nominal commander-in-chief. In
these they respectfully pointed out that the cost of living had
doubled and that their pay was insufficient to support their
families. And since it was only paid in the port of commission,
whence in war-time a ship might be absent for months and even
years, it was frequently in arrears.

As Howe was an invalid at Bath and about to hand over his
command finally to his deputy, Lord Bridport, he merely for-
warded the petitions to the Admiralty. Here they were ignored.
For in the critical state of the country's finances, application to
Parliament for a rise in naval pay seemed out of the question, and
discussion of the matter would thus obviously be undesirable. As
the petitions were anonymous no reply was made. When the fleet
returned to Spithead at the end of March the men found their
request met by silence. They were very angry and took steps to
prepare a petition to Parliament and to support it by joint action.
'They had better,' the *Queen Charlotte*'s men wrote of the government, 'go to war with the whole globe than with their own subjects.'

Of all this Lord Bridport was unaware. For through an administrative oversight the Admiralty had failed to inform him of the
petitions. But on April 12th he accidentally learnt of a plot to
seize the ships and hold them as pledges for redress of grievances.
He was naturally profoundly shocked and, hearing at second hand
of the petitions to Howe, became exceedingly indignant with the
Admiralty. In his heart he sympathized with the men's demands.
But when he raised the matter with Whitehall he was merely told
to take the Fleet to sea. For the Admiralty was determined to
sidetrack the matter.

On the morning, therefore, of April 16th – Easter Sunday –
Bridport reluctantly ordered the Fleet to weigh anchor. His signal
was ignored. In the *Queen Charlotte*, Howe's former flagship, the
men, seeing an attempt to forestall the mutiny, manned the

shrouds and gave three cheers – the pre-arranged signal for revolt.
At once the leaders put off in boats and rowed round the fleet,
ordering the crew of every vessel to send two delegates that night
to the *Queen Charlotte*. Like all the Hoods a shrewd and sensible
man, Bridport forbade his captains to resist. Instead he ordered
them to muster their men and ask them to state their grievances.

That evening the delegates of sixteen battleships assembled in
the *Queen Charlotte*'s state-room to draw up rules for the regula-
tion of the fleet. They ordered watches to be kept, drunkenness
to be punished by flogging and ducking, and yard-ropes to be rove
at every fore-yard arm to enforce their authority. Women were to
be allowed aboard as usual in harbour, but to prevent tittle-tattle
were not to go ashore till the matter was settled. Respect was to be
paid to the rank of officers, but, until the desires of the men were
satisfied, not an anchor was to be raised. To symbolize their
unanimity the shrouds were to be manned morning and night and
three cheers given.

It was a strange position. The fleet was in indubitable mutiny.
Yet the men did not regard themselves as mutineers and persisted
in trying to behave as though ordinary discipline prevailed. The
country was at war with an ideological creed which glorified revolution: it was hourly expecting invasion. Yet in the rebellious ships
there was no sign of sympathy with that revolution: on the contrary
the delegates declared that the fleet would sail at once if the French
put to sea. They even stopped the frigates and small craft from
taking part in the mutiny lest the country's trade should suffer.

Meanwhile Admiral Pole, dispatched post-haste with news of
the mutiny, had reached the Admiralty at midnight on the 16th.
In the small hours of Tuesday morning he told his horrifying story
to the First Lord. Earl Spencer was the best type of patrician – an
athlete still in early middle age, a scholar with liberal leanings, red-
haired and handsome. He acted with promptitude and vigour. As
soon as it was light he hurried to the Prime Minister and, after a day
of interviews, set out for Portsmouth with two junior Lords and the
Secretary of the Admiralty.

Here on the 18th the Board, formally sitting in the Fountain
Inn, opened its proceedings. Refusing to compromise its dignity

by meeting the seamen personally, it used the flag officers of the
fleet as go-betweens. It would have been wiser for Spencer, who
was over-persuaded by his Service colleagues, to have settled the
matter directly with the delegates, whose real weakness was not
Jacobinism but excessive suspicion. As it was, in the delays and
second thoughts born of too much coming and going, the seamen's
conditions tended to rise.

The new requests were in themselves reasonable: they were
all in the end granted without doing the country the least injury.
But, however reasonable, the ultimatum was presented at a time
when the country was in graver danger than any since the Spanish
Armada. To yield unconditionally at the pistol's mouth might
undermine the whole fabric of naval discipline and precipitate the
same tragic train of events which had brought monarchical France
to massacre and ruin. Therefore, though the Board prudently
eschewed violent counsels, it determined to make some sort of a
stand: to keep the seamen at a distance and, while granting the
substance of their demands, to make as many minor abatements as
possible.

The results of this obstinacy were not happy. Next day, while
Admiral Gardner was arguing with the delegates in the *Queen
Charlotte*'s state-room, the men – after seeming agreement had
been reached – grew suspicious and declared that a final settlement
must wait till a pardon had been received under the King's hand.
At this the admiral, who thought it high time the fleet was at sea,
lost his temper and denounced the delegates as 'a damned, mutinous, blackguard set' of 'skulking fellows' who were afraid of
meeting the French. In his fury he even shook one of them and
threatened to have him hanged. At this there was a riot which ended
in the apoplectic old man's being hustled out of the flagship and
the red flag being hoisted in all ships. The officers were placed
under confinement or – in the case of the unpopular ones – sent
ashore.

Once more, faced by urgent crisis, Spencer acted promptly.
That night he set out for London to obtain the royal pardon,
secured next morning an immediate Cabinet council, by midnight had obtained the King's signature at Windsor and had had

copies printed for circulation in the fleet. But by the time that these, galloped through the night, reached Portsmouth, the good temper of the Navy was already re-asserting itself. The astonishing delegates, while still insisting on the redress of grievances, had apologized gracefully to Bridport for the flag striking incident and begged him as 'father of the fleet' to resume command. This the admiral did on the morning of the 24th, reading the royal proclamation to the crew of the flagship and making a speech in which he promised general satisfaction of all demands. The mutiny thereupon ended. Next morning the greater part of the fleet dropped down to St Helens to await an easterly wind to carry it to Brest.

But though the country congratulated itself that a dreadful week had been attended by no worse consequences, suspicion and unrest remained. The men were not sure that the Government meant to honour its promises. The inexplicable delays attendant on parliamentary processes increased their distrust. During the next fortnight while the fleet waited for the wind, the ferment continued to work. The seamen had tasted power and learnt their strength. Moreover the recognition of their principal grievances had reminded them of others.

Grievances apart, the Fleet was ripe for trouble. The dilution of the better elements with the worse had left a dangerous sediment at the bottom of every crew. In four years of war naval personnel had swollen from 16,000 to 120,000. Ten per cent of the seamen were foreigners. Another ten per cent were Irish, some of them under sentence for political offences and illegally smuggled into the Fleet by high-handed officials. Recently an increasing number had been United Irishmen and sympathizers with the principles proclaimed by revolutionary France.

The agitation and struggle of those seven breathless days at Spithead stirred all this perilous matter into a ferment. This was no ordinary mutiny, for it had succeeded. Suspicion that its fruits were going to be filched by parliamentary chicanery was now aroused by a foolish Admiralty document forbidding captains to temporize with mutiny, and directing the marines to be kept in constant readiness for action. This was no more than a childish attempt of official pride to recover official face. But by accident or design its contents became known to the fleet. On Sunday, May 7th, when on a change of wind Bridport hoisted the signal to sail, the seamen at St Helens once more manned the shrouds and broke into defiant cheers.

This time mutiny wore a graver aspect. The seamen of the *Royal George*, swearing their officers had deceived them, seized the arms and ammunition. A broil in Admiral Colpoys's flagship at Spithead, in which a seaman lost his life while rushing the quarter-deck, nearly ended in the admiral and the officer who had fired the shot being summarily hanged. In other ships unpopular officers were bundled ashore and left with their belongings on the quay-side. Some of the marines, the traditional keypins of naval disci-pline, joined the rest. The people of Portsmouth, confronted with the spectacle of the fleet flying the red flag and of shaken captains and admirals dumped on the sea front like *emigrés*, hourly expected the arrival of the French and the guillotine.

Meanwhile the conflagration had spread. At Plymouth the crews of Sir Roger Curtis's squadron had mutinied on April 26th and turned most of their captains ashore. Four days later ominous cheering signalled an outbreak of revolt in the flagship of the North Sea Fleet waiting at Yarmouth for a wind to blockade the Dutch invasion fleet in the Texel. But in this case the admiral in command was equal to the occasion. Towering with rage, the giant Scot, Adam Duncan, called his men out of the foreshrouds and rated them like a father. The affair ended – for they adored the fine old man – in their promising to go to any part of the world with him and writing a letter thanking the Lords of the Admiralty for their compliance with the request of the Channel Fleet.

For underneath the suspicion, the smouldering grievances and agitation ran the English individual sense of humanity. A worthy officer remained in the seamen's eyes a worthy man, however much he might theoretically embody the forces of despotism. All the generalizations of French ideology or Irish logic could not persuade them otherwise.

It was this deep-rooted manliness of the British sailor that saved the day. The authorities, at last abandoning false pride, behaved with equal good sense. The supplementary estimates providing for the increase in pay were hurried through their remaining stages, and the one line of approach to the disgruntled seamen which was certain of success – the simple human one – was chosen. Someone with a flash of the inspiration which always seems to come to the salvation of England in the last ditch suggested the victor of the First of June as *deus ex machina*. Armed with full powers to redress grievances on behalf of the Admiralty and to grant pardon on that of the Crown, Lord Howe, overcoming gout and infirmities, set off for Portsmouth. Without wasting a minute he had himself rowed across the Solent to St Helens where, visiting every ship in turn, he set to work to restore the confidence of the seamen in their rulers.

By May 13th, six days after the renewed mutiny had begun, the old hero had achieved his purpose of quietening what he described as 'the most suspicious but most generous minds' he had ever met. There only remained to celebrate the reconciliation of Fleet and nation. On May 15th, after twelve hours of rowing round the cheering fleet amid the strains of 'Rule Britannia', 'Black Dick' – as exhausted as after the battle of the First of June – was carried by the sailors shoulder high to the port governor's house. Here in a perfect delirium of patriotic emotion he and his lady entertained the delegates to a grand dinner and jollification.

* * *

At the time of the Spithead mutiny Horatio Nelson was thirty-eight years old. He had been born at Burnham Thorpe in Norfolk on September 27th 1758, the son of a country parson with a large family to support. His mother was a distant kinswoman of the Norfolk squire, Sir Robert Walpole. It was her uncle, Maurice Suckling, captain of a 64-gun battleship, who had given the boy his first chance in life by offering to take him to sea at the age of twelve. 'What has poor little Horatio done that he should be sent to rough it at sea?' he wrote. 'But let him come, and if a cannon ball takes off his head he will at least be provided for.'

Though frail and delicate, the boy's sea training was as varied and thorough as it was rough and harsh. He sailed as a cabin boy in a merchant ship to the West Indies; served, like Drake before him, an apprenticeship in navigation among the shoals of the Thames and Medway and at the age of fourteen, took part in a naval polar expedition, in the course of which he and another boy risked their lives by attempting to capture a bear. By the time he was eighteen he had spent two years as a midshipman on a frigate in the East Indies and, passing the necessary examination for lieutenant, mastered every branch of the seaman's profession. For the next five years he was continuously engaged in the great naval war which followed the American Declaration of Independence when a hard-pressed Britain faced a coalition of all the maritime powers of Europe, eager to take advantage of her foolish quarrel with her colonies. He was still eighteen when he was promoted to his first independent command and by the time the war ended he was, at twenty-two, a post-captain. 'We all rise by deaths,' he wrote to his father. 'I got my rank by a shot killing a post-captain, and I most sincerely hope I shall, when I go, get out of the world the same way.'

This had been his apprenticeship: exercising command in a war when his country was fighting against desperate odds and nothing but the spirit and superlative seamanship and fighting quality of her sailors stood between her and ruin. After the war he served for several years in the West Indies, enforcing the Navigation Laws against the former American colonists, who, having with the help of Britain's enemies won their independence, were no longer as British subjects entitled to carry British goods in their ships. While there he formed a friendship with the king's naval son, Prince William, the future William IV – then a midshipman.

When he was twenty-eight, Nelson met and married a young widow named Mrs Nisbet, who was living in the island of Nevis. After his ship was paid off at the end of 1787, being unable to support a wife on peacetime service in home waters, he withdrew to Norfolk, where for the next five years he led the life of a poor half-pay officer, eating out his heart ashore, farming his father's glebe and fretting under the tedium of a respectable but, as it turned out, ill-assorted marriage. They were years in which, under its young Prime Minister, William Pitt, a long period of peace for England seemed certain, and disarmament and public retrench-ment were the order of the day. Nelson's career seemed finished and he and his friend, the future Admiral Collingwood, then in like retirement, told each other that they despaired of chance ever drawing them back to the seashore.

The unexpected outbreak of the French Revolutionary War in January 1793 found him at the age of thirty-four bombarding the Admiralty with requests for a ship, though it were only a cockle-boat. They gave him a 64-gun ship of the line – a battle-ship of the second class. For the next four years, despite his frail health, and the loss of his right eye while directing siege operations in Corsica, he was on continuous active service in the Mediterranean. Cheerfully fulfilling every mission entrusted to him, by his enthusiasm to excel in the performance of duty he won a reputation for almost foolhardy gallantry. Leading, as always, by love and example, he filled those who served under him with the same zeal as himself. There was nothing he would not do for his officers and men. There was nothing they would not dare for him.

By the end of 1796, with the conquest of Northern Italy by the young Revolutionary general, Napoleon Bonaparte, and with the whole of western Europe marshalled against her by France, Britain was forced to recall her Fleet from the Mediterranean in order to defend her own shores. Nelson, now a commodore, was sent by his Commander-in-Chief, Admiral Sir John Jervis, with two frigates to perform the sad mission of evacuating troops and stores from Elba. Off Cartagena, the main Spanish base, he fell in with two enemy frigates and at once engaged them, capturing one. Returning to the Atlantic early in February 1797, his mission accomplished, he found his way barred by a Spanish fleet of twenty-seven battleships and twelve large frigates who were sailing to join the French at Brest with the intention of jointly escorting an army of invasion to Ireland, then on the verge of revolution. Relying on his superior seamanship as they battled with the Atlantic gales, Nelson boldly proceeded to tack his way through them. While his ship was being closely pursued by two battleships, one of his men fell overboard and his First Lieutenant, Hardy, lowered a boat and went to the rescue. To save the man, Nelson, checking the course of his ship, characteristically risked almost certain destruction. But the Spaniards, bewildered by their tiny prey's unaccountable conduct, checked too, and Nelson got away. Next day he rejoined Jervis off Cape St Vincent, hoisting his Commodore's pennant in the *Captain*, 74 guns.

That night the two fleets drew near. The Spaniards were still ignorant of Jervis's presence, but he, shadowing them with his frigates, was well aware of theirs. The night was misty and the Spanish ships, strung out over many miles of sea, fell into confusion, puncturing the silence with minute guns. At five o'clock on February 14th – St Valentine's Day – they were sighted fifteen miles to the south-west: 'thumpers,' as the signal lieutenant of the *Barfleur* reported, 'looming like Beachy Head in a fog!' Jervis had been reinforced a week before by five ships from England, but he was still outnumbered by nearly two to one. Yet he was determined to bar their way and bring them to battle. For a victory at that moment was essential to his country's safety.

In two columns, imperceptibly merging into an impenetrable line with sterns and bowsprits almost touching, the British fleet bore down on the enemy, making straight for the gap – nearly three miles wide – between the main force and a straggling division to leeward. It was like the inexorable thrust of a sword into a lanky giant's careless guard.

Down in the dark of the gun decks and in the 'slaughter houses' near the mainmasts, the men waited with the precision born of long practice. As each enemy drew alongside and all was ready – the ports open, matches lighted, the guns run out – they broke into three tremendous cheers more daunting to their foes even than the thunder of their broadsides.

The climax of the battle came at about one o'clock. At that moment the head of the Spanish line was nearing the tail of the British. Nelson, flying his flag in the thirteenth ship in the British line, saw with the instinct of genius that only one thing could prevent the main Spanish division, which had suddenly turned to leeward, from rejoining its isolated ships and so confronting Jervis with a reunited fleet before he could alter course. The Spaniards were battered but they were still intact: another few minutes and the chance of the decisive victory which England needed would have passed.

Without hesitation, disregarding the letter of the orders he had received and anticipating those there was no time to transmit, Nelson bore out of the line and placed the *Captain* – the smallest two-decker in the British fleet – straight in the course of the giant *Santissima Trinidad* – the largest fighting ship in the world – and four other ships. For ten minutes it looked as though the *Captain*, her foremast shot away and her wheelpost broken in a tornado of fire, would be blown out of the water. But when the smoke cleared she was still there, and the *Excellent* under Captain Collingwood was coming to her aid. The Spaniards' line was in inextricable confusion, all hope of a junction between their sundered divisions at an end and Jervis beating back into the fight with the remainder of his fleet.

But before the victory was complete, Nelson did a very remarkable thing. Crippled though she was from her duel with the

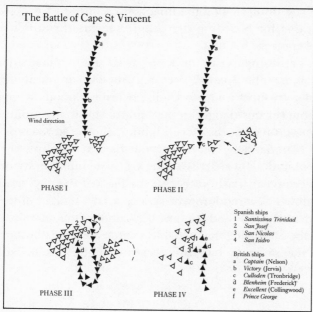

The Battle of Cape St Vincent

Wind direction

PHASE I

PHASE II

PHASE III

PHASE IV

Spanish ships
1   *Santissima Trinidad*
2   *San Josef*
3   *San Nicolas*
4   *San Isidro*

British ships
a   *Captain* (Nelson)
b   *Victory* (Jervis)
c   *Culloden* (Tronbridge)
d   *Blenheim* (Frederick)
e   *Excellent* (Collingwood)
f   *Prince George*

Santissima Trinidad, he placed the *Captain* alongside the 80-gun *San Nicolas* and prepared to board. Helped by a soldier of the 69th, the one-eyed Commodore climbed through the quarter-gallery window in her stern and led his boarders in person through the officers' cabins to the quarterdeck. Here he found Captain Barry, who had jumped into the enemy's mizzen chains, already in possession of the poop and hauling down the Spanish Ensign. At that moment fire was opened on the boarding party from the stern-gallery of the three-decker, *San Josef,* which in the confusion of the fight had drifted against the *San Nicolas*. Placing sentries at the tops of the ladders of his still scarcely vanquished prize, Nelson directed his boarding party up the side of the *San Josef*. There, as his friend Collingwood described it, on the quarter-deck of a Spanish first-rate he received the swords of the officers of the two ships, 'while one of his sailors bundled them up with as much composure as he would have made a faggot, though twenty-two of their line were still within gunshot.' Presently the *Victory*, now in the thick of the fight again, passed that triumphant group on the *San Josef*'s quarter-deck, saluting with three cheers. The cool daring of the thing tickled the imagination of the Fleet: 'Nelson's patent bridge for boarding first-rates' became the admiring joke of the lower-deck.

Four battleships, two of them first-rates, remained in the victors' hands. The Spanish fleet, still superior in numbers, withdrew under cover of night to Cadiz, bearing wounds which freed Britain from serious danger in that quarter for many months. The Government, saved at the eleventh hour, showered rewards on the principal commanders. Jervis became Earl St Vincent, the Vice- and Rear-Admirals were made baronets, and another subordinate admiral became an Irish peer. But the hero of the day was the till then unknown Commodore who was created a Knight of the Bath. His sudden exploit had caught England's imagination. For a moment the clouds of that terrible winter parted. Through them men saw the gleam of something swift and glorious and of a new name – Nelson.

*   *   *

In the summer of 1797, six months after his victory off Cape St Vincent and shortly after the end of the Nore and Spithead mutinies, Lord St Vincent sent Nelson with three ships of the line and four frigates to storm the all-but-impregnable Spanish island fortress of Tenerife in the hope of capturing the Mexican treasure fleet which was falsely rumoured to be sheltering there. A more desperate assignment could hardly have been conceived. For, since the great Cromwellian admiral, Blake, had taken it under very different circumstances a century and a half earlier, the fortress of Santa Cruz now bristled with guns and was defended by eight thousand Spanish regular troops. Against them the thirty-eight-year-old Commodore could oppose a bare thousand sailors and marines. On the night of the 24th, he had brought his landing boats to within half a gunshot of the shore before the church bells sounded the alarm and a hurricane of grapeshot swept the harbour. With his right arm shattered to the bone, he was borne half-conscious to his flag-ship, while the heroic landing party, under his lieutenant Trowbridge, fought vainly against impossible odds to capture the Mole and awakening city.

Thus, in his first independent command as a flag officer, Nelson tasted defeat – albeit glorious defeat. He returned to England a physical wreck with little hope of ever serving again. Yet by the spring of 1798, after nine months' painful convalescence, he was able to rejoin his old Commander-in-Chief, Lord St Vincent, still blockading the Spanish fleet off Cadiz, at a time when taking advantage of the prolonged absence of a British fleet from the Mediterranean, the twenty-nine-year-old Napoleon Bonaparte, had been fitting out a great armada and army to cross that sea, invade Egypt and march on India, so making himself master of the eastern world and, so he thought, cutting the overseas wealth which sustained England. And almost at the very moment of its sailing, the British government had decided to risk weakening its home defences and send a fleet back to the Mediterranean, not so much with the idea of thwarting Bonaparte's grandiose oriental designs – of which it knew nothing – as of rousing Austria and the European powers to revolt against the French Revolutionary yoke. On May 2nd Cabinet instructions had therefore been sent to St Vincent to detach part of his fleet for a sweep in the Mediterranean. They were accompanied by a private letter from Lord Spencer, the First Lord of the Admiralty. 'When you are apprised that the appearance of a British squadron in the Mediterranean is a condition on which the fate of Europe may at this moment be said to depend, you will not be surprised that we are disposed to strain every nerve and incur considerable hazard in effecting it.' And he went on to suggest that, in the event of St Vincent not commanding it in person, it should be entrusted to the junior flag-officer on the station, Sir Horatio Nelson.

Even before the First Lord's letter reached him, St Vincent had sent Nelson back to the Mediterranean with three ships of the line to discover what had been happening in that sea during the year in which Britain had withdrawn from it. Here, shortly after his arrival, to his unspeakable chagrin, Nelson's flagship, the *Vanguard*, had suffered an unexpected disaster, her newly commissioned and as yet imperfectly trained crew losing her main and mizen topmasts in a sudden gale. When she was able to sail again, coasting the Riviera, Nelson discovered that Bonaparte had sailed from Toulon a fortnight earlier for an unknown destination with 40,000 picked troops, more than 300 transports and 50 warships, with horse, foot artillery and stores of war, engineers, architects and professors of every science and art, equipped for both conquest and colonization.

At that very moment Lord St Vincent, after receiving Spencer's instructions, without even waiting for the arrival of promised reinforcements from England, dispatched his ten finest battleships and captains – the élite of his Cadiz fleet – to join Nelson in the Mediterranean. His instructions gave the latter no clue as to Bonaparte's destination. They mentioned Naples, Sicily, Portugal and Ireland – now in open rebellion – but made no reference to Egypt. Nelson had thus no reliable information as to the strength of the French fleet, though he believed it to consist of fifteen or sixteen ships of the line. He knew even less of its whereabouts. Having no frigates he could not comb the seas for intelligence. He had only the light of his intellect to follow and the strength of his will. 'Be they bound to the Antipodes,' he assured Spencer, 'your

Lordship may rely that I will not lose a moment in bringing them to action.'

On June 14th, while far away the fate of Ireland trembled in the balance and the rebel leaders in the green-bannered camp on Vinegar Hill waited for the tidings of French sails, Nelson obtained second-hand news from a passing ship that ten days earlier a great fleet had been seen to the west of Sicily. He accordingly sent the *Mutine* ahead to Naples with a letter begging Sir William Hamilton, the British Ambassador, to urge the king of the Two Sicilies and his English-born Prime Minister, Acton, to shake off their sub-servience to the dreaded Jacobins and strike while the iron was hot. On the 17th he arrived off the port to learn what he had already suspected: that the French had gone to Malta and were either about to attack or had already attacked that island stronghold.

Yet though the timorous Italians sent good wishes and a secret promise of supplies, they would dare no more. Nelson must beat the French before they would stir, even though their inertness should rob him of all chance of victory and themselves of survival. Without wasting time, though still bombarding Hamilton with letters, he pressed through the Straits of Messina and, crowding on all sail, hurried southward down the coast of Sicily heading for Malta where he hoped to catch the enemy at anchor. On June 22nd at the southern point of Sicily off Cape Passaro the *Mutine* fell in with a Genoese brig and learnt from her master that the French had already captured Malta from the Knights of St John – which was true – and, which was not true, had sailed again on the 16th eastward bound.

With the instinct of genius, though his instructions had given him no inkling of it, Nelson had already divined Bonaparte's intention. A few days earlier he had written to Spencer, 'If they pass Sicily, I shall believe they are going on their scheme of possess-Alexandria and getting troops to India.' He had been strictly cautioned against allowing the French to get to the west of him lest they should slip through the Straits of Gibraltar. But he reckoned that with the prevailing westerly winds Bonaparte's vast and un-wieldy armada had little chance of beating back to the Atlantic. Egypt on the other hand would be an easy run for it. If Bonaparte had left Malta on the 16th, he must already be nearly at Alexandria.

Nelson, therefore, decided to act and to act decisively. Though the prudent course, safeguarding his professional career and avoiding official censure, would be to await events while guarding the Two Sicilies, keeping the weather gauge and making sure the enemy could not get to windward and threaten England and her blockading squadrons in the Atlantic, to do so would be to abandon that on which he was resolved: the annihilation of the French fleet and its transports. He at once set course for Alexandria.

But the French had not sailed from Malta on June 16th. Bonaparte, whose besieging armada would otherwise have fallen an easy prey for Nelson on the 22nd, had taken possession of Valetta – 'the strongest place in Europe'. And here he remained for nearly a week. Then, leaving a strong garrison behind him to hold the strategic half-way house to France, he finally sailed on the 19th for Egypt.

Nelson was now directly pitted against Napoleon, the most dazzling genius of his age – himself the embodiment of that great and terrifying explosion of human energy, the Revolution, which England was struggling to hold in bounds. Nelson's success or failure was to depend on his ability to guess and anticipate the thoughts of his brilliant adversary. To that test he was now to bring qualities of an almost unique order: immense professional knowledge and experience, the fruits of life-long application and discipline, selfless devotion to duty, inspired courage, a great heart and the imagination with which to mobilize the evidence of the present and past to predict the future. His countrymen, slow to recognize intellect, knew his courage and ardour but as yet had little conception of the quality of his mind. They had still to realize its infinite capacity for taking pains, its knife-like penetration, its brilliant clarity. Its very lucidity, reducing every scheme and command to elemental terms such as a child could understand, tended to deceive them. They thought of him as a simple sailor-man. They never conceived of him, till his miraculous deeds were to enlighten them, as the supreme embodiment of the genius of their country. For his was that strange combination of brooding patience, study and intense concentration with a mercurial tem-

perament which rose like lightning out of storm and in the hour
chosen of destiny lighted the path to victory. Above all, his power
was based, like his country's, on adherence to moral law: once he
was convinced that a course was right, nothing could shake his
constancy to it and the tenacity of his purpose.

*   *   *

On the evening of June 22nd, the look-outs in Nelson's fleet,
bound for Egypt, saw the sails of French frigates on the horizon.
But he did not stop to investigate them for he supposed that they
could not belong to Bonaparte's main fleet which, according to his
information, had left Malta six days before. Had he possessed any
frigates of his own, he would soon have discovered his error. But
to have pursued the French frigates with his battle fleet would have
led him nowhere, for they would inevitably have lured him away
from his real quarry, the great ships and transports. So instead he
kept on his course. Shortly afterwards darkness fell, and during the
night, which was hazy, the British line of battle, swift, compact and
intent, passed unknowing through the converging track of the
French expedition. The sound of the British minute guns firing
through the mist caused the French admiral to sheer away to the
northward in the direction of Crete. Had dawn come half an hour
earlier it would have revealed him and his helpless transports. But
by sunrise on the 23rd the last French sails were just below the
horizon.

That was one of the decisive moments of history. A long train
of events had brought the two fleets to that place at that hour, of
which the most important were Bonaparte's dynamic ambition
and Nelson's zeal for duty. Had they clashed the result would have
been certain: thanks to the Cabinet's bold resolution, to St
Vincent's discipline, above all to Nelson's own inspired fixity of
purpose, the blundering, persistent patience of Pitt's England
would, on the afternoon of June 22nd 1798, have been rewarded.
Bonaparte, epitomizing the Revolutionary weakness for desperate
gambling, had staked everything on Britain's not being able to
send a fleet to the Mediterranean. And now at the moment that he

was reaching out to grasp the prize of the Orient, the British fleet crossed his path.

Crossed it and vanished. Lack of frigates alone robbed Nelson of a victory that would have been Trafalgar and Waterloo in one. Again and again St Vincent had pleaded with the Admiralty for more frigates: pleaded in vain. Treasury parsimony, the unpreparedness of a peace-loving people, above all the needs of restless, ill-treated Ireland had all contributed to this fatal flaw. It was to cost Britain and the civilized world seventeen more years of war, waste and destruction.

*   *   *

So it came about that on June 23rd 1798 the two fleets, having converged, passed out of reach of one another, the French admiral Brueys with his momentous freight edging cumbrously northwards towards the greater security of Crete, Nelson with every inch of canvas spread direct for Alexandria hoping to catch Bonaparte before he could disembark. On the sixth day he reached Alexandria and to his unspeakable chagrin found the roads empty. No one there had seen anything of Bonaparte's armada, though the sleepy Turkish authorities were making languid preparations to repel it. Still believing in his false information that the French had left Malta on the 16th, it never occurred to Nelson that they had not yet covered the distance. Without waiting he at once put to sea again, steering for the Syrian coast in hope of news of a landing at Aleppo or an attack on the Dardanelles.

As, early on June 29th, the British sails dropped over the eastern horizon, watchers at Alexandria saw those of the French rise over the western. Hampered by its lack of skill, vast size and triangular course, Bonaparte's expedition, averaging only fifty miles a day, had taken just double the time of its pursuer to reach Egypt. Once more, cruelly crippled by lack of frigates, Nelson had missed an epoch-making victory by a few hours.

Though Bonaparte had still no idea how narrow had been his escape, he wasted no time before disembarking. On July 1st he landed: on the 5th he stormed Alexandria, putting all who resisted to the sword. A fortnight later, advancing at his habitual speed across the desert, he routed the main Egyptian army under the shadow of the Pyramids. On the 22nd he entered Cairo. Another nation had been overwhelmed.

Meanwhile fretting with impatience and full of anxiety for the kingdom of the Two Sicilies, Nelson had sought in vain for his elusive quarry in the Gulf of Alexandretta. Thence, skirting the shores of Crete, he beat back against westerly winds to Syracuse. On July 19th, with his water nearly exhausted, he reached it, having in his own words gone a round of six hundred leagues with 'an expedition incredible' and being at the end of it as ignorant of the enemy's situation as at the beginning. But he reproached nobody but himself. 'Your Lordship,' he wrote to St Vincent, 'deprived yourself of frigates to make mine the first squadron in the world . . . But if the French are above water, I will find them out and if possible bring them to battle. You have done your part in giving me so fine a fleet, and I hope to do mine in making use of them.'

On July 25th he was ready once more for sea. Disregarding the protests of the Neapolitan Prime Minister, who wished him to stand sentinel over the Two Sicilies, he sailed again, this time – since all intelligence showed that the French were not to the west of him – towards the Morea. With all canvas spread the great ships sped on their search – *Culloden, Theseus, Alexander*, and *Swiftsure*; *Vanguard, Minotaur, Defence, Audacious, Zealous, Orion, Goliath, Majestic, Bellerophon*. They sailed in order of battle, in three compact divisions in case the enemy should be encountered at sea: two to tackle Brueys's battle fleet and the other to do the work of the missing frigates and destroy the transports.

Every day throughout the long chase the men were exercised at their guns and small arms. Whenever the weather permitted the captains went aboard the *Vanguard* to discuss with the admiral the precise function which each was to fulfil in battle. In the 'school for captains' on Nelson's quarterdeck they unconsciously entered into his mind till each of his ideas – lucid, precise and devised against every eventuality – became as natural to them as to him. Long linked by the comradeship of sea and service, these rough, weather-beaten men, with their wonderful professional skill, were distilled into a single instinctive instrument of war in the alembic of Nelson's mind and spirit. They became what in his love he called them – a band of brothers.

The keynote of the fleet's readiness for battle was a minute imaginative attention to detail: the sure hallmark of a great leader. 'No man,' the American historian, Mahan, has written, 'was ever better served than Nelson by the inspiration of the hour; no man ever counted less on it.' Every ship was ready day and night for action: every man schooled in an exact part. Five thousand wills and bodies moved to a single purpose infinitely diversified in individual function.

On July 28th, three days after leaving Syracuse, Nelson obtained news of the French from some Greek fishermen in the Gulf of Koron. A month before, a great fleet had been seen spread far over the seas sailing south-eastwards from Crete. With the wind in the west for the past month it was evidence enough. Bonaparte must have gone to Egypt after all. Once more all sail was set for Alexandria.

A little before noon on August 1st 1798, the Pharos of Alexandria became visible and soon after the minarets of the city and the masts of merchantmen in the port. At the masthead of the *Goliath*, leading the fleet with the *Zealous*, the straining eyes of Midshipman Elliot, scanning the low Egyptian shore in the hot haze, had caught the first sight of those heavenly masts. Fearing to hail the quarter-deck, lest keen ears in the *Zealous* should hear and gain the credit, the exultant boy slid quickly down a backstay and ran to Captain Foley with his tidings. But before the fluttering signal 'Enemy in sight', could reach the masthead, *Zealous* had guessed the meaning of the scurry and cluster of flags on the deck of her sister ship and had been before her. As the signal reached each crowded ship, a 'wave of joy' ran through the fleet. Nelson, whose inflexible will had equalled Bonaparte's had run his quarry to earth at last. 'If we succeed,' cried Captain Berry voicing his unspoken thought, 'what will the world say?' 'There is no *if* in the case,' replied Nelson. 'That we shall succeed is certain; who will live to tell the story is a very different question.'

Fifteen miles east of Alexandria the French battle fleet lay at anchor in a great bay guarded by shoals to eastward and by the batteries of Aboukir Castle at its western end. There were sixteen ships in all, thirteen of the line with the *Orient*, Admiral Brueys's giant flagship, in the centre of the line. They lay as close inshore as the sandbanks allowed, forming for nearly two miles a line of thousands of guns with 160 yards between each ship. At the head of the line, guarding it from approach from the west, lay Aboukir Island crowned with mortars.

At half-past two, about the same time as the pursuers sighted

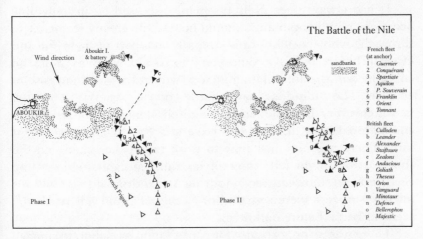

their prey, the French look-outs saw the British sails. As his van was so strongly protected and as to attack his centre or rear his assailants would have to face the concentrated fire of his whole line, Brueys felt convinced that there would be no battle that day. It was to his advantage that it should be postponed. His ships were bigger than the British and more heavily gunned, but many of his men were ashore, discipline was lax and the decks were cumbered with stores and booty. Only the most reckless of foes would be likely to attack him in so strong a position with equal or inferior force. By the time they could reach the bay and negotiate the sandbanks it would be almost dark. It would be insanity for them to attack at night.

But the British squadron never paused. It came on out of the west with all sails set. For Nelson was as eager to do that for which he had come as Bonaparte had been to land and take possession of Egypt. He saw the strength of the French centre, where Brueys had concentrated his greatest ships and of its rear where the next strongest were gathered. But he also saw the weakness of the van if he could bring his fleet round inside the island and pass between it and the leading ships. And though he had no chart of the shoals except a rough plan taken from a prize, 'it instantly struck his eager and penetrating mind that where there was room for an enemy's ship to swing, there was room for one of his to anchor.'

It had always been Nelson's plan, discussed on innumerable occasions with his captains, should he find the enemy at anchor to throw the whole weight of his strength on a part of their line and crush it before the rest could come to its aid. Only by doing so could he win the annihilating victory which it was his purpose to achieve. The ding-dong naval battles of the past two centuries, in which every Englishman laid himself alongside a Frenchman and battered away till one side tired and drew off, could not give it him. There was only just time to work round the island and the shoals before night fell; three of his thirteen capital ships – the *Swiftsure* and *Alexander* reconnoitring Alexandria, and the *Culloden* towing a prize – were some miles away and could not reach the scene of battle before darkness.

There was no opportunity for consultation or elaborate signals, but there was no need for them. Every captain knew what was in his admiral's mind. At five-thirty he flew the signal to form line of battle in order of sailing, and silently and imperceptibly without slackening their majestic advance the great ships slid into their appointed places. Within half an hour of the commencement of the action, the five leading French seventy-fours were being raked by eight ships of similar size and greatly superior to them in gunnery, while their consorts to leeward watched helpless and inactive.

Wrought to the highest tension by their long, tenacious pursuit, the British fought, as Berry put it, with an ardour and vigour impossible to describe. The French also fought with great gallantry. But the British were fighting with the certain conviction of victory and, every man knowing what to do in all emergencies, with an order and freedom from confusion absent in the Republican ships. Early in the engagement, when the issue was already a foregone conclusion, Nelson was struck on the forehead by a piece of flying iron from the *Spartiate*. Flung to the deck and blinded by the strip of bleeding flesh that fell over his solitary eye, he was carried below thinking himself a dying man. Here in the crowded cockpit he lay in intense pain, insisting on taking his turn at the surgeon with the other wounded men and constantly calling with what he believed to be his dying breath for news of the battle.

It was about nine o'clock when Hallowell in the *Swiftsure*, still fresh to the fight, noticed flames pouring out of one of the cabins of the *Orient*. He at once directed every available gun on the spot. As the great vessel, the finest in the Republican Navy, blazed more fiercely, every British ship in the neighbourhood trained her guns on her. Down in the hold of his flagship Nelson heard of the impending fatality and insisted on being led up on deck to watch; as soon as he saw her imminence of doom he ordered the *Vanguard*'s only undamaged boat to be lowered to rescue the survivors. At a quarter to ten the *Orient* blew up with a terrifying detonation. The whole bay was lit as brightly as day by the expiring flame of the great ship as she rose in the air. After she vanished, silence fell on the combatants: then after some minutes the guns opened out again. As they did so the moon rose dazzling in her Egyptian beauty over the wreckage and slaughter.

Yet though the night was still young the battle was losing momentum. With the great admiral who had conceived it dazed and disabled by his wound, the soul was gone out of it. Five of the French ships had already struck: another, the 80-gun *Franklin*, was failing fast. But the victors after sailing and fighting all day were exhausted. They would fire for a time and then desist: all night the battle flared up and then died away. 'My people was so extremely jaded,' reported Captain Miller of the *Theseus*, 'that as soon as they had hove our sheet anchor up they dropped under the capstan bars and were asleep in a moment in every sort of posture.' After the surrender of the *Franklin* the second lieutenant of *Alexander* approached Ball to tell him that, though the hearts of his men were as good as ever, they could do no more and begged him to let

them sleep for half an hour by their guns. Nelson's slightly dis-
jointed messages speeding through the night were received rather
than obeyed: in that confused interminable nightmare of weariness
nothing was ever quite carried through to an end.

As it began to grow light the magnitude of the victory became
apparent. At 5.26 a.m. Captain Hallowell noted that six enemy
battleships had struck their colours; the whole bay was floating
with charred wreckage and dead bodies, mangled and scorched.
By this time it was light enough to see that three other battleships
were at the victors' mercy: dismasted hulks aground or drifting.
Only Villeneuve's three spectators in the rear remained uninjured.
Presently these slipped their anchors and began to bear out to sea.
But one of them, the *Timoleon*, in her haste to be gone ran on to the
sandbanks. Her crew swam ashore and made off inland, a cloud of
smoke revealing that her captain had fired her. Alone of the thirteen
French ships of the line the *Guillaume Telle*, and the *Généreux*
with two frigates escaped into the blue of the Mediterranean.

In the first aftermath of battle Nelson and his men could
scarcely conceive the fullness of what they had done. All day on
August 2nd they were engaged in fishing naked prisoners from
rafts and floating wreckage. More than two thousand unwounded
prisoners were taken and nearly fifteen hundred wounded: that
night Nelson dined half a dozen wounded French captains in his
cabin. Brueys, the first admiral in France, had been cut in half by
a cannon ball before the *Orient* blew up. Two thousand more of his
men had been killed or drowned, nine of his thirteen battleships
captured, two more destroyed. Nothing like it had been known since
the day when the duke of Marlborough had entertained a French
marshal and two generals in his coach after Blenheim.

*   *   *

Because of Nelson's lack of frigates and the very depth of his
penetration into the French position, the news of his achievement
travelled slowly. Its effect was not an instantaneous explosion but
the spluttering of a charge of powder. For many days after the

battle the victors remained in Egyptian waters, remote from the world which had lost trace of them. It took Nelson a fortnight before he could make his dismasted prizes fit for sea. Three he was forced to burn: the other six he sent off to Gibraltar on August 14th under escort of seven of his battleships. Their progress up the Mediterranean was painfully slow.

So it came about that no intelligence of the victory reached western Europe till September 4th, when it was brought to Naples by the *Mutine* sloop, which Nelson, on the arrival of his long-lost frigates, had sent off with duplicate dispatches on August 14th. Before they arrived Nelson himself was on his way to Europe. On August 14th he had received a summons from St Vincent to return to save the Kingdom of the Two Sicilies from the threat of sea-borne invasion and co-operate in the capture of a British Mediterranean base in the Balearics. Accordingly, leaving three battleships and three frigates under Captain Hood to blockade Egypt, Nelson reluctantly set out on the 19th for Neapolitan waters. He was still suffering from the effects of his head wound and from perpetual headaches and vomitings. The voyage, prolonged by the derelict state of his flagship, acted as an enforced holiday.

On September 22nd 1798, towed ironically by a frigate, the *Vanguard* anchored off Naples. 'I hope,' Nelson wrote to Sir William Hamilton, 'to be no more than four or five days at Naples, for these are not times for idleness.' He had reckoned without the ambassador's lady. Accompanied by the King and Queen of Naples, this large, fascinating, vulgar, dynamic woman of thirty-three bore down on the admiral with the same spirit that he himself had borne down on the French. She had only set eyes on him once before when, five years earlier during the siege of Toulon, he had borne dispatches to Naples. But she was resolved to conquer him as he had conquered Brueys. Acknowledged as a mistress of dramatic effect – her 'attitudes' were the talk of the less exacting *salons* of Europe – she positively boarded the unsophisticated sailor on his own quarterdeck. Still bemused from that astonishing encounter he described it in a letter three days later to his wife. 'Up flew her ladyship and exclaiming, "O God, is it possible?" she fell into my arm more dead than alive.' She was followed by the

King who, seizing the admiral by the hand, hailed him as his deliverer and preserver.

It was all too much for Nelson and his poor dazed head. The loveliest city of southern Europe was in summer gala to receive him, the most voluptuous of women at his feet. After the strain and intense excitement of the summer and the dreary reaction of the voyage west, he could not refrain from yielding to all this overflow of tenderness and adulation. It seemed a sailor's due, after the hardships and deprivations of the sea. He had known little of luxury and nothing of courts. He found himself when he was least able to withstand its fatal charm the adored hero of the most luxurious and enervating society in existence. He struggled for a little while: wrote to St Vincent a week after his arrival that he was in a country of fiddlers, puppets and scoundrels: that it was a dangerous place for a simple sailor and he must keep clear of it. A fortnight later he sailed for Malta, where the islanders had risen against the French garrison at the first news of the Nile, to organize a blockade of Valetta. But he left his heart behind in Naples, and early in November, at the first stirrings of Continental war, he returned there to be the counsellor of an admiring king and queen and the hero of a lovely and designing woman, and to waste his genius in an element alien to it.

* * *

It was not until Monday, October 1st, exactly two months after the battle that the postscript of *Lloyd's Evening Post* announced that the Hamburg mail had arrived with news of a glorious victory in which Admiral Nelson had destroyed or captured all but two of the French battleships. Next morning Captain Capel of the *Mutine* delivered Nelson's dispatches to the Admiralty. Within a few minutes the Park and Tower guns began to fire and all the church bells to peal. And as the steeples started to rock, the wife of the First Lord sat down to write to the hero of England. 'Joy, joy, joy to you, brave, gallant, immortal Nelson! May the great God whose cause you so valiantly support, protect and bless you to the end of your brilliant career . . . My heart is absolutely bursting with different sensations of joy, of gratitude, of pride, of every emotion that ever warmed the bosom of a British woman on hearing of her country's glory.'

There was scarcely anybody in England who did not realize the magnitude of the victory. The *Annual Register* described it as 'the most signal that had graced the British Navy since the days of the Spanish Armada.' The old King, when the despatch reached him at Weymouth, read Nelson's opening words, then stopped and, standing silent for a minute, turned his eyes to heaven. It seemed to promise not only a lasting salvation for England, but preservation from anarchy, distress and misery for the still free countries of Europe, liberation for the enslaved, and, in the fullness of time, peace.

*　　*　　*

The two years which followed Nelson's arrival at Naples after his victory of the Nile were in some ways the saddest in his life and blemished his wonderful reputation and career. Desperately in love with Lady Hamilton – a once fabulously lovely woman whose beauty was now fast fading and who, with her melodramatic nature, was resolved to keep her last lover and hero constantly at her side – he appeared everywhere with her and her ageing husband, the ambassador. At her instigation he became involved in the treacherous politics of the corrupt Neapolitan court. It was his nature to do everything with passionate intensity, and for a time his devotion to her almost took the place of his utter dedication to his country's service. On one occasion, in his anxiety to defend Naples and Sicily against attack, he even ignored a superior's order and incurred the displeasure of the Admiralty. In the summer of 1800, pleading wounds and illness, he resigned his command and returned home. Travelling across Europe with the Hamiltons, he was everywhere lionized as a hero, with his adored Emma beside him. But when he reached England, though his carriage was drawn by a cheering mob from Ludgate to the Guildhall and the City fathers presented him with a diamond-studded sword, his wife refused to countenance his new friends and parted from him for ever, while the King, after the briefest of greetings, turned his back on him at a levee. In political and official circles it was assumed by many that his career was finished.

From this sad state of affairs Nelson was retrieved by the call of duty. The great European coalition against Revolutionary France, which had been brought about by his victory at the Nile, had by now been defeated by the genius of Bonaparte who, having escaped from Egypt and evaded the British blockade, had made himself First Consul and dictator of France. Even Russia turned against Britain and, joining with the maritime powers of Denmark and Sweden in a Confederacy of the North, closed the Baltic to her trade, cutting off the supplies of naval stores and grain on which her fleets and the factory population of her new industrial towns largely depended.

Faced with the closure of the ports of all Europe against her and by a threat of famine, Britain's rulers did not hesitate. Gathering every available warship in home waters, the Government assembled early in 1801 a fleet at Yarmouth for immediate service in the Baltic. Its command was entrusted to a sixty-two-year-old admiral, Sir Hyde Parker, who possessed more seniority than experience of active service and was known to the Navy as 'old vinegar'. But to spur him to action, the Admiralty appointed as second-in-command the youngest and most daring Vice-Admiral in the Service, the forty-two-year-old Lord Nelson of the Nile.

The effect on Nelson was electric. He reached Yarmouth on March 6th, flying his flag in the *St George*. He found his elderly admiral 'a little nervous about dark nights and fields of ice'. 'We must brace up,' he reported, 'these are not times for nervous systems. I hope we shall give our northern enemies that hailstorm of bullets which gives our dear country the domination of the seas.' For Nelson viewed England's new enemies with the same pugnacity and intensity as the old.

Sir Hyde, worthy man, did not. His chief interest at the moment was a farewell ball which his young wife was preparing to give at Yarmouth on March 13th. Nelson, knowing that every minute was precious if the Baltic Powers were to be disarmed in detail before the had time to prepare and unite their forces, was beside himself with impatience. 'Strike home and quick,' he urged. He dropped a hint of Parker's preoccupation to his old friend, St Vincent, now called to the Admiralty. Whereupon the fleet received orders to sail at once, the ball was abandoned and the two admirals started on their mission on decidedly strained terms.

But when Nelson made up his mind, there was no resisting him. Between the sailing of the fleet on March 12th and its arrival on the 19th at the Skaw, the northernmost point of Denmark, he had already half won over his superior – tradition has it by means of a timely turbot.

Not that he had yet succeeded in inspiring Parker with his own spirit. Eighteen miles north of Kronborg Castle and Helsingor (Elsinore), where the Kattegat narrows into the Sound between Sweden and the Danish island of Zealand, the fleet anchored to await the return of Nicholas Vansittart, the Government envoy, who had been sent on in a frigate to Copenhagen with a 48-hour ultimatum. Nelson was for pushing on at once into the Baltic before the Danes and their Russian and Swedish allies were ready. But until Vansittart had a chance to accomplish his mission Parker would not face the double guns of the Elsinore Straits and the responsibility for precipitating war with countries still technically neutral. Nelson's strong, realist mind told him diplomacy was now useless, that the Danes having gone so far would not draw back without the compulsion of force and that they would merely use the delay to make themselves stronger.

It was a sombre moment. The weather was bitterly cold and half the fleet seemed to be coughing. On March 23rd Vansittart returned with the Crown Prince of Denmark's rejection of the British ultimatum. Nelson was thereupon summoned to the flagship. He found all in the deepest gloom, Vansittart expatiating on the strength of the Danish defences, and Parker, appalled by his account of great batteries erected by multitudes of defiant Danes, in favour of anchoring in the Kattegat till the united Baltic navies emerged to give battle. Nelson thereupon set to work, quietly and cheerfully, to argue the Council of War round. After learning that the Copenhagen defences were in the north where the Trekronor Battery barred the approach from the Sound, he suggested that the fleet should follow the longer route by the Great Belt round Zealand

415

and so fall on the enemy where he was least expecting attack, in the rear. The manoeuvre would have had the additional advantage of placing the British between the Danes and their Russian and Swedish allies. But the great thing, he insisted, was to attack at once. 'Go by the Sound or by the Belt or anyhow,' he said, 'only lose not an hour.' I am of the opinion the boldest measures are the safest.'

Parker's yielding nature could not resist such strength. He would not, as Nelson urged, press boldly on against the Russians – the heart of the Armed League – and smash half their fleet at Reval while it was still separated from the remainder by the ice. The thought of leaving the Danish ships in his rear was too much for his conventional mind. But he agreed to pass through the Belt and attack the Danes: on that point he argued no more. On the 26th, as soon as the wind allowed, the fleet weighed and steered towards the Belt. But on learning from his flag-captain something of the danger of those intricate waters, the admiral changed his mind and decided to brave what he had refused before, the narrow entrance to the Sound between the Danish and Swedish guns. As often happens when men boldly grapple with difficulties, the initial obstacles vanished as soon as tackled. When, after being detained by head winds for three days, the fleet entered the dreaded Straits of Elsinore on the 30th, the passage proved absurdly easy.

That afternoon eighteen British sail of the line and thirty-five smaller vessels anchored five miles south of Copenhagen. The two admirals at once made an inspection of the town's defences in a schooner. They found that they had been still further strengthened during the days of waiting. But Nelson showed no sign of dismay. Next day at the Council of War he got his way, and, when he asked for ten battleships, Parker gave him twelve. The old gentleman, in spite of his longing for ease and quiet, was almost coming to love Nelson.

At a second Council of War Nelson's plan was adopted for the destruction of the Danish fleet and floating batteries. About two miles to the east of Copenhagen the water in front of the city was broken by a great shoal known to pilots as the Middle Ground. Between this and the short flats ran a swift current of deep water called the King's Channel. Along its western or inner side were anchored nineteen hulks and floating batteries with a host of smaller vessels in an unbroken line whose head was protected by the famous Trekronor Battery. Instead of attacking it from its strongest end, Nelson proposed to take the twelve lightest battle-ships and the smaller vessels of the fleet round the Middle Ground and so sweep up the King's Channel from the south with the current. This would enable him, after crippling the enemy, to rejoin the rest of the fleet without turning. It involved, however, an intricate and dangerous piece of navigation, for the shoal waters round the Middle Ground ran like a mill race, and the fleet had no charts. But Nelson spent the icy, foggy nights of March 30th and 31st in an open boat taking soundings, and he felt confident of his ability to take the battle fleet through the shoals. It was by now his only chance of over-coming the defences.

While Parker with the reserve moved up to the north end of the Middle Ground about four miles from the city, Nelson, on the afternoon of April 1st, skirted the west of the shoal and anchored at sundown some two miles to the south of the Danish line. That night he entertained his captains on board his temporary flag-ship, the *Elephant*. His instructions, unlike those issued before the Nile, were of the most detailed kind. There would be no room for manoeuvring on the morrow and little for individual initiative. Every ship was therefore allotted an exact task.

At eight the captains came aboard for their final orders: at nine-thirty the fleet weighed. As usual the British entered action without a sound. Both sides seemed awed by the solemnity of the scene: the great ships like enormous white birds, with rows of cannon bristling beneath their canvas, bearing down on the Danish line, and the waiting city tense with expectation. In that brooding silence the chant of the pilot and helmsman sounded to one listen-ing midshipman like the responses in a cathedral service. Then, as the leading ship came into range of the enemy batteries, the thunder began. For nearly four hours the Danes, with successive relays of volunteers from the shore taking the place of the fallen, kept up the cannonade. Along a mile and a half of water, with only a cable's length between them, fifteen hundred guns pounded

417

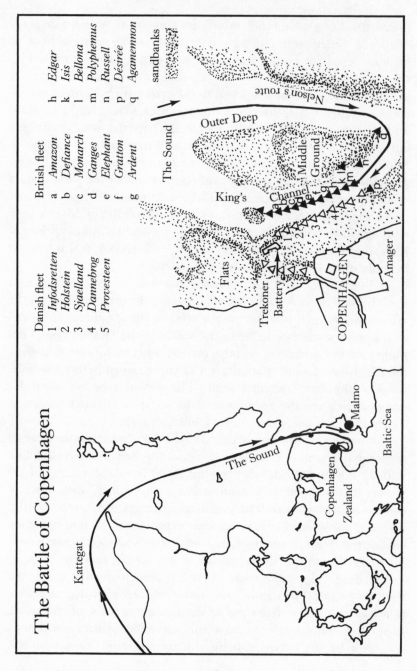

The Battle of Copenhagen

Danish fleet
1 *Infodsretten*
2 *Holstein*
3 *Sjaelland*
4 *Dannebrog*
5 *Provesteen*

British fleet
a *Amazon*
b *Defiance*
c *Monarch*
d *Ganges*
e *Elephant*
f *Gratton*
g *Ardent*
h *Edgar*
k *Isis*
l *Bellona*
m *Polyphemus*
n *Russell*
p *Désirée*
q *Agamemnon*

sandbanks

away at one another: 'I have been in a hundred and five engagements,' wrote Nelson, 'but that of today is the most terrible of them all.'

Twice the Danish Commodore was forced to shift his flag; in the *Dannebrog*, 270 of the crew of 336 were struck down. One or two of the British ships endured casualties almost as heavy: the *Monarch* lost over two hundred men. 'Hard pounding,' remarked Nelson to Colonel Stewart of the Rifle Corps, 'but mark you, I would not be anywhere else for a thousand pounds.'

At one moment Parker, seeing from his distant anchorage that three of the British ships were aground, flew the signal 'Cease Action'. But Nelson, knowing that to break off at such a moment would be disastrous, disregarded it, symbolically putting his telescope to his blind eye. 'Keep mine for closer battle still flying,' he said. 'Nail it to the mast.'

About two o'clock in the afternoon, the Danes' fire slackened. Taken at a disadvantage by the unexpected direction of the attack, and, for all their courage, over-borne by the deadly accuracy of the British fire, they could do no more. Nelson's own position was almost as precarious, with the undefeated Trekronor batteries dominating the treacherous channel between his battered ships and the main fleet to northward. With the sure psychological insight which was part of his greatness, he at once penned a letter addressed: 'To the brothers of Englishmen, the Danes', and sent it under a flag of truce to the Crown Prince. For his instinct told him that he could now obtain what he came for without further bloodshed.

The weariness of his foes and his glorious bluff did the rest. While he referred the terms of the proposed armistice back to Parker in the *London*, he cleared his ships from the shoals under the silent guns of the Trekronor batteries and drew off his prizes. His reputation as much as his crew's gunnery had broken the enemy's will to resist. And, thanks to his exquisite skill as a negotiator, the truce, prolonged from day to day, ended in a permanent armistice. The Danes were to suspend their alliance with the Russians and leave their warships in their existing unmasted state for fourteen weeks, during which time they were to supply provisions to the British fleet. In return the British were to refrain from bombarding Copenhagen.

Nelson had gained his purpose. The hands of Denmark were tied, and his admiral was free to proceed against the Russians without fear for his rear. On April 12th the fleet entered the Baltic. But to Nelson's disgust, instead of proceeding to Reval with a fair wind Parker waited off the Swedish coast for new instructions from England. A blow at Russia, Nelson saw, would destroy the whole northern Coalition, for Denmark and Sweden were merely intimidated by their mighty neighbour. And so long as the ice in the Gulf of Finland prevented the Russian squadron at Reval from retiring on its inner base at Kronstadt, Britain by striking could either destroy it or exact terms from the Czar. When Parker objected that too rapid an advance up the Baltic might expose the whole fleet to a superior Russian and Swedish combination, Nelson replied: 'I wish they were twice as many: the more numerous, the easier the victory!' For he knew that their inability to manoeuvre in large bodies would place them at his mercy.

Not till May 5th did fresh instructions arrive from England. They recalled Parker and left Nelson in command. Immediately the latter left for Reval, but too late. Three days before, the ice had melted sufficiently to enable the threatened Russian squadron to retreat to Kronstadt. There was nothing for Nelson to do but to make as firm and dignified an exchange of letters with the Czar's Minister, Count Pahlen, as circumstances admitted, and then retire.

But his work, if incomplete, was done. The shattering effect of the Battle of Copenhagen, coupled with the Czar Paul's death, had destroyed Bonaparte's prestige throughout the North. The new Czar, Alexander, like his subjects, had no wish to preserve a quarrel with a former ally of such strength and courage as Britain. On May 16th 1801, Russia raised her embargo on British ships, and a month later a Convention between the two countries affirmed the full legality both of the right of search and the seizure of hostile goods in neutral bottoms. Already Prussia and Denmark had withdrawn their troops from Hanover and Hamburg. The northern threat to Britain's security was at an end.

The tidings of Nelson's victory filled the country with relief. For the second time he became the hero of England: 'Your Lordship's whole conduct,' wrote St Vincent, 'is the subject of our constant admiration. It does not become me to make comparisons: all agree there is but one Nelson.'

CHAPTER SEVENTEEN

Blockade, Pursuit and Victory

'The wind was rising easterly, the morning sky was blue,
The Straits before us opened wide and free;
We looked towards the Admiral where high the Peter flew,
And all our hearts were dancing like the sea.
"The French are gone to Martinique with four-and-twenty sail."
The old *Superb* is old and frail and slow,
But the French are gone to Martinique and Nelson's on the trail,
And where he goes the old *Superb* must go!'

Newbolt

'Thank God I have done my duty'
Nelson's dying words

IN THE WINTER after Nelson's victorious return from the Baltic,
Great Britain and France – the one supreme on land, the other at
sea – made a truce. The makeshift Peace of Amiens of 1801 meant
for Nelson release from a purposeless task for, though in the face
of an invasion scare he had been appointed to command a defence
flotilla in the English Channel, he knew that invasion-barges would
never be able to cross the Straits of Dover unescorted. For the
next year he lived with the Hamiltons at Merton in Surrey where
he had bought a home to share with them. In April 1803, Sir
William died, leaving him in sole possession of Emma and of the
child, Horatia, which she had secretly borne him. His happiness
was shortlived, for a month later war broke out again and he was
immediately recalled to service. On May 18th he hoisted his flag
in the *Victory* and two days later sailed for the Mediterranean to
take supreme command there.

His instructions were couched in the broadest terms, for, once on his station, no orders from England could reach him under many weeks. He was to maintain watch over the French fleet at Toulon, prevent its union with the Spaniards should the latter show signs of activity, and protect Malta, Naples, Sicily, the Ionian Islands and the Turkish dominions in Europe, Asia and Africa. He was also to keep the Mediterranean and Aegean clear of French privateers and Algerian pirates. He had no ally – for the Two Sicilies and Sardinia, though secretly friendly, were far too terrified of France to offer him active help – and no base nearer than Malta and Gibraltar, respectively seven hundred and nine hundred miles from his station off Toulon. His task was complicated by the fact that his ships could not, like those of the Channel Fleet, put into Plymouth or Portsmouth to refit, but, however rotten, had to remain on the station till they could be replaced from England.

Only Nelson's inexhaustible resource enabled Britain to maintain her Mediterranean blockade at all. Dependent for supplies on the neutral islands of Sardinia and Sicily – neither of which was safe from French attack – and on a Spain which, lying athwart his communications, might at any moment enter the war against him, the British Admiral's position was one of growing jeopardy. The whole Italian mainland was under French control, with General St Cyr's army waiting in Calabria to pounce on Sicily, Greece or Egypt.

The British had needed the Peace of Amiens for trade; Napoleon in order to prepare to conquer the world. Emperor now of the French and absolute ruler of western Europe, he assembled a vast army on the Channel shore and started to mobilize the fleets of the Continent to break the British blockade. On July 2nd 1804, he ordered his finest admiral, Latouche-Tréville, to give Nelson the slip, and, escaping from Toulon into the Atlantic, release the French ships from Cadiz and Rochefort, make a wide sweep round Cornwallis's blockading force off Brest and, either rounding the British Isles or running straight up Channel, appear off Boulogne in September with sixteen sail of the line and eleven frigates. 'Let us,' he wrote, 'be masters of the Straits for six hours and we shall be masters of the world.'

But Latouche-Tréville never got out into the Atlantic because Nelson made it impossible for him to do so without fighting. Unable to remain close to the port in the Gulf of Lyons gales, Nelson tried not so much to hold him in Toulon as to lure him out. He offered him every opportunity to put to sea, believing that once he had got him there he would make it impossible for him to do further harm. This, however, was not at all what the French wanted: their object was to reach the Atlantic and Channel uncrippled and without an action. Once that summer, encouraged by Nelson's trick of keeping his main fleet over the horizon, Latouche-Tréville edged out of port with eight sail of the line and gave chase to the British frigates. After pursuing for a few miles he realized that he was running into a trap and returned to harbour. A report of the episode in the Paris Press – the only fruit of Napoleon's first naval design – almost reduced Nelson to an apoplexy. 'You will have seen Monsieur Latouche's letter,' he wrote, 'of how he chased me and how I ran. I keep it, and, by God, if I take him, he shall eat it!' A few weeks later he had his revenge when, worn out by overmuch climbing to the Sepet signal-post to watch the British fleet, Latouche-Tréville died of heart failure.

Even had he lived and contrived to escape Nelson, he could not have evaded Cornwallis's Western Squadron. The ultimate function of the great British fighting force off Ushant was not, as Napoleon, like other landsmen supposed, merely to blockade Brest but to secure the approaches to the English and Irish Channels. Absolute blockade of a port, especially in winter, was impossible: sooner or later fog or gale was sure to offer a chance of escape. British naval strategy aimed rather at making it impossible for any French fleet or combination of fleets to enter the Channel without having to fight a superior or equal force. For the Western Approaches were the key to England's existence. Through these waters passed and repassed the merchant shipping on which depended her wealth, drawn from every corner of the earth: the great convoys or 'trades' which it was the unsleeping task of the Navy to secure. As they neared the danger zone close to the French ports the arms of the Western Squadron reached out to protect them. Its frigate tentacles, stretching far out into the outer ocean and southward beyond the Bay, could feel every movement of a converging foe long before he reached the Soundings.

In a series of eighteenth-century world wars extending over more than sixty years British seamen had been engaged in thwarting every conceivable combination of hostile navies. The task had become second nature to them, and there was scarcely a senior officer who had not mastered every move of the game. Such men were not likely to forget their business merely because an amateur of genius took to mapping out the sea in his cabinet at St Cloud as though it were the Lombardy Plain. On August 24th 1804 the Admiralty issued instructions adapting the classic strategy of Britain – the 'matured tradition' of more than two centuries – to the needs of the hour. The French Brest fleet, Cornwallis was warned, sailing without troops, might try to enter the Channel and cover the passage of the Grand Army to Kent. If it evaded him, he was to fall back on the Lizard ready to follow it in any direction. Since it would be suicide for its commander, Ganteaume, to enter the Channel with an undefeated fleet in his rear, it seemed more likely that his destination would be Ireland or Sicily. Any large embarkation of troops would suggest one or other of these, and a smaller the West Indies. Cornwallis was therefore to be ready to detach a division in pursuit, while keeping sufficient force in the Bay to meet any attempt of the enemy to double back on the Channel.

Possibly Napoleon had already divined this, though he refused to admit it to his admirals and the world. Having reaffirmed his faith in his destiny before Charlemagne's tomb at Aix, he drew up a new plan against the English. Realizing that they might make the task of his scattered squadrons progressively harder as they neared their destination, he sought instead to lure them away from the entrance to the Channel. Sailing at the end of October for diversionary raids on the West Indies and South Atlantic trade routes, the Toulon and Rochefort squadrons were to present the greedy islanders with the alternative of losing the wealth of their colonies and trade or of uncovering their heart. Having drawn half their fleet away on wild-goose chases, the two French admirals were to double back to support Ganteaume, who was to escape from Brest in November, land 18,000 shock troops in Ireland and, running up Channel or rounding Cape Wrath according to the wind, convoy either Marmont's 25,000 from the Texel to Ireland or the Grand Army from Boulogne to Kent. In either case the war would then be won.

For the moment the logic of sea power was forcing Napoleon back on a policy of action not against England's heart but against the circumference from which he imagined she drew her strength. All over the world were British trading stations and richly laden merchantmen whose only protection was the thin wooden crust of the blockade along the western and southern seaboard of Europe. There was so much to defend that Britain's naval resources appeared insufficient for the task. Spain's entry into the war now further narrowed her dwindling margin of safety. By a treaty signed in Madrid on January 4th 1805, Napoleon secured the promise of thirty-two Spanish ships of the line by the spring. Till they were ready Spain, with her position athwart England's trade routes, afforded a splendid springboard for diversionary raids into the western and southern Atlantic.

Spurred on by their master's orders and aided by winter gales, the commanders of the Rochefort and Toulon squadrons sailed on their West Indian mission. Missiessy, with 3500 troops packed in his five battleships and attendant cruisers, escaped from Rochefort in a snowstorm on January 11th 1805. A week later Latouche-Tréville's successor, Villeneuve, put out from Toulon with eleven of the line and nine cruisers. Nelson, who had been praying for him to come out, was victualling in Maddalena Bay at the northern tip of Sardinia when his frigates brought the news. In three hours he was under way, leading his ships in a north-westerly gale through the dangerous Biche passage and standing along the eastern coast of Sardinia for Cagliari. With the wind hauling every minute more into the west, he had three main anxieties – Sardinia, the Two Sicilies, and Egypt, for he knew that the French had embarked troops. On the 26th, battered by the gale, he reached Cagliari to learn that no landing had been made. He at once sailed with the wind for Palermo to save Naples and Sicily.

For Nelson's duty was clear. Only by preventing the enemy

from invading the neutral countries of the central and eastern Mediterranean could he maintain the command of that sea on which Pitt's plans for the offensive depended. From this strategic principle nothing could deflect him, neither his longing for glory nor an early return to his mistress and daughter. Aching to meet the enemy, he continued to put first things first. But he refused to uncover the vital point that he had been sent to defend, and kept his eastward course for Sicily.

By the 20th Nelson knew that the island key to the central Mediterranean was safe. The French had made no attempt to

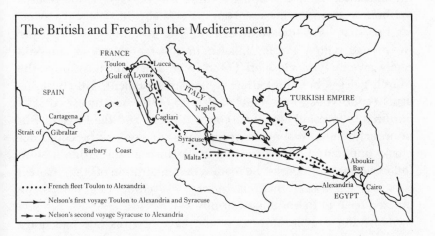

The British and French in the Mediterranean

• • • • • French fleet Toulon to Alexandria

———▶ Nelson's first voyage Toulon to Alexandria and Syracuse

➤ ➤ Nelson's second voyage Syracuse to Alexandria

attack Neapolitan territory. With the prevailing westerly gales they must either have put back into Toulon or sailed ahead of him, as in '98, to Egypt or Greece. To secure the Turkish provinces and the overland route to Egypt, he therefore pressed on through the Straits of Messina towards the Morea and Alexandria. Here on February 7th, as he had predicted, he found the Turks unprepared, the fortifications unmanned and the garrison asleep. With a week's start, he told the Governor of Malta, the French would have made the place impregnable.

But the latter, as he had guessed, were back in Toulon. Three days of storm and the fear of the victor of the Nile had been too much for Villeneuve and his untrained crews. 'These gentlemen,' wrote Nelson, who in twenty-one months had never set foot on shore or lost a spar, 'are not accustomed to a Gulf of Lyons gale.' On March 22nd Napoleon again sent urgent orders to Villeneuve to sail by the 26th. Four days later the unhappy officer stole out of Toulon at dead of night with eleven battleships and eight cruisers. He was speeded by two fears – of his master behind and of Nelson lurking beyond his watching frigates on the horizon. The 'fiery admiral', as the French called him, had been reported off Barcelona on March 17th, and, instead of hugging the Catalan coast, Villeneuve steered south to avoid him, intending to pass to the east of the Balearics before shaping course for Cartagena and Cadiz. Without knowing it, he was running straight into Nelson's arms.

For that long-thwarted seaman after his weary return from Egypt had baited a trap. Unable to cover both the Straits and Sicily save by lying close off Toulon – an untenable position in the March gales – he adopted an ingenious expedient. He chose his usual rendezvous in the Gulf of Palmas on the southwest coast of Sardinia to forestall any move towards Sicily and the Levant. But in order to deter Villeneuve from using the one exit he could not block, and tempt him – were his destination the Atlantic – to follow an easterly course, he made a demonstration off the Spanish coast. Then, aware that his quarry was embarking troops, he hurried back to Palmas to await him.

Here the French admiral would have met his fate had not a chance encounter with a Ragusan merchantman on the morning of April 1st put him wise. Learning that Nelson was no longer off Catalonia but almost straight in his course, he turned west and ran for Spain along the north side of the Balearics. He had managed to shake off the shadowing British frigates during the night, and the sudden change of direction prevented them from rediscovering him. He was by now too far to the south to meet the cruiser which his adversary had left off Cape St Sebastian in case his ruse should fail. Thus, at the very moment for which Nelson had so long waited, the French fleet vanished.

On April 7th Villeneuve anchored off Cartagena and signalled to the warships in the harbour to join him. But the Spaniards, with the gracious dilatoriness of their race, had omitted to load their ammunition and asked for time. Still haunted by the thought of Nelson, Villeneuve refused to wait and sailed with the wind that night. Next morning Lord Mark Kerr, refitting the *Fishgard* frigate in Gibraltar, was startled to see a line of ghostly warships scudding through the Straits before an easterly gale. Vice-Admiral Orde and his five blockading battleships of Cadiz had just time to withdraw as Villeneuve's nineteen ships rose over the eastern horizon. Anchoring outside Cadiz Bay at eight o'clock on the morning of April 9th, Villeneuve signalled to the single French warship and as many of the fifteen Spanish battleships as were ready for sea to join him at once. Soon after noon he gave the order to weigh and by nightfall was receding into the west with six belated Spaniards straggling after him. When Orde's cruisers reappeared off Cadiz next day the Combined Fleet had disappeared, no one knew where.

Meanwhile Nelson had been passing through a period of strain and frustration worse than any since his chase of Napoleon in 1798. On the night of March 31st when his frigates lost sight of Villeneuve, he was waiting off the Sardinian coast for the reward of his labours. But on the morning of April 4th he learnt that the French had again escaped him. He had no idea where they had gone and, true to his unfailing principle, refused to act till he could base action on judgment. Instead he took his station midway between Sardinia and the African coast in order to cover that island and the vital objectives to the east.

For twelve days he remained cruising between the two islands without the slightest news. Owing to a series of mischances no instructions had reached him from England of later date than November. At that time the position in India had seemed very grave, and he was therefore acutely conscious of the possibility of a new attempt on Egypt – a consciousness which Napoleon had done all in his power to foster by troop movements and false Press reports.

But, as day after day passed and the silence continued, Nelson's mind began to misgive him. On the morning of April 10th while cruising near Palermo he learnt by chance that a military expedition had left or was about to leave England for Malta to co-operate with a Russian force in Italy. At once his quick perception warned him of the worst. Villeneuve, evading his outlook off Cape St Sebastian, had sailed to the west, not the east, with the express object of intercepting the convoy. It seemed inconceivable to Nelson that as Commander-in-Chief in the Mediterranean he had not been warned to protect it. Yet it was just the kind of muddle that British governments made.

He at once began to beat back to the west. But the wind was now dead in his teeth. In nine days he only covered two hundred miles. On the 18th he learnt from a passing merchantman that the French had been seen off the Spanish coast eleven days before, sailing west. Next day confirmation arrived that they had passed the Straits, been joined by the Spaniards in Cadiz and had sailed again without entering the harbour.

Agonized though he was, Nelson at once made up his mind. As the Spanish Admiral Gravina had joined Villeneuve, he guessed that the object must be something more than a buccaneering raid against the sugar islands. It must be either Ireland or the Channel. He therefore informed the Admiralty that he was sailing at once for the Atlantic, proposing a rendezvous west of the Scillies where his fleet could join in the defence of the British Isles.

With his almost fretful care for all contingencies he left five of his much needed frigates to guard the Two Sicilies. Then he bent once more to the task of getting up the Mediterranean. Battling against head-winds and squally weather, in two successive days he made only fifteen miles. For nearly a month the monotonous struggle continued, while his heart all but broke.

Not till May 4th did he reach Tetuan Bay. Here all hands were set to work getting in provisions and water. On the 5th the wind came fair and the fleet stood over to Gibraltar where it stayed only four hours. While he was waiting for the wind, Nelson weighed every item of intelligence that could indicate the whereabouts and destination of Villeneuve. He still intended to close on the Channel, yet his information was beginning to point to the French having gone to the West Indies. The most significant item was that given by Rear-Admiral Campbell who, while serving with a Portuguese squadron off the Moroccan coast, had seen the Combined Fleet sailing west on April 11th. The evidence was not conclusive, and Nelson could not run to the West Indies on mere surmise. Yet if he did not and the enemy had gone there, the great sugar island of Jamaica might be lost.

In the next twenty-four hours, victualling in Lagos Bay against a long voyage, Nelson reached a momentous decision. On the evening of May 9th one of Orde's frigates reported having spoken two days before with a vessel which had left Spithead on April 27th. At that date nothing had been heard in England of Villeneuve: a homecoming convoy had also been encountered sailing across the Bay serene and unmolested. It seemed, there-fore, certain that the immediate destination of the fleet which had left Cadiz on April 9th could not have been the Channel. Nelson now felt sure it was Martinique. Next morning he wrote that his lot was cast and that he was going to the West Indies.

By May 14th Nelson was at Madeira, dipping south to pick up the long, steady trade winds to waft him to his goal. He had left one of his two three-deckers to accompany the convoy past Cartagena and twenty of his twenty-three cruisers with Rear-Admiral Bickerton to patrol the Mediterranean. Now with ten of the line and three frigates he was in pursuit of a fleet three thousand miles away and nearly twice as big as his own. He knew he was taking his professional life in his hands and that gentlemen abed in England were probably already blackguarding him for his prolonged dis-appearance. But he had weighed the chances carefully in the light of his professional knowledge. It he was wrong and the French had gone elsewhere, he promised the Admiralty he would be back by the end of June – before the enemy even knew he had crossed the Atlantic.

On the last day of June an unconvoyed merchantman from Dominica brought tidings to England that Villeneuve had reached Martinique on May 16th. It seemed that no harm had been done beyond an attack on the Diamond Rock, and Nelson was known to be in pursuit. But unlike the public, Lord Barham, the new First Lord of the Admiralty, a lifelong naval administrator, realized the significance of the news. For as soon as the fearful Villeneuve heard of Nelson's arrival in the West Indies he would be sure to sail with all speed for Europe. He would make either for the Channel or Cadiz. By the one he would threaten the British Isles, by the other the military expedition to Malta and the Mediterranean.

At that moment Cornwallis was holding Ganteaume's twenty-one battleships in Brest with twenty-two, Admiral Stirling Missiessy's returned five in Rochefort with an equal force, and Calder fourteen French and Spanish ships in Ferrol with twelve. Seven more British capital ships were in reserve in the Channel ports. Somewhere in the Atlantic Nelson's ten were in pursuit of Villeneuve's eighteen. A further eleven were on the West Indian stations, two were on their way there from Collingwood's squadron off Cadiz, and one lay on guard off Naples.

On July 7th Barham drew up a plan by which Cornwallis was to send ten battleships, or nearly half his force, to Collingwood. To guard against the risk of Villeneuve making for the Channel instead of Cadiz, Calder, having shown himself off Ferrol, was to stretch north-north-west across the Bay with a cloud of outlying frigates,

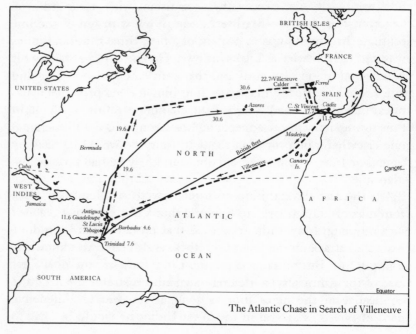

The Atlantic Chase in Search of Villeneuve

while Cornwallis, his depleted battle strength brought up to fifteen by three fresh vessels from England, was to cruise south-south-west from Ushant to meet him. If Villeneuve attempted to raise the blockade of either Ferrol or Brest, he would thus risk an encounter with twenty-seven capital ships – a force greatly superior to his own. Napoleon's idea that his Brest or Ferrol squadron would be able to join forces with Villeneuve at the crucial point and moment was based on a misunderstanding of naval warfare. For not only would it take time for the blockaded to discover that the blockaders had gone, but any wind favourable for the former would almost certainly be foul for the homecoming fleet.

But Barham's ingenious expedient was unnecessary. On the night of the 7th a sloop from the West Indies anchored at Plymouth with despatches from Nelson. All next day, while the Admiralty clerks were drafting the requisite orders, her commander, Captain Bettesworth, was posting up the Exeter road. Towards midnight his post-chaise rattled over the Charing Cross cobblestones and drew up at the Admiralty door. He brought urgent despatches from Nelson.

The story contained in Bettesworth's wallet was one of unrelenting pursuit, expectation, frustration and renewed pursuit. Nelson had covered the 3200 miles from the Straits to Barbados in little more than three weeks – an almost record average of 135 miles a day. Officers and men were on short allowance, but no one minded, for after two years of endurance and waiting they believed they were about to meet the enemy. 'We are all half starved,' wrote one of them, 'and otherwise much inconvenienced by being so long away from port, but our recompense is that we are with Nelson.'

At five o'clock on the afternoon of June 4th his fleet had reached Barbados. A fast sloop, sent ahead, had already brought news of its coming. Since Villeneuve's arrival three weeks before, the islands had been in a state of intense excitement. All through the night after his arrival, at the urgent entreaty of the local Commander-in-Chief, Nelson had embarked troops. By ten next morning he was on his way to Trinidad, taking with him two battleships of Cochrane's which he had found in the port. Five hours later he made the signal, 'Prepare for Battle'. As before the Nile every captain knew what was expected of him, for during the Atlantic crossing the tactics to be employed had been repeatedly discussed. No man could do wrong, the Admiral had told them, who laid his ship close on board the enemy and kept it there till the business was over. For though the Combined Fleet was nearly twice as large as his own, Nelson was confident he could annihilate it.

At Tobago, sighted on June 6th, there had been no word of the enemy. Brereton's intelligence had proved false. Without wasting an hour Nelson had put about for Grenada and the north. Next day he learnt that his unsuspecting quarry, having captured the Diamond Rock on June 3rd, had still been at Martinique on the 5th. Had he kept his course for that island – less than a hundred miles from Barbados – he would have encountered the man he had sailed so many miles to find.

Meanwhile Villeneuve had been in as great a state of apprehension as the planters he had come to ruin. On his arrival at Martinique on May 13th he had found that Missiessy had returned to France. Hoping daily for Ganteaume's appearance and the signal for his own return, he dared not commit himself to any major operation. On June 4th, after three thousand of his men had gone down with sickness, there arrived from France, not Ganteaume, but Magon with two battleships and orders to await the Brest Fleet for five more weeks and then, if there was still no sign of it, to sail for Ferrol, release the French and Spanish force held there by Calder, and with thirty-three sail of the line make for the Straits of Dover. There, he was assured, the Emperor would be waiting with the Grand Army.

As part of this terrifying programme Villeneuve was instructed to fill in his remaining time in the West Indies by capturing as many British islands as possible. With this intention he had sailed next day for Guadeloupe to embark troops for Barbuda, a small and, as he hoped easy, objective in the extreme north of the Leeward Islands. On his way there on June 8th, while Nelson was still three hundred miles to the south, he had had the fortune to encounter a small convoy of sugar ships off the west coast of Antigua. Capturing fourteen of them, he learnt to his consternation that his terrible pursuer had anchored off Barbados four days before. From that moment the risk of missing Ganteaume in mid-Atlantic became negligible to the French admiral compared with the infinitely more alarming risk of meeting Nelson. Ordering his frigates to take back the troops to Guadeloupe and rejoin him in the Azores, he sailed next morning for Spain and Ferrol.

When Nelson reached Antigua on the 12th he found that he was four days too late. Once more he was faced with the task of basing on a few fragmentary wisps of evidence a decision involving not only his career but the very existence of his country. If the French had gone to Jamaica and he did not follow them, Britain's richest colony would be lost; it they had gone to Europe, every ship would be needed in the Western Approaches or off Cadiz. Precipitate action would endanger the islands and the two hundred sugar ships he had saved by his timely arrival; yet delay might jeopardize England herself. He was put out of his agony, just as he was about to return to Dominica, by news that the French troops, taken a week before from Guadeloupe, were disembarking. This satisfied him that Villeneuve did not intend to attack Jamaica. His last doubts were removed a few hours later by the arrival of the *Netley* schooner which had been escorting the captured convoy. Powerless to defend his charges against eighteen sail of the line, her young captain had kept the enemy under observation as long as he could. When last seen the Combined Fleet, thirty-two strong, had been crowding away into the north-east.

Once Nelson was sure that his enemy had sailed for Europe, his course was clear. Whether they were bound for the Bay or for Cadiz and the Straits, the protection of his station was his prior duty. 'I am going towards the Mediterranean after Gravina and Villeneuve,' he wrote that night, 'and hope to catch them.' He had every hope of an action on the southern crossing, preferably close to the Straits where he could look for reinforcements. Yet even before the *Netley* had anchored in St John's Road, he had despatched the *Curieux* sloop under Captain Bettesworth for England. With her superior speed she would be able to raise the alarm at least a week before Villeneuve could molest the British squadrons in the Bay. Another cruiser Nelson sent direct to Calder off Ferrol.

At noon next day, June 13th, after little more than a week in the West Indies, he had sailed himself for Gibraltar.

*   *   *

The news Bettesworth brought to the Admiralty on the night of July 8th contained more than Nelson's despatches. On June 19th, 900 miles north-north-east of Antigua, he had sighted the Combined Fleet standing to the northward. Its course made it almost certain that its destination was the Bay. Roused from sleep early on the 9th, the First Lord, upbraiding his servants for not waking him sooner, dictated – Admiralty tradition has it while shaving – an order for strengthening the forces between Villeneuve and his goal. Like Nelson's his intention was purely offensive. The enemy was at sea and must be crippled before he could reach port. It was the only way to safeguard both Britain and the Mediterranean offensive.

On July 17th Nelson made his landfall at Cape St Vincent, having crossed the Atlantic in thirty-four days or a fortnight quicker than the less experienced Villeneuve. Next day he passed his old friend Collingwood blockading Cadiz and on the 19th anchored in Gibraltar Bay. Still cursing General Brereton, he went ashore for the first time in two years. He still had hopes that Villeneuve, labouring in the Atlantic behind him, might attempt to re-enter the Mediterranean. But he was coming to share Collingwood's belief that his enemy had gone to the northward.

On July 23rd, having revictualled his fleet at Tetuan, Nelson weighed again for the Atlantic. Two days later, while waiting for an easterly breeze off Tarifa, he received a copy of a Lisbon paper with an account of Captain Bettesworth's arrival in England. The wind at that moment freshening, he sailed in such haste that he left his washing behind. He did not even pause to exchange a word with Collingwood as he passed Cadiz. All the way north, delayed by headwinds on the Portuguese coast, he fretted lest the enemy should do his country some injury before he could arrive.

On the same day Napoleon reached Boulogne to take command of his invasion army. 'They little guess what is in store for them,' he wrote to his Minister of Marine, Decres. 'If we are masters of the Straits for twelve hours England is no more.' Only one thing was missing – Villeneuve's fleet. 'I can't make out why we have no news from Ferrol,' he added. 'I can't believe Magon never reached him. I am telling Ganteaume by telegraph to keep out in the Bertheaume Road.'

Yet the intelligence from Germany and Italy was too grave to be disregarded. Pitt's long-maturing plans for a new Coalition against France were coming to fruition; Austria plainly meant business; the Russian armies were marching south to her aid. Before leaving Paris Napoleon had dictated ultimatums to the Courts of Vienna and Naples threatening them with invasion unless all troop movement ceased immediately. They had still to be sent off, and on August 7th, still hoping that his fleets would arrive in time for him to cross the Channel, he ordered them to be held up a few days longer. At the same time he summoned the Imperial Guard to Boulogne.

Next day he countermanded the order. Nelson was reported from Cadiz to be back in Europe and to have been sailing north on July 25th. For once Napoleon was in two minds. His Foreign Minister, Talleyrand, convinced that he would have to face a superior British concentration in the Channel, was urging him not to risk a crossing. Yet the chance of destroying England, if not promptly taken, might pass for ever.

Then on the same day, August 8th, the Emperor learnt that Villeneuve had entered Vigo, claiming to have defeated Calder. He at once proclaimed a victory and sent him peremptory instructions to hurry north. Until the 13th his mind still seemed set on invasion. Then news arrived that Villeneuve, having reached Ferrol, had disregarded orders and entered the harbour. Beside himself with rage, Napoleon ordered an immediate military concentration against Austria. Yet, still hoping against hope, he dashed off letter after letter to Decres and his errant admiral, exhorting the latter at all costs to put to sea, brush aside the British naval forces in his way and enter the Channel. The army of invasion was waiting: only the Combined Fleet had still to fulfil its duty!

And on that very day, unknown to Napoleon, Villeneuve put to sea. No admiral ever sailed with a stronger sense of fear and doom. His ships were short of stores and water, their crews decimated by scurvy and dysentery, and the ill-trained Spaniards in a state of almost open mutiny. Before leaving Corunna Bay Villeneuve had sent out a frigate to find Allemand, whose squadron had left Rochefort in mid-July for a secret rendezvous with him off Finisterre. By a series of almost miraculous chances Allemand had hitherto evaded detection and was at that moment cruising between Ushant and Finisterre in search of Villeneuve. But the latter's frigate never reached him. On August 10th she fell in with a slightly smaller English cruiser, provocatively disguised as a sloop, and, on attacking, was captured with all hands. By the time the Combined Fleet reached the open sea, Allemand, having no word of it and finding the enemy everywhere, had left his station and run for Vigo.

The British squadrons were assembling automatically in the very path that Napoleon had ordered the hapless Villeneuve to tread. On August 9th, discovering that the Combined Fleet had contacted the French and Spanish ships in Ferrol, Calder had raised the blockade and hastened northwards. On the 14th he joined Cornwallis off Ushant, a few hours after Rear-Admiral Stirling had also come in with his division. And at six o'clock next evening the Channel Fleet, already twenty-seven sail of the line including ten three-deckers, was joined by Nelson with twelve more. For learning on the 13th, while bound for his Scillies rendezvous, that Ireland was safe, that officer had at once altered course to bring his fleet to Cornwallis.

It was what Villeneuve most feared. 'Your Lordship each night forms a part of his dreams,' Captain Bayntun wrote to Nelson. It was an obsession that transcended ordinary reason. For as he hurried from sea to sea and port to port on his pitiful five months' mission, the French admiral felt he was struggling against more than ordinary mortal strength and ingenuity. In Nelson this honourable, brave but mediocre man had encountered one of the great elemental forces of nature. Being a Frenchman, he had the imagination to see it.

In such a mood he left the shelter of Corunna Bay on August

13th with twenty-nine sail of the line and ten cruisers. Of the former fourteen were Spanish. Only one, the *Principe de Asturias*, was a three-decker. The crews were largely made up of landsmen and soldiers. 'Our naval tactics,' Villeneuve wrote to Decres, 'are antiquated, we know nothing but how to place ourselves in line, and that is just what the enemy wants.' The latter, he reported, was watching his every movement from the horizon; evasion was impossible. Forgetting his master's objurgation, he had already all but made up his mind to take his final option and seek refuge in Cadiz. For anything was better than to face the certain destruction lurking in the north.

Though he sailed on a north-easterly course, the French admiral never made any attempt to penetrate the British defences. At the first sight of a sail the entire fleet went about and continued on the opposite tack until the horizon was clear. Its only progress into the Bay was by night. Every hour, as it edged away from the dreaded north, it got farther into the west. There was no sign of Allemand; to reach Brest without a battle was impossible; at any moment Calder, and perhaps Nelson, might appear over the horizon. Far from dispersing the British the Grand Design, as Villeneuve had foreseen from the first, had concentrated them at the point where there was no avoiding them. A gale was blowing up from the north-east, his ships were ill-found, the soldiers and landsmen were seasick. As darkness fell on August 15th, he abandoned his enterprise and fled to Cadiz.

*　　*　　*

On August 18th 1805, Nelson anchored off Portsmouth in the *Victory*. Having chased Villeneuve for 14,000 miles and failed to find him, he was depressed and anxious about his reception. But the waiting crowds on the ramparts were cheering, and all the way to the capital the enthusiasm continued. Without knowing it the tired, ailing Admiral had become a legend. Forgotten during his long Mediterranean vigil and all but reviled when the French fleet escaped from Toulon, his dash to save the West Indies had caught the country's imagination. Once more, as in the old days before his passion for Lady Hamilton and his parting from his wife had sullied his fame, he was 'our hero of the Nile' – the wonderful Admiral whose name had swept England's foes from the seas. The unexpected popularity was like sunshine to him. As he walked down Piccadilly the people flocked about him: it was affecting, wrote an eye-witness, to see the wonder, admiration and love of every one, gentle and simple; 'it was beyond anything represented in a play or a poem of fame.'

On the evening of September 2nd the *Euryalus* frigate had brought the latest news from Cadiz. As she heaved to off the Needles Captain Blackwood went ashore to hire a chaise and four in Lymington. At five in the morning he stopped for a few minutes at Merton to see the most famous man in England. He found him already up and dressed. Like the rest of the world Nelson had been eagerly awaiting the tidings he brought. 'Depend on it, Blackwood,' he said, 'I shall yet give Mr Villeneuve a drubbing.' A few hours later he was receiving his charge at the Admiralty from the First Lord. At his first return Barham, who, scarcely knowing him, had distrusted his brightly-coloured reputation, had sent for his journals. But a few hours' perusal had resolved the old man's doubts. Nelson might be a junior admiral and unorthodox, but he was complete master of his calling. His right to return to his command – now of such supreme significance – was indisputable.

Nelson received the summons with quiet gladness. 'I hold myself ready to go forth whenever I am desired,' he wrote to George Rose, 'although God knows I want rest. But self is entirely out of the question.' His friends had never seen him so cheerful. In those last quiet days at Merton and in London, taking farewell of all he loved, he radiated hope and inspiration.

While Napoleon, his hopes of invading England thwarted, was planning under the chestnuts of St Cloud an immediate march of his army from Boulogne to the Danube to forestall the Austrian-Russian coalition which Pitt had mobilized against him, Nelson was bidding farewell to England. Much of his brief respite while the *Victory* was being made ready for sea he spent at the Admiralty, drawing up plans for his mission. Barham, who by now had completely surrendered to his fascination, offered him forty ships of the line and *carte blanche* to choose his officers. 'Choose yourself, my Lord,' the Admiral replied, 'the same spirit acuates the whole profession. You cannot choose wrong.'

Many saw him during those last days on his native soil. The painter, Haydon, watched him going into Dollond's near Northumberland House to buy a night glass – a diminutive figure with a green shade over one eye, a shabby, well-worn, cocked hat and a buttoned-up undress coat. The little Admiral 'with no dignity and a shock head' had captured the hearts of his countrymen at last: the challenging eye, the curving lip, the quick moods, the marks of exposure and battle struck deep into the popular imagination that autumn. Among those who met him was a young general, just returned from India, who was waiting for an interview in the Secretary of State's ante-room. The famous Admiral, conspicuous by his empty sleeve and patch-eye, at first tried to impress him by his histrionic address. But after a few minutes, sensing something in his expression, Nelson left the room and, ascertaining from the porter that he had been talking to Arthur Wellesley, he returned and discussed public affairs with such good sense and knowledge that this most unimpressionable of men confessed he had never had a more interesting conversation.

Yet the real core of Nelson was his absolute self-surrender. 'I have much to lose and little to gain,' he wrote to his friend Davison, 'and I go because it's right, and I will serve the country faithfully.' The shy, austere Prime Minister, William Pitt, who shared the same unselfish love, showed his recognition of it when, on the Admiral's farewell visit to Downing Street, he waited on him to his carriage – an honour he would not have paid a Prince of the Blood.

At half-past ten on the night of Friday, September 13th, after praying by the bedside of his child, Horatia, Nelson took his leave of Merton. 'May the great God whom I adore,' he wrote in his diary, 'enable me to fulfil the expectations of my country.' Then he drove through the night over the Surrey heaths and Hampshire hills to Portsmouth. He spent the morning at the George Inn transacting business, and at two o'clock, accompanied by Canning and George Rose, who were to dine with him, went off to the *Vic-*

tory. Near the bathing machines, which he had chosen in preference to the usual landing stage, a vast crowd was waiting to see him go. 'Many were in tears,' wrote Southey, 'and many knelt down before him and blessed him as he passed.'

On the following morning, Sunday the 15th, the *Victory* weighed, with the faithful Blackwood in attendance in the *Euryalus* frigate. All the way to the Scillies adverse weather continued; it was not till the 21st that the *Victory* cleared the soundings. Then with a northerly wind she ran swiftly across the Bay and down the Portuguese coast. By September 25th Nelson was off Lisbon, sending an urgent warning to the British Consul to conceal his coming from the public, and another to Collingwood to refrain from hoisting colours on his arrival.

In the Fleet they were waiting for him a little wearily. After the excitements and disappointments of the summer the prospect of another winter of close blockade was having a depressing effect. To make matters worse, Collingwood, the acting Commander-in-Chief, shunned society and seldom communicated with anyone. He himself confessed in his letters home, that he was worn to a lath with this perpetual cruising: his sole comfort his dog Bounce and the thought of his home in Northumberland – 'the oaks, the woodlands and the verdant meads.' For it was only when the guns began to sound that Collingwood grew inspired. 'Is Lord Nelson coming out to us again?' asked Captain Codrington. 'I anxiously hope he may be that I may once more see a Commander-in-Chief endeavouring to make a hard and disagreeable service as palatable to those serving under him as circumstances will admit of and keeping up by his example that animation so necessary for such an occasion . . . For charity's sake send us Lord Nelson, oh ye men of power!'

On September 28th the prayer was answered. As the *Victory* joined the Fleet the captains hurried aboard to greet the Admiral, forgetting everything in their enthusiasm. Their reception, Nelson told Lady Hamilton, caused the sweetest sensation of his life. 'He is so good and pleasant a man,' wrote Captain Duff on the *Mars*, a newcomer to his command, 'that we all wish to do what he likes without any kind of orders.' Codrington, who was also serving under him for the first time, spoke of the joy throughout the Fleet; everyone felt that his work would be appreciated and that nothing but the best would be good enough for such a commander. Soon every ship's company was busy painting in black and yellow bands after the old Mediterranean pattern and endeavouring to make her what the delighted Codrington called 'a dear Nelsonian – in all things perfect.'

For Nelson's task, as he made the Fleet aware, was to transform it into an instrument fit to do the service for which the country was waiting. Less than a third of its twenty-nine battleships had been with him in the Mediterranean. Of the remainder most, for all their companies' staunch virtues and wonderful skill, fell a little short of that flawless discipline, training and spirit which he expected of those who sailed with him. If he was to annihilate a superior enemy he knew he had to crowd into a few brief weeks, and perhaps only days, the teaching of years. And he had to school the captains, not of a mere squadron, but of the Navy itself, a third of whose fighting strength was now gathered under his command.

But Nelson in those autumn weeks of 1805 was a man exalted. On the two days after his arrival – the first of them his forty-seventh birthday – he entertained his flag officers and captains to dinner, and, as he laid before them his plans for destroying the enemy, an electric current ran through them.

Some who listened at the long table were strangers: others were old friends like Collingwood who had shared with him 'a brotherhood of more than thirty years'. But all were welded that night into one by the magic of the Nelson spirit and ritual: the gleaming silver and mahogany, the stately music, the cheerful, courtly hospitality, the friendliness and consideration, the sense which ran through all of sharing in a great adventure. Jealousy, sulking, backbiting – maladies that long confinement in over-crowded ships easily bred – could not survive in such an atmosphere.

Consciously or unconsciously Nelson in those last weeks off Cadiz was fashioning a tradition and a legend which was to be of priceless service to England. He reminded the Navy that, whatever the bonds of authority, leadership was not a mere matter of transmitting orders but of evoking the will to serve. It was this which, as an officer said, double-manned every ship in the line. Nelson was essentially a humanitarian who, wooing men to duty, trusted them and had the imagination to see into their hearts. By his reckoning the best disciplinarian was he who most loved and understood men, who remembered that they were human and treated them accordingly. One of his first acts was to order that the names and families of all killed and wounded should be reported to him for transmission to the Chairman of the Patriotic Fund and that an account of every man's case should accompany him to hospital.

All the while that he was inspiring others with cheerfulness and resolution Nelson's own heart was pining for the home which he had barely seen and for the woman and child from whom he had so long been parted. On the second night after he entertained his captains to dinner he was seized by a dreadful spasm. 'The good people of England will not believe,' he wrote, 'that rest of body and mind is necessary to me.' To comfort Emma, he told her that the brief days of happiness at Merton were only a foretaste of greater happiness.

But even as he wrote he knew that what he had come to do precluded the probability of return. To secure his country and make her victory certain – whether now or in the more distant future – he had to destroy the great concentration lying before him in the inner harbour of Cadiz. The chance would probably never occur again and, when it came, a few brief hours of opportunity would be all he could hope to snatch from the gods of wind and tide. In that day with a force of less than thirty ships of the line – a few more, perhaps, if the promises given him in England could be made good – he would have to shatter, burn and blast a superior enemy fighting with the courage of desperation. Before him in Cadiz were perhaps thirty-five or thirty-six sail of the line including the three most powerful ships in the world. At Cartagena, two days distant, were six more. And to maintain his fleet on that inhospitable coast he was under the necessity of sending it in detachments to provision and water in the Straits. Almost his earliest act had been to dispatch a first instalment of six battleships under

Rear-Admiral Louis, thus reducing his fighting strength to twenty-three.

For the menace created by the union of the French and Spanish fleets still remained – a standing challenge to England's strained resources. To keep the Fleet throughout the winter on that exposed and treacherous shore was almost impossible. Yet at the least easing of the blockade the enemy might escape either in a body through the Straits, so imperilling the whole Mediterranean position, or in detachments into the Atlantic to harry trade and the colonies.

Still graver, in Nelson's view, was the risk of Villeneuve running for the Mediterranean. His statesman's instinct warned him that Napoleon, having failed to cross the Channel, would again, as in '98, turn eastwards and try to conquer the world by breaking the ring of British sea power at its weakest point – in the Levant. When Nelson left England no news had been received of the arrival at Malta of an expedition under General Craig which was to take part in an Anglo-Russian offensive in the Sicilian Straits. France and Russia were still nominally at peace, and Austria, though mobilizing, had not declared war. Yet the explosion might occur at any moment, and Nelson knew that when it did Napoleon would try to forestall the Allies in Sicily. That he would use Villeneuve and his great concentration at Cadiz to further his purpose seemed certain.

Nelson therefore withdrew his inshore squadron from before Cadiz and moved his fleet fifty miles out into the Atlantic where he could both guard against a surprise from the north and control the entrance to the Straits without the risk of being prematurely blown through them. The task of watching the enemy he left to Blackwood's frigates and a linking division of his faster seventy-fours, which maintained hourly communications by flag and gun signals. By withdrawing over the horizon he hoped to tempt Villeneuve out.

And unknown to the British, Villeneuve was already preparing for sea. On September 27th he had received Napoleon's order to sail for Cartagena and Naples. Anxious to recover his relentless master's esteem, he had at once ordered his captains to make ready. But on October 2nd, just as they were about to sail to 'strike down England's tyrannical dominion of the seas', rumours reached Cadiz of Nelson's arrival and of his plan to attack. Immediately the port was in a tumult; the order to sail was suspended and all hands were diverted to arming a harbour guard of gunboats. At a Council of War on October 7th, though an easterly breeze offered a chance of entering the Straits before the British could engage, it was resolved, after heated debate, to disobey Napoleon's orders. The French and Spanish admirals were brave men, but they had no wish to commit suicide. And to sail with Nelson in the offing, they reckoned, was suicide.

*   *   *

With Villeneuve's failure to use the east wind, hopes of a fight fell very low in the Fleet off Cadiz. Only Nelson, buoyed up by some inner sense of impending events, remained convinced that the enemy would put to sea. And on the very day that Villeneuve and his admirals were debating Napoleon's orders, Nelson's belief became a certainty. For the *Royal Sovereign* arrived from England after a refit with news that war had broken out in Europe and that Craig's army intended to protect Sicily was on the point of leaving for Malta. The British Fleet, after securing the enemy in Cadiz, was ordered to cover his landing. Nelson now knew that Villeneuve or his successor would have to sail and what course he would take. The fate of Sicily, of the Mediterranean, of Pitt's new European coalition and, in the last resort, of England would be decided by a naval engagement at the mouth of the Straits.

For that ordeal – now imminent – Nelson summoned up all his art. The problem was to annihilate, for only annihilation would serve. He had never been content with the classic conception of a naval victory: an ordered cannonade in long, laboriously formed lines of battle in which the French, receiving an attack from windward were always able to withdraw, occasionally leaving a few prizes in British hands. A disciple of the great eighteenth-century pioneers who had first had the courage to defy the Admiralty's Fighting Instructions and break the formal line of battle, and a lifelong student of naval tactics, Nelson had long wrestled with the problem of how to transform limited into decisive victory. As a Commodore at Cape St Vincent, and then in his first independent command at the Nile, he had pointed the way. But never till now had he directed a major fleet in battle in the open sea.

On October 9th, two days after his new orders reached him, he issued instructions to his flag officers and captains. He had already outlined them verbally in those two dramatic evenings in the *Victory*'s cabin. He now committed them formally to writing. The problem, as he saw it, was to bring such crushing force against a portion of the enemy's line as to overwhelm it and to do so in time to destroy the remainder before night fell. 'To make the business decisive, I have made up my mind . . . that the Order of Sailing is to be the Order of Battle.' In other words, not only was the classical line of battle to be discarded in the heat of the fight, as it had been in earlier engagements, but it was never to be formed at all.

The spirit of the offensive was implicit in every line of Nelson's Memorandum. So was his genius. Attack was to be made in two divisions, one of which was to immobilize the enemy's van by a feint while the other broke and destroyed his rear and centre. No time was to be wasted in manoeuvring for position, for with the brief October days and the uncertain winds of that region none could be spared. Instead the approach was to be made by whatever course would most quickly bring the fleet to gunshot of the enemy's centre. Then one division under Collingwood was to break the enemy's line at about the twelfth ship from the rear, while the other, under Nelson's immediate command, after keeping the enemy's van in the maximum uncertainty as to its intentions by hovering to windward till it was too late to succour the rear, was to fall on the centre.

Nelson was confident of his ability to defeat the enemy. 'I will give them such a shaking,' he told Blackwood, 'as they have never yet experienced; at least I will lay down my life in the attempt.' But he was growing increasingly anxious lest the reinforcements promised from England should not arrive in time to achieve complete annihilation. Others, however, were straggling in as fast as Barham could dispatch them from the dockyards, and on the 13th the *Agamemnon* showed over the horizon with his old flag-captain,

Berry, in command. 'Now we shall have a fight,' Nelson cried.

The newcomer brought the immediate strength under his flag to twenty-seven of the line including seven three-deckers. Yet the ships in Cadiz harbour continued to lie at their moorings. On the 17th the wind veered into the east again; the Combined Fleet could not have finer weather for sea. But still there was no sign of life from the bare forest of masts beyond the low thin strip of the isthmus.

Yet within the port, unknown to the blockaders, the enemy was stirring. On October 11th, four days after the Council of War had decided not to fight, news arrived that Rosily was on his way to take over command and was already at Madrid. The idea of being superseded with a stigma of cowardice upon him was more than Villeneuve could bear. He knew that Louis was in the Straits: he did not yet know that reinforcements had arrived from England, for Nelson had been careful to conceal them. He therefore estimated British capital strength at twenty-three to his own thirty-three, with an equal number of three-deckers on either side. Of these one, the Spanish *Santissima Trinidad*, carried 130 guns, and two others 112 guns against the 100 guns of the largest British ships.

At six o'clock on the morning of Saturday October 19th, the *Sirius*, Blackwood's nearest frigate inshore, gave the longed-for signal. 'Enemy have their topsail yards hoisted.' An hour later the first ships were reported coming out of the harbour. At half-past nine Nelson received the news fifty miles out in the Atlantic. At once the signal was hoisted for a 'General Chase', followed soon afterwards by 'Prepare for Battle'. All day the British fleet stood towards the Straits under a clear sky with a north-easterly wind, intending to catch Villeneuve at the entrance to the Gut. Though during the afternoon the wind began to drop, the enemy's fleet was reported at sea. 'How would your heart beat for me, dearest Jane,' wrote Codrington to his wife, 'did you but know that we are now under every stitch of sail we can set, steering for the enemy.'

And just as Nelson was about to beat back to his old station for fear of being driven by the south-wester through the Straits, word came from the frigates that Villeneuve was still at sea to the northward and that a group of his ships had just been sighted in some confusion off Cadiz lighthouse. The Combined Fleet's seamanship had proved unequal to the task of getting out of the harbour in a single tide. But the ships were still coming out. Nelson, therefore, after giving orders to wear and stand to the north-west, called Collingwood aboard for consultation. Yet, though he listened to his eager advice to attack at once, he refused to do so. For, if he was to gain the victory on which he counted, he knew that he must let his foe get farther away from port. He dared not trust his courage with a bolt-hole.

Later in the day, when the British fleet had reached a point some twenty-five miles to the south-west of Cadiz, there was an improvement in the weather, and visibility became clearer. At one moment, owing to the continued confusion of the enemy's ships – it was not till midday that they were all clear of harbour – there was an alarm that they were trying to get to the westward. But Nelson, with his strong strategic grasp, refused to believe it, especially as the wind was steadily shifting into the west. He continued on his course, watching the enemy over the rim of the horizon through the eyes of his frigates. During the afternoon he spent some time on the poop talking to his midshipmen; 'this day or tomorrow,' he remarked, 'will be a fortunate one for you, young gentlemen.' Later he entertained some of them at dinner, promising that he would give them next day something to talk and think about for the rest of their lives.

* * *

October 21st 1805 dawned calm and splendid. There was a faint wind out of the west-north-west and a heavy swell rolling in from the Atlantic towards Cape Trafalgar and the Gut of Gibraltar. The British fleet was about twenty miles off the Spanish coast; the enemy nine miles away to the south-east still steering towards the Straits. The supreme moment of Nelson's life had come. The whole horizon, clear after the low clouds of yesterday, was filled with Villeneuve's ships.

Having summoned the frigate captains aboard, Nelson, a little after six, gave the signal to form order of sailing in two columns.

Shortly afterwards the signal 'Prepare for Action' was made. And the heavy ground swell and his seaman's instinct warned him that, though at the moment the wind was dropping, a gale from the Atlantic was imminent. When Blackwood came aboard at eight o'clock to congratulate Nelson on his good fortune, he found him, for all his cheerful spirits and calm bearing, deeply intent on the enemy's direction and formation. The Admiral's thoughts were running, not on victory but on the possibilities of the foe's escaping. He told Blackwood to be ready to use his frigates in the latter stages of the fight to complete the work of destruction and not to think of saving ships or men. For his end, he kept stressing, was annihilation, not prizes.

There was little need for signals, for almost everything had been determined in advance. Collingwood's Lee Division which, in accordance with the Admiral's Memorandum, was to attack the enemy rear, was on a port line of bearing steering to cut the line at a point from twelve to sixteen ships ahead of the last ship. Nelson with the Weather Division was steering a slightly more northerly course towards the centre and – since the enemy's line was moving as well as his own – aiming at a point some two miles ahead of his leading ship. It was a wonderful sight, and Codrington in the *Orion* called up his lieutenants to see it: the Combined Fleet straggling like a forest of canvas across five miles of sea, its bright, many-coloured hulls, and the scarlet and white *Santissima Trinidad* towering up in the midst. Many of the enemy ships were doubling each other in their confusion and, instead of forming a straight line of battle, were tending to move in a wide crescent with its arc to leeward. By comparison the two British divisions, though strung out a little in their haste, looked, with their black and yellow painted hulls, grim and forbidding.

About nine o'clock, with the fleets still several miles apart, Nelson made an inspection of the *Victory*. Dressed in his threadbare, storm-stained admiral's frock-coat with the stars of his four Orders sewn on the left breast and accompanied by the frigate captains, he made the tour of the low, half-lit decks and the long curving lines of guns. The crews, stripped to the waists, waited with the alert silence of the Navy's age-long ritual, but here and there a whispered aside or a legend chalked on a gun revealed their mood. Walking swiftly, Nelson occasionally stopped to speak to the men at their quarters, repeating the old counsel that they were to hold their fire till they were sure of their object. Once he tapped a powder monkey on the shoulder and warned him to take off his shirt lest a spark should set it alight. Only when he reached the quarterdeck ladder to the poop did the pent-up emotion of the ship's company break in a great cheer. He stood there for a moment, with his emaciated figure and lined face, looking down on his men.

The wind was gradually failing and shifting into the west, and the pace of the British fleet slackened from three to two knots. But it was still gaining on the French and Spaniards who, from their thickening line and resolute bearing as they forged, close-hauled, slowly to the north-north-west, clearly meant to make a fight of it. Blackwood, seeing that the flagship from her leading position would be unduly singled out for attack, suggested the propriety of letting one or two ships go ahead as was usual in line of battle. With a rather grim smile Nelson assented and ordered the *Temeraire* and *Leviathan* to pass the *Victory*. But, as the *Victory* continued to carry every stitch of sail she possessed, and as neither Captain Hardy nor Nelson would consent to shorten it, her consorts made little headway.

About an hour before the time when the opposed lines seemed likely to converge, Nelson left the poop and retired to his dismantled cabin. Here Pasco, the flag-lieutenant, coming in with a message, found him on his knees composing the prayer which was part of his legacy to England:

'May the Great God whom I worship grant to my Country, and for the benefit of Europe in general, a great and glorious Victory; and may humanity after Victory be the predominant feature in the British Fleet. For myself, individually, I commit my life to Him who made me, and may His blessing light upon my endeavours for serving my Country faithfully. To Him I resign myself and the just cause which is entrusted to me to defend.' Afterwards he made a codicil to his will, committing his child and Lady Hamilton to his country's keeping, and got Blackwood to witness it.

Shortly after Nelson reappeared on the poop, land was sighted.

At first, since the fleet had been sailing for several days on a dead reckoning, it was thought to be Cadiz, and the admiral, fearful lest the enemy should escape, signalled that he would go through the end of the line to cut off their retreat. A few minutes later it was identified as Cape Trafalgar, and he reverted to his original plan. The *Victory* was now closing towards the centre of the enemy's van where the *Santissima Trinidad* and the French flagship, *Bucentaure*, towered up among their fellows. There was no desultory firing at long range, and it became plain that the enemy was holding himself in for a grim fight.

After signalling to make 'all possible sail', Nelson remarked to Pasco that he would amuse the fleet with a signal. 'I wish to say Nelson confides that every man will do his duty.' After a brief consultation about the capacity of Popham's code, this was altered to 'England expects.' Soon after it had been hoisted, and just as the first ranging shot from the *Fougueus* ploughed up the water in front of the *Royal Sovereign*, No. 16 – 'Engage the Enemy more closely' – was seen flying at the *Victory*'s masthead where it remained till it was shot away.

The advance was over: the battle about to begin. The British fleet had been brought in accordance with the terms of Nelson's Memorandum 'nearly within gunshot of the enemy's centre'. The time had now come for the Lee Division to fall on his rear while Nelson prevented the van from coming to its aid. Judging that the disproportion of force and the enemy's inversed sailing order justified a modification of his original instructions, Collingwood decided to cut the line at the sixteenth instead of the twelfth ship from the rear. He thus set his fifteen battleships to engage not an inferior but a superior force. But he relied on British gunnery and discipline to give him the necessary ascendancy. Nelson approved, for as the *Royal Sovereign* bore down under a hail of fire on the great black hull of the *Santa Ana*, he cried out, 'See how that noble fellow Collingwood carries his ship into action!' The latter, who, a few minutes before had been muttering, 'I wish Nelson would stop signalling; we know well enough what we have to do,' was now feeling the exaltation which always came to him in the hour of danger. 'No dodging and manoeuvring,' he wrote afterwards in ecstatic recollection. 'They formed their line with nicety and waited for our attack with great composure. Our ships were fought with a degree of gallantry that would have warmed your heart. Everybody exerted themselves, and a glorious day they made it.'

The fight between the Lee Division and the enemy's rear began just before midday. At eight minutes past twelve, after enduring the fire of six French and Spanish ships for nearly a

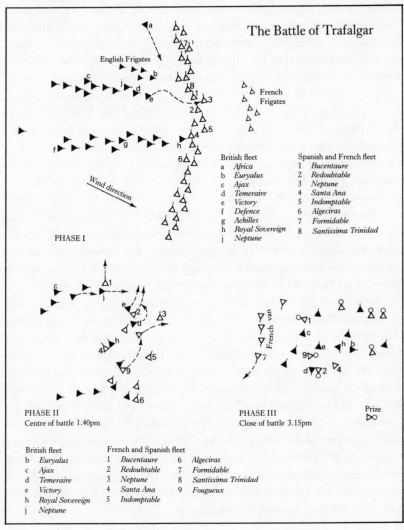

The Battle of Trafalgar

English Frigates

French Frigates

Wind direction

PHASE I

British fleet		Spanish and French fleet	
a	Africa	1	Bucentaure
b	Euryalus	2	Redoubtable
c	Ajax	3	Neptune
d	Temeraire	4	Santa Ana
e	Victory	5	Indomptable
f	Defence	6	Algeciras
g	Achilles	7	Formidable
h	Royal Sovereign	8	Santissima Trinidad
j	Neptune		

French van

PHASE II
Centre of battle 1.40pm

PHASE III
Close of battle 3.15pm

Prize

British fleet		French and Spanish fleet		
b	Euryalus	1	Bucentaure	6 Algeciras
c	Ajax	2	Redoubtable	7 Formidable
d	Temeraire	3	Neptune	8 Santissima Trinidad
e	Victory	4	Santa Ana	9 Fougueux
h	Royal Sovereign	5	Indomptable	
j	Neptune			

453

quarter of an hour, the *Royal Sovereign* broke the line, discharging as she did so one broadside into the bows of the *Fougueux*. Then she ran alongside her, with the muzzles of the guns almost touching, and simultaneously engaged the *Indomptable* to leeward, evoking from the watching Nelson a slap of the thigh and a shout of, 'Bravo! Bravo! what a glorious salute!'

By now it was half-past twelve, and the *Victory* had opened fire on the enemy's centre. For the first half hour Nelson had been performing his essential task of containing and deceiving the French van while the Lee Division did its work. He had been steering to close with the *Santissima Trinidad*, the eleventh ship in the line, meaning to break through between her and the *Bucentaure*, two ships in rear. But while he did so he retained his option of ranging up to the enemy's advanced ships, keeping their flag-officer, Rear-Admiral Dumanoir, in a state of impotent uncertainty till the last possible moment. At one time he made a feint of hauling out towards them, eliciting from Codrington the tribute, 'How beautifully the Admiral is carrying his design into effect.' Then, when it was too late for Dumanoir to save the rear, he turned again to starboard and opened fire on the cluster of great ships in the centre which he had marked as his special prey. At this point he threw prudence to the winds and, bearing up so as to pass under the lee of the *Bucentaure*, ran straight at the enemy's line, bringing down upon the *Victory*'s bows the fire of hundreds of guns.

Because of the obtuse re-entering angle at which the enemy's van was sailing, Nelson's approach, instead of being oblique like Collingwood's, had of necessity far more of the perpendicular in it than normal discretion allowed. But, having served his primary purpose, his object was now to get alongside the enemy as quickly as possible and complete the work of destruction before it was too late. He did so regardless of his own safety and left the rest of his Division to scramble into the fight as best it could. For, with the short October afternoon beginning to run, there was not a second to lose. As Blackwood left him to warn each captain to take whatever course he thought fit to get quickly into action, Nelson wrung his hand and bade him farewell. 'God bless you, Blackwood,' he said, 'I shall never speak to you again.'

When Villeneuve saw the British flagship's sudden turn he knew that his hour had come. Never, he wrote after the battle, had he seen anything like the irresistible line of the British approach. But the final charge of the *Victory*, closely supported by the *Neptune* and *Temeraire*, was something he could not have conceived had he not actually witnessed it. It unnerved him. In sudden desperation he hoisted the signal for every ship not engaged to get into action without delay but failed to give the specific order to Dumanoir to tack and come to the aid of his encircled rear and centre.

At 12.40 p.m. the *Victory*, within musket-shot of the French flagship, put her helm to port and steered for the stern of the *Bucentaure*. The line was at this point so close that the *Redoubtable*'s jib boom was actually touching her leader's taffrail. Puzzled, the flag-captain asked the Admiral which of the two ships he should run down, only to receive the reply, 'Take your choice, Hardy, it does not much signify which.' As the *Victory* passed astern of the *Bucentaure* her mainyard, rolling with the swell, touched the vangs of the Frenchman's gaff; then with a terrific explosion her port broadside opened, while the forecastle carronade, raking the crowded deck, swept down a hundred of his crew. A moment later she ran aboard the *Redoubtable* and broke the line. Behind her the *Temeraire*, *Neptune*, *Leviathan* and *Conqueror*, supported by *Britannia*, *Ajax* and *Agamemnon*, followed in quick succession.

By one o'clock the centre as well as the rear of the Franco-Spanish line was a mass of flame and billowing smoke. For nearly a mile between the two British flagships the ridge of fire and thunder continued. Codrington who, taking advantage of Nelson's order, had hauled out of line to starboard to reach the fight by the shortest route, calmly reserving his fire as he did so till he found an object worthy of it, described 'that grand and awful scene' – the falling masts, the ships crowded together, the broadsides crashing into blazing timbers at point blank range as rival boarding parties vainly sought an opportunity. For this was a sea battle of a pattern never previously attempted – more terrifying and more decisive. In the *Victory*, his mizzen topmast shot away, her wheel broken, and her sails torn to shreds, the decks were swept continuously by rifle fire from the *Redoubtable*'s tops, while every now and then a broadside from the *Bucentaure* or the *Santissima Trinidad* struck home with terrific force. A single shot killed eight marines on the poop. Another, narrowly missing Nelson, flung his secretary, a mangled heap of spurting blood, at his feet. 'This is too warm work, Hardy,' he said, 'to last long.' Down in the crowded cockpit the scene of horror was so awful that the chaplain, Scott, could bear it no longer and stumbled up the companion-ladder slippery with gore, for a breath of fresh air. There, 'all noise, confusion and smoke,' he saw Nelson fall.

As they bore him down, his shoulder, lung and spine shot through and his golden epaulette driven deep into his body, the Admiral covered the stars on his breast with his blood-soaked handkerchief lest his men should see and be discouraged. 'They have done for me at last, Hardy,' he said. In the cockpit gasping from pain and exhaustion, he told the surgeon in broken sentences that he was past help. Five minutes later, as he lay there in the blinding darkness, the *Bucentaure*'s last mast fell, and Villeneuve, 'a very tranquil, placid, English-looking Frenchman, wearing a long-tailed uniform coat and green corduroy pantaloons,' sought for someone to whom he might surrender. A marine officer with five men from the *Conqueror* went aboard the French flagship to take him, while the British Admiral was being stripped of his clothes and covered with a sheet that the surgeon might probe his wound. As each French and Spanish ensign fluttered down, rounds of cheering broke from the *Victory*'s gundecks, faintly audible amid the cries and groans of the cockpit. 'It is nonsense, Mr Burke,' Nelson whispered to the purser who bent over to fan him and give him water, 'to suppose that I can live. My sufferings are great but they will soon be over.'

By five minutes past two, little more than two hours after firing began, the action in the centre was all but done. Eight French and Spanish ships had been beaten out of the fight by five British, and, despite the heroism of their officers and crews, three after suffering appalling losses had been forced to surrender. About the same time, the *Santa Ana* struck to the *Royal Sovereign* in the Lee Division. Half an hour later the number that had yielded had increased to five, while seven more were isolated and doomed.

About this time, after repelling the last despairing attempt to board by the survivors of the shattered *Redoubtable*, Hardy went below in response to the Admiral's repeated inquiries. He found him in great pain and weakness but with a mind still intent on the progress of the battle. 'I hope none of our ships have struck, Hardy,' he said when he had been told of his captures.

'No, my Lord, there is no fear of that!'

'I am a dead man, Hardy. I am going fast; it will be all over with me soon. Come nearer to me. Pray let my dear Lady Hamilton have my hair and all other things belonging to me.'

About three-thirty the fight flared up again as Dumanoir's squadron stood down to rescue the last French and Spanish ships resisting in the centre and rear. But the *Victory*, calling a few un-damaged consorts around her, barred the way. As her starboard guns opened fire, Nelson, clinging vainly to life, murmured, 'Oh, *Victory*, how you distract my poor brain!' Within twenty minutes the counter-attack had failed, and three more prizes had fallen to the British Weather Division. On this Hardy again went below and congratulated the Admiral on his victory, telling him that fourteen or fifteen enemy ships had surrendered. 'That is well,' whispered Nelson, 'but I had bargained for twenty.' Then the prescient mind of the great sailor, reverting to the thoughts of the morning and that steady, ominous swell out of the west, began once more to range ahead. 'Anchor, Hardy, anchor!' he cried with a sudden spasm of energy. Afterwards he begged the captain not to throw his body overboard, bade him take care of Lady Hamilton and his child, and, with some flash of childhood's tenderness battling against the delirium of pain, asked him to kiss him.

After Hardy had left, the Admiral began to sink fast. His voice became very low and his breathing oppressed. His mind now seemed to be running on his private life. 'Remember,' he told the chaplain, Scott, who was rubbing his chest to ease his pain, 'that I leave Lady Hamilton and my daughter Horatia as a legacy to my country.' 'I have not,' he said a minute later, 'been a *great* sinner,

Doctor.' But towards the end he reverted to the battle, now dying around him. 'Thank God,' he kept repeating, 'I have done my duty.' About the same time Dumanoir called off his four last uncaptured ships and hauled out of the fight. A quarter of an hour later the Spaniard Gravina, mortally wounded, hoisted the signal to retire and withdrew towards Cadiz with ten crippled ships, leaving the remainder in the victors' hands. As he did so, Nelson's spirit passed and became 'one with England and the sea.'

CHAPTER EIGHTEEN

Neptune's Generals

'Napoleon's plan was always to try to give a great battle, gain a great victory, patch up a peace, such a peace as might leave an opening for a future war, and then hurry back to Paris. We starved him out. We showed him that we wouldn't let him fight a battle at first except under disadvantages. If you do fight, we shall destroy you; if you do not fight, we shall in time destroy you still.'

Wellington

ON THE NIGHT OF NOVEMBER 5th 1805, amid thick fog, blazing flambeaux and shouting coachmen, the news of Trafalgar reached London. Woken at two o'clock on the morning of November 6th by Collingwood's dispatches, Pitt could not compose himself to sleep again, but rose for the day's work. Outside, as the whisper spread, men recoiled from the shock; the turnpike keepers called out to early travellers to ask whether they had heard the bad news. 'The Combined Fleet is defeated,' was the universal cry, 'but Nelson is no more!' Down at Swanbourne the Fremantle household was startled from its rustic calm by the maid Nelly's ghastly look as she came in with the tale; little Emma Edgcumbe, at the words, fell senseless at her nurse's feet as though shot. The Prince of Wales was so affected that he could not leave the Royal Pavilion at Brighton. Even the hard-boiled underwriters at Lloyds burst into tears when the proclamation was read.

Thus it was that the greatest naval victory of all time was not so much celebrated as mourned. It took time before men could realize its meaning. The very mob forswore its customary night of jubilation and blazing windows. 'What,' they cried, 'light up because Nelson is killed!' 'This glorious dear-bought victory,' ran the typical comment in a young lady's diary, 'twenty ships for a hero!' Only a few saw from the first what the great admiral had achieved in his death. 'How truly he has accomplished his prediction that when they met it must be to extermination,' wrote Lady Bessborough. 'He could not have picked out a finer close to such a life. Do you know, it makes me feel almost as much envy as compassion; I think I should like to die so.' 'He was above pity!' wrote another, 'he died as he always wished to do in the arms of Victory after driving our Foes by the bare sound of his name from the farthest part of the earth back to their own ports.' To his old friend Minto, his splendid death seemed indeed the last favour Providence could bestow – a seal and security for all the rest.

Within a few days, too, men with their minds set on the ephemeral were seeing in Trafalgar a quick way to liberate Europe. 'The news from Cadiz,' wrote Lord Auckland, 'came like a cordial to fainting men'; old Admiral Roddam declared that it made every one alive again. A week later England learnt how on November 4th Richard Strachan, searching for Allemand off the Spanish coast, had encountered Dumanoir's four battleships flying from Trafalgar and captured all by nightfall. As Charles Paget wrote, it made the smash complete. Patriots began to pore over the map of Europe as they marked the progress of the armies with wafers stuck on pins; good wives reckoned that they might yet live to see 'that monster humbled in the dust.'

For the tide of defeat, it was felt, had been turned; courage could still redeem all things. On November 9th, after an unwonted popular triumph in which his carriage was drawn by cheering crowds through the streets, the Prime Minister spoke at the Lord Mayor's Banquet. Toasted as the saviour of Europe, he replied in the shortest speech of his career. 'Europe,' he told that glittering audience, 'is not to be saved by any single man. England has saved herself by her exertions and will, I trust, save Europe by her example.'

But though England's supremacy on the oceans was beyond dispute, it seemed that Napoleon was invincible on land. In October, Nelson's victory was almost paralleled at Ulm on the Danube, when after a lightning dash from the Channel, Napoleon surrounded the Austrian General Mack, compelling him to surrender with 70,000 men. In the face of Napoleon's speed, Austrian incompetence, Russian recklessness, Prussian greed and treachery, the intransigence of the Swedes, the servility of the Germans and rumours put about on the London Stock Exchange that the Austrian Emperor had capitulated – in the face of all this, Pitt stood firm. For it was his unshakeable belief, a belief that made him so representative a leader of his countrymen, that Britain had only to stand firm against the tyrant for his power, one day, now or in the future, to break before the forces of human decency.

Pitt's real test, and England's, was the hour when hopes proved liars. At the end of December the axe fell. The combined Austrian and Russian armies under the veteran General Kutusov were defeated at Austerlitz outside Vienna. It was one of Napoleon's most dazzling and daring victories. 'Soldiers,' he addressed the victors, 'you are the first warriors of the world! Thousands of ages hence it will be told how a Russian army, hired by the gold of England, was annihilated by you on the plains of Olmutz.' Pitt waited at Bath for confirmation of the news and for his agonizing gout, now constantly torturing him, to subside. Suddenly he resolved to attend Parliament if he possibly could, and arrived at his villa on Putney Heath on January 11th 1806. As he passed down the passage to his room, now knowing the magnitude of the defeat of his plans, he whispered to his niece, Lady Hester Stanhope, to roll up the large map of Europe hanging on the wall, saying that it would not be needed for ten years. Save to take the air in his carriage two days later, he never left the house, and declined rapidly over the next month. Though during various visits from friends the flame of buoyant life returned, he collapsed when he was left alone. 'The constitution is gone; it won't rally,' wrote his doctor, Sir Walter Farquhar from the stricken house on February 21st, 'I do not see a ray of hope. The battle of Austerlitz and its consequences are not cordials.' The following afternoon he became delirious, and all through the night his nephew and biographer Stanhope, watching by his side, heard the journeyings of his mind, worn out like his body in the service of his country. At half past two on the morning of the 23rd he grew silent and still. 'Shortly afterwards,' wrote Stanhope, 'with a much clearer voice than he spoke in before, and in a tone I shall never forget, he exclaimed, "Oh, my country! how I leave my country!"' From that time forward he neither spoke nor moved.

* * *

'Mr Pitt died this morning!' 'Mr Pitt died this morning at half-past four!' The news spread through the awakening streets of the capital in widening circles. 'Pitt is no more!' 'Mr Pitt is dead!' Arthur Young recorded in his journal. For twenty-three years this man, still only on the threshold of middle age, had been the greatest figure in England, and for all but three of those years Prime Minister. Never again would his countrymen see the eager, gaunt, imperious face and hear those deep, bell-like tones, embodying, for all his errors, the very front and voice of England. 'Now all is void and blank,' wrote Lord Aberdeen, 'in whom can we put our trust?' 'Shocked?' declared his rival, Fox; 'it feels as if something was missing in the world.'

For the remainder of the War, England would be governed largely through Pitt's legacy. Fox, now immensely the most impressive Parliamentary figure, was for a time effective leader of the government. This giant of a man – the 'incomparable Charley' to his devoted followers – was still anathema to half the nation. 'I could name you,' wrote Francis Horner, 'gentlemen with good coats on and good sense in their own affairs who believe that Fox *did* actually send information to the enemy in America and *is* actually in the pay of France.' Yet during the worst days of that terrible autumn Lady Bessborough found him the one person who could comfort her; things were bad, he said, but so long as the government remained stout, all was not lost.

For Fox was too big for political definition; too full and whole a man, as Horne Tooke said, to be consistent, and too content and wise to be a failure. At one moment he would enrage opponents and antagonize moderate men by his partisanship, at another outrage his own followers by some spontaneous act of magnanimity. Whatever he did, he did with his whole heart; so impetuous was he that, when he went shooting, he frequently put the shot into his gun before the powder. 'What,' asked a child hearing him speak

in Parliament, 'is that fat gentleman in such a passion about?'
Campbell, dining at the same table, noted that in a conversation of
eighteen persons nothing escaped his eager notice. Yet, with all his
vitality, he could be more idle than any man: at his home at St
Anne's Hill he would lie for hours on a sunny bank against a wall
covered with fruit trees, doing nothing. 'Ah, Mr Fox,' a friend
said to him, 'how delightful it must be to loll along in the sun at
your ease with a book in your hand.' 'Why the book? why the
book?' was the reply.

In his middle age this former roué and gambler had scandalized
an easy-going society by marrying the mistress with whom he had
lived for years. His unexpected domesticity was the wonder of his
contemporaries. 'You would be perfectly astonished,' wrote
Creevey, 'at the vigour of body, the energy of mind, the innocent
playfulness and happiness of Fox. The contrast between him and
his old associates is the most marvellous thing I ever saw – they
have all the air of shattered debauchees, of passing gaming, drinking, sleepless nights, whereas the old leader of the gang might pass
for the pattern and the effect of domestic good order.' A few weeks
before he assumed office Minto met him with Mrs Fox buying
cheap china.

It was from this many-sidedness – this ability to live fully and
cheerfully at half a dozen different levels – that Fox derived his
surprising good-humour and tolerance. He never bothered to read
what his enemies wrote about him and so was not annoyed by it.
'No, no,' he said, 'that is what they want me to do, but I won't.'
From the same cause, too, came his power of detachment; Lady
Bessborough once found him during a national crisis playing chess
and consigning the politics of Europe to the bottom of the sea and
all the politicians with them! He took important business in his
stride with a lightness of touch that puzzled and sometimes appalled
colleagues. As befitted a classical scholar and a considerable reader,
he was a great patron of letters and learned men; the young poet
Campbell, finding himself pacing the salon at Holland House arm
in arm with the Demosthenes of his age and discoursing on Virgil,
scarcely knew whether he was standing on his head or his feet.
Even learned political opponents benefited by Fox's liberality;

Scott wrote that, though his principles made him abhor his views, he was 'proud of his approbation in a literary sense.'

Above all, Fox was a champion of generous causes. He loved liberty and he loved peace, because he wished all men to be as happy, free and easy as himself. This gave him an appeal to millions of ordinary men and women who were repelled by Pitt's outward austerity and official correctitude, and to whom the name of the recluse, Grenville, meant nothing. For years Fox had been the hero and champion of all who hoped for a speedy end to the European conflict.

Fox led the so-called 'Ministry of all the Talents', which sought in some way to take what it thought the only realistic course – to come to terms with Napoleon. Yet Napoleon refused to deal jointly with London and St Petersburg, hoping for advantage from a tactic of *divide et impera*. Fox told Lord Holland on August 4th that he had not the slightest expectation of peace. Indeed he had little of his own life. Since the spring he had been in constant pain with the growing symptoms of dropsy. In a last conversation with Grey he stressed the three cardinal points to be observed in any negotiation with France: unswerving fidelity to the Russian connection, British security and honour, and independence of Sicily. A few days later a great poet, walking in the vale of Grasmere at the close of a stormy evening, learnt from a newspaper of the impending dissolution of Mr Fox. 'A Power,' he wrote,

> is passing from the earth
> To breathless Nature's dark abyss."

On Saturday, September 13th, 1806, surrounded by what an old friend beautifully called the Privy Council of his heart, the end came. 'The giant race is extinct,' wrote Francis Horner, 'and we are left in the hands of little ones.'

In October 1806, with all a weak man's sudden resolution, Frederick William of Prussia surrendered to the rising Gallophobia of his people and, promised support by the Czar, demanded a French withdrawal from Germany. Napoleon moved with characteristic swiftness. At one moment the Prussian officers were reported to be sharpening their swords on the steps of the French embassy, the next they were trailing past the same steps behind the victor's coach. The military state which Frederick the Great had made the terror of Europe collapsed on October 14th at Jena and Auerstadt (where Marshal Davout, Napoleon's ablest lieutenant, won a crushing subsidiary victory) in a single day. The remainder of the Prussian army, mesmerized by an exemplary cavalry pursuit, surrendered itself and its fortresses with hardly a shot being fired. 'What a people! What a country!' cried Napoleon. 'The Austrians have no energy, but they have honour. The Prussians have neither honour nor soul – sheer *canaille*!'

Yet the overthrow of Prussia was only a means to an end. While Napoleon wreaked his vengeance on her, exempting only Potsdam – in honour of Frederick the Great – from the crushing imposts laid on her cities, he launched a new thunderbolt against the real enemy. On November 21st, five weeks after Jena, he issued from Berlin a Decree to strike her to the heart. Instead of England blockading France, Europe would blockade England. Commerce and correspondence with her, whether carried in neutral or her own ships, was forbidden under pain of death in all lands controlled by France; all ships and goods hailing from her shores or those of her colonies were declared forfeit. The nation of hagglers who had made themselves masters of salt water should be left with nothing else. Against the distant and dispersed conquests of Trafalgar the new Charlemagne opposed the solid Continental *bloc* won by Austerlitz and Jena. To enlarge it he ordered his armies to advance on Russia. A week after the Berlin Decrees Murat entered Warsaw.

Because of calls on her manpower England in the West Indies and the Dardanelles had no army to spare for her allies in eastern Europe when they needed one. That winter Napoleon suffered his first setback on land since his flight from Egypt eight years before. As then, his attempt to break out of Europe to the East was meeting with unlooked-for difficulties. In his impatience to defeat Russia and close the Continent to England, he had embarked on a winter invasion of Poland without magazines or supplies. The country turned out to be a roadless wilderness of ragged hovels and ruined estates out of which even a French army could not wring a subsistence. Within a few weeks the victors of Jena were stuck fast in the mud. When, after a bloody and indecisive engagement at Pultusk, they went into winter quarters at the beginning of 1807, the Russians, ignoring the ordinary decencies of war, counter-attacked. On February 8th the armies met in a terrible encounter at Eylau. Two French columns, attacking in a snowstorm, were caught in the crossfire of Russian batteries, and by nightfall a third of the 140,000 men engaged had fallen. For the first time in his career Napoleon had been held in pitched battle.

Refusing to despair after his reverses and calling on France for a further levy of conscripts – the third in a year – Napoleon gathered together nearly 300,000 men and, as the sun returned to the frozen North, took the offensive. The Russians, who had failed to make the same use of time, saw their advantage slipping away. Impatience for help from the West became an obsession: it was openly proclaimed that if the Allies were forced to make a separate peace it would be England's fault. It was not easy for Russians and Prussians, fighting for bare existence against Napoleon, to understand the ramifications and delays of the parliamentary system. 'You English,' the Allied general Haugwitz told Francis Jackson, 'are always two months too late!'

On June 14th, 1807, two days before the first British contingent sailed from Yarmouth, the armies met at Friedland. By nightfall the Russians were in retreat with the loss of half their force. The fate of Europe was decided. The demand for peace throughout a starving and disorganized Russia could no longer be resisted. The Czar was warned by his officers that his life would be in danger if he persisted in further resistance. The suppressed exasperation of months broke out against the proud western ally who had failed to send aid in Russia's need.

To Napoleon victory was only a stage on the road to London. He at once sought out the vanquished and offered peace – on his own terms. On June 25th the two Emperors met on a raft in the Niemen, while the King of Prussia waited in the rain on the Russian bank. When three hours later they parted, they continued waving to one another as long as their boats were in sight. 'I hate the English as much as you do,' the Czar was reported to have said. 'In that case,' Napoleon replied, 'peace is made!'

A fortnight later, on July 7th, a formal treaty was signed at Tilsit. The young Czar abandoned his quixotic dream of liberating Europe and embracing Napoleon's friendship, fell back on the traditional Russian policy of expansion towards the south-east. Napoleon threw over his ally, Turkey, and promised to enforce peace in the Balkans unless the Turks accepted Russia's terms within three months. Swedish Finland and part of Prussian Poland were also to go Russia. In return the Czar recognized all Napoleon's conquests and his paramountcy over western and central Europe. Henceforward France and Russia were to rule the world between them. The English — the restless moneylenders and trouble-makers who had divided the Continent and sucked its blood and betrayed all who trusted them — were to be excluded from Europe and their trade outlawed. By a secret clause Russia was to join the crusade against them by November 1st unless they first accepted Napoleon's terms. Denmark, Portugal and Austria were to be coerced into joining the common cause and a great Northern fleet to be assembled in the Baltic to regain command of the sea.

The ring was closing. Despite an audacious expedition led by Sir Arthur Wellesley to relieve the hesitating Danes, fewer and fewer of the courts of Europe had the bottom or the men to resist Napoleon's diplomatic and military assaults. Only Portugal still gave shelter to a representative of England. A few days after the news that he had been pipped at Copenhagen by Wellesley reached him, Napoleon gave one of his famous displays of temper at a diplomatic reception. 'If Portugal does not do what I wish,' he shouted at the Portuguese Minister, 'the House of Braganza will not be reigning in Europe in two months! I will not longer tolerate an English ambassador in Europe. I will declare war on any Power who receives one after two months from this time! I have 300,000 Russians at my disposal, and with that powerful ally I can do everything. The English declare they will no longer respect neutrals on the sea; I will no longer recognize them on land!' With eastern Europe and Russia in his pocket, Napoleon was free to concentrate his entire force against the last remaining corner of the Continent where English merchants had a foothold. The Iberian peninsula, trackless and remote though it might be, was now at his mercy.

Immediately afterwards the French and Spanish ambassadors quitted Lisbon. The Portuguese Regent was in a quandary. England was his oldest ally and her Fleet could paralyse his country's trade and cut her off from her colonies. The British ambassador, Lord Strangford, representing Canning's virile policy, was urging him to defy Napoleon and, by transferring his Court to Brazil, to continue the war by England's side. A weak man, sunk in luxury, Prince John had hoped that it might somehow be possible to steer a middle course until the two adversaries had made peace. But it was now plain that a decision must be made. Early in October it became known that a French army under General Junot had assembled at Bayonne and was about to cross the Bidassoa and march on Lisbon.

As was to be expected, the unhappy man made promises to both sides. But he was too late to save his throne. On November 13th an intimation appeared in the Paris *Moniteur* that the House of Braganza had ceased to reign – 'a new proof of how inevitable is the ruin of all who attach themselves to England.'

On the last day of November, 1807, Junot, having marched three hundred miles in a fortnight over the rain-deluged hills, straggled into Lisbon with less than 2000 of his original 30,000 men. The Portuguese army made no resistance. But the Court and Fleet had gone. Two days before, Strangford, strengthened by the appearance of Sir Sidney Smith and a battle squadron in the Tagus, had gone ashore and by almost superhuman efforts had persuaded the terrified Regent to fly the country. On the 29th, taking his treasure and family with him, Prince John had embarked in his flagship and, escorted by British warships, sailed for Rio de Janeiro. Three weeks later Major-General Beresford landed with 4000 British troops at Madeira and took control of the island in his name.

One more alliance now seemed denied to Britain, and the effectiveness of the Berlin Decrees grew. In the past two years Britain's exports to northern Europe had fallen from £10,000,000 to £2,000,000; her warehouses were bursting with manufactured goods and colonial products for which there was no outlet. Her merchants had to find alternative markets or repudiate their debts and mortgages. Already there was grave unrest in the industrial towns where mills and factories were closing down. England was feeling the pinch.

Napoleon moved in for what – not for the first or the last time – he believed to be the kill. The Berlin Decrees were damaging the continental economy almost as much as they were damaging the English. He himself had been forced to wink at smuggling, and on occasion to take part in it himself: only by doing so had he been able to supply his freezing army in Poland with 50,000 West Riding overcoats and 200,000 pairs of Northampton boots. He was forced to resort to more drastic measures. His victories in northern Europe had released his immense military forces for operations exclusively against England. Once more, as in the days before Nelson and Pitt thwarted him, he felt free to revert to his dream of a drive across the Mediterranean towards the Orient – the source as he always believed of England's power and the goal of his early ambitions. The first hint of coming events was a report by the French War Minister which appeared in the opening days of January, 1808. It dwelt not only on the necessity of closing all ports to France's irreconcilable enemy, but stressed the importance of being ready to seize every chance of carrying the war into the bosom of England, Ireland and the Indies. 'The English influence must be attacked wherever it exists,' it declared, 'until the moment when the aspect of so many dangers shall induce England to remove from her councils the oligarchs who direct them and confine the administration to men wise and capable of reconciling the love and interest of the country with the interest and love of mankind.'

The new design to break the ring of British sea power envisaged a triple military drive across and round both ends of the Mediterranean. A joint Franco-Russian-Austrian host was to strike, or pretend to strike, at the crumbling Empire of the Turks and the distant approaches to India, where the English had been having trouble with their Sepoy levies. In the central Mediterranean King Joseph's troops were to invade Sicily. In the west a third and greater French army was to march through Spain, besiege Gibraltar and cross the narrow waters dividing Europe from Africa. Once the coasts of Barbary were closed to them, the British blockaders off Cadiz, Lisbon and Cartagena would be deprived of their supplies. As soon as they had abandoned their posts, French and Spanish raiding squadrons would sail for the Cape and the Indian Ocean. In the meantime the small fleet at Toulon under Ganteaume, reinforced by Allemand's squadron from Rochefort, was to escape in the spring gales, and, re-provisioning the French forces in Corfu, heighten the threat to Sicily and draw Collingwood's Mediterranean Fleet eastwards.

But the most crucial part of Napoleon's design turned on the occupation of Spain and north-west Africa. For this he had prepared the ground with the greatest care. After Godoy's presumptuous show of independence before Jena he had insisted on the dispatch of 15,000 of the best Spanish troops to police his north German conquests. In October, 1807, having reduced that petty dictator to a state of abject servility, he skilfully used a secret correspondence of his own with the heir apparent, Ferdinand, to have the prince – the one member of the Spanish royal family with any following – arrested by his father for high treason. At the same time he secured through the secret Treaty of Fontainebleau permission for French troops to occupy the principal towns of Biscay and Navarre. This they at once proceeded to do under pretence of supporting Junot.

Early in the New Year the *Moniteur* began openly to attack Godoy. On February 16th, 1808, all disguise was abandoned. On that day a French Brigade at Pampeluna rushed the gates of the citadel after challenging the garrison to a snowball match, seized the magazine and barred out its allies. Similar acts of treachery occurred at San Sebastian, Figueras and Barcelona. Then, having secured the entrances to the Peninsula, Napoleon poured 100,000 troops through the passes and proceeded to take Spain over, lock, stock and barrel, as the essential preliminary to attacking Gibraltar and invading Morocco.

For a few weeks it looked as if the Spanish adventure had succeeded. Murat, advancing from Burgos, entered Madrid, acclaimed by the populace as a liberator; at Aranjuez the mob rose, prevented the flight of Godoy and the Royal family to South America and forced the King to abdicate in favour of Ferdinand. The latter was then induced by specious promises to cross the French frontier and meet Napoleon at Bayonne. Here he was made prisoner, asked to resign the throne and, when he refused, confronted by his own father and mother who denounced him as a bastard. By May 6th his powers of resistance, never strong, were exhausted and, in return for a French pension, he joined with his father in surrendering his rights to Napoleon. A stroke of the pen, supported by a little force and treachery, had secured France the Iberian Peninsula and the Spanish Empire of South and Central America. The Pyrenees had been eliminated.

Up to this point everything had gone as Napoleon had planned. The rulers of Spain had been tricked out of their rights like those of a dozen outworn States before them. But the Spanish people now took a hand in the game. They were proud, they were ignorant and they hated and despised all foreigners. Though unanimous in their loathing of Godoy, they had a deep-rooted affection for the Throne which now took the form of a wave of irrational enthusiasm for Ferdinand. When they discovered he had been kidnapped, they became passionately angry. Instead of acquiescing in French rule they rose against it – spontaneously and without the slightest warning.

The storm broke even before the curtain had fallen on the sordid abdication scene in Bayonne. On May 2nd the Madrid mob poured into the streets to massacre the French garrison. Every French soldier found was instantly cut down or shot. After three hours the invaders' main forces began to regain control. Then it became the Spaniards' turn to be slain. No mercy was shown; an English lady whose room was invaded by eight fugitives saw them bayoneted under her eyes while her children clung to her in terror. By nightfall the French guns, sweeping every street, had restored a dreadful travesty of order. Almost every person still abroad was stained with blood, and the dead lay piled in heaps in the roadways.

Napoleon refused to take the outbreak seriously. He knew the power of artillery too well. His deputy, the bold and ruthless

Murat, closed down on the country with martial law and mass shootings. A farewell proclamation of the *ci-devant* King Charles was sedulously circulated, exposing the folly of resistance. The Junta of the Regency, a body of carefully selected grandees and Court officials, was dragooned by Murat into petitioning for Joseph Bonaparte to ascend the throne. 'Opinion in Spain is taking the direction I desire,' Napoleon wrote, 'tranquillity is everywhere established.'

But on May 20th the trouble began again when the pro-French Governor of Badajoz was dragged through the streets and killed by the rabble. Two days later the Governor of Cartagena met the same fate. At Jaen peasants murdered the Corregidor and plundered the town. Everywhere the timid Court aristocracy who had yielded to the French were hunted through the streets like wild beasts. Valencia sprang to arms on the 23rd, the Asturias – five hundred miles away – on the 24th. Here – untinged by French influence – the local squirearchy and priesthood assembled at Oviedo, ordered an army of 18,000 men to be raised and declared war on France in the name of the captive Ferdinand. Seville followed suit on the 27th. At Cadiz the mob stopped a paternal harangue by the Gallophil Governor on the power of France with shouts for arms and ammunition, hunted him through the town and dashed his brains out on the pavement.

Moved by the same impulse as their brethren, the country gentry and clergy of the remote Asturian valleys, gathered in defiant conclave at Oviedo, decided on May 30th to appeal to London. That night, armed with formal powers by this Provincial Council of Asturias, the historian Toreno and five other emissaries set out and, after an adventurous voyage, arrived at Falmouth on June 6th. The opportunity for which Pitt had sought so long, and of which his successors had grown to despair, had come at last.

* * *

Before the end of June the government learnt that the insurrection had spread to Portugal. Here, by arrogance, by unconcealed contempt for religious and national feelings and by shameless plunder,

"All agree there is but one Nelson."

The Great Duke, "who embodied the genius of his country – patience."

the French had aroused the whole population. Rebellion first broke out in the north at Oporto, where the Bishop led the peasantry against the pro-French Governor; it quickly spread to the Algarve south of the Tagus. By June 25th Junot's hold on the country had shrunk to the vicinity of Lisbon and the principal fortresses.

On June 30th, 1808, therefore, the Cabinet decided to employ Sir Arthur Wellesley and his troops stationed in Cork in a Portuguese diversion to help the Spanish patriots. Spencer's corps from Gibraltar was added to his command. The Horse Guards felt some scruples at the appointment of so young a Lieutenant-General; Wellesley was only thirty-nine, and his experience of service had been mainly Indian. But he was a member of the government, brother to one of its principal supporters and knew how to work with politicians without making trouble; Pitt in his last months had declared that he had never met a military officer with whom it was so easy to converse. And beneath his pleasant, calm, well-bred exterior the Sepoy general impressed those who knew him with being a thorough master of himself and his profession. A few days before leaving London he entertained an official named Croker who was to take over some of the work of his Irish department. After dinner the two men sat together over their wine, looking out of the tall windows on Harley Street. As Sir Arthur was silent, Croker asked him what he was thinking about. 'Why, to say the truth,' Wellesley replied, 'I am thinking of the French that I am going to fight. I have not seen them since the campaign in Flanders when they were capital soldiers, and a dozen years of victory under Bonaparte must have made them better still. They have a new system of tactics which has out-manoeuvred and overwhelmed all the armies of Europe. It's enough to make one thoughtful; but no matter. My die is cast; they may overwhelm me, but I don't think they will outmanoeuvre me. First, because I am not afraid of them, as everybody else seems to be; secondly, because, if what I hear of their system of manoeuvres be true, I think it a false one against steady troops. I suspect that all the Continental armies were more than half beaten before the battle was begun. I, at least, will not be frightened beforehand.'

By his very military ascendancy – as Castlereagh had predicted in a remarkable speech in the House – Napoleon was creating a power to which the world might one day look for deliverance.

*   *   *

Through sheer necessity the British Army had begun to climb out of the fifty years' pit of defeat and neglect into which it had fallen after the great days of Minden and Plassey. The mainspring of all reform had been the *corps d'élite* of light infantry which had been formed at Shorncliffe Camp under the first soldier in the Army, Sir John Moore. Born in November, 1761, the son of a Glasgow doctor, Moore had seen hard fighting in America, Corsica, the West Indies, Ireland, Holland and Egypt, becoming a brigadier at thirty-four, Major-General at thirty-six and Lieutenant-General at forty-three. Handsome and athletic, with broad shoulders and generous, penetrating eyes, there was something in his glance and bearing that warmed the coldest nature. He seemed made to inspire confidence and courage. 'Every one,' wrote the duke of York's Military Secretary, 'admires and loves him.'

This great soldier was at once realist and idealist. So clear was his perception of what was wrong and so passionate his resolve to set it right that he sometimes expressed himself with a vehemence that alarmed the timorous. 'My feelings were so strong and my indignation such,' he wrote on one occasion, 'as at times to bring tears to my eyes and for moments to stop my speech.' When his normal good humour and love of friendly banter were in abeyance, there was a touch of pedantry in his virtue, not uncharacteristic of his uncompromising northern race. Towards corruption and injustice he was merciless. 'Soldiers are flogged for drunkenness,' he once observed, 'I could not look them in the face if I was not to punish it equally in officers.' The chilling contempt with which he turned on those who behaved unworthily was, like the love he inspired, still remembered fifty years after his death.

Yet it was not Moore's frown that made men follow him but his example and inspiration. He expected of others only what he demanded of himself. An ambitious man, he applied to his life, at a time when wire-pulling was the bane of the Service, the unflinching principle that a soldier should not choose his lot but go wherever he was ordered. In the field he shared the lot of the meanest private; at the siege of San Fiorenzo he slept every night in his clothes on a bed of straw. Though a poor man, he on more than one occasion advanced the money to enable a deserving officer to obtain promotion. His simplicity and directness shrivelled up meanness and shabby conduct. Fearless, he shamed fear in others. 'I ordered them to leap over it,' he wrote in his diary after an engagement, 'and upon their hesitating showed them the example of getting over it myself.'

When Moore received his first command the Army was at the lowest point of its history. Its discipline was based on mechanical parades and mass firelock exercises, copied in the letter rather than the spirit from Frederick the Great's Prussia and increasingly divorced from the realities of war and human nature. It was enforced regardless of humanity and common sense; soldiers were treated as automata to be bullied and flogged into an unthinking obedience. Moore, faced by a triumph of the natural courage and enthusiasm of the Revolutionary armies, went back to nature to defeat them. He did not discard the traditional discipline of the British Service; he humanized it. Against the *élan* of the armed *sans-culottes*, so irresistible when confronted only by the 'stiff solidarity' of the old monarchical armies of the Continent, he opposed an equal enthusiasm based on common sense discipline and careful training.

His opportunity to remodel the Army arose out of the need for light infantry. The French had won their battles with a horde of highly individualized skirmishers and sharpshooters going ahead of their dense half-disciplined columns and firing from every side into the rigid Teuton lines whose only reply were machine-like volleys, imposing on the parade ground but ineffective against such invisible and fast-moving targets. By the time the columns came into range or the cavalry charged, the defenders were already demoralized, and the rather sketchy discipline of the former – strengthened by successive victories – was seldom tested. An antidote for the *tirailleur* had had to be found. At the outset the British, being almost without light infantry, had relied on hired German

475

Jägers who were little more than armed gamekeepers and foresters. The exigencies of West Indian warfare, like those of American warfare two decades before, caused General Grey and his successors, Abercromby and Moore, to train special companies as protective and reconnaissance screens. The need for more of these being acutely felt during the brief invasion of the Continent in 1799, the duke of York had ordered the formation of an Experimental Rifle Corps at Horsham to which fifteen regiments were ordered to send officers and men for courses of instruction. Trained in Windsor Forest by two brilliant leaders, Colonel Coote Manningham and Lieutenant-Colonel William Stewart, these took part in the landing at Ferrol in October, 1800, fought by Nelson's side at Copenhagen and were formed in the spring of 1801 into the 95th Regiment of the Line – a Rifle Corps with distinctive green uniform and dark buttons and accoutrements. Disbanded at the end of the Revolutionary War, they were re-formed when the war clouds regathered, armed with the new Baker rifle – a weapon of high precision compared with the smooth-bore musket of the heavy infantry – and in October, 1802, consigned to Shorncliffe Camp for special training under Sir John Moore. Here, facing across the Channel towards Napoleon's cantonments, they formed with the 14th Light Dragoons and the 52nd and 43rd Regiments – both reconstituted as light infantry – the spearhead of the force designed to repel invasion. For the next three years, until they passed overseas, they were trained by Moore in an amalgam of disciplined team-work and individual initiative unmatched since the days of imperial Rome. With the archers of Agincourt and the Brigade of Guards, they formed England's peculiar contribution to the art of land warfare.

It was with an army still in transition from old to new that Wellesley set sail from Cork in the broiling July of 1808. On the 23rd he landed at Oporto; and as soon as he heard of it, Junot despatched his best general, Laborde, with 4000 men up the river road to the north to delay the British advance until a second force, twice as large, under General Loison could move down from beyond the Tagus to join him. By August 20th Junot had assembled his forces and attacked Wellesley at Baylen. Everywhere his over-confident attacks broke on the patient discipline of Wellesley's scarlet lines. When the red-coats, following up with the bayonet, bore down on them 'like a torrent breaking bounds', the victors of Austerlitz and Jena broke and fled. But, infuriatingly, the British were prevented from following up their victory by the caution of Wellesley's nominal superiors, Sir Henry Burrard and Sir Hew Dalrymple. Castlereagh, the Foreign Secretary, had written to Sir Hew urging him, nearly twenty years Wellesley's senior, to take that officer's advice. He was damned if he would. When the news that he had failed to follow up his subordinate's victory and opened negotiations with the French for a truce reached England, he was recalled and damned by his countrymen. A wag declared that he would henceforth spell humilitation with a 'hew'.

The most unexpected result of this uproar was its effect on the fortunes of Sir John Moore. With enemies in Parliament, his career, a few weeks earlier, had seemed over. Now he was appointed to command the 40,000 British troops about to be employed in Spain. Moore moved north into Spain to support the Spanish patriot armies there of the Asturias and Aragon, leaving 10,000 troops to defend Portugal. He expected to be joined by 17,000 troops under Sir James Baird who landed at Corunna in the middle of October. Neither they nor the Spaniards expected that Napoleon would address himself to this thorn in his flesh so quickly. By November 1st he had 120,000 men on the Ebro, and by the 13th had occupied Vittoria and Valladolid and smashed the Spanish armies of Belvedere and Blake. Immediately Moore found himself in a perilous position. Baird was still detained a hundred miles to his north-west at Lugo by the rains; Major-General Hood, with the artillery, was still a hundred miles away to the south on the far side of the Guaddarramas mountains. To make matters worse, the Spanish generals Castanos and Palafox, having the insane notion of cutting Napoleon off from France, advanced on his eastern flank and were easily routed. There was nothing for it but to retreat.

So began one of the most desperate episodes in the history of the British army. Though he succeeded in joining forces with Baird, and for a month hoped Madrid would hold out against the

French Emperor, he knew it would be folly to attempt to meet him on the open plain when once again the greatest military genius in the world began to move north.

The question was whether the British could escape Napoleon's converging jaws. Already the threat to their flanks was developing fast. On December 29th, the day Paget's rearguard evacuated Benavente, Soult's cavalry, fanning out to the north, overwhelmed La Romana's disintegrating army at Mansilla. By leaving the bridges over the Esla undestroyed the Spaniards opened the road through Leon and beyond. Meanwhile it was discovered from the captured chasseurs that other forces were seeking to reach the great mountain defile at Villafranca. As soon, therefore, as he reached Astorga on the 30th, Moore sent officers ahead to watch any attempt either to cut the Corunna road from the direction of Leon or to use the track from Benevente to Orense to work round his southern flank. However bad such cross-country roads might be, he could not forget how often he had been misled about Iberian topography. Nor could he rely on the Spaniards defending their native passes; La Romana, ignoring every entreaty and his own promise, had failed to take his starving army over the Cantabrian range into the Asturias, and was now flying across the British line of retreat towards Orense. For these reasons Moore on New Year's Eve dispatched Major-General Craufurd's Light Brigade towards Vigo to guard the valley of the Minho and his southern flank.

The threat of hunger kept pace with that of encirclement. Owing to the inadequacy of Baird's commissariat only two days' provisions were found at Astorga, while the flight of the Spanish bullock-drivers and their carts made it impossible to bring up supplies from the next magazine at Villafranca. The only course was to cover the fifty miles to that place before the army starved. Shortage of rations further undermined discipline; the natural tendency of the frightened inhabitants to hide what little food they possessed led to illicit house-to-house searches, and these in their turn to orgies in the cellars. The bad characters, who according to one witness numbered from fifty to a hundred in every battalion, came into their own. The national weakness for drink – always accentuated in an army recruited at the ale-house door – found a terrible vent, and hundreds of uncontrollable and armed men roved the streets in delirium. To add to the horror La Romana's troops poured into the town while the British were still evacuating it – a starving, shivering, stinking, typhus-ridden rabble who fell on the homes and chattels of their countrymen like a wolf-pack. Their example was eagerly followed by their allies.

The renewed retreat completed the army's demoralization. In many units the sullen men became openly mutinous. The road into the mountains was knee-deep in snow and ice that became a river of slush by day and froze again at night. Boots, already in tatters, were wrenched off bleeding feet; horses could not stand and died in the snow or slid over frozen precipices. With every gust of wind clouds of snow blew in the men's faces. It was bitterly cold: there was no fuel, no shelter and nothing to drink but snow. 'We suffered,' wrote a soldier of the 71st, 'misery without a glimpse of comfort.' All the time La Romana's pitiful scarecrows kept getting in the way, swarming with famished howls through the battered doors of every wayside farm or hut.

At the top of the mountain a great pass ran through a barren waste of snow. All the way through it, for eight or nine miles, the men trudged in angry silence broken only by the groans of the dying by the wayside or the occasional report of a pistol fired at the head of a fallen horse. Afterwards at the village of Bembibre hundreds of troops left the ranks and, burning and plundering, fought their way into the wine vaults. Here, as the old year went out, horrible scenes were enacted. 'Bembibre,' wrote an officer, 'exhibited all the appearance of a place lately stormed and pillaged. Every door and window was broken, every lock and fastening forced. Rivers of wine ran through the houses and into the streets, where soldiers, women, children, runaway Spaniards and muleteers lay in fantastic groups with wine oozing from their lips and nostrils.'

Here too on the first day of the New Year came the rearguard, sounding their bugles, hammering on the doors and rousing the insensible men in the cellars and streets with blows from their rifles. Behind them – though still at a respectful distance – came the French cavalry. As the rumour of their approach ran through the plundered town the streets filled with revellers whom all the efforts of their comrades had failed to rouse, reeling, staggering and crying out for mercy. They received none from the French dragoons who, eager to avenge Benavente, slashed at drunkards, cripples, women and infants in arms. Yet even in this pit of shame the stubborn English spirit flickered; during the night and following day with a wonderful persistence many stragglers regained the retreating columns – tattered soldiers with bloodshot eyes and festering wounds and women who had been raped in barns but had fled from their violators to rejoin the colours.

It was this spirit, almost as much as the valour of the Reserve and Light Brigade, that robbed Napoleon of his triumph. 'The English are running away as fast as they can,' he wrote from Benavente; 'they have abandoned the Spaniards in a shameful and cowardly manner. Have all this shown up in the newspapers. Have caricatures made and songs and popular ditties written. Have them translated into German and Italian and circulated in Italy and Germany.' For, as his prey eluded him, the Emperor's indignation rose. He hated the British from the bottom of his soul. The man who had plundered half the cities of Europe felt genuine horror at the ill-disciplined rapscallions who had pillaged the wine shops of Benavente. He particularly disliked their barbaric destruction of bridges – one of the principal channels of civilization.

On New Year's Day, 1809, while pressing forward from Benavente to Astorga to join Soult, Napoleon learnt that Moore had reached the mountains and that his last hope of forcing a battle on the open plain had passed. He at once resolved to leave Spain. As he approached Astorga a courier galloped up with dispatches from Paris. He dismounted, read them in the presence of his troops and paced angrily up and down. Later it became known that momentous tidings had arrived: that Austria was arming for war, that there had been a revolution – incited by British agents – in Turkey, that traitors had been plotting in Paris. That night the Emperor handed over command of the army to Soult, and ordered the immediate return of the Imperial Guard to Valladolid. The English were beyond his reach. So for that winter were Portugal and southern Spain.

In the course of January 10th the hills were left behind and the main body reached Betanzos on the coastal plain. Here the sun was shining and the orange and lemon trees were in flower; there was ample provision of food, and the famished troops were able to fill their stomachs. Next day, with indescribable feelings, they caught their first glimpse of the sea and the distant masts of ships. A thorough reorganization having taken place under the supervision of the Commander-in-Chief, the army entered Corunna that night in tolerable formation, the ragged, shoeless scarecrows stumping on frostbitten, bleeding feet through the streets with every commanding officer leading his regiment and every captain and subaltern flanking his section. The high light was the performance of two battalions of the First Foot Guards, each 800 strong, who marched in perfect formation in column of sections, with drums beating and the drum-major twirling his staff.

Moore at once embarked as many of his sick and wounded as possible in the store and hospital ships and began to fortify the landward approaches to the town. In this he was aided by the townsfolk, who, regardless of their own bleak future, threw themselves, men, women and children, with whole-hearted abandon into digging trenches, strengthening the neglected ramparts and carrying ammunition to the forts and batteries. It was as though, touched by the sufferings of their allies, they had resolved by a single impulse to make amends for all the improvidence and procrastination of the past six months. Among the consequences of the latter was a huge magazine of four thousand barrels of powder, sent out in haste from England at the beginning of the war and since left undistributed and unused. This was fired on the 13th, causing an explosion which broke every window in the town, swept the harbour with a tidal wave and killed a sergeant and two men on piquet more than a mile away.

Moore did not destroy everything that he found at Corunna. From the stores he took arms and ammunition, giving to every man a new firelock and a pouch filled with fresh powder – a valuable exercise of sea power, for the French, with the long mountain road behind them and their powder and arms damaged by exposure, could hope for no such advantage. And Moore needed all the help he could get. The Rearguard after its superb performance during the retreat – in which, though continuously engaged, it had lost fewer men than any division in the army – was holding the crossing over the Mero at El Burgo, four miles east of the town. But, with the enemy massing beyond the river, the position ceased to be tenable after the 13th when a partially masked battery was disclosed commanding the broken bridge. General Paget's small force had no alternative but to withdraw in haste, leaving the French free to cross. A battle under the walls of Corunna could no longer be avoided.

It was a desperate affair. Soult had resolved to destroy the British as they embarked, Moore to meet the French on the hills surrounding Corunna. During the battle Moore himself was everywhere. Young Charles Napier, commanding the 50th foot, when the fighting was at its climax, heard above the thunder of musketry and the cries of an advancing French column, the gallop of horses, and turning round, saw him. 'He came at speed,' he wrote, 'and pulled up so sharp and close he seemed to have alighted from the air; man and horse looking at the approaching foe with an intenseness that seemed to concentrate all feeling in their eyes. The sudden stop of the animal, a cream-coloured one with black tail and mane, had cast the latter streaming forward; its ears were pushed out like horns, while its eyes flashed fire, and it snorted loudly with expanded nostrils, expressing terror, astonishment and muscular exertion. My first thought was, it will be away like the wind! But then I looked at the rider and the horse was forgotten. Thrown on its haunches the animal came, sliding and dashing the dirt up with its fore feet, thus bending the general forward almost to its neck. But his head was thrown back and his look more keenly piercing than I ever saw it. He glanced to the right and left, and then fixed his eyes intently on the enemy's advancing column, at the same time grasping the reins with both his hands, and pressing the horse firmly with his knees: his body thus seemed to deal with the animal while his mind was intent on the enemy, and his aspect was one of searching intenseness beyond the power of words to describe. For a while he looked, and then galloped to the left without uttering a word.'

Presently Moore returned and joined a group on a knoll. A

round-shot struck the ground close to his horse's feet, causing it to spin round, but he never took his gaze from the enemy. A second shot tore the leg off a 42nd Highlander who started screaming and rolling about, much to the agitation of his comrades. 'This is nothing, my lads,' Moore called out, 'keep your ranks, take that man away; my good fellow, don't make such a noise, we must bear these things better.' His sharp tone had the calming effect intended, and the ranks closed again. The experienced eye of the great Scottish soldier told him that victory was his; the sufferings he and his men had endured for so long were about to be avenged.

At that moment a cannon-ball from the threatened battery struck him from his horse, carrying away his left shoulder and part of his collar-bone, and leaving his lungs exposed and his arm hanging by a torn string of flesh. For a moment he lay motionless, then raised himself to a sitting position, and, with eyes kindling with their habitual brilliance, resumed his gaze on the smoke and turmoil ahead. So unmoved was his face that those about him could scarcely realize the deadly nature of his wound.

A little later Commissary Schaumann saw him being borne by six Highlanders through the streets of Corunna on a blood-stained blanket, with a little group of aides-de-camp and doctors walking beside. He had refused to be parted from his sword which he carried out of the field with him like a Spartan his shield. Though breathing only with intense pain, he repeatedly made his bearers pause so that he might look back on the battle. 'You know,' he murmured to his friend, Colonel Anderson, 'I have always wished to die this way.'

After Moore's departure – for Baird had also had his arm shattered by the great battery's raking fire – the command devolved on a fellow Scot, Sir John Hope. The latter, isolated on the left from the decisive events which had been taking place elsewhere, was unable to follow up the swift succession of blows planned by his fallen chief. The gallantest of men, pottering instinctively – as one of his officers testified – to wherever the fire was hottest, he was a little overawed by the weight of the responsibility that had suddenly fallen on him; England's only army was in his keeping and her fleet was waiting in a perilous anchorage. It was now growing dark and, seeing that the French attack was broken, Hope called off the pursuit and ordered Moore's instructions of the morning to be put into immediate operation. It was certain now that the embarkation would be unmolested.

In darkness and weariness the men marched to the quayside while the rearguard piquets lit bivouac fires on the abandoned ridge. Hollow-eyed and covered with blood and filth, they looked so terrible that the townsfolk crossed themselves as they passed. But the withdrawal was carried out in perfect order, so well had Moore's measures and a brush with the enemy restored the discipline of his tattered troops. Presently, on the dark, tossing water-front they were grasped by the mighty fists of the sailors and pulled into the boats. As they were rowed across the harbour to the waiting ships, their General lay breathing his last on the soil of the land he had come to save. 'I hope the people of England will be satisfied,' he whispered, 'I hope my country will do me justice.' He repeatedly inquired after his officers, urging that this one should be recommended for promotion and begging to be remembered to another. 'Is Paget in the room?' he asked, 'remember me to him, he is a fine fellow.' Then, as his wound congealed and grew cold and the agony increased, he became silent lest he should show weakness.

By the morning of the 17th the whole army was on board except for 1500 troops whom Hope, resolved to depart in dignity, had left under Hill and Beresford to cover the embarkation of the wounded. The Spaniards, stirred by the battle to a sudden ecstasy of generous enthusiasm, had volunteered to defend the ramparts while the fleet got to sea. The whole town, men, women and children had turned out; 'everybody commanded, everybody fired, everybody halloed, everybody ordered silence, everybody forbade the fire, everybody thought musketry best and everybody cannon.' 'Thus, after all,' wrote Schaumann, 'we became reconciled to the Spanish character.' About the same time Napoleon, having threatened to hang the municipality for the murder of a French soldier, was preparing to leave Valladolid for Paris. His eagles had not been planted on the towers of Lisbon after all. Nor had he destroyed the British army. As it began to grow light and the wind in the bay of Corunna freshened, a party of the 9th Foot with a chaplain and a few mournful officers could be seen making their way along the ramparts on the landward bastion of the citadel. They carried the body of their dead commander, wrapped in his military cloak. Presently they committed it to the ground, and 'left him alone with his glory.'

*   *   *

It was not until April 1809 that the government was able to draw together its disparate resources sufficiently to send Sir Arthur Wellesley once again to Portugal. He landed in Lisbon with only a few regiments that had known fighting previously in the Peninsula, and immediately resolved to strike at the strung out French forces, selecting first Soult's 23,000 veterans threatening Lisbon from Oporto. He advanced with Napoleonic boldness and threw his troops across the Douro – a manoeuvre he had perfected in his early commands in India, and of which the bemused Soult could have had no expectation – before his adversary realized he was in danger. With casualties of only twenty-three killed, two missing and ninety-eight wounded, Wellesley forced Soult to retreat, and though again he did not have the cavalry to follow up his victory, he had defeated the most urgent of the threats to Lisbon.

With the Spanish patriots in Galicia and the Asturias more than holding their own against the corps of Marshals Ney and Mortier, the government gave Wellesley the authority to extend his campaign outside the borders of Portugal. He advanced to Plascenia, hoping to take Madrid from Victor and Napoleon's brother, Joseph, the titular King of Spain. It was only when he joined the Spanish troops under Cuesta that he realized how dubious their help would be. He was forced to deploy against Victor at Talavera on the Tagus, a hundred miles from Madrid, with only 17,000 British and 3000 German troops against 46,000 French veterans. His Spanish allies, he said, though they were 32,000 strong, looked like the last army of the Middle Ages come to do battle with the French Revolution. Against the veterans of Austerlitz, Wellesley's line stood firm. When Joseph insisted on abandoning the field in the late afternoon to cover his capital against the advancing Spanish army of Venegas, the French had suffered 7000 casualties against the 5000 Allied. Wellesley could claim another victory, but he was too badly mauled to pursue the puppet king as he scurried away, and shortly the news reached him that the Spaniards of Cuesta's army, who he had left to guard his communications with Portugal, had failed to stop an advance by Soult to Plascenia, so he was forced to retreat. Thirst and hunger, suffocating dust and heat beyond conception hammered the British as they hurried westward across the wilderness of rugged and waterless hills that lay to the south of the Tagus in a dash to reach the ford at Almaraz before Marshal Ney's corps. Though he secured that position, he wrote to his brother, who had just become Ambassador at Seville: 'With the army which a fortnight ago beat double their numbers, I should now hesitate to meet a French corps half their strength.' His men were famished and discouraged. Their wives, usually decently clad and faithful to their husbands, following the army to make their comforts as many as possible, went round on starved donkeys offering themselves to anyone for half a loaf. Wellesley knew that he would have to retreat to a point at which he could be supplied from Portugal, knowing equally that Soult's troops, now occupying the ground which his men had recently denuded of every edible scrap, would also have to retreat. He answered Spanish complaints that he was abandoning Spain and leaving Andalusia open to the enemy by laying at his accusers' door their neglected responsibility to supply him. Nothing would induce him to cooperate again with Spanish generals or rely any longer on Spanish promises of food. He had lost a third of his army by doing so, and it was enough.

Wellesley knew, however, that whatever the weaknesses of the Spanish in the field, particularly after their joint armies of Andalusia and Estremadura had been demolished by Soult at Ocana in November, how invaluable they were in the hills. 'If we can maintain ourselves in Portugal, the war will not cease in the Peninsula, and if the war lasts in the Peninsula, Europe will be saved,' he wrote. 'The French may do as they please. I shall not give up the game here as long as it can be played.' He saw that so long as the guerrillas fought on and his army remained in the field, the French would be in a quandary. If they dispersed enough strength to smother the growing conflagration, they would sooner or later expose some part of their forces to a blow from him. If they concentrated against him, they would be unable to keep the flame of rebellion under control. In the dark hour after the retreat from Talavera, therefore, when almost every other Englishman despaired of Spain, he urged the government to persist. The geography of Portugal gave him the capacity to fight a defensive war successfully: the only easy approach from Spain to Lisbon was the Merida highway to the south of the Tagus. This was held by the great fortresses of Badajoz and Elvas, still in the hands of the Portuguese and Spanish.

This gave the British commander an opportunity to offset his inferiority in numbers. While he held the southern approach with a comparatively small force, he could concentrate his best troops to the north of the Tagus. Fighting a delaying action with light infantry and road demolitions, he could force the invaders to advance over the northern mountains where their supply difficulties would increase with every mile, and only give battle when they were on the verge of the coastal plain. Here, where there were several strong positions barring every track out of the mountains, his own communications, based on the sea, would be as short as theirs were long.

Even if the French with their almost inexhaustible reserves of conscripted man-power could not be held at the edge of the coastal plain, Wellesley had a further resource. His great object was to hold Lisbon and the Tagus estuary, for, so long as he did so, his army would remain in being and the enemy's dilemma only increase with every advance. The danger was lest in holding on too long, his army should be unable to escape. Situated several miles up the estuary and with its water approaches vulnerable to shore artillery, Lisbon had none of the obvious defensive advantages of Cadiz.

Yet it had others which did not escape the British commander's experienced eye. Though it could not be defended from its own ramparts without allowing the enemy's artillery to reach the river below it, the peninsula on which it stood was long and narrow and, nearly thirty miles to the north of the city was still little more than twenty miles wide. Here it was intersected by a deep chain of hills stretching from the Atlantic to the Tagus and rising in places to 2000 feet. Three years earlier Junot, preparing to defend Lisbon against a British advance from Mondego Bay, had noted 'the excellent position of Alenquer and Torres Vedras, the right of which could be extended to the Tagus, the left to the sea.' On his subsequent visits Wellington had carefully noted them too.

At the beginning of October, 1809, as soon as his troops had withdrawn to the Portuguese frontier, the Commander-in-Chief made an exploratory visit to Lisbon. For a few days he remained undecided. Then on October 20th he issued his orders to Colonel Fletcher, his chief engineer. Three lines of defence were to be constructed – an inner one at the extreme southern tip of the peninsula to cover an embarkation, a principal line twenty miles to the north based on the central massif of the Cabeça de Montechnique, and an outer line six miles farther north extending east and west from the Monte Agraça above Sobral. In all more than fifty miles of earthworks, redoubts and abatis were to be constructed under British supervision by gangs of Portuguese labourers and militiamen: precipices were to be scarped, forests cleared and stone walls piled on mountains. But fearful lest the over-confident French should hear of these elaborate preparations and, anticipating a prolonged siege, improve their haphazard supply services, the British general confided his intentions to no one but those directly concerned. So secretly were the works set in hand that months elapsed before even senior officers of the Army suspected their existence.

All this was characteristic of the man – foresight, patience, reticence. If genius is an infinite capacity for anticipating and taking pains, Arthur Wellesley possessed it in supreme measure. He left little to chance. He foresaw every contingency and took the necessary steps to meet it. While he was instructing his engineers, he was also consulting with the naval Commander-in-Chief and the Government about embarkation arrangements and transports. The latter, he begged, should be stationed permanently in the Tagus, both to give confidence to his troops and, by accustoming the civilian population to the sight, to prevent an eleventh-hour panic in the capital. In the event of failure in the field, he was resolved to embark and bring away his army safely. He therefore made sure that he could do so. 'Everything is prepared for us,' he told a colleague in the new year, 'either to go or stay.'

The distinguishing feature of this great soldier's mind was that it dwelt as much on the future as on the present. He was a strategist not merely in space but in time. 'In military operations,' he had written in India, 'time is everything.' He husbanded it not only for today's battle but for tomorrow's. In this he embodied the genius of his country – patience. He could bide his time and, unlike his passionate adversary, knew when to refrain from action. 'It will give Spain the chance of accidents,' he wrote of his Fabian plan in December, 1809, 'and of a change in the affairs of Europe.'

In his calculating, undemonstrative way Arthur Wellesley was at heart an optimist. He saw the inherent flimsiness of Napoleon's dominion: its foundations were not sound in time. 'The Austrian marriage is a terrible event,' he wrote in the spring of 1810, 'and must prevent any great movement on the Continent for the present. Still I do not despair of seeing at some time or other a check to the Bonaparte system. Recent transactions in Holland show that it is all hollow within, and that it is so inconsistent with the wishes, the interests and even the existence of civilized society, that he cannot trust even his brothers to carry it into execution.' Ephemeral disaster, however shattering, never blinded the vision of this cool, dispassionate observer. 'The affairs of the Peninsula,' he noted in March, 1810, 'have invariably had the same appearance since I have known them; they have always appeared to be lost . . . The contest however still continues.'

Yet this temperate optimism was never based on wishful thinking. An eight years' apprenticeship in the cynical school of Indian warfare, followed by the campaigns of Vimiero and Talavera, had purged Arthur Wellesley of illusions. He looked facts unflinchingly in the face, and men too. Of the latter his views were seldom sanguine: he mistrusted, he once said, the judgment of every man where his own wishes were concerned. He kept even his generals at arm's length and viewed his junior officers as slapdash amateurs who would always bungle things unless he took care to prevent them. His opinion of the rank and file was still lower: such drunken scum, he maintained, could only be schooled by the cat-o'-nine-tails and kept in check by fear of punishment. A cadet of the ruling Protestant garrison of Ireland, his vision of the world was that of an aristocrat struggling to preserve order in an untidy welter of plebeian folly, confusion and graft. Nor was it unsuited to the realities of the Iberian peninsula in a revolutionary decade.

Yet, though he was no John Moore and planted few seeds of love and growth in men's hearts, he was adept in the difficult art of shaping human materials for the purposes for which he needed them. Not expecting much of men, he seldom tried them too high and, knowing where they were likely to fail, was always ready with the necessary corrective at the right place and moment. No one was ever a greater master of cold, scathing rebuke that, without exaggeration or provocative heat, left the victim without answer or escape. 'It is not very agreeable to anybody,' he told a refractory Portuguese magnate, 'to have strangers quartered in his house, nor is it very agreeable to us strangers who have good houses in our own country to be obliged to seek for quarters here. We are not here for our pleasure.'

During the quiet winter months of recuperation that followed the collapse of his hopes after Talavera, the British Commander-in-Chief – using the respite offered by Napoleon and Joseph – was transforming his still half amateur army into a professional fighting force. Under his easy, high-bred manner he reshaped it with a hand of steel. In this he was helped by the fact that he was a man of the world and of the highest fashion. Though of frugal and even Spartan tastes, he was accustomed to the best society, kept a mistress – in her due place – and understood the lure of pleasure. He was well able to deal both with senior officers who claimed a gentleman's right to go home for the winter to hunt and manage their estates, and with subalterns who neglected their regimental duties for the charms of the Lisbon opera house. 'My Lord,' one of his brigadiers began, 'I have of late been suffering much from rheumatism . . .' 'And you wish to go to England to get cured of it,' snapped the Commander-in-Chief, turning his back: 'By all means. Go there immediately.'

The rule of such a chief was as unpalatable to gentlemen who thought themselves above discipline as to marauders who deserted for drink or left the line to plunder. Just as the malingerers and column-dodgers of the base hospital at Belem – the notorious Belem Rangers, 'noted,' according to Rifleman Costello, 'for every species of skunk' – were driven back to their regiments that winter by an icy wind, so gay sparks who tried to find in Lisbon a second Drury Lane were recalled in chilling terms to their duties. 'The officers of the army,' they were reminded, 'can have nothing to do behind the scenes . . . Indeed, officers who are absent from their duty on account of sickness might as well not go to the playhouse, or at all events upon the stage and behind the scenes.'

Nor would this unsympathetic commander permit his officers the liberty of politics. He stigmatized the croaking which prevailed in the army as a disgrace to the nation. 'As soon as an accident happens,' he complained to one of his divisional generals, 'every man who can write, and who has a friend who can read, sits down to write his account of what he does not know and his comments on what he does not understand.' Such letters, diligently circulated by the idle and malicious, not only found their way into English newspapers, encouraging the anti-war Opposition and conveying valuable information to the French, but aroused partisan feelings in the field. These Wellesley would have none of; his wish, he stated, was to be the head of an army not a party, and to employ indiscriminately those who could best serve the public, be they who they might.

Yet his discipline was never negative. He made it his business to teach his officers the same meticulous care and attention to duty in which he had schooled himself. Success, he told them, could only be attained by attention to minute detail and by tracing every part of an operation from its origin to its conclusion, point by point. An indefatigable worker, he expected every one about him to be so too. He made it a rule, he said, always to do the work of the day in the day. Regular habits, a superb constitution and a well-regulated mind had been the foundations of all his triumphs. 'When I throw

491

off my clothes,' he once remarked, 'I throw off my cares, and, when I turn in my bed, it is time to turn out.' He taught his army to do the same.

At the root of this punctilious, fastidious, clear-sighted man's nature was a deep and abiding sense of duty. It was not an inspired and burning passion like Moore's or Nelson's; Arthur Wellesley made no pretence of being at home in such altitudes. But, though his feet were firmly planted on his mother earth – one on the battle-field and the other in Bond Street – he was inherently a man of his salt. He spoke the truth, honoured his bond and kept faith. He regarded a lie as an act of cowardice and a breach of promise as a vulgar betrayal. He had learnt to eradicate these easy frailties from his own character, just as he had taught himself to be frugal and reticent, in his youth when he had had to master his Irish ebullience and artist's sensitivity in order to survive in a *milieu* of thrustful elder brothers and inadequate family resources. Adherence to bond and duty was not so much a natural bent of his rather mys-terious nature – in which ran suppressed rivers of deep emotion – as a close-fitting mask which he had early donned in self-protection and to which in due course his own features had come to conform. Yet it was one which, like his talent for economy, perfectly served his country's need. He spared himself no care or labour which could further her ends and made every man and every penny go as far as man or penny could go.

In November, 1809, at the close of his second Peninsular cam-paign, he was a slight, upright, wiry-looking man of forty with keen grey eyes and an aquiline nose. His habitual dress, though neat to the point of dandyism, was almost consciously unostenta-tious: a plain blue frock coat, a small, glazed, cocked hat without feathers, a short cape and strapped grey trousers. He eschewed plumes and gold lace, went about without a Staff, and was usually followed at a discreet distance by a single orderly. He liked seeing things for himself without fuss. 'Our post,' wrote one of his junior officers, 'was next the enemy. I found, when anything was to be done, that it was his also.'

It was his genius for being reasonable, coupled with his clarity and common sense, which enabled Wellesley, now created

Viscount Wellington of Talavera – unlike most men habituated to discipline and command – to deal with politicians. Being free from Moore's troublesome sense of moral indignation, he never made them uncomfortable with tedious reiterations of principle. So long as they ultimately came along with him, he always allowed them a way to wriggle round their difficulties. And though he left them in no doubt as to what he wanted and meant to do – there is nothing in life, he once remarked, like a clear definition – he never expected or asked them to do the impossible. 'In my situation,' he told a colleague, 'I am bound to consider not only what is expedient but what is practicable.' He remembered that ministers had to do so too. He realized that they were harried and abused in Parliament and the country, that there was a shortage of money and troops. He made no more claims on them than were absolutely essential, told them the exact truth and explained, in language which the busiest fool could understand, the commonsense reasons for his requests. He only pressed them when he had to: 'would it be fair or indeed honest in me,' he wrote to the British Ambassador at Lisbon, 'to ask for a man more than I thought absolutely necessary.'

For, frigid and almost inhuman though he sometimes seemed, Wellington had a curiously detached sense of justice. He could be just even in his own cause. Having explained to Lord Liverpool exactly why he needed transports in the Tagus, he added that none of his reasons were worth anything if the ships were needed elsewhere. Such moderation, despite the sacrifices it involved, had its reward. It established a sense of confidence between Cabinet and General: made them conscious of their mutual dependence. When Wellington really needed support from England he could rely on receiving everything that was available.

Thus it came about that, while the ordinary Englishman despaired of Portugal and expected nothing better than an evacuation, a government with a precarious majority accepted Wellington's contention that it should be held. This was the more praiseworthy in that any fighting there was bound to be defensive and could offer few prospects of political glory. But after seventeen years of almost unbroken war British statesmen were at last learning how to wage it. 'We must make our opinion,' the War Secretary wrote, 'between a steady and continued exertion upon a moderate scale and a great and extraordinary effort for a limited time which neither our military nor financial means will enable us to maintain permanently. If it could be hoped that the latter would bring the contest to a speedy and successful conclusion, it would certainly be the wisest course; but unfortunately the experience of the last fifteen years is not encouraging in this respect.' Instead of seeking in every corner of the globe like their predecessors for opportunities 'to give a good impression of the war in England,' ministers, therefore, concentrated on building up expanding strength in Portugal. In this they were helped by the fact that in the fifth year after Trafalgar and Austerlitz there was not much left outside Europe for them to conquer and nowhere inside it save Portugal where they could even hope to retain a footing. The capture of the last French Caribbean islands in the summer of 1809 released the garrisons of no less than seventeen British stations for service elsewhere. By the following summer a small but steady flow of reinforcements was heading for Portugal from every corner of the world.

Yet the growth of this confidence and support was a gradual thing and largely of Wellington's own creation. The Lord Liverpool who became the War Secretary of the Peninsular campaign was the despised Hawkesbury of the Peace of Amiens and Addington's Administration. His own and his chief's tenure of office were so slender that they had at first to trim their sails to every parliamentary wind. 'The Government are terribly afraid that I shall get them and myself into a scrape,' Wellington wrote in April 1810, 'but what can be expected from men who are beaten in the House of Commons three times a week?' Yet, though he did not expect them to last for more than a few months, he calmly took the responsibility of urging them to cling to Portugal, knowing that if he failed the full weight of the disaster would fall on his own head. At the best the defensive campaign he was planning could win him little credit – one, as he said, in which there could be few brilliant events and in which he was almost bound to lose the little reputation he had. 'I am perfectly aware,' he wrote, 'of the risks which I incur personally, whatever may be the result of the operations in

Portugal. All I beg is that, if I am to be responsible, I may be left to the exercise of my own judgment.'

*   *   *

The British army did not fire a shot for six months. While Wellington guarded the southern route into Portugal and husbanded his army, the Light Brigade, under Craufurd, guarded the northern, covering a river line more than forty miles long between the Serra da Estrella and the Douro for six months with only 3000 men. It was through this screen of patrols of riflemen and hussars, ranging far beyond the enemy's lines and into Spain, that Wellington obtained his knowledge of the French movements. Yet, though within an hour's march of 6000 French infantry and 60,000 infantry in support, they never allowed their lines to be penetrated or the slightest intelligence of the British strength and movements to reach the enemy.

This situation was not satisfactory to Napoleon. The Continental system, though it had closed 397 of the 400 sugar-boiling factories in Hamburg by the summer of 1810, had failed to prevent the expansion of British trade and the transformation of the Caribbean into a British lake. He did not feel that he kept 300,000 troops in Spain – losing them at a rate, on average, of 100 men per day – merely to shore up his brother on a precarious throne. He had beaten the Austrians again, in 1809, on the Danube at Wagram, married the Emperor of Austria's daughter to cement an alliance and, he hoped, provide himself with the heir that the Empress Josephine had so conspicuously failed to produce. To the Peninsula therefore, in his own place, he sent the most cunning and experienced of all his Marshals, Massena, Prince of Essling and duke of Rivoli. Massena was a great soldier – an old fox up to every trick of the game and worthy of Wellington's mettle. He was not a man in whose presence it was safe to take risks or to blunder. He was determined, by a methodical advance with all the correct transports over the mountains, methodically to roll the British back into the sea. His first object was to take the fortresses of Ciudad Rodrigo and Almeida, which he had done by August 1810. Wellington

withdrew down the Mondego as Massena advanced, and successfully beat him off at Bussaco outside Coimbra, on September 23rd,
though heavily outnumbered, which he regarded as a holding
battle, to help the morale of his troops and the impatience of
Parliament. But neither he nor Massena was deceived about the
realities of the war. To the incredulous consternation of the
Portuguese, Wellington continued to withdraw. On October 8th,
with Massena on his heels, he reached the lines of Torres Vedras.

Scarcely any one even in the British army had any idea of their
existence. Scores of guns disposed in elaborate redoubts and earthworks looked down from every height. Trenches had been dug,
parapets raised, palisades, abatis, *chevaux de frise* and *trous-de-loup*
made, forests, orchards, mounds and houses levelled to the ground,
every hollow and ditch that could give cover against the terrible
cross-fire of the guns filled in, and every hillside turned into a vast,
exposed, featureless glacis. In other places streams had been
dammed to form impassable marshes and defiles blasted into
precipices. Wellington's engineers had used the respite Napoleon
had given them to good advantage. For nearly a year thousands of
Portuguese labourers had been working to turn a broken range of
hills into an impregnable barrier. Every pass had been barred,
every roadway transformed into a death-trap. Behind, echeloned
in immense depth, were other forts and redoubts whose guns
covered every way to Lisbon. And on either flank of the twenty-
nine miles of mountain wall the British Navy was on guard. Already, as the enemy's left moved along the Tagus highway, the
gunboats of the river flotilla went into action.

The French were dumbfounded. Massena had had no idea that
any serious obstacle lay in his path. The Portuguese traitors at his
headquarters had told him that the approach to Lisbon from the
Mondego was through open, uneventful country. 'Que diable!' he
exclaimed when they laid the blame on those who had failed to
discover what Wellington had been doing to their familiar hills, 'il
n'a pas construit ces montagnes!'

The more he looked at it, the less he liked it. After a half-hearted
attack in the rain on October 14th against an outlying mound near
Sobral – from which the British withdrew to their main lines after

inflicting heavy losses on his men – Massena decided that any attempt to storm the heights would end in a massacre. So strong were the British works that they could be held by artillerymen and second-line troops alone, while the main army remained in the field to strike down any attackers who succeeded in scaling their slopes and penetrating through the cross-fire of their guns. And behind them, as Massena soon learnt, lay other and still stronger lines.

For the British had fallen back to their ultimate base – the sea. The French with their strung-out land communications had advanced far from theirs and were – as they had been under Junot two and a half years before – at their very weakest. Around them was a wasted wilderness. Behind them the Portuguese guerrillas were closing in on every road. Within a fortnight Massena, wishing to send a letter to Napoleon, was forced to detach half a brigade under General Foy to carry it back to Spain. Only the fact that Wellington's orders to destroy all crops and food had here and there been disobeyed, and the ability of the hardy French to live on next to nothing, enabled the Army of Portugal to retain its position at all.

Massena clung on manfully. In a starving match in which the odds were against him, he persisted where almost any other commander would have despaired. Wellington had given him a month in which to starve; he held out for three. What was more, he persuaded Soult, now pandering to his predeliction for gathering art treasures in his vice-royalty at Seville, to attempt to draw Wellington out by besieging Badajoz, one of the fortresses guarding the southern route into Portugal, whose fall would make it almost impossible ever to advance into Spain in the future without first reducing it. Soult laid seige to Badajoz and took it, largely due to the incompetence of its Spanish commander, in February 1810. But the Fabian General refused to be drawn. On March 5th Massena was forced to retreat. He took with him only 44,000 of the 73,000 first-line troops with which he had entered Portugal. As they went, the French reverted to being the pillagers they had been in the first revolutionary days, murdering, plundering, raping, retreating so fast that they outstripped Wellington's pursuit. In April they recrossed the frontier to regain their base at Salamanca.

Wellington was now faced with the prospect of retaking the fortresses of Almeida and Badajoz before he could once more proceed into Spain, and of having to divide his forces to enable him to do so. At Fuentes de Onoro on May 7th he successfully prevented Massena from relieving Almeida, which fell to him immediately. Badajoz, beseiged by Major-General Beresford, was a harder nut; and while Massena attempted to relieve Almeida, Soult made a bold dash for it, forcing Beresford to meet him at Albuera, where the British lost nearly 6000 out of 35,000 men and the French 7000 out of 24,000 in one of the most bloody battles of the war. These losses were so staggering that both sides felt they had been defeated; to make matters worse, the British siege works outside Badajoz had been reduced while Beresford was distracted and the fortress had once more to be invested. But without a proper siege-train, which did not arrive from England until August 1811, and fearing to concentrate on the plain because of the continuous superiority of numbers of the French, Wellington was unable to prevent Soult and Massena relieving the fortress again in June and Marmont reaching Ciudad Rodrigo. Wellington was not excessively worried. To his superiors in London it looked very much as if the campaign in the Peninsula had reached an *impasse*. He himself knew that he now held the initiative.

Napoleon knew it too. In the face of such maddening British obstinacy he reacted with all the violence of his passionate nature, sending repeated orders to his Marshals to make grand sweeps through the Peninsula to clear away all opposition – orders based on information often months out of date, and made with a complete incomprehension of the realities of war south of the Pyrennees. Having long been accustomed to astonish and deceive mankind, as Wellington said, he had come at last to deceive himself. Bounded on two sides of his dominions by British control of the seas, and on a third by Russian control of Asiatic Europe, he now committed a further folly, resolving to march in the summer of 1812 to Moscow, and to take with him 650,000 men. To do this he recalled forty of his best divisions from Spain, and at the same time, not believing reports that the prime struggle there was against the British, transferred a third of Marmont's force to Suchet's control in Valencia, so that it could aid the expulsion of Blake's 30,000 men and a few cruisers. It was the opportunity that Wellington had been waiting for. At the end of January – though with a thousand casualties, including, tragically, Craufurd, who fell at the head of the Light Division, leading the storming party – he took Ciudad Rodrigo, which allowed him, for the moment, to ignore the French Army of Portugal. At the end of February he marched over the lonely Beira mountains to 'proud' Badajoz, with its rich, fever-laden mists and its record of disaster to the Allied cause. On this occasion too, it took such a toll that at midnight on April 6th, Wellington gave the order to call off the attack, unaware that the bloody frontal assault which he had directed had drawn the defending French sufficiently in one direction for General Picton's division to scale the towering walls at different points and were inside the city. Badajoz had fallen, though the price was 5000 men. Instead of regarding it as a warning, Napoleon received the news with one of his famous fits of rage and then, forbidding all reference to it behaved as though it had never happened. On June 24th he turned his back on Wellington and marched into Russia.

Knowing that each of the Marshals in the Peninsula would not willingly come to the aid of any of their fellows, and that his own supplies and communications were now guaranteed by Badajoz, Ciudad Rodrigo and the sea, Wellington resolved to close first against Marmont. The two generals paced each other from the Agueda to the Tormes, manoeuvring, fencing, seeking the best ground on which to force the other to attack. Outside Salamanca Wellington caught his adversary temporarily extended without the capability to call all the parts of his army to the aid of any one division which might be attacked. It gave him his greatest victory in the war, destroying the frantic French divisions piecemeal. Foy thought that the battle raised Wellington almost to the level of Marlborough. Indeed had it not been for the failure of a Spanish officer to guard a crossing of the Tormes across which the French retreated, he would have had as complete a triumph as Ulm or Jena.

The road to Madrid was open to him. He arrived there on August 12th, with every bell pealing, palms waving and women casting shawls before his horse. But he chose not to remain there; if he did, he knew he would have to face attacks from the one remaining army in northern Spain, and possibly three from the south and east. Critically underestimating the capacity of the French forces to hold out (a surprising fault, given his experiences over the past three years) he failed to take the stronghold of Burgos, which if he had taken it would have forced the French back beyond the Ebro. As winter approached he faced the prospect of the 50,000 men of the Armies of Portugal and the North uniting with the 60,000 of the South and Centre. Soult, coming up from the south, was too wary of being worsted again to risk an engagement. Instead he tried to cut Wellington's communications with Portugal, forcing him to retreat beyond Salamanca and bring the campaign of 1812 to a close.

In the second week of December the magnitude of Napoleon's defeat in Russia became evident. Immediately he demanded from the French people a new army for the campaign he planned in 1813, against Germany, now rising against him, and his defected Austrian allies. The Spanish guerrillas, heartened by rumours reaching them over the Gulf of Lyon, intensified their activity to the extent that Napoleon ordered his brother to abandon his capital to drive them from their valleys in Biscaya and Navarre. Having carefully husbanded his troops over the winter, foddering, equipping, disciplining and augmenting, he moved not north-east, as Joseph expected, to attack over the easily-defended Douro, but due north, through the Tras os Montes – lowering his cannon over precipices by ropes in the process – and moved between him and France before Joseph was aware that he had left the Agueda. Valladolid was evacuated on June 2nd, Valencia on the 7th, Burgos itself on the 12th, the castle in the last destroyed by the French in despair. Despite news from Germany that Napoleon had defeated the Russo-Prussian armies twice in May, at Lutzen and Bautzen, and the consequent caution of his own commanders, Wellington saw that his best course now was to press on, falling back on the Pyrennees as a line of defence if necessary. His judgment was rewarded when, having crossed the Ebro on June 14th he was able to fall on Joseph's retreating army as it poured into the valley of Vittoria. The French, depressed by their long retreat and no longer with any confidence in their leaders, did not fight well that day. They left the valley of Vittoria not as an army, nor did they stand upon the order of their going. Among the spoils were Joseph's baggage wagons, full of his Spanish plunder, and Marshal Jourdan's imperial baton, found on the road. As their retreat continued beyond Pamplona, they left all but one of their 152 guns and hastened to the mountains. It was the battle that liberated Spain. For a moment Britain became the idol of resurgent German youth; Beethoven wrote an overture on the theme of 'Rule Britannia', and the Russians sang, for the only time in their history, a *Te Deum* in gratitude for a foreign victory.

As soon as he heard of the fate of his army at Vittoria, Napoleon placed Joseph and Jourdan under house arrest and sent Soult from Dresden to 're-establish the imperial business in Spain'. Wellington was now perforce strung out between Roncesvalles and Lesaca, and a bold attack by Soult almost succeeded in breaking through to raise the seige on San Sebastian. Wellington advanced only cautiously, waiting for news from Germany. When he heard of Napoleon's defeat at Leipzig in October, he knew it was sage to proceed into his enemy's heartland. By November he was on the east bank of the Nive, consolidating every advance, and making sure, as he was gradually hampered by the rains, that he would not have to detach portions of his army for the purpose of holding down the countryside, as the French had had to do so disastrously in Spain. In this he was helped by his opponents who, after twenty years of pillage, rape and arson abroad, could not deny themselves these pleasures in their homeland. This had the effect of making the invaders appear as liberators instead of conquerors. There was a little difficulty at first in imposing this conception on them; one private, tried and hanged for a rape, explained that, as he was now in France, he thought it must be in order. Most of the Spaniards had to be sent home; as Wellington told their commander, he had not sacrificed thousands of men merely to enable the survivors to rob the French. Their British comrades, who included a liberal proportion of gaolbirds, he treated in his usual realist way by sending a strong force of military police up and down the columns with orders to string up on the spot every man found pilfering. After a few examples there was no more plundering.

Such a manner of making war much astonished the French. They could scarcely believe their eyes; an innkeeper veteran of Napoleon's Italian campaigns was speechless when Brigadier Barnard of the Light Division asked him how much he owed for his dinner. Having long repudiated the idea of gentility, the people of south-western France found themselves quartering an army of gentlemen. It was worth a dozen victories to the Allies. The British Commander-in-Chief even invited the *maires* of the towns where he stayed to his table: a thing undreamt of in a French Revolutionary general. Those who had fled came flocking back to their homes: the British, it was said, only waged war against men with arms in their hands. What was more, they paid for all they needed. Before long the inhabitants were coining money; fowls were selling at 14s. a-piece and turkeys at 30s. The Commissariat was inundated with cattle, grain and fodder. Even bankers offered the British cash and credit. If this, wrote an English officer, was what making war in an enemy country was like, he never wished to campaign in a friendly one again.

This wise humanity increased the size of Wellington's striking force by at least two divisions. Lines-of-communication troops were rendered needless. Men and supplies could travel about the country unescorted, while the wounded could be billeted and nursed in French households. In vain Soult circulated proclamations exhorting the people to raise partisan bands; they declined to do anything so unprofitable. The only guerrilleros were disgruntled conscripts who took to the hills and fought, not the British, but the Emperor's recruiting officers. Instead, the people of Aquitaine looked on their nice, orderly conquerors as harbingers of peace and prosperity who had come to put an end to conscriptions and war taxes. Some even expressed a wish to be governed by them permanently.

*　　*　　*

Wellington pushed Soult back across the Bidouze, the Gave
d'Oloron and the Gave du Pau at Orthez, which the Marshal had
chosen to dispute. Thereafter there was little effective French
resistance. He was able to despatch a flying force under Beresford to take Bordeaux, the third city of France, which he did
on March 12th, meeting no resistance. On the 26th Wellington
entered Toulouse, where he was overtaken by events. Despite a
vigorous campaign along the north-eastern borders of France that
spring, in which he had shown many flashes of his old genius,
Napoleon had failed, in the face of half a million advancing Allied
troops, to save Paris. He had tried, aware of his numerical inferiority, to play the Allies off one against the other, as he had done
with his own Marshals, by negotiating for a separate peace with
Russia, but the British Foreign Secretary, Castlereagh, had held
the common purpose firmly together. Shortly afterwards Napoleon
signed an act of abdication at Fontainebleau and was exiled to the
island of Elba, off the Italian coast. It was over. 'It is like a dream,'
wrote Dorothy Wordsworth, 'peace, peace all in a moment,
prisoners let loose, Englishmen and Frenchmen brothers at
once!' For one magnanimous moment humanity seemed to stand
in the dawn before the Bastille fell.

The victory summer passed equally like a dream. In June the
Czar, the King of Prussia, the Chancellor of the Austrian Empire,
Prince Metternich and the ruling princes and statesmen of the
greater part of Europe paid a gigantic state visit to England. They
came, in De Quincy's words, to pay homage to the nation which had
'put the soul into the resistance to Napoleon' and to 'the moral
grandeur which had yielded nothing to fear, nothing to despon-
dency.' The visit was not a success, partly because the Czar took a
personal dislike to the Prince Regent, and partly because the Prince
Regent himself, in the process of estranging himself from his wife,
was the object of constant derision by the London crowds for his self-
indulgent behaviour, giving him the considerable embarrassment
of being jeered in the streets of his own capital while the Czar, as
often as not in the next coach, was cheered as a saviour. A succession
of banquets passed more and more frostily, and even the arrival
of Wellington in triumph failed to distract their fellow-diners from

the attentions that the Czar was conspicuously paying to the Prince Regent's opponents. The government granted Wellington £300,000 to buy an estate, and the Speaker of the House of Commons told him as he sat in his Field Marshal's uniform at the bar of the House 'when the will of Heaven and the common destinies of our nature shall have swept away the present generation, you will have left your great name and example as an imperishable monument, exciting others to deeds of glory and serving at once to adorn, defend and perpetuate the existence of this country among the ruling nations of the earth.'

It was a fitting, a more than fitting reception. Wellington did not claim, nor even did his greatest admirers claim for him, that the battle against Napoleon had been won by him alone. But even the role which he had played militarily in the Peninsula was not the sum total of his contribution. He had exemplified Pitt's hope that Britain would save Europe by her example. For as long as Wellington, by his sagacity, his brilliant military mind, his ability to compromise with his Allies, his superiors, the terrain of the Peninsula and the poverty of his fighting resources, had maintained his foothold on the continent of Europe, all those crushed under Napoleon's heel knew that there was yet a hope of final victory. His presence had engendered a steady growth of confidence, even as it had in his immediate presence to his own men. 'Whare's ar *Arthur*?' asked one fusilier of another as, under Beresford's temporarily errant command, they had tramped up the blood-stained hills at Albuera. 'I don't know, I don't see him,' replied the other. 'Aw wish he wore here.' Such was the effect of British constancy as the war yo-yoed up and down the Peninsula.

Sergeant Euart of the Scots Greys seizes a French eagle at Waterloo.

"Bliss it was in that dawn to be alive,
But to be young was very heaven."
Wordsworth

CHAPTER NINETEEN

Waterloo

'The British infantry are the best in the world. Fortunately there are not many of them.'

Marshal Bugeaud

WHILE THE DIPLOMATS were talking and masquerading at the Congress of Vienna, restoring the old order to the map of Europe as far as they might, the little Caesar at Elba kept a sharp eye on the Continent they were reshaping. His hope of a breach between them had been averted by Castlereagh; but Talleyrand's diplomatic victories in the drawing-room of Vienna had still to salve the vanity of defeated France. The wounds of her humiliation at the hands of her former victims were too deep: the spectacle of her inglorious Court could not be stomached by those who had so recently dictated to Europe. The possessors of national lands were scared by the foolish talk of the *émigrés*, the State's creditors irritated by the petty economies of an empty Treasury, the Army angered by popinjays in white feathers and laced uniforms who barred the democratic road to promotion and slighted the pride of the veterans of Austerlitz and Jena. A few months before, Napoleon had been reviled as the cause of all France's defeats and sufferings. Now the old *moustache*, home in his native village, quaffed the ashes of the eagles and muttered bloodcurdling oaths against the fat *coquin* in the Tuileries and the foreigners who had put him there. The Emperor, brave men whispered hoarsely, would return in the spring with the violets. And, as the hereditary boobies in Vienna undid his life's work and the London crowds queued outside the Panorama in Leicester Square to see the model representation of his island cage, the little man in the garden at Porto Ferrajo, with his telescope fixed on every passing sail, saw his opportunity. That February an English traveller was informed that Leghorn Jews were shipping eagled buttons to Elba. The British Commissioners in the island sent a warning to London that something was afoot, the French government pleaded nervously for the Emperor's removal to St Helena. But at Vienna, where the tinkling sleigh parties drove nightly home from the Wienerwald, the Congress was too busy to listen.

On the night of March 7th a great ball was to be held in the Austrian capital. That afternoon the Czar laid a wager with a lady as to who could dress most quickly. At a signal both left the room by different doors, the one returning reclad in a minute and a quarter, the other in a minute and fifty seconds. During the evening a courier arrived at Metternich's house with dispatches from Genoa. The Chancellor was tired from too much business by day and revelry by night. After resting for a while on his couch he opened the dispatch. Napoleon had escaped. In its well-bred inefficiency the *ancien régime* had let out the Corsican ogre.

Thereafter events moved at a terrible speed. On March 10th Napoleon, evading all attempts by the authorities to arrest him, appeared at Lyons, announcing that he had come to save the French from degradation and that his eagles, once more on the wing, would soon alight on the spires of Notre Dame. Unit after unit of the Bourbon army went out to stop him, and, on meeting that familiar, grey-coated figure at the head of his daring few, threw down their arms and welcomed him in a tempest of emotion. On the 14th he was joined by Marshal Ney, who had promised King Louis that he would bring him back to Paris in a cage. Six days later he reached Fontainebleau, where less than a year before he had abdicated and bade a last farewell to his veterans. That night he slept at the Tuileries, the King with a handful of courtiers tearfully scampering before him across the Flemish frontier. France had gone about again and the Revolution Militant was once more enthroned. In Italy the impetuous Murat put his army in motion and the Pope and his Cardinals fled from Rome. So, except for a few fastidious Whig aristocrats, did most of the English tourists.

The Sovereigns of Europe assembled at Vienna refused to accept the outrageous *fait accompli*. On March 18th they proclaimed the escaped prisoner an outlaw and 'disturber of the peace of the world'. Thereafter they ordered an immediate mobilization of the Continent's armies and appointed the duke of Wellington to command the advance guard in the Low Countries – the doorway to the plains of France – until the immense forces of Prussia, Austria and Russia could be mobilized. The flower of the British Peninsular Army – what remained of it after demobilization – was still in America or on the high seas returning from that country. But every man that could be raised was sent in haste to Flanders; even Ireland, despite the protests of Dublin Castle and young Robert Peel, was stripped of troops. Everywhere the trumpets were sounding again for war.

* * *

During the afternoon of Sunday, June 18th, 1815, the city of Brussels was in a state of panic. Since three o'clock a stream of fugitives had been pouring in from the plain beyond the forest of Soignes where, twelve miles south of the capital, Wellington, with 21,000 British and 42,000 Germans and Netherlanders, was barring the way of a victorious French army of 70,000 veterans commanded by Napoleon. Most of the English visitors who had invaded the city in the wake of their army had already fled to the north and were crowding the roads and waterways to Antwerp, where, on Wellington's orders, a state of siege had been proclaimed and crowds waited all day in the rain for news. But hundreds more, unable to obtain transport in the panic – for everything on wheels had been requisitioned – remained in the city without hope of escape. Every few minutes fugitives from the battlefield kept galloping into the town shouting that all was lost and that the French were at their heels. Once a whole regiment of Hanoverian cavalry poured in through the Namur gate with swords drawn and foam-flecked horses and rode through the town towards the north, upsetting everything in the streets on their way. There were other fugitives with bloody and bandaged heads, and

507

cartloads of wounded, and occasionally, towards evening, an officer of high rank, British or Belgian, extended upon a bier borne by soldiers. As the dreadful afternoon advanced and the distant cannonade grew in intensity, the rumour spread – possibly circulated by French sympathizers, of whom there were said to be many – that Napoleon had promised his soldiery the sack of the city. Every woman knew what that meant. 'I never saw such consternation,' wrote Fanny Burney. 'We could only gaze and tremble, listen and shudder.'

Yet three days earlier Brussels had seemed as securely held by British wealth and the martial power of united Europe as London. For weeks it had been a scene of gaiety and military pageantry, with the brilliant aristocracy of England flooding the city in the wake of her army and spending money with a profusion never matched by its successive Spanish, Austrian, French and now Dutch rulers. The nearest French vedettes had been forty miles away beyond the Sambre, and between them and the Belgian capital two great armies had guarded every road on a hundred-mile front, growing daily in strength and commanded by the two most famous soldiers of the European alliance that had defeated and dethroned Napoleon. The Prussian host of around 113,000 men – almost as numerous as the largest striking force Napoleon could be expected to raise from an exhausted and divided France – had entered Belgium under Blücher to hold the frontier from the Ardennes to Charleroi, while a smaller joint British, Netherlands, Hanoverian and Brunswick army had guarded it from Mons to the North Sea under the duke of Wellington. Every week the young, under-strength battalions sent out in haste from England were being joined by the veteran regiments which had driven the French from Spain and which were now returning from America. Elsewhere more than half a million men, mobilized by the sovereigns of Europe, were on the march, their vanguards already closing in on the French frontiers. The danger to Brussels and the Low Countries, so great three months before, seemed to have passed. Though no official state of war existed – Napoleon being merely treated as an outlaw under the new international system of collective security – it had been known that an invasion of France was to begin in July. It had even seemed likely that the French, republicans or royalists, would themselves throw out the usurper and so avoid the necessity of invasion. Napoleon's house, Wellington had told English visitors to the front, was tumbling about his ears.

On the night of Thursday, June 15th, there had been a ball in the city. It had been given by an English lord of fabulous wealth, the duke of Richmond, and the principal officers of the British and Allied army had attended it, including the duke of Wellington and the leader of the Netherlands forces, the Prince of Orange, heir to the throne of the new kingdom. But during its course, and even before it had begun, it had become known that something was amiss. Several times Wellington had been interrupted by messages and was seen to write orders, and at an early hour many of his officers took their leave. During the small hours of the 16th the squares and streets of Brussels had filled with troops as trumpets sounded and drums beat to arms. Presently the troops – green-jacketed Riflemen, scarlet-clad infantry of the line and High-landers, blue-coated Belgians and Brunswickers in black – had moved off, laughing and joking in the early morning sunshine, and asking one another what all the fuss was about. The stolid Flemish country folk, rolling into the city in their carts, had watched them with curious eyes as they marched out down the Charleroi road. Everyone in command had seemed very composed and quiet; old Sir Thomas Picton, commander of the British 5th Division, with top hat and reconnoitring glass slung over his shoulder, cheerfully accosted his friends as he rode through the streets.

Elsewhere – at Enghien, Ath, Grammont, Nivelles, Oudenarde and even as far away as Ghent – other troops, British, German and Netherlandish, roused from their cantonments, had assembled to the sound of trumpets and bugles, and, marching off along the hot, dusty highroads southwards and eastwards, had begun to converge on the assembly point. It had been a day of intense heat. As they emerged from the beech forests on to the great corn plain that fringed the Sambre to the north, the tramping infantrymen and jingling cavalry and gunners heard a dull, sullen sound like distant thunder and saw on the horizon columns of smoke arising.

For on June 15th, after one of his incredibly swift and secret concentrations, Napoleon had sprung like a tiger across the Sambre and driven in the outposts of Blücher's army at the point where its right touched the left of Wellington's equally scattered force. When the first news of the crossing had reached the Prussian and British commanders, they had suspected it to be a feint. The hours Napoleon had thereby gained had given him the chance to drive a wedge between them. With 124,000 men he had placed himself between Blücher's 113,000 Prussians and Wellington's miscellaneous 83,000. His object had been to defeat one or the other before they had time to concentrate and then, forcing both back on their divergent communications, to enter Brussels as a conqueror. Thereafter, he had believed, the Belgian common people would rise against the Dutch, the war-weary French take heart and unite behind him, the Tory government in London fall, and his Austrian father-in-law, deprived of British subsidies, sue for peace.

All afternoon on the 16th the people of Brussels had heard, through the hot, airless haze, the sound of cannonading from Quatre Bras, where twenty miles to the south Marshal Ney was trying to brush aside a weak Netherlands force from the crossroads which preserved front-line communication between the Prussian and Anglo-Dutch armies. By some miracle of tough, confused fighting, in which Picton's Highlanders had covered themselves with glory and the duke of Brunswick had fallen, Wellington, reinforced by successive contingents, had held the crossroads and by nightfall assembled 30,000 troops in Ney's path. But owing to the delay in ordering his concentration – the result of faulty staff work – he had failed to join Blücher in battle that day against Napoleon. By nightfall, six miles away at Ligny, 63,000 Frenchmen under the great Emperor had beaten the 80,000 Prussians concentrated against them and inflicted 15,000 casualties. The seventy-two-year-old Field Marshal had only narrowly escaped capture after being trampled on by French cavalry.

Yet Napoleon's victory had not been as complete as he had thought. Owing to the failure of one of his corps which, through contradictory orders, had marched and countermarched all day between the two battlefields without taking part in either, the

Prussians had escaped annihilation and were able to withdraw in tolerable order into the night. Next morning, when the Emperor, detaching 33,000 troops under Marshal Grouchy to pursue the Prussians, had thrown the rest of his army against Wellington, the latter had withdrawn in good time up the Charleroi-Brussels highway. And though Napoleon had supposed that he had driven the Prussians back eastwards towards their communications, Blücher had in fact withdrawn northwards towards Wavre on a road parallel to the British only a dozen miles to the east. Unknown to Napoleon, the Allied armies had thus remained in touch and, though the Emperor had reduced their numerical superiority and shaken their morale, he had not, as he supposed, divided them. Nor, though the people of Brussels had expected all day to see the victorious French emerge from the Forest of Soignes, had the British withdrawal towards Brussels been on the whole precipitate. It had been brilliantly covered by Lord Uxbridge's cavalry and horse artillery, and by nightfall Wellington had concentrated his army on the ridge of Mont St Jean twelve miles south of the city. During the afternoon Napoleon's retreat had been increasingly delayed by torrential thunderstorms which had converted the Charleroi *chaussée* and the fields on either side into quagmires. It had seemed, recalled one officer, as if the water was being tumbled out of heaven in tubs.

The two armies had spent an uncomfortable night. The rain fell almost continually, with flashes of lightning and violent gusts of wind. The ground on which the men lay, drenched to the skin and shaking with cold, was sodden with wet crops. A few old campaigners made themselves tolerably comfortable by smearing their blankets with clay and making pillows of straw. Few of the newcomers to war, who in the Allied army outnumbered the old hands, got any sleep at all.

Dawn on the 18th was cold and cheerless. Everyone was covered in mud from head to foot. Presently the clouds began to lift, and the men managed to get their camp-fires lit and to cook breakfast. Afterwards, on the officers' orders, they dried their ammunition and cleaned their arms. Later, as the sun came out, Wellington rode round the lines, accompanied by his staff. They looked as gay and unconcerned as if they were riding to a meet in England.

The ridge, or rather rolling plateau, on which the British army has halted was one which the duke had long marked as a favourable position for the defence of the Belgian capital. It crossed the highroad from Brussels to Charleroi a mile and a half south of the village of Waterloo and the forest of Soignes. It was named after the little village of Mont St Jean which nestled by the roadside in one of its northern folds. In the course of riding and hunting expeditions Wellington had carefully studied its gentle undulations and contours. It was here that twenty-one years before, when he was a young lieutenant-colonel marching from Ostend to join a hard-pressed and almost identically circumstanced army, his chief, the duke of York, had urged the Austrian generalissimo, Coburg, to give battle to Jourdan's levies after Fleurus. But Coburg had chosen to fall back eastward on his communications, leaving Brussels to its fate and the British to shift for themselves. Only now, when after a generation of disaster and servitude, a Prussian Field Marshal had learnt the necessity of unselfish cooperation between allies, Wellington was able to take his stand here. For though his only reliable troops were outnumbered by two to one and though the French had nearly double his weight of artillery, he knew that he had only to hold his ground with one wing of an international army until the other under Blücher could reach the battlefield. Then, on the morrow, the whole mighty force could take the offensive and sweep Napoleon back to France.

Unlike Blücher at Ligny, who, in the normal Continental manner, had drawn up his army in view of Napoleon, Wellington – proven the greatest master of defensive tactics in Europe – had chosen a position where his infantry could inflict the utmost damage on the attackers while suffering the least themselves. Its reverse or northern slope, in whose undulations he concealed his forces, gave him precisely the cover and field of fire needed for an active defence. Behind it lay the forest which, stretching for miles on either side of the Brussels highway, constituted, with its close-growing beeches and freedom from undergrowth, an excellent temporary refuge into which to withdraw inexperienced troops if they proved unable to withstand Napoleon's attack. Once inside it, he remarked, he would have defied the Devil himself to drive him out. But as, like his ally, he was thinking in ultimate terms, not of defence but of offensive action, he gave battle on the open plain where the full strength of the Prussian and British armies could later be brought to bear on Napoleon.

Until then, however, Wellington knew that his role must be strictly defensive. At least half the foreign troops under his command could not be trusted to manoeuvre. Captain Kincaid drew the picture of a detachment of them at Quatre Bras, behaving for all the world like Mathews', the comedian's, ludicrous sketch of the American Militia; whenever, after a careful explanation of their role, they were given the word to march, they had started blazing away at the British skirmishers ahead – 'we were at least,' Kincaid wrote, 'obliged to be satisfied with whatever advantages their appearance would give, as even that was of some consequence where troops were so scarce.' Later in the day, he admitted, when they got used to the sensation of being fired at, they behaved quite well. Many, however, having fought for Napoleon when Belgium, Holland and western Germany formed part of his empire, had little stomach for fighting against him. Many more were boys and raw landwehr, though, in the case of the Brunswickers, with good officers and NCOs. Few were adequately equipped or trained. Of the 42,000 foreign troops in Wellington's army only the 5500 men of the veteran King's German Legion – an integral part of the British army – could be described as first-line troops.

Wellington was, therefore, forced to do as he had done in early Peninsular days; to stiffen his foreign formations with redcoats. In the teeth of opposition, particularly from the King of the Netherlands, he had tried to make his force as international in organization as possible; to this end he habitually wore the national cockades of all the Allies in his hat and forbade the playing of 'Rule Britannia' at regimental concerts. As at Talavera, the most immobile troops of all he stationed among buildings and behind walls. Fortunately one of the features of his position was the presence of villages and farms on either flank of his two-and-a-half-mile front – Smohain, Papelotte, La Haye and Frischermont to the east, and Merbe Braine and Braine l'Alleud to the west. In these he

513

placed some rather uncertain Nassauers – who, however, defended them bravely – Chassé's Belgian division and the youthful Bruns-wickers who had suffered so severely at Quatre Bras. They thus served – an old device of Wellington's – both as flank guards and reserves.

The backbone of his polyglot, and what he afterwards described as 'infamous army' was its 21,000 British regulars – of whom more than 2000 had arrived from Ostend only that morning – and their comrades of the King's German Legion. Yet of this vital 26,500 – a smaller force than any he had commanded since his first Portu-guese campaign – only about half had been under fire. Several of its units were weak second-line battalions, scarcely out of the goose-step. Even most of the eighteen infantry battalions that had fought in Spain had been brought up to strength by recruiting from the plough before they left England. Probably not more than 12,000 had served in the incomparable army that had marched from the Douro to Toulouse.

Compared with his Peninsular army, Wellington's force was relatively stronger in cavalry than infantry. Its 7000 British and King's German Legion cavalry, though far outnumbered by Napoleon's cuirassiers and lancers, made an imposing spectacle, superbly uniformed and caparisoned – the Prince Regent saw to that – and mounted on the finest horses in the world. They could ride across country like a field of high-metalled foxhunters, for they came from a land where horsemanship was a passion. At a review they left Blücher speechless with admiration. 'It did one's heart good,' wrote a Rifleman, watching them on the retreat from Quatre Bras, 'to see how cordially the Lifeguards went at their work; they had no idea of anything but straightforward fighting and sent their opponents flying in all directions.' Their chief, the earl of Uxbridge, was the Lord Paget who had commanded Moore's cavalry so brilliantly during the Corunna campaign, but whose service in the Peninsula had been cut short by an elopement with the wife of Wellington's brother. Apart from his amatory exploits, he was an excellent officer, quiet and incisive, though, like his command, rather too dashing.

What the British cavalry lacked, except for the King's German

Legion and a few fine Peninsular regiments like the 23rd Light Dragoons, was experience of war and, in their high-spirited younger officers, discipline. Too many of the latter held their commissions, not because they wanted to be professional soldiers, but because a few years in a crack cavalry mess was a mark of social distinction. Their courage and dash was indisputable; their self-control and staying power less certain. The troopers, magnificent fighting material, were what the officers – so much less experienced and realist than their humbler infantry colleagues – made or failed to make of them. The same witness of the Life Guards' charge during the retreat noticed with amusement that, whenever one of them got a roll in the mud, he went off to the rear as no longer fit to appear on parade.

In artillery, though he only acknowledged it sparingly, Wellington was brilliantly served. Its mounted branch was magnificently horsed,* and, Horse and Field Artillery alike, officers and men were animated by the highest professional spirit. Only 96 of the 156 guns opposed to Napoleon's 266 pieces were British or King's German Legion, but they were probably better handled than any guns even on a battlefield where one of the commanders was the master gunner of all time. They were lighter metalled than the French guns, many of which were the dreaded twelve-pounders. Yet, thanks to the foresight of Sir Augustus Frazer, three of the seven mounted batteries had recently substituted nine-pounders for the normal six-pounders. There were also some howitzers.

In the last resort, as Wellington well knew, everything depended on his British infantry. There were far too few of them; as he carefully sent them off after Quatre Bras before the rest of his troops, he remarked, 'Well, there is the last of the infantry gone, and I don't care now.' A few weeks before, Creevey, encountering him in a Brussels square, had asked whether he and Blücher could do the business. 'It all depends upon that article there,' the duke replied pointing at a private of one of the line regiments who was gaping at the statues, 'give me enough of it, and I am sure.'

He, therefore, placed his thirty-five under-strength British and

---

* 'Mein Gott,' said Blücher, after inspecting Mercer's battery, 'dere is no von 'orse in diss batterie wich is not goot for Veldt Marshal.'

King's German Legion infantry battalions where he thought the
danger was greatest, but left no part of the battlefield without
them. He had received in the small hours of the morning, before
retiring to sleep, Blücher's assurance that he would join him in
the course of the day with not less than two corps – a force as large
as his own. His anxiety was, therefore, for his right rather than his
left. Believing it to be to Napoleon's interest to shift the battle
away from the Prussians' impending flank march, he expected him
to incline to the west, possibly even striking as far as the Mons-
Brussels road to seize the Belgian capital in his rear and break his
communications with England. For this reason he had retained at
Hal and Tubize, some ten or twelve miles to the west, 15,000
Dutch and Hanoverian and 3000 British troops to guard the
Mons-Brussels road, protect the capital and keep open his lines to
Ostend, where more veterans from America were expected. In the
event of the battle shifting to the west this force might have an
important effect, either against an offensive or in pursuit of a
French retreat towards Maubeuge or Lille.

There was a more immediate reason why Wellington felt
anxious about his right. The unobtrusive but fine defensive
position he had chosen had one flaw – a narrow, winding, shallow
depression which, passing under the walls of a country house called
Hougoumont in the plain below the ridge, afforded an approach
by which a column could climb round the west shoulder of the
plateau out of direct gunfire and debouch on to the reverse slope
where his army was drawn up. For this reason he placed near the
danger spot on the right of his front line the First or Guards
Division and behind it, in reserve and *en potence*, Clinton's fine
2nd Division which, with its two brigades of veteran British and
King's German Legion infantry, was the nearest he possessed to
his old Peninsular Light Division – a force which could manoeuvre
quickly. Beyond it he stationed at Merbe Braine and Braine l'Alleud
his less mobile reserve of Brunswickers and Chassé's Belgians. In
addition, since the winding hollow which his experienced eye had
perceived could be commanded by musketry fire from Hougoumont, he adopted the unorthodox expedient of fortifying and
garrisoning an outpost nearly a quarter of a mile in advance of his

main position on the ridge. With its château, barns, orchards, gardens, park and woods, the estate of Hougoumont formed a 500 yards square whose wooded southern border extended almost to the ridge occupied by the French. Without its possession Napoleon could neither move a column up the hollow nor, unless he divided his army in the presence of his enemy's best troops, envelop the Allied right. Wellington, therefore, placed seven hundred Hanoverians and Nassauers in the Hougoumont woods, and four light companies of the Guards, detached from the Guards' Division on the ridge behind, to hold the house, gardens and orchard and command the sunken way. To the west, defending the avenue to the house from the Nivelles road, he stationed Mitchell's British brigade with some light cavalry in rear. Thus garrisoned, the Hougoumont estate outflanked from the west the plain between the rival armies; if it could be held till the Prussians arrived, Napoleon's position would become untenable. In the meantime it would gravely delay and impede his attack.

Having secured his right, Wellington strengthened the remaining two miles of his front in his usual way by placing his formations, except for the guns and skirmishers, on the reverse slope of the ridge. They were thus out of sight, though not out of range, of the enemy's cannon. They were deployed in broken and staggered lines and so disposed as to present single rather than double targets for the enemy's round-shot. The artillery, save for the reserve batteries, Wellington placed along the summit of the ridge, with orders to reserve its fire for the enemies' columns. The skirmishers and riflemen were stationed on the forward or southern slope, concealed, as were all his troops, in the corn which, almost shoulder-high, covered the entire battlefield. By this arrangement the French masses would have to advance through three successive zones of fire – the rifle fire of picked marksmen, the round-shot and grape of the guns, and, as they came over the crest, the musketry volleys of deployed and, till then, invisible infantry.

Apart from Hougoumont on the west, Smohain, Papelotte and La Haye on the east, and the little farm of Mont St Jean just behind the British lines, there were no buildings on the open ground Wellington had chosen for battle except the farm of La Haye

517

Sainte. This lay a hundred yards or so down the slope on the southern side of the ridge, abutting on to the straight-paved *chaussée* from Charleroi to Brussels which, ascending the hill here through a cutting, intersected it and the British line at right angles. Here, in the centre of his line of skirmishers, Wellington placed a battalion of the King's German Legion under Major Baring. Behind it and at the top of the ridge the Charleroi-Brussels road was crossed at right angles by a sunken lane which following the crest from west to east, joined, north of Hougoumont, another highway that fanned out of the Brussels road at Mont St Jean and ran through a cutting south-westwards towards Nivelles. This road, like the orchards and woods of Hougoumont, had the effect of constricting the frontage on which the French could assail Wellington's right.

It was generally believed by the British – though not by Wellington, who knew his adversary's overweening confidence and impatience – that there would be no attack that day. But in the course of the morning, it became clear that the enemy advance-guard, which had bivouacked during the night on a parallel ridge three-quarters of a mile to the south, was being joined by the entire French army. Presently the sun came out, and watchers could see the long lines of massed troops, with their glittering helmets, cuirasses and arms, forming a magnificent spectacle, on the ridge of La Belle Alliance – named after the solitary, red-tiled public house of that name. At one time there was a burst of cheering as a grey figure on a white horse, accompanied by a cavalcade, rode down the lines. For the French were not only intending to attack, but in their resolve to conquer, were partaking of a sacrament. Napoleon might not have France, or even all his anxious generals behind him, but there was no question of the devotion of his fighting men. Between him and his old *moustaches* was a bond to be found in no other army on earth. For all his grandiloquent pretensions, he and they were familiars. Cam Hobhouse, watching him review the Imperial Guard just before the campaign began, was amazed at the way he mingled with his troops, leaving the saluting base and marching in time beside each column; once he went up to a grenadier and affectionately pulled his nose. He might be prodigal of his men's lives, but, unlike Wellington, who was not, he valued his command of their hearts. It was the foundation of his fortunes. At that moment as he rode along the lines amid shouts of *'Vive l'Empereur!'*, Leipzig, the Retreat from Moscow and the Abdication were as though they had never been.

Neither Napoleon nor his men doubted their ability to destroy Wellington's army and reach Brussels by nightfall. Their triumph over the Prussians two days before – achieved against superior numbers – had whetted their appetite for glory. Nor was the urgent victory Napoleon needed the key only to political salvation. It would be a revenge for all the humiliations the English had heaped on him. Wellington was the one commander with a European reputation whom he had never beaten and the British the one army. 'Because you have been defeated by Wellington,' he told his Chief of Staff, Soult, who dwelt on the British capacity for recoil, 'you think him a great general! I tell you that Wellington is a bad general, that the English are bad troops and that this will be a picnic!' His only fear was that they would vanish before he could attack them, as they had done on the previous day at Quatre Bras and seven years earlier under Moore on the Carrion. As, however, they now appeared to be calmly waiting for him, their doom was certain. 'We will sleep tonight,' he told his officers, 'in Brussels.'

Owing to the usual dispersal in search of food and plunder the last of the French only reached their battle stations at midday, three hours after the time originally ordered. Napoleon, however, was not hurrying, since to make full use of his superior artillery and cavalry, he wanted the ground to dry. Despite warnings from those who had fought in Spain, he was quite sure that, once he struck in overpowering force, there would be little need to waste time in manoeuvring. Most of Wellington's foreign auxiliaries, he reckoned, would bolt at the start, and the stiff redcoats would then break under the triple shock of his massed bombardment, veteran columns, and discharge of grape at close range. 'I shall hammer them with my artillery,' he announced, 'charge them with my cavalry to make them show themselves, and, when I am quite sure where the actual English are, I shall go straight at them with my Old Guard.'

As for the Prussians, he was so convinced that they had retreated eastwards, as he wished, that he never considered the possibility of their appearance on the battlefield at all. After the hiding he had given them at Ligny they were manifestly incapable of further fight for the present. Having detached Grouchy to shepherd them out of Flanders, he felt he could discount them. They could be trusted, as in the past, to act selfishly and leave their allies to their fate. It had never been his habit to keep faith with anyone unless it suited him. That a Prussian commander should endanger his army and strain his communications to keep faith with Wellington never occurred to him.

The Emperor, therefore, decided to open his main attack at one o'clock. In the meantime, while he massed eighty field-pieces on a spur of high ground in the middle of the valley opposite and about 600 yards short of the British centre, he ordered the troops on his two flanks to engage the extremities of the defenders' line at Papelotte and Hougoumont in order to distract attention from his impending blow, and probably – though of this there can be no certainty – to clear a way for the use, at the decisive moment, of the sunken hollow leading to the heart of Wellington's right. In that case, however, he was unfortunate in his adversary.

The first shots of the battle were fired at about half-past eleven in front of Hougoumont. After a short preliminary bombardment, four battalions of Prince Jerome's division advanced against the wood to the south of the château. During the next hour they succeeded in driving out its not very numerous German defenders. But they then went on to attack the gardens and mansion and in doing so came up against a far more formidable adversary, the four light companies of the British Guards under Lord Saltoun. The attackers not only attracted the close attention of Wellington, but brought upon themselves exceedingly heavy casualties – 1500 in the first forty minutes, both from the steady aim of the British guardsmen, firing through embrasures in the walls, and from the accurate fire of Bull's howitzer battery stationed on the ridge behind the house. When the Guards counter-attacked and drove them back, Jerome threw another brigade into the assault and tried to gain a lodgment in the courtyard of the château. So furious was his attack that at one moment a detachment of his men broke open the great gate with an axe and swarmed in, only to be surrounded and destroyed inside, while four officers and a sergeant of the Coldstream closed the door behind them by main force. Once again the British counter-attacked with four companies of the Coldstream whom Wellington sent down from the ridge. 'There, my lads, in with you,' he said as they moved off, 'let me see no more of you.'

Jerome's answer and that of the commander of the French left, General Reille, was to undertake – a quarter of an hour before Napoleon's main attack on the centre was due to begin – a third attack on Hougoumont with still larger forces. For every regiment they committed, the frugal Wellington staked no more than a company or whatever smaller force was necessary to hold the position. All the while his guns continued to shell the wood with such effect that, as one unending column of fresh attackers poured into it, another – of wounded – as continuously poured out.

So far Napoleon had been only partially successful. His diversion to the east had made little effect on the Netherlanders in Papelotte and La Haye, while the more important one to the west, though occupying Wellington's attention, had failed either to by-pass or capture Hougoumont. It was now one o'clock, the hour at which the bombardment of the Allied centre was due to begin. But before its smoke enveloped the battlefield, Napoleon, watching the preparations from a knoll beside the Brussels road, observed through his telescope a suspicious movement on the high ground towards Wavre, five or six miles to the east. It might – at first it seemed to him that it must – be Grouchy, from whom he had just heard that the Prussians were retiring, not on Liège as both men had thought, but on Brussels. Yet this was scarcely likely, as Grouchy in his dispatch, dated at six that morning, had announced his intention of following them northwards on Wavre. And, as Grouchy, like Napoleon, had been wrong once about the Prussians' movements, there was another and less pleasant possibility.

At that moment, this terrifying suspicion was confirmed. For a Prussian hussar, captured by a French vedette to the west of the battlefield, was brought to Napoleon bearing a dispatch from

Blücher to Wellington which showed that the troops visible on the heights of St Lambert were Bülow's corps, advancing from Wavre, and that the rest of the Prussian army had spent the night around that town, only thirteen miles away.

Napoleon, in other words, had been 'making pictures' – the crime against which he had always warned his subordinates. He had made his dispositions to fight under conditions that did not exist. Instead of having only the English and their feeble auxiliaries to contend with, he would have, if he proceeded with his attack, to face before nightfall the intervention of another army. The attempt to separate Wellington's and Blücher's forces had failed, at least in any but the most temporary sense. The French must either withdraw – the prudent course – or defeat the British in the next three hours. For after that they would have to contend against two foes.

Being a gambler, and being, both politically and strategically, in desperate need of an immediate victory, Napoleon decided to proceed with the battle. It still seemed unthinkable to him that the breach he was about to blast in the British centre could fail to defeat Wellington, and, with him out of the way, Blücher could be dealt with in turn. Indeed, with Grouchy in his rear and his army committed to the muddy defiles between Wavre and Mont St Jean, the old Prussian might end the day in an even worse disaster than Ligny. Napoleon, therefore, detached part of his reserve to delay the still distant Prussian advance, and ordered the attack on the British to proceed.

The eighty-gun bombardment, which opened at one o'clock, fully came up to expectations. Twenty-four of the guns were Napoleon's great twelve-pounders, with a 2000 yards range. It took away the breath of Wellington's young recruits and militia men, and surprised even Peninsular veterans by its intensity. Captain Mercer, commanding a reserve battery of horse artillery in a hollow several hundred yards and in rear of the British right flank, found, even in that sheltered position, the shot and shell continually plunging around him. One shot completely carried away the lower part of the head of one of his horses. Fortunately the ground was still wet and many shells burst where they fell, while the round-shot, instead of hopping and ricochetting for half a mile or more, frequently became embedded in the mud.

But though very alarming, owing to Wellington's skilful dispositions, the bombardment did comparatively little harm except to a brigade of Belgians, whose commander, General Bylandt, misinterpreting his orders, had drawn it up, in the Continental manner, on the forward slope of the ridge. During its half-hour of bombardment in this exposed position it lost one man in four, and, had it not been hastily withdrawn to a less conspicuous position, its loss might have been still greater. When, therefore, at half-past one, D'Erlon in charge of the French right moved his corps forward to the attack, with all the panoply and terror of a Napoleonic offensive – drums beating at the head of dense column, bearded grenadiers marching four hundred abreast shouting at the top of their voices, and clouds of *tirailleurs* running and firing ahead – the customary conditions for success seemed to have been ensured. Four divisions of infantry – more than 16,000 men – each moving in close column of battalions at a quarter of a mile's distance, tramped down the slope and up the hill against the British centre and left through clouds of sulphurous smoke. Behind came companies of sappers, ready to turn the village of Mont St Jean beyond the British centre into a fortress as soon as it was captured.

A hail of shot from the artillery on the crest greeted them. But it did not halt the men who had conquered at Wagram and Friedland. One column, supported by cuirassiers, swept round La Haye Sainte, encircling it and its German defenders and driving back the two companies of the Rifles – the most formidable marksmen in Europe – who were stationed in a sandpit on the opposite side of the *chaussée*. Another, to the west, forced the Dutch out of Papelotte and La Haye and temporarily occupied Smohain. In the centre about 8000 men approached the summit simultaneously. As they did so, Bylandt's Belgians – raw troops who had endured to the limit of their capacity – fired one hysterical volley at the advancing, shouting column and took to their heels, carrying away the gunners of the reserve batteries behind. They never stopped till they reached the Forest of Soignes, where they remained for the rest of the day.

To Napoleon, watching from the knoll near La Belle Alliance, it seemed as though, as at Ligny, his adversary's centre was broken. But as the French bore down on the gap they had opened, Picton deployed Kempt's reserve brigade in their path. It was the familiar story of every battle of the Peninsular War. 'The French came on in the old style,' said Wellington afterwards, 'and we drove them off in the old style.' The 28th, 32nd, 79th Highlanders and the 95th Rifles – all veterans of Spain – held their fire till the head of the column was only twenty yards away. Then, from their thin extended line, they poured in a tremendous, disciplined volley, and, as the leading French files tried, too late, to deploy, charged with the bayonet. At the moment of his triumph Picton was struck in the head by a bullet and killed.

Farther to the east, D'Erlon's two other divisions reached the summit. Here, after its heavy losses at Quatre Bras, Pack's brigade – Royals, 44th, 42nd and 92nd Highlanders – could only muster 1400 bayonets. Slowly, against such odds, they began to give ground, while a brigade of French cavalry on their flank, having cut a Hanoverian battalion to pieces, swarmed on to the crest.

At that moment, Lord Uxbridge, waiting behind the British infantry with two brigades of heavy cavalry ready deployed, gave the order to charge. Leading the Household Brigade in person, he drove the astonished French cuirassiers into the ranks of the infantry behind, who, seeing the big, scarlet-coated Life Guardsmen slashing at them, turned and joined in the flight. Simultaneously the Union Brigade – consisting of Royal Dragoons, Scots Greys and Inniskillings – swept down on another French column. Within a few minutes the flower of D'Erlon's corps was flying across the plain with 2000 British cavalry after it. 'Hundreds of the infantry threw themselves down and pretended to be dead,' wrote Kincaid, 'while the cavalry galloped over them and then got up and ran away; I never saw such a scene in all my life.' More than 4000 were cut down or taken prisoner. Many did not stop till they reached Genappe.

Unfortunately the pursuers did not stop either. The secret of cavalry is iron discipline. It was a secret that the British cavalry, though superlative in dash, physique and horsemanship, had never wholly mastered. According to Hamilton of Dalzell of the Scots Greys, the troopers had been served with rum before the charge. They followed the French into the heart of Napoleon's position, sabring the gunners of his great battery and riding on to the ridge of La Belle Alliance itself as though they were after a fox. Having charged in the first line, Uxbridge was unable either to stop them or to bring up reserve cavalry in support. When the French cuirassiers and lancers counter-attacked in superior strength, the scattered, breathless men and horses were powerless and became themselves the pursued. The flower of Wellington's cavalry – the striking-force of his tactical reserve – having saved his centre, was itself needlessly destroyed. Sir William Ponsonby was struck down at the head of the Union Brigade, and nearly half the personnel of the six splendid regiments which had smashed D'Erlon's columns were killed or taken prisoner. Vandeleur's Brigade, which gallantly tried to cover their retreat, also suffered severely. Those who got back to the British lines were too few to intervene with real effect in the battle again. Some of the weaker brethren never returned to the field at all.

*　　*　　*

But for this unexpected advantage, there would have seemed little object in Napoleon's continuing the battle. It was now three o'clock. Not only had one of his two corps of front-line infantry become heavily committed to an increasingly costly and still un-successful struggle in front of Hougoumont, but the British, con-trary to expectation, had repulsed and shattered the other which, untouched at either Ligny or Quatre Bras, was to have breached and pinned down Wellington's centre until Lobau's reserve infantry, Ney's cavalry and, at the end of all, the Imperial Guard, had destroyed him. Instead, Napoleon now found himself com-mitted to an impending battle on a second front, to avert or post-pone which he was forced to detach, under Lobau, the very reserve of infantry which was to have followed up D'Erlon's expected success. With the Prussians approaching from the other side, he dared not commit this now to a left-hook against the British centre, the vital approach to which was still untaken. Apart from the small portion of Reille's corps still uncommitted to the unending fight round Hougoumont, he had no infantry left for a new attack on the ridge except the twenty-four battalions of the Imperial Guard. And these, in view of the growing threat to his flank and the, to him, unexpected revelation of British defensive striking-power, he was not yet prepared to commit. For the Guard was the last card that stood between him and ruin. He kept it, 13,000 strong, the apple of his eye, unused beside him.

For about half an hour there was a pause in the battle, except at Hougoumont, where Jerome and Foy threw ever more troops into the inferno round the blazing but still defiant buildings. Wellington took advantage of the lull to readjust his dispositions. Pack's brigade took the place vacated by Bylandt's Netherlanders, Lambert's brigade came up from the second line to strengthen Picton's battered division, and two more companies of the King's German Legion were thrown into La Haye Sainte. The Prussians were taking far longer to arrive than the British commander had expected. There had been a delay in their start, aggravated by a fire in the narrow streets of Wavre and the fact that Bülow's as yet unused corps in the van had the farthest distance to march. After the rains, the cross-country lanes were almost impassable for transport, and Gneisenau, the Prussian Chief of Staff, was reluctant to attack Napoleon, with Grouchy's troops in his rear, until he knew for certain that Wellington was standing fast. Only Blücher's insistence – for the old man, oblivious of his injuries, was with Bülow's advance guard by midday – carried the tired and hungry troops forward through the soggy defiles of the Lasne and the dense woods that lay between it and the battlefield. 'I have promised Wellington,' he told them as they dragged the guns axle-deep through mire, 'you would not have me break my word!'

Meanwhile, the French gunners had taken up their position again on the central ridge and, soon after three o'clock, reopened their fire. It was more intense than anything the oldest Peninsular veteran had experienced. The range was so accurate that almost every shot told, and after a quarter of an hour Wellington withdrew his infantry a hundred yards farther back from the crest.

Under cover of the bombardment, La Haye Sainte in the centre was again surrounded. But Baring's handful of German Legionaries continued to hold the walls, and with Kempt's and Lambert's men standing firm on the plateau above, D'Erlon's mangled infantry refrained from pressing home their assault. They seemed to fear a renewal of the storm of cavalry that had struck their comrades.

Suddenly the battle took a novel and spectacular form. For, mistaking the partial withdrawal of Wellington's infantry for the beginning of a general retirement, Marshal Ney decided to take a short cut to victory by sweeping the ridge with heavy cavalry. Of these – the finest in the world – his master had almost as many as Wellington's British infantry. He therefore ordered forward 5000 of them, including eight regiments of cuirassiers, drawing them up in the plain immediately to the west of the *chassée* where the slope was easiest.

Wellington watched the splendid spectacle with amazement. It seemed unbelievable that the French would dare to assail a line of unbroken British infantry with cavalry alone. But such was plainly their intention, and, with his own heavy cavalry too weakened to counter-charge in strength, there was a danger that, if Napoleon was able to bring up infantry and guns behind them, the defenders, forced to remain in square, might be blasted out of existence by case-shot. The two divisions to the west of the Brussels road – the 3rd and 1st – were ordered to form battalion squares or oblongs in chequer-wise pattern across the gently swelling, corn-covered plateau. They were aligned so that every face of every square had a field of fire free of the next. Until the attackers appeared over the crest Wellington ordered the men to lie down. Behind the twenty squares his cavalry, including the remnants of the two British heavy brigades, were drawn up in support.

Between and a little in advance of the squares Wellington placed his guns, bringing up his last two reserve batteries of Horse Artillery to inflict the utmost damage on the advancing cavalry. As Mercer's men, on the order, 'Left limber up, and as fast as you can!' galloped into the inferno of smoke and heat on the plateau, they heard a humming like the sound of myriads of beetles on a

527

summer's evening. So thick was the hail of balls and bullets, wrote their commander, that it seemed dangerous to extend the arm lest it should be torn off. Their orders, in the event of the enemy charging home, were to run for shelter to the nearest square, taking the near wheel of each gun with them.

Mercer disregarded this order – one that could only have been given to gun detachments of the highest discipline and training – not because he doubted his battery's morale, but because he believed that the young Brunswickers in square on either side of him, who were falling fast, would take to their heels if they saw his men run. As soon as the French appeared out of the smoke a hundred yards away – a long line of cuirasses and helmets glittering like a gigantic wave on the crest of the rye – he ordered his six nine-pounders, doubly loaded with round-shot and case, to open fire. As the case poured into them, the leading ranks went down like grass before a skilled mower. Again and again, when the French charged, the same thing happened, and the Brunswickers who, before the battery's arrival, had stood like soulless logs in their agony and had only been kept at their posts by the gallantry of their officers, recovered heart.

Elsewhere, where the gunners obeyed Wellington's orders, the French cavalry, crowded in a dense mass into the half-mile gap between Hougoumont and La Haye Sainte, rode over the abandoned guns and swept round the squares beyond. They did not gallop like English foxhunters, but came, as was their wont, at a slow, majestic pace and in perfect formation, their horses shaking the earth. As they appeared the British infantry rose at the word of command, their muskets at the ready and their bayonets bristling like massed gigantic *chevaux de frise*. If the cavalry of the Empire were Atlantic breakers, the British squares were the rocks of an iron coast. The men, many of them rosy-faced youngsters from the plough, were much impressed by the splendid appearance of the hordes of legendary horsemen who suddenly encircled them and even more by their courage, but they were not intimidated by them, as Ney had intended. As their experienced officers and NCOs seemed to regard the newcomers as harmless, in their stolid, unimaginative English way they did so too. The cuirassiers and lancers made a great deal of noise and glitter, brandishing their weapons like pantomime giants and shouting '*Vive l'Empereur*', but they seemed infinitely preferable to the continuous hail of shot and shell which had poured from the French batteries till they arrived on the ridge.

Short of impaling their horses on the hedges of bayonets, Ney's cavalry tried every device to break the squares. Occasionally little groups of horsemen, led by frantic officers, would dash for the face of one, firing off carbines and pistols and hoping to draw sufficient fire to enable their comrades behind to break in on a line of unloaded muskets. But the British and Hanoverian squares preserved perfect discipline, withholding their fire until they received the word of command and then, with their volleys, bringing down everything before them. The loss of horses was prodigious; the poor creatures lay dead or dying in hundreds, their riders, many of them wounded, making their way in a continuous stream back down the hill, or sprawling in their heavy cuirasses in the mud, looking, as Wellington afterwards recalled, like overturned turtles.

Whenever he judged that the intruders were sufficiently worn down and wearied, Wellington endeavoured to push them off the plateau with his cavalry, or, in default, by edging forward his squares in echelon towards the abandoned guns. He did not hurry, for he was playing for time, and he could not afford to let his light British and King's German Legion cavalry encounter the heavier armed cuirassiers until the latter were too exhausted and reduced to retaliate. The foreign Horse which he had brought up from the flanks and reserve to take the place of Ponsonby's and Somerset's lost squadrons proved, most of it, worse than useless, refusing repeated appeals from Uxbridge to charge. One regiment of Hanoverian hussars, led by its colonel, fled as far as Brussels.

Even the British cavalry showed a reluctance at times to charge home in the face of such overwhelming weight and numbers, though several regiments, particularly the 13th Light Dragoons and the 15th Hussars, behaved with the greatest gallantry. The shock felt by men encountering for the first time the sights and sounds of battle – and such a battle – had in the nature of things a more paralysing effect on cavalry than on infantry whose men in square had the close support of officers and comrades. Once Uxbridge, whose energy and initiative throughout this critical time was beyond praise, was driven into exclaiming that he had tried every brigade and could not get one to follow him, and then, as he rode up to the 1st Foot Guards, 'Thank God, I am with men who make me not ashamed of being an Englishman.' One of the officers recalled how, while Wellington was sheltering in his square, the men were so mortified at seeing the cuirassiers deliberately walking their horses round them that they shouted, 'Where are our cavalry? Why don't they come and pitch into these French fellows?' Such resentment failed to take into account the hopeless numerical inferiority of the Allied cavalry after its earlier losses, and was based on an incomplete view of the battlefield. All the hard-pressed infantrymen could see, amid clouds of thick, eddying smoke, was the outer face of the square on either side, and the hordes of encircling French horse. They could not realize that the very presence of the decimated English squadrons in their rear helped to sustain the wavering morale of the Netherlanders and Brunswickers, and that the memory of their earlier, and heroic onslaught accounted for Napoleon's failure to follow up his cavalry with infantry and subject their squares to case-shot at close range.

Five times in two hours the French horsemen were driven from the plateau; five times, after rallying in the plain they returned. Whenever they disappeared the British gunners ran out of the squares and reopened fire, while Napoleon's guns resumed their cannonade. Some time after five o'clock Ney brought up the last cavalry from the second line – Kellermann's two divisions of cuirassiers and the heavy squadrons of the Imperial Guard. At one moment more than 9000 horse assailed the ridge in a compact phalanx. This immense body was packed in the 800 yards front between the *chaussée* and the British bastion at Hougoumont, where the ground was a morass piled with dead horses. The front ranks, including most of the senior officers, were completely wiped out by the English batteries, and the weary mounts could only proceed at a walk. Yet they still continued to return.

Throughout this time and during the bombardments which

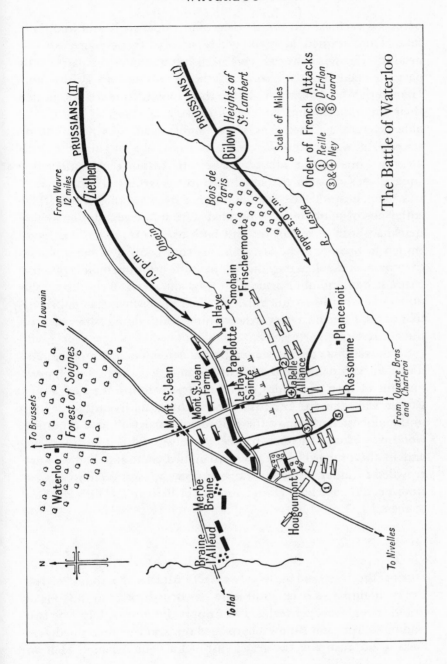

N

To Hal

To Nivelles

From Quatre Bras
and Charleroi

To Brussels

To Louvain

Waterloo

Forest of Soignes

Braine
l'Alleud

Merbe
Braine

Mont St. Jean

Mont St. Jean
Farm

Hougoumont

La Haye
Sainte

La Belle
Alliance

Rossomme

Plancenoit

Papelotte

La Haye

Smohain

Frischermont

Bois de
Paris

Heights of
St. Lambert

PRUSSIANS (II)

PRUSSIANS (I)

Ziethen

Bülow

From Wavre
12 miles

10.0 p.m.

7.0 p.m.

R. Ohain

R. Lasne

approx. 5.0 p.m.

Scale of Miles

0

Order of French Attacks
① Reille ② D'Erlon
③&④ Ney ⑤ Guard

The Battle of Waterloo

531

preceded each assault the British infantry patiently endured their fate. They seemed in their steady squares to be rooted to the ground. Though it would have been hazardous in the extreme to have manoeuvred with some of the young second British and Hanoverian landwehr battalions, they showed themselves, under their fine officers and NCOs, as capable of standing fire as the oldest veterans. Theirs, as Harry Smith said, was no battle of science; it was a stand-up fight between two pugilists, milling away till one or the other was beaten. Inside each suffocating square, reeking with the smell of burnt cartridge and powder, it was like a hospital, the dead and dying strewing the ground. The sufferings of many of the wounded were indescribable; one rifle-man had both legs shot off and both arms amputated, but con-tinued to breathe as he lay amid his comrades. Few cried out in their pain, and, when they did so, their officers immediately quieted them, it was a point of pride with Englishmen of all classes to take punishment without murmuring. Their stoicism was equalled by that of the French cavalry, who won the ungrudging admiration of the entire British army.

Nor was less courage shown by the defenders of Hougoumont. The flank companies in the burnt-out mansion among the charred remains of their comrades, the Coldstream lining the hedge and garden wall, the 3rd Guards in the orchard, all lived that day up to the highest tradition of the Brigade of Guards. Three times the wood was taken and retaken; every tree was riddled with bullets, and in the orchard alone more than two thousand bodies were crowded together. 'You may depend upon it,' said Wellington, 'no troops could have held Hougoumont but British, and only the best of them.'

*　　*　　*

During the last hour of Ney's cavalry attacks the sound of the Prussian guns had been audible on the British ridge in the lulls of firing, though few yet realized its import. By four o'clock, the two leading divisions of Bülow's corps had reached the western edge of Paris wood, just over two miles east of La Belle Alliance. Half an hour later, in view of the urgency of Wellington's messages, they went into action without waiting for their supports. Soon after five, when they had advanced to within a mile and a half of the Brussels road, Lobau counter-attacked and drove them back. But at six o'clock, two more Prussian divisions having emerged from the wood, Bülow again attacked, striking round Lobau's southern flank at Plancenoit, a village less than a mile from the French lifeline.

The situation was growing grave in the extreme for Napoleon. His troops had been marching and fighting almost continuously for four days; their losses during the afternoon had been heavier than in any engagement of comparable scale in his career. Again and again they had seemed on the point of carrying the ridge and sweeping Wellington's international flotsam and jetsam down the Brussels road. Yet whenever the smoke cleared, the stubborn red-coats were seen to be still standing. The Prussian shot, already playing on the *chausée*, brought home to the Emperor that, unless he could break Wellington's line in the remaining hours of day-light, his doom was certain.

The Emperor descended from the mound on which he had so long watched the battle. Though, like his adversary, still in his middle forties, he had so far taken little active part in the direction of the assault. After a study of the battlefield in the early hours and the issue of orders for the attack, he had delegated tactical control to Ney. Exhausted by the exertions of the last three days, he had spent part of the afternoon in what seemed to onlookers a coma, and had not even intervened to stay the impetuous Marshal's abuse of his cavalry. But he now roused himself, to snatch, as so often in the past, victory from defeat.

He had to fight on two fronts. To the south-east 30,000 Prussians were striking at his communications; to the north 20,000 Britons and as many or more Germans and Netherlanders were still barring the Brussels road. Despite his casualties he still had between 50,000 and 60,000 veteran troops, though of Grouchy's 33,000, wandering somewhere in space to the east, (unknown to him they were at that moment fiercely attacking the Prussian rear-guard at Wavre twelve miles away) there was no sign. To clear his flank and gain time for a further assault on the British, he dispatched eight young Guard battalions of the Imperial Guard to reinforce Lobau and recover Plancenoit. Simultaneously he gave Ney peremptory orders to throw in infantry and capture La Haye Sainte.

Conscious that the crisis of the battle was at hand and that the interminable and futile attacks of the French cavalry must now be followed up by infantry, Wellington had already reorganized his line. Taking advantage of the lull after the last charge, he had brought up Clinton's division of Peninsular veterans from its place in reserve to a point at which, standing between the defenders of Hougoumont and Maitland's Guards, they could enfilade any attack on his right. Feeling that Hougoumont was now secure and that, as a result, no threat could develop from that quarter, he also summoned Chassé's Netherlanders from Braine L'Alleud and placed them in rear of his centre. Simultaneously, seeing that Ney's force was spent, he deployed his shrunken battalions from square, forming them four-deep instead of in the normal two-rank line so as to give extended fire-power against infantry while preserving sufficient solidity to repel what remained of the French cavalry.

Soon after six Ney attacked the centre with two columns of infantry and cavalry. They were driven back by a terrific fire from the British guns. But the French were fighting magnificently and with the recklessness of despair, and the young Prince of Orange, in charge of the defenders at this point, was without experience of command. Repeating a mistake made at Quatre Bras, he ordered one of Ompteda's battalions of the King's German Legion above La Haye Sainte to deploy in the presence of cavalry, with disastrous consequences. Their comrades inside the farmhouse were now down to their last round of ammunition and at about six-thirty the key to the British centre was captured. Baring's remaining forty men fought their way back to the ridge with the bayonet. At about the same time the eight battalions of the Young Guard, sent to Lobau's aid, recovered Plancenoit.

This double success gave the French, at the eleventh hour, a chance of victory. Throwing sharpshooters and guns forward from the captured farm, they established themselves on the ridge and opened a destructive fire on the left of the 3rd Division and the right of the 5th. The Prince of Orange, who had by now completely lost his head, deployed another of Ompteda's battalions in the presence of cavalry with the same disastrous result. A few minutes later Ompteda was killed. His shattered brigade and that of Kielmansegge's young Hanoverians had reached the limit of their endurance and were on the point of breaking. Only the gallantry of the Rifles and a charge by the 3rd Hussars of the Legion prevented immediate disaster.

Had Napoleon been on the spot to exploit the opportunity, he might have turned the gap in the British centre into a chasm. But when, still watching from La Belle Alliance three-quarters of a mile away, he received Ney's urgent appeal for more infantry, he only asked petulantly whether the Marshal expected him to make them. At the crisis of his gamble his moral courage faltered; he was not ready to stake everything. And while the twelve remaining battalions of the Imperial Guard waited, unused, Wellington, summoned from his position with the Guards Division above Hougoumont, galloped to the spot, calling up every remaining available unit.

The British commander-in-chief had received the news with his habitual calm and decision. As all the Allied leaders in the centre had by now been killed or wounded, he temporarily took over command there himself. Leading five young Brunswick battalions into the full storm of the French batteries, he rallied them when they broke under that hurricane of shot and brought them steadily back into line. Meanwhile, Vivian, seeing a new force of Prussians moving up from the east, arrived on his own initiative from the left of the ridge. Uxbridge galloped off to fetch Vandeleur's 11th, 12th and 16th Light Dragoons, and Somerset, with the wreck of the Union Brigade extended in single rank to make the utmost show, instilled confidence and pressure from behind into Chassé's Netherlanders.

The bombardment had now reached a new degree of intensity as Napoleon brought up every available gun to reinforce his massed batteries. All along the Allied centre men were going down like ninepins; close by the crossroads 450 of the 700 men of the Twenty-seventh lay in square where they had fallen. In a neighbouring regiment – the Fortieth – both ensigns and fourteen sergeants had been killed or wounded round the tattered colours. The 5th Division, 5000 strong when the battle started, seemed to have dwindled to a line of skirmishers. Kincaid with the Rifles began to wonder at that moment whether there had ever been a battle in which everyone on both sides had been killed. The stream of wounded and fugitives towards the rear was so great that a Prussian aide-de-camp, who rode up from Ziethen's oncoming corps to investigate, returned with a report that the British were defeated and in retreat. No one knew what was happening outside his own immediate vicinity, for in the windless, oven-like, smoke-filled air visibility was reduced to a few yards.

Yet Wellington's grip on the battle never relaxed. Unlike his imperial adversary he was used to commanding comparatively small armies and to attending to every detail himself. In his grey greatcoat with cape, white cravat, Hessian boots, telescope and low cocked-hat, he rode continuously up and down the line, often alone and seemingly oblivious of the storm of shot. He neither avoided nor courted danger, but, knowing that his presence was necessary to keep his young soldiers to the sticking point, showed himself, placid and unconcerned, wherever the fire was hottest. Everywhere he infected men, near the limit of endurance, with courage and confidence. Almost every member of his staff, including De Lancey, his Quartermaster General, had by now fallen, but, though he looked thoughtful and a little pale, he betrayed no sign of anxiety. Once, chatting with the commanding officer of a square in which he had taken shelter, he was heard to say, 'Oh, it will be all right; if the Prussians come up in time, we shall have a long peace.' But occasionally he looked at his watch.

'Hard pounding this, gentlemen,' he observed, 'but we will see who can pound the longest.' And when the smoke for a moment drifted away and the scanty lines of red were seen everywhere to be standing, a cheer went up from his tired countrymen that showed him to be justified. The hour for which he had waited had come. For streaming on to the west end of the battlefield from

Smohain, driving the French from the environs of Papelotte and La Haye and filling in the two-mile gap between Bülow's men before Plancenoit and the left of the British line came Ziethen's Prussian corps. Its intervention was far more decisive than Bülow's earlier but more distant attack on Plancenoit. As the Prussian batteries, adding their quota to the inferno on the ridge, began to shell the ground near La Belle Alliance, Napoleon knew that the end was at hand. Already from his right rear news had come that the Young Guard had been driven out of Plancenoit. The field was closing in as it had done at Leipzig, and the night was little more than an hour away.

Soon after seven the Emperor took his final resolution. He sent two of the magnificent, untouched battalions of the Old Guard to recapture Plancenoit and prevent encirclement. Then, bidding his aides-de-camp announce that Grouchy had arrived from the west, he ordered a general advance of all units. As its spearhead he brought forward the remaining battalions of the Imperial Guard, keeping only three as a last reserve. With these he descended the plain, marching at their head towards the British ridge. As he did so the French guns again increased their tempo.

The Guard, fresh from its triumph at Ligny two nights before, advanced with a deeply impressive *élan*. Its men were conscious that they bore the destinies of the world. The two veteran battalions who had been sent to recapture Plancenoit did so in twenty minutes without firing a shot. Those of the Middle and Old Guard advancing against the British were inspired by the personal presence of Napoleon. At the foot of the slope, in a sheltered hollow, he halted to let them pass, throwing open his greatcoat to display his medals and repeatedly crying out, '*A Bruxelles, mes enfants! à Bruxelles!*' They answered with shouts of '*Vive l'Empereur!*' and pressed forward with solemn tread and shouldered arms. In front of each regiment rode a general, Marshal Ney – '*le rougeout*' – with powder-blackened face and tattered uniform, directing. Cavalry moved on their flanks and in the intervals between the battalions came field-pieces loaded with case-shot. Ahead went a cloud of sharpshooters.

The Guard went up the hill in two columns, the one moving

obliquely up a spur from the Brussels road towards the centre of the British right, the other using, so far as Wellington's dispositions admitted, the sheltered ground between La Belle Alliance and Hougoumont. True to the tactical conception that had dominated the earlier attacks, the frontal blow was to be clinched by a left hook. But with Hougoumont firmly held and Duplat's Hanoverians and Adam's brigade of Light Infantry deployed across the hollow way between it and the ridge, the front on which the attackers could operate was narrower than ever. And, with his unerring tactical sense, Wellington was waiting at the very spot at which his adversary's knock-out blow was aimed: on the right of the Guards Division where it touched the left battalion – the 95th – of Adam's brigade. Warned of the approach of the Old and Middle Guard by a deserting royalist colonel, he had ordered his men to lie down out of fire of the guns and *tirailleurs* until the French appeared; their long vigil of endurance, he told them, would soon be over.

In the general darkness and confusion, and because of the fire from the guns on the ridge, the leading battalions of the first column struck the British line at two points: where Halkett's battered brigade of the 3rd Division was drawn up in front of Chassé's Netherlanders, and immediately to the west where Wellington was waiting with Maitland's 1st Guards. As the huge bearskins suddenly loomed out of the darkness, the waiting British sprang to their feet in the corn and poured from their extended line a volley at point-blank range into the head of the advancing columns. The French tried to deploy but too late, and most of their officers were swept down. Then, while they were still in confusion, the British charged, Wellington himself giving the word to the Guards with a quiet, 'Now, Maitland, now's your time!'

But though the Imperial Guard recoiled, it did not break. Both parts of the column re-formed and opened fire on the oncoming British, their guns supporting them with ease. To the east the remnants of the 33rd and 69th were driven back and at one moment almost broke, but were rallied by Halkett. A Dutch battery, behaving with great coolness and gallantry, raked the French column, and Chassé's Belgians, 3000 strong, came up in support. Gradually the attackers, isolated and without support behind them, began to give ground. Meanwhile those opposed to the 1st Guards, though driven back for some distance, had also rallied. Maitland ordered his Guardsmen back, but his voice could not be heard above the firing, and some of them, mistaking his intention, tried to form square. In the confusion the two British battalions withdrew in disorder, only to re-form at the word of command with flawless and habitual steadiness on regaining their original position.

But before the battle between the rival Guards could be resumed, it was decided by the action of the most experienced regiment on the British side. Wellington always maintained that, if he had had at Waterloo the army with which he crossed the Pyrenees, he would have attacked Napoleon without waiting for the Prussians: 'I should have swept him off the face of the earth,' he said, 'in two hours.' The first battalion of the 52nd, commanded by John Colborne, afterwards Lord Seaton, had served in John Moore's original Light Brigade; Colborne himself was Moore's finest living pupil. It had gone into action at Waterloo with more than a thousand bayonets, being one of the very few British battalions which was up to strength – 'a regiment,' wrote Napier of its Peninsular exploits, 'never surpassed in arms since arms were first borne by men.' Owing to the skilful way in which Colborne had placed and handled it, its casualties during the French cavalry charges and the long hours of bombardment had been extraordinarily light.

As the second and westernmost column of the Imperial Guard after passing by Hougoumont pressed up the slope towards Maitland's unbroken line, the drummers beating the *rummadum, dummadum, dum*, of the *pas de charge*, Colborne, who was stationed in the centre of Adam's brigade to the right of the Guards, took a sudden decision. Without orders either from the Duke or any superior officer, he moved his battalion forward out of the line for a distance of three hundred yards, and then, as it drew level with the leading company of the advancing French column, wheeled it to the left with the order, 'Right shoulders forward.'

He thus laid it on the flank of the French. By doing so he took the risk both of leaving a gap in the line behind and of having his men cut to pieces by cavalry – a fate he had experienced when, as one of Stewart's brigade commanders, he had moved up the hill at Albuera.

The reward of his daring was decisive. The Imperial Guard, taken by surprise, halted and poured a volley into the 52nd which brought down a hundred and forty of its men. But the British reply of this grave Roman battalion was decisive. It seemed as though every bullet found its mark. So heavy were the casualties in the dense, astonished column that the Imperial Guard did not wait for the 52nd to charge. It broke and fled. As it did so, the 52nd resumed its advance eastwards across, and at right angles to, the British front, with the two other battalions of Adam's brigade – the 95th and 71st – moving up on Wellington's instructions on either flank. A few hundred yards on they encountered another French column re-forming – the first that had attacked – and dealt it the same treatment and with the same results. Gradually, as the recoiling units of the French army streamed back across their path from the impregnable plateau, the British Light Infantry inclined to the right towards La Belle Alliance. Round them, out of swirling smoke, scattered units of British and French cavalry appeared in charge and counter-charge.

For from the ridge above them, starting from the right, the whole British line had begun to advance as Wellington, hat raised high in air, galloped westwards from one tattered, enduring regiment to another. The time for which he and they had waited had come. 'Who commands here?' he shouted to Harry Smith, Lambert's brigade major. 'Generals Kempt and Lambert, my Lord.' 'Desire them to form column of companies and move on immediately.' 'In what direction, my Lord?' 'Right ahead, to be sure.'

It was now nearly dusk. But, as the French cannonade ceased and the smoke began to drift from the ridge, the setting sun cast a ray of light along the glinting British line, now motionless no more, and on the accoutrements of the defeated columns in the plain. The whole French army was suddenly dissolving with the landscape: entire regiments leaving their arms piled and taking to their heels. From the east the Prussians were pouring in a great flood across the battlefield, and to the south-west, where the Old and Young Guard were still fighting fiercely to keep Napoleon's life-line open, Bülow's men had swept through Plancenoit and were approaching the *chaussée*. 'I have seen nothing like that moment,' wrote Frazer of the Artillery, 'the sky literally darkened with smoke, the sun just going down and which till then had not for some hours broken through the gloom of a dull day, the indescribable shouts of thousands where it was impossible to distinguish between friends and foe.'

In that final advance, with little groups of French gunners and horsemen and the last unbroken squares of the Old Guard fighting gloriously to give their Emperor time to escape, a few score more fell, among them Lord Uxbridge, who, riding forward by the Duke's side, had his leg shattered by a shell. Most of the British regiments were so exhausted that they halted in the plain between the ridges. Only the cavalry and Adam's brigade, following the retreating squares of the Imperial Guard, proceeded through the heart of what had been the French position.

As Ziethen's Prussian cavalry from the east and Vivian's and Vandeleur's British from the north met at La Belle Alliance, the union of the armies, fought for so fiercely during three days and nights, was consummated. Shortly after nine o'clock the two men whose good faith, constancy and resolution had made it possible, met on the spot where Napoleon had launched his attack. They were both on horseback, but the old Prussian embraced and kissed his English friend, exclaiming, *'Mein lieber Kamerad'* and then, *'Quelle affaire!'* which, as Wellington observed, was about all the French he knew.

Then, in weariness and darkness, Wellington turned his tired horse towards Waterloo and the ridge he had defended. He rode in silence across a battlefield in which 15,000 men of his own army, including a third of the British troops engaged, and more than 30,000 Frenchmen lay dead, dying or wounded. The sound of gunfire had ceased, but, to the south, trumpets could be faintly heard as the tireless Prussian cavalry took up the pursuit of their inexorable enemies. As their infantry, many of whom had marched fifty miles in the past two days, debouched from Plancenoit into the Charleroi highway, where the 52nd, with its tattered colours, was halted by the roadside, they broke into slow time and their bands played 'God save the King'.

The English Vision

'It is not to be thought of that the Flood
Of British freedom, which, to the open sea
Of the world's praise, from dark antiquity
Hath flowed, "with pomp of waters, unwithstood,"
Roused though it be full often to a mood
Which spurns the check of salutary bands,
That this most famous Stream in bogs and sands
Should perish; and to evil and to good
Be lost for ever. In our halls is hung
Armoury of the invincible Knights of old:
We must be free or die, who speak the tongue
That Shakespeare spake; the faith and morals hold
Which Milton held. – In everything we are sprung
Of Earth's first blood, have titles manifold.'

Wordsworth

TRUE ARISTOCRACY, after true religion, is the greatest blessing a nation can enjoy. Early nineteenth-century Britain possessed an unrivalled capacity for aristocracy. Her troubles arose because she was ruled by a counterfeit instead of the real aristocracy which her institutions had evolved with such profusion. The subalterns and company commanders who had created a fighting force superior to Napoleon's were relegated to half-pay or placed under the command of young popinjays who had acquired their commissions by influence and purchase. Yet the rich country, which wasted natural leadership with such arrogant carelessness, continued to produce almost unlimited talent and genius. In every walk of life she threw up men who attained to the highest levels of achievement. In science and invention she towered above other nations,

as she did in commerce, colonization and discovery. Though the
State applied to aspirants to public office the narrow measuring-rod
of lineage and inheritance, men of enterprise in these years were
creating new openings in a hundred spheres of spontaneous personal endeavour. While the Liverpools and Sidmouths were feebly
governing England in the 1820s and 1830s, their fellow countrymen,
whom they regarded, except for purposes of war, as outside their
social pale, were policing Sicily, liberating Greece and Chile,
pacifying the warlike tribes of Asia and civilizing Malaya.

And if in Cabinet and Convocation inspiration was lacking, in
the arts Britain was richer than she had ever been before. Not even
in the time of Shakespeare and Milton had she produced such an
astonishing harvest of literary genius. In the decade after Waterloo
one might have met at one time or another in the London streets
William and Dorothy Wordsworth, Coleridge, Blake and Lamb,
Keats, Shelley and Byron, Jane Austen and Walter Scott, Hazlitt,
Landor, Southey, Moore, Crabbe, Cobbett, De Quincey, Leigh
Hunt, William Napier, Jeremy Bentham, Godwin, as well as a host
of lesser literary figures like the elder D'Israeli, Haydon and John
Nyren. And Thackeray, Dickens, Carlyle, Fitzgerald, Tennyson,
Borrow, Macaulay, George Eliot, Robert and Elizabeth Browning,
the Brontës, Trollope, Surtees and the younger Disraeli were
growing up – in the nursery or on the threshold of manhood.

> 'Great spirits now on earth are sojourning:
> He of the cloud, the cataract, the lake,
> Who on Helvellyn's summit, wide awake,
> Catches his freshness from Archangel's wing:
>
> 'And other spirits there are standing apart
> Upon the forehead of the age to come;
> These, these will give the world another heart,
> And other pulses . . .'

With the exception of Scott and Byron, none of these men and
women were known at the time to more than a small circle of their
countrymen. The blaze of genius was there, but it was a blaze in
the garret. The great chandelier-lit rooms below were filled with
magnificently dressed nonentities. It was her real aristocrats who,

when the nation's official spokesmen were silent, gave her the answer she needed. The poets and philosophers recalled her to the enduring truths of her being. On the political issues of the time, in the narrow party sense, these great men were divided. Wordsworth, Coleridge, Scott, Southey and De Quincey were Tories, Shelley, Hazlitt, Hunt and Cobbett were radicals, Byron a Whig. Keats and Lamb, though conservative in instinct, were born too far below the social salt in that extravagantly snobbish age not to resent the pretensions of the ruling classes and translate that resentment into opposition. Yet all were at one in their advocacy of the moral truths which had made Britain great and whose oblivion by those in power threatened to make her little.

The most penetrating analysis of the shallowness of the rulers of Regency Britain came, not from a revolutionary or radical but from the philosophic founder of nineteenth-century conservatism. Anticipating both the social-welfare Toryism of Disraeli and the socialism of Ruskin, Coleridge poured scorn on the prevailing determinism of economists and statesmen. 'It is a mockery,' he wrote, 'of our fellow creatures' wrongs to call them equal in rights, when, by the bitter compulsion of their wants, we make them inferior to us in all that can soften the heart or dignify the understanding.' Distinguishing between conservatism as inertia and as a condition of organic life, he went to the root of the controversy between liberty and authority, finding the synthesis in his unvarying starting-point, the human soul. 'Man must be free, or to what purpose was he made a spirit of reason and not a machine of instinct? Man must obey, or wherefore has he a conscience? The powers which create this difficulty contain its solution, for their service is perfect freedom.'

The repression of later Tory politicians had no part in this moralist's conservatism. 'No assailant of an error,' he wrote, 'can reasonably hope to be listened to by its advocates who has not proved to them that he has seen the disputed subject in the same point of view and is capable of contemplating it with the same feelings as themselves.' Sunk into easy and slothful living, pottering about Hampstead Heath between meal and meal, Coleridge seemed in his latter years to have become a rather futile person –

'the dear, fine, silly old angel,' as Lamb called him. Yet from 'that great piece of placid marble' flowed a never-ending stream of germinating ideas that were to stir and influence the hearts of men unborn: of a living and organic conservatism, a restored Church, and a society so morally knit that the gain of one class should automatically become that of every other.

At the opposite end of the pole to the quietist of Highgate stood, or rather rode, the radical pamphleteer, Cobbett. While the one had travelled from Jacobinism to Conservatism, the other had begun as a Tory and ended as a disciple of the republican Tom Paine. Yet the two men based their criticism of the ruling political philosophy on precisely the same grounds: that it was inhuman, un-Christian and, therefore, un-English. Cobbett's lifelong object was to restore the yeoman England of his youth in which, or so he believed, the property of the poor had been held sacred. 'Then,' he wrote, 'should I hope once more to see my country great and glorious, and be cheered with the prospect of being able to say to my sons, "I leave England to you as I find it; do you the same by your children."' He saw dying all round him, of a poverty inexplicable in the light of the growing wealth of the rich, all the things he loved – good husbandry, craftsmanship and social virtue – and threw his whole being into denouncing such poverty and those who tolerated it. For the repression of the helpless determinists in power he had nothing but a burning contempt. 'I was not born under the Six Acts; nor was I born under a state of things like this. I was not born under it and I do not wish to live under it; and with God's help I will change it if I can!'

Though secular in outlook and profession, in purpose all the great English writers of the day were religious. Where the Church failed to find an answer for the problems of an evolving society, the poets, like the prophets of the Old Testament, answered for her. When Shelley wrote 'atheist and philanthropist' after his name in the visitors' book at Chamonix and spoke of 'that detestable religion, the Christian,' it was not because he was opposed to the ideals of Christianity, but because he was so passionately in favour of their practical application that he could not bear to be classed with the hypocrites who used the Church as a cloak for selfishness and intolerance. Even Byron, writing Don Juan in adulterous exile on gin and water and announcing that he was going to be immoral and show things, not as they ought to be, but as they really were, helped to restore the moral currency. 'Go, dine,' he apostrophized the duke of Wellington

> 'from off the plate
> Presented by the Prince of the Brazils,
> And send the sentinel before your gate
> A slice or two from your luxurious meals;
> He fought, but has not dined so well of late.'

In his great political satire, *The Age of Bronze*, and in *Don Juan*, he weighed the world he knew so well in the scales of justice, and with urbane, malicious laughter, refined the snobbery, vulgar pride and inhuman callousness of fashionable society.

Unconsciously the poets and philosophers were setting standards of outlook which, though little regarded by the political and social leaders of their age, became, through the influence of their genius, the accepted canons of the next. The character of early Victorian Britain was not formed by its Prime Ministers, serving in 1822 their apprenticeship in junior Government office, or on the Opposition benches – Robert Peel, young Palmerston, Aberdeen, Lord John Russell, the future Lord Melbourne. It was profoundly influenced by the prophetic writers of the Revolutionary and Napoleonic War and the Regency. The ideals of Thomas Arnold, creator of the Victorian public school, derived from Wordsworth, denouncing amid the luxury and display of the brief-lived peace of Amiens the moral blindness of fashionable society.

> 'Altar, sword and pen,
> Fireside, the heroic wealth of hall and bower
> Have forfeited their ancient English dower
> Of inward happiness. We are selfish men;
> Oh! raise us up, return to us again;
> And give us manners, virtues, freedom, power.'

Under the solemn dullness and pomposity of the gaunt, bony Westmorland prophet, the exclusive absorption in his own work, the huge crocodile jaw working in interminable monologue, the

547

majesty of his poetry and doctrine worked like a leaven on the mind of the future:

> 'inspiration for a song that winds
> Through ever-changing scenes of votive quest,
> Wrongs to redress, harmonious tribute paid
> To patient courage and unblemished Truth,
> To firm devotion, zeal unquenchable,
> And Christian meekness hallowing faithful loves.'

No nation whose ruling class based its faith on Wordsworth's philosophy was likely to fail its destiny through frivolity or lack of faith.

To this renewal of the nation's moral fibre in the spiritual exhaustion after the long war all the great writers of the age contributed: Shelley preaching, through the flaming lyrics of his revolutionary advocacy, that men should love one another and that no society not built on love could endure; Blake, so obscure that only a few knew him, protesting against all that was rigid, unimaginative and complacent in religion and morality and bequeathing from his rambling books of prophecy an anthem for the twentieth-century Welfare State; Keats, turning his back in a worldly age on every worldly hope in order to sustain – to the consumptive's death in the garret – his poet's creed that whatever the imagination seized on as Beauty must be Truth. It was not that such men were apart from their country or possessed some superior virtue not shared by her people and rulers; on the contrary, their vision sprang directly from her common faith and civilization. Jane Austen was as organic a part of the nation as a tree, Scott as his native Tweed. Genius merely enabled them to see her true course and to check the deviation of the helmsmen with shorter vision. In a country that fostered freedom of expression, they operated as a magnetic compass. Walter Scott, wrote his political opponent, Hazlitt, by emancipating the mind from petty, narrow and bigoted prejudices, and communicating to countless thousands his chivalrous and humane ideal of patriotism, was one of the greatest teachers of morality that ever lived. Jane Austen, seeing life steadily across the quiet lawn of a country rectory, was as true a delineator of female honour as Scott of male. She once defined a lady as a mixture of love, pride and delicacy, and in six great novels, never transcending the limits of human capacity, immortalized the type. Self-assertion was the cardinal sin in her calendar; the attributes she helped to perpetuate were self-discipline, moderation, a morality founded on tenderness and constancy, a readiness to shoulder the dullest and weariest burdens for those with claims of kindred and association, a quiet but unflinching opposition to everything lawless, coarse, brutal and uncontrolled. But for these there could scarcely have been a Florence Nightingale or even a profession of modern nursing.

Even the essayists, Lamb, 'the frolic and the gentle,' and the savage Hazlitt whom Wordsworth thought unfit for respectable society, helped to shape the outlook of the lesser professional and clerical classes on whose integrity the commercial empire of the Victorians was to rest. The one humanized and invested with poetry the common round of city life for an age in which cities continually multiplied; the other exposed, with compelling clarity, the wrongs and injustices of those without land, capital or birth. Lamb, in his rusty stockings and unpolished shoes, preached the English creed of humorous and affectionate acceptance; Hazlitt, with his rapier thrusts, cleared a way for Thackeray and the young middle-class reformers of *Punch*.

Nor did the English vision stop at the sea. For thousands of patriots in his own age and for millions in the next, Britain was typified not by Castlereagh, whose foreign policy, as the event proved, was writ in water, but by Byron. The latter's championship of liberty and nationalism, his aristocratic disdain for every form of tyranny, and his realization, so moving in a fastidious and sensitive man, that a nation has a right to its freedom, whatever its faults or vices, ran through the adolescent mind of European liberalism like fire. The little limping dandy who wrote 'The Prisoner of Chillon' threw, like a lamp on the screen of the future, the form of Gladstone's speeches and Campbell-Bannerman's policy.

The splendours of Regency society, the power and wealth of early nineteenth-century Britain seemed brassy and eternal to the men and women of the time. So did the destitution and degradation which accompanied them. To poor and rich alike they appeared to be unchangeable – part of a divine, or, as many had begun to suspect, a diabolical ordinance. The poets taught otherwise. They could not change the laws or the harsh economic phenomena of the age, or arrest the cumulative evils to which those phenomena gave rise. But they could make men want to change them. 'If we are a Christian nation,' wrote Coleridge, 'we must learn to act nationally as well as individually as Christians . . . Our manufacturers must consent to regulations; our gentry must concern themselves in the education of their national clients and dependents – must regard their estates as offices of trust with duties to be performed in the sight of God and their country. Let us become a better people, and the reform of all the public grievances will follow of itself.'

SUBJECT INDEX

Act against Appeals to Rome, 1534, 31
Acts of Settlement, 33, 316
Act of Supremacy, 1563, 43
Acts of Uniformity *see* Uniformity Acts
Act of Union, 1707, 331
actors and acting, 204–6
Adamites, 251
Admiralty: Pepys at, 286, 291, 293–4;
  under Bridgeman, 326; and 1797 pay
  mutiny, 388–93; denies frigates to St
  Vincent, 404; and Nelson's movements 431, 433, 436; *see also* Navy
Agitators, 225
agnosticism, 313
agriculture, 78–9, 305, 336, 339–40
American Independence, War of, 348
Anabaptists, 225, 251
Anglicanism *see* Church of England
apprenticeships, 263
archery and archers, 13, 51
aristocracy (nobility), 14, 334, 340, 345,
  543–4
Armada, Spanish: preparation and
  composition, 130–2, 140; Drake's
  preventive actions against, 133–8,
  141–2, 146–7; sets sail, 143–5, 147;
  English land defences against, 143–4,
  172–3; conditions on board, 144, 146;
  movements and formation in Channel,
  148, 149–63; guns, 153–4; fireship
  attack at Calais, 163–5; in Battle of
  Gravelines, 166–7, 175; escapes to
  North Sea, 168–71, 175; return to
  Spain, 176–81
army: Tudor militia, 50–2; Elizabethan
  development, 115–16; and Armada
  threat, 172–3; supplies, 183; 'New
  Model', 223–4, 237; and Restoration,
  236–7; reduced under William III,
  311; and Jacobites, 325; and liberty
  under law, 344; strength at start of
  Napoleonic Wars, 376–9; reforms
  under Moore, 474–6
art, 353–4; *see also* literature

Bangorian controversy, 1717, 324
Bank of England: established, 304, 309
Belem Rangers, 491
Bible, Holy: Lollard, 2; Tudor
  translations, 33–4; King James
  (Authorised) Version, 186, 200, 202,
  218; universal reading of, 249

Bill of Rights, 1689, 301, 314
Black Act, 1723, 327
Black Death, 28
Book of Common Prayer, 34–5, 45,
  200–12, 218–19
Bond of Association, 118
Bow Street runners, 344*n*
Brownists, 251
bubonic plague, 14, 53, 186, 280

calendar: Julian reform, 328
Calvinism, 48, 86
Catholic League (France), 129
censorship: of newspapers, 316
children: family life, 262; labour, 352
Church of England (Anglicanism): and
  Prayer Book, 34, 200–1; under
  Elizabeth I, 44–5, 47; effect on
  national character, 45–6; James I and,
  216, 218; Charles I and, 223;
  re-established (1660), 250; supports
  Tory party, 312; and William III
  allegiance controversy, 312; loses
  special relationship with Crown,
  314–15; High Church Movement,
  315; and Hanoverian succession, 316;
  under Hanoverians, 324; and
  consolation of social orders, 329;
  relations with State, 356–7
Cimaroons, 93–4, 98; *see also* slaves
cities and towns, 270, 350
Civil Service, 325–6
Civil War, 1642–6, 223–4
class (social): late medieval changes,
  12–15, 28; in Pepys's Navy, 289;
  effects of Nine Years' War on, 318–19;
  and constitution, 329; landowning and
  governing, 330–5
clergy, 250–2; *see also* Church of
  England
cloth: exports, 18, 90, 269–70; and
  immigrant refugees, 80; as village
  industry, 337; *see also* cotton; wool
coaches and coaching, 272–3
coal, 78–9
coinage *see* currency
colonization: North American, 186–92,
  195–8; expansion under Charles II,
  266
Commonwealth (Cromwellian), 224
Commons, House of: composition and
  sittings under Stuarts, 256; under

PERSONS AND PLACES INDEX

557